# playing AND learning

## IN EARLY CHILDHOOD EDUCATION

**BEVERLiE DiETZE** MOUNT SAINT VINCENT UNIVERSITY

**DiANE KASHiN** SENECA COLLEGE

**Pearson Canada**
Toronto

**Library and Archives Canada Cataloguing in Publication**

Dietze, Beverlie, 1957–
    Playing and learning in early childhood education / Beverlie Dietze.

    ISBN: 978-0-13-512546-5

    1. Play—Textbooks.   2. Learning—Textbooks.   3. Early childhood education—Textbooks.   I. Title.

LB1139.35.P55D53 2011                372.21                C2010-907559-5

ISBN: 978-0-13-512546-5

Vice-President, Editorial Director: Gary Bennett
Editor-in-Chief: Ky Pruesse; Michelle Sartor
Editor, Humanities and Social Sciences: Joel Gladstone
Marketing Manager: Loula March
Developmental Editor: Rema Celio
Lead Project Manager: Söğüt Y. Güleç
Project Manager: Renata Butera, Central Publishing
Production Editors: Sudip Sinha, Aptara®, Inc.; Lila Campbell
Copy Editor: Deepak Arora
Proofreaders: Dheerandra Kumar Singh; Heath Lynn Silberfeld
Manufacturing Coordinator: Susan Johnson
Compositor: Aptara®, Inc.
Art Direction: Miguel Angel Acevedo
Interior Designer: Anthony Leung
Cover Designer: Opus House Inc./Sonya Thursby
Cover Image: Alamy Ltd.

18  17

Printed and bound in the United States of America

*I dedicate this book to my late mother, Eileen Lucy Arthurs and my late father, William Christie Arthurs, who knew intuitively the importance of their children having the freedom to play outdoors—in the woods, at the brook, on the lawn, and in playhouses. And to my childhood playmates, my sister, Myrna, and our late brother, Philip, who, collectively known as the three little ones by our siblings, shared new adventure, risk taking, intrigue, and surprise into our play and learning.*

**—B.D.**

*To the many students that I have taught over the years whose continued ability to see the learning in the play has been inspirational.*

**—D.K.**

# Brief Contents

# Contents

## 7 Language, Emergent Literacy, and Play 201

## 10 Bringing Technology into Child's Play: A New Perspective 308

# Preface

Children's play—it sounds so simple, yet it is a complex process as you will come to discover as you read the information presented throughout this book. Play is as important to children as their nutrition, family nurturing, and community. Children reap so many benefits when early learning practitioners and parents invest in providing children with a rich play environment, experiences, and opportunities to explore and discover. For example, play ultimately enhances the child's sense of curiosity and wonderment, which in turn influences each aspect of the child's social, emotional, cognitive, and physical development.

Contemporary children are growing up in fast-paced societies where many adults are replacing or reducing play opportunities and options for activities that focus on academic skills, technological gadgets, organized activities such as sports, and indoor passive activities, including computer games and television. This societal shift is eroding opportunities for children to play. Early learning practitioners and educators must collectively work with children, families, neighbourhoods, policymakers, educational institutions, children's organizations, and governments to refocus our knowledge about play and, more importantly, to bring play back into the centre of a child's world. Why? Because child's play = learning for life.

*Playing and Learning in Early Childhood Education* evolved from a number of factors. A few years ago when working with early learning practitioners, I was intrigued and distressed to discover that some early learning practitioners did not have childhood experiences such as making mud cakes, creating snow angels or snow people, or having tea parties. Some had never built a fort out of wood pieces or blocks. A large percentage of early learning practitioners felt that outdoor play was a time for children to run off energy rather than recognizing that outdoor play can be an incubator for incredible exploration and discovery. It is common for some early learning practitioners to view outdoor play as a time for a "break." And still others believed that it was far more important to offer children "academic type" exercises than play opportunities. These perspectives led me to want to create a textbook that would provide our up-and-coming early learning practitioners with an examination of how child's play impacts every part of a child's being and development—a book that would examine both indoor and outdoor play from the perspective of risk-taking skills, problem-solving abilities, interpersonal relationships with peers and others, and how the use of natural and loose materials in play: "plant the seeds, weave the ideas [and] nurture the growth" (Dietze, 2005) of children's being.

When Dr. Diane Kashin agreed to contribute to this book, she reinforced how new research is advancing government and early learning organizations to change policies and directions across our nation. In her chapters on language and literacy experiences, math and science concepts, dramatic play, and moving play to the next level, she clearly articulates the importance of developing play spaces and experiences that offer children opportunities to learn through exploration, discovery, wonderment, making predictions, and reflecting upon their experience and learning. Diane helps us examine the changing roles and responsibilities of early learning practitioners in facilitating learning and in becoming learning and play partners with the children, families, and communities.

Collectively, we wanted to offer early learning student practitioners and early learning practitioner graduates with a text that would highlight the theoretical concepts of play relative to each of the programming areas highlighted. We also sought to provide information that would bring insight into how theory informs the application of play experiences and how these two components support early learning practitioners in developing their philosophy and approach to working with young children.

We have been inspired by the knowledge and skills that we have gained from our early learning practitioner students, our graduates, the children, and our colleagues. This book represents a compilation of our learning acquired from our life journeys and being in the early learning field. We hope that by reading this text you too will gain new knowledge and skills to share with colleagues and our most precious resource in our communities—the children.

## OUR VISION FOR THIS BOOK

As we conducted research for this book, we recognized the importance of early learning student practitioners having a text that would provide an in-depth examination of how play contributes to a child's overall development. We wanted this book to

- support early learning student practitioners in exploring the "who, what, when, how, and why" about children and play;
- spark readers to engage in discussion and debate about the concepts and ideas presented;
- highlight new research for the purpose of advancing thinking and learning about the importance of child's play to learning;
- stimulate new and experienced early learning practitioners to examine their roles and responsibilities in creating stimulating, challenging, exciting, and unique play environments and experiences with children in both indoor and outdoor environments;
- offer our readers tools to support them in educating parents about how early play experiences provide children with the foundational knowledge, skills, and attributes needed for later academic learning;
- support early learning student practitioners in gaining the knowledge and skills needed to commit to ensuring that children in both urban and rural settings have access to quality play experiences;
- provide early learning student practitioners with information about the importance of play that would be incorporated into their working philosophy;
- contribute to early learning student practitioners' developing a passion for and commitment to children and their play.

# APPROACH TO THE TEXT

This text is intended to be user-friendly and a valuable resource that early learning student practitioners will use during their studies and refer back to as they enter any number of exciting career options with young children. Each chapter begins with messages from early learning practitioners to students. These messages and the application examples in each chapter are intended to help readers connect how the theoretical framework is used by early learning practitioners to inform their practice.

*Learning and Playing in Early Childhood Education* differs from other texts in several ways:

- First, many of the chapters discuss the concepts and programming perspectives from both an indoor and outdoor play perspective. This book not only has a chapter devoted to outdoor play, it also clearly weaves in the importance of outdoor play to the development of the whole child throughout the text.
- A second important feature of this book is the emphasis on play and learning from infancy to school age. Many of the examples are relevant to all phases of childhood.
- Third, this book introduces you to Canadian content and many Canadian educators, professionals, researchers, early learning practitioners, including Martha Friendly, Dr. Jane Hewett, and Dr. Charles Pascal, and children.
- Another key feature is the discussion on technology and children's play. It emphasizes the pros and cons about technology in early learning environments and its role in child's play.
- This book offers readers opportunities to see play from multiple perspectives. It introduces the concepts of reconceptualization and critical thinking about play.
- The final attribute of this book that differs from others is the approach taken in planning play space. The importance of creating a positive feeling tone within the early learning space and among the staff, children, parents, and community is emphasized.

We believe that this text has many unique features and would be ideal for use in both play- and curriculum-related courses. We envision this text to have many applications across ECE diploma curriculum as well as in the curriculum of related degree programs. Observation courses, methods or curriculum courses, as well as content-specific courses such as those focusing on art, planning, the environment, language and literacy, math and science, will benefit from the content presented in this text. We see the possibility of this textbook being used from one semester to the next, as we recognize that it is unlikely that in one course all of the chapter content topics could be addressed. We hope it will be a text that early learning student practitioners will refer to during their studies and as they launch their careers as early learning practitioners.

## The Content and Features of the Text

We believe that learning occurs when students are engaged in exploring subjects and concepts with others in their learning community. The pedagogical layout of the text is designed to support learners in exploring the theoretical concepts through stories, examples, and discussions among faculty and other learners.

The text begins with the first three chapters introducing you to the foundational information on play. Chapter 1 examines the foundations of play. Chapter 2 discusses the process of play, while Chapter 3 highlights the importance of conducting observations and documentation of children's play.

The next section of the book, Chapters 4 through 11, highlights the relationship of play to programming areas including dramatic play, outdoor play, blocks, language and literacy, math and science, art, technology, and music. Chapter 12 outlines considerations to be made when planning play space. Chapter 13, the final chapter, examines how we can take play to the next level in our practice.

The book features

- *Opening Quotes:* Each chapter begins with a quote that is intended to offer the reader "a place to begin" in thinking about one aspect of child's play.

- *Stories from the Field:* At the beginning of each chapter, practitioners share their perspective on the topical issue the chapter will address. These messages help set the stage for you to become familiar with how theory has informed practice, how new learning is essential in the field, and how the combination of theory and practice guides early learning practitioners in their daily work with children and families.

- *Learning Outcomes:* Each chapter begins with a series of learning outcomes that will be presented in the chapter. This helps the reader to become familiar with the core concepts of each chapter.

- *Words of Wisdom Boxes:* These boxes highlight perspectives on the chapter topic from Canadian experts.

- *Stop . . . Think . . . Discuss . . . Reflect Boxes:* These boxes provide probing questions that are intended for you and members of your learning community to explore and to trigger ideas, passion, and research interests beyond the content presented in the chapter.

- *Key Terms with Definitions:* Throughout the text, key terms are shown in boldface and definitions presented in the margins.

- *Chapter Summary:* At the conclusion of each chapter, there are key points identified that summarize the core concepts of the chapter and reflect the learning outcomes presented at the onset of the chapter.

- *Review Questions:* Each chapter offers the learner questions to explore based on the content of the chapter.

- *Making Connections—Theory to Practice:* Each chapter provides scenarios based on the content of the chapter. This section is intended to help the reader make the connection between theory and practice.
- *For Further Research:* This end-of-chapter section provides suggestions for further discussion, exploration, and research. The exercises are intended to trigger debate, perspectives, and connect theory and research to practice.
- *Additional Reading and Weblinks:* The listed resources support you in exploring further information on the core content presented.

# SUPPLEMENTS

*Playing and Learning in Early Childhood Education* is accompanied by the following supplements, which all instructors will find helpful:

An **Instructor's Manual** which offers case studies, teaching and learning methods for consideration, and other resources to support active learning with students.

A **Test Item File** (in Microsoft Word format) consisting of multiple choice, short answer/short essay, and essay questions.

**PowerPoint Presentations** for each chapter that help to highlight and illustrate key themes in the text.

Please note that all of these supplements are available online. They can be downloaded by instructors from a password-protected location on Pearson Canada's online catalogue (**vig.pearsoned.ca**). Simply search for the text, then click on "Instructor" under "Resources" in the left-hand menu. Contact your local sales representative for further information.

**CourseSmart for Instructors** CourseSmart goes beyond traditional expectations—providing instant, online access to the textbooks and course materials you need at a lower cost for students. And even as students save money, you can save time and hassle with a digital eTextbook that allows you to search for the most relevant content at the very moment you need it. Whether it's evaluating textbooks or creating lecture notes to help students with difficult concepts, CourseSmart can make life a little easier. See how when you visit www.coursesmart.com/instructors.

**CourseSmart for Students** CourseSmart goes beyond traditional expectations—providing instant, online access to the textbooks and course materials you need at an average savings of 60 percent. With instant access from any computer and the ability to search your text, you'll find the content you need quickly, no matter where you are. And with online tools like highlighting and note-taking, you can save time and study efficiently. See all the benefits at www.coursesmart.com/students.

# ACKNOWLEDGMENTS

We would like to sincerely thank Pearson Canada for providing us with this opportunity. We are particularly grateful to our developmental editor Rema Celio and acquisitions editor Joel Gladstone who have worked with us throughout the project. Your guidance and support have allowed this project to evolve. We thank the reviewers whose feedback helped us shape the content and the layout of the text, including the following:

Dale Long, Seneca College
Karyn Callaghan, Mohawk College
Cathy Coulthard, Sheridan College
Kathrina Lalog, Seneca College
Shivani Rikhy, Mount Royal University

We wish to sincerely thank Ingrid Timmermans for introducing us to each other. We also thank Ingrid for sharing with us her knowledge about and writing on art and young children. A major portion of Ingrid's work has influenced and is reflected in Chapter 9.

We thank Passant Elalfy for her support in assisting us with the various aspects of research required.

We would like to thank all of the children, families, and early learning centres who have allowed us to use their photos throughout the book. The photos help us emphasize key aspects of the content through the actions of the children. We would especially like to thank Diane's friend, Rosalba Bortolotti, Director of the Acorn School, for being so generous with sharing her photos and stories of children at play. We also thank Sally Kotsopoulos at Ryerson University for the various photos that she has shared with us. We are also extremely grateful to our colleagues and acquaintances who agreed to offer their words of wisdom for each of the chapters.

We would like to thank our families, extended families, and friends. A project such as this is only made possible when families and friends are encouraging, supportive, and positive. We appreciate your patience with us and your encouragement along the way. Thank you for listening to us, challenging our thoughts and perspectives, and helping us engage in and focus on making this project the best it can be.

**Diane Kashin:** In particular, I wish to thank my husband Lorne, my children Jeremy, Ben, and Dory for the space, support, and the inspiration to take on new challenges. Finally, thank you to my mother whose joy for life reminds me that play is a lifelong endeavour.

**Beverlie Dietze:** I wish to thank my brothers, sisters, aunt, and friend Sue for encouraging me to embark on new challenges and for always believing in me. Your encouragement has led me to examine, explore, and discover so many new ideas, perspectives, and opportunities. Thank you, Peter, for continuing to support me in my quest to gain new knowledge and make a difference in teaching and learning.

Without your support and encouragement these learning adventures would not occur. You are a great husband and partner in learning!

Finally, we want to acknowledge that this project brought us together as new colleagues. We are grateful to Pearson Canada for allowing us to engage in such a stimulating, collaborative learning experience. We have challenged each other, we have mentored each other, learned significantly from each other, and we have shared a collective spirit, enthusiasm, and commitment that helped us bring this project to fruition.

— Beverlie Dietze
— Diane Kashin

# 1 Exploring the Foundations of Play

## Learning Outcomes

After exploring this chapter you should be able to

- discuss five perspectives on play and describe the similarities and differences of each perspective;

- explain the relationship of the United Nations Convention on the Rights of the Child to play;

- describe how obesity, outdoor play, culture, consumerism, technology, and poverty impact the quality of play and child development;

- discuss how various theorists such as Comenius, Locke, Rousseau, Pestalozzi, and Froebel, have influenced early learning practitioner's knowledge and practice about play and learning; and

- describe the Canadian Association for the Education of Young Children's (CAYC) position on play for preschool and school-aged children.

## Stories from the Field: Practitioner to Student

When I began my college education, I thought that taking an early childhood education course would be easy—after all I had been a camp counsellor, a swimming instructor, and I was a babysitter in my neighbourhood during my teen years. I also grew up in a family with parents who believed in providing children with active learning experiences.

Prior to starting the compulsory play course, "I thought, oh this is going to be a bit boring—why do we need to study about play? Play is play—that is what children do." I soon realized that play is a comprehensive, complicated process that children engage in. Children make play look easy and natural, but it is not. Each aspect of their play has a developmental purpose—it is laying foundation for academic, social, physical, and emotional life skills.

If I have any advice for students enrolled in Early Childhood Education programs, it is to carefully explore the concepts presented in your play course. Why? Because early learning practitioners who acquire a thorough understanding about the relationship between play and child development gain incredible skills in being able to figure out the types of experiences that would be most appropriate to help children grow and develop.

I believe that understanding the various facets of play is an important investment in your time. Every day I use my knowledge about play in my work with children. Understanding play becomes your guide, your touch point, your reference, and your anchor for programming, interacting, and respecting the important work of children—that is playing.

*Melinda, ECE Graduate, 2005*

# CHAPTER PREVIEW

Play—what is it? Does play have a defined "textbook" meaning? Is child's play the same across cultures, genders, and age groups? Are there different types of play? Does it differ from urban to rural environments? Do children go through stages of play? Do all children play? Does play impact us later in life?

As you can see, the word *play* brings forth many questions. It may also generate many images in your mind. For some, we may have fond memories of our childhoods—being in dress-up clothes, making mud cakes, or playing with a favourite toy. Others may think about playing outdoors with friends and the freshly cut grass clippings while others may reflect upon the neat block structure they built with others at their child care centre. For some of you reading this, you may have vague or limited memories of play and childhood. There are many reasons for this, which may include stressful childhoods, lack of opportunity for quality play experiences, or limited exposure to other children and group play. Play is an important part of childhood. As you explore the concepts of play, we hope that it will trigger positive childhood memories. Ultimately, you will begin to connect the theory of play with the play experiences that you observe children participating in.

Child's play has long been important to early learning practitioners, parents, and professionals who have an interest in child development and human thought (Rutherford & Rogers, 2003). Throughout history, in every culture, children have played. It is a vehicle in which cultural attributes are passed from one generation to another. Through play, children communicate their feelings and ideas to other children and adults. Children gain physical development and experimentation opportunities. In essence, the subject of child's play is complex as it formulates the foundation for child development. Understanding child's play is pivotal to the role and responsibilities of early learning practitioners.

Observing children's play is one of the most important roles and responsibilities of early learning practitioners. That may seem strange to you at this point in your studies, but as you engage in your studies, you will note that the young child is at the centre of early childhood programming, and it is through play that children learn and develop. Early learning practitioners examine the types of play that children participate in and use their observations to acquire information about the child so that appropriate programming may be organized that will expand play opportunities. Examining children's play, visualizing how it may evolve, and reflecting on what has been observed and heard, sparks many questions, ideas, and pathways for the early learning practitioner and children. Play becomes part of the road map for programming. Observing children's play is discussed in depth in Chapter 3 and is a dominant theme that is presented in each of the upcoming chapters.

This chapter will introduce you to different perspectives about what play is and its importance in the lives of young children. Learning about the complexity of play will help you in understanding how a child's play becomes your guide for facilitating quality programming experiences—one that meets the child's developmental needs, learning, and interests.

## WORDS OF WISDOM

### An Expert Describes the Importance of Play to Child Development

Jane Hewes is a Canadian expert on play. In *Let the Children Play: Nature's Answer to Early Learning* published by the Canadian Council on Learning, she makes a strong case for play because of its significant contribution to young children's development. According to Hewes, being able to play is one of the key developmental tasks of early childhood. In fact, play is the leading source of development in the early years. Essential for children's optimal development, play stimulates physical, social, and cognitive development in the early years. Children need time to play for the sake of playing.

# THE ORIGIN OF THE WORD *PLAY*

Scott (2008) suggests that the origin of the word *play* is unknown. It is thought that the English adopted the word *pleien* meaning to "dance, leap for joy, and rejoice" from the Dutch in the later Middle Ages (c. fourteenth century). They translated it as *pleg(i)an*, which means "to exercise, or frolic." Throughout history, movement and motion have been synonymous with the word *play*.

Johnson, Christie, and Wardle (2005) indicate that "the Greek words for play and education were the same (*paitheia*); distinguished aurally by whether the accent was on the second syllable (pie deé ah: education) or the last syllable (pie dee ah́: play)" (p. 3). Both words are derived from the Greek word for child, *pais*.

## Defining Play

Discussions about play and learning, the definition of play, and the role of adults in children's play are essential tenets in early childhood literature. The literature clearly articulates that children in all cultures learn through play. It is through play that children acquire knowledge, skills, and abilities that become the foundation for lifelong learning and development. Play is serious business for young children (Pascal, 2009).

When we examine the literature on defining play, there is a clear distinction made between work and play. The concept of play differs from the concept of work in that play is a self-chosen activity rather than prescribed. Play is a process rather than a predicted outcome or product (Wiltz & Fein, 2006). Work has a defined intent and prescribed outcome. However, some would argue that play is a child's work.

Play is serious business for young children (Pascal, 2009).

According to Froebel (1887) children learn through play. It is serious and of significant importance to a child's development. Because play and learning are interrelated, Froebel advocated that programming for young children must be play-focused and that children have exposure to play experiences in both indoor and outdoor environments (Dietze, 2006).

There are many perspectives on what the term *play* means. Henniger (2002) suggests that it is difficult to choose one definition that clearly defines play and its attributes. We need to think of play in broader terms—from building roadways in the sand, to building elaborate block structures, to rolling down hills or playing on a structure. Rather than provide you with one specific definition, we invite you to examine the following five perspectives and determine if there is one that resonates with you or if there are parts of each of the statements that you support.

- "The generally accepted definition of play would include three large categories: (1) sensori-motor play (large and small motor activity); (2) symbolic play, which involves representational abilities and includes the fantasy play of socio-dramatic play; and (3) construction play, which involves symbolic product formation" (Wolgang, Stannard, & Jones, 2001, p. 2).
- Play is a multidimensional, developmental (Sutton-Smith, 1997) activity expressed through a variety of forms and actions (Tannock, 2008).
- "Play is the purest, the most spiritual, product of man at this stage and is at once the prefiguration and imitation of the total human life—of the inner, secret, natural life in man and in all things. It produces, therefore, joy, freedom, satisfaction, repose within and without, and peace with the world. The springs of all good rest within it and go out from it" (Froebel, 1889, p. 25).
- "I believe that play is as fundamental a human disposition as loving and working" (Elkind, 2004, p. 36).
- For educators from Reggio Emilia of Italy, whose pre-primary schools have inspired others around the world, play is highly valued for its ability to promote development, but no more so than the complex and long-term projects in which children and teachers become engaged (New, 1998).

There is no one perspective that encapsulates the importance, the breadth, or the complexities of play. As you examine the various tenets of play, you will gain insight into why play is pivotal to childhood for learning and development. Understanding the concept of play and the influence that adults have on a child's play is complicated. It requires early learning practitioners to examine it from a variety of perspectives. Schwartzman (1978) says that "[t]oday we are still flying theoretical 'kites' in the study of play—only now there are more of them. This is as it should be because play requires a multiperspective approach. . . . and resists any attempts to define it rigidly" (p. 325).

In order for an activity to be considered play, the experience must include "a measure of inner control, ability to bend or invent reality, and a strong internally based motivation for playing (Bergen, 2009; Neumann, 1971). If parents or early learning practitioners try to label experiences as play, but in reality have prescriptive requirements to the activity, this becomes work not play. For example, it is really impossible to play with flash cards whose purpose is to have a child

*Photo 1.1    Children's play is stimulated by new experiences, materials, and the environment.*

memorize something depicted on each card. This is not playing. Young children quickly develop the skills to be able to differentiate between pure play experiences and work being disguised as play.

As you read about play and begin to formulate the meaning of play for you in your role as an early learning practitioner, you will note that there are many national and international organizations such as the International Play Association (Canada) and the Canadian Association for Young Children (CAYC) that advocate for society to ensure children have the right and the opportunities to play. " 'Promoting the Child's Right to Play' is fundamental to all aspects of child development and is a key component in preserving community and culture, in the broadest sense" (International Play Association, Canada, 2006, p. 1).

Throughout this book, the multi-facets of play will be examined. Think about the following as key reasons why early learning practitioners value play.

**Play**

- is a natural activity for children;
- helps children understand their social, community, and cultural world;
- supports children in understanding how to communicate and cooperate with other children. This sets the foundation for building social competence which is linked to the development of resiliency;
- impacts the child's social, moral, and emotional development, which is essential to support stress, conflict management, and resiliency;

- is a vehicle that influences the development of creativity, flexibility, and problem solving; and
- capitalizes on a child's natural curiosity and exuberance. (Pascal, 2009)

According to Pascal (2009), when play experiences are well designed, children are given the opportunities to draw upon their imagination, individual interests, their emerging capacities, and their sense of curiosity and inquiry. Young children become highly motivated in the right play environment.

Many authors begin textbooks with a discussion on play by looking at it from a historical perspective. In this book, we highlight the United Nations Convention on the Rights of the Child followed by some of the current societal issues that impact play, before examining some of the historical perspectives. We have taken this approach because both the international treaty and our societal issues help us formulate our views and perspectives on play and its role in early learning environments. It also stretches us to think about how children's development can positively or negatively be affected by their play environment. As you review this section, we encourage you to think about how you envision our society contributes to, or erodes, children's play.

# THE UNITED NATIONS CONVENTION ON THE RIGHTS OF THE CHILD

The UN Convention on the Rights of the Child is an international treaty that outlines universally accepted rights for children. It provides countries such as Canada with a benchmark that is used to measure the treatment of children. It amalgamates a variety of agreements into one document, including the Declaration of the Rights of the Child adopted in 1959.

The Convention was officially approved by the United Nations in 1989. Canada ratified the Convention on the Rights of the Child on December 13, 1991. By ratifying the treaty, Canada made a commitment to comply with the articles of the Convention. This means that Canada has made a commitment to protect and enhance the basic rights of children through its policies, programs, and services. Article 31 refers to child's play. You will also note below other articles of the treaty that are interrelated to child's play.

**Article 31 of the UN Convention states:**

1. That every child has the right to rest and leisure, to engage in play and recreational activities appropriate to the age of the child and to participate freely in cultural life and the arts.

2. That member governments shall respect and promote the right of the child to participate fully in cultural and artistic life and shall encourage the provision of appropriate and equal opportunities for cultural, artistic, recreational and leisure activity.

*Photo 1.2   Play is the right of every child.*

**Article 3** states that, in all actions concerning children, the best interests of the child shall be a primary consideration.

**Article 12** indicates the child has the right to express his/her views freely and have them considered.

**Article 19** focuses on the prevention of child abuse and childhood injury. Adults have a responsibility to ensure that children have safe environments for their play episodes.

**Article 23** tells us that children with disabilities have the right to recreation and the fullest possible social integration and individual development.

**Article 29** states that education should be directed to a broad range of developmental areas, including the child's personality, talents, and mental and physical abilities.

**Article 30** states that children of ethnocultural minorities, or of indigenous origin, have the right to their own culture. This includes their forms of play/recreation.

# THE IMPORTANCE OF EXAMINING SOCIETAL ISSUES AND CHILD'S PLAY

There are a number of societal issues that impact play. As identified in Figure 1.1, we highlight six societal issues that have a correlation to play and active living. Early learning practitioners and student practitioners can help bring play back into the lives of young children by making a commitment to promote play opportunities. Quality play experiences are one of the most important strategies that will contribute to children developing the foundation for a healthy lifestyle.

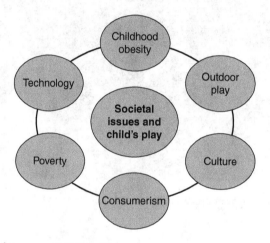

**Figure 1.1**  *Societal Issues and Child's Play*

## Childhood Obesity

There are some children living in Canada who are considered overweight or obese due to defined health conditions or genetic dispositions. Others may be labelled as overweight or obese due to environmental conditions. These environmental conditions may include family role models, parenting styles, a lack of active living experiences, a lack of availability of healthy food choices, living conditions, or poverty.

Today, overweight and obesity among children is categorized as an "epidemic" in Canada. Currently, Canada ranks the fifth highest country out of 34 Organisation for Economic Co-operation and Development (OECD) countries for childhood obesity in the developed world. Twenty-six percent of young Canadians aged 2 to 17 years are overweight or obese. About 55 percent of our First Nations children living on reserves are either overweight or obese and 41 percent of Aboriginal children living off reserves are considered overweight or obese. In 1978, 12 percent of children aged 2 to 17 years were overweight. Three percent were obese. By 2004, 18 percent of this age group was overweight and 8 percent obese (Katzmarzyk, 2004). The obesity rates continue to increase.

The increases in overweight and obesity conditions are similar among boys and girls. The number of children between the ages of 2 and 5 years who were overweight or obese has remained constant from 1978 to 2004. However, during that same period, the overweight/obesity rate for children aged 6 to 11 years increased from 13 percent to 26 percent (Katzmarzyk, 2004).

In a report prepared for the House of Commons, Canada entitled Healthy Weights for Healthy Kids, (2007), it states that "First Nations children between the ages of 9 and 11 years are twice as likely to be overweight as their 3- to 5-year-old counterparts (29% versus 13%)" (p. 2). These findings are of major concern to First Nations community leaders, governments, policymakers and children advocates.

Obesity issues during childhood fluctuate across the Canadian landscape. For example, in the Healthy Weights for Healthy Kids report (2007), it states that "In 2004, the combined overweight/obesity rate of those aged 2 to 17 years was significantly above the national average (26%) in Newfoundland and Labrador (36%), New Brunswick (34%), Nova Scotia (32%) and Manitoba (31%)" (p. 2).

Children with poor diets and lack of exercise are vulnerable to an array of health problems. The health implications for children who are overweight or obese include chronic diseases such as high blood pressure, Type 2 diabetes, heart attack, joint problems, and mental health issues. For example, a 2010 study released by Statistics Canada found that just under 1 percent of Canadians aged 6 to 19 years have high blood pressure, while 2.1 percent are on the borderline of developing the condition. Janssen, a co-researcher in the study found that elevated blood pressure levels were most pronounced among the youth who were overweight or obese and high blood pressure rates were significantly higher among overweight or obese girls aged 6 to 11 years and boys aged 12 to 19 years.

Appropriate role modelling, nutrition, and active play are vital to children and their wellness. Children require appropriate play spaces, where they can run, jump, climb, and be free to explore. Children who have access to interesting tools and resources in their play space will become intrigued and want to use them in their play. The use of the tools and resources increases the potential for children to engage in more physical movement. This ideal lifestyle must be role-modelled during a child's early years in order to establish this as a daily living practice and be continued throughout childhood.

## Outdoor Play

There are many reasons cited in the literature as to why there has been a reduction in the amount of outdoor play young children participate in. Some suggest it is because of the concerns adults have for childhood safety. Others indicate it is because children will be injured or bullied while playing outdoors (Johnson, Christie, & Wardle, 2005). Then there are those who express concern that the urban and rural play spaces are not suitable for children's play. As outlined in the previous section, despite the concerns, there is sufficient evidence to suggest that children who are not active are at high risk of becoming overweight and develop a host of diseases that may follow them into adulthood.

As you begin to examine play, you will soon recognize that there are many benefits of outdoor play for children that can't be emulated in indoor environments. For example, children's power of observation of their environment is much sharper

---

### How overweight and obesity are defined

Overweight and obesity are generally defined based on a Body Mass Index (BMI) screening tool that calculates weight and height using a standard formula. Generally the weight in kilograms is divided by the square of height in metres. Cole, Belizzi, Flegal and Dietz (2000) identify a BMI of 25 or greater is considered overweight and a BMI of 30 or greater is identified as obesity (Canning, Courage, & Frizzell, 2004).

**Photo 1.3**    *All aspects of a child's development are influenced with outdoor play.*

in outdoors than in indoors (Rudolph & Cohen, 1984). The outdoor environment has a significant impact on a child's developing
motor skills and self-concept. Outdoor play stimulates social play
because there is more space than indoors, the noise levels are less
distracting in outdoors, and there are more active play opportunities. The outdoor play environment is where children gain overall
control over their bodies—a control that is essential to their total
development.

Outdoor play impacts a child's physiological and psychological development. When children play outdoors they gain exposure
to light and sunshine. Children need the stimulation of the sun
and light to nourish the human body (Liberman, 1991). The
exposure to light decreases the heart rate, blood pressure, respi-
ratory rate, blood sugar, and lactic acid in the blood following
active movement. The active movement increases energy, strength,
endurance, tolerance to stress, and the ability of the blood to
absorb and carry oxygen (Kime, 1980). These key bodily functions
influence cognitive, physical, emotional, and social development.

Children who do not have sufficient outdoor play are at risk
of experiencing vitamin D deficiency. This is a critical vitamin
needed for the development of the healthy vertebrate skeleton
during the preschool and pre-adolescent years.

Although there is sufficient evidence to support outdoor play
in early learning programming, it continues to be one of the
major deficiencies in program design. Organizations such as the Canadian
Association for Young Children (CAYC) and The National Association for the
Education of Young Children (NAEYC) maintain that since children's physical
development is occurring so rapidly, children need daily, active, outdoor play
experiences to use large muscle skills, to learn about their outdoor environments,
and to experience freedom not always possible indoors. Hewes (2006) suggests
that adults—parents and early learning practitioners—must take the same care in
designing the outdoor play environment as they pay to the indoor environment
because of the growing body of evidence on the developmental significance of contact with nature, light, and the quality of play experiences. You will read more about
these components in Chapter 5, which is devoted specifically to outdoor play.

Outdoor play is an integral part of the early learning experiences. It requires
planning for all types of weather across our Canadian landscape. The life practices
established during the early years affect later life—children need to be exposed to
outdoor play as part of their daily living routine.

## Technology

Today's children have far less face-to-face play experiences with other children and
their natural world than 20 years ago. There are many reasons for this; one of
which is the exposure to technology. Children as young as 2 years of age are now
exposed to technology as part of their daily living experiences. In some instances,

adults are using technology to entertain children or using it as a form of play, rather than the active play experiences that are essential for children. As you will read in Chapter 10, there is great debate about the role that technology should play in childhood. Parents, educators, and policymakers continue to examine the relationship, benefits, and dangers of mixing child's play with technology. Many advocates of play continue to express concerns that technology must not erode child's play.

*Photo 1.4    There is controversy on whether children need technology in their early years.*

## Culture

Canada is home to one of the world's most diverse populations and has self-identified as a multicultural society (Canadian Heritage, 2007). It is one of the few countries with a national policy that focuses on respect for diversity, multiculturalism, and anti-racism (Friendly & Prabhu, 2010).

"Culture refers to the underlying beliefs, patterns of behaviour and assumptions of a group that are passed on from one generation to the next. Culture is developed from a society's key values" (Dietze, 2006, p. 25). Early learning and child care programs in Canada service families with differing beliefs and values on a variety of subjects, including the value of child's play to development.

Around the world, play appears to be a universal activity for most children, provided that they are not being exposed to events such as famine, war, or natural disasters. The amount of time and attention invested in child's play is influenced by family, community, resources, and beliefs about the relationship of play to development. Despite parental and societal beliefs about play, children have the innate ability to take articles such as dolls, rocks, balls, or wood and other materials within their environment and use them for play. Hughes (1999) calls play a "true cultural universal." Play is an "enculturing" process—it is the foundation for children to learn about their culture and the diverse communities in which we live.

Each family and culture brings important values and diversity to our Canadian society. As identified by Friendly and Prabhu (2010), early childhood is the prime time for young children to learn about and develop positive thoughts, feelings, and respect for diversity. These attributes are effectively illustrated in early learning programs that philosophically incorporate social inclusion into both policy and practice.

*Photo 1.5*   *Some families prefer their children not to play outdoors in the Canadian winter climate while others believe that it is essential for their child's development.*

Early learning practitioners have a responsibility to become familiar with common practices to ensure diversity is understood and appreciated. The play space and play experiences introduce children to materials and experiences that broaden a child's knowledge about life. Families collectively are brought together in an effort to build a strong family–child–community appreciation.

Parental perspectives on play may differ from one region of the country to another or from one family to another. For example, parents who have grown up in a country such as Norway, where their culture values outdoor life and freedom to explore, will have different perspectives on outdoor play during the winter months than parents who come from a warm climate and who have not had life experiences in the colder temperatures and weather conditions such as snow. Children coming from rural Canada and from farming communities have different play experiences from children living in an urban environment. Families who have immigrated from Middle Eastern countries to Canada may exhibit different beliefs about child-rearing, family values, and the use of natural resources such as water than European immigrants.

Below, you will find aspects of research findings that illustrate some of the potential cultural differences in relation to play. Examine each of the statements below. Then, think about how these differences may impact the play experiences in early learning centres, blended families with different cultural orientations, neighbourhoods, and your personal understanding of play and its importance for children.

- Whiting (1975) indicates that children play more when a culture supports them roaming about the community playing with whomever they choose.
- European–American mothers emphasize independence and self-expression. Parents of Chinese descent focus on social harmony and respect for rules (Haight, Wang, Fung, Williams, & Mintz, 1999). These parents require play to concentrate on proper conduct.
- Parents of Indonesian descent respond to an infant's needs until the child is mobile; then older siblings become the play partners with the child. The siblings scaffold the play, while the parents provide the guidance and direction for correct child behaviour.
- Parents of Japanese descent focus their child's play on social interactions and communications (Tamis-LeMonda, Bornstein, Cyphers, Toda, & Ogina, 1992).
- Parents from countries with a shortage of water, such as Jordan, may not appreciate children using water as part of their daily play experiences.

Play is influenced by a child's culture and environment. When children from different cultures come to early learning places, practitioners must consider each of the cultural attributes that children bring to the environment and determine how to best support each child. For example, in 2006/2007, in Vancouver, 55 percent of primary students did not have English as a first language (Pence & Pacini-Ketchabaw, 2008). This finding would be consistent among larger cities across Canada. This means many children come to early learning programs with their **cultural norms** and language differences; some of which may be common among families or conversely very different. Early learning practitioners work with the parents and children to provide a play environment that meets the needs of all children in the early learning centre.

For those early learning practitioners who have not been exposed to cultural diversity, it is important to learn about the children's cultures. This helps you to reach beyond your sphere of knowledge and contributes to you gaining insight into the relationship of culture to play. Networking with colleagues, families, and

**Cultural norms** are behavioural patterns or beliefs that are common among specific groups of people. Such behaviours and beliefs are generally learned from parents, extended families, peers, and other significant people in the child's life.

**Photo 1.6**    *This child shares with his mother his portfolio that documents some of his play experiences. This parent takes an active role in revisiting play experiences with her son.*

professionals internationally is a valuable strategy to acquire an understanding of how children's cultural backgrounds impact play and development and how the cultural attributes may be exhibited in play episodes.

   Early learning practitioners benefit from observing and listening to children during play. Children's conversations with their peers during dramatic play provide early learning practitioners with valuable insight into a child's cultural, family, and community celebrations and traditions (Jalongo & Isenberg, 2004). These insights guide early learning practitioners into the types of new materials and experiences that may trigger a child's interest and expand their knowledge about play, culture, and problem solving.

## Stop . . . Think . . . Discuss . . . Reflect

Think about your childhood. Can you think of experiences with children from other cultures? Did you play with children from your culture only? Were you guided in playing based on cultural norms? Were there play experiences that you engaged in that your parents indicated were not appropriate? Why or why not?

# CONSUMERISM

As young children spend more time connected to technology and television, invasive marketing to children has dramatically increased. Marketing toys, food, and entertainment is commonplace. The industry magazine *KidsScreen* suggests that advertising agencies are interested in the infancy-to-three-year-old demographic because they are trying to bombard children with understanding branding at a young age. Children today often recognize brands and status items by the age of 3 or 4. Beder (1998) indicates that in one study conducted "52 percent of 3-year-olds and 73% of 4-year-olds 'often or almost always' ask their parents for specific brands" (p. 101). Brand loyalties and consumer habits formed during childhood will be carried through to adulthood.

Canadian consumers spend in excess of $1.15 billion on toys annually (Canadian Toy Testing Council, 2001), while the toy manufacturers spend millions annually on toy advertising. The advertising of toys is generally the child's first exposure to consumerism.

The Canadian Toy Testing Council indicates that one of the biggest concerns about the marketing of toy ads is the exaggeration of the product. Young children, because of their inabilities to distinguish fact from fiction, think that particular toys have the capability of doing many neat things because of the advertising they have been exposed to on television. This is of concern, because children between 2 and 5 years of age do not have the cognitive abilities to differentiate between a TV program and a commercial, or reality and fantasy.

With advertising now being expanded to include television, print, and etailing via the internet to children, the Canadian Paediatric Society is examining the impact of advertising on the lives of children, especially as they deal with the number of children who are overweight or obese. They suggest that most food advertising during children's programming shows fast foods, soft drinks, candy, and pre-sweetened cereals. The commercials for healthy food make up only 4 percent of the advertising shown.

McNeal (1992) outlines the stages in the evolution of a child consumer.

- **Infancy to 2 years**—children accompany parents shopping where there are all sorts of products displayed. These children are usually placed in a shopping cart where items are placed at their eye level.

- **Age 2 to 3 years**—children accompany parents and begin requesting items. They begin to make the connections between television advertising and store items. The more the exposure to television, the more the children begin to express "wants." During this phase, children begin to use strategies such as whining, screaming, or tears to influence parents in providing them with desired items.

- **Age 3 to 4 years**—children accompany parents and begin selecting items that they desire. At this phase, they begin to exhibit a desire for specific brands of items. Children have made many connections—they are able to express wants—to the stores where the products are available, to finding the items in the particular stores. This is defined as the stage in which a child expresses an understanding of the want-satisfaction process in a market-driven society.

- **Age 4 to 5 years**—children accompany parents and make independent purchases. This is the phase when children choose their products and take their products to the check-out counters.

According to the Media Awareness Network (2010), the concerns about how advertising impacts children have led to some jurisdictions banning advertising to children. For example, in Québec there is a ban on all print and broadcast advertising aimed at children under thirteen. Similarly, Sweden has banned advertisements aimed at children under 12 and it is lobbying the European Union members to adopt similar policies.

**Media literacy** with young children refers to children being able to view the media messages as seen on television, in print, or on the internet and to be able to make meaning or connections with the message based on their life experiences.

Early learning practitioners play a role in educating children about consumerism and reducing the need for children to express the "I want . . . I need" statements. Materials available to support children's play should be chosen for the versatility they offer children. Products that do not promote play, such as many of the electronic toys, or materials that promote sedentary action, should be replaced with more appropriate items. Early learning practitioners discuss with children, (especially school-aged children) the intent of the advertising in relation to the characteristics of particular products. Over time, with appropriate adult guidance, children can begin to develop an understanding of **media literacy**. Further information on electronic toys will be highlighted in Chapter 10.

# Stop . . . Think . . . Discuss . . . Reflect

How does consumerism impact child's play? Why? What signs might you observe in an early learning and child care centre that would lead you to be concerned about consumerism and the children? How might your consumerism impact children and families? Do consumerism and technology depend on the socioeconomic status of children and their families? Why or why not?

## Poverty

Canada is ranked 20th out of 30 of the world's wealthiest nations, as defined by the Organisation for Economic Co-operation and Development; yet, according to the 2009 Report Card on Child and Family Poverty in Canada, more than one million children living in Canada are growing up in poverty—this translates into one in nine children living in poverty. These numbers do not reflect the one in four First Nations children who now grow up in poverty. The rate of child poverty has remained at about 12 percent for the past two decades (Statistics Canada). The Report Card also indicates that while children under the age of 18 make up 22 percent of Canada's population, they represent 37 percent of those using food banks.

Child poverty also impacts the child's levels of health and education and behavioural attributes. This is reinforced in the Determinants of Health as identified by the Public Health Agency of Canada (2010). There are 12 key determinants, which include income and social status, education and literacy, physical and social environments, gender and culture. The quality of play is influenced by these determinants. Access to play materials, peers, space, and positive role modelling are common factors that positively or negatively affect play experiences.

Poverty adds stress to families. Parental stress impacts the developing child. Families living in poverty suffer from more anxiety, depression, and irritability within the family unit (Driscoll & Nagel, 2005), which in turn impact a child's feelings of worth and the freedom needed to explore her or his environment. When parents have constant worries and stress about employment, housing, debt repayment, and needs of their children, they have less human resources and resiliency needed to nurture and support children. This in turn reduces the child's intuitive needs to express curiosity, creativity, independence, and self-control. Excessive stress, regardless of source, disrupts the neuron pathways of a child's developing brain, which can cause lifelong problems (National Scientific Council on the Developing Child, 2005). Children new to Canada and Aboriginal families are at greater risk of living in poverty (Canadian Children's Right Council, 2009).

Statistics indicate that children in low-income families suffer a higher rate of accidents during their play. One of the reasons identified is that some of the neighbourhoods where families in poverty live have more safety issues than more affluent neighbourhoods. The lack of quality play materials and equipment may also contribute to the higher level of accidents. When children do not have access to quality play experiences during the preschool years, they have reduced opportunities to develop the required physical, social, emotional, and cognitive developmental milestones during that expected phase of life. These milestones are essential for children to reach their full potential.

The simple story below as presented in *Toward a Healthy Future: Second Report on the Health of Canadians* (2006) makes linkages to health, child development, family, and play.

"Why is Jason in the hospital?

Because he has a bad infection in his leg.

But why does he have an infection?

Because he has a cut on his leg and it got infected.

But why does he have a cut on his leg?

Because he was playing in the junkyard next to his apartment building and there was some sharp, jagged steel there that he fell on.

But why was he playing in a junkyard?

Because his neighbourhood is kind of run down. A lot of kids play there and there is no one to supervise them.

But why does he live in that neighbourhood?

Because his parents can't afford a nicer place to live.

But why can't his parents afford a nicer place to live?

Because his Dad is unemployed and his Mom is sick.

But why is his Dad unemployed?

Because he doesn't have much education and he can't find a job.

But why . . .?"

## Stop . . . Think . . . Discuss . . . Reflect

Think of a 4-year-old child who lives with her mother and three siblings aged nine, three, and eighteen months respectively. They live on the tenth floor of a high-rise block in a two-bedroom apartment. How does this impact play? Is there room for the child to play? Is there room for movement? Will the child be able to keep materials in the environment so that she may return to play in an hour or the next day? If no, does that have any impact on play?

Now think of the outdoor experience. As the children go to the play area—it is the parking lot at the apartment. There is space for the child to run around, but the child is required to move each time a car comes. How does this impact play? Does the economic situation of the family influence the amount and type of play that children participate in? Why or why not?

## BRAIN DEVELOPMENT

In recent years, early learning practitioners have benefited from the brain development research that has been conducted by researchers from a variety of disciplinary backgrounds, including neuroscience, psychology, and child development. The research has confirmed that there is a relationship between play experiences and brain development. Bergen (2009) indicates that although it is difficult to find historical evidence, there has long been speculation that the evolution of the human brain and play has occurred simultaneously. During the first 5 to 6 years of life, play development and brain development have similar complementary features.

A child's brain is rapidly developing during the early years. Brain development is complex and is influenced by both biology and environment. The genes formulate the base for the development and the environment is the critical vehicle in how the brain develops (NCAC, 2007). The growth and development of the brain are influenced by a child's experiences and environment.

Human beings become a reflection of the environment in which they develop (Perry, 2004). For example, if young children are exposed to environments that are rich with experiences, safe, and predicable, "the child can grow to be self-regulating, thoughtful, and a productive member of family, community, and society" (Perry, 2004, p. 1). If a young child's world lacks supportive relationships, is chaotic, bored, and lacks limited nutrition and stimulation, "the child is more likely to become impulsive, aggressive, inattentive, and have difficulties with relationships" (p. 1). This reinforces the importance of children having access to appropriate environments.

The Canadian Institute of Child Health (2008) indicates that there are four principles of brain development:

- The child's environment shapes the brain's wiring;
- a child experiences the outside world through the senses—seeing, hearing, smelling, touching, and tasting—which enables the brain to create or modify connections;
- the brain operates on a 'use it or lose it' principle; and
- relationships with other people early in life are the major source of development of the emotional and social parts of the brain (p. 2).

Optimal brain development requires children to have positive life experiences that include good nutrition, a nourishing and stimulating environment, and quality relationships. If the child's environment is one that encourages creativity, exploration, and wonderment, there are more opportunities for optimal brain development. To be creative, to explore, and to wonder are components best achieved through quality play experiences.

The neural systems that shape our development happen during the early years. During the first four years of a child's life, his/her developing brain becomes organized based on the child's life experiences and environment. Perry (2004) indicates that the neurons, neural systems, and the brain change in a "user-dependent" way. The "synaptic connections increase and strengthen through repetition, or wither through disuse" (p. 1). The brain adapts to the experiences of each child.

Play experiences support brain development. Children who participate in consistent, enriched, and stimulating play experiences are in a position where optimal development is being fostered. Examine the following play experience. Marley, Marti, and Megan decided after reading the story of Elmer to make an elephant out of boxes. They began by discussing how they could make an elephant. They asked each other what they could use. Then finding boxes, fabric pieces, and glue they began to make an elephant. They had to determine how they were going to place the boxes. They engaged in dialogue that led to verbal negotiations among the children. They determined that they did not have anything to use for a trunk and they did not know what they could use. This required them to think about elephant trunks and then explore the types of materials that could be used to achieve their desired trunk. They also returned to the storybook so that they could examine the elephant's trunk. In consultation with their early learning practitioner, Suzanne, the children examined a variety of pieces of tubing; some of which were pliable and others rigid. They examined each to determine which would be most like an elephant's trunk. They determined that they needed to see a live elephant so that they could watch how the trunk moves. This required the children and the early learning practitioner to look up clips about elephants on the internet, as the children did not have access to a place where they could observe a live elephant. When children have opportunities for such play episodes, their play requires them to use their brain capacity to engage in language, problem solving, socialization skills, resource identification, and physical activity.

Recognizing that the child's brain is sculpted by her or his early experiences, which impact the development of the neural circuits known as the "synapses," the environment to which a child is exposed requires careful consideration by adults. As identified by National Childcare Accreditation Council (NCAC) (2007), "the architecture of the brain and skills are built in a hierarchical 'bottom-up' sequence. Foundations are therefore important, as higher level circuits are built on lower level circuits" (p. 8). When children do not have opportunities to achieve a solid foundation at the lower level, it is much more challenging for them to attain the higher-order skills because the lower-level circuits are not properly structured or wired.

When you think about children achieving optimal brain development opportunities, we ask that you reflect on play and adult–child relationships. Play is meant to be interactive so that children may respond to their environment and the environment is organized so that it triggers play. Play that is child-initiated and child-directed is more likely to meet the needs of each child than adult-imposed play. Play is one of the best investments that can be made to support the child's brain development and growth potential.

Observing child's play helps early learning practitioners know the correct timing for offering new, stimulating experiences in the play environment. For example, when children stop playing with materials, use the materials in a repetitive way, or play in particular experience centres, adults take this as a cue that there is a need to examine the child's interests and add new play options that will embrace the child with new challenges and opportunities to learn through play.

In this section, we have examined the current issues that impact child's play. Understanding these issues is important because they provide you with the conceptual lenses of why play is as essential today as it was from a historical perspective. Early learning practitioners benefit from continuously examining how play is interwoven with child development. Understanding the theory and application of play is an essential skill that early learning practitioners use in their daily practice.

## AN OVERVIEW OF THE CLASSICAL, MODERN, AND CONTEMPORARY PERSPECTIVES ON PLAY

Students frequently ask educators why there is a need to examine the classical, modern, and contemporary perspectives on subjects such as play. Does it help early learning practitioners meet the needs of young children today? The simple answer is yes. Examining the varying beliefs about play helps students and early learning practitioners explore how the historical values, beliefs, and philosophies shape and influence our practices today. The information guides us in questioning past practice, current practice, and future practice. This contributes to building new "knowledge."

For example, Froebel determined that children learn through play and that the quality of play is enhanced in an outdoor environment. Why would play be enhanced outdoors? If true, can this outdoor environment be emulated indoors? Froebel's writings indicate that outdoor environments are rich with natural surroundings which stimulate children to interact with nature and their environment while contributing to their physical environment (Dietze, 2006). The indoor environment sees children using more commercialized materials, thus changing the play focus. With this new information and knowledge, how do we change our practice?

When examining theories, they are usually classified in at least three time frames. **Classical theories** are those that were prevalent in the nineteenth century through to World War I. **Modern theories** are those that evolved after World War I (Frost et al., 2008; Scarlett & New, 2007; Johnston et al., 1999) and **contemporary theories** are those theories that are currently being examined and debated.

In Table 1.1, we present you with a brief overview of some of the more popular theorists, in chronological order, who have contributed to the literature on children's play. Each theorist has challenged previous perspectives and added new thinking and positions that lead us to ask more questions. This process brings new thinking and learning to practice.

You may have studied about these theorists in other courses and in other contexts. It is not an exhaustive listing; rather, we see it as an introduction to great thinkers. It is our intent to whet your appetite. You may become intrigued with a particular philosopher or a perspective. This may lead you to engage in further research. As you review the information that follows, we encourage you to think about what each perspective focuses on. Then, we ask that you think about your beliefs and values in relation to the position presented. Think about what play is, what it looks like, why children play, and what your role is in child's play. Examine how each theorist has influenced early learning and child care programs today. Determine if one orientation best represents your current thought processes on child's play and learning.

**Table 1.1**  *An Overview of the Classical, Modern and Contemporary Perspectives on Play*

**John Amos Comenius (1592–1670):** The family, especially the mother, has the most influence on children's learning. Children should have access to organized education in the child's language.

**Theory to Practice:** Children need to have access to active learning, and reading is a core element of play and learning experiences.

**John Locke (1632–1704):** Believed that children were born as blank tablets (Dietze, 2006) and that their life experiences determine who they are.

**Theory to Practice:** Children's play must be observed to determine the child's interests. Play experiences must be active and have acceptable role models. Children's environments need to be planned so that children are provided with pleasurable and successful opportunities.

**Jean Jacques Rousseau (1712–1778):** Distinguished childhood as a separate entity from adulthood. "Childhood has its own way of seeing, thinking, and feeling and nothing is more foolish than to try to substitute ours for them" (Rousseau, 1762, p. 14).

*(continued)*

**Theory to Practice:** Young children make intellectual and physical developmental gains when they engage in learning through exploration and discovery experiences in natural, play-based environments rather than structured formal school settings (Corbett, 1979). Children between the ages of five to twelve years of age require direct experience with nature, people and challenging objects (Frost, 1947).

**Johann Heinrich Pestalozzi's (1746–1827):** Identified that children need to be given the freedom to choose their play materials from nature-based, sensory rich environments. A natural environment provides children with the freedom to explore their natural surroundings, including plants and animals, and geography (Corbett, 1979). Children pass through developmental stages that require opportunities to learn through trial and error.

**Theory to Practice:** Children require a balance of personal exploration and input/presentations from an adult (Frost, 1947). This process triggers a child's curiosity in new directions and helps them expand their life experiences.

**Friedrich Wilhelm Froebel's (1782–1852):** Children require play based environments whereby there is a reciprocal relationship between God, humans and nature (Wellhousen, 2002). Through observations of children, Froebel determined children have an inherent need to play. This was seen as a radical discovery at that time in history (Maxim, 1993). Gardens were a major part of the children's learning environment as this allowed children to acquire scientific principles of nature and contribute to sustaining living things (Brosterman, 1997).

**Theory to Practice:** Children learn best when their experiences are grounded in quality indoor and outdoor play opportunities. Children need to connect with nature and to interact with specially-designed materials, based on their interests.

**John Dewey (1859–1952):** Children need to be in environments that "integrate with daily living, preserve social values including culture, and involve interacting with peers and adults. Children learn best by *doing* both physical and intellectual activities" (Dietze, 2006, p. 99).

**Theory to Practice:** Play experiences are planned according to children's needs, interests, and abilities. Children must have the freedom to take an active role in the play. This occurs naturally with children when the environment is intriguing and not restricted by unnecessary rules.

**Rudolph Steiner (1861–1925):** The play experiences must come from the children as this is how children spark their sense of curiosity and become motivated to play and explore. Children lead the play experiences, while the adults provide the conditions, such as the materials and opportunities.

**Theory to Practice:** Adults working with children must invest the time in getting to know the children so that the play environment reflects the children's interests and needs. The learning environment requires music, arts, and drama to be incorporated into the play environment.

**Maria Montessori (1870–1952):** A child's play is their work. Children require opportunities to make choices in the materials they wish to use. The adult demonstrates the sequential steps in using the materials.

**Theory to Practice:** Play has more of a focus on adult-child interactions and less child-initiated exploration. For example, if a child is interested in using the pink tower which is a classic stacking apparatus, the adult first demonstrates to the child the process of carrying the cubes to the area, and how the pink tower is built. Once the demonstration is complete, the child may pursue using the materials.

**Abraham Maslow (1890–1970):** Basic needs of food, safety/security; belonging/love must be met before children are able to include others in their sphere.

**Theory to Practice:** Children require environments with adults who support them in developing a sense of "belonging" and self-esteem.

**Lev Vygotsky (1896–1934):** Play is a *leading factor in development* and is impacted by one's community and culture. Group play is an essential venue for a child's social development because it is through play that children think about problems and solve them in new ways.

**Theory to Practice:** Young children benefit from mixed-age groups in their play because they gain new ideas, assistance or opportunities to explore when children with different skills and experiences come together.

**Jean Piaget (1896–1980):** Adults facilitate or guide the process of hands-on play experiences that are rich in exploration, wonderment, and discovery. Children create knowledge by being in environments that allow them to construct knowledge rather than adults providing it. Play experiences should be extended across an environment rather than confined to specific play centres.

**Theory to Practice:** Play experiences move from simple to complex, and are built and sequenced on previous experiences. Children have opportunities to repeat play experiences and in collaborative play environments rather than in solitary play spaces. If children express an interest in particular figurines that are in the block area, children should be given the freedom to take those figurines to the dramatic centre, the art area, or the garden.

**Loris Malaguzzi (1896–1994):** Culture, children, families, communities and teachers are equal partners in learning, with the play evolving in discovery-oriented environments (Henniger, 2002). Children are active participants in determining what their interests are and in their construction of learning. The learning environment is based on the belief that "things about children and for children and are only learned from children" (Edwards, Gandini & Forman, 1993, pp. 43–44). There is a balance between play and project work.

**Theory to Practice:** Using an emergent curriculum approach, the teacher carefully observes the children's interests and questions and offers concrete learning experiences. Adults and children of mixed age groups work together to choose and negotiate short and long term projects. During this process the children's learning is documented making it visible to be examined and used to provide direction for the next phase of play and learning experiences. A variety of mediums are used to document the child's learning including conversations, observations, photographs and two dimensional or three dimensional artistic representations.

**Erik Erikson (1902–1994):** Child's play supports the development of self-esteem. Through play, children learn how to manage their thoughts and feelings, without pressure from adults.

**Theory to Practice:** Children require access to peers and accessories such as those found in the dramatic centre. For example, think of a child who has just experienced one parent separating from the family unit. Through play, the child is able to act out feelings of loss, sadness, and anger that may be felt toward the parent who has left the home environment.

**David Weikart (1931–2003):** Children's play environments must be structured so that children are active learners and planners. Children require opportunities to have hands-on experiences with materials and environments that support them in planning, experiencing, and reviewing their activities and experiences. This is known as the *plan, do, and review* process.

**Theory to Practice:** Adults take on an active role in observing children and in posing questions that will extend a child's thinking and trigger their sense of curiosity to advance their exploration and learning.

**Howard Gardner (1943–):** Child's play requires exposure to the nine different intelligences. They are: linguistic, logical-mathematical, music, bodily-kinesthetic, spatial, interpersonal, intrapersonal, naturalistic, and existential.

**Theory to Practice:** Children require a variety of experiences that support all nine intelligences and that will appeal to their interests and learning styles.

Finally, as identified by Pence and Pacini-Ketchabaw (2008), when examining theoretical frameworks, we encourage practitioners to adopt "an inclusive approach that appreciates diverse theories, voices and methods" (p. 242). This will open your minds to think outside the box and examine the possibilities—the whys, the what ifs . . . or why not questions.

As you review the key contributions that each theorist has made, common themes evolve. The importance of play can be framed as

- being the natural way that a child learns;
- requiring adults to provide opportunities for children to explore and discover; and
- children requiring a combination of spontaneous and guided experiences.

Early learning and child care programs use philosophical perspectives as a foundation to determine how they will offer and execute play experiences conducive to the child. For example, in one early learning centre, the practitioners meet with small groups of children each morning and afternoon. During the meeting, each child discusses where he or she would like to begin their play. Discussion occurs on the resources that the child may require during the play episode. At another early learning centre, early learning practitioners prepare the environment by placing specific materials in each of the experience centres. The children are required to make choices about their play based on the materials available.

Research today continues to link the importance of play to child development. For example, the well-known Early Years Study, commissioned by the government of Ontario and completed by McCain and Mustard in 1999, clearly identifies the importance of the child's first six years of life. They describe this phase as critical or sensitive periods of development for particular parts of the brain. During this phase "a child's brain is exquisitely primed to receive sensory input and develop more advanced neural systems, through the wiring and sculpting process" (McCain & Mustard, 1999, p. 29). This reinforces the importance of play.

# THE CANADIAN ASSOCIATION FOR YOUNG CHILDREN POSITION STATEMENT ON PLAY FOR YOUNG CHILDREN

Children learn through play. Through their play children develop sensory motor control, eye-hand coordination, and problem solving skills. Physical, social, intellectual, and emotional development are all enhanced through play.

**CAYC believes that**
- Play is natural
- Play is essential for children

- Play is fun, exciting, adventurous, and open ended
- Play is creative and spontaneous
- Play is magical and complex
- Play is rewarding and stimulating
- Play is non-judgmental
- Play is directed by the children
- Play is full of choices and decision making opportunities
- Play is posing questions and hypothesizing
- Play is focused on the process and not on the product

## CAYC Believes That It Is Important for Children to Play

Children have a natural mechanism that enables them to make sense of their world—that mechanism is play. For over 100 years, researchers have studied play and have found that:

- Child-initiated play lays the foundation for learning and academic success. In play, children learn to interact with others, develop language skills, recognize and solve problems, and discover their human potential. Play helps children make sense of and find their play in the world (Alliance for Childhood, 2004).
- Play is regarded as interpretations of the situations of everyday life. In play, children interpret their experiences and give them life (Sandberg & Pramling-Samuelsson, 2003).
- Play is an integral part of a child's being. It is the business of childhood, and it has a unique and vital role in the whole educational process (Weininger, 1994).

## CAYC Believes That Children Need Time to Play

Studies show the links between play and many foundation skills and complex cognitive activities, such as memory, self-regulation, oral language development, successful school adjustment, and better social skills (Bodrova & Leong, 2004).

## CAYC Believes That Children Need Space to Play

We promote children's play by providing them with space, time, and materials; offering them support in building relationships, facilitating problem solving; presenting new ways of communicating ideas by attending to their spontaneous interests; and valuing their eagerness to learn about the world in which we all live together (Jones, 2003). Support for play means guiding the development of respectful interactions—CAYC believes that all children benefit from opportunities to be in safe, stimulating environments that encourage them to play.

## CAYC Believes That Children Need Certain Materials for Play

Expensive toys are not necessary, but natural materials and authentic items need to be provided tying children's experiences together, building connections of relationships within the children's world, thus helping them to make sense of their environment (Edwards, Gandini, & Forman, 1998). CAYC understands that a rich play environment happens through careful planning and observation of children. Early Childhood Educators use their knowledge about the potential play value of a variety of materials to offer children enriching play opportunities.

## CAYC Believes That Children Need Adults to Support and Enable Their Play

Adults take on many roles in order to facilitate children's play: stage manager, mediator, planner, communicator, player, and observer (Jones & Reynolds, 1992). CAYC appreciates that adults draw upon considerable expertise as they enable, support, and extend the play of groups of children in home, preschool, child care, and school settings.

# THE CANADIAN ASSOCIATION FOR YOUNG CHILDREN POSITION STATEMENT ON PLAY FOR SCHOOL-AGE CHILDREN

Developmentally, school-age children are seeking mastery and success. They want and need to acquire relevant knowledge and to learn specific skills. They enjoy testing their capabilities in realistic situations. School-age children also are developing social values and attitudes.

Play is widely recognized as a vehicle for constructing personal and collective meaning. Physical, social, intellectual, emotional, creative, and spiritual development is enhanced through play. Play enables children to internalize the concept taught in subjects such as literacy, math, science, and social studies. Play also develops empathy and tolerance between and amongst the players.

**CAYC believes that play for school-age children is:**
- Natural
- Stimulating, invigorating, complex
- Exciting, adventurous, open-ended
- Self-directed, self-selected
- Multi-sensory
- Interactive
- Inquisitiveness, wonder, and joy

- Enjoyable and fun
- Endless possibilities
- Energetic and exuberant

**Play fosters:**

- Active learning
- Control by players
- Decision-making, collaborating
- Problem solving, negotiating
- Critical thinking
- Creativity
- Hypothesizing, questioning
- Predicting, evaluating
- Risk-taking

**For quality play to occur school children need:**

- Uninterrupted time
- Partners
- Rich, stimulating environments that children can help plan and rearrange
- A wide variety of materials
- Supportive, responsive, knowledgeable adults who are partners in the learning process
- Repeated opportunities for exploring materials and ideas

**Play amongst school-age children might be:**

- Creating, writing, producing and acting out plays of their own making, re-creating everyday experiences
- Imagining themselves in a variety of roles to see what fits and works for them
- Negotiating the rules, solving problems and enjoying success and satisfaction from participating in cooperative experiences
- Creating and recreating play spaces both indoors and out

    *Source:* The Canadian Association for Young Children. Reprinted with permission.

# SUMMARY

## Chapter Preview

- Children's play is multifaceted and is directly linked to a child's development.

## Defining Play

- There are many perspectives on what the term *play* means. It is challenging to articulate one definition that encompasses the breadth, depth, and complexities of the topic play.

## The United Nations Convention on the Rights of the Child

- Articles 31, 3, 12, and 23 outline the commitment that Canada has made to support children in having the right to play.

## Societal Issues and Child's Play

- There are several societal issues that positively or negatively impact children's play.
- Many children living in Canada have been identified as obese or overweight. Children benefit from having role models who are engaged in active living principles and practice appropriate nutrition in their diet.
- Children who do not have adequate outdoor play experiences have a higher risk of not developing a variety of cognitive, social, emotional, and physical skills that are primarily gained from outdoor play.
- Children are being exposed to technology. There are differing opinions on technology and play.
- When children are exposed to cultural differences during the early years, children develop positive values towards cultures and diversity in the early learning environment.
- The more children are exposed to television, print, and emailing through the internet, the more exposure they have to consumerism.
- Poverty impacts more than one million children living in Canada today. Families who deal with poverty also suffer from more anxiety, depression, and irritability than other families. These issues have an effect on the child's play and development.

## Brain Development

- The child's environment and experiences influence brain development. Children who are not exposed to a supportive, stimulating environment are at risk of losing the opportunity for the brain to develop to its fullest potential.
- Play experiences support brain development.

## Classical, Modern, and Contemporary Perspectives on Play

- Each of the classical, modern, and contemporary theorists offers early learning practitioners insight into the importance of play to child development. Some of the common themes include play is a natural way for children to learn; children require stimulating environments and a combination of spontaneous and guided experiences.

## The Canadian Association for Young Children Position Statement on Play

- The CAYC has two distinct position statements on play—one for preschool children and the other for school-age children. These two statements provide a framework for what the Association believes is important for children relative to play.

# REVIEW QUESTIONS

1. Why is play an important concept for early learning practitioners? How do the complexities of play support practitioners in facilitating developmentally appropriate learning environments?
2. What is the significance of the United Nations Convention on the Rights of the Child to early learning practitioners and to children living in Canada?

3. What is meant by every child having the right to engage in play activities appropriate to the age of the child and cultural life?
4. Describe how the six societal issues outlined impact on children's play, family dynamics, and the roles and responsibilities of early learning practitioners.
5. Explain the key perspectives of the five philosophers outlined in the chapter. Discuss how they suggested play influences children's development.
6. What are the key features of the modern perspectives on play? How do they differ from the historical perspectives and the postmodern or contemporary perspectives?
7. Describe the similarities and differences between the CAYC position statements on play for young children and school-age children.

# MAKING CONNECTIONS

## Theory to Practice

1. What would be the benefit for early learning practitioners to be familiar with the history of play? How can the historical perspective inform practice?
2. Visit an early learning setting and examine it in relation to the historical perspectives presented in this chapter. What areas would you examine to determine if there is a historical influence? What do you expect to see? Why? Once you have visited the setting, reflect on your findings. Are there areas where you were able to clearly see the connections of the historical underpinnings? Describe these findings.
3. What is meant by the notion that the historical information about play is a catalyst for helping early learning practitioners think critically about the depth and breadth of play?
4. Based on the CAYC position statements for young children and school-age children, how might the environments be similar and different? Why?

## For Further Research

1. As identified in the Occupational Standards for Early Childhood Educators, a project funded by the Government of Canada, Sector Council Program, supporting play-based learning for children is the ultimate responsibility of the early childhood practitioner. This national publication is available at www.ccsc-cssge.ca. Examine the occupational standards and determine the specified skills, abilities, and core knowledge that relate to play.
2. Many provinces and territories are developing or have released curriculum frameworks for early learning. Conduct research in your area to determine if there is a curriculum framework. Review the framework to determine the significance of play within it. How does this impact the work of early learning practitioners? If the framework does not specifically address play, how might that impact early learning programs in your area?

   *Please note:* If your province or territory does not have a framework, research one from another part of Canada or internationally.

# ADDITIONAL READING

Canadian Paediatric Society. (2009). Are we doing enough? A status report on Canadian public policy and child and youth health. Available at http://www.cps.ca/English/Advocacy/Status Report2009.pdf

Hirsh-Pasek, K., & Golinkoff, R. M. (2003). *Einstein never used flash cards: How our children really learn and why they need to play more and memorize less.* Emmaus, PA: Rodale.

Kieff, J. E., & Casbergue, R. M. (2000). *Playful learning and teaching: Integrating play into preschool and primary programs.* Boston: Allyn & Bacon.

Mayo Clinic. (2005, April 19). Childhood obesity: What parents can do. Retrieved November, 2009, from http://www.mayoclinic.com/health/childhood-obesity/FL00058

## WEBLINKS

www.cayc.ca

www.childhoodobesityfoundation.ca/statistics

www.healthycanadians.gc.ca

www.jpacanada.org/home_childs.html

www.unicef.org/crc

> _In play the child is always behaving beyond his age, above his usual everyday behaviour; in play he is, as it were, a head above himself._
> —Lev Vygotsky (1978)

# 2 The Process of Play

## Learning Outcomes

After exploring this chapter you should be able to

- discuss the relationship of Urie Bronfenbrenner's ecological theory to a child's play experiences;

- examine what is meant by play, learning, intrinsic motivation, active engagement, and process rather than product;

- outline the seven common characteristics of play as identified by Henninger, Isenberg, and Jalongo (2010);

- discuss the six phases in the play process and how they guide early learning practitioners in their work with children;

- describe how Piaget, Parten, Smilansky, and Seagoe classify play experiences;

- explain how specified classical, modern, and contemporary theorists describe the purpose of play;

- discuss play and concerns that must be addressed with children with atypical developmental patterns; and

- describe four key roles that adults have in promoting child's play.

## Stories from the Field: Practitioner to Student

Every day the children that I have the pleasure to work with surprise me with their ability to engage in such rich play activities that evolve from an individual child or a group of children. Last week, while we were outdoors, I noticed a group of children discussing something. Then Joma, who has just turned 4 years old, asked if she could bring one of the yellow chairs from the art area outdoors. I had some choices to make. I could say "no those chairs are for the indoors;" I could ask questions such as "why do you need the chairs?" or "is there something else in the yard that you could use for chairs?" or I could have said "yes" and let the play episode evolve.

The challenge that I have in working with children is that the adult decisions we make about the early learning environment and what the children can do within the environment have such an influence on play. I believe our decisions either support the child's curiosity or impede it. Yet, when children ask us for materials or accessories, such as Joma did, often I don't always have the luxury of thinking about the open-ended questions that I should ask. Sometimes I would get so tense worrying that I was not asking the right questions. I realized that I need to be able to support the child as her needs and ideas are expressed. So over the past four years, I have worked to develop a style of relaxation with the children. When children make a request for accessories, such as the chair, my answer is always "of course." Then, I say to the child "Is there something I can do to help you incorporate this (chair) into your play?" The child usually responds by saying "no" or "no thank you". Of course, I observe the children in their play and I participate when it is appropriate.

My advice for new early learning practitioners: provide children with the freedom to be. Allow them to explore their environment and incorporate as many items as they wish from varying experience centres into their play. The least amount of restrictions we as adults place on children, the richer the play. The more the comfort that children feel within the environment, the more they will engage in quality play.

_Danielle, ECE Graduate, 2001_

# CHAPTER PREVIEW

We are living in a society whereby children are being increasingly programmed and structured (Golinkoff, Hirsh-Pasek, & Singer, 2006). We are providing little time for children to play; rather, we are asking children as young as three years of age to produce products. We are expecting important academic school type work deemed important, rather than play. If we continue to structure children's time and limit play, we as a society are taking incredible risks that will impact a child's overall development for life. Zigler and Bishop-Josef (2004) indicate "play is under siege" (p. 2). Play contributes to a child's academic, social, artistic, and creative skills that should flow naturally from within; however, the quality of these skills is threatened because many children are in environments where rich play experiences are limited. This impacts every phase of a child's development.

Broadbent (2004) indicates that the combined pressure from parents and early learning student practitioners being trained and focused on subject-based curriculum rather than play-based learning is contributing to play being eroded in the early years.

Early learning practitioners are constantly examining research and different perspectives on the importance of play in the lives of children. Our beliefs about child development and play contribute to how we facilitate children's play. To understand play and its relationship to child development, it must be examined from a variety of perspectives. The amount of time that is devoted to offering children *pure play experiences* is related to specific beliefs, values, roles, and goals for children. We continue to encourage early learning practitioners to return play to be the centre core of the child's life.

Play is a vital activity for children in all cultures (Bloch & Pelligrini, 1989). As identified in Chapter 1, each element of a child's development is impacted by play. Children's play experiences become more complex in environments that encourage and allow for exploration and risk taking. These two attributes lead to the child gaining a sense of success, especially when the play experiences are sequenced from simple to more complex.

Maja and Allie have been playmates since Allie moved into the neighbourhood six months ago. Their parents have been encouraging the girls to play together by arranging play dates for them when the children express an interest. During their last play date, Maja and Allie decided that they were going to play with the sand in the open sandpit. As Allie's mom Maggie observed the girls, she noticed the three-year-olds talking back and forth, sharing sand accessories, giving each other ideas about what they could use for various things they were trying to create, and suggested each to try "this or that." Maggie realized that the girls had been playing in the sand area for more than 30 minutes. This was interesting to Maggie, because recently an early years practitioner at Allie's centre expressed concern about Allie's attention span. The teacher, Marissa, described Allie as flitting from one activity to another, rather than engaging in play for extended periods. Marissa was concerned that Allie does not become engaged in in-depth play experiences. This news was distressing for Maggie because she knows the importance of having concentration skills for today's marketplace and she knows that these skills are developing during the early years. Maggie wondered about how she could encourage Allie to focus like she was doing today when she was at her program with Marissa.

As you continue to explore this chapter, it will be beneficial to think about Maja and Allie. Why might Allie have more concentration skills in the sand play environment than in other environments? What might be influencing her interest in the sand play? Why might her play experiences be different at the early learning and child care centre? How might play experiences be expanded to support Allie's needs?

In this chapter, you will explore play concepts that support child development. The play process, components of play, play stages, the debate about process versus product, and the role of adults in child's play are among the topics that will be discussed. A number of theoretical perspectives will be presented as a way to help you begin to formulate your beliefs and philosophy about children and play.

## WORDS OF WISDOM

### An Expert Describes the Importance of Play to Learning

"Play is serious business for the development of young learners. This is such an important understanding. During my fact-finding, I observed people recoil at that thought of spending resources on 'just having kids play.' But research and best practice indicate clearly that a deliberate and effective play-based approach supports young children's cognitive development. When well designed, such an approach taps into children's individual interests, draws out their emerging capacities, and responds to their sense of inquiry and exploration of the world around them. It generates highly motivated children enjoying an environment where the learning outcomes of a curriculum are more likely to be achieved" (Dr. Charles Pascal, 2009, p. 16).

## Child's Play: From an Ecological Theory Perspective

Early learning practitioners recognize that play is one of the most important aspects of a child's life. Play is fundamental to all aspects of the child's development. It is through play that cultural and community attributes are explored and adapted into the child's being. A child's physical movement develops motor skills necessary for life. Children who have consistent playmates enhance their opportunities to advance their social, moral, and emotional development. This developmental component is fundamental to a child's personality development and lifelong skills needed to deal with such things as stress management and conflict resolution. Children who develop positive self-esteem have an increased level of confidence to try new things. This increases a child's cognitive learning skills.

Urie Bronfenbrenner (1979) developed an influential theory of human development. This theory, known as the **ecological theory,** helps us to examine

**Ecological theory**
Bronfenbrenner's environmental-system theory of development: This theoretical framework emphasizes the relationship of environmental factors and social context through the five environmental systems—microsystem, mesosystem, exosystem, macrosystem, and chronosystem.

the relationship of how environmental influences contribute to a child's play experiences. His model outlines the relationship of a child's environment and their interactions to play, with human development. Figure 2.1 provides an outline of Bronfenbrenner's five major systems and how play is influenced by each of the system.

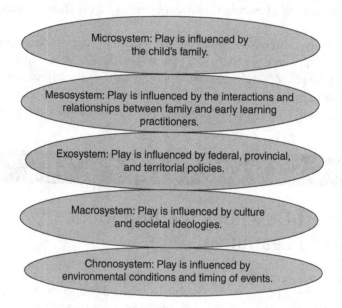

*Figure 2.1* *Bronfenbrenner's Ecological Model of Development*

**Microsystem** This refers to the setting in which children live, including the home, early learning experiences, and neighbourhood. The microsystem considers the child's direct interactions with parents, peers, and early learning practitioners and groups that apply to a child's cultural context. The child is influenced by the position that the family and the community take towards play. If play experiences are encouraged and made available, a child's development will be positively impacted. Conversely, if play is not encouraged, there will be a negative effect on a child's development (Vandermaas-Peeler, 2002).

**Mesosystem** The mesosystem refers to the people and places outlined in the microsystem. For example, when we think of children in early learning centres, the mesosystem extends to include the beliefs, interactions, connections, and relationships between the parents, extended family members, and early learning practitioners. Think about the early learning practitioner who believes in children learning through play; whereas a group of parents prefers to focus on academic preparation for their 3-year-old children. This leads to an imbalance and confusion for the child. It may cause tension between the parents and the early learning centre, to the point that the parents choose to place their child in a more academically focused setting.

**Exosystem**   This system refers to experiences or influences from other social settings or forces. These systems generally have an indirect impact on the child. For example, many provincial governments and territories have adopted new standards for playground apparatus. Because of the cost to upgrade the equipment, some early learning centres and community playgrounds have removed playground equipment. Government decisions may positively or negatively directly impact a child's access to safe play opportunities.

**Macrosystem**   This system in its broadest terms examines the level of influence that occurs from cultural values and societal ideologies. As we think about this from a child's play perspective, the culture, society, and educational **backgrounds** of parents impact the types of play and diversity of the play experiences extended to their children. For example, in some families, there is a belief that young children require play experiences. Parents make decisions about early learning experiences and settings based on that belief. Others may believe that in order for children to succeed, they must participate in academic learning rather than play. They in turn look for early learning experiences that focus on academic concepts. Or, think of the 3-year-old child who moves from a country such as Japan to a rural Saskatchewan farming community. This child may be one of the few children in the neighbourhood with a different ancestry, language, and customs. This will impact how the child integrates into the early learning environment, and hence development.

**Chronosystem**   This system focuses on the patterning of environmental events, transitions through the life process, and the time of events (Santrock, 2002). For example, preschool children who live in apartment buildings with limited or no access to outdoor play opportunities may experience a more sedentary lifestyle than those children who have access to a yard. The absence of rigorous play impacts the development of the bone and muscle systems, which contributes to health issues later in life. The lifestyle attributes established in early childhood impact the child's lifestyle throughout the life cycle.

Bronfenbrenner's (1979) ecological model provides an important framework for making the relationship between play, environment, and child development. The social systems combined with family beliefs positively or negatively impact the child's play experiences. It is beneficial for families and early learning practitioners to have discussions about how children learn through play.

When children are in environments that allow them to initiate and control their play—they learn through play. For example, when a child is in a new situation, or discovers new information, it is the play process of trying things, thinking about processes and reworking information that allows the child to integrate the new information with previous knowledge. This interactive process becomes intrinsically motivating. It contributes to children developing an understanding of their culture and their world (Fromberg, 2002; McCune & Zanes, 2001; Wolery & McWilliams, 1998). This is how children build social competence while developing resiliency.

# COMPONENTS OF PLAY AND UNIQUE FEATURES OF PLAY

There are many theories and perspectives about how children and adults learn. Modern theorists suggest that "the learner is no longer regarded as a passive receiver of knowledge, but as an active constructor of meaning" (Katzeff, 2003, p. 1). This perspective is especially emphasized within the constructionist theory. Children's rich play experiences require three key components.

- Play requires children and adult interaction with others and artifacts so that children may engage in a process of understanding new information and within a context.
- Play and learning require children to share both the physical space and opportunities for it to be a social process (Vygotsky, 1978). This requires the child to participate in both an internal process and a social construct in order to make sense of the learning.
- Play sets the stage for a learning process for not only individual learners but also within a group of learners (Lave, 1988; Saljo, 2000).

Early learning practitioners work collectively to incorporate these components into their play environments.

Many theorists who have studied play, and those theorists who have researched learning, help us to understand some of the unique features of play (Monighan-Nourot et al., 1987). As identified in Figure 2.2, we will introduce you to the following three unique features:

- Play, learning, and **motivation**
- Play, learning, and **active engagement**
- Play, learning, and **process rather than product**

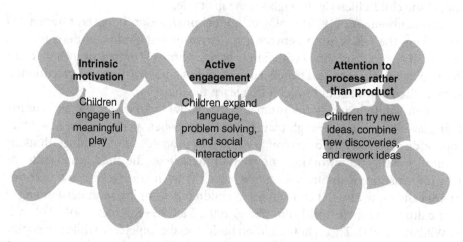

**Intrinsic motivation**
Children engage in meaningful play

**Active engagement**
Children expand language, problem solving, and social interaction

**Attention to process rather than product**
Children try new ideas, combine new discoveries, and rework ideas

*Figure 2.2*  *Unique Features of Play*

*Photo 2.1*  *Unique materials motivate children to explore and discover.*

## Play, Learning, and Intrinsic Motivation

Play and intrinsic motivation are interrelated to spontaneous exploration and curiosity. Katzeff (2003) indicates that motivation plays a crucial role in learning. Bruner (1973) suggests that there are three internal motivators that influence play and to learning:

- curiosity;
- desire to show oneself and others what you know and what you are able to do; and
- strive towards a common goal with others.

Each child is internally motivated in a different way. Their intrinsic motivational level is related to the environmental conditions including the exposure to play that the child has experienced. Some theorists define internal motivation as

- the doing of an activity for its inherent satisfaction rather than for some separable consequence. When intrinsically motivated, a person is moved to act for the fun or challenge entailed rather than because of external products, pressures, or rewards (Ryan & Deci, 2000);
- motivation to engage in an activity for its own sake. People who are intrinsically motivated work on tasks because they find them enjoyable (Pintrich & Schunk, 1996); and

> The more a child is driven by interest and curiosity, the more carefully she attends to her teachers (Bruner, 1966). But a child cannot be trained to be interested and curious (Shanker, 2009, p. 3).

- choosing to do an activity for no compelling reason, beyond the satisfaction derived from the activity itself—it's what motivates us to do something when we don't have to do anything (Raffini, 1996).

Play and its contextual principles are driven by positive emotions (Jensen, 1999). When children feel comfortable in their play surroundings, they exhibit positive emotions, which, in turn, increase a child's sense of curiosity and focus on the task. Negative emotions, such as anxiety and stress, detract from a child's motivation (Santrock, 2003) and their interest in exploring learning opportunities. Think about infants. They try to grasp, throw, get to items, and scream and squeal as they encounter new objects (Oudeyer & Kaplan, 2007). Children will continue this zest for learning and exploring when the environment allows for it. Conversely, the will to play and learn becomes problematic in structured environments that confine children to specific activities or events. Infants and young children require opportunities for exploration of personal interests. When children are placed in environments that stifle their natural interests, spontaneous play and learning become jeopardized. This influences the child's ability to develop self-regulation.

There are many ways to think about self-regulation. Pascal (2009) suggests that it is the cornerstone of development and is a central building block of early learning. He defines it as "the ability to adapt one's emotions, behaviours, and attention to the demands of the situation" (p. 1). He indicates "It is about establishing one's own internal motivation for adapting to, and understanding emotional and social demands" (p. 4). Developing self-regulation is essential because it is interconnected to attention skills, memory, cognitive flexibility, and interpretation of behaviour and social interactions. A child's ability to exercise patience, persistence, flexibility, curiosity, exploratory play, and to approach new experiences is dependent on the level of self-regulation and internal motivation that the child develops. It is thought that behaviour such as bullying stems from a deficit in self-regulation, intrinsic motivation, and self-esteem.

Intrinsically motivating activities contribute to the young child exhibiting energy and the ability and interest in taking new risks (Dietze, 2006). Play ideas, directions of play, and the will to try new ideas are present with children who are intrinsically motivated. For example, think of children who observe machinery digging holes in a neighbourhood. Tomas, who has an interest in the large machines, observes the operator and the features of the machinery. Then, in his sand play, he replicates the sounds of the machine and the motions/movements that various parts of the machinery can do. Using the back hoe, he digs holes, he piles the sand, and then he uses the grater to flatten the sand. He gets shovels and planks and uses them for other tasks. Tomas returns to this play for several days. Marley, the early learning practitioner, offered resources such as a toolbox and construction books to expand the challenge, while enhancing the play. Tomas knew so much more about the machinery than Marley. He was able to tell her about tires, levers, and how the movement of the buckets occurs. Tomas's level of knowledge about graters was sparked from his interest rather than in the programming offered at the early learning centre.

Self-regulation "the ability to adapt one's emotions, behaviours, and attention to the demands of the situation" (Pascal, 2009, p. 1).

*Photo 2.2    Children become internally motivated when they have stimulating environments.*

Intrinsic motivation is affected by challenge, curiosity, and fantasy (Malone & Lepper, 1987). Table 2.1 provides an overview of how these factors may look in an early learning and child care setting.

# Stop . . . Think . . . Discuss . . . Reflect

How do early learning practitioners know if children are being adequately stimulated and challenged? Is it their sole responsibility? If so, why is that? If not, who is responsible for children being challenged, curious, and having the opportunity to participate in fantasy?

There is a relationship between satisfying basis needs, higher needs, and motivation. Maslow (1987) suggests that children have basic needs—food, safety/security; belonging/love; achievement/prestige; and aesthetic needs. Children must first satisfy their basic physiological needs before they are able to fully engage in higher levels of intrinsic motivation. All human behaviour, including that of young children, is motivated by attempts to satisfy their human needs (Glasser, 1998).

*Table 2.1*    *Intrinsic Motivators*

| Factor | Description | Expanding Opportunities |
|---|---|---|
| Curiosity | **Curiosity** is stimulated by something in the child's environment that leads the child to have a desire to explore, discover, question, and wonder.<br><br>Curiosity is foundational to developing new knowledge, skills, creative expression, and scientific inquiry. | • Pose questions that require the child to think in new ways and reflect.<br>• Make changes to the environment so that the child explores and makes new connections.<br>• Provide new materials that will stimulate the child's cognitive curiosity and desire to explore and wonder.<br>• Develop strategies that encourage children who are timid to explore areas of interest. |
| Challenge | **Challenge** is stimulated when children work and play with materials and activities that pose a continuously optimal level of difficulty (Malone & Lepper, 1987).<br><br>Challenge expands exploration and learning. | • Provide materials and experiences that support each child's personal interests.<br>• Scaffold the activities so that as the child gains success, more advanced activities occur.<br>• Provide feedback and encouragement as required. |
| Fantasy | **Fantasy** is when children use mental images of things and situations that are not actually present to stimulate their play.<br><br>Fantasy extends children's creativity in their play. It helps children visualize what is possible. | • Facilitate experiences that support the child in exploring the fantasy or imaginary context of play.<br>• Discuss how the imaginary experiences may be in real life. |

One of the most challenging roles for early learning practitioners is to create environments that support children feeling important and that they are lovable. Children who are given the freedom to choose play activities that they wish to partake in developing a strong sense of self. Allowing children to make choices is directly related to building intrinsic motivation and self-regulation. This is how a child fosters a sense of autonomy, initiative, and industry (Van Hoorn, Nourot, Scales, & Alward, 2007). A child's self-regulation is established when children are exposed to play experiences that encourage the individual child and groups of children to plan, revise, reflect, investigate, redesign, retry, and discuss their ideas with peers and adults (Pascal, 2009).

Intrinsic motivation and self-regulation is a scaffolding process. In the early phase of brain development, a neural platform for self-regulation occurs (Pascal, 2009). The more positive life experiences a child has and the more nurturing that occurs, the stronger the self-regulation becomes.

## Play, Learning, and Active Engagement

Children are designed to climb, crawl, run, jump, swing, tumble, and twist. Active engagement in play is *children's work* during their early years. It leads children to exhibit their zest for life (Van Hoorn et al., 2007), develop skills and abilities in language development, cooperation, sharing, problem solving, expansion of curiosity, and coordination of body skills. Active play supports children in developing skills to manage stress and to formulate a healthy lifestyle. As highlighted by Van Hoorn et al. (2007), "Children's sense of autonomy, initiative, and industry are rooted in intrinsic motivation and active engagement" (p. 6). Pascal (2009) indicates that early learning systems, including the school environment, must create an environment of "child-directed activity that will mobilize the child's interest and imagination" (Shanker, 2009, p. iii).

Children, during their early years, require a balance of vigorous play and quieter activities. The combination of play experiences enhances each of the child's developmental domains.

## Play, Learning, and Play as a Process Rather than Product

Children's play experiences should focus on the process of play rather than the production of a product. For example, when we think of play and creativity, we know that creativity must be generated from within the child (Hendrick & Weissman, 2007). Children need opportunities to try new ideas, combine new ideas with current knowledge, and rethink how things were done and how they may be done differently. Salim, for example, is using large planks and the hollow blocks. It is unclear whether he intends to build an identified structure. Because Salim has access to a variety of blocks, planks, wood stumps, and cylinders, the opportunities are endless. This allows Salim to make choices about the materials he needs as his exploration evolves and his creation unfolds.

Salim has a different experience from Marine and his friends. He and the other fourteen children are required by the end of the week to make a card using the pattern pieces that the early learning practitioner has prepared. This is necessary so that each child has something to take home to the parent on Friday. The objective is to share with parents "work" that the children are completing.

***Photo 2.3*** *Building block structures evolve when children have materials and an environment that supports exploration and creativity.*

*Photo 2.4*    *An early learning practitioner's philosophy impacts children's play experiences.*

## Stop . . . Think . . . Discuss . . . Reflect

Think about children and learning. Look at the block structure that Salim created. Then look at Marine. What are the differences in the experiences? Is one experience more play based than the other? Under what circumstances might both of these experiences be considered learning through play experiences? In what context would Marine's activity be useful to his development? Why might some parents be more enthusiastic about Marine's experience than Salim's? Why? How might you share the learning that Salim engaged in with the parents?

There are two classic works that provide further insight into the debate about process versus product in early learning experiences. Sylva, Bruner, and Genova (1976) suggest that "the essence of play is the dominance of means over ends" (p. 244). They indicate that children need to be in control of their play by being given the freedom to engage in play, explore, and make mistakes without the feeling of failure. In essence, in order for a play process to evolve, it must be voluntary and self-initiated.

The second classic work is that of Helen Buckley. Her story, as found in Box 2.1, helps us put the process versus product debate into context.

# BOX 2.1

## The Little Boy

Once a little boy went to school.
He was quite a little boy
And it was quite a big school.
But when the little boy
Found that he could go to his room
By walking right in from the door outside
He was happy;
And the school did not seem
Quite so big anymore.

One morning
When the little boy had been in school awhile,
The teacher said:
"Today we are going to make a picture."
"Good!" thought the little boy.
He liked to make all kinds;
Lions and tigers,
Chickens and cows,
Trains and boats;
And he took out his box of crayons
And began to draw.

But the teacher said, "Wait!"
"It is not time to begin!"
And she waited until everyone looked ready.
"Now," said the teacher,
"We are going to make flowers."
"Good!" thought the little boy,
He liked to make beautiful ones
With his pink and orange and blue crayons.
But the teacher said "Wait!"
"And I will show you how."
And it was red, with a green stem.
"There," said the teacher,
"Now you may begin."

The little boy looked at his teacher's flower
Then he looked at his own flower.
He liked his flower better than the teacher's
But he did not say this.
He just turned his paper over,
And made a flower like the teacher's.
It was red, with a green stem.

*(Continued)*

## B O X  2 . 1  (*Continued*)

On another day
When the little boy had opened
The door from the outside all by himself,
The teacher said:
"Today we are going to make something with clay."
"Good!" thought the little boy;
He liked clay.
He could make all kinds of things with clay:
Snakes and snowmen,
Elephants and mice,
Cars and trucks
And he began to pull and pinch
His ball of clay.

But the teacher said, "Wait!"
"It is not time to begin!"
And she waited until everyone looked ready.
"Now," said the teacher,
"We are going to make a dish."
"Good!" thought the little boy,
He liked to make dishes.
And he began to make some
That were all shapes and sizes.

But the teacher said "Wait!"
"And I will show you how."
And she showed everyone how to make
One deep dish.
"There," said the teacher,
"Now you may begin."

The little boy looked at the teacher's dish;
Then he looked at his own.
He liked his better than the teacher's
But he did not say this.
He just rolled his clay into a big ball again
And made a dish like the teacher's.
It was a deep dish.

And pretty soon
The little boy learned to wait,
And to watch
And to make things just like the teacher.
And pretty soon
He didn't make things of his own anymore.

# BOX 2.1 *(Continued)*

Then it happened
That the little boy and his family
Moved to another house,
In another city,
And the little boy
Had to go to another school.
This school was even bigger
Than the other one.
And there was no door from the outside
Into his room.
He had to go up some big steps
And walk down a long hall
To get to his room.
And the very first day
He was there,
The teacher said:
"Today we are going to make a picture."
"Good!" thought the little boy.
And he waited for the teacher
To tell what to do.
But the teacher didn't say anything.
She just walked around the room.

When she came to the little boy
She asked, "Don't you want to make a picture?"
"Yes," said the little boy.
"What are we going to make?"
"I don't know until you make it," said the teacher.
"How shall I make it?" asked the little boy.
"Why, anyway you like," said the teacher.
"And any color?" asked the little boy.
"Any color," said the teacher.
"If everyone made the same picture,
And used the same colors,
How would I know who made what,
And which was which?"
"I don't know," said the little boy.
And he began to make pink and orange and blue flowers.

He liked his new school,
Even if it didn't have a door
Right in from the outside!

*Helen Buckley, 1961*

## Stop . . . Think . . . Discuss . . . Reflect

What do you gain from the poem "The Little Boy"? What does this poem tell you about the roles of early learning practitioners? How does adult role modelling impact a child's creativity and freedom to explore in their play episodes? What strategies may an early learning practitioner use to rekindle the self-directed exploratory characteristics that the little boy exhibited prior to being exposed to a product-orientated environment? Do you think that there might be circumstances in an early learning environment when product is emphasized as long as it is not to the detriment of process?

## Characteristics of Play

Henniger (2002) and Isenberg and Jalongo (2010) suggest that there are seven common characteristics of play, as outlined in Figure 2.3. Becoming familiar with these characteristics helps early learning practitioners understand the foundation of play and how it influences the roles and responsibilities of early learning practitioners.

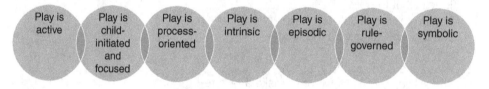

**Figure 2.3**   *Seven Common Characteristics of Play*

**Play is active (Henniger, 2002)**   Children explore, discover, experiment, become engaged, move their bodies, and make connections in environments that are designed to support children using their bodies and materials. Active play increases the child's senses, language acquisition, and interaction among peers. It facilitates children developing the confidence to explore the "what if" possibilities.

Children develop personal meaning and relevance through active play. As identified in Chapter 1, when a child is involved in active play, their neural connections are enhanced, which contribute to situations, ideas, and skills becoming part of the child's long-term memory. Conversely, when children are exposed to concepts and isolated facts that are irrelevant to them, the potential knowledge and experiences will not be transferred into a child's long-term memory (Fromberg, 2002). Think of a group of children trying to figure out what they can use for a gas pump. First they take long and short black pipes to the area. They try to attach a short pipe to a longer pipe so they have a nozzle. They use this for a short period of time. It does not provide the children with the flexibility they require. Then, in the curiosity centre, they discover a pliable hose—a vacuum hose. Suddenly, the play at the gas station takes on new meaning. This play allowed children to gain knowledge about material construction principles such as hard, soft, flexible and rigid, and the requirements needed for specific play interests.

**Play is child-initiated and focused (Henniger, 2002)**    Children's play is much richer when it is child-initiated and child-focused, than when it is adult-planned and adult-initiated. Children are intrinsically motivated when they have the freedom to choose materials and play topics. Marley is on the dramatic play platform in the garden. She thinks she would like to prepare for a wedding. She starts conversations with Tina, Tyla, and Jamill about the wedding. They decide they need chairs, flowers, and dresses. They also need to have food—Tyla asks the early learning practitioner if snack time can happen at the wedding. The children construct how the wedding will occur and they determine the depth of the play experience based on their knowledge and interests in the idea of a wedding (Dietze, 2006). If adults tried to initiate this play, it probably would not have had the same richness as what the children brought forth. They execute the play based on their life experiences and vision.

**Play is process-oriented (Bruner, 1972)**    Children require the freedom to play without adult-imposed structure. When children engage in play experiences that allow them to play for the true pleasure of the experience rather than to achieve a finished product at the end of the play episode, the play is richer in language, discovery, and movement. Children have total concentration on the play

*Photo 2.5    Children learn by trial and error.*

episode when it has been self-initiated. They gain a sense of success when play experiences and environments support active, meaningful learning with complex, challenging, and varied materials (Fromberg, 2002; Isenberg & Jalongo, 2000; Jensen, 1999).

**Play is symbolic and transformational**   Children learn about life through play. One of the purposes of play is to support children in connecting past experiences with their current world. They take on new play endeavours by trying new ideas and expanding their roles. This requires children to "step outside the box" as they use their imagination to try new ideas. The use of creativity, spontaneity, and exploration advances a child's thinking process—"*what if this happens*" or "*If I try this, I wonder if*"—which leads to a higher level of thinking. This contributes to the child developing the foundational skills necessary for critical thinking and problem solving.

# THE PLAY PROCESS

Toddler play is different from the play of preschoolers, which also differs from the play of school-age children (Jones & Reynolds, 1992). Children and their play is a progressive process, with each new phase building on previous learning and experiences (Dietze, 2006). There are a number of developmental and environmental conditions that contribute to the progression of the play process. For example, a child's age and his developmental level, combined with the materials and experiences provided, influence the play process and the level of engagement within the play experience. As a child gains experience with the play materials, a play plateau is reached. If new stimulation is not added, the play progression is affected. Children require new play materials and opportunities so that they continuously achieve new skills, perfect skills, or modify skills. Children intuitively advance to the next level of play when they have had sufficient opportunities and experiences at any given phase.

During childhood, we can expect children to advance through five phases in the play process. The sixth phase occurs during adulthood.

## Phase I: Body Play

An infant's first exposure to play occurs with his body. Think of the infant who becomes intrigued by being able to move a hand one way or another, or discovering the sounds that can be made. The infant will try to repeat the movement over and over again. This process is used by the child to gain information (Driscoll & Nagel, 2005). Piaget (1980) identifies this body play as exploration. As infants explore their environments visually, through mouthing and their senses, they quickly begin to show preferences such as for faces and patterns and textures. When the infant has gained information through the exploration process, play begins. The infant repeats movements for the purpose of combining or reconfiguring information previously explored (Dietze, 2006).

*Photo 2.6*    *The infant repeats movements for the purpose of combining or reconfiguring information previously explored.*

## Phase II: Motoring Movement Play

As infants become more mobile through creeping, crawling, and toddling, their interest in play expands. The child gains skills in being able to balance and coordinate body movements through the various movements that occur during play. The expansion of active play, the accomplishment of skills such as in running, hopping, jumping, climbing, and rolling expands a child's play while advancing skills in a variety of developmental domains.

## Phase III: Imaginative Play

Between the ages of 3 and 4, children's play becomes more advanced by combining play with movement. The freedom to move, run, jump, and climb now has an expanded purpose (Driscoll & Nagel, 2005). During this phase, a child becomes

*Photo 2.7   When the toddler has the opportunity to explore and gains more competence in her body movements, she will try new ideas and adventures.*

*Photo 2.8   Children use imaginative play to make sense of their world.*

interested in determining how high jumps can be, or how to walk on one foot. Imaginative play evolves, which is usually triggered from experiences or observations a child makes from their environment. This phase provides early learning practitioners and parents with insight as to how the child perceives the world. For example, after Jonathan's mother gave birth to a new sister, Jonathan spent many days in the dramatic centre playing mother and baby. At times, Jonathan spoke to the doll to tell her that she can go to someone else's home—she doesn't need to stay with Jonathan's family. At other times, Jonathan expressed caring, nurturing behaviours, and loving dialogue towards the doll.

## Phase IV: Intentional Imaginative Play

During this phase, between the ages of 4 and 6, the richness of fantasy play is enhanced. It is further expanded with school-aged children. Children take many objects from their environment or concepts and use them as props in their play. Children develop sophisticated role playing. They use mental images to devise plans for objects and ideas that can be incorporated into the play episode. For example, the children decide they want to be involved in catching a robber. As Jamie hears Matt and Mila discussing the robber play, Jamie decides that he will take on the role of the robber, using his trike as the getaway car. Jamie solicits help from Mandy. He and Mandy decide that she will hide the robber, by getting on the back of the trike. They think this will help Jamie not to be visible. This play moves beyond imitating an act that was previously observed. Each person has a role in the play experience. The children became involved because the play topic was of interest to them.

When children are engaged in the imaginative phase, often, the child's cultural backgrounds, life experiences, and environments will influence the depth and breadth of the play. Children who are active in their play, have the ability to engage in a variety of roles. Their level of energy and their commitment to the play experience differs dramatically from those children who have limited play experiences.

***Photo 2.9*** *Children learn about practical life skills through imaginative play.*

## Phase V: Peer Play with Rules

Play among school-aged children moves from the innovative and imaginative play experienced by the 4- to 6-year-olds, to a more structured play that is generally governed by rules. This phase sees children attracted to team-focused and competitive play. The spontaneous play seen in an earlier phase is replaced with materials and play being specific to a predetermined end result.

*Photo 2.10* *School-aged children take risks in their play while following rules with peers.*

## Phase VI: Adult Play

Play is a lifelong process. Through play, adults learn many valuable skills including relationships, communication, innovation, problem solving, and visualization. Adult play generally occurs in competitive environments such as one's workplace or at social events. For example, think about the last social gathering you were at. Many of the adults may have shared stories or reflected on experiences of the past. These processes support adults in constructing new knowledge or perceptions about issues and concepts through these exchanges (Dietze, 2006). Although play differs in adulthood from childhood, it remains as an essential life experience to maintain life-work balance.

## CLASSIFYING PLAY EXPERIENCES

Children's play is influenced by the role models, environment, and the materials available to them. Theorists such as Piaget, Parten, Smilansky, and Seagoe categorize play stages and phases. Early learning practitioners become familiar with these varying perspectives and use the information to guide them in planning an environment that supports each child's phase of development and play interests. Table 2.2 provides a summary of the types of play stages with examples.

## Piaget's Stages of Play

As identified in Figure 2.4, Piaget (1970) suggests children participate in three distinct stages of play. Each stage contributes to the child's cognitive-developmental domain.

1. **Functional/sensorimotor play (birth to age 2)** is marked by play that focuses on simple, repetitive muscle-like movements with people, objects, and sounds. Functional play is most prevalent among children to approximately the age of two. It gradually declines to about one-third of the play of preschoolers, and less than one-sixth of play of school-aged children (Rubin, Fein, & Vandenberg, 1983). Some of the more common observable play examples are:

   • A toddler stacking blocks and then unstacking them.

   • A 3-year-old pulling a wagon with handles from the front and then pushing it from the back.

   • A 4-year-old who puts on a cape and repeats on several occasions—"I am superman."

   • A 5-year-old creates structures with blocks such as a bridge and a road with a specific pattern.

   • A 7-year-old traces marks in the sand.

2. **Symbolic/dramatic play (ages 2 to 7)** is marked by the onset of children beginning to express fantasy, use props, and take on roles other than being children. Isenberg and Jalongo (2010) suggest that this play has three elements: props, plot, and roles. This phase is linked to the pre-operational phase of development. As cognitive abilities advance, children expand the depth of their play by using objects, actions, and language in various ways. The children intentionally examine and determine the social roles that will be incorporated into their play. They make plans, they create options, and

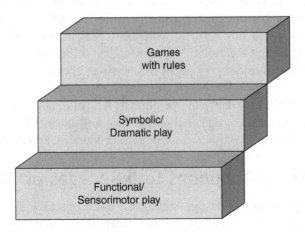

*Figure 2.4*  *Piaget's Stages of Play Development*

they express their feelings about how roles should be played out. Some examples of symbolic/dramatic play include the following:

- A toddler picks up plastic apples and pretends to eat them. As she advances in her play, she may offer the apples to other children or to her doll. This requires the child to have the cognitive skills to shift from a focus on her to others.
- The 3-year-old uses her fingers as imaginary friends and talks with them as playmates.
- The 5-year-old becomes a pilot. She lines chairs up for other children to sit on and then she makes announcements about the flight.
- School-aged children become detectives, use secret codes, use written and verbal language to make up clues and provide them to others to sort out the mystery.

Early learning practitioners encourage symbolic play for many reasons. This play increases children's memory capacity (Newman, 1990) and it provides a venue to acquire new ways of using language and vocabulary. This increases language acquisition skills. Symbolic/dramatic play contributes to children developing or enhancing their creative thinking and problem-solving skills, learning the importance of being flexible, and participating in inventive thinking (Pepler & Ross, 1981).

As children become more involved in dramatic play (as you will read in Chapter 4), the play generally includes two or more children. The children use their language skills to discuss the play episode and the direction in which the play will follow. This play is child-to-child rather than object-oriented as seen in symbolic play (Isenberg & Jalongo, 2010). Children exhibit social skills and use their knowledge and life experiences to think about the "what if" component of the play. This play may be extended for long periods of time or over several days. This extended play accommodates children trying new roles, refining roles, and adding new props based on group problem solving.

3. **Games with rules (school-aged children)** occur as children negotiate the rules before they engage in a play experience. As part of the process, the children determine how to deal with the consequences if rules are broken. Children exhibit reciprocity and turn-taking in their play. Games with rules may include outdoor play games such as street hockey or skipping games, or indoor games including board, card, and computer games. This play period is consistent with the concrete-operational phase of development. Children use more language skills, logic in their thinking, and advanced social skills, as this play requires negotiation skills, as well as cooperative and competitive skills.

## Smilansky's Contributions to the Stages of Play

Sarah Smilansky (1968) made two significant additions to Piaget's play stages. Children between 4 and 6 years of age participate in social/dramatic play that is complex and sophisticated. She labelled this as a constructive play stage and outlined six criteria for determining the level of the dramatic/sociodramatic play.

**Constructive Play Stage (4 Years of Age and School Age)**    This level of play is determined by the level of sophistication of the social/dramatic play. The level of role playing, the use of and creativity with the props, and the way in which the children use their imagination with the materials to construct the play experience all contribute to the sophistication of the play experience. Children combine functional and symbolic play (Forman, 1998) into the play episode. This play exhibits a high level of problem solving and social interaction among the children as they engage in the play.

Marshall, Megan, and Brittany visited a neighbourhood greenhouse. The children brought back many flowers and plants from the greenhouse to the early learning centre. They determined that they would like to turn the dramatic centre into a flower shop. They placed flower pots on shelves, they chose tall cups to use for vases, they took large pieces of newsprint from the easel to use for wrapping flowers and they used ribbon and string from the creative area to wrap flower packages. The children took a rectangular block and used it for the debit and credit card machine. This type of play shows how children combine construction (making the flower shop) with symbolic play (visiting the greenhouse) and then incorporating their play experience to reflect what they saw with how they created their play environment (Isenberg & Jalongo, 2010). Constructive play is about children enjoying a process of experimenting and exhibiting a sense of "what will happen if I do this" rather than creating a specific product.

Early learning practitioners observe both the level of construction play and the behaviours that are exhibited during dramatic play. This also supports early learning practitioners to facilitate advanced play options.

## Parten's Classifications of Social Play

Social play is essential for children. Social play leads children to develop skills such as sharing, turn taking, group work, and cooperative skills. Mildred Parten (1933) examined play from a social-behaviour perspective. Similar to Piaget, she identified that play progresses through a series of stages. It is interesting to note that although Parten correlated the phases of play with age ranges, more recent researchers describe Parten's phases of play as social descriptors rather than phases of play. Van Hoorn et al. (2007) and others suggest that children move back and forth in the cycles of play. For example, a 4-year-old child who is trying to figure out how to build a particular structure may require an environment that provides opportunities for solitary play experience because the child needs time to experiment, to think, and to try strategies. Once the child has figured out how to proceed, there is more opportunity to become a partner in an associative play experience.

1.  **Solitary Play**—The child generally plays alone. There is limited or no interaction with other children or with the materials that other children are using. Solitary play is influenced by the context of the play. Solitary play assists children in working out ideas, thoughts, and strategies for their play. For some children, it is easier to try ideas on their own, master them, and then share their learning with other children (Hendrick & Wiseman, 2006).

2. **Parallel Play**—Children begin to either play independently or beside peers—they do not play with peers. Children may use similar materials and play in similar ways, but they do not play together or share materials.

3. **Associative Play**—Children begin to share play materials and participate in similar activities. Children enjoy being with other children as much as the play experience itself. This is often thought of as the "bridging" phase as children transition between parallel and cooperative play.

4. **Cooperative Play**—Children participate in group play. Children determine a common goal and then each child works towards meeting the goal. Cooperative play is more prevalent among school-aged children than in preschool environments because of the experience and maturity required to negotiate roles and responsibilities, and work out strategies to complete the task. Cooperative play creates a bond with the group—children gain a strong sense of belonging.

Parten (1933) also identified non-playing as unoccupied behaviour time and onlooker play.

**Unoccupied Behaviour** is described as time when children are not engaged in play; the children appear to be wandering in the play area without a defined purpose. Mayfield (2001) indicates that "many contemporary researchers do not consider this to be a category of play, but rather a non-activity" (p. 268).

**Onlooker Play** refers to children who observe other children or adults in play but do not become involved in the play. They may ask questions of the play participants. Children may use this strategy to learn about particular materials or to determine how they may participate in a play episode.

## Seagoe's Contributions to Play

Seagoe (1970) added to the body of literature on the social aspects of play. She identified that as children approach 7–9 years of age, they participate in **cooperative-competitive play**. This involves play where children focus on team sports and victory, such as soccer and hockey (Dietze, 2006).

The transition from one stage of play to another does not mean that the child will not return to a previous stage. As each child engages in new play opportunities, new environments, and new playmates, there may be a change in the stage or phase exhibited. This is very common among children who move from one early learning care centre to another. For example, Jamie (age 4) had been in the same early learning centre for three years. He had four "buddies" that he played with on a daily basis. These buddies also lived on the same street. The children spent a great deal of time playing with one another (associative play) and were beginning to play as a group (cooperative play). When Jamie moved to a new neighbourhood, he played by himself (solitary play) for several weeks. Gradually, he began to play beside other children (parallel play) and then moved to associative play. As Jamie became more comfortable in the environment, he moved through the latter two phases more quickly than when he engaged in solitary play.

**Table 2.2**  *Types of Play Stages*

| Type of Play | Description | Example |
|---|---|---|
| **Cognitive Play**<br>Functional/<br>Sensorimotor | Simple, repetitive muscle movements, with or without materials. | Infants throw block from high chair.<br>Toddlers using a jack-in-a-box.<br>Preschoolers repeat a pattern in block structure.<br>School-age children figure out how things work. |
| Symbolic/Dramatic | Objects used in play as props.<br>Children take on roles such as being a firefighter. | Infants use blanket to disappear.<br>Toddlers pretend to eat toy as a cookie.<br>Preschoolers pretend by taking on roles such as a nurse.<br>School-aged children take on sophisticated roles such as in plays. |
| Games with rules | Predetermined rules and consequences understood before the play begins. | Infants play pat-a-cake.<br>Toddlers play peek-a-boo.<br>Preschoolers play simple games.<br>School-age children play games with more challenges, rules, and competitiveness. |
| Construction Play | Role play dominates play.<br>Creativity and imagination combined with materials are used to construct items according to a predetermined plan. | Preschool children build a bridge for goats to cross.<br>School-age children use materials to create complex items for their play such as tree houses. |
| **Social Play**<br>Solitary | Playing alone, without interaction with others. Use of materials is child's decision. | Infant plays with toys but does not acknowledge others.<br>Toddler plays beside other children but does not show an interest in other children.<br>Preschooler plays by self with own materials.<br>School-aged child plays with materials on own without peer contact. |
| Parallel | Playing independently or beside peer, but not with peers. The materials may be used in similar ways as peer. There is no sharing of materials during the play episode. | Toddlers play near others, without interaction.<br>Preschoolers play beside others, using the materials in different ways and for different goals.<br>School-aged child has a defined goal for his or her play. Is focused on achieving the goal on own. |
| Associative | Play occurs with other children. Materials are shared and playing together occurs.<br>Being with other children is as important as the actual play. | Preschool children use the same materials, but may not have the same goals in mind.<br>School-aged children may have similar goals but try different strategies to achieve the goals. |

*(Continued)*

*Table 2.2* (Continued)

| Type of Play | Description | Example |
|---|---|---|
| Co-operative | Play with other children as part of a group. Collectively the children determine a common goal and work toward achieving the goal through negotiation, role assignment, and problem-solving interaction. | Older preschools and school-age children determine the goal for the play such as building a beach resort. Each child has roles and responsibilities in the plan and execution of the play plan. |
| Co-operative-competitive | Playing occurs as part of a team. The team works together to achieve winning results. | School-aged children become members of teams; usually sport teams. Each child has a role and works with team members to achieve results. |
| Unoccupied | No engagement in play. | Children will be in the environment but are not engaged in play. They appear to be thinking or reflecting. |
| Onlooker | The child observes other children or adults in their play. | Infants watch the activity in their environment. Toddlers observe other children with specific toys. Preschoolers observe groups of children in play. School-aged children observe individual and teams in play. |

# CHILDREN AND THE THEORIES OF PLAY

Both in Chapter 1 and in this chapter, we have discussed aspects of children's play in an effort to answer questions such as "What is play?" "Why do children play?" and "What are the theories and beliefs that guide researchers, educators, and parents in understanding the purpose of play?" Exploring theories helps bring clarity to our beliefs and perceptions.

## Theories of Play

As discussed in Chapter 1, we are guided by the three groupings of theories; classical theories, modern theories, and contemporary theories. Each brings a perspective to the broad views of what play is.

## Classical Theories

Classical theorists examine play through theories of surplus-energy, recreation/relaxation, practice, and recapitulation (Ellis, 1973).

1. **Surplus-energy theory.** This theory identified by Friedrick Schiller and Herbert Spencer (Ellis, 1973) suggests that play is a mechanism to allow humans to burn off the excess energy that is not required for survival. When children are confined in their environment, they build excess energy. This causes children to become restless and unable to stay on task. Children need to expend the energy. This can best be achieved through active play experiences.

2. **Recreation/relaxation theory.** This theoretical base suggests that play is a mechanism to replenish energy after hard work has occurred. This is in direct opposition to surplus energy. When children engage in activities that are more cognitively focused, or have been alternating between quiet and active play, active play or rest is needed to replenish the child's energy. This rejuvenation allows children to refocus on activities requiring concentration. Children benefit from being in environments that support a rotation of sedentary activity followed by active play.

3. **Practice theory.** Play is a mechanism whereby the children practice adult roles and roles that are directly related to culture and community. Children will play roles of significant people in their lives such as the mother, father, or teacher, based on their observations.

4. **Recapitulation theory.** This theory differs from practice theory. Children engage in play that has them revisit the developmental stages their ancestors passed through. Children alleviate negative behaviours and develop correct processes that support current society.

## Modern Theories

Modern theorists examine play from the perspective of why play exists and the consequences of play for the child (Frost et al., 2008; Scarlett & New, 2007). Psychoanalytic theory, cognitive-developmental theory, and sociocultural theory are outlined in the modern theories grouping.

1. **Psychoanalytic theory.** This theory, supported by the work of Freud and Erikson, examines how play enhances emotional release and esteem building as children gain mastery and understanding of their thoughts, bodies, and social etiquette. Through play, children act out feelings and work through areas of challenge using the following two mechanisms:

   **Role switching.** During play, children may switch roles as a way to suspend reality and engage in behaviours that allow them to be a recipient of a bad experience or take on the dominant role of executing the experience. For example, if a child has been disciplined by a parent, a child may take on the role of disciplining a doll. This level of activity provides the child with a feeling of power while transferring the negative feelings to the doll.

   **Repetition.** When a child has had a negative experience, the child will seek out play experiences that will allow the negative experience to be replayed many times. The child gradually assimilates the actions and feelings associated with the event. For example, if a child has had a negative experience in a hospital setting, through play, each segment of the experience is played out. Gradually the child brings meaning to the event.

2. **Cognitive-developmental theory.** This theory, supported by the work of Bruner, Piaget, and Sutton-Smith, views play as a venue for children to use materials and interact with people as a way to build their knowledge about the world they live in. Children require time, flexibility, and the opportunity to practice new skills, test ideas, and amalgamate new ideas and information with previous knowledge and practices. Isenberg and Jalongo (2010) indicate "because children focus on the process of play, they engage in multiple combinations of ideas and solutions that they use to solve relevant life problems" (p. 57). Quality play experiences provide young children with the "testing ground" needed to discover ideas and transfer findings to daily living.

> **Narrative modes of thinking**
>
> refers to children figuring things out, learning-by-doing, making sense of ideas, and problem-solving areas to gain new knowledge, and then expressing learning through their narratives or storytelling.

**Bruner's theoretical construct** indicates there is a relationship between play and problem-solving abilities during childhood and later in life. In play, the means are as important as the end result because play promotes flexibility in solving real-life problems. The ability to problem solve provides a child with more behavioural options. There is a relationship between play and the development of narrative modes of thinking. Because children organize their knowledge in a sequential, narrative process, through verbal and logical play, as well as social-dramatic play, children perfect their narrative thinking skills and abilities.

**Piaget's theory**, as outlined earlier in the chapter, suggests that children engage in play experiences that correspond to their cognitive developmental levels. In order for learning through play to occur, the child must engage in an adaptation process. This requires the child to incorporate new information into existing structures (known as assimilation) and to modify existing cognitive structures (known as accommodation).

> **Adaptation**
>
> refers to an organism's ability to modify its environment or to find ways to fit with the environment (Vasta, Miller, & Ellis, 2004).

**Sutton-Smith's theory** reinforces that play impacts cognitive development. Play is important to the child's behaviour, creativity, and problem-solving skills. Through play, a child prepares to develop skills needed in adulthood, such as flexibility skills.

3. **Neurobiological theory.** With the advancement of technology, researchers continue to gain new information about the organization and functional operations of the brain. The environment children are exposed to positively or negatively impacts brain development. Children flourish in environments that are nurturing, stimulating, and responsive to their needs and interests. A child exposed to environments lacking in stimulation or with inappropriate stimulation, such as ongoing stress, is less likely to reach her potential.

Children who are engaged in quality play experiences are strengthening their neural network. This network is made up of the cells and synapses that develop during pregnancy and continue during the first three years of life. Synapses that are used regularly during play become permanent, while those that are not used are gradually eliminated (Shore, 1997).

## Contemporary Theories

Contemporary theorists examine play in relation to current societal issues such as diversity, social justice, and the relative nature of truth and knowledge.

1. **Sociocultural theory.** This theory is dominated by the work of Goncu, Vygotsky, and Bronfenbrenner. Children learn about the social and cultural contexts, such as their social world through their daily living experiences. Through play, children encounter problems and work through strategies that will support them in their problem solving.

   **Vygotsky's** (1978) **zone of proximal development** perspective suggests that through play, children stretch their boundaries to figure out situations and then construct knowledge.

   **Bronfenbrenner** indicates that a child's development is influenced by both the person and the environment, which includes family, community, culture, and the broader society. The personal characteristics as well as the interaction among people and their environment contribute to the child's development.

   **Goncu** (2000) and his colleagues examine child's play from both a cultural perspective and an interdisciplinary thinking process. Play behaviours are influenced by the economic, social, and political factors that are prevalent in larger cultures. The values and beliefs that adults have about play, directly influences the quality of the play experiences that are extended to children.

2. **Critical educational theory.** This theoretical framework examines education from the social-political and cultural context. Critical theorists examine how play is influenced by gender, class, and race inequalities within society. Children's play and learning experiences should be linked to their cultural experiences, and children should have freedom and control over their learning. Adults facilitate opportunities for children to examine the inequalities that exist within their learning environment and in society in general.

   Each theoretical framework presented is based on play as being a vital part of a child's life for optimal development, socially, cognitively, physically, and emotionally. This information causes early learning practitioners to think about values, beliefs, and philosophy about play.

> **Zone of proximal development (ZPD)** This concept developed by Vygotsky (1978) suggests that children require activities that support past learning and encourage new learning at slightly more difficult levels.

# PLAY AND CHILDREN WITH ATYPICAL DEVELOPMENT

Not all children engage in play in the same way. For example, children with atypical developmental patterns may participate in play differently from children with typical developmental patterns. Many children with atypical developmental patterns explore the play environment less. Their opportunity to participate in social play is more challenging (Jalongo & Isenberg, 2004). It is essential for children with atypical development to have environments that provide them with similar opportunities to children with typical developmental patterns. For example, in early learning centres where there are children in wheelchairs, the materials are placed in a space and at a level that will provide easy access for the child. Accommodations are made so that all children have equal access to obtaining blocks and building structures—these structures may be built on a large table top rather than on floor space.

Children with mobility disabilities have significantly reduced access to both indoor and outdoor play. For example, there are limited specialty playgrounds in early learning centres and in neighbourhoods that allow for inclusive practice. Although some physical modifications may be made to the equipment, there is a need for both physical changes and early learning practitioners to work with parents and children with disabilities to determine ways in which they can engage in safe play within the existing environment. For example, children with autism often engage in repetitive play. Over time, when the child has gained a comfort level, new risks will be taken to try new ideas (Atlas & Lapidus, 1987). Early learning practitioners continuously observe each child to understand their play patterns and needs.

We advocate that early learning practitioners develop a program philosophy that focuses on each child's developmental level and interest. This perspective allows every child to have their needs met without being centred out from other children. For example, if Jordan wishes to play in the dramatic centre but has a physical restriction of being able to manoeuvre to get the dress-up clothes on, the role of the early learning practitioner is to help Jordan problem solve as to how he can get the dress-up clothes on.

All children deserve access to an enriching play environment.

## THE ROLES OF EARLY LEARNING PRACTITIONERS IN PLAY

Throughout this book we will be discussing the roles and responsibilities of early learning practitioners in promoting play in the lives of young children. As a student practitioner you may think that **play is play**: however, it is a very complex component of a child's life. Below, we outline four key roles of adults who have an interest in promoting child's play.

1. **Adults role-model positive attitudes towards play.** Adults role-model and exhibit a positive attitude towards both indoor and outdoor play, each season. There is a balance between indoor and outdoor play throughout the year. There is a variety of active play experiences and materials that support each child's phase of development. The adult exposes children to play environments that meet established criteria for safety, risk, and challenge. The adult encourages children to engage in safe risk practices, particularly when children are trying new activities.

Play opportunities are encouraged that are free of bias and exhibit respect for gender, race, culture, interest, and abilities.

2. **Adults prepare appropriate environments.** Adults create equal opportunities for play experiences both indoors and outdoors. Children are provided with adequate options, intrigue, challenge, and freedom to explore with limited adult intervention.

   The early learning practitioners examine the ratio of children to materials. There are sufficient materials and equipment that accommodate the number of children in the play area. For example, Catron and Allen (1999) indicate that there should be 50 percent more play items and experiences available than children in the centre. This would mean, if there were 16 children in the early learning group, there are at least 32 items or experiences that children may choose from. The materials and experiences offer varying levels of difficulty according to the developmental levels of individual children and groups of children. When there are too many materials in the play space for children to choose from, the need for them to invent new uses for materials is reduced. This inhibits them from looking at the possibilities that materials may offer and it reduces the use of the child's wonderment and creativity.

   Both the indoor and outdoor experiences provide children with interest/exploratory centres, space designated for physical-movement activities, and places for children to pause and reflect or think about their next play experience. The play environments empower children to make choices and take safe risks as they explore the play possibilities.

3. **Adults observe children in their play.** Conducting observations and environmental scanning, which is an ongoing process, provides early learning practitioners with information about the child's interests, abilities, strengths, and opportunities for further learning and development. Early learning practitioners make connections about the types of materials, skills and interests that the child has by reviewing ongoing observations and documentation panels. Observations provide insight into the types of materials that may support the child in the play episode. When new play materials are offered that add new dimensions or challenge, the child engages in new discoveries through exploration and problem solving. Observations provide practitioners with insight into determining if and how the needs of the individual child and group of children are being met (Dietze, 2006). Further information on observations is outlined in Chapter 3.

4. **Adults promote play and opportunities for expansive discoveries.** Children's play is rich in experience, creativity, and imagination when it is child-initiated and reflective of the child's daily living experiences. Early learning practitioners facilitate play by encouraging children to bring their interests and experience into the play.

   One of the most challenging roles of early learning practitioners is to examine child's play and find the appropriate balance of facilitating play, engaging in the play episode, and determining the benefits of modelling particular behaviours or skills through play. Environmental scanning and careful observations help adults determine the most appropriate times and strategies to use to expand play opportunities and discoveries with children. When adults interrupt children's play, the benefits of the play experience to the development of the child's neural pathways *can* be inhibited. The child's neural pathways are influenced and advanced in their development as exploration, thinking skills, problem solving, and language expression occur during play episodes (Dietze, 2006).

Children are exposed to TV shows, videos, and violent toys through the various media. Young children are unable to discriminate between reality and fantasy (Gerbner, Gross, Morgan, & Signorielli, 1994). The more opportunity children have to use their creativity and imagination in positive ways in their play, the less they will participate in violent play. Positive play increases interactions and socialization skills.

## Adult's Participation in Child's Play

There are many perspectives on the role and level of involvement that adults should have in child's play. When appropriate, having children and adults participate in play provides opportunities for play, communication, relationships, and learning to be expanded in new ways. Children benefit from taking charge of the play with the adult. Adults encourage this by asking the child to explain each of the roles in the play episode and ensure that the child's performance or abilities are not judged. Student practitioners and early learning practitioners set aside their familiar roles and authority and follow the child's lead in the play. Adults avoid putting pressure on a child to succeed or do something the right way. They allow the play to unfold as the child wishes it to. Adults have important roles in child's play, from a coach to a partner, to a facilitator. The cues come from observing children in their play and listening to the children.

Johnson, Christie, and Yawkey (1987) identify three levels of adult participation in child's play experiences. They are parallel play, co-playing, and play tutoring.

**Parallel play** is described as adults playing beside the child, not with the child. The adult may use similar materials as the child. Adults exhibit this type of involvement when they wish to role-model positive play behaviours, without intervening in the child's play episode with words or active involvement.

**Co-playing** is used to describe play episodes that include a child or group of children and an adult. The children control the play, thus determining the role that the adult will have. Co-playing provides the adult with an opportunity to role-model particular skills and behaviours, and introduces the children to new language and problem-solving techniques.

**Play tutoring** is the third level of adult participation when the adult participates with a child or group of children and takes charge of the play episode for a short period of time. This involvement occurs when the adult recognizes, through observation, the need to shift the play in new directions. This is of particular importance if there is a level of aggressive behaviour beginning to develop, or if the play has potential to hurt a child physically or emotionally.

Heidemann and Hewett (1992) suggest that adults consider carefully when and how they become involved in children's play. The more adults become involved, the more intrusive and domineering the adults become in the play.

# SUMMARY

## Chapter Preview

- Children require opportunities to play. Children currently have little time to create play experiences. As a society, we are taking great risks in reducing children's play opportunities.

## Child's Play—from an Ecological Theory Perspective

- Urie Bronfenbrenner's ecological theory examines the relationship of how environmental influences contribute to a child's play experiences. There are five environmental systems: microsystem, mesosystem, exosystem, macrosystem, and chronosystem.

## Components of Play and Unique Features of Play

- Play requires child and adult interaction, physical space, and individual and group experiences.
- Play has three unique features: intrinsic motivation, active engagement, and process rather than product.

## Characteristics of Play

- Henniger, Isenberg, and Jalongo (2010) outline seven common characteristics of play. They are: play needs to be active, child-initiated and child-focused, process-oriented, episodic, rule-governed, intrinsically motivated, and symbolic and transformational.

## The Play Process

- Children advance through five phases in the play process: body play, motoring movement play, imaginative play, intentional imaginative play, and peer play with rules. The sixth phase of play occurs during adulthood.

## Classifying Play Experiences

- Early learning practitioners observe children's play and use information gained to plan an environment and experiences that support the developmental levels of children.
- Piaget identified three distinct stages of play: functional/sensorimotor, symbolic/dramatic, and games with rules.
- Smilansky identified, in addition to the stages of play identified by Piaget, that there is a construction play stage. She also outlined six criteria used to determine the level of dramatic/sociodramatic play.
- Parten outlined four stages of play from a social-behaviour perspective. They are: solitary, parallel, associative, and cooperative play. She also identified non-playing as unoccupied behaviour time and onlooker's play.
- Seagoe identified cooperative-competitive play as a stage that occurs between 7 and 9 years of age. This involves children focusing on team sports and victory rather than on an individual's performance and success.

### Children and Theories of Play

- There are three major groups of play theories. They are classical, modern, and contemporary.
- Classical theories focus on play from the surplus-energy, recreation/relaxation, practice, and recapitulation perspectives.
- Modern theories examine play from the perspective of the consequences of play for the child and how it impacts a child's development.
- Contemporary theories focus on the relationship of play to diversity and social justice relative to daily living and knowledge.

### Play and Children with Atypical Development

- Early learning practitioners observe children with atypical developmental needs to determine the types of environmental play space and play material modifications needed to support their play and learning opportunities.

### The Roles of Early Learning Practitioners in Play

- Early learning practitioners have many roles in supporting children's play. Four key roles are role-modelling positive attitudes towards play; preparing appropriate environments; observing children in play; and promoting play and opportunities for expansive discoveries.
- Johnson, Christie, and Yawkey (1987) indicate there are three levels of adult participation in play. They are parallel play, co-playing, and play tutoring.

# REVIEW QUESTIONS

1. How does Bronfenbrenner's Ecological Model of Development help early learning practitioners gain insight into the relationship of child development to play? Are there current Macrosystem and Chronosystem issues in your community that are impacting child's play? If so, how do early learning practitioners and families address the issues?
2. What is the significance of child's play, learning, and motivation? How do early learning practitioners and families address these components? What are the long-term challenges that could occur if children do not gain the internal motivational attributes to engage in play?
3. Describe how the seven common characteristics of play guide early learning practitioners and families in their work with children?
4. Outline the six phases of the play process. What do you envision the role of the early learning practitioner to be at each phase? Is one phase more challenging than another? Why or why not?
5. Explain the key stages of play development as outlined by Piaget, Smilansky, Parten, and Seagoe. How do these stages influence the work of early learning practitioners? How might play experiences differ in early learning environments with early learning practitioners who do not have this knowledge?
6. What are the key features of the classical, modern, and contemporary perspectives on play? Describe their similarities and differences.
7. Children with atypical developmental patterns may participate in play differently than those children with typical developmental patterns. How do early learning practitioners accommodate all children in the play environment?
8. Describe the four key roles that adults have in promoting child's play. Which are the most challenging? Why?

# MAKING CONNECTIONS

## Theory to Practice

1. You are working in an early learning centre. There is a 4-year-old boy who has been building the same type of skyscrapers for the past three weeks. If you made this observation, what recommendations do you have to handle this situation? Why?
2. In the chapter preview, we outline a play episode that Maja and Allie engage in. What have you gained from this chapter? Why might Allie have more concentration skills in the sand play environment than in other environments? What might be influencing Allie's interest in the sand play?
3. When you read the poem, The Little Boy, what information do you gain about the importance of environments supporting a process-oriented play environment rather than a product-oriented environment? How do early learning practitioners help parents understand the importance of these two concepts?
4. How do you envision a child's culture may impact imaginative play? Give specific examples. How would you support a child and family if their cultural perspectives do not include imaginative play options?

## For Further Research

1. W. George Scarlett, Sophie Naudea, Dorothy Salonius-Pasternak, and Iris Ponte (2005) indicate that there are three types of bad play. They are Risky Play, Mean-Spirited Play, and Misbehaving play. Research each of these terms and types of play to determine what is meant by them. How do early learning practitioners deal with these play categories in an early learning centre?
2. What are the characteristics of inclusive playgrounds? Where would you find one in your region? How does it differ from other playgrounds?

# ADDITIONAL READING

Canadian Child Care Federation. (2004). Supporting children to learn through play. Retrieved from http://www.cccf-fcsge.ca/pdf/RS77_ENG_web.pdf June, 2010.

Hyun, E. (1998). Making sense of developmentally and culturally appropriate practice (DCAP) in early childhood education. New York: Peter Lang. Retrieved from http://ruby.fgcu.edu/courses/ehyun/10041/culture_and_development_in.htm June, 2010.

Irwin, L., Siddiqi, A. & Hertzman, C. (2007). Early childhood development: A powerful equalizer. Final report. World Health Organization's Commission on the Social Determinants of Health. Human Early Learning Partnership (HELP). Vancouver, B.C.

# WEBLINKS

Cultural safety in practice with children, families, and communities
**www.ecdip.org/culturalsafety/**

Early Learning Report.
**www.ontario.ca/en/initiatives/early_learning/ONT06_018870**

# 3 Observing and Documenting Children's Play

## Learning Outcomes

After exploring this chapter you should be able to

- discuss the relationship of observation to play and learning;

- explain the debate relative to observations and pedagogical documentation;

- discuss the tenets of observations and the pedagogical process;

- describe 12 ways of acquiring information that supports student practitioners in understanding the whole child;

- discuss the use of specified observation and documentation tools;

- explain why it is important to conduct observations in both indoor and outdoor play settings;

- describe the process outlined of ways to discover information and understanding children and their play; and

- describe the types of discoveries that can be made through watching, listening, and discussing play with children.

## Stories from the Field: Practitioner to Student

I learned early in my studies and practice that there are differing perspectives on the purpose, methods, and usage of observations. I recall one professor during my college days indicating that without proper observational data, it was difficult to design and offer children an environment that supported the child's learning, interests, and phase of development. Some of our placements required us to plan activities specific to the observations made. If there were no observations, activities could not be planned or implemented. I still have mixed emotions about every experience planned needing to be based on observations. However, my feelings on this do not negate the importance of observation to early learning practice.

Learning to observe effectively is a process—and one that evolves and is refined as our knowledge about children and programming develops. I believe my observational skills and use of the information has been achieved not only through the ability to document what I see, using a variety of methods, but also to discuss my information with colleagues, the children, and parents and then reflect upon the discussions that have taken place as a result of sharing my recordings or interpreting what I see.

In essence, I believe that observations are like *painting* a picture or *weaving* a blanket. You need to look at the child and appreciate the vibrant rays that the child brings to the environment. Each discovery the child makes, changes the colours in the picture or the patterns in the blanket. I combine my observations with my knowledge of child development, my philosophy about play and learning, and most importantly with what I hear the children say and see them do. This strategy allows me to appreciate the strengths that each child brings to my life on a daily basis rather than making judgments about the child.

*Katrina, ECE Graduate, 2003*

# CHAPTER PREVIEW

Play is the vehicle for children's learning. When children use blocks, they may compare size, shape, height, and weight, one-on-one relationships, and related mathematical concepts. They may create interesting patterning and build structures that exhibit intriguing architectural designs. They may use blocks as cell phones in the dramatic area, and they may engage in social play, where they exhibit partnerships in play, cultural competencies, and language. How, as early learning practitioners, do we figure out what children know and what they are learning? When we observe children at play, we see children negotiating with others, having conversations with peers and adults, trying new ideas, and seeing their frustration levels. This information helps us to unlock the discoveries of children and their learning.

Friedrich Froebel (1782–1852) was one of the early theorists to identify the importance of the role of adults guiding and supporting children in developing knowledge, skills, and abilities that are essential tenets for them through their lifespan. Early learning practitioners examine the environment and children's play through observation. Practitioners develop effective observation skills and reflective practice strategies as a way to guide them in their work with children. "Observation is essential for understanding and responding to children" (Jalongo & Isenberg, 2004, p. 85). The results of observations help us to create nurturing environments. How we support children in their environment influences their desire to learn and develop.

The literature on observations and early learning is being examined, discussed, and redefined by many early learning practitioners, researchers, and educators. For some, conducting observations of children has been used as a strategy to assess the children's psychological development and behavioural patterns in relation to normative or documented developmental milestones (Kirova, 2009). It has been an accepted practice with specific tools intended to gain information about the child's development. The information discovered becomes the framework for the types of experiences offered to children that would complement their next phase of development. Based on the growing body of literature addressing the importance of understanding the whole child and the educational approach used in Reggio Emilia, Italy, there is an increased interest in adopting a contemporary perspective on pedagogical documentation processes. Many educators and researchers are suggesting that this practice provides valuable information that helps adults learn about and understand each child.

In this chapter, we provide information on both observations and pedagogical documentation. Early learning practitioners benefit from having a combination of skills and knowledge about observations and pedagogical documentation. Both these practices have merit as you prepare to become partners in learning with children and families. As you examine the information on observation and pedagogical documentation, you will note that one's philosophy and beliefs about how children learn will continue to be the foundation that guides our practice.

Planning play-based environments for young children requires early learning practitioners to have knowledge about and interest in each child. Understanding the child, child development, culture, and programming enhances the experiences and opportunities that may be extended to children. This requires early learning practitioners to use a variety of ways of knowing each child in order to make the connection with the children with whom the environment and program are being planned for.

Elizabeth McGill, an Early Childhood Education Instructor at Assiniboine Community College in Brandon, Manitoba, helps us examine how observations support the parent and early learning practitioner partnership.

## WORDS OF WISDOM

### How Observations Support the Parent and the Early Learning Practitioner Partnership

Research validates what early learning practitioner know intuitively: Children learn best through play. The terms for the types of programs change with academic trends—child-based curriculum, child-centred environment, and the latest, emergent curriculum.

Whatever you call it, play is back in vogue and it's all right. The challenge is in convincing parents that although what they may perceive as "just play" results in valuable learning. In the days of computer software for children preparing our babies to be future academic superstars, some parents may feel uneasy with the concept of play. The first few years are crucial for children to develop to their fullest potential. Are those years of opportunity squandered through play? Definitely not.

Every learning domain is enhanced through authentic play experiences. Authentic play experiences have these essential characteristics: intrinsically motivated, freely chosen, pleasurable, non-literal, and actively engaging the child.

An early learning practitioner observes, documents, and plans experiences that further a child's sense of wonder. This sets the stage for learning that intrigues a child. An early learning practitioner acknowledges the importance of interacting not only with the child but the child's family. Share and discuss observations with parents. A little time spent in learning what parents value and want for their children will help the early learning practitioner develop a program satisfying to both parent and child. It is well worth the effort!

## THE RELATIONSHIP OF OBSERVATION TO PLAY AND LEARNING

The work of Vygotsky and others helps us to understand how a child's perspective is merged and rooted in social behaviour (Ivich, 1994). A child's environment directly impacts how they learn, grow, and develop. For example, children use their cultural tools to change themselves; "the most powerful of which is language" (Broadhead, 2006; Vygotsky, 1976, 1978, 1986). In early learning and child care environments, it is the combination of materials, experiences, language among children and adults, cultural artifacts, and adults who are facilitators and coaches that stimulate a child's thoughts, experiences, and ultimately their play. The early learning environment and children's experiences are directly linked to an early learning practitioner's knowledge and understanding of child development, learning processes, environmental design, and the roles and responsibilities that adults exhibit in facilitating play and learning opportunities.

Children require environments where adults view play as a kaleidoscope—children playing with peers, engaging in creative and investigative work, participating in simple and complicated problem-solving activities, and where children are encouraged to take responsibility for their play choices and learning (Broadhead, 2006; Tyrell, 2001; Whitebread, 1996; Gura, 1992; Isaacs, 1929). Knowing how children play, investigate, explore, engage in peer-to-peer and child–adult relationships provide early learning practitioners with insight and understanding into the whole child.

There are some experts, including Broadhead (2006) and Nutbrown (1994), who encourage early learning practitioners to create a play "environment where [children] can access a **thinking curriculum** that allows them to develop their understanding of the world in conjunction with their own preoccupations, experiences and emerging schemata" (Broadhead, 2006, p. 192). To facilitate this, children require environments "where they can take their intuitive ideas about the world around them and, with scaffolding from adults and peers, test them against other theories and possibilities" (Broadhead, 2006, p. 192). In addition to examining the child's phase of development, adults use their observations and collaborative experiences with the child, family, and colleagues to guide them in understanding the child's knowledge, curiosity triggers, play partners, and the types of play experiences that support new exploration opportunities relative to the child's zone of proximal development. Early learning practitioners require strategies that will allow them to consistently examine children's play and learning.

**Thinking Curriculum**
A thinking curriculum weaves in the experiences and knowledge that children bring to the environment with new discoveries. Children connect the new discoveries with life experiences and transfer this knowledge to different settings or perspectives as required.

*Photo 3.1   Children need interesting experiences and materials for a thinking curriculum to evolve.*

***Photo 3.2*** *Adults need to allow children the opportunity to look, think, explore, and examine for a thinking curriculum to evolve.*

***Photo 3.3*** *Children benefit from different experiences in their settings. This is how they build upon the knowledge they bring to the environment.*

***Photo 3.4*** *Children engage in a thinking curriculum when they explore their discoveries together with their peers.*

***Photo 3.5*** *A thinking curriculum evolves when children have time to explore their environments.*

# AT A CROSSROADS: REDEFINING OBSERVATION PROCESSES

Conducting child observations as a way to develop an understanding about children is not new. In early learning and child care environments, child observation strategies have long been practiced as a guiding principle for program development. G. Stanley Hall determined that child observations provided a scientific method for educators to understand children. He incorporated observations into the child study movement in the late nineteenth century (Weber, 1984). His premise for observing children in the play settings was to collect data about each child so that the "true needs" of the child could be gained. On the basis of the data collected, Hall advocated that "the data of child development should provide the content of the curriculum" (Weber, 1984, p. 49).

Observation theory and application have been embedded into the early learning practice as a way to inform the development of child-centred, play-based programming (McAuley, 1993). Early learning practitioners conduct observations to gain information and insight into the children that they are working with in programs. In essence, as identified by Perry (1997), we need this information "in order to build a more complete picture of them" (p. 27). Early learning practitioners combine the data gathered with their knowledge of child development, so that they make connections between the child's interests, skills, and programming (Perry, 1997) that should be made available to children.

Many early learning and child care programs have used observation documentation not only for programming but also as a form of assessment. Observation documentation has offered support for the child when some external services are needed to further enhance specified areas of development such as speech and language. In recent years, observations have become part of some external organizations' expectations for accountability factors and program standards (Grieshaber, Halliwell, Hatch, & Walsh, 2001; Hatch & Grieshaber, 2002). Although seen as important by many policy and funding groups, educators, researchers, and practitioners are now questioning whether this practice is best for the child. Some suggest it has the potential to put pressure on children to perform to a set of predetermined standards. It may reduce our need to listen to the children, to appreciate their strengths and interests, and to authentically view the contribution each child makes to the early learning environment.

As we examine the literature today on pedagogical documentation, some may suggest that this is a new methodology and process for understanding children. Alcock (2000) indicates that researchers such as Susan Isaacs and Jean Piaget used a form of pedagogical documentation in their work with children. They used the documentation as a "tool for studying and *understanding* the whole child within an open paradigm, where preconceived standards such as developmental norms did not frame the observations" (Alcock, 2000, p. 5).

If Piaget used a form of pedagogical documentation in his work, why are we at a crossroads? Why is there a debate about which is better—the use of observations or pedagogical documentation? What we understand is that in the 1920s and 1930s, a "scientific expert" psychological perspective (Alcock, 2000) evolved. This started a shift in how observation data was interpreted and used. Instead of being used to understand the whole child, gradually the observations began to focus on looking at individual children's behaviours based on documented developmental norms for cognitive, social, emotional, and physical development.

The Reggio Emilia early childhood programs in Italy have provided educators, researchers, and practitioners with great insight into working with children and families. "Reggio leaders understand that no theory is the absolute truth, but is just a starting point for further investigation and discussion" (Pence & Pacini-Ketchabaw, 2008, p. 247). Early learning practitioners who are influenced by Reggio and Reggio-inspired programs find a need to "open up" their minds to a multitude of perspectives (Rinaldi, 2006) so that we do not become rigid in using one framework of thinking in our practice. This is changing how early learning practitioners approach their work with children. We are again seeking out practices that help us understand the whole child.

Pence and Pacini-Ketchawaw (2008) indicate that those who have been inspired by the nature of the programs in Reggio Emilia are transforming their practice. This has resulted in "re-imaging the child and the role of early childhood educators and institutions" (p. 247). Early learning practitioners, children, researchers, and educators collectively engage in **reflective practice** (Dahlberg, Moss, & Pence, 1999) in an effort to acquire a mutual understanding of both the adult and children's experiences of learning within their play environment.

There are many reasons to incorporate reflective practice into our work. For example, the reflective process of a situation or experience changes over time. As we gain new knowledge, our perspectives change. When we engage in collaborative reflective practice, our thoughts and perspectives may change. This allows us to construct shared knowledge and experiences. This enhances our knowledge and learning environment. Reflective practice is now a vital part of early learning practitioners' practice in gaining a sense of understanding the whole child.

Early learning practitioners require knowledge about the relationship of child development to play, observations to play, documentation to play, and reflective practice to advancing play. These knowledge touch points are essential in your role as the architect: the person who creates diverse learning environments to support each child's needs. Gathering information about children and being able to effectively use the information acquired from observations and discussions flourishes when the early learning practitioner looks at child's play from an inquiry/wonderment perspective. Think about what makes this child interested in play with puppies. Why does a child usually gravitate to the block area at a particular time each day? Is there a reason why Sammy and Jake find it so difficult to allow Markas into their play? Why does Markas have a need to play with Sammy and Jake?

Ross-Bernstein (2001) describes each child as an *ever-changing* puzzle that early learning practitioners try to make sense of. She describes observations and data gathering as an "art form, which takes practice, skill and persistence" (p. 3). It is our role to develop an understanding of what each child brings to the play environment. All children are different. Some are exuberant, leading them to be explorers, and risk takers; other times they are introverted and reserved; their emotions range from happy to sad, quiet to loud. Because each child is packaged differently, one of our roles as early learning practitioners is to become partners with children as co-inquirer and

**Reflective Practice** with children is a continuous process involving the early learning practitioner and the children reflecting on significant discoveries or experiences that occur during play episodes. Drawing from the work of Schön (1983), early learning reflective practice involves children and adults by thoughtfully considering the child's experiences in applying knowledge to practice. The early learning practitioner may coach the child through a questioning process. Reflective practice brings to light a child's individual strengths, learning styles, and ways of knowing.

co-investigator. Think about your role as trying to gather information to crack an important mystery or case. Each time you gain information about the child, more questions will evolve and that will lead to more observations and further investigations, providing more clues to the mystery of development. In essence, it is a continuous process. You are always trying to gain insight into the child's play so that you can create an environmental framework that will support the child in his quest to discover new knowledge.

In the next section, we highlight information on observation and pedagogical documentation. As you review this information, we suggest that you think about how observation, reflective practice, and pedagogical documentation strengthen the knowledge and skills of early learning practitioners and ultimately the experiences extended to children.

*Photo 3.6   Pedagogical documentation of a human body project.*

# OBSERVATION AND PEDAGOGICAL DOCUMENTATION

## Defining Observation

Early learning practitioners have many roles throughout the day—one of which includes observing children at play from a variety of perspectives. Observing is more than watching children play. It includes skills in (a) watching and observing, (b) documenting, (c) coaching, (d) facilitating, (e) reflecting, (f) planning, and (g) analyzing the observations with children, parents, and colleagues so that appropriate play experiences may be offered.

More specifically, observation is defined as a systematic process used to listen to and watch children in their play. Its purpose is to gain information about a child's or group of children's stage of development compared with documented developmental norms or behaviours that are expected for a particular age group.

Observation tools are considered informal; they are not diagnostic. If more formal assessment tools and screening tests are required for children, they would be conducted by a specialist in assessment and child development.

Observations may take many forms—from pictorial documentation to predefined charting methods. The information gained from observations is used to plan an environment for children with potential experiences that support their interests and phase of development.

## Defining Pedagogical Documentation

**Pedagogical documentation** may be a new term for some early learning environments. You may find that it has a different meaning for early learning practitioners, depending on one's educational background, work experience, and philosophy.

According to Alcock (2000),

> Pedagogical documentation can be defined as all documentation that has pedagogy as its focus. The documentation may be thought of as content and the pedagogy as process. In this way pedagogical documentation can be used as a tool for mediating the understandings of both adults and children. By making children's thinking visible, documentation facilitates teaching and learning. (pp. 1–2)

Kirova (2009) indicates that pedagogical documentation is a way in which early learning practitioners examine, see, and understand what is going on in the work and what the child is capable of. This orientation looks at the child for what he or she brings to the environment rather than having a predetermined framework of expectations.

**A content of documentation** refers to the materials or tools which represent the child's activities such as what they are doing, what they are discussing, what they are involved in, what triggers their curiosity, and the work of the children. Content documentation may include

- children's works;
- audio/video recordings of children and their early learning practitioners engaged in action;
- photographs and documentation of work in progress;
- children's illustrations; and
- storyboards with comments and pictorial information.

**A process of documentation** refers to how the documentation encompasses what is to be reflected on, discussion points, and action that is generated from the documentation, as well as the reflective process, including what is seen, what is heard, and what interests the children generate. The reflective process brings together parents, children, and early learning practitioners to engage in dialogue, exploration, questioning, and charting ideas for new directions. The documentation process tools may include

- Cameras
- Audio/video recordings

*Photos 3.7, 3.8, and 3.9   Children learn by exploring, discussing, and reflecting on experiences.*

- Computers
- Pictorial elements
- Notes by children and adults

Pedagogical documentation extends beyond the observational stage. It is a cyclical process, which brings children and early learning practitioners back to a new beginning point (Pence & Pacini-Ketchabaw, 2008). Pence and Pacini-Ketchabaw (2008) indicate that those who use pedagogical documentation as a tool "are not fixed in guidelines that provide one view of the child; rather they are opened to multiple voices, multiple interpretations—opened to diversity" (p. 248). In Reggio Emilia, the term used to describe curriculum is *progettazione*, which means to project to the next steps. Pedagogical documentation is not only concerned with project topics but with constructing *progettazione* in the process of each activity or project. Throughout the process of documentation, the program is adjusted accordingly through a continuous dialogue among the teachers and with the children (Gandini & Goldhaber, 2001).

# Stop . . . Think . . . Discuss . . . Reflect

What does it mean to you when you read about becoming partners in play in early learning environments? As partners, who does the program planning? What is the role of an early learning practitioner in being a partner? Is it the same as the role children have? Why or why not? How would your role with children be examined? Who would examine what you do in your role? What tools would be used to do this?

# EXAMINING THE DIFFERENCE BETWEEN CHILD OBSERVATION AND PEDAGOGICAL DOCUMENTATION

There are differences between observation processes and pedagogical documentation as identified in Figure 3.1. Observations generally focus on concentrating on one aspect of a child's play for a specific purpose. Observation data is generated so

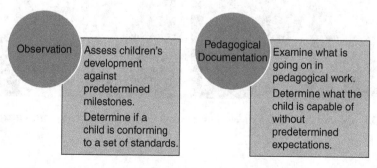

*Figure 3.1 Differences between Child Observations and Pedagogical Documentation*

that the practitioner may gain insight into a child's developmental phase and interests. Pedagogical documentation focuses on the child's process of learning and the interconnectedness between the child's ideas, partners in learning, and play. It looks at what the child brings to the environment as an individual rather than making a comparison of the child to others.

Dahlberg et al. (1999) help us gain further insight into the difference between child observation and pedagogical documentation. They indicate:

> As we understand it, the purpose of "child observation" is to assess children's psychological development in relation to already predetermined categories produced from developmental psychology and which define what the normal child should be doing at a particular age. The focus in these observations is not children's learning processes, but more on the idea of classifying and categorizing children in relation to a general schema of developmental levels and stages . . . "Child observation" therefore is mainly about assessing whether a child is conforming to a set of standards. "Pedagogical documentation" by contrast is mainly about trying to see and understand what is going on in the pedagogical work and what the child is capable of without any predetermined framework of expectations and norms. (p. 146)

Dahlberg and Moss (2005) as cited by Pence and Pacini-Ketchabaw (2008) indicate that

> Documentation is not . . . "child observation" that assesses children's progress (usually in terms of development) against predetermined and normative categories . . . Instead, (Reggio Emilia educators) have shown how documentation, used in a critical way, can make us observant of the contingency of our constructions, and hence, make it possible to destabilise the meaning of that which we take for given and see as natural and true about the child . . . [Documentation] has helped [teachers] to refuse to codify children in prefabricated developmental categories, and hence they have been able to transgress the idea of a lacking and needy child. (p. 248)

## Moving Forward

In the preceding section, we have introduced you to information on the traditional observation process and pedagogy documentation. As early learning student practitioners, you will have the opportunity to discuss, debate, experience, and reflect on the most appropriate process for acquiring information about the children that you are working with. No matter what your philosophical orientation is or becomes, there is a need for you to develop observation skills that look at children's play from a variety of perspectives and to engage in dialogue with children, parents, and colleagues about your reflections and perceptions of what you see. There is also a need to work with children to document their learning and to have them revisit their learning and their experiences.

Early learning practitioners require skills in observing and in becoming a documenter—the documentation process communicates the important stories about our work with young children and families. It allows us to capture and share children's learning and experiences. When we are transparent in communicating this valuable information, it helps both the children and early learning practitioners share with parents the types of play experiences children engage in, how the learning occurs, and how children use one learning experience as a jump-off point to embark on new learning options. As early learning practitioners develop documentation processes and reflective practice, they also advance their skills for being able to understand children and being able to communicate with them through information sharing and questioning. These strategies lead children to collaborate with other peers and adults in ways that brings new options for learning. Dahlberg et al. (1999) suggest that pedagogical documentation is a "vital tool for the creation of a reflective and democratic pedagogical practice" (p. 145). Documentation as described by Gandini and Goldhaber (2001) is a way of democratizing early childhood education through the collaborative and collective voices of children, teachers, and families.

## Ways of Acquiring Information to Support Student Practitioners Understanding the Whole Child

Early learning practitioners have an obligation to acquire knowledge about the children in their care. Various aspects of their play are examined in order to develop an understanding of the whole child. The following guidelines are intended to help you develop strategies to gain information about children that will support you in your work with them.

**Organize your observation tools**   Develop a system to determine the type of observation you will conduct and how you will track your observations in a way that is efficient for you. These tools, combined with discussions with the child, early learning practitioners and parents guide you in planning experiences.

**Develop purposeful observations**   Generally, observations have a purpose. Knowing the purpose of the observation helps observers collect the information that will be useful in gaining insight into the question that triggered the observation. For example, if you are interested in observing a child new to the centre, for the purpose of determining the child's interest, would it be valid to observe the child on the first day and then determine what the child's interests are? Or, would it be reasonable for you to observe the child on your first day working at the centre and then make statements of what the child's interests are? It would be unlikely that we could gather accurate information about the child under these conditions. Neither of these cases would provide purposeful observations because of the conditions in which the observations were carried out. Observations are not useful if conducted under challenging conditions—either for the child or the early learning practitioner.

**Involve children and adults in observations**   At times, it is beneficial to have children as active participants in observations. You need to determine why you are conducting the observation and then determine the level of involvement of the children. For example, when appropriate, asking probing questions and listening to the children provides insight into what children say about their learning, their activities, their experiences, and their interests. Involving children also provides opportunities to discuss their vision for play and learning.

**Examine information from varying perspectives**   There are many ways to view children's play. By having more than one early learning practitioner observe a child at the same time, you may acquire varying perspectives on the same situation. Think about the child playing in the sandbox and three practitioners conduct an observation. Most likely there will be aspects of the observations that differ. Through dialogue and reflection, you each gain new insight and understanding into the child.

**Recognize what your biases and perceptions are**   We all have biases and perceptions. As early learning practitioners, it is important to be aware of the biases and perceptions that we bring to the environment. For example, if you determine that you do not like completing observations, this will impact what you see, the way in which you record your findings, and how you use the information gained from your observations. When you find yourself in a compromising position, it is important to develop a strategy to manage your biases so that every child has the opportunity to play and learn in a comfortable environment. Our personal life experience, culture, and philosophical orientation towards working with children influence our observations.

Think of 3-year-old James. James has had a temper tantrum on a daily basis for the past week when his dad drops him off at the centre. You observe the dad as being patient, offering words of comfort to James, yet he gets on the floor, he kicks, and screams. You may think to yourself—this child is "spoiled" and the father should not allow James to get away with this. Once we label the child as "spoiled," we have expressed our bias and reduced our ability to see the child with an objective lens. This has the potential to interfere with seeing the strengths of the child and understanding the needs that would support the child.

**Listen to the children**   Listening to the children helps early learning practitioners document useful information about each child and their play. This, combined with what you see, provides rich insight into the child's play and learning. It is useful if the observer has the opportunity to record specific quotes from the child's play. Read the play episode of Nabil on pages 90–91. Then think about how his direct quotes help to discover insight into his knowledge about the use of a cell phone and business etiquette evidenced by his comments of "Nice doing business today."

**Review documented observations many times to seek meaning**
When you review observations at different times, important details evolve that lead you to make connections about the child and their play. Think about 3-year-old Damian. In reviewing a video observation you notice that he is using red and black play dough. You note that he extracts a piece of play dough from the large

play dough ball with his thumb and forefinger on his right hand and then rolls it into a smaller ball. He alternates between the red and the black play dough. Upon review of the video three times, you notice that the more Damian used the play dough, the more efficient he became in the process. For example, instead of making one ball at a time, near the end, he divided both the black and the red play dough into pieces. Then, he rolled all of the red play dough into the balls and then rolled the black ones. This change in process led him to eliminate the movement back and forth from one end of the play dough table to another. Although we can't determine from this observation if Damian made the decision to change the process or if it just happened, it would be helpful to pose probing questions to Damian to gather his thought process on the play dough experience.

**Examine children's play patterns and actions**  By reviewing observations and documentation, early learning practitioners and student practitioners gain insight into the ways in which children approach problems and problem solving. For example, when a child has determined a strategy to figure something out to achieve the desired effect, generally the child will proceed with confidence. However, if it does not unfold as the child thought it might, there may be a pause or change of directions. This tells us that the child has engaged in a different thinking pattern.

Think about Melissa, a 4-year-old child playing with connector blocks. According to your observation Melissa has spent seven minutes picking up long connector tubes, placing the connectors on them, and trying to make them stay upright. Each time the structure fell, she rotated the connectors. She then stopped working with the blocks and walked away from the area. Melissa went to the block area and then returned. Why do you think Melissa left the area? Why might she have gone to the block area? What might she have gained from going to the block area? When Melissa returned, she tried a couple of new actions. In the end, she added long connector pipes and connectors both lengthwise and crosswise on the bottom portion of her structure. This gave her structure the stability that was needed.

**Examine how children co-construct knowledge**  We encourage children to play and learn together. As identified in Chapter 2, there are different levels of social play that children participate in. Children may collaborate with one another on a particular play project or several play experiences. Think about Maryellen and Mattie at the sand table. You heard Mattie indicate that she would like to make an underground tunnel between castles. As she began to dig out the sand, she made more of a roadway than a tunnel. Mattie then announced to Maryellen "It is not working." They tried a couple of ways without success. Then Maryellen suggested they needed something for a base. Maryellen went to the block centre and brought back pipe pieces. They dug a hole, put the pipe in between the castles, and then covered it with sand. Mattie identified that they needed to scoop out the sand at both ends. Together, Mattie and Maryellen co-constructed knowledge that led them to figure out how to build the tunnel between the castles.

Early learning and child care programs that use a **co-construction** of knowledge philosophical orientation will benefit from early learning practitioners being participant observers. This allows the early learning practitioner to participate

**Co-construction** is defined as the generation of new knowledge by two or more people, that neither would be able to generate alone (Damon, 1984; Rafal, 1996). Co-construction results in the partners in play to internalize the knowledge, use the knowledge independently, and to use the knowledge with others.

*Photo 3.10    Co-constructing a play experience.*

in the play through discussions about play ideas, in the construction of ideas, and listening to the children's thoughts. The adult discovers possible future paths of interests and opportunities for learning.

**Examine how children express meaning and representation**    One of the purposes of child's play is to help a child bring meaning to their world. As you review the observations of Fritz and Gunter in the block centre, you note that both children are building structures. There is no verbal communication between the children as they build their structures. Fritz's structure has three levels to it, while Gunter's building has only one level. When Fritz's structure was complete, he said to Gunter, "Me, my Oma and Opa live here." Gunter responds saying that "me live here and my Oma and Opa live far away. They need a plane to see me." Later that day, the early learning practitioner found out that Fritz, Gunter, and families had spent the weekend together with their grandparents. Gunter's grandparents returned to Germany on Monday. When children are able to express meaning and representation in a visual format, they begin to develop the skills to be able to verbally express their thoughts. Expressing representations is interrelated to a child being able to think about life experiences and bring meaning to her thoughts.

**Examine the observations to determine the level of meta-cognition the child exhibits**    When we think about meta-cognition, we are seeking insight into how children express knowledge about their thoughts, their thinking process, how they approach a task, and what success is. Shammin is 5 years old. You observe him and his buddy Matthew at the art centre. Shammin says to Matthew, "I don't like drawing faces. It's too hard. I can't get the eyes and the nose right." Matthew says, "I draw a circle, and then I put the nose in the centre of the page." As you review the children's comments, you realize that such a comment reveals that Shammin has evaluated his ability to make faces; he has also brought feelings from a past experience to his present situation. This illustrates how Shammin thinks about his abilities and how he has worked it through to be able to communicate his feelings and the challenges that he has with producing a face. You also note that Matthew tries to help Shammin by sharing his process.

**Examine children's play and determine if and how it should be documented** Children and early learning practitioners benefit from documenting experiences and learning about what children engage in. As you observe children in their play, it is beneficial to determine if the play episode should be documented, what might the benefits be and how would be the most effective way to document it.

When children and/or early learning practitioners are able to document and share learning, it helps to tell stories of their learning. This is an important strategy that brings meaning to the play for both the child and adults. Most often, documentation and storytelling provide insight into interests and potential direction that will bring forth further wonderment to the child.

*Photo 3.11* Early learning practitioners and children need to determine what aspects of their projects and their daily experiences should be documented.

# OBSERVATION AND DOCUMENTATION TOOLS

There are many observation tools and documentation methods that are used by early learning practitioners to gain information about an individual child and groups of children in their play.

Early learning practitioners need to become skilled in using the tools, documenting findings or insights, and discussing perspectives with colleagues, children, and parents.

Some of the tools presented in Table 3.1 are more focused on pedagogical documentation strategies. Some of the tools do not necessarily support the perspective of using observations to understand the whole child from multiple perspectives (Alcock, 2000), as they generally focus on one aspect of the child's play. As part of developing your practice, you will need to try a number of tools in order to gain an understanding of different ways and perspectives that help you to acquire information about a child. Remember, observations and documentation help you learn about children as you make connections to growth and development, learning styles, children's interests, knowledge, diversity, and abilities.

Early learning student practitioners try different tools to become familiar with how to use the tool and the benefits of each. Over time, gathering data becomes more comfortable and efficient. Active involvement with the children in observations and documentation is a practice that we strongly advocate be practiced. When children and early learning practitioners are partners in the play environment, including observations and documentation, there is less emphasis on early learning practitioners seeing the child from a behavioural perspective or in comparing one child to another. Using a variety of methods is a more inclusive practice and it allows adults to look at situations and each child from multiple perspectives. This creates rich data that will help plan for children's experiences and our facilitation strategies with children.

## Where Do Observations Occur?

There is a great debate about what the most appropriate environment is for observing children. Are observations better suited to be conducted indoors or outdoors? The answer depends on one's philosophical beliefs. For example, if you are working in an early learning and child care environment that focuses more on the indoor portion of the program than outdoors, or if there are less materials available for outdoor play, and if children spend more time indoors than outdoors, then it is likely that there is a perception that indoor play is more important than outdoor play. If you have an attitude that outdoor play is for a child's recreational needs, then this too will influence where and when you will engage in observations. Conversely, if you recognize the richness of play, language, and creativity that evolves in the outdoor environment, you will want to ensure that you engage in observations when children are involved in outdoor play.

*Table 3.1* *Observation and Documentation Tools*

| Tool | Use of Tool |
|---|---|
| **Portfolio**<br>The purpose of a portfolio is to be an active, living document that assists in planning potential experience centres and learning opportunities for an individual child and groups of children. | A portfolio is a parent–child and early learning practitioner document that is made up of a collection of observations, creative samples, pictures, anecdotes, recordings, and other artifacts that documents a child's experience while in the early learning centre.<br>The portfolio records an array of experiences and achievements that informs how learning occurs through play. It supports children, early learning practitioners and parents in capturing and understanding the child's experience.<br>Early learning practitioners and children collectively examine information to determine what learning is best to document and what strategy best documents the learning episode.<br>These should be a living document that children have access to on a daily basis. |
| **Photographs**<br>The purpose of photographs is to be able to capture particular moments in time. They support children, parents, and early learning practitioners in revisiting previous play and learning experiences. They may become part of public documentation of learning. | The photographs provide a record of a specific action, interests, skills, and developmental levels.<br>Photographs are a useful tool to help children recall experiences, reflect on experiences, and project how new experiences could evolve.<br>Often, photographs become valuable parts of stories of learning and may be transferred to a child's portfolio.<br>When children have access to photographs instantaneously, they spontaneously describe activities and explanations about their play. This level of engagement is rich with information about the child's play. |
| **Brief Notes**<br>The purpose of a brief notation is a beginning strategy used in observation. They are also used to record important information that may be used to trigger other ideas or to examine specific information with children. | Using a form of shorthand, the early learning practitioner records a brief note that depicts an action or experience observed. These brief notes may be discussed with the children, included with photos, or placed in the child's folder on his own.<br>Early learning practitioners may ask children specific questions about what they would like to do in the environment. Brief notes may be used to record this information and then used later to share with the children as part of a plan and review process. |
| **Peer-to-Peer Observation**<br>The purpose of the peer-to-peer observation is to observe the types of interactions between adults and children, and approaches used by practitioners to facilitate play with children. | Designated early learning practitioners and/or children may take part in a peer-to-peer observation, either as the observer or being observed. Generally, focused questions are formulated prior to the observation. The questions may focus on how children and adults manage in particular situations such as peer interactions, or how children manage in their environment.<br>The early learning practitioner team examines the responses to the questions and extracts themes of best practices and areas for further exploration. |
| **Video Recordings**<br>The purpose of video recordings is to capture a child's activity and actions exhibited during play. | Similar to the portfolio, the video recording is a way to record data that illustrates the child's play. It provides insight into the communication process among the children and adults. The data may be transferred to |

**Table 3.1**  (*Continued*)

| Tool | Use of Tool |
|---|---|
| These recordings support groups of practitioners and children in examining the same data and discussing their perceptions of what they see both from a child and an early learning practitioners perspective. | written records, as it provides insight into a sequence of events that helps to understand attributes that the child brings to the environment.<br><br>The video recording allows the early learning practitioner and parents to view the child in her play. It helps parents to see how play contributes to the development of the whole child. |
| **Learning Stories and Journeys**<br>The purpose of learning stories is to document a particular activity or experience or group of experiences that a child or group of children participate in. | Learning stories capture a child's or a group of children's play and the related aspects of learning and development. Learning stories are a form of documentation that may be referred to when examining the current and previous interests of a child. It provides insight into the sequence of experiences and timing of interests. They are often used in conjunction with photos or video recordings. |
| **Running Records**<br>The purpose of these records is to provide a detailed narrative account of a child's play or behaviour written as it happens. | These comprehensive records are completed as you see a child engaged in an identified play experience or behaviour. They provide insight into targeted areas of investigation. For example, if a child is having difficulty adjusting to the program, a running record may be completed to seek answers into specified periods/activities of the program that causes distress. |
| **Anecdotal records**<br>The purpose of anecdotal records is to record in-depth, targeted information about a particular event or experience after it happens. | This method requires observation and recording of observations in detail as to what you saw. These longer narratives can be collected over a period of time. They are specific in describing detail of an observed event. |
| **Frequency Count**<br>The purpose of this observation method is to record the frequency of a specific play experience, event, or behaviour. | This method is used to determine how often a child participates in a particular event or behaviour. For example, how often does a child use the dramatic centre? Who uses the dramatic centre? What are the challenges with children in the dramatic area? How often do the challenges occur? |
| **Checklists**<br>The purpose of a checklist is to record specific traits or behaviours that are observable. The observed behaviour is checked off as seen. | This tool requires the observer to have an in-depth understanding of the developmental milestones of children. The checklist tools are useful for recording developmental abilities and growth that children achieve over time. |
| **Learning Journals**<br>The purpose of the learning journal is for children and early learning practitioners to be able to record any information about their learning, their feelings, and their reflections. It may be done in word or pictorial format. This is a working, fluid document that may be public or private. | A learning journal is a tool that is used to explore and record self discoveries or to generate new ideas. It is often used to record experiences or events that include reflection and commentary. |

In order to acquire an understanding of the whole child, early learning practitioners conduct observations in both the indoor and outdoor environments. Early learning practitioners gain different information about the child *and* with the child, in the two settings. Although most observations are conducted indoors, we advocate that early learning practitioners give children equal access and consideration to both environments. Wellhousen (2002) indicates the following reasons to observe children during their outdoor play experiences.

- Outdoor play provides an opportunity to observe the gross motor developmental milestones of the child. Skills such as jumping, running, and climbing are less likely to be allowed indoors. This is an authentic environment for such activities where accurate observations may occur.
- The outdoor play environment sees children exhibiting different strengths or new challenges from those observed indoors.
- Conducting observations outdoors, communicates to colleagues and parents the need for, and the value and benefits of outdoor play to a child's development.
- Children's outdoor play is different from indoor play. New interests are discovered in outdoor play.
- Outdoor play contributes to experiences that support the child's overall developmental domains.

As we continue to support children in developing healthy, active lifestyles, the need for outdoor play experiences will only increase. Observing children outdoors is crucial to understanding the child, their play interests, and the environment that will support their exploration and discovery.

## Stop . . . Think . . . Discuss . . . Reflect

How does observing outdoors differ from indoors? Do you think you get better information about a child from observing their play indoors or outdoors? What are the challenges of observing children outdoors? Why? How would you conduct outdoor observations during the winter months? Is the process different from the spring? Why or why not?

## Discovering Information and Understanding Children and Their Play

There are a number of ways to get to know and understand children. It is a process that develops with time, experience, and guidance. The information outlined in Table 3.2 is intended to provide you with a starting point of ways to discover information about children and their play.

*Table 3.2*  *A Process for Discovering Information and Understanding Children and Their Play*

**Preparation.**   What do I already know about this child? Is there specific information that I would like to try to discover about the child? What information is missing that would help me understand the child in more depth? How might I collaborate with the children, colleagues, and parents to acquire the information?

The early learning practitioner determines what information is known about the child and what may be helpful to understand the child more fully.

**Selecting an information gathering tool.**   What methods or tools are available that would help me capture the information that I seek? Why would one method or tool be used over another?

The early learning practitioner examines the various tools and methods and determines which one is most efficient relative to the information being sought. Pertinent materials are prepared.

**Gathering information.**   How will I gather the information? Where will I gather the information? What role will I play? What role will the children play? Is there a role for colleagues? If so, what is that role? How will I record the information?

The early learning practitioner determines what strategy and resources to use to gather information about a child or children in their play. The strategy should support the type of information being sought.

**Review of information.**   What can I glean from the information gathered? What new information has been acquired? How do my perceptions align or differ from my colleagues and children? What connections can I make to my previous understanding of the child? What did I notice about the child that I have not previously noted? What did the child learn through play? How do I share the information with the children? What information from this process is valuable to communicate to the child, other practitioners, and family? What is the best way to do so?

The early learning practitioner examines the information and discusses it with experienced practitioners to collectively interpret the data in terms of making connections, seeing themes, or examining gaps. Discussions assist in developing a program that is supportive of a child or group of children's needs and interests.

**Sharing learning.**   What new information have I gained? How will it inform and guide my practice in the role of an early learning practitioner? What questions may help me clarify information with the child? What are some of the questions that I may seek to answer in my reflective process? Are there aspects of my information that I would like to move to story format for the child or with the child? What core questions may an experienced early learning practitioner help me clarify? How do I isolate the correct information that will help me in determining the types of experiences to provide an individual child and groups of children? How do I share the information with the various audiences?

The early learning practitioner uses the results of the data analysis to guide one's practice, and in working with the child to determine the types of experiences that will support the child in being stretched just beyond their knowledge and skill level.

**Reflective practice.**   How do I use the information gained to support the child or groups of children? How do I know if the new types of experiences that I wish to offer a child or children support their learning? How do I know that my perceptions are correct? Why do I feel that I am missing some aspect of information that would help me understand a particular child better? Why do I feel a disconnect? How does this information inform my practice? What might I do differently next time?

The early learning practitioner continues to seek out information that will answer questions and support a child or group of children. The practitioner continuously seeks information and answers from the children, colleagues, parents, and the environment to ensure that expanded play experiences contribute to learning and development.

## Stop . . . Think . . . Discuss . . . Reflect

Are observations and data gathering always planned and analyzed? Why or why not? What might you consider doing if you see a child engaging in a play experience that you have not seen before but you do not have observation tools ready? How do you gather the information and move it to a sharing process?

## The Types of Discoveries Made through Watching, Listening, and Discussing Play with Children

Children are influenced by people, places, experiences, and environments. By watching, listening, and discussing play, early learning practitioners may make many discoveries about a child. When early learning practitioners examine play episodes from the perspective of a child's life experience, developmental milestones, and the environment, as outlined in Figure 3.2, new insight into the child—what they know, what their interests are, what is important to them, and their ways of knowing—is gained.

Read the play episode below. As you do, think about the type of information you can gain from observing such a play episode.

Nabil is an only child. His parents own a successful plumbing store business. Nabil often plays "business" in the dramatic centre. Today Nabil comes to the dramatic centre with his briefcase and cell phone and sits down at the table that he is using as his desk. He announces to Mohammed, "We need to get the plumbing

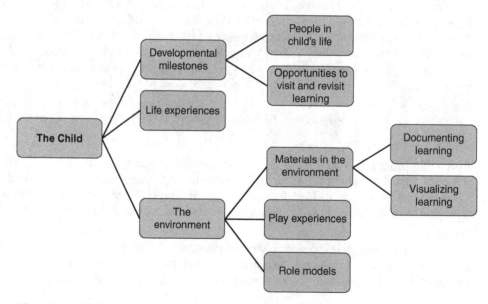

**Figure 3.2** *Life Experiences, Developmental Milestones, and the Environment Influence Children's Learning and Ways of Knowing*

order in by noon today." Next he goes into the briefcase and brings out a pad of paper. He reaches for his cell phone. As he begins to play with the cell phone, his briefcase begins to slip off the table. He says to Mohammed—"help!" As he catches the briefcase with this knee and his hand, he turns to Mohammad and says, "that was close." After he reshuffles the placement of the briefcase, he picks up the cell phone again. He presses numbers and then places the phone to his ear. He begins talking. Then he turns to Mohammad and appears to ask a question. The conversation between Mohammad and the person that Nabil is speaking with on the phone is not audible to the early learning practitioner. Mohammad sits at the chair, with a pad of paper and crayon. Each time Nabil says something to him, there is movement of the crayon on the paper. As Nabil concludes the conversation, he says, "Nice doing business today." He sets the phone down and turns to Mohammad, "Let's get some hoses, wrenches and tape for our truck." Then, the two boys go to the block centre and begin using the large van trucks that have been placed in the area.

When early learning practitioners observe play episodes such as that of Nabil and Mohammed, there are many important discoveries that can be made. For example, reread the play episode and then think about the following questions.

### Developmental Milestones

- What does Nabil learn as he plays?
- How does Nabil's play support his social, cognitive, and emotional development?
- What do we know about Mohammed from this play episode?
- Why might this play episode be important to Nabil and to Mohammed?

### Life Experience

- What life experiences does Nabil bring to this play episode?
- How might Nabil's play be different from other children in his group?
- What life experience insight can be gained about Nabil and Mohammed from observing their play?
- What is the value of sharing this play episode with Nabil's parents?
- How can Nabil's parents help early learning practitioners gain information about their child?
- What learning is evident?
- How are role models impacting the play?

### Environment

- How does this play setting contribute to Nabil's play?
- How can this setting further support Nabil's play? Why is it important to do so?
- How might additional material support the play for Nabil and Mohammad?
- What learning options could be extended?

### Facilitating Play

- What strategies would be best to facilitate opportunities for Nabil and Mohammad to extend the play?
- How might early learning practitioners support Nabil's interests in the business play role?
- How might Mohammad's role change?
- How might the early learning practitioner engage in the play to extend it further?

### Documenting Play

- How could you document this play?
- How might you get the children involved in documenting this play?
- What key elements of learning might you wish to explore with the children and document?
- How might the documentation inform practice?

All these questions provide us with rich information that can help us to understand children and provide us with the impetus for the framework for program planning. When children participate in programs where a thorough examination of their play has not been conducted, potential play opportunities are missed, which causes children to miss "teachable moments" (Bredekamp, 1991). Early learning practitioners and children learn about play by examining what is and what it could be.

# SUMMARY

## Chapter Preview

- Early learning practitioners require skills and tools in gaining information that will help them understand the whole child.
- Observations and pedagogical documentation support early learning practitioners in examining children's play and learning.

## The Relationship of Observation to Play and Learning

- Observations lead early learning practitioners and children into creating environments that support children in play that is rich in investigation, exploration, peer-to-peer relationships, and problem solving.

## At a Crossroads: Redefining Observation Processes

- Child observations were initially implemented to figure out the "true needs" of children and to determine the content of the curriculum.
- Over time, observations began to focus on behaviour attributes of children relative to a prescribed set of norms.
- Research today indicates the need for early learning practitioners to study and understand the whole child rather than aspects of developmental domains, using a pedagogical documentation approach.

## Observation and Pedagogical Documentation

- Observation is a systematic process used to listen to and watch children in their play for the purpose of gaining information about the child's stage of development compared to documented norms or behaviours expected for the particular age group.
- Pedagogical documentation involves strategies used to examine, see, and understand child's play and what the child is capable of.

## Examining the Difference between Child Observation and Pedagogical Documentation

- Observations focus on one aspect of a child's play to gain insight into the developmental phase and interests.
- Pedagogical documentation focuses on the child's process of learning and interconnectedness between the child's ideas, the environment, partners in play, and the play experiences.

## Ways of Acquiring Information to Support Student Practitioners Understanding the Whole Child

- There are many ways to gain information about children. These include organizing observation tools, involving children and adults in observations, examining information from varying perspectives, developing purposeful observations, recognizing biases and perceptions. Listening to the children, reviewing observations to seek meaning, examining children's play patterns, examining how children co-construct knowledge, examining how children express meaning, determining how children exhibit meta-cognition, and determining how and what should be documented provide valuable insights about a child and groups of children for early learning practitioners.

## Observation and Documentation Tools

- The common types of observation and documentation tools include portfolio, photographs, brief notes, peer-to-peer observations, videotaping, running records, anecdotal records, frequency counts, learning stories and journeys, checklists, and learning journals. Each tool has its strengths, depending on the purpose and the environment in which the tool is being used.

## Where Do Observations and Documentation Occur?

- Observations and documentation should occur in both indoor and outdoor environments.
- Outdoor play provides early learning practitioners with uniquely different information about the child than what is gained from indoor play observations.

## Discovering Information and Understanding Children and Their Play

- There are a number of ways to get to know and understand children. One process includes preparation, selecting an information-gathering tool, gathering information, reviewing information, sharing learning, and reflective practice.

## The Types of Discoveries Made through Watching, Listening, and Discussing Play with Children

- Early learning practitioners make many discoveries about children and the environment by becoming familiar with the child's life experiences. Formulating questions and exploring the answers to them provides rich information about a child's developmental milestones, life experiences, environment, and ways to facilitate play.

# REVIEW QUESTIONS

1. Describe what is meant by children requiring environments where adults view play as a kaleidoscope.
2. Describe the evolution of child observation and discuss why we are at the crossroads of redefining observation processes.
3. Explain the similarities and differences between observation and pedagogical documentation. Do early learning practitioners need to know the principles of observation to engage in pedagogical documentation? Why or why not?
4. Why is it important for student practitioners to acquire information about children in various ways? What are the dangers if only one or two methods are used? What are the benefits for student practitioners to use one or two methods? Why?
5. There are a variety of observation and documentation tools available. How do early learning practitioners determine which tool to use at any given time?
6. Why should observations and documentation processes be carried out in both the indoor and outdoor environments? What types of information might you gain from outdoors that would not be evident in an indoor environment?
7. Why might early learning student practitioners benefit from establishing a systematic process for discovering information and understanding children and their play? How does a process help practitioners focus on gathering useful data?
8. How do life experiences, developmental milestones, and the environment influence children's learning and ways of knowing? Why do early learning practitioners examine play episodes and then re-examine them?

# MAKING CONNECTIONS

## Theory to Practice

1. If you were working in an early learning environment and interested in exploring how observations and pedagogical documentation differ, what are the types of questions that you would ask of your host teacher or field mentor? What do you envision the differences will look like? Is there a difference in the role children play during observations and pedagogical documentation? If so, what are the differences? We outlined a play episode of Nabil and Mohammad. What information did you gain from that episode about each of the children? How would you prepare for their upcoming play experiences based on that episode? How would you involve parents? What learning story would you wish to tell? How would you get the children involved?
2. If you were asked to document a play episode in the dramatic centre for three days, what tools and process would you use? Why? Describe in detail.
3. Throughout this chapter many questions have been posed for the early learning practitioner to consider. How do such questions guide early learning practitioners in their practice? Using the play episode of Nabil and Mohammad, answer the questions and then record your new learning about the children. You may want to use a reflective practice journal to write down your answers.

## For Further Research

1. Deb Curtis and Margie Carter identify that the curriculum framework for reflective practitioners is one that requires them to be learning together with young children. Research what this means and how it will

change the current practice of early learning practitioners. What does it look like in an early learning environment? What are the roles of the children? What are the roles of the early learning practitioner?

2. Some researchers suggest that pedagogical documentation is a process of visualization and social construction. What does that mean?

# ADDITIONAL READING

Alcock, S. (2000). *Pedagogical documentation: Beyond observations.* Wellington, New Zealand: Victoria University of Wellington, Institute for Early Childhood Studies.

Carr, M. (2003). *Assessment in early childhood settings: Learning stories.* London: Paul Chapman.

Dahlberg, G., & Moss, P. (2005). *Ethics and politics in early childhood education.* London and New York: RoutledgeFalmer.

Dahlberg, G., Moss, P., & Pence, A. (2007). *Beyond quality in early childhood education and care: Languages of evaluation* (2nd ed). London: Falmer Press.

# WEBLINKS

For more information on the work of Deb Curtis and Margie Carter, particularly as it relates to observation and reflective practice, go to

**www.ecetrainers.com**

# 4 Dramatic Play

## Learning Outcomes

After exploring this chapter you should be able to

- discuss the importance of dramatic play and relate it to the theories of Vygotsky, Erikson, Piaget, and Gardner;

- define dramatic play and explain its scope;

- describe the relationship between development and dramatic play as children progress through stages and the criteria identified by Smilansky;

- describe the role of the early learning practitioner supporting and scaffolding children's dramatic play experiences;

- explain the types of dramatic play; and

- discuss issues related to dramatic play such as gunplay and superhero play.

## Stories from the Field: Practitioner to Student

As a college student, I thought that dramatic play took place only in one area of the room. I thought that the "house" centre was the only place where dramatic play occurred. I learned that you could change the "house" centre into something else, like a doctor's office. I stopped children from taking play dough into the house-keeping area and putting it in pots and pans to make pretend food. I told them that play dough belonged at the play dough table. Then one day I arrived late to work and saw that the children were collectively and collaboratively moving the furniture from the dramatic play area to across the room. I was so shocked that I was rendered speechless and did not jump to stop the children. Instead I listened to their conversation. They were talking about "moving day" and as they brought the furniture to the carpeted area they discussed and negotiated where each piece would be placed. We decided that day to leave the furniture where it was and we took the opportunity to set up the dramatic play area as a store. Now children could buy their groceries, go home, and put them away. The whole room changed that day and I too changed as I discovered that dramatic play is everywhere!

*Jema, Graduate, 2000*

## CHAPTER PREVIEW

Dramatic play is one of the most important forms of play (Smilansky & Shefatya, 1990). It is a common activity of young children that you should see in most early learning programs because it is one that children enjoy and will do spontaneously, and it supports them in combining their ideas and thoughts to bring meaning to their world.

Think back to your own early childhood experiences. Did you like to play house? Did you enjoy playing "cops and robbers"? You may have liked to play "school" or "race cars." Can you recall a time when you lined up your dolls or stuffed animals and then taught them a lesson? This may reflect your earliest image of a teacher! Can you recall driving your small cars and trucks on pretend roads? This may have been your introduction to developing an interest in vehicles. You may not have known it at the time but you were learning while you were playing. In this chapter we will introduce the theories, stages, and types of dramatic play. You will gain insight into how early learning practitioners encourage dramatic play because as you will find out, dramatic play is a very important play and learning experience that children require in their early years.

Theoretical frameworks provide students and early learning practitioners with a foundation in which to explore one's thoughts and beliefs. The theories of dramatic play are very important for you to consider as you read this chapter. Think carefully about what you are reading and relate it to your own experiences as a child as well as those you are having now as a student practitioner. Think of what you believe about children and play.

# THEORETICAL FOUNDATION

Dramatic play and social play are interconnected. We introduce four theories that have made significant contributions to the understanding of the relationship between dramatic play and social development. They are Piaget's cognitive developmental theory, Erikson's psychological theory, and Vygotsky's social cultural theory (Frost, Wortham, & Reifel, 2001). We also highlight the contemporary perspective developed by Howard Gardner (1993) that connects a child's dramatic play with theories of multiple intelligences.

For Piaget, play provides children with opportunities to develop social competence through interactions. Children learn to be social as they play out different perspectives. When engaged in dramatic play, children start to make sense of their world. In Piagetian theory, children assimilate concepts and ideas, practice, and expand on their ideas during play with others. Play interactions contribute to children developing perspective-taking, especially when they can put themselves in another's shoes while role-playing (Chaille, 2008). They begin to understand that other players have perspectives different from their own (Frost, Wortham, & Reifel, 2001).

Erikson (1963) stressed the relationship between dramatic play and children's ability to learn about the social world. Play facilitates the understanding of cultural and social norms and provides an avenue for learning social skills. Erikson maintained that there is a relationship between dramatic play and wider society. Through play, children integrate acceptable social and cultural norms into their own personalities. Erikson and Piaget believed that children who have exposure to rich play experiences become socially competent (Frost, Wortham, & Reifel, 2001).

Vygotsky's sociocultural theory sees play as a significant venue in helping children to separate fantasy from reality, to control impulses, and to follow social rules. Dramatic play is vital for the acquisition of social and cognitive skills. "Vygotsky suggested that make-believe play required children to initiate an imaginary situation and follow a set of rules to play out the situation; the child is able to act separately from reality" (Frost, Wortham, & Reifel, 2001, p. 182). Children learn to choose between courses of action when engaged in pretend play. They learn to control their impulses as they subject themselves to the rules of play (Bodrova & Leong, 1996).

Experiences with dramatic play tap into three kinds of intelligences as espoused by Gardner in his theory of multiple intelligences. Gardner suggests that children, like adults depend upon different areas of their brain in different situations, at different times, and for different reasons. When children act out stories, situations, and ideas, they use their body-kinesthetic intelligence to express themselves. They do this through gesture, voice, and/or movement. They use their interpersonal intelligence to work cooperatively to determine how to dramatize a story or to interact with an audience; they use intrapersonal intelligence to assess their own feelings and mood. They can do this through role play and pantomime (Isenberg & Jalongo, 2001). Table 4.1 lists the three types of intelligences and relates the theory to practice with examples.

*Table 4.1*   *Types of Intelligences and Dramatic Play*

| Intelligence | Examples in Practice | Theory to Practice |
| --- | --- | --- |
| **Bodily-Kinesthetic**<br>The ability to use the body to express thoughts and feelings and to problem-solve. The ability to use hands to handle objects skillfully | Role play<br>Acting out stories<br>Pantomime<br>Dramatic play<br>Dance and movement | A concrete, hands-on, specific, and personal way for children to develop abstract and representational skills |
| **Interpersonal**<br>The ability to distinguish the intentions, moods, and feelings of others by being sensitive to voice, gesture, facial expressions<br>The ability to respond sensitively to others' feelings and moods | Improvisation<br>Pantomime<br>Role play<br>Pretend<br>Puppets | An opportunity to explore feelings, moods, and points of view of others and to respond to them |
| **Intrapersonal**<br>The ability to detect one's own moods, needs, desires, and to look both inwards and outwards | Dramatic play<br>Pantomime<br>Improvisation<br>Readers theatre<br>Puppets | A socially acceptable way for children to reflect on and explore their own feelings and to test out their feelings and emotions as well as their responses to others |

Early learning practitioners examine dramatic play from a broad perspective. We begin by examining core definitions for dramatic play. You will note that there are interchangeable terms related to this area of development. These definitions are intended to help you think about the complexity of dramatic play and introduce you to the expansive possibilities of programming in this area.

## WHAT IS DRAMATIC PLAY?

Dramatic play is also known by terms such as *pretend play, imaginative play, symbolic play, make-believe play*, and *sociodramatic play*. The terms may vary, however, they all refer to a type of play that involves pretending or using symbols to stand in for that which is real. You can probably recall such experiences from your own childhood. When a child acts like a puppy while another child takes on the role of the dog owner, they are pretending. When the dog's owner spontaneously produces a block to represent the dog's water bowl, a symbol representing something real is being exhibited. Figure 4.1 illustrates the scope of dramatic play.

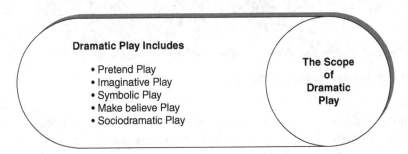

*Figure 4.1*   *The Scope of Dramatic Play*

Dramatic play connects to the whole child and contributes to multiple developmental domains. For example, puppets are an example of a prop that encourages pretend play. While using a puppet all areas of a child's development can be engaged. Small muscles manipulate the puppet to make the mouth move—that is fine motor development. Expressive language comes into play as the child makes the puppet speak. Deciding how the puppet will interact with other puppets gives the child control over his play—this is important for emotional development. As two puppets speak to each other, children are practising their social skills.

Dramatic play also offers children a forum for cognitive development as it helps them create a mental picture or schema of events. If the children decide to take the puppets shopping, they are developing a mental picture of what it means to shop. After repeated experience, the schema becomes complex. Davidson (1996) maintains that "once created, this mental picture of shopping will help children to understand future experiences." The schema is not static as it continues to expand with each shopping experience. "In dramatic play children reenact and adapt their schema, or concepts, about the events they are enacting" (pp. 5–6). Look at Photo 4.1. Could this be a child who has a new sibling in the family?

*Photo 4.1    Changing the baby: A child pretends.*

Sometimes, it is necessary to consider the child's developmental phase through their play. Children who use a pile of blocks to represent a cave or a mountain are using symbolism in their play. Children who assume the identity of hibernating bears or mountain climbers are assuming a role, relating to other persons or objects (Olsen & Sumsion, 2000). These kinds of play experiences tell us about a child's level of development, interests, and potential capabilities. Early learning practitioners do not take these experiences for granted as purely child's play.

Children in the beginning stages of dramatic play probably wouldn't enact a scene with a make-believe cave or mountain. That level of play is exhibited among children with more dramatic play experience. During the beginning stages of dramatic play, children most often take on the roles of those who are meaningful in their lives; mommies, daddies, doctors, storekeepers, etc. If a child takes on a role alone, they are engaging in dramatic play. If a child takes on a role with others, they are engaging in sociodramatic play. Whether it is with another child or an adult, the dramatic play becomes social play when the other person also takes on a role. This level of play requires the ability to transform objects and actions symbolically. The play is enhanced when there is dialogue and negotiation; and it involves role taking, script knowledge, and improvisation (Bergen, 2002).

In the transcript in **Box 4.1** three children are playing hairstylist. They decide to play out a scene together, taking on roles of hairstylists and customers. They are not using real props or even realistic toy props. They are using other objects for the scissors and mousse.

*Photo 4.2*    *Let's go to the mall. A child is dressed and ready to go "shopping."*

## BOX 4.1

ANTHONY:    It's a hair salon here! We're doing the hair salon.

JOEY:    Is that mousse?

ANTHONY:    Yeah!

JOEY:    I'm going to be scared of it!

ANTHONY:    Oh you want me to do your hair? It's for boys too; I can give you a haircut.

REBECCA:    No I'll make you look like a Backstreet Boy.

ANTHONY:    These are not real scissors.

REBECCA:    Ok, ready to put your cap on?

ANTHONY:    No wait, we don't have real water in here.

**Master players** refers to children who are skilled in representing experiences symbolically in their self-initiated improvisational dramatic play.

These children are 4 and 5 years old. They have had many experiences with dramatic play and their enactment is more symbolic than what it would have been when as toddlers they began to pretend. They are skillful and proficient in their dramatic play enactments. They work well together. You could say that they were **master players**.

## Characteristics of Dramatic Play

As children gain more experience with dramatic play it becomes more complex. You will observe variations of breadth and depth of play within each age group. For example, some children provide a leadership role for other children during play (Davidson, 1996). Reynolds and Jones (1997) refer to these children as "master players." The children in the aforementioned scenario had the skills of master players as they self-initiated the experience and represented the play symbolically.

Prior to advancing to this level of sociodramatic play, master players learned their craft when as toddlers, or even in some cases as infants, they used symbolism in their solitary play. Between the ages of 8 to 12 months, children develop memory and begin to play symbolically. To play symbolically means that the child is able to represent objects mentally and engage in pretend actions. Toddlers can do this by themselves. Preschool children are able to play with others in symbolic ways. Children of kindergarten age become so skilled in their dramatic play enactments that they are seen as master players, enacting scenes that are more exotic than the previous store, house, or doctor's office. School-aged children take dramatic play to a new level of sophistication. Generally, they re-enact components of shows from television or movies. Their props are like realistic and they take on the roles of characters in books and in actions.

As identified in **Figure 4. 2**, Smilanksy (1968) characterized six criteria of dramatic play, which are described in Chapter 2. The first is *imitative role play* and this criterion, along with the second, *make-believe play*, regards children and objects; the third, *verbal make-believe*, regards actions and situations and the fourth criterion, *persistence in role play*, involves children playing alone; the last two are the criterion of *interaction*, where there are at least two players within the context of a play

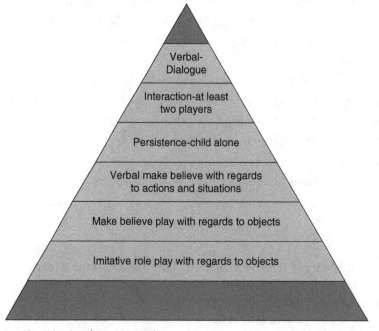

*Figure 4.2    Six Criteria of Dramatic Play*

episode, and the criterion of *verbal communication*, where there is dialogue between children (Smilanksy & Shefatya, 1990).

As with all areas of development, children progress through stages. The more experience children have with dramatic play, the more involved and interactive it becomes. In order to become master players, children require environments and materials that offer various types of dramatic play opportunities. Having the right materials and environment, combined with adults who encourage and facilitate dramatic play opportunities, increases the sophistication of a child's dramatic play experience.

## Stages of Dramatic Play Development

Young toddlers from 12 to 15 months of age perform auto-symbolic actions. These are pretend acts that are familiar to the child, however done outside of the act's usual context and directed to self. For example, in the photograph below a child pretends to drink from an empty cup. Since the child cannot direct the pretend act to a partner but only to the self, the social play is constrained by the child's capacity to pretend. Older toddlers have the ability to enact events that they have directly experienced, such as diapering and feeding.

Preschool children add to these incidents with more imaginative and make-believe situations, such as preparing meals for a family or taking care of a baby (Isenberg & Jalongo, 2001). By age 4, children are capable of engaging in "mature" or "high-level" pretend play. This usually involves sustained pretend scenarios, multiple roles, and symbolic use of props. They become particularly adept at

*Photo 4.3   Passing the carrot and "drinking" juice—toddlers are playing house.*

enactment and are master players. School-age children are able to structure their pretending for presentation to an audience. Usually the more formal aspects of the dramatic arts—acting, directing, scene and costume design, playwrighting, and stage management are left to the high school years.

Enactment occurs when children adopt actions, feelings, thoughts, and behaviours of people in particular situations. This ability emerges around age 3 and signals the child's developing imagination. According to Isenberg and Jalongo (2001), enactment in early learning occurs in three forms: (1) informal drama, (2) story or interpretive drama, and (3) formal or scripted drama. During **informal dramatic play,** children spontaneously enact roles and behaviour of familiar people or characters. Little preparation time is needed and simple familiar props are the only materials necessary. With **story or interpretive drama** some rehearsal is necessary and therefore it requires some preparation time. Simple props are necessary. In **formal or scripted drama,** memorization of a script is required and extensive preparation time is necessary. In the first two types of enactment, children have an active role. In formal or scripted drama, the role of the child is passive, as she must rehearse as directed. This latter type of enactment is not considered developmentally appropriate for the early learning settings, as it is product-oriented and focuses on technique rather than spontaneous self-expression.

You may remember experiences in childhood with theatre arts or creative drama. The distinction between these experiences and sociodramatic play is that the former are directed by an adult and occur in the later years. Smilanksy (1968) placed "games with rules" at the highest level in her division of play. Theatre is a more structured form of dramatic play or creative drama. It fits Smilansky's definition but is not usually associated with the very young. Theatre has rules; it follows a script, it has a director, and an audience. Children can bring these elements of theatre into their dramatic play but "the effort necessary to rehearse staged performances and the skills required to portray characters consistently are within the range of a very few preschool children" (Furman, 2000, p. 175).

The term *product versus process* is one used often in the field of early learning. In dramatic play the process is what counts. In creative drama, it is the product. As a point of reflection, consider that in practice it is not always so cut and dried. Some preschool children may be interested in a staged performance or to have more formality attached to their dramatic play experience but, developmentally, what is important is the process of the play.

## Experiences for Children in Dramatic Play across the Ages

By now, you have realized that dramatic play is something a very young child can experience. Early learning practitioners incorporate dramatic play every day for all children regardless of their age and interests. Building dramatic play skills begins in toddlers and advances throughout childhood. Early learning practitioners scaffold the dramatic play experiences with children according to their ages and stage of dramatic play. For instance, given the skills necessary to participate in staged performances, school-age children are given more ownership in their dramatic play experiences. Older children can make their own decisions about roles to take and stories to enact.

Trister Dodge, Colker, and Heroman (2002) suggest that when preschool children are engaged in dramatic play, there is a beginning level and an advanced level. When role-playing, the beginning-level child imitates the familiar—mommy, daddy, baby, pets. The child who is at a more advanced level will select roles from the outside world, such as doctors, police officers, and firefighters. When children begin the first level of using props, they generally use real objects or replicas of objects. Advanced-level players use any object as a prop, i.e. a block stands in for a phone. Children at advanced levels will sustain their dramatic play experiences, while those beginning may engage only fleetingly. As children advance in their dramatic play, their verbal communication increases and is related to the play theme. At this stage, children are constantly discussing roles. They are interacting cooperatively, whereas the beginning player often engages in solitary play and verbalizes around the use of props—"I had that doll first."

After reading about the complexities of dramatic play and how rich the experiences gained through it can be for children, you might be surprised to learn that it has been discouraged in recent years. More emphasis has been placed on academic preparation for younger children. Paley (1986) is a strong supporter of children's pretend play and is concerned that we are moving away from encouraging dramatic play. She encourages a return to a time when fantasy play was practiced leisurely and openly. For children, "fantasy play is their ever dependable pathway to knowledge and certainty" (p. viii). As you read on, there will be further evidence of the importance of dramatic play in the lives of young children.

## The Importance of Dramatic Play

In dramatic play, children use a number of developmental attributes including cognitive, language, and social skills in carrying out a play theme or event. For example, Bergen (2002) maintains that new research findings indicate that there are many connections between cognitive competence and high-quality pretend play. Many cognitive strategies are exhibited during dramatic play such as joint planning, negotiation, problem solving, and goal seeking.

> If children lack opportunities to experience such play, their long-term capacities related to metacognition, problem solving, and social cognition, as well as to academic areas such as literacy, mathematics, and science, may be diminished. These complex and multidimensional skills involving many areas of the brain are most likely to thrive in an atmosphere rich in high-quality pretend play. (Bergen 2002, p. 5)

Dramatic play enhances children's emotional development. Unlike adults, children generally are not able to verbalize feelings. They experience the same feelings as adults; however, they express their feelings through play. Children feel safe in play. According to Sigmund Freud (1856 to 1939) play can be cathartic. Children may use play to reduce anxiety and understand traumatic experiences. They may re-create an unpleasant experience over and over to assimilate it and thereby reduce the intensity of the feelings. Sociodramatic play promotes emotional development. Children also use play to express positive feelings of joy and contentment. Children who have aggressive or negative feelings are able to develop a sense of mastery and control during their sociodramatic play. Sociodramatic play helps children acquire a greater feeling of power, sense of happiness, and positive feelings of self (Frost, Wortham, & Reifel, 2001).

As identified in Chapter 2, there continues to be a great deal of research being conducted on *self-regulation* in early childhood education. According to Bodrova and Leong (1996) the key ingredient to developing self-regulation is play; specifically *mature* dramatic play. This level of play is complex. It may include, extended make-believe scenarios involving multiple children and lasting hours, even days. Throughout the play experience, children get to practice skills in both self-regulation and in being regulated. Dramatic play supports children in developing self-regulation; as it requires them to gain skills in controlling their emotional and cognitive impulses. It becomes part of a child's **executive function.**

Learning to be both the regulator and the object of regulation is important to the development of higher mental functions. Vygotskian theory proposes that other-regulation precedes self-regulation. Children learn to regulate the behaviour of others before they can regulate themselves (Bodrova & Leong, 1996). Vygotsky maintained that at 4 or 5 years, a child's ability to play creatively with other children is a better gauge of future academic success than any other indicator, including vocabulary, counting skills, or knowledge of the alphabet (Bodrova & Leong, 2009). Vygotsky is quoted in the *New York Times* article "Can the Right Kinds of Play Teach Self Control?" as saying that dramatic play, "is the training ground where children learn to regulate themselves, to conquer their own unruly minds" (Tough, 2009, p. 5). According to Vygotsky children are guided by the basic rules of dramatic play which involve taking on a role and sticking to the role. When children follow the rules of make-believe and push one another to follow those rules, Vygotsky believes that they develop important habits of self-control (Tough, 2009).

**Executive function** refers to "the ability to think straight: to order your thoughts, to process information in a coherent way, to hold relevant details in your short-term memory, to avoid distractions and mental traps and focus on the task in front of you" (Tough, 2009, p. 2).

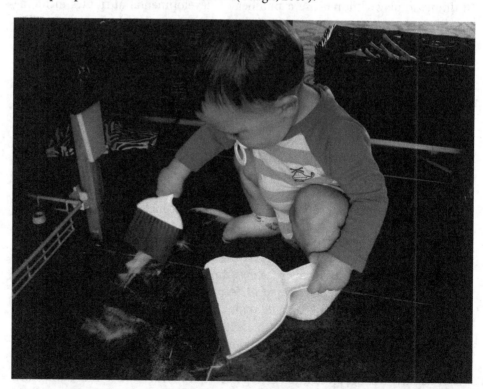

*Photo 4.4 Mommy's and Daddy's helper? A young child is given realistic props and takes on a role.*

Research supports the use of dramatic play to develop skills across the domains. It is an excellent whole child experience. Some researchers suggest that dramatic play provides opportunities to challenge social norms that may be marginalizing to children. Guss (2002) views dramatic play as an impetus for reconceptualizing play. This concept will be discussed further in Chapter 13.

# Research Connections

Guss (2005) describes a dramatic play scenario where two young children Tessa, aged 3 years and 8 months, and Hilde, aged 5 years and 1 month enact a 40-minute dramatization about a wolf. Through this experience these two girls had the opportunity to symbolically enact power, as the characters they portrayed overcame the threat of the wolf. They could actualize a life experience for themselves as powerful children/girls. Guss (2005) suggests that if early childhood education is reconceptualized as a time when children can counter accepted cultural norms of girls being docile and obedient it can be transformative. Girls need not always take on the role of the stay-at-home mother during enactments and boys need to be encouraged to play more often in the dramatic play centre. When you reflect on dramatic play enactments, you need to be conscious of variations in play that might be due to gender but can also be explained by other factors.

## Variations in Sociodramatic Play

Just like there are differences in children's social development, there are variations in children's social play. Studies have shown that variations in sociodramatic play can be explained by parenting style, child care quality, attitudes of early learning practitioners, children's temperaments, and socioeconomic differences. Parents who encourage and model pretend play give their children a chance to practice playing. Parents who arrange play activities for their children are creating opportunities for their children to display pro-social behaviours with their playmates. On the other hand, families who do not provide young children with mentoring or opportunities for social play inhibit them in acquiring the background to engage in advanced social play. Similar to parents, early learning practitioners can positively or negatively affect a child's socially competent play. When children have positive role models who support dramatic play, they gain skills in executing dramatic play and in turn they become more socially competent. The socially competent child is more skilled in understanding the play cues exhibited by peers and can engage in higher levels of fantasy play (Frost, Wortham, & Reifel, 2001).

Often, in low-quality early learning and child care centres, there is a lack of complex social play interactions (Frost, Wortham, & Reifel, 2001). There are a number of reasons to account for this correlation including an absence of equipment, furniture, and props, and an environment that would support and provoke children's dramatic play. Another reason may include the attitude of the adults in the room. Attitudinal barriers largely derive from the value early learning practitioners place on play. As identified earlier in the chapter, early learning practitioners may be under pressure to provide a more academically oriented and less play-based curriculum. This often results in children being exposed to more teacher-directed academic instruction (Olsen & Sumsion, 2000) rather than having the freedom to learn through play.

Some research suggests that children from lower-income families engage in less and in poorer-quality sociodramatic play. This is due in part to their not having as many play opportunities (Frost, Wortham, & Reifel, 2001) as other children. Yet, studies indicate that children from all socioeconomic levels respond well to opportunities for sociodramatic play. Not only do they learn pro-social behaviours but their language performance improves (Furman, 2000). Dramatic play can be an equalizer for all children regardless of gender, culture, and background. It is important for early learning practitioners to encourage dramatic play for these reasons.

## THE ROLE OF THE EARLY LEARNING PRACTITIONER

An adult's participation in dramatic play provides a scaffold to raise children's social interaction to a higher level. An adult's involvement may also extend the length of the interaction (Davidson, 1996). The more time children engage in sociodramatic play, the more likely their opportunity to become master players. An early learning practitioner's involvement communicates approval and support for the children's pretend play. When children see that an early learning practitioner is excited about the pretend play, it becomes a stimulus for them and triggers other children to become involved. If the adult takes on a role that supports the children's play, it will show children that pretend play is a fun and valuable activity (Davidson, 1996).

Unfortunately, in some early learning settings the early learning practitioners may not become involved in the dramatic play episodes. They may choose to become involved only when children are having trouble maintaining their play smoothly. They may intervene to tell children to play more quietly, to reduce the number of children in the area, or to remind children to use materials correctly. This type of negative intervention sends a message to the children that adults do not like or approve of this play (Davidson, 1996).

When an adult intervenes in a dramatic play experience it alters the nature of the play. The objective of the play changes as it is no longer for the pleasure of the participants, but to fulfill the goals of a third party (Furman, 2000). However, when an adult acts as a facilitator during the play experience a number of learning outcomes are possible. Sometimes the early learning practitioner's role is to set aside space, provide props, and make time in the schedule for dramatic play. Other times, early learning practitioners take on active roles that are intentionally focused on a goal such as language and literacy enhancement. Isenberg and Jalongo (2001) recommend that early learning practitioners find a balance between not becoming too intrusive and directing children's play and not completely ignoring the children's dramatic play experiences. They suggest three strategies early learning practitioners can use to avoid being caught in these two extremes. They are:

1. **Ask thoughtful questions that provoke creative thinking.** Before dramatic play experiences, find out from the children what they know or want to know about the content and roles. During the experience, the early learning

practitioner's role is to be curious and a good listener, challenging the children's thinking, and helping them to enact a more complex scenario.

2. **Reflect with the children.** By talking about specific roles and situations during and after the dramatic play experience, children can clarify their thoughts and actions. They can reflect on their actions and discuss the ideas of other children.

3. **Model a behaviour or attribute.** Empower children through drama by modelling certain behaviours for the children while being mindful of not becoming too intrusive.

Pedagogical documentation, as described in Chapter 3, is an excellent strategy that provides support to the early learning practitioner and to the children as it enables them to reflect on the play experiences. Documentation gives children the visible evidence of their past play experiences and it encourages reflection and discussion.

Davidson (1996) reflected on each of Parten's (1932) stages of play as introduced in Chapter 2 and suggests specific adult roles for each. Table 4.2 provides an overview of these roles and a description of the enactment you might see in the dramatic play centre.

**Table 4.2** *Types of Play and Early Learning Practitioner's Role*

| Type of Play | Children's Enactment | Role of the Early Learning Practitioner |
|---|---|---|
| **Solitary Play** | Stories | Express enjoyment. Provide space. |
| **Parallel Play** | Object play | Provide multiple sets of the same object. |
| **Associative Play** | Scenarios—independent and interactive | Provide materials and themes that allow for a balance of interaction/independence. |
| **Cooperative Play** | Scenarios with multiple roles | Help children to negotiate roles. Support children in finding the necessary materials to enhance the complexity of the play theme. |

For solitary play, early learning practitioners can help individual children re-enact complex stories. This play may be more elaborate than when done with peers because the child can devote total concentration to the development and creation of the story without having to negotiate ideas with others. The early learning practitioners "can support the children's right to play in this manner by expressing enjoyment of the child's play, by providing space where the child will not be interrupted and by recognizing the validity of such play" (Davidson, 1996, p. 22).

With 2-year-olds who are just beginning to develop parallel play, early learning practitioners provide many duplicates of the same materials; because in parallel play the main form of interaction is doing the same thing next to a peer. "It is essential to have multiples of objects so children can join in with each other" (Davidson, 1996, p. 23).

When children are involved in associative play, the early learning practitioners promote the play by using themes that allow for a combination of some interaction, and independent play. For example, playing store is a theme that encourages this balance. Paying for purchases requires some interaction. The independent play occurs when children select what they wish to purchase (Davidson, 1996).

An airplane-themed dramatic play area produces more cooperative play. The early learning practitioner encourages the child who is acting as the pilot to talk to the children acting as the air traffic controllers. If the early learning practitioner and children turn the dramatic play area into a fire station, a map area is set up for the dispatchers to direct the drivers to the fires. A beauty salon offers different stations including a waiting area, a shampoo station, a cutting and styling station, and an area for manicures and pedicures. The adult may explain the roles to the children and support them in negotiating the direction of the play, and assist in resolution if conflicts arise (Davidson, 1996).

As you read about different themed dramatic play areas, be careful not to confuse this concept term with the term *theme* used in program planning. In the case of program planning, the term theme usually means a broad concept or topic such as *seasons* or *animals* and is often based on holidays. These themes are usually teacher-directed and teacher-owned, which involve planning the children's experiences in advance with limited or no input from the children. Often these themes have questionable meaningfulness for the children. For example, holiday themes run the risk of being little more than a convenient backdrop for classroom decorations and craft displays. Young children usually come away from such experiences without having expanded their concepts or increased their skills across the curriculum (Jalongo & Isenberg, 2000). It is suggested that the key to programming should be an emphasis on meaning making. A meaningful programming experience is relevant to children (Wortham, 1992). Children need to be involved in the programming process and the experiences extended to children reflect the various learning styles and interests of the children. Since themes are often short-lived (one week in duration), there is also potential for a lack of depth (Kashin, 2009).

Dramatic play concept themes differ from the thematic approach to programming employed by some early learning practitioners. When an early learning practitioner sets up the dramatic play centre based on the emergent curriculum concept, children have input into how the dramatic play evolves, diverging along new paths as choices and connections are made, and it is always open to new possibilities that may not have been thought of during the initial planning process (Kashin, 2009). The early learning practitioner responds to the children's exploration of the theme by adding props and making connections to other areas of the indoor and outdoor play space.

## OBSERVATION AND DOCUMENTATION

When children are playing in the dramatic play area, the priority for the practitioner or student is to observe the play in order to know how to facilitate, expand, and support the play. How do you know what props or themes to incorporate in the children's dramatic play experiences? The only way you will know is by first carefully observing their play, by listening to the children and documenting key play episodes. Begin by observing children in the dramatic play centre prior to transforming the centre using a different theme and adding new materials or props. There are a number of observation tools available to assist you. You may wish to begin by using a basic anecdotal observation technique, as described in Chapter 3 and then analyze what you have written and answer these questions:

- Are the children using the props that are there?
- What types of play are the children engaging in?
- Are there any children in an onlooker role?
- What roles are the children taking?
- Is there any evidence of metacommunication?
- What materials are needed to encourage scaffolding to the next level of play?
- What role could you take during this future play episode?
- How might you document the upcoming play episode and how might you use the documentation with the children to further expand their opportunities?

After your observation and analysis are completed, it is beneficial for you and the children to set up the dramatic play centre that will take the children's play experiences in new directions. This leads you to begin the cycle again—observe, reflect, analyze, and program plan.

## Planning and Facilitating Dramatic Play

When planning for and facilitating dramatic play, early learning practitioners consider the interests, dramatic themes, and props that are familiar to children and those that will add a new level of curiosity and exploratory opportunities. Children, who are beginning players rather than the master players described earlier, find it easier to pretend around familiar themes. Davidson (1996) suggests that the same is true for the adults who are beginning players. If the early learning practitioner is not experienced in facilitating dramatic play, it makes sense to begin with a familiar theme, such as playing house. If a child tries to enter the dramatic play centre while other children are playing house, it is a comfortable starting point for the early learning practitioner to generate the role that the newcomer can take (Davidson, 1996). The early learning practitioner is able to suggest alternative scenarios if conflict arises because of the familiarity with the theme. As the adult and the children become more skilled at dramatic play, the themes chosen can become more complex and exotic.

Some children have difficulty entering into dramatic play enactments with their peers. In sociodramatic play (dramatic play that involves others), children must be able to use language "to plan, explain, negotiate, and create imaginary situations" (Weitzman & Greenberg, 2002, p. 185). Children with language delays generally have more difficulty than others when trying to enter, or initiate play. These children become the watchers of others until they build the problem-solving skills and self-confidence to figure out how to enter the play. Parten (1932) suggests that at this phase the child is at the beginning of a continuum of social participation in play. She indicates that the child is taking on an onlooker role (Van Hoorn, Nourot, Scales, & Alward, 2007). It is the role of the adult to assist children to move along this continuum through solitary, parallel, associative, and group play.

Children who have not yet developed the necessary cognitive and language skills to analyze a social play situation may try to enter the play of others but their interactive behaviour will often be inappropriate. This may lead to them being rejected by their peers. Older peers may label them and call them names such as "mean" or "weird." "Some children become aggressive and non-compliant when they are rejected by their peers, resulting in a cycle of poor relationships with peers and increasingly problematic behaviours" (Weitzman & Greenberg, 2002, p. 193). This may have a negative impact on their social, intellectual, and language development in the long term (Weitzman & Greenberg, 2002). The adult's role in this circumstance is to facilitate positive peer interaction so that the child who is watching learns how to approach a group and to enter the play with the group. By setting up opportunities for interaction and giving a socially isolated child a specific role to play, the early learning practitioner extends the potential for the child to join in the play using appropriate sociable behaviours.

*Photo 4.5* *Cooperative play: setting the table for lunch.*

Setting up an interaction in the dramatic play centre to encourage social play involves knowing what topical themes to offer, selecting and arranging appropriate props, keeping the area neat, and ensuring there is time and space for play. Davidson (1996) refers to this role as a stage manager. The early learning practitioner as *stage manager* provides background experiences, such as books, trips, group discussions, or classroom visitors, which can serve as a prompt for dramatic play. In addition, to stage manage Davidson (1996) suggests other possible roles for adults to include being *players* or participants in the play or a *mediator* who helps children resolve conflicts and misunderstandings. The early learning practitioner may assume the role of *interpreter*, and help children to understand other children's points of view. As a *social director*, the early learning practitioner supports the child who is the onlooker find a role. The early learning practitioner also becomes the observer and documenter for the children's dramatic play episodes.

Early learning practitioners look beyond a dramatic play centre to see how and where children pretend because, when given the opportunity, pretend play takes place anywhere and everywhere! Children will engage in pretend play outside, in the block centre, when using manipulatives, or even "as they look through a pretzel at snack, pretending it is a pair of glasses" (Davidson, 1996, p. 70). Observing children pretending and by transcribing their dialogue, early learning practitioners become aware of the children's level of dramatic play. This guides us in determining ways to scaffold the children's experiences. Once the nature of the children's play is identified, you can make meaningful programming decisions which may include introducing them to specific types of dramatic play such as story play, pantomime, puppets, story drama, and early teacher theatre, as well as a specific program based on Vygotsky's theories entitled "Tools of the Mind."

## Types of Dramatic Play

**Story Play**    A young child's sense of story and drama are closely connected to dramatic play. Story play is suitable for preschoolers to school-aged children. Paley (1981) suggests that when children share their own stories by acting them out, they "feel that they are playing together inside a story" (p. 167). For example, In the *Boy who would be a Helicopter* (1990), Paley describes the experience of Jason, a child who is an outsider or onlooker in the classroom. Jason eventually becomes the inspiration for a technique Paley developed to build on the children's sense of story and drama called *story acting*. Even very young children, as Paley (2001) demonstrated in *Mrs. Tully's Classroom,* can participate. There is a connection between this technique and the constructivist theory approach because the experience begins with the children's own stories and dramatizations. The children construct their own knowledge by making meaning and representing their stories. Children also learn to be part of an audience and to perform for an audience. The technique is summarized below:

- The child initiates by telling a story.
- The adult writes the story down exactly as dictated by the child who becomes the author.
- The children in the classroom take on the parts of the characters in the story.
- The author may pick the part that he/she wants to play.
- Additions and revisions to the story may be made in process if parts are unclear or incomplete.
- Only the author has the right to make changes in the story.

Older children document their own stories and collaborate with others to create jointly composed stories and dramatizations. Through these experiences children develop a sense of story. Children discover that a story has a beginning, middle, and end and that they have a setting and a plot. There are characters in stories including the main character or protagonist. Usually, the plot involves some sort of conflict or problem that the protagonist has to overcome (Waite-Stupiansky, 1997). Creating an environment for storytelling is a gift an early learning practitioner or student can give to children, as it enhances their development in so many areas.

**Pantomime**    During pantomime experiences children do not speak, they communicate through gesture or movement. They express themselves by "miming." In pantomime children communicate ideas, feelings, and actions—without using words. Pantomimes are the starting point for creative drama. They help children to feel comfortable using their bodies to express themselves. Because pantomimes begin with physical experiences, it makes concepts more concrete. Pantomimes are particularly useful for children in the early learning centre whose first language is not English. Pantomimes are also valuable for children who have speech or hearing problems, or are very shy. "In pantomime, all children can be successful because they do not have to be concerned about verbal communication" (Isenberg & Jalongo, 2001, p. 226). Some appropriate mime activities for children include:

- Acting out a familiar nursery rhyme.
- Showing what it is like to ride a bike or climb on the jungle gym.
- Being a character or an animal in a favourite song. "I'm a Little Teapot" is a good example of a song to mime to.
- Modelling familiar actions like brushing teeth, washing hands, eating lunch. The early learning practitioner can mime the action and the children guess the action and then they mime it as well.
- Imagine that they are animals performing specific actions, such as a lion stalking through the jungle looking for food or a kitten lapping up some milk or a wiggling worm (Isenberg & Jalongo, 2001).

**Puppets**    The word *puppet* is derived from the Latin word for doll. However, puppets are much more than dolls—they are powerful teaching and learning tools that invite children to explore their imaginations and share their imaginings with others. Puppets add life to an early learning environment. They are a natural prop for toddlers, preschoolers, kindergarteners, and school-aged children. Puppets offer them opportunities to exhibit creativity, imagination, and self-expression (Isenberg & Jalongo, 2001). Jalongo (2000) describes four reasons for using puppets in the early learning environment:

1. **Puppets improve communication skills.** Children often will talk to or through a puppet when they feel uncomfortable talking to another person.
2. **Puppets speak a universal language.** Children with hearing problems or limited English can watch a puppet play and usually can infer the meaning of the performance.
3. **Puppets encourage cooperation.** Coordinating one's puppet's behaviour with other children's puppets helps children to work together.

4. *Puppets help to integrate curriculum.* Learning through all the developmental domains can be explored through puppetry.

Children may experiment with puppets that are provided or make their own. Children are encouraged to have their puppets vary the pitch of their voice and make a variety of sounds such as animals growling or chirping. Children can be involved in discussing what puppets can be used for. For example, puppets can be used for "talking with one another, creating a puppet show, or retelling a story" (Isenberg & Jalongo, 2001, p. 231).

Introducing a mirror so that the children can see the puppet's movements and gestures will help children learn the art of puppetry (Isenberg & Jalongo, 2001). Younger children find it easiest to use puppets that have moving mouths so that it makes sense to add dialogue if they choose (Hunt & Renfro, 1982). Creating a puppet centre with puppet-making materials such as fabric, paper plates and bags, recycled buttons, yarn, and Popsicle sticks may trigger an interest in children creating their own puppets.

Puppets also provide early learning practitioners with an opportunity to discuss with children the limits and responsibility for puppet use. For example, puppets thrown carelessly in a corner of a room can send a message to children that caring for the puppets is not important. This could lead to children throwing the puppets around or using them for "hand-to-hand" combat. Puppets are important props and therefore require careful consideration when displayed and when being stored.

**Story Drama**   Sometimes referred to as story retelling, story drama is a type of interpretive drama based upon the re-enactment of familiar stories, poems or fables. Often story drama involves a facilitator-led group experience with children creating scenes from familiar literature that use both dialogue and movement. Story drama is used in the early learning environment as a way to help children understand the structure of a story and see how language affects others. For early learning practitioners, it offers a natural and authentic way to promote literacy learning. Research shows that enacting stories improves reading comprehension, promotes speaking, listening, critical, and creative reading skills. It heightens children's interest in reading and enables children to experience the feelings and behaviours of others (Isenberg & Jalongo, 2001).

**Teacher Theatre**   Carter and Curtis (2008) describe another dramatic play strategy called teacher theatre. By using stories and props to convey ideas, early learning practitioners coach children in grasping certain concepts. "Stories captivate children's attention, and playing out the details with dramatic play and props helps them internalize the concepts and strategies" (Carter & Curtis, 2008, p. 132). The topics for teacher theatre can be chosen in response to a particular or recurring interpersonal issue that is happening among the children. For example, using three rubber dinosaurs an early learning practitioner demonstrates to children the issue of excluding others from play. The children suggest ideas and solutions to help the protagonists in the story solve their problems. By early learning practitioners and children acting out the situation, the children involved revisit their problems and receive some coaching without feeling singled out or criticized (Carter & Curtis, 2008).

# Stop . . . Think . . . Discuss . . . Reflect

Carter and Curtis (2008) suggest that "whenever children are invited to pretend, they seem to be able to access skills and concepts that are more difficult for them to grasp when they are in the middle of a real situation" (p. 134). Teacher theatre coaches children to think constructively about social problems. The issues being conveyed are one step removed from the emotion and intensity of their own play. Stop and think about teacher theatre. What theory are you bringing to the classroom if you give children an opportunity to constructively think and discuss social problems? Discuss with your classmates other skills that children can be coached to practice with teacher theatre. Reflect on a situation that you might act out with another student or practitioner. What are the skills that you need to employ in order to do this? Write the skills out and share your responses with a classmate. You may try to simulate teacher theatre during class with pairs of students acting out potential real situations like bullying, issues around sharing or inclusion, separation anxiety, and so on.

**Tools of the Mind** Tough (2009) describes a Tools of the Mind classroom where "every morning, before embarking on the day's make-believe play, each child takes a coloured marker and a printed form called a play plan and draws or writes his declaration for the day's play: "I am going to drive the choo-choo train"; "I am going to make a sand castle"; "I am going to take the dollies to the beach" (p. 6). For the Tools of the Mind program it is important at the beginning of the day for children to be coached on dramatic play. This is called Make-Believe Play Practice—with the early learning practitioner leading the children, in a step-by-step process. For instance, the example of coaching a child to feed a baby doll is used: "I'm pretending my baby is crying. Is yours? What should we say?" (p. 6). As children progress to kindergarten they carry around a clipboard with the day's activities on it and each Friday, every child has a 5- to 10-minute "learning conference" with his or her early learning practitioner that is viewed as a mini-performance review where the children discuss what they accomplished in the week, where they fell short, and what skills they want to work on. Tough indicates that these practices reinforce habits of self-control using pretend play.

According to Bodrova and Leong (1996), when children are engaged in dramatic play scenarios, the early learning practitioner's suggestions and guidance are most important when any of the following things happen:

- Children do not talk to each other.
- Children exclude a specific child.
- Few roles emerge.
- Children do not pretend.
- Children do not use objects to stand for other objects.
- Play is fleeting, lasting only for 2 to 3 minutes.

Early learning practitioners do not discipline children for not playing well in the dramatic play centre. Rather, their role is to guide play more directly by suggesting how to include other children, proposing a "plot" or roles, asking questions, or even coaching specific children. It may include role-playing with children to practice cooperation and conflict management skills. Children practice the social skill of joint decision making and negotiating. These skills helps children become better prepared to handle conflicts when they arise, reducing the need for the early learning practitioner to intervene. Through role play, children confront conflicts. These conflicts can be both internal and external to the story. Either way, the child is becoming more experienced at conflict resolution (Wheeler, 2004). In the transcript in **Box 4.2,** three preschool children negotiate during a sociodramatic play experience. Notice how rules are chosen and disagreements are quickly resolved.

## BOX 4.2

| | |
|---|---|
| SAM: | No, look we need one, two, three. |
| SARAH: | No, no let me! |
| SAM: | And one for you, and the baby, one for you. |
| SARAH: | No, no! |
| SAM: | This is gross, let's play water table. |
| SARAH: | No, no! Wait, wait! |
| SAM: | I get to play house. |
| SARAH: | Ok, ok, put some tea in here. |
| SAM: | Done. No maybe a little more. Hey Sarah, we need water in here. |
| SARAH: | Is this finished? |
| SAM: | It's finished. More, more, more, |
| LILY: | Sarah, Sarah let's go to get more coffee. |
| SAM: | It's a treat. Ta da! |
| LILY: | The baby needs a small spoon. I'm going to get some. Dad, don't do that. |
| SAM: | But I need a lot! |
| SARAH: | I did give you lots. |
| SAM: | Let me do it. Everybody does it by themselves! |
| SARAH: | Stop. Stop I said! |
| SAM: | It's my idea. |
| SARAH: | You want me to put more water? |
| SAM: | Yeah put more water please. |
| SARAH: | You want me give you a cup? |
| SAM: | Yeah. Uh, could I have some more please? A lot more, could I have the whole thing please? |
| SARAH: | I've got more! |

When early learning practitioners view dramatic play as an opportunity to enhance learning during the experience, they create and stimulate simulations that children can learn from. For example, in the above scenario, the children were able to solve their own problems during the play. Early learning practitioners need to know what materials to provide and ideas to present that will give children the opportunity to practice negotiation, problem solving, and collaboration skills. You could refer to this as a provocation for dramatic play.

## Provocations for Dramatic Play

**Provocation** is a means for provoking further action. A provocation can be anything that arrives by surprise and sparks interest, such as a collection of interesting scarves or pieces of materials that children find by surprise in the dramatic play centre one morning.

Educators from Reggio Emilia, Italy, focus on provocation as a way of helping children to think more deeply or broadly about a topic, question, or issue. As described by Gandini (1998) **provocation** is something arriving by surprise.

Chaille (2008) describes provocation as "an intentional sparking of interest" (p. 63). A provocation can be as simple as reading a book that might spark an interest to dramatize an event described in the book. There are many possible provocations for dramatic play in the early learning environment, including the much overlooked treasure chest of dress-up clothing and early learning practitioner-created prop boxes that are built around topics. **Table 4.3** provides suggestions for the contents of 5 prop boxes focused on dramatic play. These types of boxes are offered on a rotating basis or in response to children's expressed interests.

*Table 4.3*    *Five Prop Boxes*

**Prop Box 1: The Office**—Stapler, tape, old adding machine, old fax machine, telephones, computer keyboards, old computer monitors, paper, pencils, pens, paper clips, Post-it notes

**Prop Box 2: Flower and Fruit Stand**—Plastic flowers, vegetables, fruits, boxes, crates, bags, table for display, cash register, play money, credit cards, chalkboard to list prices, baskets for carrying produce once purchased

**Prop Box 3: A Bakery**—Cookie sheets, muffin tins, play dough, oven, telephone, labels, chalkboard for prices, cash register, play money, credit cards, beads for decorations, cookbooks, blocks for display cases

**Prop Box 4: Dining Out**—Aprons, chef's hat, menus, tablecloths, silverware, dishes, play food, chalkboard and chalk for "specials" order pads and pencils, cash register, play money, credit cards, telephones

**Prop Box 5: The Shoe Store**—Shoes and boxes, foot measure, tape measure, rules, socks, telephones, receipt book, price labels, cash register, play money, credit cards

## Setting Up for Dramatic Play

Dramatic play centres are recommended for all early learning settings. Children require both a permanent space designated for dramatic play and other space that may be converted as play ideas evolve. Space constraints make it difficult for most early learning settings to include more than one area devoted to dramatic play; however, think of the possibilities for children to extend and expand their experiences. Dramatic play options occur indoors and outdoors.

The "House" is the central theme in children's dramatic play and very often you will hear the dramatic play centre referred to as the housekeeping area. This is because playing house is a familiar family theme for all children. Early learning practitioners provide familiar props and storylines on this topic and other topics based on the children's interests. Ideally, the concept theme areas that would be represented by the prop boxes listed in Table 4.3 would be in addition to a specific "house" area. Can you imagine children playing house and then going to the bank for money to purchase a new pair of shoes at the shoe store? The house centre, if remaining static, becomes a symbol of lost opportunities for children when this is their only exposure to dramatic play.

The house centre is set up to encourage and invite children to engage in various types of play. Davidson (1996) suggests some guidelines that should be considered when arranging the house area.

**Allow Enough Space.** Children require enough space to move around easily; however, the area should not be so large as to complicate negotiations over roles, props, and the direction of the play. The larger the group the harder this becomes. Having two areas that accommodate smaller groups works best.

**Clearly Define the Space.** The furniture in the dramatic centre, i.e. fridge, stove, and sink should be used to define and enclose the space along with backs for shelves from adjacent areas. Clearly defining the space decreases disruptions from children not currently in the area. If possible, the dramatic play centre should be beside the block centre, as children often use the two together.

**Provide Dress-Up Clothing.** Since dressing up is an integral part of pretend playing for children, there should be a variety of clothes for both boys and girls. Ethnic and cultural clothing is included. Consideration is given to how easily the children may independently put the clothes on and take them off. Clothing with Velcro fasteners, large buttons, skirts with elastic waists, and pre-tied ties will give children a sense of independence.

**Provide Props.** Props often set the direction of the play. Too few props will create disputes and too many will result in dumping and clutter. Younger children require realistic props. As the children get older less realistic props will allow for more creative use of materials.

If the early learning environment has space, the house area can have more than one room or the house area can be set up in addition to another area in the environment so that children may expand their play such as shopping in a grocery store. They will have a place to put the groceries once they are purchased. It provides more room for pretending and can accommodate a large number of children at a time.

Space is usually at a premium so it is often unrealistic to suggest that there should always be a housekeeping centre in the environment. Early learning practitioners support children's impulses to play house and take on the related roles. They recognize that at times children will need to extend their play beyond the designated play space. Children will assume, pretend, and take on roles readily in the outdoor environment. For more on dramatic play outdoors refer to Chapter 5.

## Time to Play

Finding the time for children to play in the schedule of the day is extremely important. Children need ample time to plan, carry out, and sustain their dramatic activity (Isenberg & Jalongo, 2001). The role of the early learning practitioner is to ensure the schedule for the day allows for long periods of time for play. Christie and Wardle (1992) conducted a study on 4- and 5-year-olds' play behaviour and found that the length of the play period affected the amount and maturity of play. How much time is adequate? Frost, Wortham, and Reifel (2001) suggest that at least one hour of uninterrupted free play is recommended in a daily schedule and that may not even be adequate. Some "children spend 45 minutes to an hour planning their play—designing play sets, negotiating roles, and discussing themes" (p. 301).

# Stop . . . Think . . . Discuss . . . Reflect

Why do you think that some early learning practitioners stop children's dramatic play experiences so that the children may move to the next scheduled activity? Is it more beneficial to keep children on a timed schedule than to allow the play to continue? Why or why not? What are the advantages of allowing the play to continue? What are the disadvantages?

*Photo 4.6    All dressed up and ready to go, baby in tow.*

# WEAVING DRAMATIC PLAY INTO THE EARLY LEARNING ENVIRONMENT

Pretend play can occur in all parts of the early learning environment, and at all times of the day. The types of materials provided will influence the direction and quality of pretend play. When children are pouring water into pots at the water table and shaping "cakes" from sand at the sand table, they are pretending to be cooking. Adding boats to the water table, the children pretend that they are sailing on the seas. Including dump trucks in the sand table could trigger children to pretend that they are construction workers.

In the outdoor setting, larger equipment such as playhouses, slides, climbers, boxes, and hallow blocks will prompt children not only to develop themes involving the ever popular house but also pirate ships, secret hideouts, and camping trips (Davidson, 1996). Science and dramatic play intermingle when children are encouraged to act out seasonal changes with their bodies (Isenberg & Jalongo, 2002). Children have fun pretending to be babies and illustrating with their bodies their own growth and development from an infant who crawls and cries to someone who can run, jump, and ride a tricycle. Art materials lend themselves to dramatic play in two significant ways. Children create stories to accompany their pictures and they can act them out. A second way is in the construction of props to be used in their pretend play (Davidson, 1996).

If children need a sign to add to the gas station that they have created in the block centre, they can create their own from art materials made readily available. By placing props in the block play, pretend play may be extended into that area. For example, imagine children who have blankets and dolls in the block area creating beds for their babies. Including signs and labels in the block and dramatic play centre will integrate literacy in both. Using other written language props to support the play, such as maps, tickets, magazines, or letters, will support a print rich environment that promotes dramatic play, language, and literacy. Books can be used for both building and pretending.

When writing experiences are associated with dramatic play, they become more meaningful than if children are given lessons or seatwork in which they practice their letters. The connection between emerging literacy and dramatic play is significant. For example, when children set up as a restaurant and take orders from printed menus as a waiter and customer, they are writing within a meaningful context. Meaning is given to literacy learning. Through play, literacy becomes an enjoyable and satisfying experience for young children. Whenever children are exposed to an environment that makes use of everyday written language, such as taking orders, filling out forms, making shopping lists, jotting down appointments, dramatic play will encourage literacy development (Furman, 2000).

It is during dramatic play situations that fantasy and collaborative storytelling can spontaneously occur. Children practice using language during play. By describing other worlds, events, and characters they begin to *decontextualize* language and learn to assume multiple perspectives (Ahn & Filipenko, 2007). It is through this play that children are most likely to expand their language skills or engage in pretend reading or writing.

## Guns, War Play, and Superheroes

It would be very uncommon to find toy weapons in early learning settings. Given the opportunity, predominately boys will fashion guns from blocks, Legos, or other construction material. Children use guns and weapons to carry out fantasy play. The research does not suggest that this type of play leads to aggression and violence, but early learning practitioners are generally uncomfortable with the play and tend to ban children from using items as guns (Frost, Wortham, & Reifel, 2001). Here is an opportunity for you to reflect on a perspective that you may not have considered before. Think about children who come from families with parents involved in the military, police, or conservation professions who are required to use guns as part of their jobs. Or, think about children who have parents that engage in hunting as a sport. Think of children who immigrate with their families from war-torn countries and how they would need to play out their experiences. Guns may be part of children's lives. Are we disrespecting these children's play if we ban guns from the environment?

An early learning practitioner can spend a great deal of energy trying to enforce a ban on gun play and restricting superhero play as it is natural that children will use play guns and weapons to enact superhero scenarios. Is it so terrible for children to engage in superhero play even if it involves gun play? Many longtime practitioners will tell you that even when you ban guns, children will be inventive at making their play more acceptable to adults, for example, "This isn't a gun, it is a laser camera" (Barnes, 2008). Early learning practitioners are cognizant that their values and beliefs about weapons such as guns must not interfere with a child's play. As identified in the following "Words of Wisdom," Shawna Lee, an early learning practitioner who conducts workshops on superhero play provides us with insight into the importance of this type of play.

# WORDS OF WISDOM

## Ask an Expert

Sometimes the line between appropriate, action-oriented, rough-and-tumble play and true aggression in children can be difficult to decipher. When the two are confused, it is more likely that restrictions which stop superhero play will be imposed on the children. Instead, it would be valuable for adults to guide the children to participate in healthy, safe superhero play. One of the best ways that they can do this is by jumping in from the sidelines and becoming *engaged* in the play with the children. Often, it is the physical action of the play that is most appealing to the children. By developing their own superhero, adults can reinforce the values and beliefs of the classroom by role modelling methods of active play and attending to the positive, appropriate behaviours that they see occurring. For example, try introducing "The Manners Monster" or "The Incredible Hug" as characters that grow bigger and stronger when children see examples of manners (physical and verbal) and consideration of others. When lots of attention is given to the children for these behaviours in their play, it is more likely that they will demonstrate this behaviour again in this and other settings.

*Shawna Lee*

Superhero play is a form of dramatic play in which children use figurines, costumes, or other props as accessories to imitate the superheroes they admire. Children are drawn to the power, strength, and special attributes of superheroes. It gives them a sense of feeling in charge of their world. It provides children with a safe way to achieve a sense of power and play out violence they may have observed, whether it be on television or in their own homes. There are positive attributes to this type of play. It is active, creative, and empowering. Having clear guidelines about appropriate behaviour will support superhero play in a positive way. This is different from aggressive behaviour. Children should know that aggressive behaviour is unacceptable and that everyone needs to feel safe.

Dramatic play involves risk taking. Acting out a role is going beyond here and now. It is a challenging but rewarding experience for children and adults. As early learning practitioners we need to be aware of the inherent benefits of taking risks in our practice to give children a sense of empowerment. Further discussion on risk taking occurs in Chapter 5.

# SUMMARY

## Chapter Preview

- Dramatic play is one of the most important forms of play for young children.

## Theoretical Frameworks

- Theoretical frameworks provide students and early learning practitioners with a foundation to explore ones thoughts and beliefs. Piaget, Vygotsky, Erikson, and Gardner's theories are lenses from which to view dramatic play as it relates to child development.

## What Is Dramatic Play?

- Dramatic play is known as pretend play, imaginative play, symbolic play, make-believe play, and sociodramatic play. All refer to a type of play that involves pretending or using symbols to stand in for that which is real.
- Dramatic play is an important developmental experience as it relates to multiple domains.
- When a child takes on a role alone, she is engaging in dramatic play; with others it becomes sociodramatic play and requires the ability to transform objects and actions symbolically. With experience, children develop their dramatic play skills, eventually becoming master players.

## Characteristics of Dramatic Play

- The complexity of dramatic play varies across the ages. There are variations of breadth and depth of dramatic play within each age group.
- Smilanksy (1968) characterized six criteria of dramatic play: *Imitative role play* and *make-believe play* which are in regard to children and objects, *verbal make-believe* regarding actions and situations, *persistence in role play* involving children playing alone, *interaction* with at least two players, and *verbal communication* where there is dialogue among children.

## Stages of Dramatic Play Development

- With experience, dramatic play becomes more complex. Toddlers have the ability to enact events. Preschools take these experiences and add complexity and by age 4 children are capable of sustained pretend scenarios, multiple roles, and symbolic use of props. School-age children are ready for an audience.
- Enactment occurs when children adopt actions, feelings, thoughts, and behaviours of people in particular situations. According to Isenberg and Jalongo (2001) enactment in early learning occurs in three forms: (1) informal drama, (2) story or interpretive drama, and (3) formal or scripted drama.
- Theatre is a more structured form of dramatic play or creative drama. It fits Smilansky's definition of "games with rules."

## Experiences for Children in Dramatic Play across the Ages

- Trister Dodge, Colker, and Heroman (2002) suggest that there is a beginning level and an advanced level when preschool children are engaged in dramatic play involving role playing and the use of props.

## The Importance of Dramatic Play

- There is connection between cognitive competence and high-quality pretend play. Cognitive strategies exhibited during dramatic play include joint planning, negotiation, problem solving, and goal seeking. It can provide opportunities to challenge the social norms that may be marginalizing children.
- Dramatic play is the key ingredient to developing self-regulation as it requires children to gain skills controlling their emotional and cognitive impulses. It becomes part of a child's executive function.

## Variations in Dramatic Play

- Studies have shown that variations in sociodramatic play can be explained by parenting style, child care quality, attitudes of early learning practitioners, and socioeconomic differences. There is also a correlation between low-quality early learning and child care centres and a lack of complex social play interactions.
- Dramatic play can be an equalizer for all children regardless of gender, culture, and background. It is important for early learning practitioners to encourage dramatic play for these reasons.

## The Role of the Early Learning Practitioner

- An adult's participation in dramatic play can provide a scaffold to raise children's social interaction to a higher level. Early learning practitioners and students become involved in children's dramatic play beyond just intervening because of children's play issues. Practitioners are facilitators of play, and they ensure there is space, props, and time set aside for the purpose of expanding children's development.
- Early learning practitioners use observation tools and pedagogical documentation to encourage reflection and discussion about dramatic play with children. The early learning practitioner asks thoughtful questions to support the child in provoking creative thinking.
- For solitary play, early learning practitioners can help individual children re-enact complex stories. With 2-year-olds beginning to develop in their parallel play, early learning practitioners provide duplicates of the same materials. When children are involved in associative play, the play can be promoted by the use of themes that allow for some interaction, but also independent play. An airplane-themed dramatic play area encourages more cooperative play.

## Observation and Documentation

- When children are playing in the dramatic play area, the priority for the practitioner or student is to observe and document the play in order to know how to facilitate, expand, and support the play.

## Planning and Facilitating Dramatic Play

- When planning for and facilitating dramatic play, consider the interests, dramatic themes, and props familiar to children and those that will trigger curiosity and add new exploratory opportunities. If conflicts arise suggest alternative scenarios.
- It is the role of the adult to assist children to move along through solitary, parallel, associative, and group play.
- There are multiple roles for the early learning practitioner to take in dramatic play including stage manager, player or participant in the play, mediator, interpreter, social director, observer, and documenter.

## Types of Dramatic Play

- Early learning practitioners and students make meaningful programming decisions which may include introducing children to specific types of dramatic play such as story play, pantomime, puppets, story drama, and early teacher theatre, as well as a specific program entitled "Tools of the Mind," based on Vygotsky's theories.

## Provocations for Dramatic Play

- Provocation is a means for provoking further action. A provocation can be anything that arrives by surprise and sparks interest such as a collection of interesting scarves or pieces of materials which children find by surprise in the dramatic play centre one morning. Early learning practitioners use prop boxes to provide provocation for dramatic play.

## Setting Up for Dramatic Play

- Children require both a permanent space designated for dramatic play and other space that may be converted as play ideas evolve in both indoor and outdoor environments.
- The "House" is the central theme in children's dramatic play. In setting up the housekeeping-themed dramatic play, early learning practitioners allow enough space, make sure the space is clearly defined, and provide dress-up clothing and props.

## Time to Play

- Finding the time for children to play in the schedule of the day is extremely important. Children need ample time to plan, carry out, and sustain their dramatic activity.
- The role of the early learning practitioner is to ensure that there is at least one hour of uninterrupted free play in the schedule for dramatic play.

## Weaving Dramatic Play into the Early Learning Environment

- Pretend play can occur in all parts of the early learning environment and at all times of the day. The types of materials provided will influence the type of pretend play.
- Dramatic play connects to art, math, science, blocks, language, literacy, music, and movement. Dramatic play occurs both outdoors and indoors.
- Dramatic play offers the young child opportunities to use symbolic representation: the ability to use one thing to represent another. It is during dramatic play situations that fantasy and collaborative storytelling can spontaneously occur.

## Guns, War Play, and Superheroes

- Children use guns and weapons to carry out fantasy play. The research does not suggest that this type of play leads to aggression and violence. Early learning practitioners are generally uncomfortable and tend to ban this type of play.

- Superhero play is a form of dramatic play in which children use figurines, costumes, or other props as accessories to imitate the superheroes they admire. Children are drawn to the power, strength, and special attributes of superheroes.
- There are positive attributes to this type of play. It is active, creative, and empowering. Having clear guidelines about appropriate behaviour will support superhero play in a positive way. Children should know that aggressive behaviour is unacceptable and that everyone needs to feel safe.

# REVIEW QUESTIONS

1. Explain the theories of Piaget, Erikson, Vygotsky, and Gardner as they relate to dramatic play.
2. What are the interchangeable terms for dramatic play? What does having so many terms tell you about dramatic play?
3. Explain the stages of dramatic play beginning with a young toddler and continuing to school-age children. Relate each stage to the criteria developed by Smilansky.
4. Why is dramatic play known as an equalizer for all children regardless of gender, culture, and background?
5. Explain the multiple roles for the early learning practitioner to take in dramatic play.
6. List the types of dramatic play and give examples for each.
7. Name five provocations for dramatic play and explain why these fit the criterion of a provocation.
8. What would be the most familiar dramatic play theme for most children? How would you set up the environment to reflect this theme?
9. Why is it important for children to have ample time for dramatic play?
10. Give examples of how your dramatic play can be woven into other areas of the early learning program.
11. Discuss the pros and cons of war play and superhero play.

# MAKING CONNECTIONS

## Theory to Practice

1. Relate the concept of self-regulation to Vygotsky's theory about dramatic play. Can you find any further research that supports a focus on executive function in early learning? In Ontario, for example, the curriculum developed for the implementation of full-day learning for 4- and 5-year-olds pays particular attention to self-regulation.
2. The next time you spend the day in an early learning classroom check the schedule—how much time is given to dramatic play? What do you think can be done with the schedule to encourage longer periods of play?
3. There are many internet articles and magazines geared for parents of young children. Write a short article for parents on the importance of dramatic play as it relates to child development. What do you need to remember when you are communicating with parents? Style, length, language? Remember to consider how your article appears visually.

## For Further Research

1. Conduct an internet search for Howard Gardner's theory of multiple intelligences. How many intelligences or ways of knowing are listed? Why are only three related to dramatic play in this chapter? In your search you should be able to find an online survey that will assess your way of knowing. After completing the survey, relate the answer to your childhood experiences in dramatic play.

2. Children are drawn to the power, strength, and special attributes of superheroes. Can you find any research related to empowerment and children? Why are the issues of power important to understanding child development?

3. Vivian Gussin Paley has made many contributions to early learning around the world. Her many publications not only celebrate the joys of story and drama in kindergarten, they bring to life the kindergarten experience itself. Discover the work of Paley by reading one of her many books or the many articles written about her work, for instance, Patricia Cooper (2005), "Literacy Learning and Pedagogical Purpose in Vivian Paley's Storytelling Curriculum," published by the *Journal of Early Childhood Literacy*.

# ADDITIONAL READING

Elkind, D. (2007). *The power of play: How spontaneous, imaginative activities lead to happier, healthier children.* Cambridge, MA: DaCapo Press.

Fromberg, D. (2001). *Play and meaning in early childhood education.* Boston: Allyn & Bacon.

Hoffman, E. (2004). *Magic capes, amazing powers: Transforming superhero play in the classroom.* St. Paul, MN: Redleaf Press.

# WEBLINKS

Creative Drama & Theatre Education Resource Site
**www.creativedrama.com**

The Role of Pretend Play in Children's Cognitive Development.
**http//ecrp.uiuc.edu/v4n1/bergen.html**

Pretend Play and Young Children's Development
**www.ericdigests.org/2002-2/play.htm**

Ask Dr. Katz: What Does the Research Say about Dramatic Play Including Gun Play?
**http//illinoisearlylearning.org/ask-dr-katz/question006.htm**

The Association for the Study of Play - TASP
**www.tasplay.org**

> **"** Must we always teach our children with books? Let them look at the mountains and the stars above. Let them look at the beauty of the waters and the trees and the flowers on earth. They will then begin to think, and to think is the beginning of real education. **"**
>
> —Davis Polis

# 5 The Power of Outdoor Play

## Learning Outcomes

After exploring this chapter you should be able to

- discuss three reasons why children living in Canada today have limited outdoor play experiences;

- explain the historical perspectives on outdoor play, starting from Froebel's perspective to today's implementation of playground safety standards by the Canadian Standards Association;

- explain five reasons and give examples why outdoor play is important to a child's development, health, and wellness;

- explain how a child's adult role model impacts a child's outdoor play experience;

- discuss what is meant by risk taking and outline its benefits to child development;

- explain seven areas that an early learning practitioner may consider when examining outdoor play space for infants, toddlers, preschools, and school-age children;

- define what is meant by loose parts and describe why they are important to outdoor play; and

- explain five roles of early learning practitioners in outdoor play.

## Stories from the Field: Practitioner to Student

When I became a student in an early childhood education program I was determined that I was going to develop skills in programming with children. I assumed that this would allow me to concentrate on working effectively with children indoors. I felt that the outdoor playtime was purely a time for the practitioners to have a coffee break and for the children to "run off their energy" so that they would settle down indoors to focus on the important parts of their program. During my first placement, I always volunteered to clean up or set up for new activities while the children were outdoors. I hated the thought of having to go outdoors.

During my second placement I was assigned to an early learning environment where the children had at least four hours of outdoor play each day. I dreaded going there! After the first day of observing the staff and children in the outdoor environment, I began to reflect on my attitude about outdoor play and I engaged in some self-talk as I needed to develop some coping strategies. Eight weeks was a long placement!

It was the best placement that I had because I began to see the merit of outdoor play for children and staff. Over time, I began to recognize the different attitudes and abilities that children exhibit when they are playing outdoors. The children were more spontaneous and energized. I enjoyed the children's laughter, and I realized there was very little fighting—rather children played together. I also liked that there were less rules for the children to remember—they could run, or hop, or glide. They could climb, jump, and squeal with excitement; they could dig in the dirt, they could explore the puddles, and they could use blocks, tricycles, wagons, books, boards, and pipes to create play options. Their play was rich with creativity, language, physical activity, and partnership. They seemed busy and content.

I learned that outdoor play is influenced by the attitudes of early learning practitioners. When early learning practitioners embrace outdoor play, they listen to the children, they offer programming that supports the play interests and options of the children, and they document play episodes so that children may examine their play, discuss their play, and imagine how to expand the play. Developing an effective outdoor play experience is as challenging as planning for the indoor portion of the program. The rewards are significant. And yes, I learned that outdoor play is not a time for practitioners to have a coffee break. It is a time to observe, facilitate, discuss, and play with the children.

*Amaz, ECE Graduate, 2004*

# CHAPTER PREVIEW

As you begin to review this chapter, you may be thinking about when you grew up playing with mud, rocks, at the brook, or up in the tree house. You may reflect on the amount of time you spent being outdoors. It may have been for most of the day, with some of the time being supervised, while other times being in the neighbourhood with groups of children. Or, it could have been in your backyard. For some of you, outdoor play may have taken place in parks with supervision or while you were at your early learning centre. Young children's outdoor play experiences are very different today from 15 years ago and 30 years ago. Why and how do you think they differ?

Many children living in Canada today have limited outdoor play opportunities or experiences. This, combined with the reduction of unstructured outdoor playtime, changes the scope and breadth of a child's play experiences. These changes have an impact on child development. For example, since World War II, a large percentage of our population has settled in urban areas. Urban areas offer limited access to natural outdoor play spaces for children. The increase of access to technology and the concern for the security and safety of children have reduced a child's freedom to play. Many kindergarten and school-aged children are in school settings that are replacing outdoor recess for gym activities, or reducing the amount of time allocated for outdoor play. Many before and after school programs, do not have an outdoor play component.

It is estimated that about half (49 percent) of Canadian children aged 5 to 12 years are not physically active enough to receive health benefits (Craig, Cameron, Russell, & Beaulieu, 2001). On average, young children under 5 years of age spend less than 10 hours per week playing outdoors versus 20 to 30 hours per week in sedentary activities. This lack of active play negatively impacts children's health, wellness, and development. As identified in Chapter 1, there is an increase in type 2 diabetes and heart diseases. These health and lifestyle practices follow children into their adulthood.

At the same time, we have growing numbers of children who are involved in structured activities such as swimming and gymnastics. Although these activities are beneficial, when children have a significant amount of time structured, it reduces their opportunities to participate in open-ended, self-initiated free play. Children need time and the freedom to participate in play.

Expanding children's outdoor play is essential. This requires early learning practitioners to acquire the knowledge about and skills in planning outdoor play. Early learning practitioners who expand their knowledge base about outdoor play will enhance their comfort levels about its importance and strategies for facilitating quality outdoor play options.

This chapter focuses on the various elements of outdoor play including information on ways to facilitate outdoor play so that children are offered a wide spectrum of experiences to support their identified interests, as well as their cognitive, social, emotional, and physical development.

As you review this chapter, think about Johah, a 3-year-old child, wanting to make a structure using plywood pieces, longboards, and cedar blocks in the outdoor play area. Think about why this outdoor play experience may be important to him. Why does Johah benefit from the freedom to build his structure outdoors? What type of learning might Johah engage in from a math and science perspective? Why? How might Johah's language requirements differ from indoors? How might this experience be different from constructing indoors? How might the weather impact the play experience? Why? These are all valuable questions that we hope you will gain insight into as you explore this chapter.

# WORDS OF WISDOM

## The Importance of Outdoor Play

**Sally Kopsopoulos**
*Ryerson University, Toronto, Ontario*

Outdoor play has been of paramount interest in the field of early childhood education over the last few years. While the *Day Nurseries Act* in Ontario guides early learning and care facilities to provide approximately two hours per day in outdoor play, it is up to the early childhood educator to ensure the quality of learning during that time. Outdoor play spaces are an extension to the indoor learning environment and consequently need to be incorporated into the teacher's plans for the program.

Early childhood educators do provide for excellent opportunities to build strong bodies through activities that challenge a child's gross motor development. But outdoor learning should also involve a child's understanding of nature, her position in nature as a living thing, social interactions with peers, and muscle development. In fact, the outdoor space can provide a comprehensive learning environment.

Opportunities to learn about nature, local plants, birds, animals, and the changing seasons, extend the child's learning and foster an understanding of the natural world and their place in it. The implementation of a thoughtful curriculum based on listening to the children's queries, observing their demonstrated knowledge, and considering their developmental needs provides opportunities where children can experience collaborative learning, challenge themselves physically, extend their understanding of the natural world, participate in team activities, and treasure precious solitary moments of thought and imagination.

Activities such as digging into sand, piling up blocks, carrying water, constructing magical places, planting gardens, pounding nails, collecting rocks, splashing water, and creating tunnels help to create a child's sense of ownership and responsibility. Outdoor play allows the child to develop their body, their mind, and their spirit.

While you may not have an ideal outdoor space, a container of vegetables or herbs can always be added. Consider how the children use the space. What works, what fosters curiosity, what curbs it? Plan changes with the children that allow for a space for water, sky gazing, someplace to dig, even if it is just a box of dirt, and loose materials (stones and logs) can always be added. A walk in the neighbourhood provides endless opportunities for observing nature that are relevant to a small child's world. There is always the sky and weather, ants, sand and weeds, that, under the tutelage of a thoughtful early childhood educator, present opportunities for learning. It is essential that early childhood educators maximize the outdoor learning experience. A child's natural curiosity leads them to smell the flower, poke the dirt, consider the spider, and gaze at the clouds floating by and to ask "Why?"

# HISTORICAL PERSPECTIVE ON OUTDOOR PLAY

The value of outdoor play has long been recognized by theorists including Piaget, Montessori, Dewey, Rousseau, and Froebel. For example, Froebel believed that children require time to play in gardens. He suggested that outdoor play brings a depth and breadth to learning that is not emulated in other settings. Outdoor play is essential for the child's whole development, not just physical development.

Froebel determined that outdoor play is a place where children find natural places to play—this includes trees and tree trunks for climbing or for imaginative play, gardens for scientific concepts including germination, water sources such as brooks, and areas of grass for games. Froebel advocated for outdoor play environments to have natural elements and free-flowing materials.

In the 1880s, piles of sand were placed in public parks in Berlin, Germany. This was the beginning of the Sandgarten (sand garden) movement (Johnson, Christie, & Wardle, 2005). By 1897, sand play became a valuable part of childhood. G. Stanley Hall noted that sand play benefited young children and school-aged children, both from a developmental and psychological perspective.

In the early 1900s, many early childhood programs across North America began to recognize the importance of outdoor play. Froebel's outdoor play blueprint became the standard model that programs worked to achieve. Over time, educators advocated for additional open-ended props and play experiences to be incorporated into the child's outdoor play experience. These included items such as

- carts, wagons, playhouses, and related materials for dramatic play;
- woodworking;
- cardboard boxes; and
- balls, ladders, and sandpiles (Frost, 1992).

As nursery schools evolved in the 1920s, the importance of outdoor play for the young child was further expanded. Similar to Froebel and the kindergarten movement, the nursery school movement emphasized the relationship of outdoor play to child development. Nursery school programs known for their quality ensured that there were natural grassy areas, places for dramatic play, trees, contact with animals, and commercially prepared climbing and play apparatus available. Frost (1992) identified that "the total array of materials and certain program practices were impressive" (p. 118) for that time in history.

In the late 1940s and early 1950s, nursery schools and kindergartens added paved areas for wheeled toys. Shelters were added for use in times of inclement weather. Safety issues also became a focus, leading programs to add soft surfaces under equipment, restricting the height of climbing apparatus, and offering a variety of soft and hard play surfaces (Johnson, Christie, & Wardle, 2005).

Up until the early 1950s, the playground equipment was generally made from steel, iron, or wood. It included swings, rope swings, sliding surfaces, teeter-totters, and monkey bars. Most equipment was set in concrete or asphalt with no other ground cover. At the same time, health care professionals began recording data on children's playground injuries. This led to some cities and municipalities examining the conditions of the playgrounds, resulting in a number of changes over the decades.

In the 1960s, manufacturers devised new features in the playground equipment. During this period, known as the "novelty era," play structures were created to exhibit various fantasy characters, animals, or related societal experiences such as nautical and rocket themes. Swings, slides, and climbers remained popular. From a manufacturing perspective, the look of the structure became more important than the child development features or the versatility for play.

During the 1970s and 1980s, there was a resurgence of wooden play equipment. The structures combined physical play features by incorporating swivel swings, tires, slides, and climbing apparatus with dramatic play areas by adding hiding places and shapes to the architecture, such as castles and ships. The structure, combined with sandpiles, tricycle paths, and space for materials with loose parts became the standard. These play works were intended to provide rich play experiences for children.

In the early 1990s, the Canadian Paediatric Society brought forth alarming statistics on the number of children injured at playgrounds. They estimated more than 28,500 children per year were treated in emergency departments and hospitals for playground injuries. The majority of these injuries occurred with elementary school-aged children falling from equipment. The most common diagnoses included fractures, followed by soft tissue injuries and lacerations. For children younger than 5 years of age, the head and face were most commonly injured.

In response to the number of childhood injuries, in the early 1990s, the first set of playground safety standards were developed by the Canadian Standards Association (CSA). These standards, known as CAN/CSA-Z614-07, are the only nationally recognized ones for children's play spaces and equipment. The standards are guidelines that are intended "to promote and encourage the provision and use of play spaces that are well-designed, well-maintained, innovative, and challenging, and, in so doing, contribute to the development of healthy children in the broadest sense of the word" (Canadian Standards Association, 2008, p. 2). The standards are continuously updated and are applied to public playgrounds, such as on school grounds, parks, early childhood learning centres, and motels. Some provinces, such as Ontario, require early learning and child care centres to meet the CSA Standards before an operating license is issued.

Box 5.1 provides a listing of the breadth of the information and standards for play spaces as outlined by the CSA. Further information on the CSA Standards is found in the final section of the chapter. In addition, each of Canada's provinces and territories provides legislation or guidelines for early learning and child care programs that address the recommended outdoor playtime required daily, the minimum types and standards of the equipment for outdoor play, and the maintenance regime required for equipment and outside play space.

---

## BOX 5.1

### CSA Standards Information for Play Spaces

**The CSA Standards provide information on**
- materials and specifications for play equipment;
- playground installation;
- surfacing for under play areas;
- play space layout;
- maintenance;
- guidelines for including water features in children's play spaces;
- surfacing materials comparison chart; and
- making play spaces more accessible to children with special needs;

---

During the first decade of this century, there continued to be a reduction in outdoor play opportunities for young children. Our family values and cultural beliefs are shifting towards the promotion of academic preparedness, the excessive use of TV and technology, and the feeling of the need to protect children in their neighbourhoods. These shifts are reducing children's access to outdoor play. Most outdoor playtime is now organized at specific times and in most cases in playground settings with adult supervision. The play space footprint given to children has been drastically reduced. And, the play spaces and opportunities to play in a naturalized outdoor setting have been greatly diminished for commercialized play centres.

Yet, the research is clear. Outdoor play is critical to the development of healthy children.

## THE IMPORTANCE OF OUTDOOR PLAY TO CHILD DEVELOPMENT

Never in Canadian society has outdoor play been so important in early learning and child care environments. Children achieve many developmental milestones through outdoor play. Outdoor play enhances exploring, risk taking, language development, social competence, fine and gross motor development, creativity, imagination, problem solving, and thinking skills (Fromberg & Gullo, 1992). It enriches children's language and is often a venue where a different vocabulary from the indoor setting is used. Outdoor play encourages children to learn about their natural environment (Bredekamp & Copple, 1997). It provides a setting for formulating informal networks, exploring cultural identity, and building learning communities (Woolley, 2006). For example, Fox (1993) observed a group of 4- and 5-year-old children during their outdoor play. She noticed that they used a variety of cognitive skills including examples of addition and subtraction, shape identification, patterning, one-to-one correspondence, number sense, sequencing of events, use of ordinal numbers, knowledge of prepositions, and identification of final and initial consonants. She also observed examples of problem solving, creative expression, language, and gross and fine motor development.

Frost (1992) states that "play is the chief vehicle for the development of imagination and intelligence, language, social skills, and perceptual-motor abilities in infants and young children" (p. 48). A rich outdoor play experience contributes to each of the developmental tasks that children must achieve, especially the physical development attributes.

Children who do not have sufficient outdoor play experiences generally have "poorer ability in motor tasks, lower levels of physical activity, poorer ability to deal with stressful or traumatic situations and events, poorer ability to access and manage risk and poorer social skills, leading to difficulties in negotiating social situations such as dealing with conflict and cultural difference" (National Playing Fields Association, 2000, p. 14).

Outdoor play is for all children. Children with disabilities value outdoor play because this is where children both with and without disabilities play. Outdoor play is a natural place for children in inclusive programs to make friends (Petrie & Poland, 1998) and learn from one another. Early learning practitioners plan and assess outdoor play space to ensure that all children have equal access to an array of play experiences. It is not acceptable for children with disabilities to be segregated at any time; especially so during outdoor play.

Outdoor play and child development are clearly linked. Figure 5.1 provides an overview of the skills children gain from outdoor play. Further discussion on the relationship of outdoor play to child development follows.

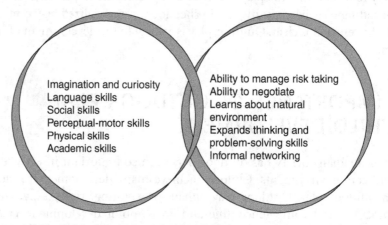

*Figure 5.1* *Skills Children Gain from Outdoor Play*

## Cognitive Development

Studies indicate that young children who actively participate in play, including outdoor play, are advanced in cognitive development, score higher on tests of imagination and creativity, and have an enhanced ability to think inventively (Freyberg, 1973; Pepler & Ross, 1981). These findings are aligned with Piaget's (1962) perspective that play is vital to cognitive development. Through play, children practice skills that they have observed and acquired in non-play situations. If the skills are not practiced in a play context, the learning opportunity is diminished. Play episodes allow children to assimilate the information that they gather and then, by using it in play, make sense of it. This contributes to a child creating his "own" knowledge.

*Photo 5.1   Outdoor play and child development are closely linked.*

Aimie, who is 4 years of age, and her family have just experienced the death of their pet cat named Mussie. When Aimie entered the outdoor play area today, she began playing "Kitty Kitty." This play had Aimie walking on her hands and knees. She moved towards people, meowing. She tried to jump up on children's laps. She tried to curl up and have a catnap. She announced to the children and the early learning practitioner "I'm dead." This play was repeated daily by Aimie for more than a week. Then, as quickly as the play idea began, it was replaced by an intense interest in the butterflies that she had observed in the garden. Aimie needed the time, support of her early learning practitioners, and the activity to be able to work through the loss of her pet.

## Social Development

Smilansky (1968) indicates that play helps children develop socially. Generally, play becomes more social as they get older. For example, 3-year-old children may play together with two or three children. By the time the children become school-aged, there are usually five or more children playing together. When outdoor environments are rich with sociodramatic play opportunities (dramatic play that involves more than one player), their social skills including cooperation, negotiation, sharing, problem solving, self-regulation, and appreciation of another's play efforts are enhanced. Children who consistently play develop the skills and abilities to be more "socially competent than those who play less frequently" (Frost, 1992, p. 34).

Generally, there is less structure during the outdoor play portion of the program than what is experienced in the indoor program portion. The outdoor play environment supports children in learning self-regulation skills. Early learning practitioners support and encourage children in developing the various skills needed to sustain play episodes. They also help children learn to express themselves and their emotions in socially acceptable ways. This is the beginning phase when children develop turn-taking skills and exhibit flexibility towards ideas

*Photo 5.2 Children extend their networking skills with playmates during outdoor play.*

and behaviours that other children express. Because children are generally more relaxed outdoors, they extend their networking skills with children who they may not necessarily connect with indoors.

## Emotional Development

Children express their feelings through play—it is their natural way to communicate. The more limited a child's vocabulary and understanding of emotions, the higher the need for play (Landreth & Hohmeyer, 1998). Self-initiated play helps young children "play out" their experiences and express their feelings (Landreth, 1991). Outdoor environments provide the setting for vigorous play to occur and for relationship connections to be made among children and adults.

Outdoor play is designed to support the emotional needs of young children. It is a place where children may explore new ideas, express new thoughts, and try new expressions and feelings that may not be tried in the indoor environment. Each of these experiences contributes to children developing their positive self-concepts and greater feelings of power and control over their actions and environment (Frost, Wortham, & Reifel, 2001).

## Physical Development and Movement

Children's movement is an essential activity that impacts all facets of their development. A child's physical development, competence, self-esteem, and knowledge about their environment and their world (Bilton, 2002; Gallahue, 1993) are interconnected to movement and outdoor play. During the early years, outdoor play provides children with opportunities to develop and refine basic motor skills, including walking, running, jumping, climbing, hopping, skipping, sliding and peddling; manipulative skills such as throwing, catching, kicking, striking and bouncing; and stability abilities including bending, stretching, swinging, twisting, and beam-walking (Gallahue, 1993; Poest, Williams, Witt, & Attwood, 1990). The movement skills and abilities acquired during the early years provide the foundation for the more specialized movement skills needed in later life, which are used in such activities as games, sports, dance, and recreation (Gallahue & Ozmun, 1995; Hihiko, 2004). Young children who do not master the required physical developmental milestones are less often active, play less on large playground equipment, and spend less time interacting socially with peers (Bouffard, Watkinson, Thompson, Dunn, & Romanow, 1996, cited in Hands & Martin, 2003, pp. 47–48).

There are a growing number of children who are suffering from **motor illiteracy.** Children who are not active outdoor play consumers do not develop a proficiency in motor skills necessary to support active play (Neto, 1997; Pereira, Fale, & da Guia Carmo, 2002). This becomes a lifetime issue that impacts a variety of physical development requirements such as skeletal and muscular development. As you will

**Motor illiteracy** refers to children not having developed the motor skills needed to support the required body movements necessary for various active play experiences.

read later in the chapter, motor development is directly related to a child's level of participation in safe risk outdoor play experiences.

Children should be encouraged to engage in stimulating activities that require them to move all parts of their bodies. Children that do not achieve their physical development needs may not be able to master more complex movements. This puts them at risk of acquiring an increased number of injuries (Sutterby & Frost, 2002).

Stephenson (1998) outlines three common types of physical play that preschool and school-age children participate in during outdoor play experiences. They include

1. **Coaching:** Children seek the assistance from early learning practitioners in the development of a skill or participation in an activity.

2. **Physical/Dramatic Play:** Children combine physical activity with various roles in dramatic play episodes, such as Duck, Duck, Duck, Goose.

3. **Physical Challenge:** Children combine activities with physical challenges while extending their skills, such as climbing up a large hill and rolling down it as quickly as possible.

When the environment is appropriate, children will participate in a healthy risk-taking behaviour, test their own limits, and exhibit their physical skills (Stephenson, 1998). Children require environments where adults encourage risk-taking behaviour. This supports the development of new physical development skills necessary to master the required motor movement.

## Outdoor Play and Exposure to Natural Light

There are many studies now being conducted to determine the benefits of children being exposed to natural light during outdoor play. Evidence suggests that natural light increases children's cognitive and academic performance, social skills, calmness, and overall psychological wellness.

The lack of outdoor play reduces children's exposure to sunlight (Downing, 1988). The human body is nourished directly by the stimulation of sunlight. There is a concern that Canadians, particularly new Canadians, who do not participate in regular outdoor exposure, are at risk of acquiring diseases due to vitamin D deficiency. Vitamin D requires exposure to sufficient sunlight in order for it to be absorbed. Canadians native to the northern latitudes have lighter skin, giving them the natural ability to absorb vitamin D. Many new immigrants require more exposure to the sun because of their skin pigmentation. For example, Vieth (2010) indicates, "people from India or equatorial Africa require six times the sun exposure to make the same amount of vitamin D as a white person" (p. 22).

Vieth (2010) indicates that clinical trials suggest that calcium and vitamin D reduce bone fractures. Children who have vitamin D deficiency may suffer from rickets, heart disease, depression, autoimmune diseases, chronic fatigue, and possibly autism. "Higher vitamin D levels are associated with a lower risk for multiple sclerosis, breast cancer and colon cancers, and juvenile and adult-onset diabetes, as well as lower rates of cardiovascular disease" (Vieth, 2010, p. 22).

It is important to protect children's skin from the sun. However, children require a minimum of 10 minutes per day without sunscreen for vitamin D absorption. Early learning practitioners benefit from taking the children out in the early morning without sunscreen to meet this requirement.

## Stop . . . Think . . . Discuss . . . Reflect

We hear the need for children to have sunscreen to protect them from skin cancer. Parents are putting sunscreen on their children before they come to the early learning centre, and the centre is also applying sunscreen. How do we help parents examine the literature on sunscreen and the need for children to have some exposure to the sun rays? What is your role in this situation?

## Developing an Appreciation for Outdoor Play

During the early years, children who are exposed to adult role models who exhibit an appreciation for the outdoor environment have a higher probability of developing an interest in outdoor play. Research in eco-psychology and evolutionary psychology disciplines suggests that humans have an affinity for outdoor play (White & Stoecklin, 2008). Evolutionary psychologists use the term **biophilia.** This term refers to an innate, hereditary emotional attraction that humans have to nature. It means that we are born with genetic coding and instincts that require us to participate in the outdoor environment (White & Stoecklin, 2008).

In more than 100 studies conducted on outdoor experiences, the results consistently indicate that outdoor experiences produce "positive physiological and psychological responses in humans, including reduced stress and a general feeling of well-being" (White & Stoecklin, 2008, p. 2). This new direction is being sought by professionals across a variety of disciplines including education, health, psychology, and ecology (Moore, 1990; Nabhan & Trimble, 1994; Rivkin, 1997; Wilson, 1999). Early learning practitioners are in a position to positively influence children in acquiring an appreciation for outdoor play and our environment.

Children require adult role models who have an interest in and appreciation for outdoor play. As identified in Figure 5.2, the outdoor play environment must provide children with many key characteristics that differ from indoor environments. Outdoor play must be diverse with opportunities for children to explore and discover in a safe environment. Children also require opportunities for solitude and wonderment. The freedom to play and explore thoughts and feelings, although complicated, allows the child to have a sense of choice, become self-motivated and self-regulated, spontaneous, and imaginative based on the child's interest rather than adult-imposed perspectives. Early experiences with a natural play space contribute to the child developing positive feelings about the outdoor environment, nature, science, each other, and the world around them.

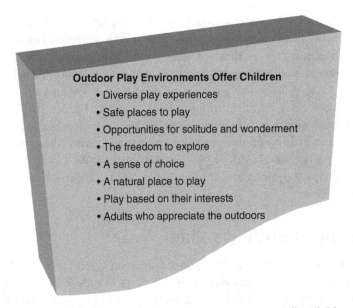

**Outdoor Play Environments Offer Children**
- Diverse play experiences
- Safe places to play
- Opportunities for solitude and wonderment
- The freedom to explore
- A sense of choice
- A natural place to play
- Play based on their interests
- Adults who appreciate the outdoors

**Figure 5.2**   *Characteristics of What Outdoor Play Environments Offer Children*

As identified at the beginning of this chapter, Froebel believed that children require a garden as part of their environment. The garden is where the children and nature meld together, creating an appreciation for play and nature. The play garden is the place where children gain a sense of observation and respect that is difficult to emulate in other settings. Over time, we have separated the playgrounds and gardens, each having a different focus. Early learning practitioners and children would benefit from realigning these elements of the outdoor play space.

*Photo 5.3   Children have an infinity for nature including playing in tall grasses.*

Appropriate play space contributes to children learning about their natural world such as the food chain by growing fruits and vegetables. For example, children discover about insects that are attracted to the fruits and vegetables. This allows children to scaffold and connect their learning about the relationship of ladybugs eating aphids or birds eating particular insects. We encourage children to learn about butterflies and hummingbirds by planting bushes that attract them. And, sunflowers bring an array of birds such as goldfinches and chickadees. Children have an affinity for tall grasses, trees, tunnels, butterflies, sunflowers, and natural loose parts. These outdoor play areas not only hold a child's interests, they also extend the play options and the opportunities for creativity and spontaneity (Hefferman, 1994).

## Risk Taking and Child's Play

Risk taking is part of child's play. It was once seen as an important part of a child's life (Furedi, 2001). Now our society has a focus on ways to reduce a child's opportunity for risk-taking experiences for the sake of safety. For example, families try to keep children safe by driving them to their destinations, teaching them not to speak to strangers, and reducing their freedom to explore outside of their family home. Most children are no longer outdoors without adult supervision. Many school-aged children are required to return to their homes after school and remain indoors until an adult returns home. These children, labelled as *latchkey* children, often choose to watch television or play with electronics in place of outdoor play. Parents express their fears for their children's safety more than in the past. This may be contributing to children growing up in over-protected environments. These types of restrictions on children change their play, reducing their freedom to explore and discover.

As you will study in this section, young children benefit in numerous ways when they grow up in environments that offer physical challenge and risk-taking opportunities. The freedom to provide children with risk taking is being overshadowed by strict standards and regulations that are being put in place to reduce childhood injury, despite the need for children to engage in healthy risk-taking opportunities. Some advocates suggest that the constraints limit early learning practitioners in being able to provide a balance of healthy freedom and exploratory opportunities to young children (Fenech, Sumsion, & Goodfellow, 2006). Some practitioners indicate that the more restrictions there are the more detrimental it is to children's learning and well-being. For example, according to Fenech et al., (2006), "all the equipment has become so supersafe that the children don't have any risk-taking activities [and] we are so restricted by things like safety all of the time that it really restricts your pedagogy" (p. 55). Early learning practitioners are required to adhere to standards, while offering children risk-taking opportunities.

As we advocate for children to engage in active play, varying levels of governments and associations are making a concerted effort to establish play space regulations to remove the possibility of hazard (danger of serious injury or death) to young children. As a society, we need to understand the importance of outdoor play and risk taking so that children are able to learn about appropriate risks associated with outdoor play. In essence, there is a need to reconsider the attitudes, approaches, and policies to our early learning and child care practice to ensure safe risk is an acceptable practice.

When we hear the term "**risk taking**" it is often thought of as having a negative connotation. In fact, from the perspective of children, child development, and outdoor play, risk taking is a necessity. Children learn about new skills, try new ideas, and achieve new knowledge and skills by taking risks. Risk taking is an essential part of the process of "becoming at home in the world" (Smith, 1998, p. 182). Children who do not have opportunities to engage in play with risk taking are living in a world that is inhibiting their development—children have a need for challenge (Stine, 1997).

Often risk and hazard are viewed as synonymous terms (Lupton & Tulloch, 2002). Greenfield (2003) makes a distinction between the two terms. A **hazard** is described as an act or experience that the child does not see or predict. A **risk** refers to an experience whereby the child has some uncertainty about being able to achieve the desired outcome, requiring a choice whether to take the risk or not.

Risk taking is a complex issue and differs from indoor to outdoor environments. Risk taking in the indoors is more cognitively based; whereas in the outdoor environment it contributes to children testing their physical limits while advancing their social, emotional, and cognitive skills. Children who are confident physical risk takers in the outdoor environment are more likely to take risks during indoor activities (Stephenson, 1998). In effect, children who have developed the confidence to embrace the challenges of the environment and accept that learning occurs with mistakes will further explore new possibilities. Risk taking must be thought of in healthy terms—providing children with the opportunity to discover, be adventurous, and build confidence in using their bodies—rather than as a possibility of injury. This can be achieved by managing safe risk opportunities.

There are many ways to manage an environment so that safe risks are present. For example, early learning practitioners examine the environment to distinguish between hazards and risks. They try to eliminate hazards. They examine the potential risks involved, the skills of the child, the likelihood of success or failure in relation to the child's skills and confidence levels, and the severity of the risk outcome, if the child is not successful. This requires practitioners to know the skills that each child has and determine the level of risk that is suitable for each child based on the environment, the governing regulations, and the child's personality.

Children need the freedom to take risks in their play, experience new challenges, and have opportunities to test ideas as part of the risk management process (Tranter, 2005). Children that do not gain healthy kinesthetic and physical skills are at risk of having their level of physical confidence, judgment, competence, and self-esteem negatively impacted (Children's Play Council, 2004; Greenfield, 2004; Duberry, 2001). Children's decision-making processes correspond to making accurate risk judgments (Goodyear-Smith & Laidlaw, 1999) and exercising independent thinking skills. Children learn to take calculated risks by being in environments that allow them to have appropriate experiences.

Safe risk does not equate to non-challenging play equipment or experiences. There are implications when the play space becomes hazard free and sterile. Children may become bored, lose interest in play, or engage in negative behavioural activities.

**Risk taking** Safe risk is defined as the opportunity for the active child to carry out an action involving risk in an environment that decreases the potential for harm (Crossley & Dietze, 2002).

Children will find ways to make their environment more challenging, often by taking inappropriate risks (Greenfield, 2003), using equipment in inappropriate ways, and exhibiting behaviour towards peers that may not normally be exhibited. For example, children will jump from one place to another on the equipment or go backwards on sliding apparatus as a way to add interest to their play. These child-initiated challenges become hazardous (Walsh, 1993) and contribute to unnecessary accidents.

The attitude towards risk taking is influenced by our cultural experiences (New, Mardell, & Robinson, 2005). For example, adults living in northern Canada consider children's outdoor play risk factors different from those adults living in downtown areas. Children in the north have experience playing in open spaces, moving from one yard to another, and climbing on natural items such as rocks and trees. Children in cities are more restricted in their play for many reasons, one of which is the difference in the environmental attributes and the need to keep children safe by keeping them close at hand.

Adults who view play as an essential element and learning process of childhood, provide more freedom to children than those who have not made the connections of play to learning and development. These differences exist not only in our Canadian society, but in other cultures as well, such as in the European and Scandinavian countries. New et al. (2005) identify that the practices in Reggio Emilia, Italy, differ from many North American perspectives. There, teachers support and encourage children to engage in active activities and experiences that allow them to test their limits. The teachers assert that children generally have intuitive monitoring skills that guide them in knowing when they have met their limits.

Other countries such as Norway provide children with the freedom to explore from a very early age. They value and use the natural environment as part of the child's natural play world (Fjortoft & Sageie, 2000) by establishing outdoor early learning programs where children hike, climb trees, use ropes, play on the forest floor, and incorporate materials such as water and beacons to trigger advanced play. These child-initiated play experiences provide children with opportunities to develop an understanding of their environment and their body mechanics (Fjortoft, 2000; Fjortioft & Sageie, 2000).

As identified in Figure 5.3, it is important for early learning practitioners to consider ways to support risk taking while reducing hazards.

Greenfield (2003) suggests, when early learning practitioners develop the skills to assess children's play for potential risk, they are well-placed to positively influence adults to understand the importance of positive safe risk opportunities to child development. The challenge is to balance the safety regulations with environments that are free from hazard while providing them with the level of risk taking that satisfies their natural curiosity. This becomes complicated because "what is challenging for one child may be a hazard for another owing to the developmental range of skills and abilities" (Stine, 1997, p. 28). Early learning practitioners develop ways to manage risk in play rather than eliminating it, as safe risk is essential for the child's optimal health and development. Ultimately, the outdoor play environment provides appropriate levels of risk, while encouraging creativity, challenge, and new learning options.

***Figure 5.3*** *Risk Taking and Children's Play*

# Stop . . . Think . . . Discuss . . . Reflect

How can we meet the safety requirements that govern outdoor play equipment and still provide children with opportunities for physical challenge and risk taking?

What are the impacts for children if they do not have opportunities to participate in physical activities that require risk? Is there a long-term implication on their development? If so, how?

## Planning Outdoor Play Spaces

The outdoor play space and play opportunities are important features in the lives of young children. Preparing an outdoor environment that is stimulating, challenging, and a safe place to play is difficult to accomplish without understanding play, learnings, the concept of safe risk, and child development.

Outdoor play spaces are designed to offer children different play experiences with a balance of skills and concepts that promote active movement, exploration of the unknown, experiences with unpredictable events, and new discoveries. Early learning practitioners prepare outdoor play space in similar ways to the indoor play experiences. There is versatility with the space, coupled with equipment and materials that stimulate children's senses, curiosity, opportunities for intrigue, interests, and abilities. These attributes help children flourish in outdoor play spaces.

The outdoor play environment correlates with the experimentation that children will engage in, which in turn is intended to contribute to their expansion of or reconfiguration of their knowledge base. The theoretical principles of child development, the learning styles of children, and the related level of developmental milestones that children are ready to achieve become pivotal in creating effective play spaces. In the programming process, early learning practitioners ensure that there are opportunities for children to have both solo play and group free-flowing play experiences (Shipley, 1998).

Similar to the indoor environment, the outdoor play space flows from one area to the next. It is open-ended, versatile, and as simple as possible because this type of play space provides opportunities for children to use their imaginations and to make the space "theirs." Quality outdoor play spaces are measured on the openness and diversity of the space rather than on the physical attractiveness. "Materials that can be moved, manipulated, and changed feed developmental needs" (Nicolson & Shipstead, 2002, p. 352) and therefore offer the flexibility that children require.

Early learning practitioners consider the following when examining space:

- Accessibility for all children, ease of entry and exit, and safety guide the play-space design and experience centre options.
- Provisions for play are made that address the environmental conditions such as ozone ratings, temperatures, and weather conditions.
- The different play zones may include: a nature zone, adventure zone, active play zone, quiet learning and play zone (Nicolson & Shipstead, 2002). The play zones offer consistent types of activities, special features, and opportunities for child-initiated experiences.
- The play zones are placed according to dry, wet, noisy, and quiet categories (Dietze, 2006) (see Chapter 12 for further information on this concept).
- The placement of the experience centres and the pathways between the play zones are clearly visible and designed to allow children to observe peers at play or the potential materials that may trigger an interest in the play zone (Dietze, 2006).
- There is open space for gross motor play and quiet spaces for observation or solo play.
- The outdoor storage units display materials at the child's level attractively. Other storage allows unused materials to be removed from the play space so that children are not confronted with clutter.

Guddemi and Eriksen (1992) and Wilson (2004) provide an overview of the types of materials and experiences that are common in the different play zones. Each will be described.

**Nature Zone** The nature zone includes trees, grasses, water, boulders, gardens, and plants. This is an ideal location to include mounds of earth for the children to climb on or to dig in. Children have options to combine items with water and natural items such as mud, leaves, feathers, and rocks in the child's play. This zone provides opportunities for both quiet and active play.

**Adventure Zone** This zone is designed to support the more active experiences that children engage in, including construction activities, dramatic play, and new play possibilities. Many types of materials are combined in this area to support the

*Photo 5.4    Children benefit from having places to dig and explore in their environments.*

development of adventure play. For example, boards, planks, wheelbarrows, dirt, rocks, and cedar blocks may trigger children to create ramps, bridges, and roads.

**Active Play Zone**   This zone includes opportunities for children to run, jump, use tricycles and wheeled toys and games. This area has a variety of ground surfaces—hard surfaces for the wheeled toys, grassy areas for rough and tumble play, and a combination of surfaces for pathways.

**Quiet Learning and Play Zone**   These zones are usually protected from the weather elements and are used for experiences such as puzzles, reading, storytelling, and creative arts experiences. Tables, blankets, benches, baskets of materials, and lawn chairs may be available to support children in their play options. Children are provided with a place to engage in solo play or less active experiences with peers.

Rich outdoor play environments have materials such as:

- sand and water;
- trees, bushes, flowers, and long grasses;
- places and features to sit in, on, under, lean against, and provide shelter and shade;
- places that offer privacy and views;
- structures, equipment, and materials that can be changed;
- loose parts;
- props for dramatic play and construction;
- materials that support children in adding to permanent structures; and
- apparatus that encourages children to roll, run, and climb.

# PLAY SPACES FOR INFANTS, TODDLERS, PRESCHOOLERS AND SCHOOL-AGE CHILDREN

Most early learning and child care programs divide their outdoor play spaces into at least three areas: one for infants and toddlers, one for preschool children, and one for school-aged children.

The infant and toddler space is designed to accommodate a wide range of movements. Frost (1992) indicates the need for infants to have confined space which is "gentle for crawling, kind for falling and cool for sitting" (p. 260). The space ensures opportunities to accommodate the emerging developmental attributes of sitting, crawling, standing, toddling, and walking. A combination of hard and soft surfaces is necessary to support the varying motor developments.

**The infant and young toddler** play spaces provide a variety of materials intended to stimulate their senses. The different ground textures such as grass, chimes blowing in the wind, and soft music support sensory development. Grass, blankets, and mats are useful surfaces for crawling experiences. Early learning practitioners incorporate novelty and challenge into the infant and toddler environment on a gradual basis. Too much stimulation may have a negative effect on the child. Infants need time to learn about the world around them by exploring sounds, sights, smells, and textures gradually.

**As toddlers** become more confident with their mobility skills, they require space that will allow them to be active in toddling, jumping, running, and darting. Toddlers benefit from environments that provide them with the freedom to explore without impeding the needs of infants or older preschoolers. As children gain confidence in their motor movements and with the adults in their environment, they expand their scope of the play space. Toddlers require

- easy access to places to dig or jump, such as sand areas;
- open areas to run through, roll in, or hop in, such as grass and tall grass plants;
- hard surfaces for pull and ride-on toys, such as asphalt;
- places to rest, such as a covered area; and
- places with inclines so they can crawl up, run or roll down, such as hills.

**Preschool children** further expand the use of their play space. Preschool children require

- areas for equipment such as swings, climbers, balance beams;
- areas to explore the natural environment, such as trees, insects, gardens, and animals;
- places for running, rolling, playing games, such as large grassy areas;

*Photo 5.5  Children will engage in adventure play when they have time, space, peers, and materials that trigger their curiosity.*

- hard surfaces for trikes, wagons, constructive play, and dramatic play, such as asphalt and wooden platforms;
- space to separate active play and quiet play; and
- places with inclines for active movement, such as hills.

**School-aged children** have different space requirements from the younger child. Wardle (1998) indicates school-age children are

> Moving from the physical play of climbing, running, crawling, and swinging to specific challenges like overhead rings and chin-up bars; they are progressing from cooperative play younger children enjoy to hanging out in groups and cliques; and they are now more interested in competitive athletic activities such as baseball, basketball, soccer, football, hockey, and volleyball. (p. 29)

School-aged children require

- space for challenging physical activities, such as open space that accommodates competitive games, skateboarding, and various types of exercise;
- space that allows them to socialize with their friends, such as picnic tables, benches, and space under a tree; and
- space to hang out.

## Examining the Use of Play Space

It is challenging to predict how children will use a play space because there are many influences that contribute to how the play space is used. For example, a child's imagination, life experiences, space availability, the play surface, the play space design, the materials, and the attitudes and types of the adult role models all impact on how play space is used. The child's level of risk taking (as discussed in the previous section), willingness to take risks, interactions with each other, and ability to explore their environment also contribute to how the play space is used.

Findings from studies of indoor environments indicate that open designs with partial shelves and dividers that define space, promote positive cognitive behaviours. For example, when children are in an open designed space with designated zones, children stay on task longer, explore more, and spend less time in solitary play or withdraw from other children (Moore, 1987). These findings are transferable to the outdoor environment.

Children prefer integrated outdoor play spaces to those that have isolated experience centres (Friedberg & Berkeley, 1970; Mason, 1982) or those that are all open. Children participate in outdoor play longer when there is a combination of both open space and semi-private spaces. For example, children often prefer to play underneath a pirate ship play structure. Children use the area "under the ship deck area as a private gathering, resting, and even dramatic play area" (Ihn, 1999, p. 4) as much as using the top of the play structure. Children who have access to semi-private space in the outdoor play environment play more persistently and the types of play are expanded. Semi-private play spaces act as a venue for children who need to have time to recuperate from their active play (Frost, Wortham, & Reifel, 2001).

The organization of play space requires careful examination and consideration because the placement of play components either helps or hinders the flow of play. For example, if children have access to a play stage and block centre with various materials, as well as a tricycle path, opportunities for dramatic play to flourish is more likely than if the play stage is a distance from the blocks and tricycle path. The closer the proximity of defined centres and materials, the more likely children will integrate a combination of materials, ideas, equipment, and play options. When integration occurs, there is a higher potential for such play to evolve that includes rich dialogue, new play partners, creativity, and new knowledge development (Frost, 1992).

## Analyzing Play Spaces

The play space design has an impact on children's social play behaviour. As outlined in Table 5.1, when the play space meets the needs of children, they will engage in positive social play. Conversely, when the play space requires some adjustments or is not meeting the needs of the children, negative behaviour is evident. Early learning practitioners watch for signs of behaviours such as children wandering, rough play, or aggressive play. These are important clues that adjustments to the play space are needed.

The arrangement of outdoor play space considers play being symbolic, free flowing, and fluid. Children require outdoor space that allows them to create, play on structured equipment, and have opportunities to create, recreate, and restructure play spaces.

There are a number of variables that early learning practitioners consider when arranging materials and experiences and maintaining fluidity into the play space. The considerations include, but are not limited to

- the terrain including the slope and water runoff areas;
- the sun, shade, and areas where children are protected from rain and wind;

*Table 5.1*   *How Play Space Impacts Children's Behaviour*

| Evidence of Positively Engaged Social Play | Evidence of Negatively Engaged Social Play |
| --- | --- |
| Social conversation | Arguing |
| Cooperative play | Object possessiveness |
| Child initiated play | Unilateral decisions |
| Sharing of materials | Aggressiveness towards others and with materials |
| Friendly, caring play | Aggressive play |

- ground surfaces including the asphalt, sand, grass, and required gravel;
- visual supervision;
- the safe risk elements;
- storage of materials; and
- the garden space.

Early learning practitioners examine space from the perspective of how young children may wish to use it (Dietze, 2006). Box 5.2 provides a guide that early learning practitioners may wish to follow when examining children's play space.

## BOX 5.2

## Examining Children's Play Spaces

Where do children go to do the following?

- Be up high or be down low
- To dig worms
- Plant flowers
- Build a wooden structure
- Observe friends rolling balls or throwing frisbees

- Yell
- Be alone
- Play with only three children
- Use boards to practice balance
- Find shade
- Play in the leaves

Kritchevsky, Prescott, and Walling (1977) analyze play spaces by considering the complexity and variety of play units (Wellhousen, 2002) available to children. This is important because when there are insufficient materials or lack of stimulating play options, it is more likely that disruptive behaviour will occur.

**A play unit** is described as a single unit item that allows items to be incorporated into the play. The unit may or may not have defined boundaries. For example, a sandbox with only sand would be considered to have a visible boundary, whereas a dramatic stage near the blocks and playhouse may have less boundaries.

**Complexity** refers to "the extent to which [the play units] contain potential for active manipulation and alteration by children" (Kritchevsky, Prescott, & Walling, 1977, p. 11). Early learning practitioners examine the complexity of the play unit, as this guides the number of children who may potentially use the area and how it may be set up for play experiences.

A **simple play unit** generally has a defined use, such as a swing or a tricycle. A simple play unit may become complex by adding materials that will advance the play opportunities (Kritchevsky, Prescott, & Walling, 1977). For example, by adding a tent and picnic baskets, dramatic play may be stimulated or enhanced.

A **complex unit** allows children the opportunity to engage in play with two or more play support materials, such as a water table with rubber ducks or a cash register with pots of flowers.

A **super complex unit** is considered as play area that accommodates one or more play materials, such as adding tables, cell phones, order pads, and a computer keyboard to the playhouse.

**Potential units** refer to empty spaces found within identified boundaries. These spaces provide children with opportunities to use the space to meet their play requirements.

Each play space is to be accessed for their complexity and assigned a corresponding value rating. Simple units are given a value rating of one, complex play units have a value of four, and super units have a value rating of eight. The complexity of the play unit of each area is determined. Then, the assigned values are totalled and divided by the number of children playing during the play episode. The goal is to have at least 2.5 play spaces available per child, per day. These play spaces offer children opportunities for intrigue and curiosity with the variety of materials and play option potentials.

Table 5.2 provides an overview of how the play space may be analyzed to determine if there are sufficient play spaces available for the number of children in the environment.

Assume you have 16 preschool-aged children. Our current playground choices have a total value of 42. Then 42 is divided by the number of children playing in the environment (16 children). This indicates that there are 2.6 spaces available for children. Think about what additions could be made to the play space that would provide children with a variety of play experiences and challenge and increase the play

*Table 5.2*  *Analyzing Play Space*

| Play Unit | Complexity Rating | Value |
|---|---|---|
| One sandbox with vehicles, cones, plastic tubing, buckets, and sieves | Super complex | 8 |
| Drama platform with tables and chairs and prop boxes | Super complex | 8 |
| 3 swings | Simple | 3 |
| One adventure play area with slide, gates, and lookout | Complex | 4 |
| One bicycle path with six tricycles | Simple | 6 |
| One bench under the tree | Simple | 1 |
| A set of cedar blocks of varying sizes with plywood strips and accessories | Super complex | 8 |
| One basket of balls of various sizes | Complex | 4 |
| Total | | 42 |

spaces to a minimum of three spaces. For example, Brent wanted to increase the complexity of the play environment. He felt that his group of 4-year-olds needed to have an equal ratio of complex and super complex units. In his plan, he was thinking about Brittany who uses a wheelchair for mobility and her excitement about watching the wheelchair athletes during the Olympics. Brent determined that if he added a small basketball hoop, balls, a parachute, pillowcases, three child-sized wheelchairs (borrowed from a local supplier), and created roller paths with masking tape for children in the wheelchairs, new play options would be created. These additions would offer both complex and super complex units for the children. It also supported children's creativity, imagination, and experience in diversity. The more opportunities children have to wonder, be curious, and make connections with their environment and the people in their environment, the more their creative thinking and appreciation of others will be enhanced (Sutterby & Frost, 2006; Tovey, 2007). Box 5.3 provides a sample of how the calculations are completed.

## BOX 5.3

## How to Calculate Play Space

1. Identify the number of:
   - Simple units (X 1)
   - Complex units (X 4)
   - Super units (X 8)
2. Calculate the total number of play spaces (based on the totals in calculations above).
3. Identify the number of children usually playing in the outdoor play space.
4. Calculate the complexity of the play relative to the environment by dividing the total number of play spaces by the number of children in the environment.

The purpose of analyzing the play space is to determine if there are sufficient play spaces, the complexity of the materials and play spaces, and how the play spaces support the children's expressed interests.

## Outdoor Experience Centres

Children play differently outdoors from indoors. One of the major differences is the level and variety of experiences that encourage motor and social skills. Other differences include the sensory experiences, the types of activities, the interaction among children, and the natural environmental attributes. We often visualize outdoor play experiences as being anchored around the climbing apparatus and tricycle paths. These are important, but quality outdoor play environments offer much more to children. The play equipment is a small portion of the play experiences.

Depending on the structure of the outdoor play space, there may be more diversity in a child's play because of the combined landscape and natural materials made

*Photo 5.6* *Children require unique materials for in-depth exploration to occur in their play.*

available such as soil, sand, and water. Natural elements facilitate open-ended play opportunities, which lead to creative exploration.

There are many ways to create outdoor play environments that support children exploring new ideas or refining their learning. Similar to the indoor environment, early learning practitioners plan experience centres that offer complexity and variety for the outdoor play space. When indoor experience centres are taken to the outdoor environment, you will note that children use the materials differently. There are many factors contributing to the differences, which include

- Children having a feeling of a broader sense of freedom to explore with messier and noisier materials;
- There being more space for the children to spread out their play, such as when using large hollow blocks, boxes, or planks;
- The natural light and natural environment offers children different sensory stimulating factors; and
- The ability to be more active increases risk taking and exploration.

Various adaptations to the experience centres are required to support children with disabilities. The supports implemented depend on the disability. For example, large cardboard boxes or snap-together blocks support children with visual impairments success. Depending on the physical disability, children may benefit from modifications made to materials such as blocks (Wellhousen & Kieff, 2001), so that they may manipulate them with success. All children deserve the opportunity to experience a variety of play options.

Outdoor play provides a host of opportunities. Early learning practitioners may expand children's play potential by ensuring active play, constructive play, sociodramatic play, and games with rules incorporated into the various opportunities available to children.

## CHOOSING MATERIALS FOR OUTDOOR PLAY: WHY LOOSE PARTS

Children require outdoor play environments to have open-ended and loose parts as standard materials. The more open-ended the materials, the more flexibility and divergent thoughts children express (Fisher, 1992). *Loose parts*, a term coined by architect Simon Nicholson, refers to natural or synthetic materials or objects that give children choices in their play and will empower creativity. Because loose parts lack structure, they offer children endless possibilities to use their imagination and engage in creative play and new discovery.

**Loose parts** may be used as a singular material or combined with other materials. There are a number of loose parts materials that enhance outdoor play. For example, in a natural play area, water, sand, dirt, sticks, branches, leaves, tree stumps, pine cones, feathers, and stones provide children with numerous play options. Other loose parts may include items such as a variety of balls, hoops straw, parachutes, blankets, buckets, cups, hoses, digging tools, boxes, shovels, brushes, wind chimes, baskets, kites, and plastic pipes.

Children who have access to loose parts in outdoor play use them to initiate or maintain dramatic play episodes (Frost, 1992). For example, children who have access to a realistic pirate ship, as well as loose parts, participate in dramatic play more often than children who only have exposure to the shape of the play equipment (Ihn, 1999). "In any environment, both the degree of inventiveness and creativity and the possibilities of discovery are directly proportional to the number and kind of variables in it" (Nicholson, 1971, p. 39).

Four important reasons why we incorporate loose parts into play environments include:

1. Loose parts encourage children to create their play options within the environment.

2. Loose parts expand the play options that increase the variability of the play and the potential for active movement.

3. Loose parts support the child's developmental level, as each child will use the loose parts in ways that are age-appropriate and reflective of their interest.

4. Loose parts stimulate children in their play, thus increasing appropriate play behaviours (Strickland & Dempsey, 2009).

Early learning practitioners encourage children to use materials from one experience centre to another, as this helps make learning connections. Children who integrate loose parts within their play express an increased use of creativity and flexibility needed for discovery learning.

> **Loose parts** are materials that can be moved, redesigned, put together and taken apart in a variety of ways.

# Stop . . . Think . . . Discuss . . . Reflect

You are in an early learning centre that has a structured outdoor play space. Children have access to ride on toys, climbers, and a sandbox. You are interested in adding loose parts to the environment. How will you discuss this with your cooperating practitioner? How will you decide what loose parts to introduce to the children first? How do you envision the children will respond? How will you manage with your cooperating practitioner if the introduction of the loose parts causes children to not share the materials? Do you think it is best that early learning student practitioners not try these ideas, but perhaps wait until you are on staff at a facility? Why or why not?

# ACTIVE PLAY

## Constructive Play Experience Centres

Preschool and school-aged children are drawn to constructive play opportunities. Constructive play gives children a sense of being able to determine how the play will evolve and how they will control it (Ihn, 1998). The constructive play area offers sufficient flexibility to accommodate the needs of the individual child and groups of children. Outdoor constructive play encompasses a variety of materials including, sand, water, and vehicle play. Woodworking, blocks, art, and science experience centres add great value to outdoor play.

## Blocks

As you will read in Chapter 6, hollow blocks, planks, crates, cedar solid blocks, and related accessories are essential outdoor play materials. Blocks support children with a range of skills, abilities, and interests. For example, when blocks are combined with resources such as outdoor magazines, road signs, masking tape, construction hats and vests, children will often incorporate building items such as forts or fancy walls into their play. These structures have the potential to become the backdrop for imaginative play episodes that may include rough and tumble play, rescue play, or acting out of fairy tales.

## Woodworking

Another important outdoor constructive play centre is the woodworking centre. Although this is an experience centre that many early learning student practitioners question the benefit of, it is one that is interrelated to block construction, scientific principles, and the expression of creativity. Working with real materials suggests to some that there is an increased risk of injury. Huber (1999) indicates that for similar risk-taking experiences, there is a need for rules to be established such as ensuring safety goggles are worn, adult supervision is present when tools are being used, and that the tools are returned to their specified holding place once the child has used them. The woodworking experiences offer children opportunities to follow a design, pattern, or model. Children require appropriate wood and tools in order for the experience to be positive and constructive.

## Art

Children's art takes on new dimensions and processes when completed in the outdoor environment. Three contributing factors to this are

- the natural light, giving children a realistic view of colours and textures;
- the natural environment offers a sense of calmness; and
- the freedom to use messier materials such as clay and sculpturing materials.

Children intuitively are attracted to objects such as sticks, acorns, and leaves that become natural materials incorporated into their art experiences. Their art process and problem-solving skills are uniquely different when they are creating on flat surfaces with the wind blowing, or on the grass or a rock, or up against a fence or building.

*Photo 5.7 Children benefit when early learning practitioners pose questions or make comments that lead the children to new thinking and exploration.*

## Discovery and Science

Outdoor play provides a natural introduction of science and discovery to children. Children require a variety of hands-on experiences that support scientific principles. As identified earlier in the chapter, a garden is an essential element of outdoor play. Children learn about vegetation, germination, growth cycles, the importance of sun and rain, and harvesting. They gain information on outdoor creatures such as worms, snakes, toads, and rabbits. This centre should be well equipped with measurement tools, items such as bicycle pumps and tires, a variety of hoses, clamps, and tools for taking things apart. Combining art materials such as paint and clay with science support children in making connections such as the shading of colours and how rainbows and light shadows are made.

Constructive play requires materials to be changed on a regular basis and the materials need to offer a sense of intrigue and flexibility in their usage. Boards, blocks, plywood, sticks, mounds of mud, sand, water, boxes, and accessories supports a child's development and interest in constructive play.

*Photo 5.8 Children experiment with their play differently when indoors and when outdoors.*

## Sociodramatic Play

Similar to other outdoor play experiences, the composition and arrangement of components in the outdoor play environment may foster or hinder dramatic play. The traditional playground space with climbing apparatus does not facilitate dramatic play. Materials, time, and space are needed to spark dramatic play.

Outdoor sociodramatic play offers young children a combination of imaginative and active play. Playhouses, tents, forts, dramatic play platforms, canopies and related accessories provide children with the opportunities to create symbolic play episodes. Dramatic play requires props—if not, the play area may become an environment that experiences high levels of aggression and conflict because children wish to play, but there are not sufficient resources to support an important role in the play. The more loose parts available, the better the dramatic play opportunities, as children may manipulate and incorporate various loose parts into their play (Frost, 1992).

Movable materials contribute significantly to supporting children in active movement. For example, slides, fire poles, clatter bridges, large planks, tables and chairs, ride-on toys, and materials such as umbrellas, boots, and dress-up clothes support active movement and dramatic play. Dramatic play platforms, forts, and panels also add unique opportunities for dramatic play to evolve.

Sociodramatic play may be stimulated by adding materials in various parts of the play area. For example, you may place dolls that may be washed near the water table with towels, brushes, and clothes in a nearby basket. You may place a restaurant sign and tables and chairs near the trike path. These items become triggers for young children, which helps children connect with their peers and participate in sociodramatic play.

Similar to other play centres, early learning practitioners examine the outdoor dramatic play area to ensure that there are culturally relevant materials and structures available to the children. For example, if an early learning and child care setting is located in an area such as a fishing village along the Atlantic or Pacific Oceans, children benefit from having realistic materials such as nets, traps, rope, and perhaps even a boat to use for their play. Or, if you are in an environment that is rich with a natural play space, then children require opportunities to design authentic dramatic play space rather than adults placing plastic items such as houses or forts in them. We want children to learn with authentic materials and experiences.

## Games with Rules

When young children are introduced to games, they must be sequenced appropriately. Early learning practitioners examine children's skill sets and correlate the type of game with the skills, interests, and capabilities of the children. Children require games to move from simple to complex. For example, the first phase of game playing with rules would include Simon Says or Follow the Leader. More complicated games such as Duck, Duck, Duck, Goose follow, as children need to be able to follow two or more instructions in the game progression. Generally, games that have one instruction are the first to be introduced, then two and three instructions, etc. Games are considered the highest level of cognitive play (Piaget, 1962). School-aged children are ready for complicated games with many more rules.

## The Roles of Early Learning Practitioners in Outdoor Play

The role of the early learning practitioner is multifaceted. Figure 5.4 provides an overview of the scope of this component of the practitioners' role and responsibilities. Each is described as follows.

## Early Learning Practitioner's Attitudes and Abilities

Studies suggest that there are significant changes in practitioners' attitudes and abilities after participating in specialized studies in outdoor play. Some of the changes include practitioners posing more in-depth questions, extending opportunities for the child's knowledge base to be enhanced, and providing encouragement with the total group of children. Practitioners who are comfortable with outdoor play generally exhibit more smiling and positive contact with the children and they offer more types of play experiences and time for outdoor play.

The attitude of the early learning practitioner directly relates to the quality of the play experiences and the duration of outdoor play (Crossley & Dietze, 2003). Early learning practitioners are role models. Therefore, it is essential that we think about outdoor play as a healthy experience, no matter what the weather is. This

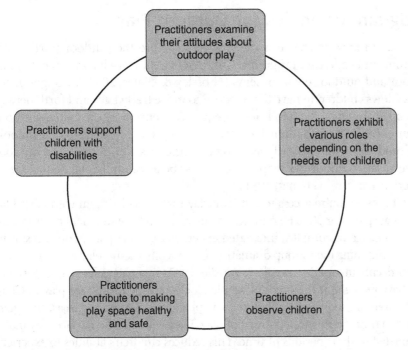

**Figure 5.4**  *Roles of Early Learning Practitioners in Outdoor Play*

requires children and adults to have the correct clothing for the cold and inclement weather. Think about the learning that occurs when children have opportunities to be in the rain, or wind, or snow. Think about how they respond when they discover the toad or the rainbow or the snowflake hitting their faces. Box 5.4 provides strategies to support the early learning practitioner in facilitating outdoor play.

---

## BOX 5.4

## Strategies to Support Early Learning Practitioners in Facilitating Outdoor Play

### Ten Strategies for Facilitating Children's Play Outdoors
- Provide long uninterrupted play periods (40 to 60 minutes).
- Provide opportunities for indoor/outdoor play to flow between the two areas.
- Provide a variety of open-ended, loose parts materials with stationary materials.
- Provide opportunities for challenging, safe-risk play to evolve in play.
- Encourage the play to flow from the children.
- Provide all children with equal access to rich play experiences.
- Become partners-in-play at the appropriate times.
- Pose questions and make comments that will facilitate discussion and wonderment with an individual child or groups of children.
- Observe a child's play and provide materials that will scaffold and expand learning opportunities.

---

## Program Schedules for Outdoor Play

There are many perspectives on how to structure the outdoor portion of early learning and child care programs. Children benefit from having access to both the indoor and outdoor environments (Crossley & Dietze, 2003) throughout the day. This allows children to have the freedom to move freely back and forth between the two environments. It establishes an equal concentration on indoor and outdoor experiences. When children have two learning environments—one indoors and one outdoors—it helps early learning practitioners view indoor and outdoor play equally. The outdoor play experiences must be as carefully planned as the indoor experience centres (Hymes, 1981).

Children require access to outdoor play that provides them with large blocks of time that span over 30 to 60 minutes. When children have sufficient playtime, they are able to engage in complex, integrated experiences. Short play periods result in children abandoning their group dramatizations or constructive play just when they begin to get deeply involved (Christie & Wardle, 1992) in a particular play experience. You will have read about the need for ample blocks of time for indoor play in Chapter 4. If children are required to disrupt their play on a continuous basis, they generally abandon more sophisticated forms of play. They will settle for surface play that can be completed in short periods of time. This reduces children's abilities to experience the many attributes of play, such as persistence, negotiation, problem solving, planning, and cooperative play. Children who are given time to play advance the complexity of the play, which in turn makes play more productive (Christie & Wardle, 1992).

## Early Learning Practitioner's Facilitation Roles

Children benefit most when early learning practitioners offer facilitation strategies that meet the needs of the children. The most effective strategies are: Practitioner-supported involvement; child-initiated exploration; and practitioner–child-guided discovery opportunities.

**Practitioner-supported involvement** refers to short- and long-term experiences or projects that the children and practitioner engage in. The practitioner's role is to support the child in gaining information through questioning, describing, modelling, repeating, or imitating actions (Dietze & Crossley, 2003). These actions support children in exploring new experiences and in learning from one another. For example, early learning practitioners may offer children warm-up experiences at the onset of outdoor play. This supports the child's muscle and motor development, and it sets the tone for feeling psychologically secure. Or, the practitioner may take the children indoors for five minutes during a winter's day for a quick story and warm-up and then return to the outdoors.

**Child-initiated exploration** refers to the area of concentration for exploration and activities that a child initiates or participates in. When the environment meets the needs of the child, a variety of approaches will be explored through trial and error, and ultimately problem solving, to master the challenge. For example, a child who serendipitously discovers how a sand mold works may be motivated to use other materials to see if a similar pattern occurs from the initial mold.

When outdoor environments provide a range of materials and experiences for play, children's powers of observational skills become more attuned to their play space. This increases the child's ability to build on their observations, experiences, and depth of dialogue with other children and adults. Children's observational skills are thought to be enhanced in outdoor play because of their freedom to explore, the open space in which to explore, the reduction of noise levels and the distractions caused by classroom stimuli (Dietze & Crossley, 2003).

**Practitioner–child-guided discovery** is described as experiences that the practitioner and child initiate. The partners in play use questions and suggestions to formulate the foundation for discovery. For example, the child may ask the practitioner, "Can you roll down the hill just like me?" or the practitioner may pose questions or offer a sequence of suggestions that will support the child in learning how to walk on tiptoes backwards. The practitioner may guide or role-model certain behaviours when the play becomes frustrating for the child or if the child requires further information in order to proceed with the play.

As identified earlier in the chapter, outdoor play is paramount for children in constructing knowledge. Young children acquire more opportunities to experience outdoor play with early learning practitioners who collaborate with an individual child or group of children to support them in their exploration, experimentation, and manipulation of their environment. This allows children to build on what they know. Through child-to-child and adult-to-child interactions and active experimentation, children discover new knowledge, skills, abilities, and interests.

*Photo 5.9 Children discover many science and mathematical concepts from their outdoor play experiences.*

# OBSERVING AND DOCUMENTING CHILDREN'S PLAY OUTDOORS

Children's use of space, time, materials, and the type of play episode differs from indoor and outdoor environments. Early learning practitioners conduct observations outdoors to acquire information about a child's learning styles, capabilities, and interests. For example, through observations early learning practitioners may gain insight about children's social interactions, cognitive and language abilities, motor skills, and emotional development. And, early learning practitioners may acquire information that may suggest differing skills of children, plan for future play experiences and materials, or obtain an overall perspective on a child's overall interest in outdoor play.

The outdoor play environment requires a level of monitoring and observation that differs from indoors because of the increased potential for risk taking, more rigorous exploration, and safety concerns. Practitioners examine children's behaviours, the quality and the quantity of the play, and the level of physical play. Early learning practitioners determine the relationship between the child and her environment by watching, listening, and engaging in play. This requires early learning practitioners to

- develop skills in recognizing the developmental and individual variations in play;
- complete an assessment on the risk and harm potential of the potential play experiences;
- identify the child's level of competence and independence (National Childcare Accreditation Council, 2005); and
- observe the social interactions among children.

Children expand their quality of play experiences when they have opportunities to be decision makers such as being able to choose where they play, what to play, and with whom to play. Early learning practitioners may need to support children who wish to join in a play episode, modify behaviour, or assist in negotiating a disagreement. Early learning practitioners scan play episodes to determine when and how to intervene in child's play so that it is a positive experience for children.

Observing how children use their outdoor play space provides adults with insight into individual, cultural, and social needs of children (David & Weinstein, 1987). These insights guide early learning practitioners in identifying individual and group needs and interests that may be incorporated into the play space. For example, children from rural communities use space differently—they are used to having large spaces to play. They use more space and their play generally consists of more vigorous gross motor play than urban children. Children living in apartments may only have designated playgrounds in which to play. Children from different cultural backgrounds will use space and materials differently. Young children coming from countries where water is scarce may have had role models who have helped them learn to conserve water. These children may find it difficult to use water for play experiences.

As identified in Chapter 3, there are many observation and documentation strategies that may be used by early learning practitioners. Tools are chosen depending on the information that you are trying to obtain. For example, early learning practitioners are interested in knowing how children use the play space. Table 5.3 provides an example of how space utilization may be examined.

**Table 5.3**  *Observing How Children Use Outdoor Play Space*

| Area of Observation | Child I | Child II |
| --- | --- | --- |
| What play spaces are used? | | |
| What play zones are used? | | |
| What types of equipment and materials are used by each child? | | |
| What type of play is each child engaging in—solitary, parallel, associative, cooperative? | | |
| In what situations does the child initiate play? When is there a need for an adult to encourage one of the children? | | |
| What is the duration of the play experience in the various play zones? | | |
| How does the child exhibit creativity in using the materials and equipment? | | |
| What risk-taking and problem-solving techniques are evident? | | |

As you think about observations, documentation, and outdoor play, keep in mind that the purpose of observations and documentation is to provide you with insight into a child's strengths, interests, and capabilities. Observations allow you to monitor a child's growth and to plan experiences that will support specific areas of development. Observations and documentation help you manage the outdoor play environment. Through observations and documentation, early learning practitioners can become familiar with their understanding of their role during the outdoor play experiences and become attuned to how children create play when given the freedom, space, tools, and materials to do so.

## Examining the Environment for Health and Safety Issues

As much as we want children to have the freedom to play and explore, we need to take the necessary precautions to ensure the play space supports children being safe. The Canadian Standards Association (CSA) provides early learning practitioners with guidelines for creating safe play space. Early learning practitioners ensure

- proper child/adult ratios and supervision as a vital component to outdoor play;
- ongoing maintenance of the play space, equipment, and surfacing;
- opportunities for children to take risks and explore;
- appropriate shelter for the children and precautions are taken such as applying sunscreen appropriately;
- plants in the play space are non-toxic and safe for children to have access to; and
- safety checks of equipment and materials are completed as per standards.

Early learning practitioners should become familiar with the Ministry guidelines and standards for licensing or approving early learning and child care environments in their jurisdiction. This information informs our practice as it helps us become familiar with the required standards of practice that must be adhered to. Table 5.4 provides an overview of the standard 11.2.7 for equipment, facilities, and surfaces as outlined by the CSA.

As identified by the CSA in **Children's Playspaces and Equipment Standards** (April, 2008), there are a number of plants that are not appropriate for children's play space. The plants that are appropriate require regular inspection for sharp edges, broken branches, and pest infestation. As a general rule of thumb, the CSA identify that any plant with white berries should be avoided. The standards should be consulted to obtain a listing of the plants that are not suitable for play spaces.

Another important area that early learning practitioners should become familiar with is toxic fungi. For example, all mushrooms that appear in the play space should be removed for safety reasons. The *Amanita virosa* (Destroying Angel) mushroom is responsible for the majority of fungus poisonings in Canada. This mushroom (the cap, gills, and stem) is white in colour and should be removed immediately from the play space.

**Table 5.4**   *Standards for Equipment, Facilities and Surfaces as Outlined by CSA*

| Item | Precautions |
|---|---|
| Access | Check for missing or broken rungs, steps, or treads; loosened or missing planks; splinters in handholds; and blocked exits. |
| Crush Points | Check for broken covers exposing crush points and exposed mechanisms. |
| Decay, deterioration | Check for rust, cracks, decay or rot, heavy wear, and evidence of insect attacks. |
| Drainage | Check for plugged drain holes; drain holes in tires, equipment, or hollow components. Special attention should be paid to heavy-use areas such as those under swings and slide exit regions. |
| Edges | Check for protrusions, sharp points, or sharp edges. |
| Emergency equipment | Ensure that the telephone is in working order, emergency numbers are up to date, and emergency access is not blocked. |
| Enclosures and fences | Check the enclosures and fences are not broken, tilted, or otherwise damaged. |
| Equipment protective surfacing | Check for obstacles in equipment-protective surfacing zones. |
| Foundations | Check that foundations are not eroded, beginning to rot, loose in ground, or exposed. |
| Guards, handrails | Check for missing, bent, broken, loosened, burnt, or wobbly guards and handrails. |
| Hardware | Check for loosened, missing, bent, worn, or open hooks or rings; protruding nails or hardware; and missing protective caps. |
| Lead paint | Use non-lead-based paints in all new equipment and when repainting existing equipment to eliminate the risk of childhood lead poisoning from playground equipment. |
| Lubrication | Check for noisy or squeaky motion. |
| Moving parts | Check for worn bearings, jammed or non-functioning equipment, lack of lubrication, excessive motion, noisy motion, missing protective pieces, or loose spring castings. |
| Needles | Remove needles in a safe manner. Do not handle them directly; use a tool such as pliers. Contact local authorities for disposal of needles. |
| Other general hazards | Check for potential clothing entanglement hazards and open S-hooks. Check for trip hazards, such as exposed footings on anchoring devices, or rocks, roots, or any other environmental obstacles in the play area. Children should remove helmets, other than those worn for medical reasons, prior to play on equipment. Remove all ropes and skipping ropes tied to equipment. |
| Other surfaces | Check for uneven, worn, poorly drained, or otherwise damaged surfaces. |

*Continued*

| | |
|---|---|
| Other surfaces and pathways | Check for worn patches, holes, and cracks. |
| Park furnishings | Check for broken, unturned, or otherwise damaged furnishings. |
| Plastics, fiberglass, rubber | Check for splitting, cracking, breaking, discoloration, scorching or burnt areas, abrasion, or wear. |
| Protective surfacing | Check for compacted, eroded, unsanitary, or littered surfacing; surfacing that has been displaced to an ineffective level; and surfacing that is not extensive enough to cover the recommended area. |
| Roads, sidewalks, and pathways | Check for unevenness, frost damage, and poor drainage. |
| Ropes, cables | Check for worn spots, fraying, vandalism, degradation, deteriorating joints and splicing, insecure attachments, and ropes or skipping ropes tied to equipment. |
| Sand facilities | Check for rancid sand, signs of stained clothing or skin, debris, insufficient sand, and need for raking. Check that the lid is in good condition. Change sand at least once a year in areas where there is a high incidence of animal excrement deposits. |
| Seats | Check for missing, damaged, or loosened seats; sharp edges or corners; and insecure fittings or attachments. |
| Site | Remove foreign objects such as nails, glass, ponding water, sharp objects, litter and syringes, and any entanglements such as scarves, skipping ropes, shoelaces, and belts. |
| Structure | Check for bending, warping, scorching, cracking, loosening, breaking distortion, vandalism, uneven surfaces, splintered or decaying wood, corroded or damaged metal, exposed footings, and unstable anchoring of equipment. |
| Supervision | Determine volume of use relative to maintenance costs, costs of vandalism, success of measures to reduce injuries. |
| Surface finishes | Check for missing protective coats, splinters, and initial signs of rust or corrosion. |
| Water facilities | Check for leaks, clogged drains, improper drainage, debris, and growths. Check for non-functioning water sprayers on other components. |

## Children Play Spaces and Equipment for Children with Disabilities

As identified by the CSA (2008), children's play spaces and equipment must be accessible to children with disabilities. Early learning practitioners are encouraged to become familiar with the standards and apply them accordingly so that children with disabilities have equal access to play experiences. In order to meet the needs of children with disabilities, early learning practitioners incorporate specified criteria for ground-level play components, elevated play components, ramps and slopes, transfer systems, and ground surfaces.

## MOVING FORWARD

Outdoor play experiences are as important to a child's development as indoor play. Planning and implementing effective outdoor play experiences is complex and challenging because a well-designed outdoor play environment supports the varying interests, abilities, and stages of play of young children. When outdoor play experiences are developmentally appropriate and offer young children variety, the child's cognitive, social, emotional, and physical development are impacted.

Early learning practitioners actualize opportunities for all young children to have the freedom to explore nature, run, hop, jump, climb, take safe risks, and participate in dramatic play during their outdoor playtime.

# SUMMARY

### Chapter Preview

- Outdoor play is an essential component of childhood. Early learning practitioners require knowledge about the relationship of outdoor play to child development.

### The Historical Perspective of Outdoor Play

- Outdoor play has long been recognized as an important component of the lives of young children.
- Froebel identified that outdoor play can't be emulated in other settings. It is essential for the child's whole development. This was supported by the nursery school movement in the 1920s.
- The standard play equipment has evolved over the decades and the range includes steel, iron, plastic, and wood. In response to the number of childhood injuries, a set of playground safety standards was developed in the early 1990s by the Canadian Standards Association.

### The Importance of Outdoor Play to Child Development

- Outdoor play enhances a child's cognitive, social, emotional, and physical skills including exploration, risk taking, language development, social competence, fine and gross motor development, creativity, imagination, and thinking skills.

### Developing an Appreciation for Outdoor Play

- Children who are exposed to adult role models with an interest in outdoor play have a higher probability of developing an interest in outdoor play and the environment, including plants, animals, and environmental sustainability components. This is now recognized by a variety of experts in disciplines such as education, health, psychology, and ecology.

### Risk Taking and Child's Play

- Risk taking is complex and is an important component of outdoor play as it allows children to learn about new skills, try new ideas, and achieve new knowledge and skills through risk taking. It needs to be balanced with safe risks.

### Outdoor Play Spaces

- Early learning practitioners examine space to ensure that it is accessible for all children, that it addresses the environmental conditions, and that there are defined play zones.

### Play Spaces for Infants, Toddlers, Preschoolers, and School-Age Children

- Play spaces are generally divided to support the developmental needs of each age group. There are different space requirements needed for each of the age ranges to accommodate their developmental milestones.

### Examining the use of Play Space

- How children use play space is influenced by a number of factors including a child's imagination, life experiences, space availability, play space attributes, and adult role models.

### Analyzing Play Spaces

- There are a number of ways to examine the effectiveness and versatility of play space. One of the more popular methods is by considering the complexity and the variety of play units in an environment, as identified by Kritchevsky et al.

### Outdoor Experience Centres

- Outdoor play experiences differ from indoor play experiences. The motor and social skills, the sensory skills, the types of activities, and the interaction among children are some of the more popular differences between the two settings.
- Early learning practitioners devise active play opportunities with experience centres such as construction, blocks, woodworking, art, discovery and science, sociodramatics, and games with rules.

### Choosing Materials for Outdoor Play: Why Loose Parts

- Children require outdoor play environments that are open-ended and have loose parts as standard materials because of their flexibility in being able to be moved, redesigned, put together, and taken apart in a variety of ways.
- Loose parts encourage creativity, expand play options, support a child's developmental level, and stimulate children in their play.

### The Role of Early Learning Practitioners

- Early learning practitioners exhibit various roles, depending on the needs of the children. These roles include practitioner-supported involvement, child-initiated exploration, and practitioner–child-guided discovery.
- Observing a child's play outdoors provides the early learning practitioner with insight into a child's interests and capabilities, most often differing from the indoor environment.
- The early learning environment and experiences extended to children must adhere to appropriate health and safety concerns.

# REVIEW QUESTIONS

1. Describe how the novelty era of play structures impacted child's play. What were the benefits of the play structures? How did they negatively influence the child's outdoor play?
2. Why is it important for early learning practitioners to be familiar with the Canadian Standards Association guidelines for children's play spaces?
3. Describe some of the challenges that children face in their daily living if they do not acquire sufficient outdoor play experiences.
4. How does the role of the adult impact a child's outdoor play experiences and appreciation for outdoor play?
5. Describe what is meant by risk taking and outline why it is an important component to outdoor play and a child's development.
6. Describe seven factors that should be considered when planning for children's outdoor play space. Discuss how play space differs for infants, toddlers, preschoolers, and school-age children.
7. Why is it necessary for early learning practitioners to analyze play space? What are some strategies that may be used to accomplish this?
8. What types of experience centres are effective for children to have in their outdoor environment? Why?
9. Describe five key roles of an early learning practitioner in preparing the outdoor play space and in facilitating play.

# MAKING CONNECTIONS

## Theory to Practice

1. Visit an early learning outdoor play setting. Examine the space to determine if a child who uses a walker to assist him with mobility will have the same access to the play experiences as children with independent mobility. What changes might you recommend to support the child in having equal play opportunities? Why?
2. Visit an early learning centre. Using the seven considerations for examining space and the potential experience centres outlined in this chapter, examine the play space. Are there areas of the play space that may need attention? If so, what areas? How might you change the space to support advancing the use of the play space? How might you increase the opportunities for additional experience centres to be incorporated into the play space?
3. Using the model for examining the complexity and variety of play units as outlined by Kritchevsky, Prescott, and Walling, examine a play space to determine if there are sufficient play spaces available for children in the setting. Make recommendations based on whether there is a need for simple, complex, or super complex units. Justify the reasons for your recommendations.
4. You are required to set up an information documentation panel for parents on the importance of risk taking in outdoor play. What would you highlight? Why? How would you document examples of children engaging in play that is risk taking rather than unsafe play?

## For Further Research

1. As identified by Froebel, children should have exposure to a naturalized outdoor environment. Conduct research on the key principles of designing a naturalized outdoor play environment. What research has been conducted to identify how a naturalized outdoor environment supports children's play? How does

it support children with disabilities? What training and development are required by staff to support children in a naturalized environment?

2. Some early learning programs are now designed to be implemented outdoors year-round. Research the philosophy and programming strategy used with these outdoor programs. Are they suitable for our Canadian climate? Why or why not?

## ADDITIONAL READING

Canadian Child Care Federation. (2002). *Outdoor play in Early Childhood Education and Care Programs*. Ottawa, ON: Canadian Child Care Federation.

Sobel, D. (2004). *Children's special places: Exploring the role of forts, dens, and bush houses in middle childhood*. Detroit, MI: Wayne State University Press.

Wellhousen, K. (2002). *Outdoor play every day. Innovative play concepts for early childhood.* Albany: NY: Delmar Thomson Learning.

Wells, N., & Evans, G. (2003). Nearby nature: A buffer of life stress among rural children. *Environment and behaviour, 35*(3), 311–330.

## WEBLINKS

www.bing.com/search?q=outdoor+play+Keith+chistensen

www.whitehutchinson.com/children/articles/outdoor.shtml

www.youtube.com/watch?v=Fp4Nny_rIiw

# 6 Blocks and Child's Play

## Learning Outcomes

After exploring this chapter you should be able to

- define block play;
- discuss the historical perspectives of block play;
- compare Reifel and Greenfield's stages of block play with Hirsch's stages of block play;
- explain what is meant by table blocks and floor blocks;
- discuss how block play supports child development, creativity, and children with disabilities; and
- discuss the various roles that an early learning practitioner has in facilitating block play.

## Stories from the Field: Practitioner to Student

Four years ago I graduated from an early childhood education program at a local college. During my studies I had terrific field placements that provided me with insight into how the theory of early childhood education looks in the field. As I participated in the field placements, I found myself developing an interest in the block area. I always seemed to gravitate to that area so naturally—I began watching the children. Soon I gained confidence to ask children questions about their structures, or pose questions about their structures. I began completing a number of observations in the block centre. I started taking photos of children and their structures, and then I started using a video camera to further document the structures that the children were making. Like many of the children, I became hooked on block play. I believe as a result of my interest and enthusiasm for this play, I invested time in listening to the children, adding new, innovative materials, such as large planks, cedar blocks, and flexible and rigid pipes of various dimensions. I was always intrigued to see what the children would do with the new materials, and how they would extend their sense of exploration and learning.

Over the four years of working with children with blocks, I have learned that using blocks is a versatile medium that may be used by infants, toddlers, preschool and school-aged children. I have also learned that children need time, space, and unique materials to support their expansion of ideas. As an early learning practitioner, I have a responsibility to thoroughly review how children use the materials and to visualize with them . . . what will happen . . . or I wonder about . . . or if you do this . . . what do you think may happen?

My advice to early learning practitioners who are just beginning their career, is to develop areas of passion and share that passion and enthusiasm with the children because your passion will become positively contagious. When this occurs, there is no predicting what the children are capable of doing with their blocks and support materials.

*Avril, ECE Graduate, 2007*

# CHAPTER PREVIEW

Most young children are exposed to blocks. Blocks are one of the simplest, yet most important play materials that we can offer children. The play value in blocks contributes to a child's whole development. Children learn skills and knowledge through block play that sets the foundation for later academic studies. And for some children, block play leads them to engage in careers such as architecture, construction, and design.

Let's think about block play. What do children gain from these materials? Block play enhances a child's understanding of patterning, objects, forms, systems, and designs. They allow children to recreate their world around them. They promote children having a free flow of creativity into using their imaginations to design, construct, recreate, and expand their creations. "Block experiences support children in practicing sorting, grouping, comparing, arranging, making decisions, cooperating and role-playing—all of which form the foundation for mathematical and scientific skills" (Dietze, 2006, p.180). Blocks are materials that contribute to a child's understanding of social communication, literacy, physical science, language, art, mathematics, creativity, and problem-solving techniques.

Although blocks are made available to young children, many early learning practitioners may not fully be familiar with the educational or developmental value that they contribute to a child (NAEYC, 1996; Wellhousen & Kieff, 2000; Zacharos, Koliopoulos, Dokomaki, & Kassoumi, 2007). Many young children are provided with worksheets or other academic tasks to "teach" children math, literacy, or social studies concepts (Park, Chae, & Foulks Boyd, 2008) rather than concrete materials, such as blocks. Paper-pencil tasks are not considered appropriate or effective because preschoolers and children in kindergarten are in the preoperational or concrete-operational stage of cognitive development. Children learn best when they are exposed to hands-on, experiential learning and free-flowing materials (NAEYC, 1997). Children who are provided with materials such as blocks and block-building experiences gain the skills and concepts more quickly and with more enthusiasm for learning than if they are required to do so in a structured "teacher led" process.

Young children and school-aged children require access to blocks in both the indoor and outdoor environments. Both types of spaces offer unique opportunities for creative experimentation. The use of different materials, the social interaction, and development that is inherent in both of these settings offer different types of problem-solving techniques that are needed to execute block play. For example, using blocks outdoors invites children to experiment with building materials such as crates, rocks, logs, sticks, and bricks that aren't easily negotiated indoors. The structures that children create may be longer and wider and accessories such as ride-on toys and the natural environment may be integrated into the structure. School-aged children, when given the opportunity, expand the block building to include a variety of elaborate structures.

As you explore this chapter, you will discover how block play provides children with the opportunity to develop a variety of skills and abilities that are transferable to other learning domains. Early learning practitioners and student practitioners have an important role in continuing to examine strategies that will advance the use of block play with young children. We begin this chapter by outlining in Table 6.1 an overview of the types of concepts and related learning that occurs when children have exposure to quality block play.

We also share with you the words of wisdom from Victoria Smith who works as a consultant with early learning facilities in southern New Brunswick.

**Table 6.1**  *Concepts Gained through Block Play*

| Cognitive/Language | Creative |
| --- | --- |
| **Emergent Concepts** | **Emergent Concepts** |
| Use of symbols as a communication tool | Use of imagination and pretend play |
| Comparison and matching of the same and different concepts | Understanding of symmetrical principles |
| Vocabulary development through interpreting pictures, and making up stories | Relationship of creating pictures and designs to the production of structures |
| Relationship of symbols and labels to words and reading | Use of problem-solving skills to advance discovery and results |
| Oral language development through exposure to new words | Discovery of the results that occur when two or more mediums are used together |
| Understanding of principles such as estimation, distance, patterning, comparing sizes, shapes, and numbers, seriation, and mapping (mathematics concepts) | Use of design, representation, balance, and stability concepts |
| Understanding of concepts such as matching, comparing, balancing, the impact of weight and height, inclined plane, gravity, negative space, and balance (science concepts) | Expansion of divergent thinking |
| Relationship of creating a plan prior to construction of the end product | Use of mixed media |
| Understanding of the concepts of combining technology with production | |

| Social/Emotional | Physical |
| --- | --- |
| **Emergent Concepts** | **Emergent Concepts** |
| Understanding how culture and community are represented in play | Understanding spatial relationships |
| Sharing space, resources, knowledge, and skills | Experiencing visual perception/discrimination skills such as stacking, dropping, grasping, lifting, and swaying |
| Practicing negotiation and leadership skills | Understanding body awareness and how the left and right sides of the body move as one |
| Forming friendships | Developing eye–hand coordination and fine and gross motor control |
| Examining roles and responsibilities, including gender roles and adult–child roles | |
| Expressing feelings and communicating them through words | |
| Releasing stress/regression in meaningful ways | |
| Developing an appreciation of aesthetic principles | |
| Developing feelings of autonomy | |

**Victoria Smith**

Through the world of play, blocks are a creative outlet for individual expression. As with all meaningful creative activities, it is the process involved in block building that is significant rather than the product. In an environment where children are provided with an assortment of blocks, sufficient and appropriate space, accessories, the freedom to explore and experiment, and above all the time to construct, design, and dismantle, important skills are developed.

As an educator, consider the problem solving that occurs, the relationships that develop and the individual and group successes that are celebrated. Language skills are enhanced, new vocabulary emerges, and wonderful new ideas surface. Observe and truly listen to the children as they engage in block play. Challenge yourself to discover new ways to encourage, support, interact with, and document children at play in the block area. Recognize the importance of block play in children's play and take advantage of every teachable moment to inspire your children and gain insight into their world.

## DEFINING BLOCK PLAY

Block play can be defined in a variety of ways. Cohen and Uhry (2007) defined it as "any time a child manipulates proportional wooden [or related product material] blocks, using actions and/or language to represent realistic or imaginary experiences" (p. 302). Block play is what children do when they engage in handling, stacking, or manipulating blocks (Provenzo & Brett, 1983).

## THE HISTORICAL PERSPECTIVE OF BLOCKS

### Beginning in the 1700s

Children and blocks are not a new phenomenon. Block building appears to have evolved simultaneously with the movement towards establishing a child-centred culture in the late 1700s. Philosophers and educators including John Locke, Richard Lovell Edgeworth, Frederich Froebel, Maria Montessori, Carolyn Pratt, and others recognized the importance of young children requiring materials that would support them in using their imaginations and creative abilities (Provenzo & Brett, 1983). Their contribution to block history is detailed below.

**Friedrich Froebel**   Froebel (1782–1852) introduced the first systematic use of blocks as part of children's early learning experiences. He believed that blocks were an educational material that would lead the child to increase her understanding of her world.

As part of Froebel's block system he created "gifts" known as the wooden sphere, a cube, and a cylinder. He ensured that the sphere with its rounded sides was opposite to the cube. The cylinder had the roundness of the sphere and the clearly defined edges of the cube.

According to Provenzo and Brett (1983), Froebel described the use of building blocks using the "gifts" in the following way:

> The material for building in the beginning should consist of a number of wooden blocks whose base is always one inch square and whose length varies from one to twelve inches. If, then, we take twelve pieces of each length, two sets—e.g., the pieces one and eleven, the pieces two and ten inches long, etc.—will always make up a layer an inch thick and covering one foot of square surface; so that all the pieces, together with a few larger pieces, occupy a space of somewhat more than half a cubic foot. It is best to keep these in a box that has exactly these dimensions; such a box may be used in many ways in instruction, as will appear in the progress of a [child's] development. (p. 12)

Froebel suggested that blocks were the foundation materials to support children in acquiring the skills to distinguish, name, and classify (Wright, 1951). He designed the block system consisting of four specific cubes. Each of the cubes contributed to children being able to build complicated structures that supported their creativity, while advancing their knowledge about classification, balance, and related architectural, scientific, and mathematical principles. For example, the cube (known as the third of eight gifts) was divided equally down the middle. This allowed children, through their play, to engage with the blocks having eight equal parts, which would lead them to discover the principles of size and the internal and external characteristics of cubes.

The next cube in the series (known as the fourth gift) is split four times, which allows children to have oblong bricks or blocks. This next cube (known as the fifth gift) is made out of 27 cubes. These cubes could be subdivided into half and quarter triangle forms. The sixth cube, (known as the sixth gift) consists of 27 oblong blocks, 3 being divided lengthwise and 6 across (Provenzo, and Brett, 1983).

As the kindergarten movement became more widespread in the 1870s, the use of blocks became an important part of children's play experiences. Educators examined ways to bring blocks into both indoor and outdoor environments as part of the core experiences and curriculum.

## Late-Nineteenth-Century Block Systems

**Richter Building Blocks**    As society moved to understand and accept the importance of play, the use of blocks became an important component of childhood. The Richter Building Block systems were created out of wood, cardboard, and related materials. Many of these initial block systems remain prevalent today such as the *nesting blocks* and *alphabet blocks*. The nesting blocks continue to support children in classifying colours and sizes and concepts such as large, larger, largest, small, smaller, and smallest. These types of blocks will be explained further in the chapter under the section on table blocks.

## The Twentieth Century

**Maria Montessori**    During the twentieth century, there was a further societal development that focused on the development of programs that supported the academic and play attributes of young children. Maria Montessori, (1870–1952), an Italian educator, recognized that block play was an important component of educational programs for young children.

Montessori believed that children needed to be exposed to a series of didactic materials. She suggested that these materials helped the child develop his inner self. When children are comfortable with their inner self, they have increased skills and abilities to observe their world, make decisions about their world, and express their thought processes. Concentration skills are further enhanced.

Like Froebel, Montessori created a set of structured block materials that graduated from simple to more complex. *The pink tower* consisting of ten pink wooden cubes was designed to be sequenced from 10 centimetres to 1 centimetre. As part of the learning, preschool children were guided to examine each of the cubes and then place them from largest to smallest or in descending order to create a tower.

Another popular Montessori block apparatus is *the brown stairs*. These 10 oblong blocks provide the child with the opportunity to examine the blocks and position them from the thickest to thinnest, or by ascending or descending order. The objective is to construct them to resemble a set of stairs.

*The color rods* add to the block construction apparatus that is prevalent in an environment following Montessori principles. These are graduated oblong rods that are intended to be placed in ascending order by the child.

The Montessori apparatus is designed with specific learning outcomes. These outcomes support the child in gaining the knowledge and skills that are fundamental constructs of math, science, and literacy.

**Carolyn Pratt**    Carolyn Pratt, an American educator during the late 1800s, is known for her philosophical orientation of **learning from the children.** She identified the importance of block play during the early years, suggesting that "a child playing on his nursery floor, constructing an entire railroad system out of blocks and odd boxes he had salvaged from the wastepaper basket, taught me that the play impulse in children is a work impulse" (Provenzo & Brett, 1983, p. 27). Children flourish in environments that provide them with materials that allow them to design their play experiences based on their imaginations.

Flexible, open-ended materials that have multiple uses position children to engage in play that does not require adult intervention. Children require blocks that include a variety of sizes, pillars, wheels, and rods because the different shapes and dimensions provide children with unlimited play opportunities. For example, a simple oblong block becomes the foundation for a house, a slide in the park, a race car, etc.

In the early 1900s Carolyn Pratt made one of the most significant contributions to children's play when she created *Unit Blocks*. They consist of a set of hardwood, natural blocks that are in proportions of 1:2:4—half as high as they are wide and twice as long as they are wide. We will explore further information on unit blocks in the section on floor blocks.

## Stop . . . Think . . . Discuss . . . Reflect

How does the historical perspective of block building influence our perspective on making blocks available to children today? Is there a relationship to early learning today? Why or why not? How important is it for early learning practitioners to think about how blocks were used historically when thinking about how to use them with children today?

## The Stages of Block Play

There have been a number of studies conducted that suggest children progress through sequential stages in their block play. For example, Gesell (1940) examined how young children play with blocks in his work related to maturational timetables. His findings suggest that infants and toddlers to approximately eighteen months use a block as a single unit rather than for constructing anything. As children move towards the 24-month-old range, they begin to place blocks in a row and make simple towers. The 3-year-olds experiment with vertical and horizontal construction. The 4-year-old engages in more sophisticated construction, illustrating a two-dimensional approach to their construction. As children gain more information on architectural, mathematical, and scientific principles, the complexity of their construction exhibits further intricacies. This would be particularly evident in school-aged children's construction. This age group increases the level of detail to the structure and the types of secondary materials that are integrated into the structures.

*Photo 6.1   Unit blocks provide children with opportunities to engage in architectural design while gaining mathematical skills.*

The complexity of children's block play increases as children gain more experience (Reifel & Greenfield, 1982). Children between the ages of 4 and 7 incorporate both spatial relationships and symbolism into their representations. Reifel and Greenfield (1982) suggest that early learning practitioners assess the symbolism and the spatial complexity of the structures created by children in the block area. They use the following guidelines:

The symbolism consists of three levels:

    0 = children use blocks simply as blocks
    1 = children use blocks to represent a real-world object such as a car
    2 = children use blocks to represent roles of people or things in imaginative play such as a circus

Through observation, the early learning practitioner examines spatial complexity by looking at the level of detail and the represented dimensions that children use to integrate blocks into their play. This process provides early learning practitioners with insight into how the children are using blocks and how adult guidance may advance the child's growth opportunities through play.

Hirsch (1996) also outlines stages of block building that children engage in. She indicates that children pass through seven stages in block building:

- **Stage I: Carrying**—Children carry blocks around, but they are not used for construction. Children typically gather blocks and dump them. This is the beginning of children exploring concepts such as—more, less, thin, thick, large, and small. This helps the young toddler refine her fine and gross motor skills.

- **Stage II: Rows and Stacks**—Children begin to place blocks in rows or vertical stacks. Repetition is visible. This is a time when toddlers repetitively make stacks and towers. Over time, they take more risks and their stacks and towers become more imaginative.

- **Stage III: Bridging**—Children's structures begin to have two blocks with a space between them, spanned or connected by a third block. During this phase, a child uses his problem-solving skills as he explores spatial relationships. They examine ways to support two blocks and join them together with a third block.

- **Stage IV: Enclosures**—Children's structures now exhibit using blocks to enclose a space. Enclosures require children to look at space, connections, patterning, and internal and external positioning. Children repeat and refine the process as they experiment with joined enclosures and consider how the varying shapes and sizes of blocks impact their enclosures.

- **Stage V: Decorative Patterns**—Children express competencies with block building and now take risks and express more imaginative attributes, including defined symmetry, in their construction. They discover how spatial relationships impact building.

- **Stage VI: Naming Structures for Enactment**—Children name the structure, based on what they have attempted to create, such as skyscraper, space station, zoo, etc. These structures are complex with bridges, enclosures, towers, and complicated designs.

- **Stage VII: Resembling or Naming for Play**—Children reproduce and construct structures based on their daily life experiences. The names of the structures correspond with the intended function of the structure. Children may express what they intend to build prior to acquiring the blocks to start construction.

Early learning practitioners examine how children use blocks and discuss with the children the types of interests they have in creating block structures. This provides insight and information that assists in ensuring that the appropriate blocks and accessories are provided which are reflective of the children's interests.

*Photo 6.2    Children learn mathematical and scientific principles through block building.*

## TYPES OF BLOCKS

As you begin to examine early learning environments, you will note that there are a number of different types of blocks, although they are primarily divided into two categories: tabletop blocks and floor blocks. **Tabletop blocks** are generally used by one child or two children who choose to work together. The **floor blocks,** much larger in size, generally attract two or more children to work together to create a particular structure. Tabletop blocks, although versatile, are generally used more as indoor blocks.

As you explore the different types of blocks available to children, you will become familiar with which blocks are best suited to be placed specifically in the block area, those that are more useful to be placed in the manipulative area, those that are specific for indoor use, and those that offer intrigue in both the indoor and outdoor environments. Examining the different types of blocks and discussing with children and colleagues the potential types of play that may occur with the blocks, helps you visualize and generate ideas to support children using blocks in their play to their full potential.

### Table Blocks

These are small coloured blocks that come in a variety of sizes. They support a child's fine motor development. Table blocks may include unique shapes that trigger children's curiosity (Isenberg & Jalongo, 2010). Children use these blocks most frequently on a tabletop or small carpet. Because table blocks are usually used on a flat surface, children often spread their structures out rather than building their structure up high.

## Picture and Alphabet Blocks

These picture and alphabet blocks date back to the seventeenth century. They continue to be some of the first blocks that are provided to children. These cube blocks have pictures or letters on each of their sides.

## Parquetry Blocks

These blocks are straight-edged geometric shapes such as triangles, squares, rectangles, and diamonds. Children generally use these flat blocks for creating patterns. Children's visual perception is enhanced by using pattern cards as a guide for creating intricate patterns.

## Bristle Blocks

These blocks come in rectangles, oblongs, squares, and circle shapes. They have bristles on each of their sides and they interlock. Children create structures by sticking them together in various configurations. These blocks provide children with more flexible possibilities than traditional blocks.

## Duplo® Blocks

Duplo blocks are used with toddlers because they are larger blocks. They are easy for a toddler to manipulate. These blocks contribute to children gaining skills at grasping, stacking, and experiencing the concept of pulling apart and putting back together.

## Foam Blocks

These blocks are usually introduced to toddlers. They are easy for toddlers to carry and stack.

## Floor Blocks

Floor blocks are large blocks that come in a variety of sizes. They are generally made from wood and are sturdy. Because of their size, children use these blocks to build replicas of buildings, enclosures, and structures that may be used for a number of purposes.

## Unit Blocks

Unit blocks are made of carefully finished hardwood. Their lengths are based on a single unit and other blocks are based on two, three, and four times the unit. The blocks are made with precision so that children may combine three half units to match one three-unit-block. Unit block sets include the unit blocks, pillars, angles, and ramps that may be large and flat.

## BOX 6.1

### Accessories for Block Play

Cardboard cylinders from carpet rolls

Traffic signs

Large pictures of buildings, bridges, farms, towers

Wheelbarrows

Human and animal figures

Metal pipes

Plexiglass

Flower pots

Moving boxes

Construction hats

Tape measures

Plywood

Logs

Gates

Steering wheels

The versatility of the unit block supports children in gaining the foundational skills in mathematics and gives them the flexibility to create with patterns and designs.

## Stop . . . Think . . . Discuss . . . Reflect

Assume you have a child who has expressed an interest in clocks and in using tape measures. How do you support the child in exploring these concepts in the block area? What types of props might you add to the area? What thought-provoking questions might you use with the child to gain new information on the child's knowledge level and depth of interest? How would you document your findings?

## Hollow Blocks

These blocks offer children a different type of play experience from that of unit blocks, due in part to their increased size. These blocks bring versatility to the children's play because large structures may be constructed. Because of the size of the blocks, children are required to use large motor manipulation when picking them up and in using them in their construction. Often, two children will manoeuvre the blocks together to the construction area or children will put them in wagons to transport them.

Hollow blocks support children's creativity in constructing enclosures that may be used for dramatic play. They solve real-life construction challenges (Cartwright, 1995). Hollow blocks, like unit blocks, are built in mathematical proportion. The square is $5\frac{1}{2}$ inches by 11 inches by 11 inches. There is a half square, a double square, and a half double square. Typical sets of hollow blocks include ramps as well as long and short boards. Cartwright (1990) suggests about 20 hollow blocks plus

*Photo 6.3*   *A child concentrates on building a specific structure with her blocks.*

10 boards for indoor play. The outdoor play area requires at least double this amount. Children also require accessories such as large packing boxes, sawhorses, long planks, hoses, and related materials to advance their block play options.

Because the structures that are usually created are large, there is a tendency towards a higher level of cooperation among children than in other types of play. Dramatic play is enhanced when hollow blocks and accessories are made available to the children.

## Cardboard Bricks

These blocks are large, lightweight, and easy to stack. Children use them as they venture into building bridges and enclosures.

# ACCESSORIES

As identified in Box 6.1, block play is enriched when children have access to blocks and accessories. Early learning practitioners choose accessories based on the expressed interests and developmental levels of children. The accessories encourage the children to move from simple to more complex play. The accessories trigger children to participate in more problem-solving skills, language, cooperation, and creativity as their play becomes more complex. The accessories contribute to more imaginative play among children, which in turn leads them to play out family roles, occupations, and community events.

# Stop . . . Think . . . Discuss . . . Reflect

Some early learning environments may not have access to the commercial blocks that have been described above. What alternative materials could be provided to children that would support them in creating structures?

Table 6.2 provides an overview of the types of skills developed and the typical types of blocks used by children at each phase of their block play.

***Table 6.2*** *Typical Skills Developed and the Types of Blocks Children Use at Each Phase of Block Building*

| Age | Skills | Recommended Blocks |
|---|---|---|
| Infants to 12 months | Transfers blocks from one hand to the other. Dump blocks from containers. Puts blocks in mouth. | Small wooden blocks that may be washed. Foam blocks covered in fabric that may be washed. |
| Toddlers (12 to 24 months) | Carries blocks to a variety of areas. Puts blocks in containers. Dumps blocks. Begins to stack blocks. | Small wooden blocks that may be washed. Foam blocks covered in fabric that may be washed. Brick blocks made from cardboard. |
| Pre-Preschoolers and Preschoolers (24 to 48 months) | Makes rows, towers, bridges and enclosures. Names simple structures. Begins to form patterns. Discusses what is being built. | Unit blocks Hollow blocks Planks Cedar blocks Cardboard blocks Accessories |
| Kindergarten (48 months to 60 months) | Incorporates rows, towers, bridges, enclosures, and special forms and items such as ramps, doors, gates into structures. Incorporates literacy skills by adding signs and maps into work. Buildings are sophisticated and built over several play episodes. Uses plans and ideas from other sources such as the internet. | Unit blocks Hollow blocks Planks Plywood Cardboard blocks Cedar blocks Accessories |
| School aged—Over 5 years of age | Uses a variety of blocks with accessories. Incorporates several types of accessories into the structure. Draws out or discusses with peers a plan for the complex structures. There is usually more than one structure incorporated into the overall construction. Each child may be assigned a specific role in the construction phase. | Unit blocks Hollow blocks Planks Plywood Accessories |

# HOW BLOCKS SUPPORT CHILD DEVELOPMENT

Erikson (1902–1994) emphasizes the importance of blocks in relation to children, play, and development. Block building helps children construct their context related to adult life (Provenzo & Brett, 1983). For example, when children build roadways out of blocks and use vehicles to travel along them, the children are playing out their life observations of how adults drive on the road. Building paths, forts, or using blocks as cars provides children with strategies to gain an understanding of their world.

Block play contributes to children's development in numerous ways. Play theorists suggest that block play helps children practice and consolidate skills, and develop flexible and abstract thinking capabilities (Conrad, 1995; Piaget, 1962; Vygotsky, 1976). Vygotsky (1978) suggests when children are valued and offered rich play experiences, that they will collectively exceed their own capabilities (Rogers & Russell, 2003).

Exposing children to blocks supports Vygotsky's concept of children engaging in activities that contribute to stretching a child's zone of proximal development. Think about 4-year-old Natioka who has been using blocks at an early learning centre for two years. She has developed skills in planning and building complicated structures. She can build enclosures, she has the ability to build large structures with bridges and towers that exhibit symmetry, and she has the language skills to tell stories about her structures. She also reproduces parts of her stories, using pictorial and written formats. Recently, 4-year-old Inika came to the centre. This is his first exposure to group care. It appears as though he has had limited experience using blocks. Over several weeks, he watches Natioka and gradually asks if he can play. Natioka, welcomes Inika to play with her. Within two months, Inika developed skills and competence in using the blocks. He mimics the language descriptors used by Natioka and uses construction strategies similar to those modelled by Natioka. Inika, bringing some technology skills to play, now uses the camera and computer to document the structures. As Wandnita, the early learning practitioner, reviewed the block construction and the camera work that Inika had presented, she was soon reminded of how, through the block play of the last two weeks, these children constructed knowledge about science, mathematical principles, language, technology, and social skills. They collectively solved problems and shared knowledge, which added to their block-building capabilities. Both children were stretched to incorporate new accessories and knowledge building into their play.

As outlined in Table 6.1 at the beginning of this chapter, children who participate in quality block play experiences, develop knowledge and skills that are foundational for understanding language, science, and math concepts and processes. Block play builds a child's confidence in working individually and in groups, which is essential for later social and academic settings. When children use blocks for pretend play, they are enhancing the use of their imaginations more than when they are participating in other experience centres such as the dramatic play area, because blocks are an open-end, less structured material (Hendrick & Weissman, 2007).

*Photo 6.4* *Children may work together to build a structure or work independently initially and then add an aspect of the structure to the group project.*

Although early learning practitioners focus on the development of the whole child, in the next section we provide an overview of how block play supports each of the child's developmental domains. For many early learning practitioners, it is helpful to become familiar with how block play supports each of the domains and then transfer that knowledge to the development of the whole child. Early learning practitioners combine the knowledge of developmental domains with the vision of what the child is interested in and capable of achieving.

## Blocks and Cognitive Development

Block play can be the catalyst for children to expand their sense of math, science, and language skills. For example, as children use blocks, their skills of sorting and classifying are integral to the structure that they create (Rogers & Russo, 2003). When children create a structure, they develop the ability to select and group blocks according to shape, size, weight, and use. As they become more experienced, their classification skills are expanded to include the relationship of size to balance, area, volume, and ordinal and cardinal numbers. They match blocks with the same attributes and they estimate the number of blocks required for their construction. This leads children to acquire counting and numeration skills. The classification and comparison skills support children in creating patterns and graphs, as well as acquiring spatial and measurement skills (Worth,

***Photo 6.5*** *Boys and girls benefit socially and cognitively from block play.*

1990). This requires children to think, experiment, communicate, problem solve, and strategize.

Think about a group of children building a structure using hollow blocks. What might children discover if they place the hollow blocks by height rather than width? Children may learn that they can build their structures taller and more quickly than if they lay the hollow blocks flat. What happens when children add ramps to their structures? They learn about velocity. And what do children learn if they drop blocks from the top when standing on a staircase, versus when they drop them when using them for construction? Children begin to experiment with the concepts of speed and distance (Rogers & Russo, 2003). When children take photos of objects and use them as a guide, they are transferring imagery to production. This requires the child to visualize, use problem-solving skills, creativity and critical thinking skills along with the attributes of the blocks.

## Blocks, Language Development and Mathematics

Block play is rich with language development. Both language and reading skills are practiced in block play. When children make signs for their structures, they discover the relationship of letters and words as symbols. As children create interesting structures, new language is acquired. For example, both Jana and Janelle will be celebrating their fourth birthday in the upcoming weeks. As they participate in building a tall structure, Anita notices the girls using words such as *uneven, tipsy, collapse, expansion,* and *shattered.* Anita was amazed at how their vocabulary has expanded and how their sentence structure has evolved to include five to eight words.

Rogers & Russo (2003) indicate that the language used during block play helps children "describe the actions that they are performing (present), predicts ideas or expectations of what will occur (future), and recapitulates what has been done (past)" (p. 18). Generally, children communicate with others as their construction takes form. The dialogue focuses on **what, why**, **and how** they build (Rogers & Russo, 2003). This communication process helps children use scientific and mathematical terms such as *height, weight, width, big, bigger, biggest, length, thick, pattern,* etc. This contributes to children constructing the language related to math and science principles.

When children are exposed to blocks, even during the phase of free exploration, they engage in mathematical actions, expressing mathematical terms, discovery of mathematical concepts, and they begin to relate objects to their personal life experiences. Children start to understand the relationships of counting, comparing, measuring, and reasoning during the play (Park, Chae, & Boyd, 2008).

Children from families with limited economic resources benefit from exposure to block play (Park, Chae, & Boyd, 2008) because blocks support the development of mathematical skills. For example, many research studies identify that children from economically deprived families have lower levels of mathematics achievement than children from more affluent families (Jordan, Huttenlocher, & Levine, 1992; Saxe, Guberman, & Gearhart, 1987). Children's mathematical understanding is enhanced when they have hands-on experiences with blocks because they need to exhibit higher levels of thinking skills and make more complex mathematical conclusions than are achieved through paper-pencil tasks (Park, Chae, & Boyd, 2008).

The early learning practitioner extends children's math, science, and language skills by facilitating or coaching the children to explain and document their play episodes. Using a digital camera to capture photos of children's structures and having the children tell their stories, helps them to connect words, objects, construction, and pictures to storylines. When early learning practitioners encourage children to develop mapping skills, it further supports them in connecting creativity and design principles through the use of language, math, and science requirements.

## Stop . . . Think . . . Discuss . . . Reflect

**Observe:**

**What** children can do . . . what do they produce with blocks?

**Why** do children begin the construction process? Why do they use particular materials?

**How** do children build . . . how do they achieve their intended structure? How do they communicate with their peers? How do they interact with adults?

The response from the early learning practitioner impacts the richness of the play episode as illustrated with Alukik and Equik. Alukik and Equik spent a considerable time in the block area. Using hollow blocks for the foundation and unit blocks for the remaining structure, they have created a large structure that has a tower at each corner of the structure. When Alukik had difficulty getting her final blocks on the top, she announced to Equik that she was going to use a hollow block to stand on so she could reach the top. Equik quickly indicated that he was tall and he did not need a block. As Alukik moved the hollow block into position, Equik tried to put his rectangle block on top. He announced that he did it by himself.

As Alukik continued to stand on the hollow block so that other blocks could be added, Equik soon said, "My tower is bigger than yours." Then Alukik added more blocks and said, "Mine is bigger now." As the two children continued to add blocks, Equik's additions became more difficult. As he stretched to add another block, his tower swayed. And as he added another block it swayed again. Equik took a few minutes to observe Alukik's success, then he announced that he too was going to use a hollow block to stand on.

The early learning practitioner Anita, approached the children. The children announced, "We're making our towers the largest they can be without falling." Anita replied, "This is interesting, but you must not stand on the hollow blocks." Although safety rules are essential in early childhood environments, Anita, missed a *teachable* moment. There are a number of other approaches that she could have used to redirect the play and get the children talking about their structure. For example, she may have suggested that the children come off the hollow blocks and look at the different shapes of the blocks they used. She may have redirected them to obtain a large plank each so that they could measure the structures with their feet flat on the floor. Or, she could have asked them to stand by their towers so that she could measure them against the tower and take photos of it. Any one of these strategies would have had the potential to enhance the play at the same time as guiding them to use safe building practices.

## Blocks and the Affective Domain

We think of the affective domain as the domain of the internal emotions and feelings. The process of block play contributes to children developing affective attributes of socially appropriate behaviours and attitudes, self-development, creativity, esteem, and motivation.

Block play and the affective domain can effectively be aligned. Block play nurtures a child's imagination and creativity. When children create from *their inner child,* the process and the product differ from when they create from a more structured experience. Blocks, with their open-ended characteristics provide children with the flexibility to try new strategies and ideas. These applications lead children to discover the possibilities of the blocks as well as explore with feelings and roles. Children gain a sense of their feelings and working out those feelings, similar to when they participate in dramatic play. For example, think of the child who has just returned home from spending three days in a hospital setting. By creating the hospital with the emergency entrance and having ambulances for props, the child can work out feelings of being afraid, lonely, and unwell. Or, think of Marquette who has just returned from being on an airplane. Having airplanes as accessories and providing a variety of blocks may lead Marquette to create an airport experience.

Block play is an experience centre where cooperative play, problem solving, and communication skills emerge as children create and construct. These components support the development of the affective domain.

## Block Play and Creativity

Block play enhances creativity and problem solving. As children enter the block area, they begin to construct with the blocks. They may generate their own idea, use resources, or use an idea from a peer. Creativity requires children to try a variety of thinking patterns that will connect previous experiences to a new idea or new way of manipulating blocks.

Early learning practitioners and student practitioners support children's creativity with blocks by visualizing with the children as many new and creative ideas as possible. When children have a variety of blocks and props, they are motivated to look beyond their usual use of the blocks. Newness requires children to look for as many new solutions as possible. The more solutions and creative ideas the children generate, the more likely new interesting solutions will be developed. This advances the types of learning experiences and opportunities for children. Early learning practitioners examine the play, listen to the children, and support them when appropriate in planning and executing their ideas. The more freedom children have to explore their ideas, the more likely they are to take risks to try their thoughts and rethink their ideas to reach their ultimate goal.

It is normal for children to have periods when they build and rebuild the structure over and over again. This could occur because children are trying to perfect a process or they could be "stuck" in trying to generate new ideas. When early learning practitioners observe that the block play is stagnating, they work with the children to spark new ideas. They may offer new materials, they may become play partners, or they may ask the child to assist them in building a particular structure. They may also share with the children documentation that exhibits the structure that the children have been reconstructing over and over again to have them talk and tell stories about the structure and then pose *what if* questions. The important part is that early learning practitioners need to examine and reflect upon how they may stimulate the child to move beyond the plateau, into a phase of new block-building creativity and discovery.

## Physical Skills

Block play helps children develop physically. Blocks contribute to the child's large and fine motor skills, as well as eye–hand coordination. Fine motor and eye–hand coordination skills are precursors to being able to formulate the letters in hand writing. The physical skills developed through block play support later physical development milestones.

## Block Play and Gender

There is controversy in the literature on whether block play is dominated by one gender over the other. According to Conrad (1995), empirical studies examining block play and gender conclude that there is inconclusive information to suggest that block play is dominated by one gender. Other empirical studies suggest that there is no significant difference between the ways in which boys and girls manipulate or use blocks. These findings differ from anecdotal perspectives expressed by some early learning practitioners. There is a perception that the block centre attracts more boys than girls. The block area requires blocks and accessories that reflect the interest of both genders, so that all children have equal interest in the area.

## Blocks and Children with Disabilities

Phelps and Hanline (1999) indicate that early learning practitioners often overlook how block play can support children with disabilities. As identified earlier in this chapter, block play generates opportunities for all children to engage in social interaction, creativity, problem solving, and language development. Quality block experiences for all children require space, time, and materials.

There are a number of strategies that may be implemented in the environment to support children with disabilities without singling them out. For example, if building space is an issue, by placing large pieces of painted plywood in areas, the space that may be used for building is defined. Arranging blocks that are within easy reach and are displayed with cues to support children returning them to the shelves is important in managing the block environment.

# THE ROLE OF EARLY LEARNING PRACTITIONERS IN BLOCK PLAY

Block play is an important aspect of the early learning environment. Early learning practitioners and student practitioners have many roles and responsibilities in preparing the environment for block play and facilitating the play experiences. Similar to other areas of early learning experiences, children require play environments that allow them to have the freedom to explore, based on their interests, skills, and ideas. Early learning practitioners who advance their knowledge and professional attention to the benefits of block play will be able to offer children a learning environment that will support their play. Let's look at some of the key roles that early learning practitioners engage in when facilitating play opportunities with blocks and accessories. Figure 6.1 provides a snapshot of the roles and responsibilities that early learning practitioners may participate in with children and block play.

## Determining One's Philosophical Perspective

One of the most important guidelines that early learning student practitioners embark on is trying to figure out how your interactions with and decisions about a child or children with whom you are working, impact their play, their desire to try new things, and their motivational levels to engage in new learning opportunities. A core question that needs to be asked when thinking about children and

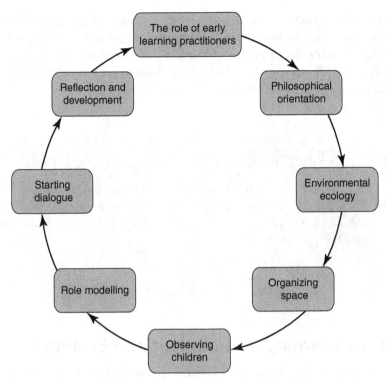

**Figure 6.1** *The Role of Early Learning Practitioners in Block Play*

block play is "How can I foster a young child's play, thinking, exploration, and visualization through block play?"

The impact of the role of the early learning practitioner can be significant to a child's learning. For example, Piaget (1971/1974) says that children develop relationships, such as logico-mathematical ones, when they *think,* "to understand social and physical phenomena, and to solve social and physical problems" (Kamii, Miyakawa, & Kato, 2004, p. 56). Thinking means supporting the children in being able "to make mental relationships about objects, people, and events" (Kamii, Miyakawa, & Kato, 2004, p. 56). Blocks support this complex area of thinking.

Student practitioners benefit from investing in the time to get to know each child and to think about their strengths and opportunities to support them in play. This helps you to focus on the child's needs and to determine strategies that will encourage children to advance the complexities of their block play. For example, think of a child Mallia who is building a tower. She has tried to get the blocks to stay piled one on top of the other. Each time Mallia attempts to add a new block she needs to think about where to place it—does it go in the middle or to one side? Does it go to the front or to the back? As part of the process, Mallia participated in a physical-knowledge activity as she tried to figure out how to produce the desired result. If you were supporting Mallia, what would your role be in this? You may either tell Mallia that if she places the block in a certain position her tower will remain standing, or, conversely, fall, or you may ask her, "What is it you need to do to make the tower stand? If your philosophical orientation is to support children in the development of thinking, which of the two strategies might you wish to transfer to your practice? Why is it important to think about the relationship of your philosophical orientation and block play?

## Stop . . . Think . . . Discuss . . . Reflect

There are five 4-year-olds building a large structure. How high should the children be able to build? Are there dangers that need to be considered? Is there a way that children can build the structure as high as they want? What happens if adults curtail their desire to build high?

## The Early Learning Environment and Ecology

Environmental factors influence children's interest and their use of blocks. Providing children with the right environment and adequate time to work on projects that extend beyond one play episode is essential (Conrad, 1995). Children's

*Photo 6.6*    *Children need opportunities to use blocks in a variety of ways in their play and experimentation.*

depth of play is expanded when structures remain standing for long periods of time. This allows children to experience cycles of planning, reflecting, making changes, researching, and developing new ideas to incorporate into the structure (Conrad, 1995). It allows them to review documentation, visualize what could be, and how they may change the structure to reflect new ideas.

Block play generally attracts three to four children to the area which can create vigorous, social, and loud play. At times, there may be a child who will benefit from having time to explore and build with the blocks on his own. This requires early learning practitioners to be aware of children who benefit from this solitary play and determine how this may occur without other children interfering with the solo play. The environmental design must be flexible enough to accommodate solitary and group play. Children may be encouraged to find spots away from the block area, such as under a table, inside a large box, or in a quiet area in the playground.

## Stop . . . Think . . . Discuss . . . Reflect

Is block play found in every culture? If so, is it always with wooden blocks? Why or why not? What might children in the far north, where wood is scarce, use for blocks? How might children in countries such as Jordan, where wood is imported, experience the concepts of block play without necessarily having wooden blocks? Why might some cultures such as Japan provide children with large blocks that require two or more children to move them? Why do some cultures and early learning program philosophies suggest that children should be presented with plain wood blocks rather than coloured blocks? Does this impact the beauty of the structures or the quality of play?

## Organizing the Space

The physical space allocated for block play impacts the depth and breadth of children's play. When children move materials between experience centres and mix the use of materials, they test and produce more innovative play ideas. Block play requires space and materials if our goal is to have children participate in play that promotes divergent thinking.

Placing the block centre near the dramatic centre has many advantages, including increasing the interchange among centres (Hirsch, 1996; Vergeront, 1996). When blocks are placed in a creative discovery zone, symbolic thinking skills are used. This is an ideal strategy that promotes children transferring creative ideas and problem-solving skills of visual arts with scientific and mathematical concepts. For example, young children who have the opportunity to use the block and dramatic area may engage in block building that builds roads to apartment buildings or castles. Some of the blocks may be used to create furniture. Children may incorporate props such as dolls and vehicles into their structural designs.

Young children require the block centre to be a place where the materials are presented in an orderly way and are accessible. Initially, children may require a reminder on the roles and responsibilities of children in the block centre.

There are a number of factors that early learning practitioners consider when preparing the block play area. Box 6.2 provides guidelines for early learning student practitioners to consider when setting up a block centre.

## BOX 6.2

## Environmental Considerations for Block Play

### Location of the block experience centre

- The block centre is most utilized by children when it is located in an area that gets limited traffic and is three-sided.
- Placing the block centre in a corner of both the outdoor play area and indoor area supports children playing for longer periods of time.
- A space of about 8 by 10 square will accommodate four to six children. Children require space to build structures up and patterns out (such as roadways or train rails).
- The floor or ground surface should support block structures while reducing the noise.
- The space should be large enough so that children may create block structures and allow them to remain standing so that they may add to their structure at a later time (National Association for the Education of Young Children, 1997).

### Quantity of Blocks

- 200 blocks for 3-year-olds
- 300 blocks for 4-year-olds
- 500 for 5-year-olds

### Displaying Blocks

- Low, open shelves are used so children have access to the blocks.
- Shelves may have block shape templates affixed to the shelf as a way to assist children in locating and replacing blocks. Sandpaper may be used as a way to support children with visual impairments.
- Large, heavy blocks are placed on the lower shelves to help stabilize the storage unit.
- Blocks should be placed on the shelves neatly so children may exhibit their independence during the building and clean-up process.
- Block storage encourages children in matching and sorting.

### Blocks and Accessories with Loose Parts

- A combination of open, see-through containers and shelving is used for accessories. Storage containers, bins, or deep boxes reduce children's interest in block building. Being able to see the materials enhances a child's interest in using the blocks and accessories.
- Interlocking blocks and accessories are available.
- Duplicates of popular props and accessories are displayed.

## Observing Children's Block Play

Observing children during block play helps early learning practitioners and student practitioners see how children use the area. For example, observing a group of children building a playhouse may provide insight into their level of problem solving, how they predict the type and quantity of blocks required, how they plan for constructing the structure, and the roles and responsibilities that each child takes on. Observations familiarize us with the environmental conditions that support children in being able to effectively participate in quality play. Table 6.3 provides examples of children's behaviours that alert early learning practitioners when children may require adult support.

Early learning practitioners and student practitioners gain insight into a child's interests and strengths through observation. For example, some children engage in block play as a social experience outdoors, whereas others prefer to use

**Table 6.3** *Examples of Children's Behaviour Observed in Block Play*

| Observation | Role of Facilitator |
| --- | --- |
| The noise level in the block area starts to escalate | Facilitator becomes part of the play with one or two children. A soft voice is used with the children. This encourages the children to use their softer voice and to listen to one another more attentively. |
| A child begins to interfere with the structure of others or the play becomes destructive and unsafe | Facilitator becomes part of the play by encouraging the child who is interfering with others to refocus on adding to the structure or developing a structure with the facilitator. Guidance to other areas of the play area may be required. |
| A child becomes tense or begins to cry | The facilitator examines areas that may be contributing to the child's stress. Open-ended questions are used as a strategy to refocus the child. Comfort strategies and dialogue are used with the child. The facilitator may suggest the child expand the play by using the video camera or graphs for documenting the structure. |
| A child begins to lose focus on the structure | The facilitator has dialogue with the child about the structure. Open-ended questions are used as a strategy to expand the play. If the child appears to have lost interest, the facilitator works with the child to move to another area of interest. |
| Children begin to argue | The facilitator listens to the dialogue to determine if it is animated discussion or children arguing. The facilitator may offer open-ended questions that will bridge the opinions expressed by the children. The facilitator helps children use critical thinking skills while building on their socialization strengths. |
| Children say "We need help." | The facilitator asks the children to put into words how they **identify** what the problem is. Discuss the problem. Using open-ended questions, help the children **brainstorm** possible solutions. Advance children's thinking by having them examine the advantages and disadvantages of possible solutions before selecting the one that they use. Support the children in **implementing** the solution. Help the children verbalize their evaluation of the solution. Did it work? Why? If it did not work, why not? (Miller, 1997). |

blocks as a solitary play episode indoors. Some children gravitate to the unit blocks, whereas others prefer the table top blocks. Practitioners gather information about how the children use the blocks from a building perspective as well as a tactile and sensory experience.

Observations provide early learning practitioners with information about the child's knowledge and skills about block play. By listening to the children and observing their play, adults are able to determine the most appropriate time to facilitate or support a play episode. For example, if there is a child who expresses an interest in trains, you may provide train props and pose cognitively challenging, open-ended questions that will help the child build a particular item, such as a train station or a train track. As you observe and support the child through play, you note the types of blocks that the child uses. Are they the unit blocks, the tabletop blocks, soft blocks, or cardboard blocks? Are there props involved? If so, how are they used? Who do children play with in the block area? Are they generally the same children? Do you need to pose open-ended questions to advance the play? Are there special materials that may lead the child to new discoveries? Or, are there ways in which you and other children may become involved to reduce a child's level of frustration? These questions are important, as they guide our practice in acquiring information about the whole child, which leads you to offer materials and experiences that support the child. Practitioners determine the opportune moments to expand the child's play experience and trigger new investigations and learning.

As identified in Chapter 3, observations and pedagogical documentation are important practices of early learning practitioners. These provide information that gives us a more holistic view of what the child knows about block building and how the child uses her problem-solving and creative thinking processes during block play. The type of observation methods and tools used are chosen based on the practitioner's style and the purpose of the observation. The examples below are data collection samples of methods used by early learning practitioners. As identified in Chapter 3, the process of collecting data and using the information effectively is a developmental process that is impacted by a personal philosophy as well as the early learning centre or classroom philosophy.

**Anecdotal records** provide a brief description or "word picture" of the event (Cartwright & Cartwright, 1974). These records are generated from a direct observation. They describe the behaviour observed. For example, Marick entered the block area at approximately 9:15 a.m. He went to the block shelf and obtained a container of table blocks. He took all of the red rectangle blocks and laid them on their edge. Then he placed them to make a rectangle enclosure. Andrew approached Marick to ask if he could play; Marick said no and returned to building an enclosure inside the enclosure. All of the blocks used for the inside enclosure were blue in colour. Marick starts another enclosure on the outside of the original enclosure. He is focused on his structure. Other children approach him wanting to play, but he keeps building.

**Checklists/rubrics** provide an overview of a child's skill level with that of typical developmental profiles of children of a similar age. Table 6.4 provides an example of how a checklist supports understanding a child's level of development, by recording the specific example observed.

**Table 6.4**  *Sample Checklist/Rubric for Stages of Block Play*

| Child's Name: Sara 3.5 years of age | | | | | | |
| --- | --- | --- | --- | --- | --- | --- |
| Carrying Blocks | Rows and Stacks | Bridging | Enclosures | Decorative Patterns | Naming Structures | Resembling or Naming for Play |
| | | 09/09 Took six blocks to make bridge over roadway. Had people figures walk across bridge. | 09/10 Used 24 blocks to make a corral for horses outside of the barn. | | | |

This observation identifies that Sara has an interest in walking across bridges and in horses, barns, and corrals. If an early learning practitioner added *lincoln-*type blocks (lincoln-type blocks are those that are long, log-like, connecting blocks) to Sara's choices, this may lead Sara to build a corral that combines open space with enclosures. Books about barns and bridges may also spark some additional block-building experiments.

**Conversational notes** is a strategy frequently employed in Reggio-inspired settings (Cadwell, 1997). These notes are acquired from discussions that early learning practitioners have with a child or groups of children about their block structures, including the process used to create the structure. The notes may be recorded and placed with digital documentation. An example of a conversational note is given below:

> I was observing Mila, Ben, Sara, and Maggie in the block area. Ben and Sara went to the dramatic centre and brought back binoculars, plants, and boots to the block area. As the four children were participating in conversation, I approached them and asked "What's happening in this area of construction?" They said they were building a path to the forest. So, I started asking questions that related to the path and the props that the children had brought to the area. I wonder why you wish to have binoculars in the forest. Mila described how binoculars help you see things that are far away. Then I asked, "what kinds of things do you think you will see in the forest?" Ben and Sara said they would see little animals like rabbits and ground hogs and little white flowers, while Mila and Maggie said that this time of year they would be looking for big bears and deer and all the trees that are green.

This conversation provides insight into the children's knowledge about the forest. It helps practitioners determine interests that children have and how additional props may expand the depth of the play experience.

**Digital documentation** provides photos or videos taken at each phase of the project or investigation. The documentation is dated and used with children to facilitate discussions, help them identify their knowledge and skills of block building, and tell stories about what they see. Practitioners may also use the documentation to acquire further information about the child.

## Role Modelling

Early learning practitioners are role models to the children in the block area. It is through encouragement and experimentation that children gain the sense that it is acceptable to try new ideas. For example, the early learning practitioner monitors negotiations, poses thought-provoking, open-ended questions that will support children in problem solving, makes comments such as "How does this . . . or explain to me . . . or tell me about. . . ." These types of comments enhance the child's problem-solving skills while supporting thinking in divergent ways. This facilitation strategy also supports children in the process of building rather than focusing on the defined product.

Early learning practitioners play an important role in working with children who may not use the block area as much as other children, by inviting them to become partners in building a structure. This can begin by stacking a couple of blocks and then inviting other children to come to the area. The purpose is for children who do not use the block area to gain success. This requires you to be an encourager, guide, and partner in play. You listen to the children and, most importantly, support their ideas. If the childrens' ideas do not work, the mistake is turned into a learning opportunity. Through open-ended questions and discussion, you help children analyze why an idea may not have worked and what they could do differently next time. As the child or children become engaged in the structure, you gradually move away from the area.

Facilitators guide children who exhibit signs of unsafe building practice, becoming destructive with the blocks or to other children, or using the blocks inappropriately. One of the most effective strategies to change the behaviour is for the early learning practitioner to become involved in the play directly with the child. This may take on two formats. The first is to have dialogue about how you can help with the construction, the types of blocks that are being used, and questions such as, "What would happen if . . . ?" as a way to refocus the child. The second strategy is to share with the child, through words or body language, your interest in block play.

## Starting Dialogue with Children About Block Play

Many factors contribute to a child's success and experience with blocks. Dialogue among the children and early learning practitioner is one of the most influential activities that contributes to children taking risks in the block area. In quality programs, the involvement with the children, the verbal exchanges, and interactions among children and adults is evident. It takes practice to facilitate discussion with children while using the blocks. Box 6.3 provides some phrases that may be used to start a conversational exchange between the child and practitioner.

## BOX 6.3

## Ways to Start Conversations about Block Play

Tell me (about)

- the blocks' shapes that you are using . . .
- the blocks on top of, beside . . .
- how you got the blocks underneath the . . .
- how you made the space for the trucks to go under the bridge . . .
- why you used the squares and triangles in this part of your construction . . .
- what will happen if you take your hand away . . . will the structure stay standing or fall . . .
- your structure
- how people get inside your structure . . .
- what happens if two cars try to pass on the roadway . . .
- how many steps the prince needs to climb to get into the building . . .
- how you balanced the planks . . .
- how I can help you use the plank to . . .
- tell me about the problem with . . .
- what happens when . . .

## Stop . . . Think . . . Discuss . . . Reflect

Marti and Hunter are using blocks. Marti sees that Hunter is building a structure that she thinks she could go in and out of. She wants to make one too. Marti starts by getting long boards and some of the cedar blocks. Her blocks tumble. Two facilitators take different approaches to responding to Marti.

**Donna responds:** You need to take your cedar blocks and place them on their side into the shape of a square. Then you need to place cedar blocks at each corner to put your planks on.

**David responds:** I'm not sure. Tell me what you are thinking as your strategy. How do you think this strategy will work?

Block play requires experimentation and discovery learning that occurs through trial and error. Which of the two responses requires the child to take the lead in her exploration and discovery? Why?

## Reflection and Development

Block play is essential for young children because it contributes to a variety of domains. Early learning practitioners continuously seek out new knowledge and strategies that will help them facilitate meaningful block play with children. When practitioners come to a point whereby they observe the children are building similar structures and not taking risks to create more elaborate structures, there is a need to examine the environment, the materials, and the interaction among children and adults. Often, by reviewing documentation of the children's play, practitioners gain insight into where the child is and what strategies may support the child in trying new adventures.

When practitioners find themselves placing the same types of props and blocks in the block area, or when children's creativity in the block area wanes, it is essential that practitioners participate in further reflection and seek out opportunities to engage in further development. Practitioner's stagnation reduces the potential for children gaining growth and development opportunities from the block area. Collaboration among practitioners helps to facilitate new directions for the play experiences.

# SUMMARY

### Chapter Preview

- Block play provides children with a variety of skills and abilities that are transferable to other learning domains. These concrete materials support children in acquiring knowledge about math, literacy, and science principles more effectively than paper-and-pencil worksheets.

### Defining Block Play

- Block play refers to children manipulating blocks by handling them, stacking them, and using actions and language to represent realistic or imaginative play.

### The Historical Perspectives of Blocks

- Children and blocks are not a new phenomenon. They evolved at the same time that a child-culture occurred during the late 1700s.
- Philosophers and educators including Froebel, Montessori, and Pratt have contributed to understanding the importance of play in early learning environments.

### The Stages of Block Play

- Reifel and Greenfield provide a three-level evaluation process to assess the symbolism and the spatial complexity used by children in the block area, while Hirsch outlines seven stages of block building. They include carrying, rows and stacks, bridging, enclosures, decorative patterns, naming structures for enactment, and resembling or naming for play.

### Types of Blocks

- Blocks fall into two categories; table blocks and floor blocks.
- Early learning practitioners provide children with a variety of blocks, space, and accessories.

### How Blocks Support Child Development

- Block play contributes to children's mathematics, science, and language development as well as their affective domain.
- Empirical research indicates that there is inconclusive information to suggest that block play is dominated by one gender.
- Children with disabilities benefit from resources and space being organized so that they may use the blocks with ease, without being singled out from other children.

### The Role of Early Learning Practitioners in Block Play

- Early learning practitioners' roles include determining one's philosophical perspective, examining the learning environment and ecology, organizing space, observing children's play, role modelling, engaging in dialogue with the children, and participating in training and development.

# REVIEW QUESTIONS

1. Why is block play an important programming area for early learning practitioners to know about? How does block play inform your work with children?
2. What is the significance of examining the historical perspectives of block play? How does it impact your approach to block play with children today?
3. Reifel and Greenfield, as well as Hirsch, indicate that there are stages to block play. What are those stages and how do you use that knowledge in your work with children?
4. Describe the types of blocks that would be considered table blocks and those that would be considered floor blocks. How does each category impact a child's block play?
5. Block play contributes to the development of children in a variety of ways. Describe how block play supports child development, creativity, and problem-solving skills.
6. How can early learning practitioners ensure that children with disabilities have access to block play without be singled out by other children?
7. Describe the key roles that early learning practitioners have in facilitating block play.

# MAKING CONNECTIONS

### Theory to Practice

1. You have been asked to reorganize the block centre that will be used with a group of 3- and 4-year olds. Based on what you have gained from this chapter, what key attributes would you include in the centre?
2. How would you ensure that children have an opportunity to use blocks in the outdoor environment? What would need to be considered in having a block centre outdoors?
3. What would you need to consider if you were setting up a block centre in an after-school program for 5- to 7-year-old children? How might it differ from one for 3- and 4-year-old children?
4. Documentation is an important part of block play. How do you envision gathering documentation from the block play? What will you do with the documentation? How does it inform your practice?

### For Further Research

1. Many educators and researchers indicate that the findings of boys using the block centre more than girls are inconclusive. Research three articles on the topic and then observe children in the block

centre six times. Are your findings similar to the research you reviewed? If so, how? If not, what are the differences?

2. Visit an early learning centre or kindergarten classroom and observe how children use blocks. Give particular attention to how, when, and where the children use the blocks. Determine the role of the early learning practitioner or teacher. How is block play facilitated, discussed, and documented? How do your observations compare to best practices outlined in the literature?

# ADDITIONAL READING

Cherney, I., Kelly-Vance, L., Gill Glover, K., Ruane, A. & Oliver Ryalls, B. (2003). The effects of stereotyped toys and gender on play assessment in children aged 18–47 months. *Educational Psychology,* Vol. 23(1).

Cohen, L. & Uhry, J. (2007). Young children's discourse strategies during block play: A Bakhtinian Approach. *Journal of Research in Childhood Education.* Vol. 21 (3).

*National Association for the Education of Young Children.* (1996). The block book (3rd ed). Washington, DC: Author.

Wellhousen, K. & Kieff, J. (2000). *A constructivist approach to block lay in early childhood.* New York: Thomson Delmar Learning.

# WEBLINKS

Block play performance among preschoolers as a predictor of later school achievement in mathematics. **http://findarticles.com/p/articles/mi_hb1439/is_2_15/ai_n28877649**

# 7 Language, Emergent Literacy, and Play

## Learning Outcomes

After exploring this chapter you should be able to

- define language development and emergent literacy;

- explain the stages of language and literacy development and the reasons why children communicate;

- describe how children's play is interconnected with the development of language and literacy skills;

- explain the theoretical foundation of language, emergent literacy, and play;

- describe the roles of early learning practitioners related to language and literacy; and

- discuss the role of the environment to children's language development and emerging literacy skills.

## Stories from the Field: Practitioner to Student

As a longtime practitioner in the field, parents have asked me so many times to tell them "what is my child learning?" Often I ask them in response, "What do you want them to learn?" Then they tell me, "I want them to learn their ABCs." This is where I have had difficulty reconciling what I learned in college with the realities of my practice. In college I learned that what is important is children's social and emotional development. I learned that my role is to facilitate play. Teaching the ABCs is the role of teachers in the school system. This never felt right to me but neither did incorporating the formalized, structured instructional strategies used in later school years. As I began to incorporate a literacy-rich environment into my practice, I was amazed by the evidence I observed every day of children learning the real meanings of letters, sounds, and words through their play. When I took pictures of the children in the process of learning, collected their work samples, and created documentation panels, I could finally tell and show parents that the children were learning their ABCs!

*Susan, Graduate, 1990*

## CHAPTER PREVIEW

Can you imagine a world without language? Language is everywhere. Children are exposed to language in their homes, schools, and in their communities. Language and the corresponding literacy skills are essential developmental milestones that impact a child's lifelong cognitive, social, and emotional attributes. Play experiences are essential to children developing language and literacy skills. Play is often the motivator for a child to expand their language and literary knowledge and skills.

Young children use and learn language in a variety of ways. For example, the simple acts of children exploring sounds, inventing language, and using symbols to link play and language help them in their quest to become familiar with words and meanings (Van Hoorn, Nourot, Scales, & Alward, 2007). Language is essential for communication. Communication is required for children to have their basic physical needs met and it is important for the human function of socializing.

From the first babbles of an infant to the complex sentences of a 4- or 5-year-old, early learning practitioners have important roles in supporting the development of children's language skills in their play experiences. The early learning environment that is rich with play will support children on this incredible journey that sees babbles evolve into a vocabulary of 5000 words at 5 years of age. Early learning practitioners require an understanding of the relationship of appropriate play experiences and programming options that support literate behaviours, language development, and literacy skills.

This chapter will introduce you to language development and literacy processes. You will gain insight into the significance of a child recognizing her first letter of the alphabet or printing her name for the first time and making the connection between the sounds a letter makes with what appears before her in print. You will also examine how the early learning practitioner's use of language supports children as they develop theirs.

As you explore the chapter, we ask that you think about the questions that follow. What can you do to inspire children to want to learn to read and write? How do language and literacy concepts in a playful environment motivate children? Think about it; how would you want to learn about new words, reading, and writing? Would you want someone to instruct you on how to read and write? Or, would you want to discover reading and writing and language concepts while playing within a literacy-rich environment?

Sheree Fitch is the multi-award-winning author of more than 20 books for children and adults, plays, poetry, chapter books, and educational literature. Fitch wrote her first book of nonsense verse, *Toes in My Nose*, for her 2-year-old son Jordan when she was 20. After years of rejection, it was published when she was 30 and it became a best-seller. Fitch believes that play and literacy should be jointly and joyfully intertwined. Read what she says about playing with words.

# WORDS OF WISDOM

## Ask an Expert

**Sheree Fitch**

The wordplay we call nonsense is not just so much silly stuff. The joy in the musicality of language, the surprise of feeling words slide off the tongue, the delight in sounding out a lipslippery spill of syllables, this dancing in the world of words is play that lays the very foundation for children developing faith in their own voices. This play is literacy and fluency in action.

# THEORETICAL FRAMEWORKS

Theoretical frameworks of language development provide students and early learning practitioners with a foundation in which to explore thoughts and beliefs. These in turn influence our practice. You will find it beneficial to think about your knowledge and beliefs about language and literacy at this point, and then revisit your ideas after you have reviewed this chapter. We introduce you to three theorists who have influenced how adults work with children in supporting language and literacy.

**Behaviourist Theory:** B.F. Skinner initiated this theory. He proposed that language is acquired through operant conditioning. Operant conditioning occurs when parents or early learning practitioners reinforce a child's efforts at language. As the child progresses from infancy, adults reinforce the child each time the most correct form of language to say words is expressed. For example, a child may be given a treat each time the word *kitty* is verbalized correctly. Practitioners who follow this theory suggest that a child will learn language through imitation. This requires adults to create an environment where children are conditioned or rewarded each time they use correct language forms, including imitating adult language (Frost, Wortham, & Reifel, 2008).

**Nativist Theory:** Noam Chomsky suggests that very young children can take charge of learning language. His theory was labelled *nativist* because he believed that children have an innate ability to acquire language. Chomsky indicates that all children have a biologically based innate system for language learning called language acquisition device (LAD). The LAD contains a set of rules that is common to all languages. Children use these rules to understand their native language (Frost, Wortham & Reifel, 2008). When children are exposed to language, they will figure out the rules such as grammar because of their LAD.

**Interactionist:** The interactionist theoretical approach as initiated by Lev Vygotsky is based on the assumption that language is acquired in a social context. This perspective proposes that children's acquisition of language and literacy skills takes place when a child interacts with others. Vygotsky tells us that cognition is always socially mediated or influenced by others. Higher mental functions, such as memory, attention, and self-regulation occur in the context of shared tasks between individuals. Thinking begins on the interpersonal or social plane before it is internalized as intrapersonal knowledge. The active and creative roles of individuals further influence language development.

## Operant Conditioning

Built on the work of Ivan Pavlov, Skinner's theory of operant conditioning is based on the premise that reinforced behaviours will tend to continue, while those that are punished or are not reinforced gradually end.

## Language acquisition device

*Language acquisition device* is the term Chomsky used to refer to the system of language that children are born with in their brains.

## Intrapersonal knowledge

As opposed to interpersonal knowledge which is derived from others, intrapersonal knowledge is that which exists or occurs within the individual self or mind.

Vygotsky indicates that every child is part of a social construct, actively experiencing and internalizing the environment, making meaning of it, and in turn, influencing the environment, just as the social situation influences the child. Vygotsky's view of the way social, individual, and creative growth is intertwined helps us further understand his idea of the *zone of proximal development* (Kashin,

**Scaffolding** is a fundamental principle of nature
whereby one concept is
built upon a previous
learning structure, thereby
ensuring its stable integration into the child's
knowledge or skill base
(Dietze, 2006).

2009). The term **scaffolding** (Wood, Bruner, & Ross, 1976) describes the transition from interpersonal to intrapersonal knowledge. Through *scaffolding*,
learners are able to cross the zone of proximal development. "The distance
between the actual developmental level as determined by independent problem
solving and the level of potential development as determined through problem solving under adult guidance or in collaboration with more capable peers" (Vygotsky,
1978, p. 86).

## Stop . . . Think . . . Discuss . . . Reflect

How do you think children acquire language? How do you think children learn to
read and write? The answers to these questions form your current beliefs about
language and literacy. Now relate your answers to play. How do you value play as
a vehicle for language and literacy learning? Is play part of your values and beliefs?
It will be helpful to write down your answers and save them. Share your answers
with a classmate and continue to reflect on your values and beliefs as you review
this chapter. At the end of the chapter, you may want to stop and think if you have
changed or adjusted any of your values and beliefs.

## FROM THEORY TO TRENDS

Throughout the decades, we are able to trace certain types of language learning
methods that have become trendy. In the past 50 years, there have been shifts back
and forth between whole language approaches to reading and writing and the
phonic approach. For example, Flesch (1955) proposed that the best way to teach
a child to read was through a phonic or direct instruction approach. At the time a
whole-word method was dominant in schools. There continues to be debate
among educators and the media about the merits of both approaches. The disagreements on how to teach reading have been characterized as the "phonics wars"
(Fisher, 2008). The two methods are featured below.

> **Phonics and Whole Language Approaches:** Generally, there are two
> approaches to reading: *Phonics* and *Whole Language*. These approaches
> reflect different underlying philosophies and stress different skills. The
> **Whole Language** approach stresses that reading "is a natural process,
> much like learning to speak, and that children exposed to a great deal of
> authentic, connected text will naturally become literate without much in
> the way of explicit instruction in the rules and conventions of printed text.
> The philosophy underlying the **Phonics** approach suggests that in order to
> learn to read, most children require explicit instruction in the rules of the
> printed text" (Wren, 2001, p. 1).

*Photo 7.1    A child is experimenting with print.*

Today, the research in early literacy is providing new approaches and understandings that differ from the tenets of both traditional Phonics or Whole Language philosophies. Now, early learning practitioners are encouraged to look beyond the restrictions of the traditional approaches. Practitioners, using research evidence on language and literacy development are now making clearer and more purposeful programming and experiential experiences for children based on interests, capabilities, developmental needs, and milestones. Children benefit most in environments where experiences are customized to meet the individual learning styles and needs of children, rather than implementing activities based on a particular philosophy or approach. Similar to other programming areas, early learning practitioners observe each child, examine a child's development phase, engage in discussion with the child, and respond with appropriate materials and experiences that will support their developmental phase and interests (Wren, 2001). This approach values both the child's and the early learning practitioner's input and suggests that individuals whether they are adults or children have substantial influence on what happens in the environment and how they execute their learning options.

The scope of the research and knowledge about language and literacy for children is immense. We begin by examining core definitions for language and literacy. These definitions are intended to help you think about the complexity of language and literacy development and introduce you to the breadth of this area of programming.

# DEFINING LANGUAGE DEVELOPMENT

Researchers and educators define language development in a variety of ways. Broadly defined, language development is viewed as the process by which children come to understand and communicate language during early childhood. Language is speech, the written symbols for speech, or any other means of communication. Language development follows a predictable sequence. It requires individuals to engage in communication strategies.

Language development is categorized as receptive and expressive language. **Receptive language** development is the ability to listen and understand the spoken, signed, or written word. **Expressive language** is the ability to communicate; to use language. It is what a child says or signs and this eventually includes what the child writes. Expressive language is also referred to as productive language. Usually receptive language develops faster than expressive language (Bowen, 1998).

# DEFINING LITERACY DEVELOPMENT

**Literacy** is commonly defined as the ability to read and write the printed text that represents spoken language—that is, to be literate (McVicker, 2007). **Emergent literacy** refers to the earliest signs of interest in and abilities related to reading and writing (Whitehurst & Lonigan, 1998). These early signs of literacy are the precursors of literacy development; they precede conventional reading and writing (Halle, Calkins, Berry, & Johnson, 2003).

Learning to become literate is a gradual process that begins at birth and continues throughout life. Literacy is continually evolving through interactions with others and the environment. While the sequence of literacy development follows the same general pattern, individual rates of growth may vary depending on life experiences and cognitive processes. "Children cannot become literate alone. They need the help of others to claim their own unique literacy" and early learning practitioners along with parents can rise to this challenge (McVicker, 2007, p. 18). Play is a key factor in developing literacy skills.

## Play and Language

**Oral language** is identified as the process used in developing communication skills and in facilitating both early reading and writing skills (Goswami, 2002; Watson, 2002). Early learning practitioners have a major role in providing learning environments that promote interpersonal communication among children and adults. The role modelling that occurs through body language, conversations, and print format in the various experience or learning centres and during play episodes helps children connect oral language, reading, print, and play to daily living.

As you begin to make the connections between play, language, and literacy, it is helpful to think about "literate behaviours." These are precursors to more specific literacy skills (Heath & Mangiola, 1991). **Literate behaviours** are methods of communication that are used, either verbal or nonverbal and that help the child identify needs or interests (Van Hoorn et al., 2007). For example, it is common for young toddlers to combine sounds with pointing at objects to communicate their desire for a particular object.

Vygotsky makes the connections between play, early learning experiences, and language development. Language development requires the child to have experiences that unite thoughts with language through inner speech. We describe **inner speech** as the silent speech that becomes part of our thought processes (Bruner, 1976). This internal process is influenced by the child's social network and psychological state. As the child engages in play, there is an internalization process that contributes to many facets of speech development (Fang & Cox, 1999). For example, when we observe children talking to themselves, they might be working out a problem, developing a plan or trying to figure out how something works. This process helps children to self-regulate their thoughts and actions. In essence, children are expressing literate behaviours that assist them in developing the framework for literacy development. Play and life experiences, including social skills and family interactions, add to the opportunities that children have for language and literacy skills to evolve (Berk & Spuhl, 1995).

Play experiences are essential for literate behaviours to develop. The examples below illustrate how children's play and language are connected.

1. Play provides children with the venue to express themselves in specific play experiences or as they explore an element of their environment. For example, Martin is trying to figure out how to build a tower that will be stable. He says, "If I place this big board on the block and then put smaller blocks on it, maybe my tower will stay." He is talking through possible solutions.

2. Play, such as solitary, parallel, and cooperative play (see Chapter 2 for further information) supports children in developing language, literacy, and communication skills. For example, in the sand area, Melinda and Max are using pails and shovels. Melinda fills hers and uses a wooden spoon to compact the sand. Max watches and then says, "Why do you want the sand to stick in the pail?" Melinda responds, "I don't know." Then a few minutes later she says, "I think it makes a pattern."

3. Unique play experiences help children incorporate new language into the play, which may further expand the quality and complexity of the play experience. For example, as Melinda thinks about the pail and the sand and as she tries to remove the sand from the pail, she realizes that it is compacted. She then says to Max, "Look what I did." Max and she then use other types of containers to get different shapes. With each success they giggle. When they had four different shapes Max said, "What will we make?" Melinda said, "Let's make a tower with a turret and a bridge that goes up and down."

4. Play leads children to explore and discover new knowledge, reframe information, or confirm knowledge including language and literacy skills. For example, Mia, a 4-year old child from China is learning English. Her peers help her with the pronunciation of words and matching words with objects.

Later in the chapter, we will examine the role of the early learning practitioner in supporting children with their language and literacy development. Children require early childhood environments and play experiences that will create and support opportunities for them to establish literate behaviours and make the interconnections of play to communication and language to culture and community.

# Characteristics of Language Development

Language development is a complex process. It is a gradual, sequential process. Early learning practitioners influence a child's vocabulary development and communication process through role modelling. They facilitate development through the play and language opportunities extended to children throughout their day. Children's language development flourishes in environments where language and literacy experiences are integrated into every aspect of the day's programming and experiences. In the block centre, for example, early learning practitioners provide paper, magazines, signs, and tools for writing signs. This approach supports children in linking play and learning to language and literacy development.

Language development includes the development of grammar, vocabulary, and pragmatics. Understanding the framework of each of these components helps early learning practitioners to incorporate language experiences into programming. Understanding the framework of each of these components helps early learning practitioners to incorporate language experiences into programming that reflects the developmental milestones common among each of the age groups and interests of individual children.

**Morphology** is the study and structure of the form of words including the use of plurals, possession, and tense in nouns and verbs (Frost, Wortham & Reifel, 2008).

**Syntax** refers to a set of grammatical rules that include word order and use of inflections. Children learn to ask questions and to make negative statements (Santrock, 2001).

**Semantics** involves the knowledge of meanings of words demonstrated through an expanding vocabulary (Frost, Wortham & Reifel, 2008).

**Grammar** By the age of 2, toddlers typically speak in two-word utterances mostly composed of nouns and verbs with some adjectives and adverbs. For example, "me go." By age of 5, a typical sentence can contain four or five words. For example, "I want to ride my bicycle." As children begin to use longer sentences, they demonstrate that they know grammatical rules such as the use of plurals, possession, and tense in nouns and verbs. These are considered the rules of **morphology,** which involves the structure of words. As children learn the order of words in a sentence, they are learning **syntax.** Morphology and syntax rules relate to the understanding of sounds and grammar of language. A third system of rules in language development is **semantics.** Semantics involves the meaning of words and vocabulary development (Frost, Wortham & Reifel, 2008).

**Vocabulary** When children are in stimulating play environments that offer challenge, new opportunities for exploration, and rich with language, they will acquire vocabulary at an astonishing rate of an average of five new words per day. As words are added to their vocabulary, children make basic assumptions about a word's meaning. Children use the words and hear them used in different contexts. Then, they refine their understanding of the meaning of a word (Berk, 2002). For example, Katie, age 3, said to her mother one day "The butterfly was astonishingly beautiful." Such vocabulary at the age of 3 is unusual. The exposure to butterflies and language had a significant impact on Katie's vocabulary.

**Pragmatics** The pragmatics of language refers to the rules for carrying out a conversation or communicating. Young children learn the rules of conversation such as eye contact and taking turns from their role models. By the age of 4, children have learned the acceptable way to communicate in their language community. They are able to adapt their language to different situations (Frost, Wortham & Reifel, 2008).

Early learning practitioners are guided by a language developmental milestones timetable, so that when observations are made of each child's language, their developmental phase relative to the timetable is determined. Table 7.1 provides the stages of language development as outlined by Weitzman and Greenberg (2002).

## Hanen Centre Stages of Language Development

Typically, children advance through the following six stages of communication and language development (Weitzman & Greenberg, 2002). The Hanen Centre stages of language development focus on children up to age 5. Below Table 7.1, information is provided on language development and older children.

*Table 7.1*  *Stages of Language Development*

| Stage | Time Frame | Characteristics |
| --- | --- | --- |
| Stage 1 Discover | Birth to eight months | At first, reflexive responses to physical needs, i.e. crying, fussing, and smiling. Interested in others but messages not sent directly. Feelings expressed through behaviour that you interpret. As the infant develops the ability to look at what or whom she wants, to move towards or reach for objects and produce a variety of sounds, interpretations are made easier. Between six or seven months babbling occurs (long strings of consonants and vowels repeated endlessly, i.e. "dadadadadadadada"). |
| Stage 2 Communicator | Eight to thirteen months | Messages are sent to others with a goal in mind. Very sociable and communicate with others because it is enjoyable. There is a willingness to share emotions, intentions, and interests—they have developed joint attention. Use conventional gestures like pointing, shaking her head "no," and waving "good-bye." Communicators also use sounds like they were words. "Guh" may mean "Look at that!" They may begin to use a few words. |
| Stage 3 First Words User | Twelve to eighteen months | First Words Users begin by using one or two first words, often accompanied by gestures, expanding to about 50 words. Capable of very brief conversations because receptive language abilities have developed. Some of their first words may be simplified versions of adult words, i.e. "baba" means "bottle." Particular words may have different meanings in different contexts. "Mama" could be a question ("Is that mama's purse?"), a comment ("There is Mama"), or a request ("Pick me up Mama"). Some words are used too broadly, i.e. "doggie" refers to all animals or too narrowly, i.e. "baba" is used to refer only to her bottle. |

*Continued*

| Stage | Time Frame | Characteristics |
|---|---|---|
| Stage 4 Combiner | Eighteen to twenty-four months | Vocabulary expands to about 200 words. Combiners first use single words, followed by combining single words into two-word sentences. Can engage in conversation. May be able to provide new information about a topic or ask a question. Responses may be inconsistent. One sentence can have different meanings in different situations (i.e. "Mommy car" can mean "That's Mommy's car" or "Mommy, I want to go in your car," or "I went home in Mommy's car." Negatives expressed by using the words "no" or "not," often at the beginning of a sentence (i.e. "no bye-bye"). They use "yes/no" questions by saying words with a questioning intonation, i.e. "Go bye bye?" They use "Wh" question words, like "Where?" or "What dat?" |
| Stage 5 Early Sentence User | Two to three years | Use two- to five-word sentences and can hold short conversations. They begin to ask "why" questions even though they themselves cannot answer "why" questions. They begin to tell stories, often with their narratives being disjointed and hard to follow. They begin to use language imaginatively and to express feelings. At this phase, children begin to understand that a pause in a conversation is a signal for them to take turns. |
| Stage 6 Later Sentence User | Three to five years | Can use long, complex sentences, most being more than four words long. They can hold conversations for extended periods of time. The use of grammar becomes more complex and correct. Use language to connect two or more ideas together. They produce sentences with verbs like think, wish, wonder, hope, remember, and pretend. Can use pronouns (I, you, she, we, and they) correctly and use auxiliary verbs (like are, is, can, do, and will) in questions, "You help me?" becomes "Will you help me?" Vocabulary is up to 5000 words. |

Adapted with permission from Weitzman and Greenberg (2002), *Learning Language and Loving It.* Toronto, ON: The Hanen Centre.

After 5 years of age, children's ability to use language increases rapidly including:

- Reaching a vocabulary of 40,000 words by grade five
- Understanding grammar by age of 6
- Becoming adept at pragmatic uses of language—they choose words, modify sentences or change voice inflections to fit the listener in a particular situation—i.e. simpler words and shorter sentences when talking to a younger sibling, code switching simpler words and shorter sentences when talking to a younger sibling, code switching when speaking to an adult (i.e. inserting the word "please") (Click, Parker, & Stone-Zukowski, 2006).

When children enter middle childhood, practitioners continue to have a responsibility to encourage language and literacy skills. Remember that language is crucial because it is the basis for social interactions. Early learning practitioners incorporate many opportunities for children to interact with others including shared reading, role playing, discussions, and debates. However, not all children will be as equally amenable to hold conversations. Some children are more social than others.

# CHILDREN'S CONVERSATIONAL ROLES

Weitzman and Greenberg (2002) indicate there are four conversational styles typical of young children. They are

- the sociable child
- the reluctant child
- the child with own agenda
- the passive child

These conversational styles are outlined in Table 7.2. They evolve from birth and are influenced by life experiences, role models, and how children see themselves through other people's eyes and—in later childhood—as they compare themselves to others. Understanding children's conversational styles helps you gain insight into why some children communicate naturally and why others find it difficult to do so. A child's conversational style guides the early learning practitioner

*Table 7.2*  *Children's Conversational Styles*

| 1. The Sociable Child | 2. The Reluctant Child |
|---|---|
| The sociable child initiates interactions constantly and is very responsive to others' initiations. Even in early infancy, sociable children initiate interactions to draw attention to themselves. | The reluctant child seldom initiates conversation and is often on the outside of group activities and interactions. He may take a long time to "warm up" when approached. Peer interactions may be more difficult for him than the social child. |
| 3. The Child with Own Agenda | 4. The Passive Child |
| The child with her own agenda spends a lot of time playing alone, appearing uninterested in interactions with adults and peers. She may initiate when she needs something, but she frequently rejects or ignores efforts to engage. | The passive child seldom responds or initiates conversation and demonstrates little interest in the objects or people around him. It can be very hard to elicit a smile or to engage the passive child in any sort of playful interaction. |

Adapted with permission from Weitzman and Greenberg (2002), *Learning Language and Loving It*. Toronto, ON: The Hanen Centre.

in how to approach each child. It also assists us in determining which strategies will be most effective in facilitating language experiences among individual children and with groups of children.

## OBSERVING, WAITING, AND LISTENING (THE HANEN CENTRE OWL STRATEGY)

You will note throughout this text that we advocate for observation and use of pedagogical documentation to be a consistent role that early learning practitioners incorporate into their practice. (Refer back to Chapter 3 for observation and documentation tools). Observing, waiting, and listening are not considered an observation tool but rather a strategy that students and practitioners employ to help children reach their fullest potential for conversations. **Observing** means paying close attention to the child so that you can gain insight into what the child is interested in and what they are trying to tell you. **Waiting** is a powerful tool because it gives the child an opportunity to initiate and to take control of their role in the conversation. **Listening** means paying close attention to what the child is saying so that you can respond appropriately (Weitzman & Greenberg, 2002). Sometimes practitioners are too quick to respond to children's actions with a question, and often it is a testing question, such as "What colour is it?" When the objective is to enhance conversation, testing questions can be a conversation stopper. Early learning practitioners employ the strategy of *observe, wait,* and *listen,* and watch children closely to determine the child's interests and then focus comments or questions on those interests. Sometimes by just pausing (waiting) before speaking, the child will have an opportunity to speak and will actually tell you their interest and aspirations. For more information about the Hanen Centre, see Box 7.1.

## BOX 7.1

### Profiling Learning Language and Loving It—The Hanen Centre
### www.hanen.org

The Hanen Centre is a Canadian charitable organization founded in 1975. The mission of the Hanen Centre is to provide the important people in a young child's life with the knowledge and training they need to help the child develop the best possible language, social, and literacy skills. Learning Language and Loving It™: The Hanen Program for Early Childhood Educators/Teachers is a research-based developmental approach to promoting children's social, language, and literacy development within everyday activities and conversations in a variety of early childhood settings including child care, preschool, and nursery and kindergarten programs. This includes children who are at risk for language delays, who have language disorders, or who are learning English as a second language.

Adapted with permission from Weitzman and Greenberg (2002), *Learning Language and Loving It.* Toronto, ON: The Hanen Centre.

# Language Skills and Play

As identified by Susan at the beginning of the chapter, early learning practitioners are often asked by parents how children will acquire the language and literacy skills needed if the children are *only* playing all day rather than receiving specific lessons and instructions. One of the key roles for early learning practitioners is to provide parents with meaningful examples of how children use drawings, scribbling, pretend writing, storytelling, and invented spelling in their play as precursors to the more formalized language and literacy skills that will be acquired in school settings. We describe the scaffolding process of language development and discuss the need for children to have a foundation in the use of language gained through tangible, concrete play before they are able to produce words in the printed format. When children are exposed to experiences that offer them a sense of curiosity and intrigue, such experiences motivate children in their play, which enhances their competency in their communication strategies during their play episodes.

**Children, play, and communication skills**   During spontaneous and guided play, children are communicating. They are involved in interaction among the people in their presence and in gathering information. Weitzman and Greenberg (2002) identify that children have seven reasons to communicate throughout their play processes. They are outlined in Table 7.3.

**Table 7.3**   *Reasons for Communication*

| Reasons for Communication | Examples |
|---|---|
| 1. To make a request | A toddler extends, holds his empty cup and says, "dah." The practitioner can interpret this as the child requesting more juice. |
| 2. To protest about something (complain, reject) | An infant cries in her crib because she is teething. |
| 3. To greet or take leave of someone | The preschooler waves good-bye at child care when her mother leaves. |
| 4. To respond to another person's communication | When the practitioner asks the 3-year-old, "What does your baby want to eat," the child responds "cookie." |
| 5. To ask for information (question) | A toddler points to the family cat and says, "Ah?" His mother responds, "The cat's name is Puffy." |
| 6. To think, plan, and problem solve | Two 4-year-olds, dressed as firefighters, are in the block centre. They have used hollow blocks to construct an enclosure. One child says to the other, "I'll yell, "FIRE!" and then you come and say, WHERE'S THE FIRE? and put it out." |
| 7. To share feelings, ideas, and interests | A child holds up a picture that she has painted and says, "Look what I made!" |

Adapted with permission from Weitzman and Greenberg (2002), *Learning Language and Loving It.* Toronto, ON: The Hanen Centre.

Halliday (1975) calls this process "learning how to mean", as children discover what they say translates to what can be done (Isenberg & Jalongo, 2001, p. 62). Children use communication to meet a variety of goals. For example, they communicate to think, to plan, and to problem solve. During pretend play, these communication strategies are evident because of the varying roles that children engage in. When children use language to plan a storyline for their dramatic play, they are using **metacommunication,** which is communicating about communication (Sawyer, 1997). Each of the seven communication areas are important for children to practice during their play because they formulate the foundation for their communication abilities and their abilities to express social/emotional attributes.

**Metacommunication** is when children communicate about how an interaction will take place. They constantly negotiate what and how they are playing, how they will continue to play, and often even negotiate interpretations of past play events (Sawyer, 1997).

**Children learn purposeful verbal interaction during play**    While children are playing they use language. They ask for materials. They express ideas or ask questions of others. For example, when children are role-playing during dramatic play, they plan the play, manage the play, problem solve, and maintain the play by verbal explanations, discussions, or commands. This process indicates highly developed language (Isenberg & Jalongo, 2002). A child learns verbal language best when the experience is meaningful and purposeful such as in sociodramatic play. Play is a meaningful context in which to embed language opportunities.

**Children learn to play with language**    Children use language during play and they play with language. As children grow, language play becomes more complex. Younger children playfully experiment with words, syllables, sounds, and grammatical structure. School-age children joke, make riddles, and use jump rope rhymes in their play with language. "These forms of language play require the transformational ability to explore the phonological, syntactic, and semantic rules of language" (Isenberg & Jalongo, 2002, p. 62). The words and meanings children learn depend on their experience and the language they hear (Roskos, Christie & Richgels, 2002). As a child's vocabulary expands, there is a need for many opportunities to use words. This requires early learning practitioners to develop opportunities to expose children to more complicated language and to be able to use it as required.

## Characteristics of Literacy Development

Play in the early years significantly impacts a child's literacy skills. Developmentally appropriate play experiences allow children to gain extraordinary powers that are essential foundational skills needed for later reading and writing. For example, sociodramatic play and literacy require children to utilize cognitive processes such as imaging, categorizing, and problem solving (Christie & Roskos, 2009). These cognitive processes are foundational to literacy development. As you examine the next section, think about your role as an early learning practitioner or student. Explore your thoughts about literacy and reflect on how the early learning environments that you have been exposed to have supported literacy practices. What aspects of literacy stand out for you?

Literacy development is related to language development. Children initially communicate most often through oral language. When children gain the ability to read and write, it extends their possibilities to transmit and receive information. From a development perspective, children are first exposed to print and written language through books. Initially, children are unable to interpret words in print or to write using adult forms of the alphabet or to use the standard spelling. As children become familiar with books and print in their environments (home and early learning settings) as well as oral language, they are making the connections between pictures, print, and language, while being exposed to principles needed to become literate. Children gradually understand that the print and not just the pictures give meaning to books. They begin to recognize print, as well as the spacing between words, and learn that individual letters are used to form words (Frost, Wortham & Reifel, 2008). Think about the excitement of children when they begin to recognize their names or produce their names on their artwork. When this occurs, it is a signal that a new phase of the child's language and literacy development is unfolding.

In 1966, New Zealand researcher Marie Clay introduced the phrase *emergent* to describe what children know about reading and writing before they begin to read and write in the conventional way. Clay created the *Reading Recovery Program,* a well-established intervention scheme for children with reading difficulties. The program identifies those having difficulty with reading early in their school career. The work of Marie Clay affirms the importance of the preschool years in the development of literacy skills. The more exposure younger children have to books and print, the less likely that they will need intervention. However, Clay reminds us that some children need extra resources and supportive interventions from practitioners to get to the stage of self-managed learning. The key to Clay's suggestion for intervention is that it is supportive and that an adult helps to *scaffold* children's learning and development (Yaden, Rose, & MacGillivray, 1999).

## Stages of Literacy Development

Children progress through stages as they develop literacy skills. The famous Bank Street College of Education identifies four stages of literacy development: *emergent literacy, early literacy, early fluent literacy,* and *fluent literacy.* Children as young as 3 years of age start to discover the printed word; they are in the stage of emergent literacy. Children begin to identify and reproduce letters. Then, they focus on the sounds within words (phonological awareness). They may even be able to write their own name and mix scribble, some letters, and drawing in "writing" notes and stories. When this occurs, they have moved into the **early literacy** stages somewhere between the ages of 3 and 5. Figure 7.1 illustrates the stages of literacy development.

Children between the ages of 5 through 8 begin to develop **early fluent literacy.** They figure out how the alphabet works. They learn to sound out words on a page and to write words phonically. As they attain more **fluent literacy,** reading becomes easier. As in most other areas of development, children do not follow one clear sequential path in a lock-step fashion. Rather, each child has the option of taking a variety of routes to reading and writing mastery. Literacy learning is circular or "recursive";

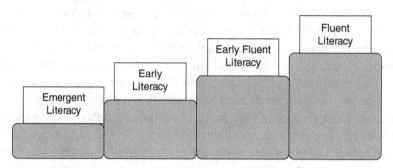

***Figure 7.1*** *Stages of Literacy Development*

learners may move forward in some areas and seem to step back as they consolidate understanding in other literacy areas. Thus, reading and writing may not develop evenly. A child may be fluent in one area and emergent in another. This is directly related to the child's brain development process.

## The Importance of Child Participation in Emerging Literacy

Children learn to construct meaning and comprehend text from exposure to books. Parents and early learning practitioners who read aloud to children are supporting emerging literacy. The way children respond to being read to provide adults with information on how to scaffold the language and literacy experiences for optimal development. How children respond when listening to books becomes more and more complex and varied as they get older. McVicker (2007) identifies three modes of reader response for preschoolers. They are:

1. **Imitation:** of language, language patterns, action, emotion, art, peers, literacy behaviours, and story.
2. **Imagination:** predicting, pretending, and creating props.
3. **Interaction:** group talk, questions, agreements and arguments, empathy talk, literacy talk, idea sharing, and role playing.

For school-age children there are seven modes of reader response as described by McVicker (2007). They are:

1. **Listening behaviour:** stretching to see, spontaneous laughter, chanting repetitive phrases, and nudging closer to the book.
2. **Contact with books:** browsing and choosing, attention to books, and proximity of books.

3. **Impulse to share:** reading together, telling about a book, sharing discoveries, and sharing connections.

4. **Action and drama:** echoing the actions, dramatic play, and reader's theatre.

5. **Making things:** visual representation, constructions, cooking, and musical response.

6. **Oral response:** retelling/storytelling, prompted responses, and literature discussions.

7. **Written response:** literature, response journals, and answers to teacher prompts.

It is important to understand that "child development is uneven" and that "many preschoolers also use some of the seven modes described for 5 to 12 year old children" (McVicker, 2007, p. 20).

# LITERACY SKILLS AND PLAY

Most children's first attempts at reading and writing will occur during sociodramatic play if appropriate reading and writing tools are present. Imagine setting up the dramatic play area with grocery story flyers, pictures of food with written labels, and paper and pencils to create shopping lists. Children can practice reading and writing as they play in the "grocery store." According to Isenberg and Jalongo (2002), their play can reveal the following literacy understandings:

1. **Interest in stories, knowledge of story structure, and story comprehension.** When children show eagerness to hear stories read aloud and they retell the stories in their own version, they are demonstrating interest in stories. When they retell the story and it has characters, a plot, a setting, goals and conflict, they show knowledge of story structure. Opportunities to act out the stories contribute to children developing or expanding their story comprehension skills.

2. **Understanding fantasy in books.** During dramatic play, children can enter the play world "as if" they were another character. When children develop the ability to transform oneself in play, it enables them to enter the fantasy world of books (Isenberg & Jalongo, 2002). This leads children to be exposed to *decontextualized* language. The benefit of supporting children in engaging in decontextualized language experiences is that it facilitates children experiencing the here and now and moving into the imaginary world of fantasy.

3. **Symbolic representation.** As children reinvent or create their own versions of stories it helps them to understand the world around them. Through play, children represent their understandings symbolically. They are able to represent their knowledge (Isenberg & Jalongo, 2002).

*Photo 7.2*    *A child retells a story about the seasons in a two dimensional representation—* *"the seasons change because they blow away."*

# NARRATIVES OR STORYTELLING

A narrative is the telling of a story. Between the ages of 3 and 4, children begin to develop their narrative skills. Narratives are thought to form from oral language to literacy. Stories require more complex language skills than are needed for daily conversations. Children begin to tell stories by recounting personal experiences. Stadler and Ward (2005) have identified five levels that children go through in the development of narratives.

1. **Labelling:** Giving labels to people and objects is a necessary stage for the development of narratives.

2. **Listing:** Children move from labelling to listing when their story focuses on a list of things, like a character's actions.

3. **Connecting:** At this stage the character's actions are linked to a central topic or certain events.

4. **Sequencing:** Once a child is able to use correct temporal sequencing and cause and effect, then he or she has moved from connecting to sequencing.

5. **Narrating:** This stage combines all of the components of the previous stages but now the child's story has a predictable beginning and end. Plots are more developed.

Early learning practitioners can encourage narrative development in children by the use of props such as pictures, sequences of pictures, wordless picture books, puppets, blocks and other constructive play materials, dramatic play props, and drawing and painting (Stadler & Ward, 2005) as catalysts for storytelling.

Vivian Paley is famous for telling stories of her practice as a kindergarten teacher, where she encouraged children to tell and act out their own narratives. She has written a dozen books on the topic including *Mrs. Tully's Room*, which illustrates that children as young as 2 years of age are capable of enacting their own stories, and *A Child's Work*, which explores the importance of fantasy play in the growth and development of young children. Fantasy play is the work of children. It is through this type of play that they learn. Paley illustrates that it is not only important to provide children with opportunities to tell and enact stories but when practitioners listen and try to make sense of the children's stories, they too are joining in an experience that scaffolds learning. Paley refers to Vygotsky's perspective, which indicates that children rise above their average behaviour in fantasy play and practitioners develop alongside as they encourage storytelling and dramatic play in their classrooms (Paley, 2004).

## Variations in Language and Literacy Development

While language and literacy development follows a predictable sequence, not all children will progress through the stages at the same rate. The variations are due to many factors, such as motivation, culture, gender, developmental delays, family background, and the child's native language. Early learning practitioners become familiar with each of these areas so that they can work with individual children and their families in appropriate ways.

**Motivation**    The research indicates that there are critical content areas for early literacy: oral language comprehension, phonological awareness, and print knowledge. Another critical factor that is emerging from the research is referred to as dispositions and these are not considered content areas. Katz (1993) suggests that a disposition be defined as a tendency to exhibit frequently, consciously, and voluntarily a pattern of behaviour that is directed to a broad goal. For example, if the goal is early literacy, the assumption is that children require the motivation to read and write. Print motivation is the frequency of requests for shared reading and engagement in print-related activities, such as pretend writing (Roskos, Christie, & Richgels, 2002). Early learning practitioners cultivate children's disposition to early literacy by creating environments that role-model literacy principles and practices. This would include facilitating, reinforcing, and becoming aware of "teachable moments" such as the following:

- willingness to listen to stories
- desire to be read to
- curiosity about words and letters

- exploration of print forms
- playfulness with words
- enjoyment of songs, poems, rhymes, jingles, books, and dramatic play (Roskos, Christie & Richgels, 2002)

**Atypical development**    Some children experience language delays for various reasons related to developmental abnormalities. Children with language delays follow the predictable sequences of development but may stay longer at individual stages. However, they may not necessarily become later sentence users in the preschool years (Weitzman & Greenberg, 2002). For example, children who are hearing-impaired face steep barriers to the acquisition of literacy skills. Children who are visually challenged are also at a higher risk for developing delays (National Strategy for Early Literacy, 2009). Speech and language delays may be the first signs of reading difficulties. Children with poor language skills are disadvantaged in learning to read because written language builds on a foundation in oral language skills (Snowing & Hulme, 2006). The early years are vital to support children with language delays.

**Culture**    Children enter early learning and child care environments with different family structures and cultures. Many families living in Canada today speak languages other than English or French in the home environment. As a result, children may enter early learning and child care programs and kindergarten programs with vast differences in their language skills (Frost, Wortham & Reifel, 2008). Regardless of the child's cultural background or first language, early learning practitioners should respect the diverse language skills that young children present.

Early learning practitioners appreciate that young children need to develop proficiency in their native language as well as English or French. While some children are *bilingual* or even *multilingual*, speaking more than one language should be seen as beneficial for all children (Jalongo, 2000). Early learning practitioners and children celebrate each child's cultural background and reach out to involve the parents in the program. This partnership not only supports the children, it also helps parents and practitioners in developing strategies to facilitate each stage of the child's language development in the languages that the child is learning. Preschool children may become frustrated because of their limited communication skills in a particular language. Often they will exhibit their frustration through unacceptable behaviours such as biting, bullying, and temper tantrums.

Exposing young children to the various languages spoken by the children is an effective strategy in modelling an atmosphere of respect and appreciation of cultural diversity. Early learning practitioners acknowledge the social nature of language. This means that children will want to communicate with their peers. School-aged children will not only want to learn the language but they will be striving to gain cultural knowledge as well.

**English language learners**   The term English Language Learners (ELLs) is used to identify children whose native language is not English and who are learning English as a second or third language. When working with preschoolers whose first language is not English, it is important that the child receive input that is comprehensible and above their level of competence. This method of scaffolding is an important technique when working with second language learners because it advances the child's ability to figure out words and their meanings in various contexts. Early learning practitioners, through observations, offer experiences that build on the strengths of each child. The environment reflects the language and culture of the children present. Children are encouraged to continue to develop their first language at the same time as they develop a second language.

**Family**   The family is the earliest learning environment (Haney & Hill, 2004) that children are exposed to. Parents play a crucial role in their child's early learning experiences, including building strong language and literacy skills. Jalongo (2000) suggests that of all the influences of children's language growth, parents and families are the most important. The environment that parents provide, combined with their attitude towards learning language and literacy skills, makes a substantial contribution to the child's development. Early learning practitioners can encourage *family literacy*, as this contributes to providing children with the optimal emerging literacy development opportunities.

Family literacy programs focusing on developing literacy within the family as a whole help parents to create literacy-rich home environments (National Strategy for Early Literacy, 2009). In 1999, ABC CANADA Literacy Foundation acclaimed January 27 as Family Literacy Day in Canada. The purpose of Family Literacy Day is to encourage families to read and learn together because it is well documented that literacy begins at home. Thousands of Canadians take part in Family Literacy Day events and activities at early learning and child care programs, schools, libraries, and literacy organizations. In 2003, Robert Munsch, the famous Canadian author of more than 50 children's books, became the Honorary Chair of Family Literacy Day.

**Other variations**   Researchers who have studied familial and cultural differences in the language that children hear indicate that mothers talk with daughters more than with sons. This suggests that there are gender variations in language development. Middle class parents use more elaborate language with their children than parents from lower socioeconomic environments. This means there can be socioeconomic variations in language development. Parents generally talk more to first-born children than later-born children and multiple-birth children. This suggests that there can be birth-order variations in language development (Frost, Wortham & Reifel, 2008). Research helps early learning practitioners understand variations in language and literacy.

# Research Connections

## Emerging Knowledge about Emergent Writing

According to Mayer (2007), the research on the importance of early writing experiences pales in comparison to research on early reading. "To focus on reading alone disregards the importance of children's experiences with writing. Reading and writing skills develop simultaneously and are interconnected" (p. 34). Theorists suggest that children begin to explore writing by drawing and scribbling. "*Emergent writing* means that children begin to understand that writing is a form of communication and their marks on paper convey a message" (p. 35). Research shows that children who have opportunities to learn about writing through interactions with peers and practitioners will provide a base for literacy development that supports reading *and* writing.

# THE ROLES OF EARLY LEARNING PRACTITIONERS

Similar to other aspects of play and learning, early learning practitioners have a variety of important roles to execute in order to support language and literacy experiences and opportunities for young children. Early learning practitioners are important role models for children. Because language and literacy skills are being developed at an incredible pace during the early years, and are influenced by the adults in their lives, early learning practitioners must exhibit appropriate language skills. As you examine this section, you will note the influence that you, the environment, and the experiences within the environment have on a child developing foundational language and literacy skills.

## Early Learning Practitioner Interactions

The Learning Language and Loving It program identifies seven different "teacher roles" related to the development of language and literacy. The way an early learning practitioner interacts with a child is likely to vary, depending on every child and situation.

**The director role**    In this role, the practitioner maintains tight control over the children and their activities. The focus is on making suggestions, giving directions, and asking questions. The adult behaviour tells children that they are not expected to initiate, just to respond as directed. While an early learning practitioner needs to direct children some of the time, if this is the predominant role, it makes it very difficult for children to be spontaneous and to play an active role in interactions.

**The entertainer role**    In this role, the early learning practitioner is playful and fun to be with. She typically does most of the talking and playing, giving children few opportunities to get actively involved in the interaction.

**The timekeeper role**    In this role, the early learning practitioner rushes through activities and routines in order to stay on schedule. Busy schedules are a fact of life but this role can and does result in very limited interactions.

**The too-quiet teacher role**    In this role, the early learning practitioner sits with the children but hardly interacts with them, even when they initiate dialogue.

**The helper role**    In this role, the early learning practitioner thinks that a child won't be able to express his thoughts so the adult speaks for the child or offers help before the child has shown any need for it. This may reflect an early learning practitioner's desire to help a child or to reduce frustration. It may result in the child learning not to expect much from himself or herself.

**The cheerleader role**    In this role, the early learning practitioner gives the child lots of praise and gets very excited when a child accomplishes a task, large or small. Words of encouragement such as "Good", "Good job!" are often expressed. Positive reinforcement is evident. Children seem to get pleasure from praise. The disadvantage of praise is that children can become too dependent on it and may not develop their own motivation to learn new skills or take on new challenges. In addition, cheerleaders often end the conversation with their praise—the interaction seldom continues after the child has been praised.

**The responsive partner role**    In this role, the early learning practitioner is tuned into the children's abilities, needs, and interests. The adult responds with warmth and interest to each child, which encourages them to take an active part in interactions, both with the adult and with their peers.

**Interaction and information**    The experiences that an early learning practitioner provides to encourage language and literacy development are as important as how the practitioner responds to children's words and stories. The more opportunities children have to speak in the environment, especially with adults, the more extensive and advanced their vocabulary will be when they enter kindergarten (Dickinson, 2001). Children need to progress from *learning to talk* to *talking to learn*—the latter is dependent on the ability to use decontextualized language, which is language removed from the here-and-now (Dickinson & Tabors, 2001). An example of a here-and-now context is a practitioner speaking to a child about a snack. An example of the use of decontextualized language is an adult sharing a storybook with young children. Here, children have the opportunity to use language in more complex and abstract ways not connected to their current context. Written language is also decontextualized, that is, the sender and receiver of a written communication usually do not share the same space (Roskos et al., 2002).

Early learning practitioners encourage interaction and provide information when they share books with children. As a student, it is beneficial to take every opportunity you can to read to children. Reading aloud is one of the most successful strategies for promoting emergent literacy skills among preschool-aged children. Small group interactive reading improves children's vocabulary and print awareness and in some cases emerging writing skills (Halle et al., 2003).

# Stop . . . Think . . . Discuss . . . Reflect

If small group interactive reading was successful in improving children's vocabulary, print awareness, and emerging writing skills, do you think a large group reading activity would be equally as successful? Imagine reading to a group of four preschool children. Now imagine reading to a group of 24.

Students and early learning practitioners can encourage interaction and provide information by asking children questions. There are two common types of questions we use when conversing with children: closed questions and open-ended questions.

**Closed Questions:**

- Require a nonverbal response or a one- or two-word answer from children
- Tend to have right or wrong answers
- Are ones for which adults already know the answers
- Require a "quick" response
- Focus on facts and similarity in thinking
- Ask for information and focus on labelling or naming
- Require the child to recall something from memory

**Open-Ended Questions:**

- Promote multi-word, multi-phrase responses from children
- Have more than one correct answer
- Are questions for which adults don't know what children's answers might be
- Allow children time to formulate and collect their thoughts
- Focus on ideas and originality in thinking
- Ask for reasoning
- Focus on thinking and problem solving
- Require the children to use their imagination

What type of questions do you think are preferable? Many students are guided to use open-ended questions to encourage children's language. However, early learning practitioners should strive for natural conversations with children. Sometimes it is alright to ask a closed question within the context of a back and forth dialogue. Perhaps, preferable to both the closed and the open-ended question is the **cognitively challenging** or **thought-provoking question.** Instead of asking a child "What shape is the structure?" ask the child to tell you what the structure is. When the child replies that it is "a house," ask "Who lives in the house?" When a child holds up a shell to his ear, don't end the conservations by asking the closed question, "What do you hear?" Continue the conversation by provoking the child's thinking by asking, "How did the sound of the ocean get into the shell?" These types of questions challenge the child to think deeply. When you test children's knowledge and ask questions such as, "What colour is it?" or "What shape is it?" children will have their comfort reduced in the environment. They will feel as though they are always being tested. An early learning environment that supports language and literacy development is about encouraging conversations to occur during play and providing opportunities to support these experiences with print.

# THE EARLY LEARNING ENVIRONMENT

Adding literacy-rich areas to the child's play environment improves children's phonological awareness (Halle et al., 2003). Increasing the amount of environmental print in the play space increases the likelihood of children engaging in literacy-related play activities (Neuman & Roskos, 1993). There is a need to find balance with print materials. When the environment becomes saturated with print materials, it will detract from a child's ability to engage with the print. Roskos, Christie, and Richgels, (2002) suggest that early literacy experiences should be embedded in the basic activities of early learning—these include reading aloud, group time, small group activities, adult–child conversations, and play. When early learning practitioners partner with children in their play experiences, there are opportunities to enrich literacy. A literacy-enriched play environment exposes children to valuable print experiences and lets them practice narrative skills (Christie & Roskos, 2003).

## Creating a Community Culture for Language and Literacy

How can you create a community culture in an early learning environment that supports language and literacy? Consider the following principles to support a literacy-rich environment:

- Reading and writing are tools. Adults and children should read and write to accomplish many goals. Reading and writing should be incorporated in activities throughout the day. When literacy is seen as a tool, it becomes an integral part of life, not just an isolated skill to be taught.

*Photo 7.3   Children playing with letters and numbers.*

- Children learn about written language by being in an environment where it is used. Adults model their use of written language for the children in their care. Seeing the power of written language makes children want to have this power.
- Children are provided with opportunities to experiment with print.
- Children need to see that written symbols can communicate, can stretch their knowledge, and that they can gain meaning from these symbols.
- The environment and the programming schedule provide time, space, and materials to the children while the adults respond to the children as members of the literate community.
- Children are provided with opportunities to share their writing and ideas with each other.
- Children are exposed to free-flowing child-initiated and child-directed activities, rather than a structured program.
- Children are encouraged to link symbols with having meaning in order to comprehend the meaning of letters and words.
- Children are given the opportunity to read and use pictorial symbols in the early learning environment so they can become confident in their ability to interpret symbols.

**Observations**   An early learning practitioner should be able to observe children experiencing language and literacy, every minute of every day. A good way for an early learning student practitioner to begin to learn about language and literacy is through books. Can you remember a particular book from your own childhood? From Dr. Seuss to Robert Munsch, we probably all have books that resonate within each of us. What is your favourite book? What draws you to that book? What questions do you have about the story? Did you ever wonder about the story—about what happens to the characters after the book is finished? Did the story make you think? In Chapter 8, we discuss the topic of wonder in children's play experiences. Books can be wonders too. Books can be provocative—they can make you think, question, speculate, predict, and theorize. Introduce a small group of children to your favourite book. Create a schematic map or web with the children about what they wonder about the book. Give the children opportunities to draw their theories. Then record their ideas, questions, and theories to create a documentation panel that illustrates the children's learning.

When choosing books to read to children, consider these guidelines:

1. Select books that you enjoy. Children know when you are reading something you don't like (you lack enthusiasm). Starting with your favourite childhood story is one way to ensure that you are enthusiastic about reading the book.

2. Choose a book with appropriate content for the children. Be sure they can identify with at least some parts of the book and its characters.

3. Analyze books for unfavourable racial stereotypes and sexism.

4. Consider the length of the text (not too long), the illustrations (bright, colourful), the size (big enough for everyone to see in a group setting), and the content (is it too complex, can children "participate" in the story?).

5. Consider the author's style. Is it enjoyable? Is the vocabulary clear? Are the phrases memorable? Look for repetition and rhyme in the story. Consider the climax and end of the book. Do these exist? Are they satisfying? Is there humour in the book?

6. Pick a book with educational value. Be sure the book expands children's knowledge in some way (new vocabulary, new understanding).

7. Be sure the illustrations in the book match the text. Do they coordinate with the text and explain what is happening in the story?

Reading to children can be a most enjoyable experience for an adult, but it can also be challenging. How do you hold the book so that a group of children can see the illustrations? Often it is preferable to hold the book in front of you and read upside down. This is a skill that requires practice. During the reading of the story, you can also pause when illustrations appear and slowly move the book so that it scans the whole group. This way, you may not hear the children exclaim over and over, "I can't see!"

**The dramatic play centre**   Literacy-related play has its roots in the theories of Piaget (1952) and Vygotsky (1978), who both suggest that children learn through play. Dramatic play has been of most interest to literacy researchers (Yaden, Rose, & MacGillivray, 1999). Dramatic play fosters communication, conversational skills, turn-taking, and perspective-taking as well as the skills of social problem solving, persuading, negotiating, compromising, and cooperating. Play requires complex communication skills: children must be able to communicate and understand the message, "this is play." A great deal of child-initiated play involves acting out life experiences. These experiences often involve printing, drawing, "reading," and "writing." When a group of children engage in play, it almost always requires speech. Children use speech to direct the play and act out these life situations. When we consider these simple aspects of play, it begins to become evident that language is a key part of play and play is a key part of language development.

Children are eager to talk to one another so that they can choose characters and settings ("Let's play house in the kitchen centre. I'm the mommy!"). Language is used to establish roles and direct action. As the children take on different roles, they experiment with the language that fits the role. Communication is used to assign roles, define objects, and define action. Children become very adept at moving in and out of roles; first they are director, then an actor. Eventually the children will become such good communicators that they will be able to direct play without leaving their acting role.

Written language is a system of symbols and so is dramatic play. Children use objects and symbols to represent the things they are imagining. This practice with symbols is a good basis for later language development. Finally, dramatic play is child-directed, allowing each child to move at his or her own pace. This means that children are able to participate comfortably at their own level of literacy. Here is a list of items to include in your dramatic play centre to encourage language and literacy:

- Note pads for doctor's prescriptions or grocery lists
- Phone message pads for secretaries and notebooks for waiters
- Maps, tickets, letters, and blueprints in the block centre and lots and lots of books
- Clothing, tools, and utensils to spark dramatic play

**Writing and book centres**   Experience centres can be set up to have a specific language and literacy focus. Provide ample tools for printing and writing. Label bookshelves and other equipment. Help children make their own books. Encourage children to "write" notes, lists, or letters to one another, the early learning practitioners, and their families. Provide writing materials and print in different forms: phone books, coupons, magazines, resource books, etc. Include office supplies, such as envelopes, in your writing centre that would encourage the children to communicate in print.

**Shared group reading with children**   Reading with children is an important support for their language development. The smaller the group, the more likely the early learning practitioner will be able to interact and provide information to scaffold the children's learning. However, many educators use the commonly referred to "circle" experience as the only time to read to children. These group experiences are often uncomfortable for children if they are forced to sit for long periods of time. "Reading aloud with children is a time-honored and effective way to introduce books and promote literacy skills" (McVicker, 2007, p. 19). Reading to children is most successful when early learning practitioners and students read to smaller groups of children as well as individual children, as much as possible throughout the day's schedule.

*Photo 7.4   Art and literacy are connected.*

**The art centre**   Children love to talk about their artwork. Asking them to describe what they have drawn or painted is a way to encourage children to use language. When children are creating their artwork, they are also practising the fine motor skills necessary to develop the ability to print. All types of art materials support language and literacy development. Offer children a variety of art forms, techniques, and materials, and make them readily available to use. Children can describe to you the materials they are using or the picture or structure they have created. Consider transcribing the children's stories about their art. Have books about art and artists available for children in the environment.

**Math and science**   When writing materials are added to math and science experience centres, it is easy to make literacy connections. Early learning practitioners label materials and provide resource books and reference materials. Cooking with children is a great way for children to practice language, math, and science skills. The use of recipe cards with both pictures and words provide the opportunity for the child to see how the printed word connects to a concrete object. There are many cookbooks geared towards young children. These can be displayed in the classroom along with cookbooks created by the practitioners and children. Materials can be labelled with both written words and diagrams. As children observe nature (plants, animals) and perform experiments with materials, they can graph growth and changes.

**Blocks**   When reading and writing materials are introduced in block play, children's language and literacy development is enhanced. Children can make signs and labels for their structures. If drawing materials are provided they can sketch their structures. Blocks enhance literacy development because children can practice symbolic representation—the blocks can become whatever the child likes. Children can use blocks, boxes, and other materials to create structures that represent a fantasy world. Ask children to tell the story of the world they created. Books about buildings and building things and architectural magazines add print to the block centre.

*Photo 7.5*   *Creating a graph—math and literacy connected.*

**Outdoor play**   Outdoor play provides opportunities for children to use language playfully as they run, jump, climb, and explore. Encourage children to describe their actions expressively. Add materials to the outdoor environment to encourage exploration. Consider bringing traditional indoor activities such as reading, writing, and drawing outside.

**Music and movement**   Children can learn language and develop literacy skills by listening to music, moving to music, and creating their own music. Offer children a variety of instruments and materials to make instruments. When songs have accompanying movements, children learn to connect the words of the song to the movement, much like making the connection between the words of a book and the illustrations.

# SETTING UP A LITERACY-RICH ENVIRONMENT

When designing areas in the early learning environment that promote language and literacy, early learning practitioners examine where to place a learning or experience devoted to

*Photo 7.6*   *Diagrams and photos added to the block centre—blocks and literacy connected.*

reading in the play environment. The library or reading centre is generally placed in an area that is visually and physically accessible, and is partitioned from the rest of the room to encourage quiet exploration of books and other print materials. The area could have a rug, pillows, and a rocking chair (to encourage adults and children to share books). Bookshelves are used for storing books and a system to organize the books such as by genre or reading level is evident. Generally, there are five to eight books per child available and there are a variety of types of books to represent different reading levels and interests, such as big books, board books, and chapter books for older children. These could include picture books, poetry, informational or resource books, biographies, magazines, newspapers, and brochures. Felt boards with story characters and puppets enhance the reading experience. Books and print material are rotated so that children do not become bored with the resources. A good library centre would also have multiple copies of the same book to encourage shared reading among children. The area would be further enhanced with a system of checking books out and in as well as a way to record books read (Morrow, 2001).

To encourage literacy knowledge and skills, a writing centre is recommended. The writing centre has a table and chairs for the children to sit on, and writing posters and bulletin boards for the children to display their writing themselves. There are a variety of writing utensils such as pens, pencils, crayons, markers, and coloured pencils; writing materials include paper in all sizes and types, booklets, and pads. Materials for writing stories and making them into books, as well as folders in which to place writing samples, are made available (Morrow, 2001). A message board or mailboxes, as you find in a Reggio-inspired classroom, are known to encourage the children to write (Fraser & Gestwicki, 2001). A computer is another tool that supports children writing stories.

The early learning play space has literacy materials in all centres. Materials are changed often to reflect the children's interest. For example, in the science centre there will be books on the current project topic and in the music area posters of songs related to the topic. All centres offer environmental print, such as signs, webs, charts, and graphs related to the project topic. Each centre has a set of rules that are developed in collaboration with the children as well as functional messages. Every centre has appropriate books, magazines and newspapers, writing utensils, a variety of papers and clipboards to make the writing process more mobile. A word wall is an excellent example of the way to promote children's vocabulary (Morrow, 2001). A calendar is included in the classroom but students and practitioners should exercise caution when using the calendar (see Chapter 13).

# SUMMARY

## Chapter Preview

- Language is everywhere. Children are exposed to language in their homes, schools, and their communities. Language and the corresponding literacy skills are essential developmental milestones that impact a child's lifelong cognitive, social, and emotional attributes.

- Early learning practitioners and families have important roles to play in supporting young children to use language in a variety of ways.

## Theoretical Frameworks

- The three common theoretical frameworks that influence the work that adults do with children associated with language and literacy development include behaviourist theory (B. F. Skinner), nativist theory (N. Chomsky), and interactionist theory (L. Vygotsky).
- According to the theories of Vygotsky through *scaffolding,* learners are able to cross the zone of proximal development.

## From Theory to Trends

- Generally, there are two approaches to reading: Phonics and Whole Language. The trend has been that these are the only two approaches. Debate continues over which method is preferable.
- Today, the research in early literacy is providing new approaches and understanding that differ from the tenets of both traditional Phonics or Whole Language philosophies.
- Early learning practitioners are being encouraged to base their choice of approach on observation of children and respond with appropriate materials and experiences that support the child's developmental phase and interests.

## Defining Language

- Language development is categorized as receptive and expressive language. **Receptive language** is the ability to listen and understand the spoken, signed, or written word. **Expressive language** is the ability to communicate; to use language; what a child says or signs and eventually this includes what the child writes.

## Defining Literacy Development

- **Literacy** is commonly defined as the ability to read and write the *printed* text that represents spoken language—to be literate.
- Literacy is continually evolving through interactions with others and the environment. While the sequence of literacy development follows the same general pattern, individual rates of growth may vary depending on life experiences and cognitive processes.

## Play and Language

- **Oral language** is identified as the process used in facilitating both early reading and writing skills.
- Literate behaviours are the precursors to more specific literacy skills. Literate behaviours are methods of communication used, either verbal or nonverbal that help the child identify needs or interests.
- Play experiences are essential for literate behaviours to develop because they provide children with the venue to express themselves. Play supports children in developing language, literacy, and communication skills, and play experiences help children incorporate new language into the play. Play and knowledge are also closely aligned.

## Characteristics of Language Development

- Language includes the development of grammar, vocabulary, and pragmatics. When children use longer sentences, they begin to demonstrate grammatical rules such as plurals, possession, and tense in nouns and verbs.
- When children are in stimulating play environments, they will acquire vocabulary at an astonishing rate of an average of five new words per day.

- The pragmatics of language refers to the rules for carrying out a conversation or to communicate. Children learn acceptable ways to converse and are able to adapt to different situations.

## Hanen Centre Stages of Language Development

- The Hanen stages of language development include six stages focused on children up to age 5 and the characteristics of their development. After age 5, children continue to develop vocabulary, grammar, and pragmatics.

## Children's Conversational Roles

- There are four conversational roles for children. They can either be sociable, reluctant, a child with their own agenda, or passive.
- A child's conversational style guides the early learning practitioner in how to approach the child. It helps us to determine what will be most effective in facilitating language experiences among individual children and with groups of children.

## Observing, Waiting, and Listening (the OWL strategy)

- The OWL strategy can help children reach their fullest potential for conversations. Observing means paying close attention to the child to ascertain the child's interest and what he or she is trying to tell you. Waiting involves pausing so that the child has an opportunity to initiate and to take control of their role in the conversation. Listening means to pay close attention to what the child is saying to respond appropriately.

## Language Skills and Play

- During spontaneous and guided play, children are communicating. Children have seven reasons to communicate throughout their play processes: to make a request, to protest, to greet or to take leave, to respond to another, to ask for information, to think and plan, and to share feelings, ideas, or interests.
- When children use language to plan a storyline and assign roles, they are using metacommunication, which is communication about communication.
- While children are playing they use language. They ask for materials. They express ideas or ask questions of others. Children learn purposeful verbal interaction during play.

## Characteristics of Literacy Development

- Children initially communicate most often through oral language. When children do gain the ability to read and write, it extends their possibilities to transmit and receive information.
- Children are first exposed to print and our written language through books. By building on oral language development with books and environmental print, young children are exposed to principles needed to become literate.
- Initially when children are exposed to books they are unable to interpret words in print or to write using adult forms of the alphabet or to use the standard spelling. With exposure they make the connections between print and language.
- Children progress through stages as they develop literacy skills. The four stages of literacy development are *emergent, early, early fluent,* and *fluent* literacy.

## The Importance of Child Participation in Emerging Literacy

- The way children respond to being read to offers parents and early learning practitioners opportunities to scaffold language and literacy development. Reader response becomes more and varied as they get older. McVicker (2007) identified three ways preschoolers and seven ways school-age children respond when listening to books.

## Literacy Skills and Play

- Most children's first attempts at reading and writing will occur during sociodramatic play where the appropriate reading and writing tools are present. Their play can reveal the following literacy under-standings: (1) Interest in stories, knowledge of story structure, and story comprehension; (2) Understanding fantasy in books; and (3) Symbolic representation.

## Narratives or Storytelling

- A narrative is the telling of a story. By age of 3 or 4 children begin to develop their narrative skills. Narratives are thought to form from oral language to literacy. Stories require more complex language skills than are needed for daily conversations.
- There are five levels children go through in the development of narratives including labelling, listing, connecting, sequencing and finally, narrating.

## Variations in Language and Literacy Development

- While language and literacy development follow a predictable sequence, not all children will progress through the stages at the same rate. The variations are due to many factors such as motivation, culture, gender, developmental delays, family background, socioeconomic levels, birth order, and whether English is the child's native language.

## The Roles of Early Learning Practitioners

- There are seven different "teacher roles" related to the development of language and literacy. The way an early learning practitioner interacts with a child is likely to vary, depending on the child and situation. These roles have been identified as the director, the entertainer, the timekeeper, the too-quiet teacher, the helper, the cheerleader, and the responsive partner role. The final role of responsive partner is the most effective in supporting children's language development.
- The more opportunities children have to speak in the environment, especially with adults, the more extensive and advanced their vocabulary when they enter kindergarten. Children need to progress from *learning to talk* to *talking to learn*; the latter is dependent on the ability to use decontextualized language, which is language removed from the here-and-now.
- Closed, open-ended, cognitively challenging or thought-provoking questions are all questioning tech-niques that early learning practitioners use with children. Each technique encourages different responses and language.

## The Early Learning Environment

- Adding literacy-rich areas to the child's play environment improves children's phonological awareness. Increasing the amount of environmental print in the play space increases the likelihood of children engaging in literacy-related play activities. Early literacy experiences are embedded in the basic activities of early learning—these include reading aloud, group time, small group activities, adult–child conversa-tions, and play.
- An early learning practitioner should be able to observe children experiencing language and literacy; every minute of every day. A good way for an early learning student practitioner to begin to learn about language and literacy is through books.

# REVIEW QUESTIONS

1. Explain the importance of oral language development.
2. What is the difference between literacy and emergent literacy?
3. Outline the relationship of play to language and literacy development.
4. If a child that you are working with is not engaging in conversation with others, how would you scaffold the child's oral language development?
5. Describe each of the Hanen Centre stages of language development.
6. Name and describe the three theories of language acquisition. Why do you think that at least one of these views is controversial?
7. Describe the three stages of reader's response in preschoolers and the seven stages in school-age children.
8. What guidelines are used when choosing a book to read to children?
9. Give three examples each of closed, open-ended, and thought-provoking or cognitively challenging questions.
10. What is meant by decontextualized knowledge?

# MAKING CONNECTIONS

## Theory to Practice

1. Look at the description of the practitioner's roles in this chapter. Do you see yourself in one of these roles? How about others that you have observed in early learning classrooms? Write a few paragraphs to reflect on the roles that you have seen both in yourself and others.
2. Can you remember your favourite book as a child? Do you still have it? If not, see if you can find a copy in the library or purchase it from a local bookstore. Think about why it is meaningful to you. Share your favourite book with your classmates or colleagues and discuss why you have chosen this book. Reflect on whether this book would be suitable to share with the children that you are currently working with. If it isn't, reflect on why. Record the names of the books that were shared. You now have a list of book titles to add to your own personal library.
3. Try to visualize the last early learning environment that you spent time in. Was the environment set up to encourage language and literacy? If your answer is yes, write down the ways in which it supported language and literacy? If your answer is no, write down what could have been done in the environment.

## For Further Research

1. Beyond the Journal is an online free source of *Young Children* articles, columns and Web resources from the American organization, NAEYC (National Association for the Education of Young Children). In "Beyond the Journal," May 2007, you'll find articles related to the theme "Beyond the Library Corner: Incorporating Books throughout the Curriculum." Go to the website http://www.naeyc.org/files/yc/file/200705/ClusterResources.pdf and create a list of books that you could use in your work with children.
2. The quote that begins this chapter comes from the National Strategy for Early Literacy prepared by the Canadian Language and Literacy Research Network and can be found at http://docs.cllrnet.ca/NSEL/finalReport.pdf. The report details the importance of language and literacy, identifies the challenges and barriers and makes recommendations. Download a copy and look at the recommendations on pages 38 and 42. Based on these recommendations, pick one and come up with an action plan for what you could do on a local level to help children develop their language and literacy skills?

3. The Canadian Language and Literacy Research Network offers a resource kit available to early learning practitioners. This resource kit is based on research into how young children develop the ability to use language and to read and write. Download the kit and see if you find effective ways to enhance the support you give to children in developing their language and literacy skills. The kit is available at http://frombirthforlife.ca/index.php/Main_Page.

## ADDITIONAL READING

Clay, M. (1998). By *different paths to common outcomes*. York, ME: Stenhouse Publishers.

Dickinson, D. K., & Sprague, K. E. (2001). The nature and impact of early childhood care environments on the language and early literacy development of children from low-income families. In Susan B. Neuman & David K. Dickinson (Eds.), *Handbook of early literacy research* (pp. 263–280). New York: Guilford Press.

## WEBLINKS

Halle, Tamara; Calkins, Julia; Berry, Daniel; & Johnson, Rosalind. (2003, September). Promoting language and literacy in early childhood care and education settings. *Child Care and Early Education Research Connections.*

**www.abc-canada.org**

**www.bnkst.edu/literacyguide/early.html**

**www.ccl-cca.ca/pdfs/ECLKC/bulletin/ECLKCBulletinLanguage.pdf**

**www.childcaresearch.org/childcare/resources/2796**

**www.famlit.ca**

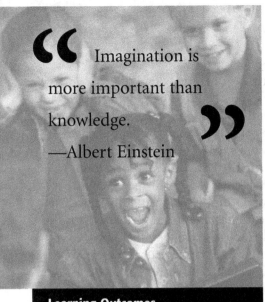

# 8 Math and Science

## Learning Outcomes

After exploring this chapter you should be able to

- define math and science and relate them to development, play, and academics;
- explain the importance of math and science in learning;
- describe what is meant by wonderment with young children and compare this to adults;
- describe the processes of the scientific method and relate them to play;
- explain mathematical concepts and the relationship of the environment to math learning; and
- describe the role of the early learning practitioner in relationship to programming for math and science.

## Stories from the Field: Practitioner to Student

I always hated math and found science difficult in school. I don't remember talking much about either subject when I studied early childhood education. I feel strongly about professional development and I have been taking workshops for years on the areas that really fascinate me but to be honest I have largely ignored math and science experiences in my programming. Yes, I put out math manipulatives every day and I have a small discovery centre in the play space that I change seasonally but that is about all. I know this is not enough. I am secure enough in my abilities as an early learning practitioner to admit that I need to change in order to better address all areas of children's learning. I need to overcome my negative disposition to math and science as this reduces my ability to facilitate the math and science discoveries that can happen every day in my early learning environment.

*Fariba, ECE Graduate, 2007*

## CHAPTER PREVIEW

Do you think that math and science as content areas belong in early learning programming? It has been our experience that these programming topics are often overlooked in the early years. Why do you think this might be? Could it have something to do with how students and practitioners feel about math and science? Perhaps, it is because early learning practitioners associate math and science with a level of difficulty they experienced while in secondary school. Some may view these as academic subjects that are best left for children to learn about when they enter their formal school experience.

Math and science experiences at an early age can offer young children power-ful ways of knowing about the world. The earlier children have opportunities to explore and discover the array of math and science topics, the better prepared they will be for more formal study in later years. For young children, these experiences do not have to be rigid or formal. Math and science experiences for young children should not be equated with formalized structured programming; it should involve hands-on exploration and discovery through their play experiences. Young children, when given the opportunity, will naturally engage in thoughtful and challenging mathematical concepts and scientific theory. It is the process of science and mathematics learning, not the content, that really counts with young children. By playing with scientific and mathematical concepts, children are learning. Think of the children using blocks and planks for construction. Through this play, children are learning about measurement, balance, formulas, symmetry, weight, height, and inclines. These are the foundational skills that are used in more advanced math and science experiences. When young children are not afforded the opportunities to gain these principles during their early years, through hands-on experiences, it influences their abilities to grasp the concepts from an abstract thinking process.

There has been a large demand for academic-focused early childhood curricula to improve learning of the knowledge and skills necessary for success in school and life (Morrison, 2004). Efforts to increase science and mathematics learning in young children coincide with a push towards incorporating academics in early learning settings. Early learning practitioners can mistakenly equate science and mathematics as subjects that have to be taught formally, not realizing the foundational concepts are best learned through play. Structured experiences will not improve math and science skills for early learners. Building more focused opportunities for children to play with science and math concepts is a more natural way for children to engage in the sense of wonderment and discovery that then leads them to learn these skills. Expanding opportunities for children to experience preschool science and math discoveries does not conflict with children's need for playtime. Science and math require a discovery-based environment and therefore require the principles to be embedded in the context of play (Hirsh-Pacek, 2010).

This chapter will help you to become more familiar with early learning experiences in mathematics and science. We will introduce you to the importance of including such experiences in early learning environments and outline the connection between math and science to play and development. Beginning with theories of math and science, you will learn why they are important experiences for children to have with opportunities to engage in exploration and discovery. Once again, as we have seen in other chapters, theories influence our practice.

## THEORETICAL FOUNDATION

Children's understanding of math and science and interest in these subjects in later years grows from the fundamental concepts they develop during early childhood. Our understanding of how and when this development takes place has been influenced by theories of concept development as put forth by Jean Piaget and Lev Vygotsky. These theories support a constructivist approach, which places the emphasis on children as intellectual explorers who make their own discoveries and construct knowledge (Lind, 1999) based on their life experiences. According to Piaget's theory, children acquire knowledge through their interactions with the environment. Piaget distinguished between three types of knowledge:

- **Physical knowledge:** This type of knowledge includes learning about objects in the environment and their characteristics, such as colour, weight, size, texture, and other features that can be determined through observation and are physically within the object.
- **Logical-mathematical:** Knowledge that includes the relationships each individual constructs or invents (such as same and different, more and less, number, classification, and so on) to make sense out of the world and to organize information. It is more abstract than physical knowledge.
- **Social (or conventional):** This type of knowledge includes information created by people, such as rules for behaviour in various social situations. (Charlesworth, 2000)

In practice, the three types of knowledge are not easily separated from each other. Just about every learning experience uses physical, logical-mathematical, and social conventional knowledge. Understanding the way Piaget classified knowledge helps us to facilitate and plan learning experiences, especially in math and science. Providing children with an opportunity to enhance one type of knowledge also offers the opportunity to develop all three types of knowledge.

Lev Vygotsky, like Piaget, was a cognitive development theorist. Unlike Piaget, Vygotsky placed more emphasis on the role of the adult or more mature peer as an influence on children's mental development. While Piaget placed emphasis on children as intellectual explorers making their own discoveries and constructing knowledge independently, Vygotsky promoted a more social context for constructivism. Vygotsky believed that "it is through others that we develop into ourselves" (1981, p. 181). It is through the influence of others, according to Vygotskian tradition, that children's math and science development can be scaffolded to higher levels.

Higher levels of learning coincide with higher order thinking skills. Benjamin Bloom (1956) identified six levels of higher order thinking which form a hierarchy, from lowest to highest. Each higher level requires all the thinking levels needed at the lower ones (Warner, 2005). Social constructivists who identify with the theories of Vygotsky could consider these levels when focusing on scaffolding children's development across Vygotsky's zone of proximal development, as described in Chapter 2. The six levels appear in Table 8.1 (Warner, 2005).

Early learning practitioners can use probing questioning techniques with children to support the scaffolding process for experiences and knowledge building. Bloom's taxonomy of higher order thinking is an appropriate basis for questioning. Warner (2005) recommends that early learning practitioners focus on levels 2 to 6. Level 1, calls for memorization and, according to Popham (2002), does not encourage higher-order thinking. Knowledge questions are at the rote level and

***Table 8.1***   *Bloom's Levels of Thinking*

| 1 | Knowledge | remembering basic information (rote learning) |
|---|---|---|
| 2 | Comprehension | understanding the basic information and being able to phrase it in one's own words |
| 3 | Application | using the information in a concrete way to solve a problem or complete a task |
| 4 | Analysis | breaking apart the information, sorting out facts, and drawing conclusions |
| 5 | Synthesis | putting together knowledge in novel, creative ways |
| 6 | Evaluation | judging content based on standards, which may be set by the learner or the teacher |

just require children to give the right answers. Children are naturally curious about the world and want to find out as much as they can. They don't want adults to give them the answers. They don't want math and science to be something that is imparted to them; they want it to be something they manipulate, discover, and do (Neill, 2009).

As you read further in this chapter, you will benefit from examining the scope of math and science. We begin by examining core definitions for these topical areas. These definitions are intended to help you think about the complexity of children's development as it relates to math and science. The definitions help to make the interconnection with play. You will learn that in order to optimize development in math and science, you will need to think carefully about how to apply this knowledge to practice.

# DEFINING SCIENCE AND MATHEMATICS

There are many complex definitions available for both math and science, but these may not be particularly helpful to early learning practitioners. Science, simply put, refers to a system for acquiring knowledge. The system involves processes, content, and concepts. It involves observation and experimentation to explain natural phenomena. Children gain competence in the processes of science while participating in meaningful scientific activities. Concurrently, children are developing an understanding of scientific concepts: the "big ideas" in science. Scientific content are the facts of science and while these are still a basic part of science education, they should not be the primary goal of science education (Van Hoorn, Nourot, Scales, & Alward, 2007).

Mathematics, or arithmetic for some, is nothing more than a subject in school that has no relationship to the outside world (Colvin, 2005). Mathematics, defined simply, is about numbers. However, children don't necessarily know their numbers just because they can count to 10. "Mathematics is not just counting and naming numerals. It involves a combination of conceptual knowledge (the ability to understand things) and procedural knowledge (the ability to do things). Children should come to understand mathematical concepts, such as numbers and space, and how concepts are related" (Clements, 2005, p. 16).

Mathematics is a particular way of thinking and children everywhere do it quite naturally (Davis & Keller, 2007). Providing science and mathematical experiences for children within a play-based learning environment is not as hard as one would imagine. There are plenty of opportunities to encourage thinking in these content areas. In fact, math and science are very much interrelated. Read the words of Louise Jupp, a professor who teaches students like you. Professor Jupp asks you to consider the potential of an apple to promote math and science!

## WORDS OF WISDOM

### An Expert Describes a Play-Based Constructivist Approach to Math and Science

An apple is truly a beautiful piece of fruit, but its potential for learning the fundamental concepts of math and science are so easily lost when we slice it up without thought and pass it out to a group of children anxiously awaiting a tasty snack. Some of us surely will take the opportunity to count the number of children sitting around the table and encourage them to indicate the number of apple slices needed to equally share the fruit, a simple but effective math lesson. Others will cut the fruit in half to reveal the seeds inside and perhaps initiate a conversation about seeds, taking advantage of a routine moment to teach a fundamental lesson in science. Good teachers take advantage of these everyday moments to integrate math concepts and scientific investigations throughout the day but how many of us consider the richness of approaching these essential programming areas by taking a more constructivist approach? For young children learning is about wonder combined with their quest for knowledge, achieved through observation and their interaction with materials. Constructivism is a way of coming to know one's world, scientifically through observing, predicting and analyzing; mathematically by establishing meaning and relationships using number, measurement, shape, line and form. Consider cutting the apple through the middle next time. Inside you will discover the most beautiful five-pointed star, the same star that you will find in a pear and of course a star fruit. Is there a star inside a banana or an orange? What other differences are there amongst fruit? Where does the fruit come from and how does it grow? Who grows the fruit? Suddenly we wonder along with children, we foster a community of learners who care about the world around them and we create an environment where math tools and science inquiry are utilized. Constructivism is about asking questions, considering "big ideas," trying to answer similar but not necessarily identical problems and it can start with an object as uncomplicated and everyday as an apple.

Some students and practitioners are comfortable providing math and science experiences because they recognize the potential of everyday materials and objects, like apples, as described by Professor Jupp. Others feel that they are complicated and abstract subjects and not as important as other experiences. However, if provided in a way that connects to children's play, math and science explorations become real, meaningful, and authentic. Consider the importance of math and science as you read on in the chapter.

## The Importance of Math and Science

David Hawkins, an American philosopher of science spent most of his life providing professional development to teachers that illustrated the importance of math and science experiences for young children (Lehmann-Haupt, 2002). He emphasized the need for math and science to be experiential and to be introduced in the early years. In Saracho and Spodek (2008), Hawkins is quoted as saying:

> The kind of experiential background in children's lives before schooling begins or along the way is more uniformly adequate to math and science than to most other school subjects. The poverty or richness of social background matter less here in the early years than in other school subjects. Math and science should therefore be the great equalizers, whether they are now seen to be or not. (p. 175)

Hawkins and his wife, Frances, an early childhood educator, developed a relationship with the Boulder Journey School in Colorado. They recognized that in order to enhance and promote math and science experiences, there was a need for adults working with children, including early learning practitioners and teachers in the school systems, to acquire opportunities to explore and experiment with math and science materials and the principles that are inherent in the everyday lives of children. In June 2007, the *Hawkins Room for Messing About with Materials and Ideas*, inspired by David and Frances Hawkins, was created as an adult studio and think tank. The room and its underlying philosophy serve as a place for adults to experiment with materials. By doing so, adults are better able to understand and support children's learning when they dedicate ample time to "messing about" with the materials that children utilize to co-construct and represent their hypotheses and theories. Additionally, this messing about with materials proves to be more fruitful when assumptions, challenges, thoughts, and ideas are shared with others.

In Table 8.2, you will see a list of the types of materials that can be found in the Hawkins Room for Messing About.

When children play with materials they are building their understanding of mathematical and scientific concepts. Adults, who understand the unlimited possibilities of materials are better able to provide children with opportunities to explore, discover, and create. Scientists know that in order to learn science you have to experience science. Van Hoorn et al. (2007) believe that science programs in the early years should be based on similarities between scientists involved in doing science and children who are involved in play—"an interest plus the energy, knowledge, and skills to pursue that interest" (p. 242). It is the same for mathematics.

*Photo 8.1*    *Two practitioners explore the science and math play potential of everyday materials.*

*Table 8.2*    *Materials from the Hawkins Room*

| Materials found in the Hawkins Room for Messing About | | |
|---|---|---|
| Plants | Large tubs | Coloured water |
| Tubes | Small tubs | Tools |
| Water | String | Pegboard |
| Dirt | Peas | Large tubes |
| Bottles | Rice | Hardware |
| Popsicle sticks | Rocks | Shovels |
| Test tubes | Shakers | Air pumps |
| Flashlight | Sieves | Syringe |
| Beans | Squeeze droppers | Tinker toys |
| Wood | Ice cube trays | Lumber |
| Hammers | Electronics | Clay |
| Nails | Screwdrivers | Pulleys |
| Rulers | Metal materials | Batteries |
| Wire | Clothes pins | Wood scraps |
| Pipe cleaners | Rubber stoppers | Pot lids |
| Paper cups | Measuring cups | Sticks |
| Styrofoam | Seeds | Glasses |
| Sand | Squirt bottles | Unit blocks |
| Rocks | Colour gels | Magnets |

Copley (2000) states that "to *know* mathematics is to *do* mathematics" (p. 15). Math experiences for children should also be play-based as it is through play that children begin to construct understandings of basic mathematical concepts (Van Hoorn et al., 2007). In early learning settings, it is the early learning practitioner's role to make math and science come to life.

## Stop . . . Think . . . Discuss . . . Reflect

Pick 10 items from the list in Table 8.2. Can you think of how you would present these to children to encourage exploration and discovery through their play? Discuss your list and related ideas for math and/or science experiences with another student in the class. What have you learned about math and science from sharing your ideas? How do you envision transferring your math and science knowledge to your work with children?

## Concept Development in Science and Mathematics

Concepts are the building blocks of knowledge. They allow children to organize and categorize information (Charlesworth, 2000). According to Gallenstein (2004), concepts help children to organize their world, serving as a mental filing cabinet. As information is discovered and organized, similar concepts are filed together. Categories are formed by observing and identifying similarities and differences of objects and ideas. During the early years, children actively engage in acquiring fundamental concepts and in learning fundamental process skills (Lind, 1999). Processes enable children to apply their newly acquired knowledge about concepts. By being involved in the process of math and science, children enlarge their current knowledge, skills, and abilities about specific concepts and develop new ones (Charlesworth, 2000).

## Science, Mathematics, and Development

Concept growth and development begins as early as infancy. In *Scientist in the Crib*, Gopnick, Metzoff, and Kuhl (2001), refer to an infant as "the most powerful learning machine in the universe" (p. 1). Babies explore the world with their senses: looking, touching, smelling, hearing, and tasting. Children are born curious creatures who want to know more about their environment (Lind, 1999).

As children learn to crawl, to stand, and to walk, they have freedom to discover on their own and to learn to think for themselves. Very early on, they begin to learn ideas about *size*. As they hold and examine objects they discover their larger size relative to what they are holding. When they go over, under, and into large objects they see their size as smaller. Infants learn about *weight* when they cannot always lift items of the same size. They learn about *shape* when they notice that some things stay put and others roll away. As babies first look and then move, they discover *space*. Some spaces are big and some are small. They learn *time sequence* when they

*Photo 8.2*    *What are the concepts this young girl is acquiring as she studies the plant and represents her understanding two dimensionally?*

wake up and feel wet and hungry. They cry. The caregiver comes and they are changed and then fed. Next they play, get tired, and go to sleep (Lind, 1999).

As toddlers, children sort things and put them in piles—of the same colour, the same size, the same shape, or with the same use. They are developing classification skills. When they are piling up blocks into tall structures and watching them tumble down, they are practising the concept of cause and effect. The solitary tall structure becomes many small parts again. When they are paying for food in an imaginary store, they are learning about money concepts and adding and subtracting concepts. When they pretend to cook imaginary food, they are measuring imaginary flour, salt, and milk. When they set the table in their play kitchen they are practising the concept of one-to-one correspondence. Children need these types of opportunities for free exploration and discovery as a basis for future learning (Charlesworth, 2000).

As children grow older, they are able to understand more abstract, relational concepts such as ideas about motion, light and shadows, changes, and relative position (Van Hoorn et al., 2007). They acquire these fundamental concepts through active involvement with their environment. They learn about what something is and what it is not especially when presented with examples and non-examples of a concept (Gallenstein, 2004). Children learn that cows, pigs, cats, and dogs are animals. Eventually, they will be able to subdivide the animals into categories such as those that can be pets and those that are usually not.

As children develop, their thinking related to mathematical and scientific concepts goes through four distinct stages involving representation: *concrete, semi-concrete, semi-abstract,* and *abstract.* For an experience to be concrete it must be part of a child's immediate world and it must be real. An example of a concrete experience related to math would be a fruit graph. Each child in an early learning centre group is asked to bring their favourite fruit from home. The children then place each piece of fruit on a grid forming a graph that would show the fruit preferences of all the children in the group. "The children see the actual fruit. They can touch and manipulate the fruit to organize their thoughts. They can use the visualization and manipulations to make direct comparisons of the different varieties" (Davis & Keller, 2009, p. 90). At the semi-concrete level the children draw the piece of fruit. The drawings could then be taped on a grid on a chart. The children can still visualize the different types of fruit represented, but they do not have the benefit of the three-dimensional tactile experience. Semi-concrete experiences require more complex reasoning by the children (Davis & Keller, 2009). At the semi-abstract level, the fruit drawings would be replaced by an abstract form or symbol, such as a square. The children can see that certain columns have more square forms (representing fruits) than others. However, they must translate in their minds that each square represents a fruit. They must also be able to reason to themselves that each column represents a different type of fruit. At the abstract level, usually experienced by school age children, the chart would not give any visual support to the children. The shape of an abstract representation would not relate to the shape of the object represented. It would be a theoretical representation. To help children develop understanding, children experiences are initiated at the concrete level. Over time, they can work towards the abstract level. However, "many experiences must be given at each level before moving towards more abstract levels" (Davis & Keller, 2009, p. 90).

## HOW DO PRESCHOOLERS LEARN SCIENTIFIC AND MATHEMATICAL SKILLS?

According to Ramsey and Fowler (2004), there is agreement amongst researchers that there are developmentally appropriate practices for children to learn science and mathematics. Such practices include the belief that skills in science and math are best learned when the following principles are in place:

1. The concepts are based on the children's informal knowledge;
2. The concepts involve the use of concrete materials;
3. The child is an active rather than passive learner;
4. An adult is present to provide structure, guidance, and assistance when necessary in order to extend learning; and
5. The programming is integrated across subject areas (p. 32).

Adults do not have to be present in order for children to learn concepts. Concepts can be acquired through *naturalistic* (or spontaneous) experiences that are initiated by the children themselves. These are important experiences for children because they control the choice and action. If the environment is rich in opportunities for children to explore, wonder, experiment, and discover, there will be plenty of naturalistic experiences that children will become involved in. When adults provide assistance to the child involved in natura-listic experiences, they are initiating *informal learning*. These experiences are not pre-planned. They evolve from the child. The adult through observation takes advantage of a **teachable moment.** *Structured* learning experiences are pre-planned. They involve the adult choosing the experience for the child (Lind, 1999).

**Teachable moment**
That point in a learner's development at which time it is appropriate for an adult to intervene and in some way build on the learning that is occurring (Dietze, 2006).

Early learning practitioners recognize the importance of children needing to be active rather than passive learners. Through active play experiences children develop mathematical and scientific knowledge. To help children with concept attainment Gallenstein (2004) recommends that early learning practi-tioners follow Jerome Bruner's stages of knowledge representation and work with children at their developmental level, as illustrated in the chart below. See Figure 8.1.

| LEVEL | TEACH WITH: |
|---|---|
| 1 CONCRETE | ACTIONS ON OBJECTS |
| 2 PICTORIAL/TRANSITIONAL | PICTURES/IMAGES OF OBJECTS |
| 3 SYMBOLIC | NUMERALS, OPERATIONAL SIGNS, LETTERS WORDS |

*Figure 8.1*    *Bruner's Stages of Knowledge Representation*

# PLAYING WITH SCIENCE IS TO CELEBRATE WONDER

Children are scientists at play. When you see a child make mud pies for baking or construct worm playgrounds, they are conducting playful experiments (Ross, 2000). Children are natural wonderers; they are full of wonder. They approach life with an openness and eagerness to know and to experience (Greenman, 2007). One of the most important roles that early learning practitioners have is to encour-age and support children's wonders. It is an opportunity to give children the chance to explore and discover scientific and mathematical concepts. "Wondering is one of the professional missions of childhood, and children don't hesitate to wonder out loud. Why? How? Where? When? As early learning practitioners we may often feel the impulse to simply respond with answers" (Ross, 2000, p.12). This response will not encourage children to discover and construct their own knowledge based on their wonders.

"To wonder is to question, to imagine, and speculate on what is and what isn't."
—Greenman, 2007

It is sometimes difficult for adults to break away from the need to provide children with the right answers. This might relate to an early learning practitioner's own experiences as young learners and what they have come to view as being the role of the educator. In early childhood education, there is no question that focusing on rote learning limits children's quest for knowledge and their learning. What would be the purpose of giving children the right answer? Is it so they could try to remember the answer and recite it to their parents? Rather than memorizing the right answer, early learning practitioners challenge children to speculate, make predictions, and create theories. This skill will serve them far better over time than any soon-to-be-forgotten answer from a teacher (Kashin, 2009). "If we let go of our image as suppliers of answers, we too can become immersed in the act of wonderment." If you can simply affirm that you share the children's curiosity and sense of wonder, it is better than trying to give them answers. "Join in the wonder and go where it takes you" (Ross, 2000, p. 12).

Wilson (2010) cautions adults to recognize and honour children's way of knowing and strive to keep the children's and their own sense of wonder alive. If children are placed in structured environments, without the freedom to explore, their wonder will dissipate over time. Visualize a group of young children playing in a pile of leaves. They will be engaged with their whole bodies, laughing with exuberance and joy. Adults are more likely to respond to a pile of leaves with thoughts about what comes next. They may spend little time immersing themselves in the

*Photo 8.3    Children looking through the fence, making observations.*

moment and in the sensory experiences of the collection of leaves. Most likely, the adults are thinking about all the raking they have to do. According to Wilson (2010) children relate to the world based more on wonder than adults because wonder dissipates over time as we get older. If adults could restore their sense of wonder and learn alongside of children, imagine the possibilities!

# THE SCIENTIFIC METHOD FOR YOUNG CHILDREN

Science is about exploration and inquiry. Early learning practitioners encourage children to engage in an inquiry process rather than memorizing isolated scientific facts. Modelling the use of "I wonder . . ."; "What if . . .?" and "How can we find out?" introduces children to the basis of science inquiry (Bosse, Jacobs, & Anderson, 2009, p. 12). Hill, Stremmel, and Fu (2004) describe inquiry as an art that involves instilling in children a sense of wonder, curiosity, asking questions, looking for answers, and making sense of the world in different ways. Inquiry skills involve questioning, planning, and investigation and are closely aligned with the scientific method.

As children investigate their world, they use the same processes that scientists use: observing, classifying, experimenting, predicting, drawing conclusions, and communicating ideas. With the support of students and practitioners children become more systematic and logical in how they use these processes (Neill, 2009). The processes are described below:

1. **Observing.** Observation is an important feature in the scientific method. Observation is the foundation of the inquiry process. When making observations, children are learning to gather evidence, organize ideas, and propose explanations (Anderson, Martin, & Faszewski, 2006). Observations trigger children to see different viewpoints and perspectives. According to Neill (2009), early learning practitioners remind children to take the time to use all of their senses to interpret the world. The world is rich with sensory experiences: sounds like thunder, smells like perfume, textures such as the rough sidewalk or the prickly pine cone and tastes aplenty—salty popcorn, sour grapefruit, sweet peaches.

2. **Classification.** Classification is the process of grouping similar things together. Classification is a basic concept experienced in science and math (Gallenstein, 2004). In the scientific method, children identify the relationships between things, and the categories that they do, and do not, belong to. For example, a child may discover during an outdoor play experience that some of the balls provide bounce and some do not.

3. **Wonder, predict, and hypothesize.** This is the process of questioning and speculating. At this point, a child might wonder why a vegetable is not a fruit or what makes a ball bounce? To predict is to describe what you expect will happen. Predictions are based on knowledge, observations,

***Photo 8.4***   *A child playing in the sand is experimenting with the concepts of empty and full.*

experience, and experimentation. For example, if I build my structure too high, it will fall down. The child is predicting what will happen based on experience (Church, 2003; Neill, 2009).

4. **Experiment, test, and explore.** The child at this point tries out ideas and tests predictions. Every time a child encounters a problem and seeks to find the answer, he is experimenting. Children may find that the glue in the bottle won't come out. They can predict that it is because the sticky substance is too hard. The child can experiment by running the bottle under warm water because his theory is that a warmer temperature will soften the glue. This experiment is an example of testing the hypothesis which is the prediction (Neill, 2009).

5. **Drawing conclusions.** Concrete evidence confirming a prediction leads to one type of conclusion; contradictory evidence requires the child to change his thoughts and ideas, and possibly gather additional information before reaching a different conclusion. Children can make generalizations and form theories about how the world works based on their observations and experiments (Neill, 2009).

6. **Communicating ideas.** At this point, children can share their questions, observations, predictions, and conclusions with others. Communication takes place through spoken language, drawings, written words and symbols, demonstrations, gestures, or documentation panels (Neill, 2009).

Remember that all the processes interconnect. Early learning practitioners who provide rich experiences that encourage observation, prediction, and experimentation are reinforcing an image of children as capable and competent scientists. As such, children are given the opportunity to predict and build theories. They are given the chance to draw conclusions and to communicate with others. The experience becomes one of social learning when families and the community are included (Jordan & Smorti, 2010).

---

# Research Connections in Science

The *International Journal of Science in Society* published an article in 2010 entitled "Fearless Science in the Early Years: Co-Construction in a Rural Childcare Centre," written by Barbara Jordan and Sue Smorti from New Zealand. The researchers tell the story about a rural child care centre in New Zealand, where children are viewed as capable and competent scientists, and the science program that is implemented there is referred to as "fearless science." The collaboration with families and community generated supplies of materials and animals, which lead to authentic science investigations that were documented into learning stories. The study illustrates the learning experienced by all: the children, their families, the community and the teachers. The teachers inspired by the interests of the children did their own research at their level of understanding, and thus developed their personal bank of science knowledge and appreciation.

---

## The Role of the Early Learning Practitioner

Early learning practitioners are constantly trying to balance their knowledge and beliefs about how young children learn and develop with parental expectations and the philosophies of early learning centres. Often, they feel pulled between "preparing children for school" and "providing rich play environments."

If early learning practitioners equate math and science with subjects in school that require work in order to learn, they may feel that a structured environment where the early learning practitioner presents specific math or science concepts will better prepare the child for the formal instruction they will receive in the school system. This may include incorporating more structured methods such as worksheets for children to complete into the program. As we have identified throughout this text, worksheets are developmentally inappropriate and do not support a play-based approach to learning. Early learning practitioners who use worksheets say that parents expect them. "Perhaps parents expect photocopied worksheets because that is what they recall from their own early schooling experiences" (Hendrick & Weissman, 2011, p. 241).

Worksheets designed to provide children with math and science experiences are part of a teacher-led and directed classroom that involves scripted teaching. The teacher's input is low because he or she is using resources developed by others. The teacher's role becomes photocopying sheets from a book and providing these to the children. The children's input is low, as they are the passive recipients of these worksheets. Young children generally prefer opportunities for hands-on experiences with real materials. Quality early learning programs provide rich documentation of children's learning experiences during play and displaying the results of the various play experiences and children's discoveries helps parents and families to understand the value of learning math and science within a play-based, constructivist approach. Worksheets don't work.

Play is children's work (Paley, 2004). However, play does not mean that "anything goes" in the early learning space. Miller and Almon (2009) in *Crisis in the Kindergarten: Why Children Need to Play in School*, describe a healthy kindergarten as one that does not deteriorate into chaos. Nor is it so tightly structured by adults that children are denied the opportunity to learn through their own initiative and exploration. The authors call for a balance of "child-initiated play in the presence of engaged teachers and more focused experiential learning guided by teachers" (p. 12). The key is finding the balance between child-initiated play with the active presence of the practitioner, combined with intentional teaching through playful learning. The line between the two should be thin and porous; the two can reinforce each other (Miller & Almon, 2009). Adults in the early learning play space make this happen by developing open, experiential, fun places to explore, discover, and play. Wendy Mitchell, a professor who teaches about the value of science, offers an expert's view on this balance and how it can be incorporated into play spaces in an authentic and playful way.

# WORDS OF WISDOM

## An Expert Describes the Value of Science

While I was working at a parent cooperative nursery school a number of years ago, I needed to park my car on the other side of the park from where the school was located. Each day as I crossed the park, I picked up a bit of "science" to bring into the classroom. In the fall it might be an acorn from the old oak tree; in the winter a piece of ice from a puddle that had frozen overnight; and in the spring part of the discarded shell from a robin's egg. Each item made its way to the science table where other treasures had been carefully placed. Magnifying glasses and other scientific tools were made available for closer examinations. Resource books, both for children and adults, were handy to help answer the many why, what, and how questions posed by the children. Science at the nursery was an everyday part of the curriculum.

Jean Piaget, the noted cognitive development theorist, called children "little scientists" as he realized their innate curiosity about the world around them. A newborn, in a very short time, reaches out to begin to understand the world. The first discovery of toes is followed by many hours of intense exploration. When mobile, the young toddler eagerly moves towards anything that captures his attention from a small moving insect on the floor to the mixing of colours while creating a masterpiece for the fridge. Preschoolers test the laws of physics as they manipulate blocks. School-age children begin to formulate hypotheses and test them while constructing clay volcanoes with baking soda and vinegar lava.

At its very basic level, science is the understanding of why the world is the way it is. Science concepts such as observation, hypothesis, inference, and communication are also intertwined with mathematical concepts like classification, comparison, and measuring. When young children are exploring they do not differentiate between the two sets of concepts. Think of the child who is experimenting with warm water mixed with salt and sprayed onto a block of ice. Why does the ice melt faster where the mixture is sprayed? What happens if more salt is dissolved in the water to make a stronger solution and then sprayed on the ice? What happens if just water is used? The children are challenged to use their skills of observation, prediction, communication, comparison and measuring. They talk to the interested adults about what they see. They are encouraged to mix up new solutions and test to see if the results are similar.

The value of including science as part of the everyday curriculum is that it fosters healthy cognitive development in young children. Children are never too young to introduce science. From a very early age children can participate in developmentally appropriate activities that foster basic scientific as well as mathematical skills. Ask yourself: "What can't they investigate?" and go from there. Encourage the children to ask the "why" and "what if" questions even if you do not immediately know the answers. Make searching for them a shared experience. Allow the children time to explore at their own pace. Many scientific discoveries took years of observation and research. As young children are primarily concrete thinkers, the more they can use all of their senses to explore their environment the better. Finally, tap into children's natural curiosity, enthusiasm, with a hands-on approach. Seeing the world through these fresh young eyes is very rewarding!

## Setting up an Environment to Support Scientific Inquiry

In the chapter on language and literacy, it was recommended that early learning practitioners create a print-rich environment to encourage language and literacy development. An easy way to incorporate science into the early learning environment is to provide materials that are rich in scientific possibilities through the use of a discovery area. The key to designing a quality discovery area is to "carefully select a variety of age-appropriate materials (such as magnifiers, a balance scale, prisms, and plants, and unique materials that are new to children) that will introduce children to the wonders of the natural world" (Bosse et al., 2009, p. 10). If the additional natural materials, books, and manipulatives are rotated into the discovery centre, they will continue to be of interest to the children and can also reflect seasonal changes.

The type of materials provided for children will depend on the type of science being explored. *Physical science* relates to physical knowledge and involves hands-on exploration of materials to investigate the properties of objects. In the water table, tubing, measuring cups, funnels, turkey basters, and eyedroppers will foster an understanding of volume, weight, gravity, and force. *Life science* involves children observing and formulating questions about the characteristics of things that are living. Caring for a classroom pet or observing birds, squirrels, insects, and worms in the natural habitat will help children develop a deeper understanding of living things. *Earth science* relates to the properties of earth materials such as rocks or shells. *Technology* involves distinguishing between natural and man-made items. Simple machines like apple peelers, clocks, or egg timers invite hands-on investigations on how machines function. *Social science* focuses on a social perspective and involves discussion and activities about conserving and recycling. By brainstorming ways to repurpose discarded objects, children can develop both problem solving skills and higher-order thinking (Bosse et al., 2009). There is more information about environmental science that focuses on sustainability (recycling, reusing, and repurposing) in the final chapter in the textbook.

**Sand and Water Play**  Having opportunities to play at the sandpits and water tables provides children with experiences rich in mathematical and scientific learning. Knowing this, would you be surprised to learn that, according to Miller and Almon (2009), classic play materials such as sand and water have largely disappeared from children's play spaces? When adults don't recognize the play value inherent in sand and water, they can be the first to go, especially if there is a move towards a more academic classroom. Sometimes, early learning spaces do not have the equipment for sand and water play. Other times, the sandbox and water table are neglected areas stocked with cast-off materials and odd containers (Van Hoorn et al., 2007).

Children love to play with sand and water. Sand and water play is messy. Messy play is appropriate for children but sometimes adults have difficulty with it. Imagine being at a beach. The experience that you are visualizing is probably soothing and relaxing. It is for children as well. Children can be up to their necks in sand caked onto wet bodies. Just because an experience is messy does not mean that it doesn't have enormous play and developmental potential. Some practitioners position the sand and water play tables close to the door of the classroom to help ease children who are experiencing separation anxiety into the program. Children find these experiences soothing when they are stressed, just like a day at the beach, usually helps adults unwind. These sensory experiences are easily incorporated into both the indoor and outdoor early learning environments, as the right equipment is readily available. In addition, sand and water play lays the foundation for logical mathematical thinking, scientific reasoning, and cognitive problem solving (Hewitt, 2006).

Sometimes, early learning practitioners shy away from sand and water because they can be messy and because they don't understand the developmental significance of messy play. Sand and water play allow for scientific inquiry and the opportunity to apply knowledge and skills of mathematical concepts such as measuring, volume, size, shape, and weight. They provide children with natural materials that provoke wonder while they pour, pound, sift, drain, and pack the water and sand. Ideally in the early learning environment, sand and water tables are placed side by side, as the effectiveness of the mediums will improve when combined.

*Photo 8.5    A sand experience outside combined with rocks, bark, logs, and even dried clay pieces!*

Outdoors, children require access to water when playing in the sandbox, as this helps them gain skills in discovering the creation of three-dimensional sculptures that advance their math, science, and creative attributes.

The materials and supplies for sand and water play should be carefully chosen. Consideration should be given to safety (i.e. nontoxic, smooth edges), quality and durability (withstand the use by multiple children), flexibility (for multiple usage), and play value (what the child can do with it). Students and early learning practitioners planning for a sand and water experience have many options for materials and supplies. In Figure 8.2, you will find some suggestions.

## Stop . . . Think . . . Discuss . . . Reflect

Refer to Figure 8.2 and reflect on the supplies and materials listed. What else can you add? Can you think of any other materials, besides sand and water that could be used to sift and pour? If you thought about cornmeal, beans, rice, and dry pasta, why do you think these items do not appear in the list? What is common amongst these items? How many reasons can you come up with for why they were excluded? Are there any parallels between your reasons and culture? Do you think there may be a connection between the recommendation that these items do not belong in the sand and water centre with child poverty?

**Materials for Sand and Water Experiences**

Natural materials such as shells and rocks

Sifters

Funnels

Plastic tubing

Plastic connectors for tubing

Shovels

Pails

Measuring cups and spoons

Garden tools

Pitchers

Pumps

Eye droppers

Water wheels

Bottles

Trays

Watering cans

Hand beaters

Sponges of various shapes and sizes

Spray bottles

Containers of various sizes

Strainers

Plastic animals/fish

*Figure 8.2    Materials and Supplies for Science and Discovery*

**Math and Science Rocks**    Finding a focus for projects that integrate math and science activities is an effective early learning play strategy. For example, rocks are materials found in nature that children instinctively are drawn to. Children can sort rocks and minerals by colour. This activity simulates one of the ways that scientists identify minerals and gems—by colour. Colour is an important

*Photo 8.6    Rocks promote scientific and mathematical learning.*

diagnostic characteristic in mineral identification (Danisa, Gentile, McNamara, Pinney, Ross, & Rule, 2006). Rocks and minerals can also be sorted by texture and size. Children can create patterns using rocks and minerals. Children can count rocks and match a grouping to a number, demonstrating one-to-one correspondence. Rocks are natural wonders that can be used to explore both science and math concepts.

> Rocks and minerals are abundant and intriguing to all. Each rock that we find has properties that make it unique, yet at the same time, it has characteristics that it shares with others. We can embrace this natural affinity for rocks as we observe, explore and investigate the many curiosities we have about them. (Davis & Keller, 2009, p. 236)

## The Development of Mathematical Concepts

As presented in the section on science, young children have a natural desire to explore and understand the world around them. Mathematics is another means by which they acquire information about their environment and begin to understand the world. Well before kindergarten, children have the "interest and ability to engage in significant mathematical thinking and learning" (Clements, 2004, p. 11). According to the Canadian Child Care Federation's (CCCF) *Foundations for Numeracy: An Evidence-Based Toolkit for Early Learning Practitioners* (2010), research has shown that "knowledge of quantity emerges early in life and develops significantly during a child's first three years." Infants can tell the difference between small quantities, for example, between two items as opposed to three, and toddlers typically learn their first number word (usually "two") at around 24 months of age. By the time they reach 4 years of age, children are able to compare quantities. They become experienced with using math words like "more" or "less" (p. 13).

The awareness that young children develop math concepts from a very early age is significant to early learning practitioners. In recent years there has been an emphasis on literacy readiness, and in comparison mathematical readiness has had a minimal focus in home and early learning environments. There is strong evidence that mathematical readiness is also important. Sarama and Clements (2004) argue that a complete mathematics program may contribute to children's later learning of other subjects, including literacy. "Much of the recent research has reported that mathematics does in fact support the development of literacy" (CCCF, 2010, p. 13). Recognizing that mathematical concepts develop early in a child's life, early learning practitioners have a responsibility to create opportunities that will support young children in engaging in play experiences that are rich with mathematical concepts.

The term *numerosity* is used to describe "the ability to discriminate arrays of objects based on quantity of presented items" (Geary, 2006, p. 780). The research suggests that infants have an "intuitive sense of approximate magnitude (i.e., how much there is) called *ordinality*" (CCCF, 2010, p. 13). The ability of a child to learn the concepts of numerosity and ordinality depends on two important cognitive

> "Some mathematician, I believe, has said that true pleasure lies not in the discovery of truth, but in the search for it."
> —Tolstoy

factors: mental representation of information and the memory of information. At age 2, "children can mentally represent and remember one, two, and sometimes three items." Between the ages of 2 and 3, "children are not only aware of the concept of small numbers," they can "also begin to learn how to solve simple nonverbal calculations involving one and two items." This is basic *arithmetic*. The older preschool child can solve problems involving three or even four items and by the time a child reaches four years of age they can begin to understand the more complex arithmetic problem of inverse relation between addition and subtraction. If one item is added and one item is taken away, the answer is still that there are two items ($2 + 1 - 1 = 2$), "adding one and taking away one cancel each other out" (CCCF, 2010, p. 14).

**Counting procedures** Between the ages of 2 and 3, children begin to use language related to mathematics, incorporating number words into their play experiences. "Children appear to know very early that number words all represent different quantities and that the sequence in which they say these number words is important" (CCCF, 2010, p. 14). There are "five implicit principles that are thought to guide a preschool child's development of counting procedures," as illustrated in Figure 8.3 and described below:

- **Stable Order** refers to the fact that number words are always used in the same order (i.e. counting in the order of "1,2,4" is incorrect).
- **One-to-one correspondence** means that one and only one number word can be assigned to each counted object in a set (i.e. an item in a set that has been assigned "2" cannot also be assigned "5") (CCCF, 2010). When each child has a cookie at snack, there is one cookie per child. This is one-to-one correspondence. It is still one-to-one correspondence when each child has two cookies. When a child understands that for snack each child will have one or two cookies, then he is beginning to understand the concept that one group has the same number of things as another.
- **Cardinality** refers to the act that the value of the last number word used when counting indicates the quantity of items in the set (i.e. counting "1,2,3,4" means there are four items in the set).
- **Abstraction** means that any set of items can be counted (i.e. a book, two bananas, and three pencils can be counted together as a set of six items).
- **Order irrelevance** means that items can be counted in any order (i.e. counting from right to left, left to right, or in no particular sequence results in the same total number of items (CCCF, 2010).

### The difference between counting by rote and rational counting

While children may be able to count to 10 by rote memory, they may have difficulty understanding that they can have two cookies each. Reciting the numbers from one to ten may appear easy for the child. When asked to point and count the 10 blocks that are lined up, the child may point to the same block more than once. It takes time and experience for children to develop the one-to-one correspondence

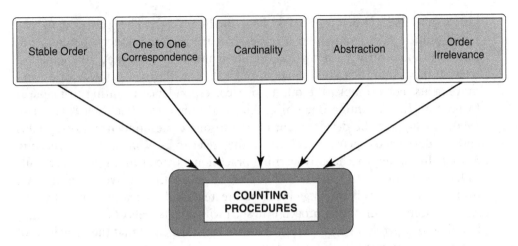

*Figure 8.3*  *Counting Procedures*

concept so that they can move from rote to rational counting (Davis & Keller, 2007). There is a difference between rote counting and rational counting. Rote counting involves the memorization of numbers. Rational counting tells children "how many there are." For children to count rationally, they need to demonstrate one-to-one correspondence. This is a skill that generally does not occur until the kindergarten years because relating the concept of one-to-one correspondence to rational counting is a complex skill. In order to do this a child must be able to keep track while reciting a stable order of numerals to their one-to-one counting (Davis & Keller, 2007). Children require practice in order to develop number sense, which is the way numbers and tools of measurement work within a given culture. Toddlers and preschoolers encounter numbers every day. They celebrate birthdays as they blow out three candles on a cake and hold up three fingers to demonstrate their age. They see numbers on appliances, on the television, by their front door and on car licence plates. They experience numbers of children at each of the experience centres. In order to count, children must have language. Some of the earliest language experiences involving counting come from nursery rhymes, finger plays, and counting books (Sperry Smith, 2009).

By the end of kindergarten, most children can count sets that contain a quantity of items for which they know the number words: if they know the numbers up to twelve, they can accurately count a set with twelve items. Not all children develop these essential principles and some still struggle even into the higher grades. "Those who are not proficient counters and who do not know the essential principles by the time they enter Grade 1 may be at risk for difficulties with mathematics" (CCCF, 2010, p. 14). Researchers have identified counting as a worthwhile focus in early learning programming.

## Research Connections in Mathematics

Donna Kotsopoulos, a professor in mathematics education, and Joanne Lee, a professor of developmental psychology, have developed a program called

LittleCounters™ (Kotsopoulos & Lee, forthcoming). The purpose of the LittleCounters™ program is to teach early learning practitioners, parents, and caregivers about early mathematical cognition and how to integrate mathematical relevant input into their child's play through the use of songs, games, stories, and movements. For example, the one-to-one correspondence counting principle is focused on (i.e., counting one object once and only once) (Gallistel & Gelman, 1990). To support the development of one-to-one correspondence, Kotsopoulos and Lee developed a play strategy which they refer to as *Name it, Say it, Touch it, Move it*. In this approach, early learning practitioners are encouraged to use multiple-modal forms to endorse counting such as fingers, voice, and toys. Additionally, physically moving objects and recreating the set is also a key strategy. A key concept within this approach is to start with smaller sets of objects to count, building to larger sets when there is evidence from the child that the principles of one-to-one correspondence are understood.

The research regarding the program provides evidence that play is an important opportunity for developing mathematical concepts. In the LittleCounters™ program, Kotsopoulos and Lee emphasize "purposeful play," which is an outgrowth from free play or play-based learning. According to Kotsopoulos and Lee, purposeful play involves interaction between the early learning practitioner and the children. The goal of the interaction is to (*a*) scaffold learning and (*b*) to engage in an assessment of/for learning.

Concrete mathematical experiences are essential to the development of counting skills. Children need to touch and feel the items they are counting. They should also be encouraged to count with their fingers. *Finger gnosis* is the term used to describe counting with fingers. Introducing children to the use of their fingers to count will help the development of their mathematical abilities (Butterworth, 1999). There are so many opportunities to do this every day in the classroom from counting items to reciting finger plays. These strategies reinforce the development of the most important area of mathematical learning: counting. In addition to counting procedures, early learning practitioners emphasize a number of other mathematical concepts during children's play episodes such as geometry and measurement, pattern, sequence, seriation, comparison, and classification, as described below.

**Geometry and measurement** "Geometry and measurement have been called the second most important area of mathematical learning" (CCCF, 2010, p. 15). What makes geometry and measurement important is their real-world connections. Geometry is about shapes and children in preschool and kindergarten should be given rich opportunities to explore shapes in their world (Clements, 2004). "Each object in the environment has its own shape" (Charlesworth, 2000, p. 97). According to Charlesworth (2000), much of the play and activity of an infant revolves around learning about shape. As children grow and develop they continue to learn about shape when they handle objects. Some objects are easier to grasp than others. Some roll, some don't. Some objects are smooth like a spoon, while others are sharp like a fork (Sperry Smith, 2009). When children are classifying, shape is often a basic attribute for comparison.

Children usually enjoy having opportunities to experience shapes in their world. They love to experiment in creating representations of shapes either two dimensionally in drawings or three dimensionally from clay, sand, and play dough (Charlesworth, 2000).

Measurement is an often neglected mathematics topic for young children (Copley, 2000), even though it is one of the easiest concepts to incorporate into a child's play. Measurement involves assigning numbers of units to physical quantities such as height, weight, length, and volume. It also can involve no physical quantities such as time and temperature (Sperry Smith, 2009). Not only does measurement help describe and compare things, it also helps record and keeps track of information. This allows children to capture and make predictions of how things may grow and change (Davis & Keller, 2009). There are tools available to measure and these can be divided into categories: linear measurement (rulers, tape), weight and mass measurement (scales, thermometers), and those that measure volume or capacity (cups and spoons). Measurement brings math and science principles together, such as when children plant seeds and then measure their growth on a daily basis.

**Pattern**    As children explore the world around them, they develop other mathematical concepts including pattern. "Mathematics is the science and language of patterns" and is basic to all mathematical thinking (Copley, 2000, p. 83). If infants are cared for in a predictable way, they begin to recognize and anticipate the rhythm or pattern of their care. Toddlers experience patterns with movement and rhythm. For example, early learning practitioners share a clapping pattern and encourage children to clap along (Taylor-Cox, 2003). Preschoolers are able to predict and anticipate events because they have learned about pattern. A pattern is a regular arrangement of objects, numbers, shapes (Copley, 2000). "If children see patterns in their world and connect them to mathematics, they are better able to remember what they have learned and transfer the knowledge to new situations or problems" (Copley, 2000, p. 89). Certain materials like blocks, beads, mud puddles, and shapes lend themselves to patterns. See Figure 8.4 for an example of a pattern with shapes and colours. During play experiences children can be encouraged to identify patterns, to practice repeating a pattern (circle, square, circle, square, circle, and square) and grow patterns. "*Growing patterns* are patterns that change from one value to another in a predictable manner." A child can start with a certain number of objects which represent the first *term* of the pattern. "Then more objects are systematically added to the previous term, with the pattern that is established." Children can generate growing patterns with beads, blocks, and marbles. Think about a pattern of 5 rocks in a linear vertical line. That is the first term of the pattern. Then the child adds 4 rocks horizontally to form a cross (Copley, 2000, p. 91).

*Figure 8.4*    *A Pattern of Shapes and Colours*

**Sequence**    Like pattern, sequence is a mathematical concept that children internalize early in life. Sequence refers to the organization and order of successive events and experiences. When children recognize sequences, they are developing a sense of order, logic, and reason. When in stable environments, children recognize the sequencing of their day and they become able to predict what will happen next. They can observe sequences in nature such as the melting of snow or the falling of leaves. As children listen to stories, they begin to understand the sequence of events and are able to consider how the story unfolds or what comes next (Davis & Keller, 2007).

**Seriation**    Lining up blocks in order of largest to smallest is an example of seriation, and in doing so children exhibit sequencing words, such as first and last, beginning and end, and next to (Sperry Smith, 2009). Of the four blocks in Figure 8.5, which one is the smallest and which one comes last? This is an example of a question you can ask children to challenge their seriation skills. Seriation is a mathematics concept that involves organizing or ordering things in a logical way. As children play with different sizes of teddy bear counters, they may put them in order from the "baby" to "daddy" bear. In doing so, they can be encouraged to tell a story connecting play to math and language. Outdoors, children can spend hours moving and making rows of rocks from smallest to largest or vice versa. They can tell stories about building roads and paths leading to special places.

**Comparison**    In order to be able to pattern, sequence, and seriate a child must be able to compare. When comparing, the child finds a relationship between two things or a group of things in connection with a specific attribute. A child may compare by size, quantity, length, age, or other attributes. During play experiences, look for times when you can note that a child may be comparing. If during block play, a child builds a larger garage for a truck that is bigger, and a smaller one for one that is shorter, he is comparing. Help the child by modelling basic comparing words, such as large and small, big and little, long and short, fast and slow, cold and hot, near and far, thick and thin, to name a few. Can you think of any others (Charlesworth, 2000)?

**Classification**    In math as in science, an understanding of constructing logical groups and classifying is essential (Charlesworth, 2000). Classifying is a way of comparing. Classification refers to putting things together and naming the group, such as smooth rocks and rough rocks or rectangular blocks and square blocks (Davis & Keller, 2007). Children naturally engage in sorting activities during play. When adults participate as a play partner, they help children identify the attributes by which they sorted the materials. This facilitates children in gaining or developing

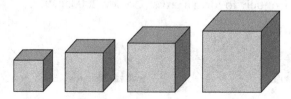

*Figure 8.5*    *How Do These Blocks Represent Seriation?*

their classification skills. There are many attributes that distinguish items in a collection or the different ways objects can be sorted. These include colour, shape, size, material, pattern, texture, and function (Charlesworth, 2000).

## THE LANGUAGE OF MATHEMATICS

The language of mathematics is part of the development of verbal communication skills. People all around the world, of all ages, speak math (Sperry Smith, 2009). Can you think of any math words that you could use with preschoolers?

## Stop . . . Think . . . Discuss . . . Reflect

How many "math words" (any words that relate to math) can you think of? Write them down. Discuss your list with a classmate. Who had the longer list? When you compare your lists you are using math language. Identify the math words you used to compare. How might you incorporate this type of language into a conversation with children? Are there some early learning experience centres where it is easier to incorporate these words than others? If so, which ones? Why? How might you try to incorporate math into experience centres that normally don't focus on math, such as a music and movement centre?

When you were comparing your lists of math words, did either of you come up with words beyond "plus," "minus," and "equals"? Would you consider "down," "between," and "to the left" as words describing mathematical relationships? There are different types of math words. *Positional* words are those that describe place. The most difficult positional word concepts for young children are left and right. These are also sometimes the most difficult for adults, too! Do you rely on a ring or watch to help sort out your left hand from you right? Some other examples of positional words include *in, out, outside, apart, over, under, top, bottom, middle*, and *together*. Other types of math words are *directional* words. As a child uses a pulley to move an object, he/she may describe the experience as moving the object "forward." This is an example of a *directional* word. Can you think of others? *Sequence* words are very important as they help children to develop a sense of order. The ability to sequence is a skill needed to solve more complex problems found in number systems. Lining up farm animals will give a child a chance to use sequence words such as *first and last, beginning and end, before and after*, and *next to. Shape* words help children to categorize and identify everyday objects. They can use the word *round* to describe a clock. They can also call it a *circle*. Other shape words would include *sides, corners, flat, box, carton, tube, triangle*, and so on. The final category of math language words are *number* words which describe our numbers system. These words help children to compare quantities and to recognize relationships. Examples of number words include *more* and *less, the same, many, fewer, greater than* and *less than* (Sperry Smith, 2009). How might you use number words at snack time? What about when children are playing with blocks or are in the dramatic play centre?

# A NUMBERS-RICH ENVIRONMENT

In order to promote literacy the early learning environment needs to have literacy materials distributed throughout, so should there be numbers and math materials (Clements & Sarama, 2005). Early learning practitioners set the stage for children to develop mathematical concepts by providing sufficient materials that will intrigue children to explore them. The materials and the environment are rich with objects that can be used to explore shape and number concepts during everyday play experiences (Van Hoorn et al., 2007), in both the indoor and outdoor play spaces. Counting books should be available. Other books, such as "*Three Little Pigs*," also reinforce math concepts. Blocks, rocks, sand, water, large boxes, plastic containers, and digging materials should be easily accessible to children during their outdoor play.

Just as labelling in the environment with words will support children's language and literacy development, early learning practitioners can write down numbers, just as they write down words. Children may find labelling with numbers to be easier than writing words. The number *one* really only involves a short stroke of a marker or crayon. Having math materials available will reinforce children's explorations with concepts. Manipulatives are easily handled concrete objects, such as puzzles, pegboards, and objects that can be used as counters (beads, rocks, buttons), that children can work with in ways that help them understand or explore mathematic concepts (Benson, 2003). These materials support children's quest to gain knowledge in sorting, classifying, comparing, and counting. Of course, an early learning environment that supports mathematical concepts will always have a substantial set of unit blocks, as they naturally promote shape and number concepts. For a list of materials and supplies that could be added to the indoor and outdoor play space that encourages mathematical experiences, refer to Figure 8.6.

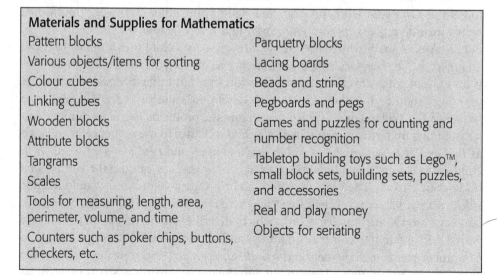

| Materials and Supplies for Mathematics | |
| --- | --- |
| Pattern blocks | Parquetry blocks |
| Various objects/items for sorting | Lacing boards |
| Colour cubes | Beads and string |
| Linking cubes | Pegboards and pegs |
| Wooden blocks | Games and puzzles for counting and number recognition |
| Attribute blocks | |
| Tangrams | Tabletop building toys such as Lego™, small block sets, building sets, puzzles, and accessories |
| Scales | |
| Tools for measuring, length, area, perimeter, volume, and time | Real and play money |
| Counters such as poker chips, buttons, checkers, etc. | Objects for seriating |

***Figure 8.6*** *Materials and Supplies for Mathematics*

The best way to approach math with young children is to make it a meaningful part of their day (CCCF, 2010). Creating flexible schedules in early learning environments, as described in Chapter 12, are considered an important feature of the practitioner's role. How the flow of the day plays out determines the availability of opportunities to learn through play as well as during routine and transitional times. When mathematical concepts are interwoven into the daily routine, it provides many experiences that will involve children using their number concepts. Think about a normal day in the life of a preschool environment. Begin at arrival time. What could you do during this time to incorporate numbers? The process of getting ready for lunch involves mathematical concepts, what do you think they might be?

## Stop . . . Think . . . Discuss . . . Reflect

Write down as many ideas you can come up with for incorporating math concepts into arrival and lunchtime. Consider other times of the day such as tidying up, snack time, and when children are picked up by their parents. How many ideas do you have for involving numbers or other math concepts? Write these down. What about group experiences or what many practitioners describe as "circle time"? Can you think of ways to involve math. Again, write them down and then compare your list to another student. Compare your answers and reflect on what you have learned about creating a math-rich environment. Is there ever a time that we can oversaturate the environment with math concepts? If so, how? How might our actions impact the child's play positively and negatively?

## OBSERVATION

Any time you observe children's play, you will probably see that "they are naturally attracted to mathematical features in their environment. For example, they spontaneously compare the size of objects, they use number words often, they make attempts at counting, and they pay attention to characteristics of patterns and shapes, including symmetry when they build with towers and blocks" (CCCF, 2010, p. 6).

In order to address children's developmental needs and scaffold learning in mathematics, observation is an essential tool for the practitioner and student. Take notes of children as they play with mathematics. How do you know that children are at the level they should be for math learning? There are standards for mathematical learning that can be referred to when observing children's experiences with math; however, we caution that if your jurisdiction has such standards, you should avoid testing children's mathematical abilities. Testing children will take the joy from the learning and is not necessary in preschool.

Standards are developed according to ages of children and should be research-based. Standards and indicators should focus on skills that children should know and be able to do. The skills should be grounded in the discipline of math and science. When the focus is on values and activities in lieu of skill-indicators, they are not well-grounded in the discipline and not related to later achievement (Newman, Roskos, Vukelich, & Clements, 2003). An example that highlights these differences involves counting. "Preschool children should count the items in a collection of one to five items and know the last counting word tells 'how many' (skill-indicator)." Preschool children should take delight in the simple joy of counting (value). Preschoolers participate in counting games and lessons involving numbers (activity) (Newman et al., 2003, p. 2). Early learning practitioners require additional training in order to become assessors. Standards can be used as guides and opportunities to articulate the learning that is happening in your pedagogical documentation, not for testing.

Early learning practitioners gain an understanding of the different developmental levels of children in any discipline so that you have age-appropriate expectations. When you observe school-age children playing with math concepts, the expectations would be that they have higher-level skills. Since school-age children will be tested in the formal system, we recommend that math and science, when delivered in early learning settings with school-age children, should be based on experiential learning. School-age children have the ability to engage in divergent thinking, therefore, they can think of alternative strategies and possibilities when working with mathematical and scientific concepts. However, they are still concrete learners and need hands-on experiences with real materials (Click & Parker, 2008).

## Science and Math Connections

Science interactions support vocabulary development by exposing children to a variety of new words in meaningful contexts. The practice of the scientific method involves practices described using verbs such as *observe, predict, estimate, sort, experiment, etc.* As children engage in these practices, they learn new nouns to label what they are seeing—*roots, pods, stems;* and adjectives to describe attributes—*sticky, pointy, more than* and *less than.* The National Institute for Early Education Research published a Preschool Policy Brief in 2009 that cites research suggesting that exposure to uncommon vocabulary words predicts vocabulary development, which predicts reading achievement, "and that participation in sustained science experiences results in vocabulary gains for preschoolers" (p. 4).

**The literacy connection**    Discussing objects that are not present or events in the past or future support the development of abstract reasoning and are related to literacy skills. While engaged in a science activity children make predictions and plan explorations. When they plan what they should do to find out whether seeds need water to sprout, they use the language in the future tense. When talking about seeds sprouting children are required to reason and talk about changes they have not yet experienced.

Children's literature is a tool to provide hands-on opportunities to apply science and mathematical skills. Integrating these areas of exploration into the programming creates an interweaving rather than a compartmentalization of math and science concepts. Math and science can be learned during play. Cutler, Gilkerson, Parrott, and Browne (2003) suggest creating games from books is a good way to provide math experiences. They identify a number of types of games that can be adapted from a

*Photo 8.7* *Children explore shapes at a light table illustrating an experience that combines math, science, and literacy!*

children's story. Games with spinners allow for numeral recognition and counting practice. Lotto games let children use their matching skills, practice one-to-one correspondence, and build on early counting skills. More complex games involve circular paths, both short (10 to 20 spaces) and long. Taking these types of games as examples and creating your own game based on a book would be an excellent way to incorporate literature and math. Take the children's story the *Prince Child* by Maranke Rinick. In it are vibrant illustrations of animals; each describing the gift they are bringing to the prince child who, the story reveals, ends up being a toad with a crown. A lotto game can be created and the children inspired by the story can match up each animal to the gift being brought to the prince. Using the same book, children can spin a wheel and move a game piece around a circle representing each animal, and they could collect cards representing the gifts.

Math and science can be used to support literacy development. The content of children's literature can serve as the basis for conversations between children and adults around concepts. Creating science charts, producing graphs, recording numerical data, and recording findings in journals provide an important connection between math, science, and language and literacy development (Brenneman, Stevenson-Boyd, & Frede, 2009).

**The music and movement connection**    There are so many finger plays, nursery rhymes, and children's songs that use math words. How many monkeys are jumping on the bed? What happened to Humpty Dumpty? Children love to move their bodies and it isn't difficult to relate their movements to mathematical language.

In Chapter Eleven on page 351 there is a photo of children playing. What do you think they are doing? Imagine children singing "Ring around the Rosies." What movements might the children be making? What math words could you use as a early learning practitioner to reinforce the children's understanding?

**The art connection** Through art children can experiment and practice with a number of mathematical concepts. *Thinking With A Line* is an interactive CD and guidebook that demonstrates to early learning practitioners how to use line printing to explore mathematical concepts such as repetition, spatial orientation, shape formation, patterning, and design. It begins with a small rectangle of cardboard dipped into paint and becomes a tool for making lines. Children can print vertical, horizontal, and diagonal lines. They combine lines to form shapes. This is just one example of combining mathematics and art. Can you think of others? What happens when children mix paint colour? When red and yellow are combined they equal orange. This is an illustration of a math concept. How would you document this for the children?

*Photo 8.8   Child is "thinking with a line."*

**The cooking connection** Cooking with children is an experience that can involve all the senses: hearing, touching, tasting, smelling, and seeing. Cooking is a hands-on experience. Children who participate in cooking may feel like they are role-playing adult behaviours. Children learn from imitating the adults in their world. Cooking is an excellent way to encourage and reinforce many skills. These include mathematics (measuring, counting, ordering, etc.). Cooking clearly involves science.

Children can observe and identify the parts of a raw egg (the shell, the yolk, the white). Depending on the cooking method and recipe chosen, children can see the egg transform to hard-boiled, soft-boiled, scrambled, and fried. Encourage the children to predict changes and then to test the accuracy of their prediction. "What will happen when we cook the egg for ten minutes in boiling water?" Lead the children into an investigation of the origins of the egg. Imagine the possibilities. Cooking also involves language, art, health, safety, and nutrition. Cooking provides opportunities in social/emotional development (such as taking turns, sharing, trying new experiences) and physical development (including small muscle actions like chopping and stirring, and large muscle actions such as kneading and mixing). It is the ultimate learning experience and can produce delicious results. As with all experiences with young children, it is the *process* of cooking that leads to learning, not the finished product.

# SUMMARY

## Chapter Preview

- Mathematical and scientific experiences are significant to a child's development and can be best facilitated during play.
- Math and science experiences at an early age offer young children powerful ways of knowing about the world. The earlier children have opportunities to engage in math and science, the better opportunity they have to formulate the foundational skills needed for more formal instruction given in the school system.
- Early learning practitioners can mistakenly equate science and mathematics as subjects that have to be taught formally, not realizing these concepts can be learned through play.

## Theory

- Our understandings of how math and science concepts are presented to young children are based on the theories of Piaget and Vygotsky.
- According to Piaget's theory, children acquire knowledge through interaction with the environment and distinguish three types of knowledge: physical, logical-mathematical, and social knowledge.
- Lev Vygotsky promoted a more social context for constructivism—that "it is through others that we develop into ourselves" (Vygotsky, 1981, p. 181).
- Higher levels of learning coincide with higher-order thinking skills. Benjamin Bloom (1956) identified six levels of higher-order thinking, from knowledge at the lowest level to evaluation at the highest.

## Defining Science and Mathematics

- Simply put, science involves processes, content, and concepts, and mathematics is about numbers.

## Concept Development in Science and Mathematics

- Concepts are the building blocks of knowledge. They allow children to organize and categorize information.

## Science, Mathematics, and Development

- Concept growth and development begins in infancy.
- As children develop, their thinking related to mathematical and scientific concepts goes through four distinct stages involving representation: concrete, semi-concrete, semi-abstract, and abstract.

## How Do Preschoolers Learn Scientific and Mathematical Skills?

- Preschoolers best learn math and science concepts when they are based on the children's informal knowledge, involve concrete materials, and the child is an active learner.
- Concepts are acquired through various experiences including naturalistic, informal learning, and structured learning experiences.
- Bruner's stages of knowledge representation guide early learning practitioners in supporting children's concept attainment.

## Playing with Science to Celebrate Wonder

- Children are natural wonderers; they are full of wonder. They approach life with an openness and eagerness to know and to experience, as long as the environment allows them to have the freedom to explore.

## The Scientific Method for Young Children

- As children investigate their world they use the same processes that scientists use: observing, classifying, experimenting, predicting, drawing conclusions, and communicating ideas. These processes are interconnected.

## The Role of the Early Learning Practitioner

- Worksheets are developmentally inappropriate and do not support a play-based approach to learning math and science.
- Documenting children's work will help parents and families understand the value of learning math and science within a play-based constructivist approach.
- The key is finding the balance between child-initiated play with the active presence of the practitioner, combined with intentional teaching through playful learning.

## Setting up an Environment to Support Scientific Inquiry

- An early learning environment is set up with materials that are rich in science possibilities and that will introduce the child to the wonders of the natural world.
- The type of materials depends on the type of science being explored. There are six different types identified, including physical, life, earth, technology, social, and environmental sciences.
- Sand and water play provides children with experiences rich in mathematical and scientific learning.
- Early learning projects which integrate math and science are easy to find. Rocks are materials that children are instinctively drawn to.

## The Development of Mathematical Concepts

- Mathematics learning begins in infancy. A complete mathematical program in early childhood contributes to children's later learning of other subjects, including literacy.
- Between the ages of 2 and 3, children begin to use language related to mathematics, incorporating number words into their play experiences.
- The five implicit principles that are thought to guide a preschool child's development of counting procedures are stable order, one-to-one correspondence, abstraction, cardinality, and order irrelevance.
- There is a difference between rote counting and rational counting. Rote counting involves the memorization of numbers. Rational counting tells children "how many there are." For children to count rationally, they need to demonstrate one-to-one correspondence.

- Other mathematical concepts that should be introduced to children during their play experiences include geometry and measurement, pattern, sequence, seriation, comparison, and classification.

## The Language of Mathematics

- Math has its own language. There are different types of math words including positional, directional, sequence, shape, and number words.

## A Numbers-Rich Environment

- Early learning practitioners set the stage for children to develop mathematical concepts by providing sufficient intriguing materials. The environment is rich with objects that can be used to explore shape and number concepts during everyday play experiences.
- Early learning practitioners label things in the environment with numbers, in addition to labelling with words for literacy.

## Observation

- Reflection is an important part of observation. Early learning practitioners and students observe the environment and consider where mathematical concepts can be introduced, supported, and reinforced.

## Science and Math Connections

- Math and science are naturally connected to other areas including literacy, art, music, movement, and cooking.

# REVIEW QUESTIONS

1. Describe Piaget's three types of knowledge and give an example of each.
2. According to the theories of Vygotsky, how do children learn best? What implications does this have for math and science?
3. Benjamin Bloom identified six levels of thinking. How does this relate to teaching and learning about math and science?
4. What are the simple definitions of math and science?
5. What is meant by concept development in math and science? Describe some math and science concepts. What are some of the first concepts children encounter as infants and toddlers?
6. What are the five principles that should be in place so that children can best learn scientific and mathematical concepts at a young age?
7. Why do you think that our sense of wonder dissipates over time and that there is a distinct difference between a child's and an adult's sense of wonder?
8. Describe how the processes that make up the scientific method are interconnected.
9. Why are worksheets inappropriate? How would you explain to parents that there is a better way to support the development of math and science skills in their children?
10. Explain what a child needs to know in order to count rationally as opposed to rote counting. What is the difference?
11. What is meant by the language of math? What types of math words are there? Give an example of each.
12. Highlight how an early learning practitioner-created game board based on a children's story connects literacy to mathematical concepts.

# MAKING CONNECTIONS

## Theory to Practice

1. Find a suitable container for classification. You would be looking for something that has equal compartments for sorting. Get a collection of natural items for sorting—small rocks, small shells, acorns, etc. Practice sorting yourself by different attributes—colour, texture, shape, and size. Can you think of some cognitively challenging questions that you could ask children while they are in the process of sorting these items? Once you have practiced this experience, present it to some children and record your observations of their processes for classification. Did your questions lead the children to higher-order thinking?

2. Visit your local museum or science centre to get inspired. What did you learn? How can you take your learning and create a developmentally appropriate experience for children? Would you take children on a field trip to a museum or a science centre? Why or why not?

3. Look around your house and find an item that you wonder about. Perhaps you wonder where the item came from or how it works? Perhaps you don't know the history of the item and wonder about who owned it before you? Perhaps you wonder about how it was made? Look at the wonder closely, from all angles. Notice details. Now sketch the wonder with pencil and paper. Are you able to capture the details? Now add colour to your sketch with paints, pencils, pastels, or markers. After that you can represent the wonder three dimensionally with plasticine or clay. What scientific processes and mathematical concepts were explored while you conducting this experience? Now take your wonder to the children and recreate the experience.

4. Take the time to observe children whenever you can. The next time you are in an early learning environment, walk around the room and take digital images of potential areas where math can happen in meaningful ways. Reflection is an important component of observation, so view the digital images you have taken and choose two different areas or experience centres to practice observing children as they play. Take some notes and more images and reflect on your findings. What could you do to encourage mathematical experiences for children? Remember not to limit your observations to just the indoor environment. Consider the potential for math in the outdoors!

## For Further Research

1. One thing that early learning practitioners and students sometimes struggle with is writing learning outcomes or objectives for children. How can you use Bloom's taxonomy to help you? For more information, check out this article posted online: http://www.childcarequarterly.com/winter05_story4.html

2. There are many reference books for children that can support math and science experiences in the classroom. Go to your local library or bookstore and find some of these books. See if you can find developmentally appropriate topics for the children that you are currently working with. Try matching up one of these books with a book of fiction, for example, if the reference or non-fiction book is about birds, can you find a children's (fiction) storybook about birds? In addition to these two books, what else could you provide children that would support hands-on exploration and discovery?

3. Conduct a Google search for "Constance Kamii," a professor of early childhood education who has done extensive research on mathematics learning. What have you learned from your research? Did you find articles and books written by Kamii? Choose one and read, summarize, and critically think about what you have read. How can you apply this learning to the classroom?

# ADDITIONAL READING

Chaille, C. & Britain, L. (2002). *The young child as scientist: A constructivist approach to early childhood science education.* Boston: Allyn & Bacon.

Foundations for Numeracy: An Evidence-based Toolkit for Early Learning Practitioners, Canadian Language and Literacy Research Network, CCCF, 2010. http://foundationsfornumeracy.ca/pdf/EY_NumeracyKit09_ENG.pdf

# WEBLINKS

The Esso Family Math Project is a community-based program for families who would like their children to experience success in math.

www.edu.uwo.ca/essofamilymath

www.naeyc.org/files/yc/file/200905/BTJMathResources.pdf

www.naeyc.org/files/yc/file/200911/ClusterResourcesWeb1109.pdf

http://gse.buffalo.edu/org/buildingblocks/index_2.htm

# 9 Art and Play

## Learning Outcomes

After exploring this chapter you should be able to

- describe why Dewey, Froebel, Steiner, and Malaguzzi advocate for art experiences in early learning programs;

- examine how art influences a child's physical, social, emotional, and cognitive development;

- discuss the benefits of children being exposed to both the principles of design and elements of art in early learning programs;

- describe the four principles that support children in developing their visual language through art experiences;

- explain the stages of children's drawing and use of clay;

- describe why children's art is more than the production of a product;

- examine common strategies used for encouraging creativity with art experiences;

- describe common types of open-ended art materials; and

- examine seven early learning practitioner characteristics that benefit children in the arts.

## Stories from the Field: Practitioner to Student

When I began my ECE studies I realized that I had very limited memories of enjoying art in my early years. When I think of art, I reflect back to a time in grade one when the Art Director for the school district visited our rural school. I think he was probably there to offer us some enrichment. I recall that he stood over me trying to guide me to draw a gingerbread man. I don't believe I accomplished the task to his standards. The experience has stayed with me and has become a guiding force in how I support children in their art. I do not want children to feel the same way I did that day. I was embarrassed and ashamed. I truly believe that children require experiences that allow them to create whatever they so desire. It is not fair to try to guide a child to represent something the way the adult wishes it to look. Providing children with models or precut materials of what they should produce is not part of my practice.

As a practitioner for more than eight years, I continue to find one of my biggest challenges in my practice is working with colleagues who prefer to cut shapes for children, prepare craft products and call it art, or wish for children to collectively sit at the art table and complete a "look alike teacher led" project. Art and crafts are so different, yet they seem to be thought of as one and the same by some early learning practitioners.

I believe that art expression must evolve from within. Our role as early learning practitioners is to provide an array of art materials in various sections of the early learning environment that will trigger children's interest in experimenting with them. Art may be a solitary experience or group, as long as the group evolves from the children. If children choose to create "look alikes," so be it, but it is not something that, as an early learning practitioner, I am going to specifically prepare for.

I encourage new early learning practitioners to view art as an incredible creative thinking process for the children. It must be representative of the child's thoughts, feelings, and experiences to be truly creative.

*Cheree, ECE Graduate, 2001*

# CHAPTER PREVIEW

Historically, art has been a major component of early learning and child care programs. Dewey, Steiner, and Froebel all discussed the importance of art to the development of the whole child. The educators from Reggio Emilia, Italy, also place a high value on art experiences. However, since the late twentieth century and during the first decade of the twenty-first century, the wide spectrum of art experiences for young children is continuously being reduced and replaced with activities that have a more academic focus. This attitudinal shift in programming is influenced by both parents and early learning practitioners. Korn-Bursztyn (2002) explains that "as the pressures for early exposure to formal academic work increase, the arts receive an ever shrinking amount of time and attention from teachers . . . In more and more early childhood settings, the arts occupy a niche on the outskirts of classroom life" (p. 39). One of the main reasons for this shift is the focus that society puts on academic preparation rather than children's play.

Currently, educators are under pressure to focus on programs and experiences that will enhance a child's literacy and numeracy skills. Although we agree that these are important, it is a disconcerting phenomenon because increasingly children have fewer opportunities to participate in spontaneous play and creative discovery. Art play has a pivotal role in a child's development. Exposure to art enhances a child's verbal and nonverbal expression, cognitive and physical development, social and emotional skills, creativity, and problem-solving attributes. Art stimulates memory, it enhances symbolic communication, it promotes relationships, and it provides a venue for building competence and self-esteem. Art is one of the most natural components of play. These attributes support children in developing innate talents and a level of sophisticated play experiences that cultivate curiosity and develop self-identity (McFadyen Christensen, & Doty Kirkland, 2009–2010).

When art is integrated appropriately in early learning programs, children are given a venue to express themselves visually in ways that they may not be able to do so verbally. Art and the expression of creativity provide young children with a medium that supports their development of independence, confidence, pride, and self-expression.

Early learning practitioners offer children opportunities to see things with a different and new perspective. Children require changes to their environments so that new ideas are generated. When they have exposure to the same art activities and materials daily, their minds begin to stagnate and they lose their zest for exploration and curiosity.

This chapter introduces you to what is meant by "the arts." It explores how art provides richness in a child's development, including how it positively influences the child's whole development. A brief discussion on the importance of open-ended materials occurs as well as a discussion on the process versus product debate. We highlight the role that early learning practitioners have in facilitating opportunities for children to be exposed to art experiences that support their interests and capabilities. We begin by sharing the words of wisdom from Professor Ingrid Timmermans.

## WORDS OF WISDOM

When I worked with young children in a College lab school I was amazed to see how the children used visual arts in their daily lives. I learned very quickly that early learning practitioners who embrace visual arts have ways and practices that motivate children to create and experience incredible art forms and elements such as balance, symmetry, and ideas. These experiences contribute to the child's whole development.

I also learned some valuable lessons from the children. Early learning practitioners require knowledge, skills, and practice about the importance of visual arts during the early years. It is not as simple as mixing paint and putting it at the easel. Early learning practitioners require a wide spectrum of information on visual arts processes and ways in which children may become immersed in the visual arts. Think about what visual arts means . . . think in broad terms . . . listen to the children . . . and look at what could be possible.

*Photo 9.1    Children engaging in sculpture.*

# DEFINING ART

There are many ways to define art. Pear, Cohen and Gainer (1984) defined art as "the conscious efforts of human beings to express their ideas and feelings about themselves and their world by arranging colours, shapes, lines, sounds, movements, and other

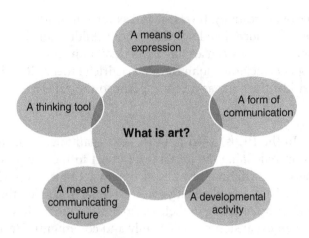

*Figure 9.1*  *What Is Art?*

sensory phenomena" (p. 17). Cornett and Smithrim (2001) describe it as the "means of thinking through our senses . . . Art is hands-on and tangible. We touch materials to make art and manipulate colour, line and shape . . . the symbols used in art are also thinking tools. These sensory-rich symbols form a special language . . ." (p. 137).

According to Lowenfeld and Brittain (1987), art is primarily a means of expression. "Art is . . . meaningful communication with the self as children select and organize parts of their environment into a new whole" (p. 34). As you read the definitions presented, you will note that art is more than an easel with paint at it. We view it as exploration, discovery, and a creative process that helps children make sense of their world. Contemporary perspectives define art as requiring the development of both a body of knowledge and as a developmental activity.

As identified in Figure 9.1, art contributes to a child's communication processes, organizational skills, and self-expression. It is a process that contributes to the development of the "whole child."

# Stop . . . Think . . . Discuss . . . Reflect

What types of art experiences do you remember from your childhood? Was there one particular art medium that you enjoyed? If so, do you know why you enjoyed it? Was there a medium that you found challenging? If so, do you know why?

# Educational Approaches Influencing the Visual Arts in Early Childhood Programs

Understanding the importance of art to the development of young children has been a process that has been challenged throughout history. For example, prior to the early 1920s, many adults, including educators, viewed children's art as clumsy and without personal creativity. It was viewed as version of adult art. As educators and philosophers expanded their knowledge about children and learning, they recognized the connection between art and child development.

Key philosophers including John Dewey, Friedrich Froebel, Rudolf Steiner, and Loris Malaguzzi identified art as a centre point to the experiences that children require.

**John Dewey**   In the 1920s, when John Dewey began to examine education, he took an interest in redefining the importance of art to the development of children. He indicated that children must be viewed as active learners. Children have a need for inquiry. Their creative energies are essential in helping them figure out who they are and bring meaning to their world around them. He suggested that a school setting be an expansion of their family and community. He advocated for adults to help children participate in group experiences, problem solving, and collaborative learning. In *Art as Experience,* Dewey indicated that "a beholder must create his own experience. And his creation must include relations comparable to those which the original producer underwent. . . . Without an act of re-creation, the object is not perceived as a work of art" (1934, p. 54).

As other educators examined Dewey's approach, a progressive movement in education for young children evolved. Art experiences began to have prominence as a tenet in new programs for young children. It was noted that given the correct experimental environments, children had abilities to be creative, engage in self-expression, and be authentic through their expression of art. Chapman (1978) suggested that Dewey's influence helped educators recognize that a child's self-expression is an essential need for maturity to occur. Children require experiences that would help them clarify their ideas both from an individual and group perspective. This generated opportunities for children to create murals, charts, and use puppet shows as a means of communication and expression—all of which are a form of art. At the time, this was a radical approach. It continues to be important—free flowing art experiences are essential in early learning and child care programs.

**Friedrich Froebel**   As identified in earlier chapters, Friedrich Froebel believed that children learn best through play. "Children in the Froebel Kindergarten are not 'schooled', they are developed. The aim is not merely mastery of content, but the nourishment of the whole child—physically, mentally, emotionally, socially, and spiritually" (Corbett, 1979, p. 17). Froebel emphasized that the nourishment of the whole child is best realized in an environment that is play based because play provides children with transforming power (Timmermans, 2005). This power process is necessary for children to explore their creative and imaginative abilities (Corbett, 1979).

Froebel advocated for young children to have stimulating, creative activities in all aspects of the program. Creative activity is the foundation for learning. Each child's creative expression comes from within and that each child, when given the materials, the environment, and encouragement, is a creative being in likeness to the creator (Timmermans, 2005).

As identified in Chapters 2 and 6, Froebel developed 10 "Gifts" for children to use in their play environment. These gifts consist of colourful wooden balls, rings, geometrical shapes, cubes, and tablets. The "Occupations" are the art activities. The Gifts and Occupations complement each other. Through play with the Gifts, children explore solids, surfaces, lines, and points. This exploration corresponds to the Occupations through the active manipulation of clay, plastercine, play dough, woodcarving, woodwork, papier mâché, sand, snow, or rocks. Further, Occupations include art activities such as painting, colouring, drawing, weaving, paper folding, sewing, and collage (Corbett, 1979). Froebel insisted that if children did not have exposure to art materials, they would not develop to their fullest potential.

**The Waldorf approach**   Rudolf Steiner (1861–1925) is the founder of the Waldorf approach, which has gained international attention. With an emphasis on creative play, Waldorf schools are often described as arts-based (Upitis, 2005).

Steiner saw the image of the child as a "threefold human being—body, soul, and spirit" (Easton, 1997, p. 2). The purpose of art is to foster opportunities for young children to "deeply engage in art and to strengthen their spiritual sense, feelings, and imaginative power" (Lim, 2004, p. 117). He believed that the whole child must be nurtured. This can best be realized when preschool children are involved in creative play and healthy work activities. Creative play experiences require children to use their imaginations through the manipulation of open-ended materials such as blocks, puppets, painting, drawing tools, clay, and working with articles from nature (Edwards, 2002). The healthy work activities refer to daily chores such as sweeping, wiping tables, and assisting in the upkeep of the environment.

The Waldorf program exposes children to a wide range of artistic activities such as water colour painting, drawing, colouring with beeswax crayons, modelling, puppetry, gardening, storytelling, and playing musical instruments (Edwards, 2002). These visual and tactile arts are integrated in programming from preschool to high school (Easton, 1997). For example, children experience curriculum areas such as math and literature "by means of drawing, storytelling, chanting and body movements known as eurhythmy" (Upitis, 2005, pp. 6–7). This approach is intended to "extend and deepen a child's intellectual experiences with images, sounds, and textures that stimulate the senses, enrich feelings, and discipline activity" (Easton, 1997, p. 3). The Waldorf approach teaches "others how to utilize the arts to enrich cognitive learning and educate the child towards becoming more fully human" (Easton, 1997, p. 6). For example, there is a relationship of visual arts to later cognitive skills such as reading, logic, and abstract thought.

**Reggio Emilia**   As identified in earlier chapters, the Reggio Emilia preprimary schools evolved from a small community in north central Italy, under the vision and guidance of educator Loris Malaguzzi (Cadwell, 1997). The Reggio Emilia approach is based on the belief that children are competent, intelligent, curious, and social beings (Timmermans, 2005). "There is a shared belief in Reggio Emilia that children have within them an innate understanding of how

## Project-based approach

Children and early childhood practitioners design projects that explore concepts and principles that support the topic of interest. The projects provoke children's thinking, inquiry, wonderment, skills, and collective knowledge.

A project may be for a short period of time or extend over several weeks, depending on the complexity of the project, the authentic questions that evolve, and the resources available to maintain the child's interest and intrigue in the topic.

to relate to the world" (Bennet, 2001, p. 2). Children co-construct knowledge in relation to other children and adults (Mesher & Amoriggi, 2001). As co-constructors of knowledge, children become "producers of cultures, values and rights" (Rinaldi, 2001, p. 51). It is through the principles of art that children express their knowledge.

In Reggio schools programming requires relationships among children, teachers, and parents. It is co-constructed with the early learning practitioner and the child, based on the interactions between them (Cadwell, 1997). The focus is on a projected curriculum which translates into Italian as the word "progettazione" and not necessarily a *project curriculum*. Documentation is not only concerned with project topics but with constructing *progettazione* in the process of each activity or project (Kashin, 2009). Throughout the process of documentation, the curriculum is adjusted accordingly through a continuous dialogue among the teachers and with the children (Gandini & Goldhaber, 2001). This approach provides children with opportunities to develop inquiry skills and to deepen their curiosity for learning. "Through project work, children produce 'art' that astounds most viewers and reflects the creative, communicative and intellectual potential of young children" (Mesher & Amoriggi, 2001, p. 245). While the Reggio Emilia preprimary schools use project work, *The Project Approach*, is a set of teaching strategies that enable teachers to guide children through in-depth studies of real-world topics (Katz & Chard, 2000). The two approaches are similar in that children are involved in project-based learning.

Reggio Emilia schools emphasize the importance of art by ensuring that there is an *atelier* (art studio) adjacent to each classroom and an *atelierista* (art teacher) to support children in their work. The *atelierista* specializes in the visual arts and assists the teaching team and children as they relate to the materials. In the *atelier*, children will find an array of open-ended materials that include a variety of paints and brushes, a wide selection of paper, drawing tools, clay, wood, coloured glass, bits of mirrors, and natural materials. Children use the materials to express symbolic representation and communication, while the teachers use the arts "as a vehicle to understand the child's thinking process" (Bennett, 2001, pp. 2–3). The collaboration amongst the teachers, the children, and the environment strengthens the depth and breadth of the visual arts experiences.

The Reggio Emilia environments position visual arts as a pivotal element to programming. Art experiences are intended to trigger the child's curiosity, which leads the child to explore new options and in new domains. This exploration combined with the interactions among children and adults, lead children to discover in-depth knowledge and skills about areas of interest that may otherwise be neglected. Tarr (2001) indicates that the Reggio approach has shown how partnerships between artist-teachers and early learning practitioners can have a powerful impact on children's learning.

Reggio and Reggio-inspired programs view the environment as a "third teacher." Care is taken in the preparation of the environment because it acts as a third teacher (Fraser, 2000). There is an underlying order and beauty in the design and organization (Lewin, 1995). All of the early learning space has an identity and purpose, is rich in potential to engage in and to communicate, and is valued and cared for by children and adults (Cadwell, 2003).

Recognizing the importance of art to the development of young children, plants, natural light, and the children's own artwork are prevalent in the environment. The environment offers a sense of order and intrigue for each child. Commercial posters are not part of a core Reggio-inspired environment. When children's art becomes the focal point of an environment rather than commercially prepared materials, the children's environment becomes a learning incubator for them. Children's own art increases their curiosity and sense of wonderment. It may lead children to expand upon previous work and to try new ideas.

*Photo 9.2    Children's art includes painting.*

Early learning practitioners constantly examine the art medium's potential to determine how it may support a child's interest and influence development. When early learning practitioners engage in this exploratory process, they are less likely to provide children with inappropriate art experiences.

## Art and Child Development

As you explore the benefits and contributions that art makes to a child's development, you will note that we stress the need for art experiences to be open-ended and process based. Why? Open-ended, process-based experiences support children's creativity and development. Open-ended materials and experiences facilitate opportunities for children to express their own thoughts and ideas about how things look to them in their world. Children gain a sense of success from open-ended materials because there is no one right way to do something and no need to specifically produce something. This freedom to explore contributes to motivating children to have independence, confidence, and an interest in taking risks to try new experiences. At the same time, we learn from the work of the educators from Reggio Emilia that teachers can help children to learn basic artistic techniques if done in a natural and authentic way. Consider a child who is trying to affix two balls of clay. The early learning practitioner scaffolds the learning by working with the child to determine what happens when small amounts of water are applied to the structure. Art is not something taught outside of the experience and it is more than just technique. Art contributes to the child's development in all of the developmental domains.

**Physical development**    Young children learn through motor experiences and sensory exploration (Schirrmacher, 2002; Timmermans, 2005). Art experiences contribute to the development of both fine and gross motor skills. For example, gross motor development is influenced when children use paint or clay. When children paint at an easel they use their entire arms and upper torso as they make large, sweeping motions with their brush (Schirrmacher, 2002). The wider the brush, the more movement the child must exert. Like painting, clay is also valuable for gross motor development. When children tear or roll or twist or flatten clay, they are using their entire arms and hands. Generally, these types of experiences allow children to gain control of the gross motor muscles prior to perfecting fine motor development.

There are many ways in which children develop fine motor skills through art experiences. The most popular materials that contribute to fine motor development include cutting with scissors, collage, painting, and drawing. Art activities also contribute to a child developing their hand and finger muscles that are needed to hold a pencil, manipulate a computer mouse, or make other related fine motor movements. Kail (2002) indicates that "a better grip improves preschoolers' drawing and results in progressively more complex drawings" (p. 222).

# Research Connections

Greer and Lochman (1998) conducted a study to determine whether preschool children grip a pen adaptively. They observed sixteen 3-year-olds, sixteen 5-year-olds, and sixteen college students. During the observations, the participants were required to draw a line from a rectangle placed in one corner of the paper to the far side of the paper. The researchers concluded that out of the three age groups, the 3-year-olds consistently experimented with different grips. By the age of 5, most children have mastered an "adult-like" grip.

Early learning practitioners gain insight into how a child's physical development is progressing. Through observation, early learning practitioners learn about children's thinking patterns and how children examine and understand what they see and experience in their environment.

**Cognitive development**    During the early years, a child's brain is making neural connections at a rapid rate. A child's play that includes movement, language, drawing, and related forms of art, contributes to all of their senses being engaged. This supports the wiring of the brain process needed for successful learning. There is a strong connection between art, thinking, and what the child knows (Eisner, 1976). "Arts serves as an index of a child's thinking. Look at a child's work and you will find out what they know about their world, what they consider important, and how they choose to represent it" (Schirrmacher, 2002, p. 79). This is prevalent when children begin to draw representational objects (Craig, Kermis, & Digdon, 2002).

Art contributes to the development of essential thinking and learning skills such as pattern recognition and development; mental representations of what they observe or imagine from their world; and symbolic and metaphorical representations. Children and adults create symbols of their experiences in order to think about them, problem solve, and make sense of experiences. This symbolization process is necessary for thought to take place (Timmermans, 2005). Drawing is a way in which children can represent what they know about the world. It illustrates how they choose to translate ideas and experiences into a visual language. This is their way of *thinking out loud*.

When children are exposed to visual arts materials at an early age, their problem solving skills and abilities emerge (Cornett & Smithrim, 2001). Problem-solving skills become apparent as children use symbols to represent their ideas in art and when they begin to develop rules about how they work with the materials (Craig et al., 2002). For example, when children work in specific sequences (drawing of head, eyes, nose, and then mouth) and have specific rules about space and location of elements in their drawings, a problem-solving process is being used. Similarly, when children work with paints and modelling materials, they explore the attributes of the materials. This leads them to discover cause and effect, balance,

*Photo 9.3    Children's art brings meaning and beauty to their play space—it becomes an inspiration to them and for them.*

symmetry, solidity and fluidity, and concentration and dilution (Craig, Kermis & Digdon, 2002). As children use art materials they discover that ideas can take form.

As identified in Figures 9.2 and 9.3, children require a variety of art experiences in order to learn about the concepts of the elements of art and the principles of design. While children experiment, discover, and create they are scaffolding their knowledge about art.

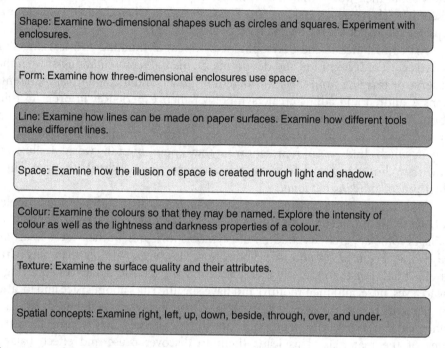

Shape: Examine two-dimensional shapes such as circles and squares. Experiment with enclosures.

Form: Examine how three-dimensional enclosures use space.

Line: Examine how lines can be made on paper surfaces. Examine how different tools make different lines.

Space: Examine how the illusion of space is created through light and shadow.

Colour: Examine the colours so that they may be named. Explore the intensity of colour as well as the lightness and darkness properties of a colour.

Texture: Examine the surface quality and their attributes.

Spatial concepts: Examine right, left, up, down, beside, through, over, and under.

**Figure 9.2**  *Elements of Art*

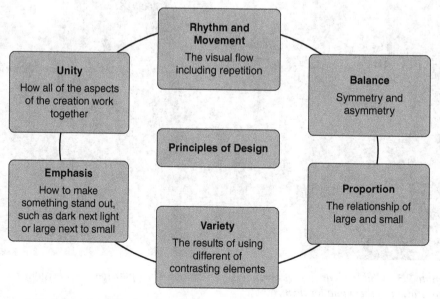

**Rhythm and Movement**
The visual flow including repetition

**Unity**
How all of the aspects of the creation work together

**Balance**
Symmetry and asymmetry

**Principles of Design**

**Emphasis**
How to make something stand out, such as dark next light or large next to small

**Proportion**
The relationship of large and small

**Variety**
The results of using different of contrasting elements

**Figure 9.3**  *Principles of Design*

The concepts that children learn during the preschool years are crucial to later cognitive development (Schirrmacher, 2002). According to Piaget, "the acquisition of cognitive skills relies on the nonverbal operations of manipulating, sorting, constructing, interpreting shapes and symbols, and appreciating different points of view" (Pear, Cohen, & Gainer, 1984, p. 89). Active involvement with art materials develops and strengthens these skills.

**Social development**   Learning through play requires young children to be involved in observation and interaction with others in the environment. A child needs to observe something, try to recreate what is seen, and match their vision with reality. Environments where children are encouraged to manipulate and interact with materials (Kail, 2002) help them to learn about themselves and others. Through art "children validate their uniqueness by making a personal statement through art. Art is rarely a solitary endeavour" (Schirrmacher, 2002, p. 73). Art experiences allow children to observe the uniqueness of others and develop an understanding of the individuals within the social environment. For example, when children are engaged in art, they develop the pro-social skills of sharing materials, taking turns, and interacting positively with others. These socialization skills are necessary for relationship building, interpersonal communication, and civic life.

Art introduces children to social and cultural constructs. For example, children learn about other cultures when they see and share artifacts, such as various forms of drawing and painting, pottery, jewellery, and related items from their family and culture. This is one way in which children build an appreciation for diversity and accept other cultural and social perspectives (McArdle & Piscitelli, 2002). As children explore artifacts and have discussions about them, they share information that supports them in becoming valuable members of a learning community.

When children are in art supportive environments, they build self-esteem. Children, if encouraged appropriately, take pride in the works of art they create. Art also contributes to children developing their problem-solving skills, especially when children are challenged with experiences such as three-dimensional problems that are inherent in sculpting experiences.

**Emotional development**   Social and emotional development are influenced by childhood experiences (Timmermans, 2005). Henniger (2002), and Kostelnik, Stein, Whiren, and Soderman (1998) indicate that self-concept has three dimensions: competence, worth, and control. As identified in Table 9.1, each of these dimensions has a positive or negative impact on a child's artwork. For example, the child who is encouraged and believes that a rainbow can be created similar to the one seen coming to the early learning centre, will more likely have the ability to try to recreate the rainbow, than a child who says they are making a rainbow and the early learning practitioner says, "It doesn't look like a rainbow to me." When children are in a caring, nurturing environment, they view art as an emotionally pleasurable experience.

Art is a venue that allows children to express their feelings, fantasies, fears, and frustrations (Schirrmacher, 2002). "Art is an outlet for ideas and feelings—a

**Photo 9.4**    *Children learn from one another and build self-esteem when they achieve what they have set out to do.*

**Table 9.1**    *Dimensions of Self-Concept*

| Competence | Worth | Control |
|---|---|---|
| Believe that you can accomplish a task | Know your sense of belonging | Feel that you can influence events within your environment |

release, a safety valve—and can give an emotional catharsis" (Cornett & Smithrin, 2001, p. 137). It also enhances a child's self-image and feelings about the self. When a child is exposed to a variety of open-ended art materials, such materials encourage the child to be creative, use originality, and express individuality. The stronger the sense of self-identity, the better the child develops skills for being able to cooperate in solving disputes over objects, playing games, and solving simple problems (Berk, 2002). Art experiences provide the motivation for the development of the whole child: physical, social, emotional, and cognitive development. Based on this reality, quality art experiences continue to be emphasized in early learning and child care programs.

Figure 9.4 provides an overview of how art and creativity support children in developing self-regulation skills.

Strategies for Helping Children **Develop Self-Regulation in the Creative Area**

Early learning practitioners

- Identify the general rules that children practise while using art materials.
- Examine the space available in the art centre and determine the ideal number of children for the space at any one time.
- Guide children when they join the early learning environment on a) the use of an artist apron and how to wear the apron; b) how to care for the art materials including washing the paintbrushes, storing the glue, putting lids on markers, and placing materials on the storage shelves.
- Encourage children to share materials and to conserve materials; using only what they require to support their creative project.
- Role-model with children how to maintain a tidy art centre so that it is ready for the next child wishing to use the area.

***Figure 9.4*** *Strategies for Supporting Self-Regulation in the Creative Area*

## Principles of Children Developing Their Visual Language through Art Experiences

As identified earlier in the chapter, children's art experiences should contribute to them gaining a sense about both the elements of art and the principles of design. Children also benefit from developing their **visual language.** A child uses her visual language to communicate ideas and to make sense of her world.

The following principles support children in developing their visual language:

**Principle 1:  Children follow a sequential process in creating art.**

> **Impact on programming:** Children require time and experience to explore and practice various skills and techniques used to accomplish tasks such as drawing or creating with clay. (See section on stages of clay development.) When adults rush children to draw or produce items before they are ready to do so, there is the potential that the child may not adequately develop the foundational skills needed to engage in more complicated art experiences (Isenberg & Jalongo, 2010).

**Principle 2:  Children's visual language evolves from their thinking and experience.**

> **Impact on programming:** Children require open-ended art materials and time to explore them. This helps children develop ways to express their thoughts and feelings. Through art, young children work through and make creations that reflect their thinking patterns, how they bring meaning to their world (Goodenough, 1954; Kellogg, 1979), and the environment in which they live. This means that many times the work that children share with adults may not be a recognizable object. Early learning practitioners observe

**Visual language** is a process whereby a child communicates an idea through the use of art mediums such as pictures and images, shapes, structures, and words as a way to make sense of the world.

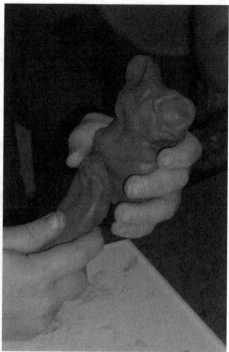

*Photo 9.5    Working with 3 dimensional materials requires the child to engage in thinking and problem solving.*

each child working with the materials and use effective discussion points to stimulate dialogue that is intended to advance the child's inquisitive exploratory options.

### Principle 3: Children's visual language is influenced by their environments and their experiences.

**Impact on programming:** Children's learning is influenced by the context in what they know (Isenberg & Jalongo, 2010; Lowenfeld & Brittain, 1982). Children flourish when the experiences are sequenced from simple to more complex. Each child's brain assimilates new information or processes based on previous knowledge (Isenberg & Jalongo, 2010). A child explores his environment based on life experiences and the exposure to new learning opportunities. If children do not have "newness" in their environments, then their level of curiosity and wonderment is compromised. This directly affects their level of exploration.

### Principle 4: Children's exploration and experiences in art are positively influenced by a guide or facilitator.

**Impact on programming:** There are times when children "get stuck" at a particular juncture, which inhibits them from moving forward. When this occurs, early learning practitioners offer assistance and guidance in the form of questioning, demonstrating a particular technique, or researching an idea or process with the child. It is important that this be a guiding process rather than simply provision of predetermined models or ideas to the child.

# STAGES OF CHILDREN'S ARTWORK

Viktor Lowenfeld (1978) connects intellectual growth, psychosocial stages of development that fall into predictable age groups, and stages of development in children's drawings. Similar to Lowenfeld, Brown (1984), and Stokrocki (1988) provide insight into the common progression or stages of clay that children progress through. Each of the stages will be outlined.

# STAGES OF CHILDREN'S DRAWING

## Scribble Stage (2–4 years of age)

This scribbling stage begins as disordered scribbles. As the child gains more experience and practice, the marks become orderly. Then the child begins to name the scribble and forms and shapes are evident. See Table 9.2.

## Pre-Schematic Stage (3–4 years of age)

During this phase, children begin to draw the human figure. The figure generally has a circle and two lines that are used for the legs. This is often referred to as a tadpole drawing. Occasionally, children will include a rectangle shape for the body. It would appear as though the child has little understanding of space—as the objects are placed in a haphazard position. As the child gains more experience, other forms develop, some of which are very complex. They seek out ways to represent ideas and items in their environment. The child's thinking process becomes more evident.

**Table 9.2**    *Stages of Scribbling*

| |
| --- |
| Disorder scribble—uncontrolled markings that could be bold or light, thick or thin, depending on the mood of the child. There is little or no control over motor activity. |
| Longitudinal scribble—controlled, repetitive motions and movements. There is a visual awareness of the lines. |
| Circular scribble—expanded exploration of controlled motions that demonstrates the ability to create more complex forms. |
| Naming—the child begins to tell stories about the scribble. The child is moving towards using imaginative thinking to represent their world. |

*Photo 9.6 Children make sense of their world through art.*

## Schematic Stage (5–7 years of age)

Children have an increase in the use of symbols. Their drawings are referred to as X-ray drawings because the picture is being seen from both the inside and the outside. For example, if a child draws a child on a bicycle, both legs are shown to the front, even though we should only see one of the child's legs. The sky may not meet the ground at the horizon. There is an increase in the details such as hands and figures and special effects such as glasses or jewellery. There is also an exaggeration between figures—such as the human being taller than the house, or the flowers taller than the person.

## The Gang Stage: The Dawning Realism (8–10 years of age)

During this phase, the child's art is becoming increasingly more realistic and is expressed with more detail for individual parts. Dawning realism becomes the child's objective. Space is discovered and is depicted with overlapping objects and the use of both small and large objects is evident. The human is depicted as a girl, a boy, a woman, or a man with details that often depict a "stiffness" in the representation. Three-dimensional effects are achieved. Children also experiment with shading and colour combinations. During this phase, children begin to compare their work and they also become more critical of it. They try to conform to the level of their peers (Donley, 1987).

## Stages of Clay Development

Brown (1984) and Stokrocki (1988) conducted three significant studies to acquire information on the stages of clay making that children engage in. Note that Brown used the same titles for the stages as Lowenfeld (1947) used for the stages of drawing.

**Scribbling (3–4 years of age)**   During this phase, children make coils, snakes, and mud pies (Brown, 1975). As children gain more experience they progress from making flat objects to upright creations such as snow people. There are limited details on their creations. Children often create items while verbalizing what they are making. For example, as Martina took a ball of clay she explained that "I am making an ice castle with a chapel for my mummy's wedding." Children begin to exhibit seriation by making simple "cookie forms" and connecting them.

**Pre-Schematic (4–5 years of age)**   During this phase, there are more recognizable forms. Children use the clay as a palate for drawing. The head has eyes, a mouth, and limbs that are attached.

**Schematic (5–8 years of age)**   Children exhibit new skills during this phase. Objects may now be in standing positions, tilted positions, or a combination of both. People sculptures include necks, hair, fingers, etc. Animals have prominent features as well. For example, cats will have tails and elephants will have trunks. Children make letters to write their name or names of important people in their lives.

***Photo 9.7***   *Pre-schematic stage (3–4 years of age).*

**Dawning realism (9–11 years of age)**   During this phase children concentrate on facial features, patterns, sexual characteristics, and special effects such as hats and a scarf. Clay forms look realistic.

The stages presented for drawing and clay are guidelines only. Some children may progress through the stages more quickly than others. Some children may overlap between more than one stage at any given time. You may find some children who prefer painting to clay and vice versa.

Although these stages are used as guidelines, early learning practitioners benefit from examining each child's artwork and use the findings as a guide to devise programming experiences that will enhance experiences and challenge the child to make new discoveries. It provides an overview of how the child is progressing—within the age ranges and stages or if the child is exceeding or is not meeting the stages and the predictable progression. For example, children with certain types of autism may develop their art talents more quickly than other children. Many children with learning disabilities may also have advanced creative and visual talents in drawing.

*Photo 9.8    Gang stage.*

At each stage of development, early learning practitioners gain insight into a child's perception about the world they live in. A child's use of colour, materials, and the art medium provide information about the child's sense of self-worth and self-expression.

## THE PROCESS OF ART VERSUS THE PRODUCT

Children's art is more than the production of something recognizable to the adult or a specific product—art is a process. Our role as early learning practitioners is to support young children engaged in exploring and creating a painting that evolves from the child mixing colours, rather than only using the three paint colours placed at the easel. We become more intrigued by how a child makes a sculpture that combines play dough and sticks than a creation that can be clearly labelled as an item, such as a cup. In essence, it is the **process of exploring and creating,** rather than a finished, recognizable product that is important to us. Open-ended art experiences require a child to use their imagination and their abilities. This is how they explore the "what if's." These are keys to nurturing creativity.

Just as there are ways to encourage creativity, there are also some practices that discourage creativity. For example, when children are given precut shapes to create a specific item such as a rabbit, or pictures to paste onto a paper bag for a puppet, these become "dictated art." Jenkins (1986) indicates such experiences lead children to lose their creativity, sensitivity, self-confidence, and free-flow or independent thinking. These types of assembly tasks lead children to become conformists and perfectionists as they try to meet the expectations of completing the task to the required standard. Think back to the story of *The Little Boy* highlighted in Chapter 2. Clearly dictated art impacted the little boy's creativity.

Similar to the assembly tasks outlined above, colouring books and sheets of paper with lines on them for colouring negatively impact a child's opportunity for creativity. These products do not support a child's individual expression or emotional release. Fill-in art is often "doing without thinking" and promotes mindless obedience to authority, rather than creative problem solving. The sense of achievement and pride that should come from art is lacking in dictated art (Jenkins, 1986; Timmermans, 2006).

Cornett and Smithrim (2001) indicate that "dictated art" can frustrate children's development. When children are not involved in a creative problem-solving process, they are not stimulated or encouraged to engage in higher-order thinking. We encourage higher-order of thinking because it advances children's ideas, perspectives, and opportunities to explore in new ways. Jalongo (1999) advises that "teachers should resist the mindless activities that are ubiquitous in our field. It is a waste of children's time. Such stereotypes are the opposite of creativity and art" (p. 205).

*Photo 9.9    Dawning realism.*

One of the key purposes of providing children with art experiences is for them to learn to express their feelings and ideas; it is not to have children duplicate adult ideas. Jalongo (1999) says, "If you choose an activity and most of your time is spent reminding children about the instructions, or worse yet 'fixing up' children's work, that is a clear indication that it is neither art nor a developmentally appropriate activity" (p. 206). Children require the freedom to engage in appropriate art process experiences that are fluid in nature. This will lead them to intertwine art, play, and real-life experiences. For example, Matt, since the age of 3, has exhibited an interest in vehicles. He carries cars in his pockets, he draws cars, and he makes the sounds of the engines. Often, his play is vehicle related, as identified in the scenario that follows.

When making trucks from cardboard boxes, Matt was joined by Justyn, Patrick, and Mohammad. They each made the trucks by using the boxes, a paper punch to make holes, string to attach them, and a knife and scissors to cut out doors to the cab. Two of the children discussed painting the trucks but decided that they needed to "get on the road." As they started to push their trucks on the floor, out of the art area, Matt yelled, "I need gas." Jamie, who had been standing on the sidelines immediately said, "My gas station is open." Quickly, the children pulled into the pretend gas stations with their vehicles. As Matt's tank was filled, he turned to Mohammad and said, "I'm hungry . . . Let's pull in at the Pizza House." The children proceeded to the play dough table where a small group of children were making pizzas with the play dough (Bhroin, 2007). The truck drivers said, "We want pizza to go." Archie responded by saying, "You got it. Will that be with cheese?" This illustrates how art influences play and how play influences art. Early learning practitioners encourage the overlap between the play and art processes because this interconnectivity allows children to explore ideas, see things in new ways, and "remake reality" (David, 1999, p. 47).

It is common practice for children to have recurring themes in their art and their play. For example, as identified earlier, Matt has a keen interest in vehicles. For him, vehicles are prominent in his drawings, in his stories, with clay, and in the sand. Each time he draws a vehicle, there are different details. It is as though he is trying to perfect one aspect of the reproduction. In one drawing, he had lines drawn that he identifies as roads. Weeks later, his drawings had roads with curves. And some more weeks later his drawings illustrated roads with curves, a truck, and dots on the windshield that he identified as snow. When children combine art and play, they are developing the conceptual framework that supports them in expanding their abstract and higher-order of thinking. This higher order of thinking provides children with resourceful options for learning.

The following questions help guide student early learning practitioners in determining if potential experiences are creative art experiences or dictated art experiences.

1. Is the early learning practitioner preparing precut pieces, patterns, or models? This implies that the children are required to produce a product even though early childhood practitioners may suggest that the children may create whatever they wish.

2. Will each child's work be original or look nearly identical to another child's creation? Do early learning practitioners need to "fix" the child's work? When a child's art looks like another, originality and creativity has been stifled. Such experiences become "busy work" rather than art. If an early learning practitioner fixes a child's work, it undermines the child's self-esteem and confidence.

3. Are children given the choice of when to engage in art experiences or are they required to participate in the art experience at an assigned time? If children are required to come together for art in a group, or if children must complete an art activity over a specified period of time, then this is not art. If art experiences are designed to be used as display pieces for parents, then this is not art; rather it is a marketing strategy for parents.

4. Are you offering children products such as food items to use as creative materials? Children require authentic art products. When children are given items such as macaroni, beans, or finger painting experiences with pudding, early learning practitioners are sending children mixed messages—first, artists do not generally use these types of products to express creativity and secondly, it says to children that it is ok to play with food.

5. Are early learning practitioners offering art experiences that may only be completed one way? If so, this implies that a structured product is necessary.

6. Are the art materials and experiences offered at one interest centre indoors? If so, this implies that art is a solitary activity, rather than one that spans across play. It also indicates that indoor programming is more important than outdoors. This reduces the opportunity for children to incorporate natural items from their environment into their creative experiences.

## Stop . . . Think . . . Discuss . . . Reflect

Think about being a student practitioner in an early learning centre. The centre is using a theme of 101 Dalmatians. The story has been read, the movie shown, and there are many photos of Dalmatians in the play space. Because a group of children seemed interested in the photos of the dogs, you thought it would be neat to provide children with cut out paper shapes of Dalmatians, black crayons, black tissue paper, and black and white construction paper.

Is this an activity that should be offered to children? Why or why not? What are the potential impacts on children? Are the impacts positive or negative? Why? Are there other ways to support the children's interests in the dogs?

## STRATEGIES FOR ENCOURAGING CREATIVITY WITH ART EXPERIENCES

Early learning practitioners are continuously incorporating ways to support and encourage a child's creativity with art experiences. There are many strategies that support creativity, such as

- Encouraging children to examine possibilities, think about options, and solve problems in creative ways. Encourage children to take risks and make mistakes. Support growth by providing idea options for the child to consider.
- Providing children with an array of materials and choices for exploration both through their senses and by the questions that the early learning practitioner poses.
- Providing children with an environment that has established routines that support and encourage children to think and explore without adult direction.
- Providing children with opportunities to observe, explore, and experience aspects of other cultures relative to their life experiences.
- Creating changes to the indoor and outdoor early learning environment so that children are stimulated to explore their environment in new ways.
- Encouraging children in ways that help them build their skills and expand their sense of accomplishment and experimentation.

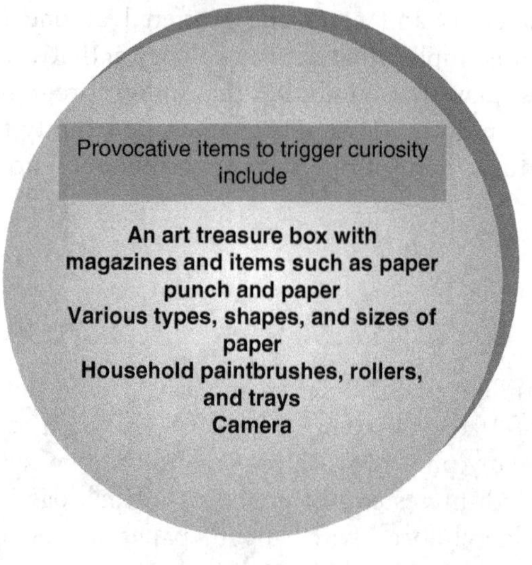

**Figure 9.5** *Provocative Items to Trigger Curiosity*

- Displaying children's artwork at their eye level, in an aesthetically pleasing format.
- Offering art experiences in both the indoor and outdoor play environments.

Figure 9.5 (above) provides ideas for materials that will trigger creativity.

## TYPES OF OPEN-ENDED ART MATERIALS

Early learning practitioners examine materials to gain an understanding of the core attributes that each material has. This helps early learning practitioners and student practitioners explore how a child may potentially use the materials and it guides the questioning process used to advance a child's thinking skills and exploration of materials. For example, Mattie and Akik were at the easel. There were jars of red, blue, yellow, white, and black paint available. Suddenly Akik says, "Mattie, I made pink!" Mattie says, "How did you do it?" Akik says, "I don't know?" Brent, the early learning practitioner hears the conversation and walks over to Akik to ask, "Akik, what paint colours did you use—did you use any yellow?" Akik thought for a moment, looked at the colours on his page and then said, "No, I did not use yellow—red and white make pink." Then Mattie said "I am going to try it. Yes, it does!" Then, Brent said, "What happens if you add another colour such as yellow to it? What colour do you think you will create?" Other children gathered around to watch as Mattie and Akik mixed different colours. Brent wonders aloud what will happen when they mix other colours. Children observing made a prediction, as did Akik and Mattie. Then they proceeded to see the results.

The above example illustrates how open-ended experiences lead children to discovery learning or hands-on learning. One child made a discovery about what happens when you mix two colours—a new colour is formed. Then other children participated in the discovery. The children learned by doing. These are the types of experiences that children should engage in during their early learning experiences. There are many types of open-ended materials to have in an early learning and child care environment, such as the following:

**Potter's Clay:** Clay offers children opportunities to be creative while providing a release for energy and stress. Clay requires children to pull, push, squeeze, and punch it. These actions support the child's fine motor development. Popular accessories with clay include rolling pins, and various containers, dull knives, and sticks.

**Paint:** Painting is one of the most popular materials that support children in exploring colours, patterns, and art forms. Children benefit from having painting activities occur on a variety of surfaces and places such as at an easel, on the floor, on a tabletop, in a sandbox, and on plywood on a fence. The paint needs to vary in colour, texture, and thickness. Children benefit from using several shades of the same colour. Painting instruments including paint brushes of different thicknesses, paint rollers, straws, cotton balls, cotton swabs, sponges, feathers, and string provide unique experiences for the children.

**Sand:** Sand provides children with an unstructured medium. Sand exploration supports children in mixing, pouring, stacking, moulding, sifting, and combining. Sand tools include buckets, cups, sifters, moulds, vehicles, pipe pieces, and boards. This medium supports children in creating art sculpture. Dry paint added to sand expands the opportunities for creativity.

**Chalk:** Chalk has many uses. Children benefit most when they have large surfaces to use the chalk on, such as driveways or surfaces that may be washed off.

**Crayons:** Similar to chalk, crayons support children in exploring line and drawing formation. Tools such as textured surfaces under paper or over paper, screens, and corrugated cardboard offer children intrigue with the crayons.

**Materials for Collage:** A variety of materials and bases are presented for collage. Collage activities lead children to examine the qualities of design, colours, textures, and forms that the materials exhibit. Materials that have similar qualities and materials that are unique and different offer curiosity triggers. Collage bases may include scraps of wood, trays, discarded mat boards, and cardboard. Fabric pieces that are soft, stiff, and net-like are also provided.

**Paper:** A variety of paper including tissue, construction, corrugated, fancy paper doilies, and specialty papers are made available. Boxes of all sizes and shapes are present as well as rolls of paper and paper cylinders.

Figure 9.6 provides ways to display materials that will trigger curiosity.

***Figure 9.6*** *Ways to Display Items to Trigger Curiosity*

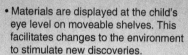

- Materials are displayed at the child's eye level on moveable shelves. This facilitates changes to the environment to stimulate new discoveries.
- Materials such as crayons, felt markers, pencil crayons, and paper are sorted by colour and size.
- Materials are sequenced from simple to more complex. For example, large paint-brushes are introduced before small intricate brushes.
- The work space is well-presented each day. For example, the easels, paint brushes, and paint containers are cleaned daily so that children have a "clean slate" to use.
- New provocative items that trigger curiosity are available at strategic points.

## THE ROLE OF THE EARLY LEARNING PRACTITIONERS IN ART EXPERIENCES

The quality of the art experiences and the strategies used to support children in their quest with art experiences must be of high quality and developmentally appropriate (Eckhoff, 2008). Children benefit most from early learning practitioners who have an interest in art and know how art experiences may span across the experience centres in the early learning and child care environment.

As early learning practitioners and student practitioners, we need to be concerned about building our knowledge level about the arts. Why? Because our knowledge levels or lack of knowledge influences the types of art experiences children are exposed to. There is a body of literature that indicates practitioners may not receive sufficient educational experiences about the relationship of arts to child development. For example, Jalongo (1999) describes her experiences on visits in the field. "When I visit classrooms, even classrooms of teachers I greatly admire, it appears to me that the arts are the least well taught of all curricular areas" (p. 205). One of the reasons for this reality is that undergraduate students have had negative experiences with arts and creativity in their early childhood training. Jalongo highlights the following comment received from students:

We only had one class for all the arts-music, art, drama, dance. It was so easy to get an "A" in this class . . . Every week, we would have to bring in some object, like a milk carton, a sock, or a clothes hanger to make it into something during class. Whoever could come up with the most creative idea (according to the teacher) had their work held up for the rest of us to admire. It felt like I was back in grade school again because mine still wasn't good enough. (p. 205)

Jalongo (1999) states that in order "to bring out the best in children, teachers first need to get over their negative experiences and feelings of inadequacy in the arts" (p. 208). Understanding the core elements of art requires early learning practitioners to explore these elements, to play with these elements, and to make discoveries about these elements (Spodek, 1993). Similarly, children flourish in environments that provide them with opportunities to experience art experiences, aesthetic experiences, and encounters with art. Children also benefit when their practitioners engage in observations, reflection, and dialogue to support children in their construction of art based knowledge (Eglinton, 2003).

Throughout your studies, you are gaining new knowledge and skills that are intended to help you develop a working philosophy. Your philosophy guides you in your observations, interactions with children and adults, how you prepare the environment, how you embrace the sense of curiosity that each child brings to the environment, and what you believe about professional development and lifelong learning opportunities. Thinking about art and its presentation to children is directly related to your beliefs about how children learn.

## Stop . . . Think . . . Discuss . . . Reflect

When you think about children and art experiences, what do you wish for them to gain from the experiences you provide? Why? How do you envision your philosophical beliefs about art experiences supporting the needs of children? Are there conflicts between your beliefs and ideas presented in this chapter? If so, how might the conflicts be resolved? What are the impacts on children when there are conflicts in philosophy and programming?

There are many strategies to support you in exploring your philosophy about art and young children. What we believe about play, learning, and the arts influences the early learning and child care environments. Hermon and Prentice (2003) encourage practitioners to incorporate each of the following into their art programming practice: enable, empower, engage, and extend. Figure 9.7 describes what is meant by each of these powerful words.

The following suggestions will help you think about what you believe about the arts. The framework is intended to further enhance your understanding and an appreciation for the arts with young children.

## Children Require Early Learning Practitioners Who View Themselves as Embracing Play, Creativity, and Art

Children require early learning practitioners to gain the knowledge and skills about art and play. Meaningful art activities are extended to children. There are

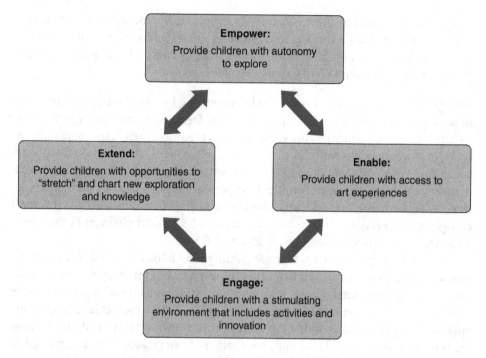

*Figure 9.7* *Hermon & Prentice's Powerful Words for Art Programming Practice*

opportunities to combine art with other play experiences. Early learning practitioners offer children various types of stimulus, time, and materials that will create an environment to fuel creativity.

Five core questions help you determine how you view yourself as a creative early learning practitioner: What are my beliefs about children and art? What types of open-ended opportunities should I provide children? How will I encourage and support children who exhibit an interest in art? How do I personally view my creative talents? How will my attitudes impact the children?

Early learning practitioners who gain a sense of their philosophical orientation are able to model appropriate attitudes towards art and play. They show respect for the interesting ideas that children create and they have the ability to ask probing and "what if" questions that help children move to a deeper level of thinking and exploration.

## Children Require Early Learning Practitioners Who Have an Understanding about the Elements of the Materials

Early learning practitioners who develop an understanding of the technical information of the materials used by children are better able to discuss ideas with the children and plan potential learning opportunities. For example, how are soft, gentle colours such as light blue and pinks made versus harsher colours of browns and blacks? What are the primary and secondary colours and how do they blend? What are the differences between newsprint and glossy paper? What is the best paper for the various mediums? How will these paper choices impact a child's work? What is the difference between plasticine and potter's clay? What is the difference between white clay and red clay? Why would you use one over the other? What are the safety concerns of the paints and the various materials that may be introduced to children? How do the various brushes impact a creation? Knowing information about the materials builds the early learning practitioners' confidence in their program planning and facilitation skills with children.

## Children Require Early Learning Practitioners Who Know When to Be Supportive and When to Allow Children to Be Free and to Problem Solve the Area of Challenge

When children explore new materials that they do not have any experience with, they may become frustrated; this interferes with the child's creativity and play. Early learning practitioners, through observation, are able to see signs of concern or frustration building. Technical guidance is offered when required, recognizing that it is proffered without imposing our ideas on the children.

Another area of support that children benefit from is by them having enough **time** to engage in experiences and with sufficient materials to support exploration. For example, think back to Matt, Mohammad, and Justyn. Think what would have occurred had the children not been given enough time to make their vehicles and then exercise the play episode of requiring gas and having pizza.

## Children Require a Learning Environment with a Variety of Materials and Places to Use the Materials

Early learning practitioners view the environment as a safe place for children to explore, experiment, and create new knowledge. Creativity is enhanced when children have access to a variety of materials, plenty of materials, space, and opportunities to use the materials. Children gravitate to play spaces that are aesthetically pleasing. Carefully arranged art materials help children exercise independence and self-regulation. Children must not be rushed so that other children can be accommodated.

When we think of variety we need to think beyond the materials that are presented. Using a variety of spaces in the play space allows children to observe different ideas, possibilities, and material attributes. For example, in an observation conducted with eight 4-year-old children who had access to a variety of materials including pipes and wooden pieces, the children's creativity differed significantly among the children who used the materials outdoors from indoors. Children using the materials outdoors had life-size creations that were built in upright positions and they incorporated a variety of materials into the creation. The children using the material indoors used smaller pieces of materials, the creations were flat, and only three types of materials were incorporated into the design (Dietze, 2009).

## Children Benefit from Early Learning Practitioners Who Encourage Children to Discuss Their Creations

When children discuss their art experiences and those of other children and professional artists, they begin to develop an art-focused and a self-focused vocabulary. They connect vocabulary related to the medium. For example, when Brent was discussing the clay experience with 4-year-old Marti, he was amazed to hear Marti say that he began by using a slab, then he had to pinch the clay, and then he rolled it. He said he was not going to fire his sculpture today. The language expressed by Marti is commonly used among potters. Marti has mastered the language at this very young age because of exposure to it and having the language context.

Early learning practitioners and children record the children's information that the children share. Throughout discussions, there is an emphasis on the process rather than the product.

Early learning practitioners take their lead from the children. For example, if the child says, "I made very thick lines," the practitioner may expand on that idea and ask, "How did you make those thick lines?" If appropriate, discussion may also occur on how to make thin lines or how curved lines may be created.

## Children Benefit from Early Learning Practitioners Who Observe Children and Engage in Documentation

Observing children using art materials provides the early learning practitioner with insight into the child's interests and skill levels. For example, knowing the child's pincer grasp ability will help early learning practitioners determine which sizes of brushes are most appropriate for the child to gain success. A child first beginning to use brushes needs large-handled brushes. A child who has a more developed pincer grasp will use both large and small brushes. Children who you notice are intrigued by sculpturing would be offered materials such as potters clay, plastercine, and play dough. The tools are chosen based on the child's interests and opportunities for new discoveries.

As identified in Chapter 3, there are a number of observation and documentation methods that early learning practitioners may use to gain information to support knowing the whole child. Implementing participation charts, profiles, and creating portfolios are effective tools that provide an overview of how a child engages in arts. By working with the child to collect pieces of their creations and by taking photos for submission into the portfolio (see information on portfolio development in Chapter 3), early learning practitioners and children gather data over a period of time on a child's skills and interest, the environment, and how groups of children use the materials. Figure 9.8 provides a participation chart sample.

Examining participation charts and compiling the data provides early learning practitioners with information on how and where children use the creative materials. Early learning practitioners examine the information to determine clues to the following:

- The number of times a child uses creative materials over a period of time
- The types of materials the child uses
- The social aspect of the experience—solitary or with other children
- The duration of the time that the child spends creating. Does the child complete the experience at one time or does the child add to the creation over time?

Participation charts help us to gain information about how children use the creative centre and the materials within it. You are able to see the types of interests children have and how you may be able to further enhance their interest through dialogue or with items and tools that may further spark a child's creativity.

| Participation Chart for Art Experiences | | | |
|---|---|---|---|
| Observer: Martha | | Date: Week of February 15 – Day 1 | |
| Indoors: X    Outdoors: X See note | | Time: Mornings and afternoons | |
| Child's Name | Easel | Creative Centre | Combined Creative and Other |
| Brit | | | Box structure created in block area |
| David | X | | |
| Marti | X | | |
| Mary | | X | |

**Notes:** David and Marti worked together at the easel. They were there for more than ten minutes but less than twenty. Mary took the paper and paints from the easel and created a painting on the tabletop. Later she put her items in the cart and took her painting outside to work on. When outdoors she set up her painting under the cedar tree. She used green and white paint. She appeared to try to match the shade of green from the tree with her paint mixing.

Brit took the creative materials to the block area. It appeared as though he needed the box structure to support his work with the blocks.

*Figure 9.8*  *Profile of Participation in Art Experiences*

The profile of skill development, as outlined in Figure 9.9, is an effective tool to record information about the skill the child exhibits in a particular area. You will note in the example provided that the child has incorporated her knowledge about the sizes of paintbrushes in relation to line development. Dusty has also illustrated using mixed media in her work by attaching shapes cut from other paper into her

**Profile of Skill Development in Art Centre**

Observer: Martha                                        Date: Week of June 15–19

Indoors:      Outdoors: X

Child's Name: Dusty      Age: 4

Experience Centre: Art—Easel and Creative Centre

Behaviour Observed:

Mixes primary and secondary colours—verbalizes how to make green

Uses large and small paintbrushes to make thick and thin lines—appears to know the smaller the brush, the more refined the lines are

Prints name with marker on upper right-hand corner

Uses scissors to cut shapes in rectangles and circles

Incorporates shapes, using glue into painting

Takes painting off easel and places on drying rack without assistance

Tells the early learning practitioner about parts of her drawing

*Figure 9.9*  *Profile of Skill Development*

work. She is demonstrating creative attributes that may differ from other children her age. Profiles assist student early learning practitioners in seeing what capabilities children bring to their play and learning.

## Children Require Early Learning Practitioners to Have Rich Dialogue with Them about Their Art Creations

Children's art experiences and creativity are dependent on materials, the environment, the facilitation, and the time allocated for creative expression. Early learning practitioners focus on advancing a child's confidence to explore new materials and methods. Dialogue between the early learning practitioner and the child must be correct. The questions posed by the adult are intended to lead the child to think about what was done and what possibilities exist. The questions are open-ended, nonjudgmental, and stimulate intrigue. As identified in other chapters, it is challenging to develop questions that encompass intrigue, problem solving, wonderment, and potential new directions for exploration. Student practitioners require practice in observing the child's art and in formulating questions that advance children's thinking, exploration, and learning. In Figure 9.10, conversational ideas are outlined.

*Figure 9.10*
*Conversational Strategies for Discussing Children's Art*

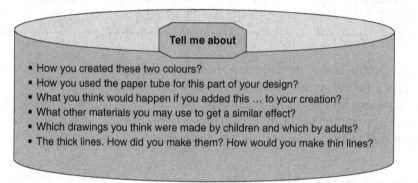

**Tell me about**

- How you created these two colours?
- How you used the paper tube for this part of your design?
- What you think would happen if you added this ... to your creation?
- What other materials you may use to get a similar effect?
- Which drawings you think were made by children and which by adults?
- The thick lines. How did you make them? How would you make thin lines?

## Children Benefit from Early Learning Practitioners Who Know about the Relationship of Art to Child Development

Jalongo (1999) indicates if early learning practitioners are not being exposed to "educationally worthwhile art experiences" in their college or university programs, then it must be available through professional development opportunities. "If the arts mission of early childhood education must be to provide high-quality arts experiences for all children . . . then, professional development in the arts is not a frill, it is a necessity" (Jalongo, 1999, pp. 206–207). As Krishnamurti (2000) states, "Education can be transformed only by transforming the educator. Throughout the world, it is becoming more and more evident that the educator needs educating. It is not a question of educating the child, but rather the educator" (p. 60).

Early learning practitioners require access to ongoing professional development so that they continue to gain an understanding of the relationship of visual arts to child development, and in the design and delivery of appropriate visual arts experiences for children during their early years. Children are more likely to explore the medium when the materials and the environment allow for fluidity.

Early learning practitioners have a key role in expanding their knowledge and skills about the benefits of art experiences. The more the practitioners know about the creative process, materials, and the development of an environment that supports the arts, the more likely children will integrate art into their daily living.

# SUMMARY

## Chapter Preview

- Research indicates art enhances a child's creativity, problem-solving skills, language skills, and their cognitive, social, emotional, and physical developmental domains. Yet, many early learning programs have a focus on academic instruction rather than art.

## Defining Art

- There are many ways to define art. Art is a means of expression, a form of communication, a developmental activity, and a way to understand culture and community. It is interconnected to the development of the "whole child."

## Educational Approaches Influencing the Visual Arts in Early Childhood Programs

- Educators and philosophers including John Dewey, Friedrich Froebel, Rudolf Steiner, and Loris Malaguzzi identified the benefits of young children participating in early learning experiences with art as a core focus. They suggest that children who are not exposed to developmentally appropriate art experiences will not develop to their fullest potential.

## Art and Child Development

- Open-ended art experiences facilitate children gaining a sense of success because they create as they desire, rather than needing to produce a specific product.
- Art advances the child's fine and gross motor development.
- Art is deeply cognitive; as there are many mental processes that occur through the thinking and problem-solving activities, many of which are essential for later academic learning, such as pattern recognition and development.
- Art provides children with the venue to develop social and cultural constructs. Children develop their self-identity, competence, worth, and control through their interactions with art experiences. Art helps children to develop and release their ideas and feelings.
- Children develop their visual language through art experiences in environments that recognize that children follow a sequential process in creating art; that it evolves from their thinking and experience; and that it is influenced by their environments, experiences, and their guides or facilitators.

## Stages of Children's Drawing

- Lowenfeld identifies four stages of drawing that children pursue. They are scribble, pre-schematic, schematic, and the gang stage.
- Brown and Stokrocki use the same classifications as Lowenfeld to identify the stages of clay development.

## The Process of Art versus the Product

- The process that the child engages in to create something is more important than producing a recognizable product.

- Open-ended art experiences require young children to use their imagination and curiosity.
- Precut shapes and structured art activities are known as "dictated art"—these types of activities negatively impact the flow of independent thinking and learning.

### Strategies for Encouraging Creativity with Art Experiences

- Children require environments that have established routines; have art experiences both indoors and outdoors; display artwork at the child's level; provide children with encouragement; have faith in the children's abilities, and encourage children to take risks and make mistakes.

### Types of Open-Ended Art Materials

- The more common open-ended materials include potter's clay, paint, sand, chalk, crayons, materials for collage making, and paper.

### The Role of the Early Learning Practitioners in Art Experiences

- Early learning practitioners benefit from determining their philosophy as it relates to the arts. Herman and Prentice suggest early learning practitioners incorporate *enable, empower, engage,* and extend into their practice.
- Children benefit from early learning practitioners who view themselves as embracing play, creativity, and art, understand the elements of the materials; know how to support and when to let the children problem solve; provide a variety of materials and places to use the materials; encourage and discuss the children's creations; consistently observe children; know about the importance of art to child development.

## REVIEW QUESTIONS

1. Describe how art experiences contribute to a young child's development.
2. Explain why Dewey, Froebel, Steiner, and Loris Malaguzzi advocate for children to have access to a variety of art experiences in their early years.
3. Discuss how art experiences support children in learning about the elements and principles of design.
4. Outline the four principles of children developing their visual language through art experiences.
5. Highlight the stages of children's artwork and clay work.
6. Describe the debate among educators on process versus product related to children's art.
7. Outline ways in which early learning practitioners may encourage creativity with art experiences.
8. Discuss a minimum of seven roles that early learning practitioners have in providing art experiences for young children.

## MAKING CONNECTIONS

### Theory to Practice

1. Visualize your ideal play space for children using art materials. In what ways do you think your philosophy about how children learn and your thoughts on process versus product influence your view of the ideal space for children's art?
2. There are many early learning centres that establish an art centre for the children in the indoor environment. How might you move the art experience to the outdoor environment? How do you envision

the experience will be for the children? Will it be different from indoors? If so, how? What different practices would you need to think about if your art centre was outdoors? How might the materials differ? Why?

3. Imagine that you are required to prepare a presentation for parents on the importance of art for young children. How would you present the information? What key messaging would you wish to share with the parents? Why? What role would children have in the presentation?

4. Examine your early learning centre. Then, visualize how you would incorporate art experiences into one of the experience centres. How would you set it up? Why? What considerations are required? How would you encourage the children to combine the two experience centre play opportunities?

## For Further Research

1. McKean (2000) and others suggest that the formal training of early learning practitioners and their experiences with art as children influences early learning practitioner's attitudes towards art and children. Conduct a literature research on this to acquire further opinions based on research on the influencers of early learning practitioners' attitudes towards art experiences for children.

2. There is debate among school teachers and early learning practitioners on the process versus product perspective. What is the research saying about children's art and process versus product? Is there sufficient documentation on these two areas that allow you to formulate your perspective based on your philosophical orientation?

3. How does creative thinking evolve from art experiences?

# ADDITIONAL READING

Coates, E., & Coates, A. (2006). Young children talking and drawing. *International Journal of Early Years Education.* 14(3), 221–241.

Isbell, R. T., & Raines, S. C. (2006). *Creativity and the arts with young children.* Clifton Park, NY: Delmar.

Kemple, K. M., & Nissenberg, S. A. (2000). Nurturing creativity in early childhood education: Families as part of it. *Early Childhood Education Journal,* 28(1), 67–71.

Schirrmacher, R. (2002). *Art and creative development for young children* (4th ed.). Albany: Thompson Learning Inc.

Upitis, R. (2005). *Architecture, complexity science, and schooling in the early years.* Hawaii International Conference on Arts and Humanities. Unpublished manuscript.

# WEBLINKS

Children Art Foundation
**http://childrenartfoundation.org/aboutus.html**

The wonder of learning—the hundred languages of children
**www.thewonderoflearning.com/?lang=en_GB**

Waldorf painting water colour
**www.youtube.com/watch?v=oBAi29Fy6yg**

# 10 Bringing Technology into Child's Play: A New Perspective

## Learning Outcomes

After exploring this chapter, you should be able to

- explain various perspectives about the use of technology with young children, including the recommendations of National Association for the Education of Young Children (NAYEC) on the responsibility of early learning practitioners and the use of technology;

- highlight the benefits of using technology;

- explain the stages of using a computer among preschool children;

- discuss how the placement of the computers in early learning centres impacts how the children use them;

- describe how technology supports child development, including children with atypical development;

- explain the concern of technology and related equitable issues;

- describe the three broad categories of adult involvement in computer play;

- discuss strategies that early learning practitioners use to facilitate play with computers, choose software, and observe children while using the technology; and

- discuss principles of training and development for early learning practitioners and technology.

## Stories From the Field: Practitioner to Student

As I think about my beginnings as an early learning practitioner and then examine societal changes, I realize it is time to face reality—I am living at a time where there is a cultural/digital divide.

Today's children are exposed to technology from birth. I know from Statistics Canada that Canadian children rank among the highest in the world in terms of living in households with computers; I also know that there are gaps within our society. These gaps create a digital divide.

I know early learning practitioners who have adapted to the technological era and those who have not embraced technology. For example, I have a friend who works at a centre where parents can view their children throughout the day on their computers through the network. Some preschool-aged children manipulate the computers with ease; some better than adults. For example, the children draw on them, they play memory games, they document their stories, and they are able to go to sites that they were familiar with. In the school aged program, children carry their cell phones, they text message, and they use computers with an ease that fascinates me. They use new language that comes with this technological age.

One of my colleagues Raquika uses technology with her group of three-year-olds. Recently she used it as one strategy in extending play. She and the children used it for research on towers, first examining the CN tower because Randall had just been there. They used a camera to take pictures and then had children document their stories in their electronic portfolio. They printed out images and compared towers that they had previously constructed. They connected with their parents in real time through email, as the towers were being built. They read the responses about the structure and considered the questions the parents had emailed back. They used software to build towers that clearly illustrated to the children what happens when the structure is not wide enough or stable at the bottom. They drew towers with the software and as they did, they predicted whether they would stand or fall. They were engaged in the activity. The children incorporated technology into their play with ease. It complemented their play experience. Throughout the process, Raquika documented each child's level of interest and the observable developmental milestones. She made notes on the new language that she heard expressed and she recorded ideas that the children expressed about other subjects for use in future programming.

As I observe Raquika and the children using technology, I am in disequilibrium. Is technology appropriate for children? Is it play based? Would children be better off returning to play without technology? I am unclear if there is a correct answer. I am thinking that this subject will cause debate among the experts for years to come. I believe as an early learning practitioner I need to continue to observe and explore the issue. Perhaps, I need to begin using some technology in the early learning environment so that I become better able to join the debate on how technology impacts children's play—for the better or worse!

*Amela, ECE Graduate, 1998*

# CHAPTER PREVIEW

In this chapter, we introduce you to the topic of technology in the lives of young children. We explore the controversies, the benefits and challenges of technology in early learning environments, and the roles early learning practitioners face in using technology to expand play experiences. We look at how technology contributes to the development of social, physical, language, and cognitive development of children. We examine the placement of computers in the environment and the role that early learning practitioners have in integrating technology into child's play.

Creating child-initiated, responsive play environments is one of the most challenging roles of an early learning practitioner. As we think about technology we need to think about how it fits with play. If it is being used, how does it support quality and active play experiences?

Technology brings inequalities into our environments. There are areas of our country and family circumstances that prohibit access to technology. This in turn impacts young children having equal access to play and learning opportunities. For example, some communities do not have access to the internet. Other children and families do not have the financial resources to support having access to computers, and still other families do not have computer knowledge that allows them to role-model the use of this type of technology to young children. These inequities in home environments place pressure on early learning settings to offer all children exposure to computers as a tool for play enhancement. Children who do not have access to computers and are not in early learning programs do not have the same skills as their peers when they start their formal schooling.

Your role in facilitating play with technology includes assisting children and colleagues in experiencing technology in a positive light. To be effective, you must have a thorough understanding of children's play and how technology can enhance the play experience. Providing support to children, while using technology, requires knowledge about play, technology, software, and roles of early learning practitioners. Effective observation skills, and abilities to pose questions that will support the children in exploring and problem solving with the software are essential. Helping children to be successful with technology in their play is an important aspect of your role. Although working with technology may be controversial and challenging, many early learning practitioners also find it a rewarding area of their role.

## VARIOUS PERSPECTIVES ABOUT THE USE OF TECHNOLOGY WITH YOUNG CHILDREN

There is controversy about the role that technology should play in the lives of young children. Examining the varying perspectives helps you understand the various positions that you may come across in your work with children. It also assists you in thinking about your beliefs and philosophy of how play and technology fit in early learning environments.

Some researchers and early learning practitioners suggest that there is a role for computers in the lives of children. And, there are researchers who suggest that computers and other forms of technology negatively impact the type of play and the quality of play experiences that children engage in. Pendleton (2001), for example, is convinced that the fast pace of the visual stimulation of the computer games causes damage to children in visual strain, obesity, and related sedentary issues. Elkind (1996, 2007) emphasizes that the computer is not a substitute for play experiences; children benefit far more from block building and dramatic play experiences than from using a computer. These perspectives are consistent with the findings in the report *Fool's gold: a critical look at computers in childhood* by Cordes and Miller (2000), who indicate that computers negatively impact a child's health, creativity, and sociocultural development.

Many early learning professionals oppose the use of computers in early learning environments because of its correlation to obesity, lack of physical development, and aggression behaviour. There is concern that the use of computers and the exposure to television can stifle children's learning and creativity, leading children to become passive consumers (Miller, 2005; Oppenheimer, 2003; Cordes & Miller, 2000). These opponents also claim that "computers are two-dimensional, calling for formal operations and thus outside [young children's] stages of development" (Mitchell & Dunbar, 2006, p. 244).

Many child development specialists and educators do not support the use of electronic play as part of a child's world. Experts debate whether television, computers, and videos take time away from children participating in quality play experiences with other children (Weber, 2006). Others question how technology supports child development or whether children need to be exposed to these mediums during their early years.

There are other researchers and advocates that indicate the need for young children to be exposed to technology as part of their early learning experience. For example, more than 15 years ago, the National Association for the Education of Young Children (NAEYC) published a Position Statement: Technology and Young Children—Ages Three through Eight (1996a) that indicated early learning practitioners "take responsibility to influence events that are transforming the daily lives of children and families" (Driscall & Nagal, 2005, p. 335). Recommendations stated that early learning practitioners take responsibility to examine

1. the role of the practitioner in assessing and evaluating the appropriate use of technology;
2. the potential benefits and challenges of technology with young children;
3. strategies for implementing technology in an early learning environment; and
4. equitable access to technology.

Since then, NAEYC has stated that as early learning software becomes further advanced, and as children become more exposed to technology, they will become more proficient in using it. Computers now need to be thought of as a tool that supports the learning process (Nikolopoulou, 2007). In ensuring an appropriate early learning environment for young children, early learning practitioners are required to critically examine the impact of technology in early learning centres and determine the most effective use of technology with children.

The use of computers should not be lumped into one domain. Drill and practice, developmentally appropriate software, educational games, and drawing programs have very different goals and objectives and therefore require different considerations of how they impact the lives of young children (McCarrick & Xiaoming, 2007). This helps us to determine how computers fit into the lives of children and into their play.

Similar to young children learning more than one language at a time, children explore the computer without the same fears that adults may exhibit. When computers are introduced into a nurturing environment, young children have a venue to explore a sense of control, independence, problem solving, and motivation (Liu, 1996; Clements & Swaminathan, 1995; Ainsa, 1989; Lee & Houston, 1987; Burg, 1984). For example, Nigel has grown up in a home where he was exposed to computers from birth. His parents have had him on their knees while communicating with Gramma who lives more than 1500 kilometres away. By the age of 2, Nigel and his parents transferred pictures that Nigel had drawn to Gramma through the computer. At three, Nigel had his own pictorial icon that he used to get into his programs and email. Nigel, now four, is competent in manoeuvring around the computer at the sites that have been designated for him to use. He is able to draw, edit, and play

*Photo 10.1    Children are growing up with technology as part of their daily living.*

games on the computer with competence. He goes to the computer for ideas for his play. And, he uses the camera and computer to record his special play episodes.

Educators and researchers have valid concerns about the role of technology in early learning environments, and its impact on play. Yet, there are several studies that suggest computers can be effective tools for young children. For example, Haugland (1992) highlights studies conducted that indicate 3- and 4-year-old children who used computers and software that supported their play interests, made significant developmental gains in areas such as knowledge, long-term memory, problem solving and conceptual skills than children without computer experiences. The success and benefits of computers with young children is directly related to early learning practitioners choosing appropriate software (Fischer & Gillespie, 2003). Computers are appropriate as long as the software is engaging and encourages interaction among the children (Mitchell & Dunbar, 2006). The challenge we face is finding a balance.

Although there are differing viewpoints on the use of technology, it is part of our society. In the upcoming sections, we have taken the position that there is a need for early learning practitioners to incorporate technology into play, when it is developmentally appropriate. We will introduce you to a number of perspectives about the relationship of technology to children's play and learning.

This chapter is intended to provoke discussions about how technology, using developmentally appropriate practice, can be adopted effectively in early learning centres.

## Stop . . . Think . . . Discuss . . . Reflect

How do you think technology has changed the way children play today from when you were growing up? Should children be exposed to technology during their early years? Why or why not? How do we know what is best?

## WORDS OF WISDOM

When I became a kindergarten teacher fifteen years ago in a small, rural school, I had no training or education on the use or the importance of computers in early learning environments. I personally had limited experience with them. Now, as an educator and promoter of children learning through play, I know that technology strengthens literacy and family connections. I invite children to write morning messages. It can be about any topic as long as it begins with the foundation of formulating a message such as "I saw a deer waiting for the bus." I use this message to build vocabulary and stories. The children and I send the messages home electronically. I encourage the parents and the children to read the messages and to respond to us about their thoughts. It is the same principle as a blog. This is using technology to advance the children's language and technology skills.

Myrna McPherson, Kindergarten Teacher, St. George, New Brunswick

# TECHNOLOGY AND EARLY LEARNING

In the opening *Stories from the Field*, Raquika identified aspects of how technology was being used within early learning centres. She reminded us that societal developments have influenced the need for technology to be incorporated into the lives of children. Raquika's perspective is similar to current research on young children and technology. For example, some parents and educators believe that children must become technically fluent, thus requiring children to have exposure to technology from a very young age. Adults, interested in helping children thrive and compete in today's society, view exposure to screen media and technology as a necessary strategy (Garrison & Christakis, 2005). Others suggest in order for this generation of children to be ready for the workforce in 2025, they need to have their cognitive skills programmed from an early age to manage technology.

Technology is here to stay. As identified by Resnick (1996), those of us who do not use technology need to change our thinking. He says:

> Computers will not live up to their potential until we start to think of them less like televisions and more like paintbrushes. That is, we need to start seeing computers not only as information machines but also as a new medium for creative design and expression. (p. 192)

Technology opens new learning opportunities. Marshall McLuhan suggested that electronic media would change our way of thinking, similar to when societies were introduced to the print media. Electronic media includes such devices as cell phones, blackberries, iPhones, iPods, and computers. Electronic media should be viewed as another form of communication, similar to both oral and print methodologies.

From an early learning perspective, Scarlett, Naudeau, Salonius-Pasternak, and Ponte (2005) indicate that electronic play, whether it is on computers or with toys with motors, is the first qualitatively different form of play to be introduced since before the turn of the twentieth century. They suggest that electronic play, like most forms of play, requires interactions among peers and adults. It can offer diversity and expansion to a child's play experiences; thus positively influencing a child's cognitive and social-emotional development. No matter what questions or concerns we have about technology, it is part of the lives of young children.

# DEFINING TECHNOLOGY IN A CHILD'S WORLD

## Technology

The term *technology* is often associated with computers and related electronic devices. More specifically, we describe technology as any device that increases or assists a child's ability to play, explore, discover new learning, and extend their potential. These include, but are not limited to, computers, cameras, DVD's, iPods, and electronic toys. Children are active participants in manipulating the devices or tools while they explore concepts, perform activities, and develop problem-solving and decision-making abilities.

As a way to illustrate how play and technology can be integrated into early learning, we share the story of Jamill and Liam. They use the resources made available to them to explore, create, experiment, and discover new opportunities in their play.

Jamill and Liam, both 4 years of age, have different play interests and styles. For example, Jamill participates in computer games, the creative area, using paints, clay, and other mixed media materials to create fascinating work. Liam frequently uses the block, construction, and climbing areas.

Anita, the early learning practitioner brought a variety of new materials to the block centre: there were planks, cylinders, large cedar cubes, measuring sticks, and cars. She also placed a computer in the area.

As the children explored the area, it appeared as though they were intrigued to find the computer set up in the block area. Anita had loaded a number of unique block structures on the screen for the children to examine. As Jamill scrolled through the images, Liam became interested in one of the images that had amazing ramps. The children engaged in rich discussion about what they saw and how they may begin a construction project.

The two children began a construction project. They used the planks to develop ramps, they incorporated the cylinders and large cedar cubes into the structure. They sought out other materials such as ropes, funnels, and containers and incorporated them into the structure.

Jamill and Liam referred to the images on the computer screen periodically, especially when they seemed to be at a standstill with ideas. Jamill at various stages, with the help of Anita, took photos and then transferred them onto the computer. Each time a new image was taken, the children told Anita about the structure. They verbalized what they had done and how they were going to add to the structure.

Over the next several days, the children brought additional materials from home to add to the structure. They returned to the computer file to examine the initial photos of the structure, as well as the documentation that was taken throughout the construction. The children had conversations about the structure and why it had been built in the specific manner. As more children and adults became interested in the structure, they incorporated new ideas, they had other children provide suggestions, and parents provided input. One father who was working on road construction brought photos of the three highway ramps that he was involved with constructing. This sparked the children to add a garage area with graters and cranes near the structure.

The children used email to send photos to their parents. Anita and the children continued to add new resources, including a couple of transformers.

Although the project began from the interests of Jamill and Liam, over the next few weeks, it became a project that received input from other children and their families. A number of children experimented with new configurations, new uses for the structure, and ways of adding new features. They took pictures, they shared them with parents, and they received immediate feedback about their structure. Parents made comments at the beginning of the day, through email during the day, and again at the end of the day. The children continued to extend and make modifications to the structure. They used the internet to search for more ideas.

Throughout the project, many design principles were examined, ideas tried, research completed, new language learned, and rich child-to-child and adult–child communication occurred. This project brought play and technology together. The use of the internet for research, the digital photos combined with transferring the photos to parents' emails, contributed to the children extending their play. The questions and suggestions about how the structure may be further enhanced by adults and other children expanded the depth of the project. Parents and early learning practitioners collectively supported the children's interests and learning.

This reinforces how play and technology enhances a play episode. Children are able to extend their play over several days and it opens up opportunities for adults to become part of the children's play and learning community.

## Stop . . . Think . . . Discuss . . . Reflect

How did the computer support Jamill and Liam in their play? What was the role of the early learning practitioner in combining technology with play? Were the children negatively impacted by using technology? If so, how and why? If not, why not?

For many early learning practitioners, mixing play and technology may be a new process, even though it is not a new phenomenon. For example, in 1837, Frederich Froebel used the technology available to him at that time to develop his "Froebel gifts" learning materials (Resnick, 2006). He designed and created precise gifts that would support children in gaining skills in mathematical and scientific concepts such as numbers, sizes, and shapes. Similar to the technology today, early learning play resources evolve and are influenced by the societal, political, and cultural attributes and needs at particular times.

## THE BENEFITS OF USING TECHNOLOGY WITH YOUNG CHILDREN

The use of incorporating technology with child's play is guided by practitioners' beliefs or philosophy about how children learn. Often, we examine our beliefs and assumptions by reviewing positions taken by experts in the field. Since technology began being available in early learning centres, experts have examined the impact

*Table 10.1*    *The Benefits of Technology*

- Computers are intrinsically motivating for young children, and contribute to cognitive and social development (National Association for the Education of Young Children [NAEYC], 1996).

- Computers can enhance children's self-concept and improve their attitudes about learning (Sivin-Kachala & Bialo, 1994).

- Children demonstrate increased levels of spoken communication and cooperation during computer use (Clements, 1994; Haugland & Wright, 1997).

- Children share leadership roles on the computer, and initiate interactions more frequently (Clements, 1994; Haugland & Wright, 1997).

- Computers contribute to enhancing the lives of children with disabilities. They improve their self-esteem, mobility, and sense of control (Schery & O'Connor, 1992).

- Technologies that are interactive and allow children to develop their curiosity, problem-solving, and independent thinking skills are very powerful for brain development (Perry, 2009).

- Contemporary programs must provide activities and situations that are close to the real world, including educational software (Nikolopoulou, 2007).

of it on child's play. As illustrated in Table 10.1, some experts indicate that there are benefits to incorporating it into early learning environments. For example, children may bring music to the screen, they can draw shapes and pictures on the screen, and they can receive immediate feedback when using letter recognition software. Early learning practitioners and student practitioners benefit from examining the literature as a way to help determine your philosophical position on technology and play.

When using technology with children, early learning practitioners examine it with the same merits as other forms of play. The core question to be asked is "How does technology contribute to a child's quality play experience?" For example, if a child is interested in music, and you are able to find software that is rich in sound, music, child action, and voice, then is it appropriate to use technology with the child? If the child is interested in climbing opportunities, then, is it appropriate to require that the child engage in activities using the computer or other technology type devices?

Having technology in the early learning environment is a strategy that may be used to promote exploratory learning in a collaborative setting. Children communicate with others, use the technology tools to write information, talk with peers, listen, and read either from the pictorial icons or written words. As you will note later in the chapter, the use of computer may be one tool that positively contributes to advancing children's literacy skills and it supports children with varying disabilities.

Constructivists who support computers in early learning centres remind us that preschool children learn through the experience gained from the use of "concrete objects." For example, Brekekamp and Copple (1997) compare children manipulating figures on the screen to Cuisenaire rods. They suggest if children learn to use the computer in developmentally appropriate ways, there are ample opportunities for children to manipulate objects and gain similar learning to that of traditional objects. The computer requires children to think in new and in different ways from the thinking that occurs with concrete play materials. Children require software that provides them with activities and situations that make demands on them to explore in groups, engage in autonomous learning and that it takes into account the sociocultural context of the learning experience (Nikolopoulou, 2007).

# COMPUTERS AND PLAY

Mildred Parten's (1932) classic work on children's stages of social play provides further insight into how computers support quality play experiences (Freeman & Somerindyke, 2001). As described in Chapter 2, play is categorized into six categories: unoccupied, onlooker, solitary, parallel, associate, and cooperative. Parten's categories, combined with Vygotosky's constructivist, social-cultural perspective, including the positive influences of peer learning and zone of proximal development, reinforces that computers provide a venue to promote collaborative learning during the preschool years. There is merit in examining the relationship between Parten's play and Vygotosky's perspective on how children learn.

## The Stages of Using the Computer among Preschool Children

Preschool children progress though stages of using the computer. Haugland and Wright (1997) identify the stages as: discovery, involvement, self-confidence, and creativity. Using these stages, Table 10.2 provides an overview of some of the behaviours that an early learning practitioner may observe of a child at each stage.

Early learning practitioners can use a combination of developmentally appropriate practice guidelines, the characteristics of the child, and the capabilities of the child to blend children's active play with computers. For example, Gage, a 3-year-old, who loves to sing, initially had the early learning practitioner assist him in going to YouTube for karaoke. Three months later, using the icons on the computer, Gage goes to the site independently. He has progressed through the first three phases of using the computer.

## The Placement of Computers in Early Learning Environments

Where computers are placed in the early learning setting influences how children use them. For example, computers placed away from the core play area reduces the opportunities for children to integrate play and technology. Placing computers in the centre core of the play area increases the social aspects of play and technology. Laptops that may be moved from one interest area or experience centre to another enhance the integration of technology with play.

**Table 10.2** *Stages and Activities of Using a Computer*

| Stage | Activity |
|---|---|
| I. Discovery | Child observes interesting images and sounds<br>Adult models the use of the mouse<br>Child begins to use the mouse<br>Adult provides physical and verbal support<br>Child begins to explore the software<br>Child may observe how peers use the software<br>Child examines specific features of the program |
| II. Involvement | Child uses the mouse and the keyboard<br>Child manipulates the software<br>Child follows pictorial directions<br>Child participates in social interaction with others including turn-taking<br>Child begins to remember how to use the software |
| III. Self-confidence | Child begins to use the computer on one's own<br>Child is able to find icons for programs<br>Child provides guidance to others<br>Child is willing to explore new software with confidence<br>Child talks about what they are doing with the computer<br>Child moves between one site and another or between programs |
| IV. Creativity | Child uses the computer in a variety of ways<br>Child combines personal expression with creativity<br>Child tries new ways to create materials |

Placing more than one computer together in the core early learning space, at eye level, with adequate space for two or more children to move chairs and materials in and out of the area (Swaminathan & Wright, 2003), enhances the breadth of the children's experiences. Providing space to accommodate children who wish to stop and observe other children at the computer is an important strategy used to spark a child's curiosity and promote learning through observation. This also expands children's collaborative learning opportunities.

Children thrive in environments that support their need to satisfy their sense of curiosity and wonderment. Environments that introduce children to items, ideas, and materials are most beneficial in triggering or expanding a child's curiosity (Dietze, 2006). The placement of the computers requires as much consideration regarding traffic flow and potential uses as other experience centres. One of the core questions that is addressed when placing the computers in the early learning centre is "How will the placement of the computers in this area enhance learning and peer collaboration?" This is supported by Bruner and Vygotsky. Bruner (1986) suggests that children learn in early learning environments where "most learning in most settings is a communal activity, a sharing of culture" (p. 127). And Vygotsky (1978) identifies that children's knowledge is created socially by communicative interaction with others, through practical tasks and speech. Using technology with young children is more effective in a group situation, than as a solitary activity. Placing computers in a central location invites children to stop by, observe, pause, and participate in the computer activity.

*Photo 10.2  Children use the computer to do research on topics that they then incorporate into their play.*

The presentation of the computer centre and related experience centres that support the computer centre, and those near the computer centre, impact how children use the centre. For example, if the computer centre is located near the block or dramatic area, it is more likely that the children will cross-pollinate the use of play and technology than if it is next to table toys. When the children can use the camera, transfer photos, or use the computer for research, technology enhances play. As outlined in Figure 10.1, placing the computer as a focal point in the early learning environment increases the social networking among children than when computers are placed in a lab or in a less visual place.

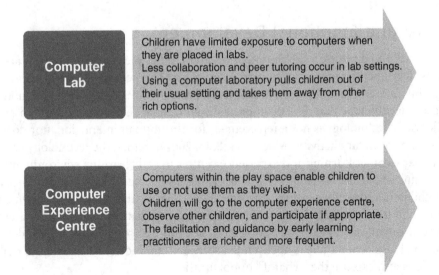

**Computer Lab**

Children have limited exposure to computers when they are placed in labs.
Less collaboration and peer tutoring occur in lab settings.
Using a computer laboratory pulls children out of their usual setting and takes them away from other rich options.

**Computer Experience Centre**

Computers within the play space enable children to use or not use them as they wish.
Children will go to the computer experience centre, observe other children, and participate if appropriate.
The facilitation and guidance by early learning practitioners are richer and more frequent.

*Figure 10.1  How the placement of the computer centre impacts the child's experiences.*

To become one of the many learning experiences, computers and related technology are intended to be placed in the core of the learning environment (Clements, 1999). When children between the ages of 2 and 5 years are exposed to stimulating environments, conducive to their developmental needs and interests, they will be attracted to the computers for short periods of time; then they will move to other experience centres. Children typically move from one experience centre to another when given the freedom to explore and engage in play that is of interest to them.

# TECHNOLOGY AND CHILD DEVELOPMENT

Advocates of technology indicate that it positively impacts a child's development. If presented appropriately, technology supports the social, emotional, cognitive, and physical development of children between infancy and 6 years of age (Seng, 1998). For example, technology may enhance a child's verbal and written language skills and increase their social-emotional development. If used appropriately, it also enhances the child's self-esteem. Technology may support children with special needs in ways that enhance their development better than other strategies.

## Social and Emotional Development

The social and emotional development of children between infancy and 6 years of age is developed primarily by human interaction. The peer-to-peer and adult-to-child interactions, including conversations and reading, create the social role modelling and feeling tone that directly impacts the emotional development through early childhood. Technology is not a replacement for this human interaction, nor does it need to be a solitary activity (McCarrick & Li, 2007). Rather, the technology centre is similar to other learning and experience centres in early learning environments.

Think about the developmental task of initiative versus guilt for 4- and 5-year-old-children, as described by Erikson (1963, 1982). During this phase of development, young children require a variety of materials and experiences that offer children a sense of direction (McCarrick & Li, 2007). Technology contributes to this developmental task, when there is open-ended software that motivates children to make decisions and explore the "what if" opportunities.

*Table 10.3*  *Social Interactions and Characteristics of Social Play and Computers*

| Type of Social Interaction | Characteristics |
|---|---|
| Active Navigators | Children have experience/expertise on the computer<br>Children appear to be child experts at using the computer<br>Children have access to computers at home<br>Children provide support to other children |
| Vicarious Navigators/<br>Super-on-lookers | Children watch from the sidelines<br>Children show interest in the program operation<br>Children do not claim control over the computer<br>Children do not share their knowledge with others<br>Children do not exhibit leadership skills |
| Spectator | Children show an interest and sense of curiosity in computers<br>Children may not actively engage in the use of computer |

Freeman and Somerindyke (2001) outline three categories of children's social play that occur with computers. These include active navigators, vicarious navigators/ super-on-lookers, and spectators. Table 10.3 provides an overview of the type of social interaction and common characteristics that children may exhibit at each phase.

Freeman and Somerindyke (2001) indicate that the active navigators can be categorized into three categories:

- *consolidated navigators* use the computer independently and explore how to solve problems.
- *mouse navigators* are able to manoeuvre the mouse to reflect items on screen and to meet their needs.
- *program navigators* use the program with proficiency.

Each of these phases contributes to the level of socialization that children engage in. For example, the active navigators, because of their comfort with the technology, are more likely to share their knowledge and help other children, than the child who is its *super-on-looker* or *spectator*. As children become more comfortable with their technology capabilities, they are more likely to connect with other children.

Vygotsky (1978) advocated that children learn with peers, not in independent or isolated environments. Peers influence the young child's learning, especially if the task can be explored with a more experienced partner. The computer experience centre provides a natural place for children to create a **shared problem space** in which the children solve problems together (Freeman & Somerindyke, 2001). Figure 10.2 provides the backdrop for how shared problem space evolves.

Technology can serve as a catalyst for social interaction and conversations related to what the children are exploring. For example, as identified in Figure 10.3, Plowman and Stephen (2005) indicate that children socialize significantly when using the computer.

**Shared problem space** is a way to organize the technology resources available to children that support their curiosity or area of exploration. The early learning practitioner facilitates discussions that help the children explore answers to their questions and incorporate their findings into new learning.

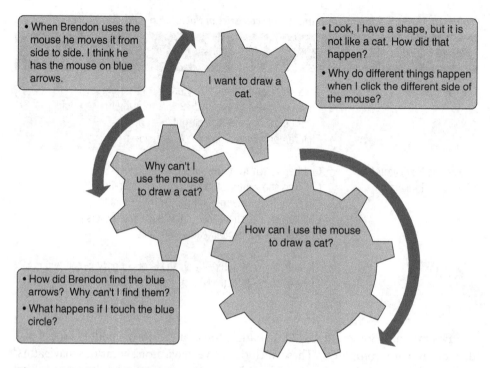

**Figure 10.2**  *Shared Problem Space Process*

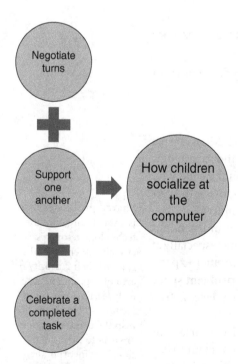

**Figure 10.3**  *How Children Socialize at a Computer*

First, children negotiate turns. Second, they support one another by helping each other's use the software, such as deciding what icons to click. And thirdly, they celebrate when they have completed a task or created something of interest. The computer experience centre facilitates friendships, and more teamwork is fostered, even during the preschool years. Forming friendships among young children is higher in a computer experience centre than when children are engaged at *table work* (Clements, 1993). Children at the computer spent nine times as much time talking to peers while on the computer than while doing puzzles (McCarrick & Li, 2007). For example, McCarrick and Li (2007) indicate that

> Peer interaction was present during 63% of the computer play and only 7% of the puzzle play. In addition, 11% of the time was spent in solitary activity at the computer and 55% of the time was spent in solitary activity with the puzzle. (p. 80)

Think about children who may not have experience with different kinds of technology and how it works. For example, Johnston, the early learning practitioner, provided four children with a video camera to use. The children initially took pictures of each other. When the video was played back to them, they realized there was audio capacity. This new learning extended the children's play. They made up a story, they used props, and they recorded it. They played it over and over again. Then Johnston transferred the viewing of the video to the television. Suzanna Maria was heard, "Look, we are movie stars!" The children made the connection between the video and television. They also became interested in other ways to use the video camera.

Children take different initiatives with technology than in other areas of play. This contributes to increasing one's self-concept and self-esteem. For example, when children, with the support of early learning practitioners, explore the software, share ideas, ask their peers for assistance, and observe how peers use the computer, they gain knowledge, which leads to self-confidence. These actions contribute to social and emotional development attributes and personal self-esteem.

*Photo 10.3    Children learn to document parts of their play for later review.*

Software that requires children to use a variety of thinking and problem-solving skills increases the likelihood that the young child will work with a peer. For example, software such as *Facemaker* has children making faces. In observing Mahamad and Parker, the more faces they made, the more they giggled and the more they shared with one another how they were going to add to their drawing. Parker asked Mahamad how he got the thick, green squiggle line on the drawing. As they created new ideas, more children walked over to the area to observe what they were doing and to join in the activity. This illustrates the socialization and communication skills consistent with preschool

*Photo 10.4    A child uses technology when needed, with confidence.*

*Photo 10.5    Children learn about using computers and the information on the computers in a social setting.*

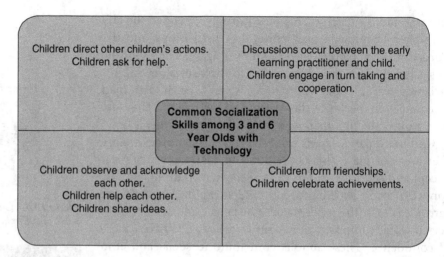

*Figure 10.4* *Common Socialization Skills Children Exhibit When Using Technology*

development. There is an emergence of unique learning and proficiency that evolves as children use technology effectively.

As shown in Figure 10. 4, technology offers children opportunities to develop a variety of socialization skills.

Examine the story of Jamill and Liam presented earlier in the chapter. Note how the initial project began with two children and then expanded to include more children and adults. Look at how Jamill and Liam had discussions with other children and adults. Examine how the children asked Marcelle for help and how at times children helped each other. These actions support the foundation of socialization skills. It is interesting to note that children appear to seek help from one another and seem to prefer help from peers over help from the teacher (King & Alloway 1992; Nastasi & Clements 1993).

Children, when using a computer and related technology, regardless of age or disability status, exhibit more positive social interactions in environments that are effectively facilitated with early learning practitioners than in environments without adult interaction (Lau, Higgins, Hong, & Miller, 2005). This reinforces why the computer experience centre is placed so that early learning practitioners may observe and facilitate dialogue when beneficial to the children. The development of socialization skills is critical during the early years. Understanding these needs and examining how the use of computers and related technology may contribute to this development guides early learning practitioners in advancing their skills in facilitating social play with technology.

## Language Development

Technology provides a rich venue to support language and literacy development of young children. Computers may be integrated into existing language experience centres or be set up as a separate

*Photo 10.6* *Children may use technology for many facets of play and learning.*

experience centre, depending on the interests of the children. For example, art/graphic software, as well as word processing software, allows children to combine written words with images. These tools support the preschool child in making stories, creating notes, and in some cases devising pieces of work that illustrate language and art. Using scanning options or documenting pictures with the computer and camera, opens new learning opportunities for children and parents.

Computers and related electronic media have contributed to the resurgence of **iconic literacy.** For example, the pictorial representations help young children manipulate the electronic media. Because preschool children are preliterate, they bring an intuitive ability to memorize the icons (Elkind, 1996), which in turn leads to the foundation skills of literacy. This is similar to preschool children who play games such as memory games with adults. Generally, they have an ability to memorize the placement of the cards more successfully than adults.

Children think by using language as their foundation; they see relationships, make classifications, draw inferences, predict outcomes, formulate conclusions, and solve problems through language and literacy skills (Dietze, 2006). The language component is integrated across the program and the use of technology contributes to this process.

During the early years, children require software that promotes written and expressive thoughts and has visual representation (Labbo, Love, & Ryan, 2007). For example, software that encourages the young child to use symbols or discover and invent with symbols, increases both language development and creativity (Isenberg & Jalongo, 2010). Children require opportunities to write stories about their creations and then verbally share them with adults and peers. Children benefit from participating in an experience, photographing the experience, telling the story, and participating in follow-up experiences (Labbo et al., 2007).

When children "create" their personalized stories, their sense of curiosity, inquiry, and problem solving is further developed. For example, when children use pictorial icons, words, colour menus, and unique characters, their language and thinking skills are stimulated because they are using more than one or two dimensions in their learning. By recording their stories on the computer, using a combination of words and pictorial representation, children experience how words and pictures are used to tell a story. They also see how print carries a message. Children appear to edit their stories and verbalize what they are doing when they move or create objects on the screen.

Research suggests that children initiate interactions more frequently and in different ways at the computer centre than when engaged with traditional activities, such as puzzles or blocks. They also show high levels of language and cooperative-play activity.

Some of the research on the relationship of computer play to language development is more than 15 years old; the findings continue to be relevant.

- Computer play encourages longer, more complex speech, and the development of fluency (Davidson & Wright, 1994).
- Children tend to narrate what they are doing as they draw pictures or move objects and characters around on the screen (Bredekamp & Rosegrant, 1994).

**Iconic literacy** is described as reading by way of pictorial representations such as on signs, on labels, or in games.

- Young children interacting at computers engage in high levels of spoken communication and cooperation, such as turn-taking and peer collaboration. "Compared to more traditional activities, such as puzzle assembly or block building, the computer elicits more social interaction and different types of interaction" (Clements, Nastasi, & Swaminathan, 1993, p. 60).

- The use of email further enhances children's interest in reading and writing; they appear to write more and in greater detail (Salmon & Akaran, 2001).

- By combining technology and play, children become more competent in verbal and written language and increased imagination (Clements et al., 1993, Haugland & Wright, 1997).

There are many ways to enhance language development with computer technology. For example, Martina, a Director of an early learning centre that is within a school setting, has the preschool children visit a grade four class once per week. Over the past several weeks, the preschoolers Marella, Kia, and Adam have been taking drawings that they have made to their grade 4 buddies. They scan the picture as they tell their buddy the story about their picture. The buddy records the story into the computer. This helps young children associate letters with spoken language. Children begin to understand the possibilities of technology.

There are many examples that illustrate how technology opens up new avenues for children with language impairments. For example, software such as *Fast ForWord*™ supports children in skill improvements. This software is used to acoustically alter speech sounds so a child can more likely distinguish them. Children who have language impairments are able to hear the rapidly changing sound elements and sequences of normal speech over and over. As children master the skills, the activities become progressively more advanced. This enables them to continually increase their rate of speech processing, which in turn leads to normal speech perception.

Children, who have autism, may also benefit from using computers to support their language development. Many children who are autistic are visual learners; they think in pictures. A combination of verbal instructions and visual cues, such as facial expressions and hand gestures, help them understand language acquisition. Software that provides virtual peers helps children produce more "contingent" sentences than when they were paired with real-life children (Cassell, 2008). Other software that requires the child to elicit socially skilled behaviours helps in the development of communication and social skills (Cassell, 2008).

As early learning practitioners bring technology into the environment, they examine it to determine how the software supports varying levels of play and opportunities to advance children's learning.

## Cognitive Development

There are many perspectives on the relationship of the use of computers to the cognitive development of young children. Based on Piaget's perspective that children learn best in environments with direct experiences and active involvement in a play-rich world (Sheltz & Stremmel, 1994); computers and related technology allow children to explore and discover new ideas and skills. Computers, when used appropriately, promote young children being in control of their learning, which is consistent with Piagetian theory (Clements, 1993). The success of computers as a learning tool is based on the software being connected to what the child already knows and offers the potential to lead the child to achieve greater motivation and self-direction.

Computers and related technology essentially provide children with another venue for learning. They support a variety of learning styles, which through observation, allows the early learning practitioner to observe a child's strength and interests. Different skills may surface from the traditional play experience observations. The computer may lead children to examine the task in very different ways than when they are using concrete material such as blocks. Their cognitive processes follow various paths to reach a goal (Clements, 1999). These processes may expand thinking and learning opportunities which become transferable to other play and learning experiences.

There are a number of significant studies that help us examine the relationship of cognitive development and computer technology. We highlight three such studies.

> **Haugland** (1992) examined the impact of children between the ages of 3 and 5 years of age having access to computers with developmentally appropriate software and supplemental hands-on activities with children who either had access to developmentally appropriate software with no supplemental activities or access to non-developmentally appropriate software. Children exposed to developmentally appropriate software and materials scored significantly higher on cognitive subtests than those children without the combination of software and materials. Children who were exposed to non-developmentally appropriate software did not exhibit any significant cognitive gains.

> **Li and Atlins** (2004) examined the impact of computers on children 3 to 5 years of age who had computer use in the home environment. They determined that the children with exposure to computer access scored significantly higher on both cognitive and school readiness assessments.

> **Mitchell and Dunbar** (2006) had preschool children complete a number of tasks on the computer that would have previously been conducted in a more traditional learning environment. The children were required to complete tasks such as "identifying letters, words and sounds; sequencing; prediction; color, shape and pattern recognition; and problem solving" (Laverkic, Heider, & Gay, p. 128). The children using the computer had an increased attention span—they worked until the task was complete—compared to those who did not use the computer. The children exposed to computers collectively solved problems, they discussed their ideas and questions among one another, they made predictions, and they provided each other with possible solutions to the problems. Mitchell and Dunbar suggest that "the joint construction of knowledge was well demonstrated in those settings where children were encouraged to engage in collaborative problem-solving and where adult intervention facilitated discussion and helped children to make their thought processes explicit" (p. 253). Children in early learning environments who are exposed to engaging

software, opportunities for social interaction, and early learning practitioners who embrace technology have an advantage over those children who are not afforded the same opportunities.

Computers alone do not improve a child's learning. Computers are one tool used to support cognitive development. Computers contribute to advancing interaction within the social contexts and may be preferred for linear and sequential organization of thought. Computers are less likely to offer children the best model for human thinking, such as in the relational, emotional, and spiritual domains.

## Physical Well-Being and Motor Development

When we think of physical development, we are generally drawn to active play. Technology can positively impact physical development. For example, using a mouse, a joystick, or a keyboard contributes to increasing hand–eye coordination and fine motor skills (Mitchell & Dunbar, 2006).

Fine and gross motor skills develop at varying rates, and learning to write can be tedious and difficult as children struggle to form letters. A word processor allows them to compose and revise text without being distracted by the fine motor aspects of letter formation (Davis & Shade, 1994). Think about the previous example of Gage. Using the computer for karaoke had Gage singing and dancing. When children have opportunities to use computers to seek ideas for their block play, their physical development is indirectly impacted.

## Technology and Equitable Issues

The use of technology causes equity issues among children and families, early learning centres, community groups, and regions. The literature on equitable access and use of technology indicates that children from diverse ethnic backgrounds, children living in inner cities, children living in rural communities, females, children with disabilities, and children whose first language is not English are disadvantaged (American Library Association, 1998; Milone & Salpeter, 1996). These inequities may disadvantage children in both their general cognitive skills and their ability to function in our digital society (Brown, Higgins, & Hartley, 2001). This causes early learning practitioners to ensure that they think about who is using the technology, how they are using it, and if they are using it.

> Early learning practitioners have a role to examine the software in relation to supporting children's diversity, culture, and language. Young children flourish when they have access to software that reflects their world. This requires the software to reflect gender equity, diverse families and culture. (Derman-Sparks & A.B.C. Task Force, 1989; Haugland & Shade, 1994)

The attitudes of the adults may hinder a child's access to computers. Children who are better behaved or show an interest may obtain more time than children who have lower-achieving attributes (Haugland & Shade, 1994). Early learning practitioners benefit from reflecting on their attitudes and behaviours about the use of computers and related technology with young children. This reflective process helps to identify how some situations have the potential to lead to inequity among the children and to examine processes and procedures that will reduce or create barriers that may have the potential to lead to inequitable issues. For example, it would be beneficial for early learning practitioners to maintain a list of the children who use the computer centre, the types of software they use, and the duration for which they use it. If children are not using it or using it for small periods of time, then early learning practitioners may wish to examine the children's interests and related software that may encourage children to explore the centre.

Early learning practitioners benefit from seeking information from parents on the level of access to technology in the home environment. Then they are able to enhance the use of technology in the early learning setting. Children who do not have access or have limited access require exposure to computers and encouragement to explore how technology can support their play. The opportunities for using the computers must be meaningful to the child.

The computer encourages participation. It can be viewed as a tool to enhance social inequities. For example, LaFrance and Meyer (2009) indicate that in some villages the computer is being used as a tool to enhance the interest and skill in reading and writing with Inuktitut children. A group of children whose education is conducted in their native language until grade three are being introduced to English with the computer. The children use the computer to bridge language and culture. They use the sounds, pictures, and related software capabilities to illustrate stories in their language and typography and add English to it. They can record the stories in their own language. If they choose, they can type the story in their language or in English. The entire platform contains culturally relevant elements. The computer provides the child with familiarity of culture and skill and it expands their opportunity to learn other life skills.

## Children with Atypical Development

Children with atypical development also benefit from having access to technology. Often it enhances inclusive practices. For example, technology may contribute to increasing fine motor skills, language acquisition, and expression of creative thought. Some computer technology may also empower young children to engage in participatory practices. This leads to social development skills.

Technology provides children who have motor impairments with a sense of control over technology, when adaptive components are available. Early learning practitioners examine the interests, learning styles, and needs of the young child and align them with the required computer technology.

Computers provide opportunities to convert written text to spoken audio playback. Computers accept spoken input as an alternative to keyboarding information, thus enabling children with physical challenges to use technology to support their development. Computers have the capacity to bring digital sound, live video, and other concepts forward. The diversity of technology can play a supporting role for children with special needs.

Children with atypical development benefit from opportunities to have computer programs that reflect their pace and skill level. This requires early learning practitioners to provide software that is levelled to meet the needs of specific children.

# GENDER DIFFERENCES

The type of play that children participate in can be influenced by gender and role modelling within a learning environment. Some studies suggest that boys use computers differently from girls. Boys tend to have more positive attitudes towards the computer and to display greater exploration with discovery-type software. They prefer to use more competitive drill software than girls (Shade, 1994). They take more risks than girls in exploring the software (Wilder, Mackie, & Cooper, 1985) and they use it more often than girls. Preschool-aged girls appear to respond more positively to software (Shade, 1994). Girls have more social interaction at the computer than boys and they seek out more help than boys (Busch, 1996). Early learning practitioners ensure that young children have exposure to gender neutral software and that both boys and girls have equal access to the computer.

## The Role of Early Learning Practitioners in Integrating Technology into Early Learning Centres

When early learning programs value child-centred, experiential learning, early learning practitioners can guide children's use of technology in similar ways they facilitate learning in other experience centres. Children require freedom to explore, based on their interests and developmental levels.

The success of integrating computers into early learning environments is influenced by the early learning practitioners' ability to guide and to be a learning partner with children (Clements, 1996; Samaras, 1996). There are a number of ways this can be achieved. Below, we present you with three examples:

- Using the computer, the early learning practitioner supports the children in making pricelists for the flower shop that is set up in the dramatic centre. The children use various flower clip art for the visuals and then include the prices, which supports them in their mathematical knowledge.
- The early learning practitioner extends a child's interest in making shapes on the computer. Imagine a child who is making shapes, in the sand area or drawing centre. Bringing children to the computer allows them to stretch the shapes, make them larger or smaller, and combine lines with other shapes.
- The children and the early learning practitioner invent storybooks with sounds such as bells and whistles and vocabulary. The children tell the story and have it played back. Together, the early learning practitioner and children edit the stories and the related sounds.

Although the above examples seem reasonable, the role of the early learning practitioner in advancing technology into the environment is unique to the other experience centres. In this section, we examine the various roles and responsibilities related to advancing technology in the early learning environment that early learning practitioners have.

# Facilitating Children's Play at the Computer Centre

Early learning practitioners are responsible for supervising and facilitating play at a number of experience centres in the play area. The time allocated for the technology area is similar to other experience centres such as the block or science area (Plowman, 2005). Generally, practitioners become involved with computer play when the child asks for help or if there is a need for intervention. In other experience centres, the early learning practitioner observes the children and moves into the area when there are opportunities to expand the child's play. This can be more challenging to do in the computer area because of the diversity of technology and children's skills.

In a study conducted by Plowman and Stephen (2005), their observations suggest that there are three broad categories of adult involvement in computer play. They identify them as reactive supervision, guided interaction, and a hybrid approach. An overview of each follows.

**Reactive supervision**    Reactive supervision is described as keeping a check on the children at the computer. It includes monitoring turn taking and the amount of time children use the computer. Practitioners may become involved with the children if there is a request for help or to have a turn at the computer. This supervision does not provide practitioners with a clear understanding of the skill level that children exhibit with the computer. Practitioners may not see how a child is transferring an active play experience to the computer (Plowman, 2005) or vice versa. However, excessive monitoring and interacting to correct a child's use of the computer prevents the child from feeling comfortable to explore or take risks.

**Guided interaction**    This category refers to the child–adult interaction that occurs as children use the computer. For example, early learning practitioners may work with a group of children to explain how to use a particular piece of software; they may pose questions that lead a child to explore alternative strategies, or they may illustrate how a particular tool is used. Effective guided interaction is one of the most powerful strategies that early learning practitioners use with children. To be effective, it requires small groups of children and time. In Box 10.1, Ramona illustrates how she uses guided interaction with Jan and Raqe.

Providing guidance to preschool children increases the expansion of the experience and learning (Klein, Nir-Gal, & Darom, 2000). It helps practitioners gain an understanding of the child's needs, interests, and abilities so that there is connectedness between the experiences provided to the child and the interest and skills expressed.

**Hybrid**    This model combines the reactive supervision with guided interaction. Early learning practitioners engage in observations to determine the competency levels, the needs of the children, and required resources. This guides the approach that the early learning practitioners use with the children in the computer centre.

---

# BOX 10.1

## An Example of Guided Interaction among Early Learning Practitioners and Children

Ramona observed Jan using the paint brush software last week. She was intrigued how he used the colour chart to incorporate various colours into his creation. Today, she observed Raqe using the software. Raqe asked Ramona how to find the colour wheel. Ramona and Raqe sat together. She said, "What would happen if you clicked on this icon?" Then, they tried another. This brought success. Raqe tried three times to find purple but was not successful. He left the area.

Ramona, observing that Jan was about to leave the science area, approached him and asked if Raqe was interested if he would show them how to get to the purple portion of the colour wheel. Jan said yes. Jan went to Raqe to tell him that he may be able to help him and Ramona find the purple. Ramona and Raqe went to the computer where the three of them sat as Jan found the purple. Jan went directly to the site. Ramona asked him questions about how he got there. Then, she asked him to "talk" Raqe and she through the process. As Jan did so, Ramona encouraged Raqe to follow the directions. She asked questions of Jan. When Raqe was successful, she had Raqe show her how to get to the purple. Ramona shared her enthusiasm with the children.

---

# CHOOSING SOFTWARE

There is an abundance of computer software available on the market. Early learning practitioners should examine the software to determine how it meets the needs, learning, and interests of an individual child and groups of children. For example, they look at its unique features such as how the children will learn through exploration, imagination, creative problem solving, and self-guided instruction. They ensure that it reflects and builds on what children know. They examine it to determine how many senses it involves and the potential versatility that it brings to the play experience. They examine it relative to how the software will expand concrete play experiences in the other play centres available.

Early learning practitioners should choose software that is scaffolded to support each child's needs including: (a) phase of development; (b) personal interests; (c) cultural background; and (d) linguistic needs of young children (Robinson, 2003). As in other forms of children's play, children require software that moves from simple to more complex, based on a child's performance (Shute & Miksad, 1997). Software that has many levels of difficulty increases a child's ability to take risks and to expand their sense of exploration and self-worth. It provides the child with the freedom to engage in using the software without always requiring adult support.

Choosing software that promotes discovery enhances learning. Children work best with software that is **open-ended** because it provides them with opportunities to discover, make choices, and to experience the impact of their decisions. Children flourish at integrating technology with play when they have projects to engage in rather than merely "free explore" time (Lemerise, 1993). Discovery-type software motivates children to actively search for diverse ways to solve tasks. This differs

**Open-ended software** refers to software that encourages children to explore, discover, wonder, make choices, problem solve, collaborate, and view the results of their choices. Children make real choices rather than choosing from a menu with options. It encourages the child to try again and problem solve by using the software in other ways. For example, two children decide to create a picture. They determine what they are going to create, how they are going to create it, and when they will complete it.

*Table 10.4*  *Questions to Consider When Choosing Software*

| Questions to Consider When Choosing Software for Young Children |
| --- |
| • How will the purchase of this software support the early learning play philosophy? |
| • How does the software support the child's interests and developmental phase? |
| • How does the software support the child's background, experiences, and what they already know? |
| • How much physical manipulation is required for the child to use the software? |
| • How does the use of the software connect with the child's learning? |
| • How does the software encourage exploration, imagination, and wonderment? |
| • How many senses, such as sound, music, and voice are used? |
| • How will the software support cooperation and child interaction? |
| • How does the software support open-ended discovery? |
| • How simple are the instructions to understand? |
| • How does the software support children completing concrete tasks? |
| • How will the software adjust to the level of difficulty required? |
| • Does the software provide children with positive verbal and visual cues? |
| • Does the software support a child working alone or in a group? |

from drill-and-practice software that leads children to gains in certain rote skills (Clements & Nastasi, 1993).

Early learning practitioners examine the developmental levels and interests of the children for whom the software is intended. For example, how does the software reflect how children think? The opening menu of software for 3-year-olds would be pictorial, whereas the opening menu for a 5-year-old may require some word recognition. Likewise, what are the choice of characters and the level of action? This will influence how the children use the software. The intended purpose of the software is examined. For example, is the software usage intended to support language development? Is the purpose to provide children with opportunities to create pictures or stories? Practitioners examine the software to ensure that it accomplishes the intended purpose. There are a number of guidelines that can be followed when choosing software. Table 10.4 provides potential questions to guide the selection of software.

## OBSERVING CHILDREN

Early learning practitioners have the unique advantage of acquiring information about children's interests and levels of developmental milestones as they interact with computers. It provides practitioners with a window into a child's thinking process (Weir, Russell, & Valente, 1982). Observing children using the computer provides insight into a child's strengths that may not be observed in other play episodes. For example, Marley, at the age of 4, does not show any interest in books and has limited contact with the other children. However, while at the computer, she recognizes words, she documents words to support her art, and she communicates with other children. The level of socialization and literacy skills are much more pronounced at the computer centre than in other experience centres. As identified in Chapter 3, the observation method chosen is dependent on the purpose of the observation. One observation method that supports early learning practitioners in understanding how children use the software is known as **contextual inquiry** (Beyer & Holtzlatt, 1997).

The contextual inquiry method is a semi-structured process used to obtain information about how the children use the software. The children are asked a set of standard questions and then observed and questioned while they work at the computers. This technique provides insight into how children manipulate the software and the social aspect that occurs at the computer centre.

Contextual inquiry is based on the following four principles:

1. **Focus**—Establish a clear understanding of the purpose of the observation.
2. **Context**—Adults participate with the children at the computer experience centre or where they are using the laptop.
3. **Partnership**—Adults discuss with the children about their activity. They help them extend their knowledge and skills about the software.
4. **Interpretation**—The children and adults develop a shared understanding about the software and how it relates to their interests.

This method focuses on the child's actual behaviour when using the computer. It helps practitioners identify the features and functions of the computer that the child is using and those that are available, but are not being used. This method requires early learning practitioners to understand the functionality of the software and become an active participant with the child (Druin et al., 1997).

The early learning practitioner can devise a set of questions that are asked of the children. The questions are directed at what the child is doing at the moment. Examples of questions to consider include:

What is the reason you are doing this?

Why do you use this function?

What does this mean?

How will this take you to . . . ?

The questions chosen avoid steering the child to specific activities or direction. Questions such as "Could you show me this?" or "What would happen if?" or "Have you tried this?" will reduce you acquiring the child's knowledge and ability of using the software. Contextual inquiry observations give us an opportunity to view how children use the software and how to support them in using added functionality of the software.

## Becoming Familiar with Other Types of Technology

Although we have primarily concentrated on computer technology, there are many other types of technology that can be used to extend children's play. Collaborating with the children to determine their interests and skills will provide practitioners with information about how play may be enhanced with technologies. Depending on the play experience, children may benefit from having access to recorders, cameras, televisions, keyboards, electronic boards, and other devices, if available.

# TRAINING AND DEVELOPMENT

Early learning practitioners play a key role in the integration of technology with child's play. One of the biggest challenges or roadblocks to integrating technology into early learning environments is training.

Practitioners, who participate in continuous training and development on the use of technology and how it may benefit the individual child and groups of children, appear to be more successful in integrating technology into a child's play (Chen & Price, 2006, Gimbert & Cristol, 2004) than in programs where this professional development activity has not occurred. When practitioners know the software and the technology, there is an enhanced level of interaction among practitioners and children.

Early learning practitioners go through three distinct phases when integrating technology into the early learning centre (Chen Chang, 2006; Sandholtz, Ringstaff, & Dyer, 1997). The first phase is to learn technical procedures. Then, the practitioner uses the technology to support learning. Finally, practitioners think about how technology advances or enhances child's play and how children engage in using technology in the learning environment. Novice users are more likely to integrate technology into the early learning environment if they have a role model to whom they can turn for knowledge about computers, as well as for emotional support and reassurance (Pearson, 1994; Persky, 1990).

The following are key training and development issues that should be addressed so that technology is effectively integrated into programs for young children.

> **Time:** Early learning practitioners require time to explore technology and acquire the skills necessary to effectively infuse technology into early learning environments (Boe, 1989; Hawkins & MacMillan, 1993; Kinnaman, 1990). There is merit when early learning practitioners have opportunities to explore the software without distractions.

> **Training Structure:** Early learning practitioners require a variety of teaching and learning opportunities related to child's play and technology. The training process provides opportunities for practitioners to determine the competencies required to support the integration of technology into child's play.

> **Collaborative Development:** Just as young children learn best in a collaborative computer area, early learning practitioners also benefit from this type of setting. Because early learning practitioner's skills and interests may vary, a non-threatening environment where the software can be explored leads to enriching the children's technology opportunities. Stager (1995), Browne and Ritchie (1991), and Persky (1990) suggest that collaborative problem solving and cooperative learning are the underpinning for supporting early learning practitioners with learning about technology. Role modelling can be part of this process. It allows practitioners with less experience to observe and then gradually build their confidence.

**Linking technology with children's interests and program philosophy:**
How technology is used in the early learning centres should support the
centre's philosophy. This helps to guide how technology is integrated into
the child's play (Guhlin, 1996; Persky, 1990). Technology must be relevant
to the program philosophy and intended learning outcomes for the children (Boe, 1989). This provides a meaningful context for the learning
about technology and transferring it to the early learning environment.

# SUMMARY

## Chapter Preview
- The role of technology in the lives of children requires an examination of the controversies, challenges, and perspectives as it relates to play.
- Technology brings inequalities to children's lives.

## Various Perspectives about the Use of Technology with Young Children
- Many early learning professionals oppose the use of computers because of their fear that it erodes a child's play and will lead to childhood obesity and aggressive behaviour.
- The NAYEC's position statement outlines that early learning practitioners have the responsibility to assess, evaluate, and develop strategies for implementing technology, while providing each child with equitable access to technology.

## Technology and Early Learning
- Technology is part of children's lives.

## Defining Technology in a Child's World
- Technology is any device that increases or assists children's ability to play, explore, discover new learning, and extend their potential.

## The Benefits of Using Technology with Young Children
- Computers are motivational for some children. If used appropriately, technology will enhance child's play and children's self-concept.
- Children share leadership roles and initiate interactions.

## The Stages of Using the Computer among Preschool Children
- There are defined stages that children go through when learning to use a computer.

## The Placement of Computers in Early Learning Environments
- The placement of the computer in the early learning environment impacts how children use them.

## Technology and Child Development
- Technology contributes to the cognitive, social, emotional, language, and physical development of children.
- Technology can cause equity issues among children, families, and genders.
- Children with atypical development benefit from access to technology.

### Facilitating Children's Play at the Computer Centre

- Early learning practitioners participate in a variety of ways with children using computers. Reactive supervision, guided interaction, and a hybrid approach provide different types of guidance to children.
- Choosing software is challenging. Children require open-ended software that supports their interests, skills, and capabilities. There are key questions that can guide practitioners in determining the needs and types of software to support children's use of computers.
- Early learning practitioners use a variety of methods to observe children using computers, including contextual inquiry.

### Training and Development

- Early learning practitioners require training and development in technology. This requires time, training structure, collaborative development, and having a clear philosophy about technology and children's play.

## REVIEW QUESTIONS

1. Outline the key reasons why some researchers suggest that computers and other forms of technology negatively impact the type of play and quality of a child's play experience.
2. Discuss six benefits of using technology with children.
3. Describe how Parten's stages of social play relate to children's social behaviours when using computers.
4. Discuss how the placement of the computer impacts the child's play positively and negatively.
5. Highlight how technology supports a child's cognitive, physical, social, and emotional development.
6. Describe how shared problem space supports a child in learning a particular task with the computer.
7. Outline the common socialization skills that preschool and school-age children gain from using computers.
8. How do computers support children with special needs?
9. Describe the roles and responsibilities of early learning practitioners in integrating technology into early learning centres.

## MAKING CONNECTIONS

### Theory to Practice

1. Interview an early learning practitioner to gain information on how technology is used in the early learning centre. How is it used to enhance the play experiences of children? Is it used by more than one child at a time? How do children use the technology? What is the value of having technology in an early learning centre? What are the challenges?
2. View six websites that have software available for infants, toddlers, preschoolers, and school-age children. Examine the software using the questions outlined in the chapter. What are your findings? Are you able to effectively evaluate software online? If not, how do early learning practitioners ensure that the software they are purchasing is suitable for their children?
3. Visit an early learning centre that uses technology. Examine the software that is available to children. How, as an early learning practitioner student, do you prepare yourself to know about the software so that you may support children when using the computer centre?
4. You are required to develop a poster board for parents that links children's play and the use of technology. What key messages would you incorporate onto the poster board? Why?

## For Further Research

1. The National Association for the Education of Young Children (NAEYC) has a position statement on children and technology. Research early learning organizations in Canada, such as the Canadian Child Care Federation (CCCF) and the Canadian Association for the Education of Young Children (CAEYC), or provincial associations to determine if they have a position statement. If they do, compare it to the NAEYC statement. What do you conclude if there are no Canadian position statements on technology and children's play?
2. Research the latest information on children's interactive media. How does the literature support play and child development? What does it tell you about the next phase of technology with young children? Does the literature focus more on children under 5 or over 5?

# ADDITIONAL READING

Elkind, D. (1996). Young children and technology: A cautionary note. *Young Children*, 51(6), 22–23.

Elkind, D. (2007). *The power of play: Learning what comes naturally*. Philadelphia, PA: DecCapo.

Li, X. & Atkins, M. (2004). Early childhood computer experience and cognitive and motor development. *Pediatrics*, 113(6), 1–8.

McCarrick, K. & Li, X. (2007). Buried treasure: The impact of computer use on young children's social, cognitive, language development and motivation. *AACE Journal*, 15(1), 73–95.

# WEBLINKS

Introducing technology to young children e-clip
**www.easternct.edu/cece/e-clips_Technology.htm**

Young children and computers
**www.naeyc.org/files/tyc/file/TYC_V3N4_Blagojevicexpanded.pdf**

Technology and young children interest forum website, technology with children
**www.techandyoungchildren.org/children.html**

# 11 Music, Movement, and Play

## Learning Outcomes

After reviewing this chapter, you should be able to

- describe reasons why music and movement may not be presented to children in the same way as other programming experiences;

- describe the historical influence of music and movement, including the contemporary perspectives;

- describe why music and movement are important for children during their early years;

- explain how music and movement support the child's psychomotor development, social and emotional development, cognitive development, and aesthetic appreciation;

- outline the considerations that early learning practitioners make when introducing songs and related music and movement experiences to children;

- describe the value of music and movement to children with atypical development; and

- describe the roles of early learning practitioners in presenting music and movement to children.

## Stories from the Field: Practitioner to Student

When I was first hired at an early learning centre after graduation, I was surprised to observe that children were exposed to music all day long. For the first few days I thought "wow" this is neat—I am hearing music from the local radio station—the golden oldie hits. I would sing along to the song. It gave me a sense of comfort. After a few days, I found myself feeling less comfortable. When we took children on walks, the radio was attached to the buggy. When children were outside, music played through the speakers, and when the children were trying to settle down for their nap, the station was still on, but lowered. It was adult music and it seemed out of place in the space devoted to play.

By the end of my second week, I was using much of my energy to deal with the music. I was constantly fighting with a feeling of disequilibrium. I began to question if children also needed to use some of their precious energy to block out the music which I had now determined to be noise. I also wondered if this was healthy for children—were they acquiring a sense of and appreciation for music. Finally, I determined that I needed to speak with my colleagues. My colleagues were interested in my feelings and open to discussing this practice. One colleague indicated that she thought because so many children now grow up in homes with music and the television playing constantly that this was more of a comfort to the children than hindrance. Another colleague thought that because, in her opinion, most early learning practitioners were not musically inclined that this was a way to expose children to music.

We collectively determined that we would try an experiment. We would reduce the times when the music was on and we would reduce the volume of the music. We decided to include calming children's music when the children were settling down to rest and nature-related music when they were outdoors. Over a month-long period, we noticed significant changes in the children. They were calmer, they participated with the music with movement when it was children's music and seemed less frenetic outdoors with the natural themed music. We also noticed that, some children were using the music centre more frequently and talking more about musical concepts!

My advice to new practitioners—music like all early learning experiences, should be developmentally and inclusively appropriate for all children. Experiences should be child-initiated and practitioner framed. Music is as important as all the other experiences. It must be incorporated into the environment at appropriate times so that children develop an appreciation for it. Choose how to present music with the same care as blocks, outdoor play, math, or science.

*Katie, ECE Graduate, 2008*

## CHAPTER PREVIEW

Many researchers have reported the benefits of music and movement to a child's whole development. Music and movement are important components of the experiences extended to children during their early years. Music play involves children in physical, social, cognitive, kinesthetic, and communicative challenges. Music and movement is a multi-sensory experience where "we hear sound, see movement-based and notation-based representations of that sound, and are kinesthetically responsive to what we hear and see as we play instruments, sing, and move" (Custodero, 2002, p. 3).

Movement opportunities help children become more aware of their bodies, what their bodies can do, and how they may use their bodies in their space. Music develops auditory discrimination, phonemic awareness acquired from rhyming words, and abstract thinking related to mathematics. Despite the importance of music and movement, there is growing concern among researchers that early learning practitioners are not emphasizing this part of the program to the extent of other programming areas (Kim, 2000). Sharpe, Harris, & McKeen (2010) indicate that there is a broad range of practices, beliefs, and attitudes regarding music and movement education in early learning settings. Some see them as "add ons" or secondary to other programming. There is a consensus among many researchers that early learning practitioners do not have sufficient training to fully support this programming area, which results in there being less emphasis on music and movement than on other programming areas.

As outlined in previous chapters, early learning practitioners are increasingly being put under pressure to offer young children under the age of 5 experiences that appears to support them in academic preparation, rather than to engage in the broad spectrum learning that occurs through play. If parents have not been exposed to music in formal ways such as taking singing lessons or instrument lessons, there can be a gap in their knowledge about how music play relates to child development and learning. Many parents do not know the connection between music and movement, language development, mathematical concepts, and overall brain development. If early learning practitioners would discuss musical attributes with parents and use the example how parents instinctively use music to comfort the child through song or humming, it might help them to think of music in new ways.

As you explore this chapter, think about the music and movement experiences you have had in your life. Think about the kind of music that you are attracted to. Are there particular musical pieces where you find your body movements react instantly to the sounds and beat of the music? How are music and movement related to play?

In this chapter, we highlight the relationship of music to movement and how music and movement are integrated into child's play, such as in dramatic play.

# HISTORICAL INFLUENCES OF MUSIC AND MOVEMENT

The importance of music and movement to play has long been identified as important features of childhood. For example, in *Principles of Psychology*, Herbert Spencer (1896) identified four types of play: physical play, artistic-aesthetic play, games, and mimicry. The artistic-aesthetic play included music and movement as a key element.

Jean Jacques Rousseau and Maria Montessori both advocated for children to be given the opportunity to experience music in their lives. Rousseau stressed the importance of adults providing environments that respected children's natural ways of knowing and learning. Music and movement are natural for children and interconnected from a growth and development perspective. Children cannot flourish without access to both. He indicated that adults have a role in singing to children, starting with simple songs. He believed by exposing children to music and singing that their voices would, over time, become accurate, uniform, and flexible (Isenberg & Jalongo, 2010).

Montessori incorporated sound exploration activities into the children's environment. For example, one piece of apparatus that she developed was a set of mushroom-shaped bells so that children could discover various musical concepts. These bells offer children many musical discovery options. They learn about sounds, patterning, how to create music, how to vary sounds, and what happens when you combine bells with other musical instruments.

Another leader who has influenced our understanding of the importance of music in the lives of young children is Carl Orff (1895–1982). Using a child-centred approach, he established a school that incorporated movement through gymnastics with music and dance. He believed that children needed the freedom to spontaneously react, create, and produce their own music, and rhythmic responses. Orff role-modelled and supported children in using their imaginations to explore making music with their voices and simple instruments.

Howard Gardner (1996) provides a contemporary approach, identifying music as one of the eight types of intelligences. The others are linguistic, logical-mathematical, spatial, bodily-kinestic, interpersonal, intrapersonal, and naturalistic intelligences.

Gardner indicates that music appreciation offers heightened perceptual discrimination, body awareness, and a sense of pitch and melody. He suggests that "musical intelligence is an almost structural parallel to linguistic intelligence" (Smith, 2008, p. 3).

According to Gardner's theory, musical intelligence, bodily-kinesthetic intelligence, linguistic, and spatial intelligences are identified in the following way:

> **Musical intelligence** involves skill in the performance, composition, and appreciation of musical patterns. It is having the capacity to recognize and compose musical pitches, tones, and rhythms.
>
> **Bodily-kinesthetic intelligence** entails the potential of using one's whole body or parts of the body to solve problems. It includes using mental abilities to coordinate bodily movements.
>
> **Linguistic intelligence** involves the skills of words, spoken or written. It is the ability to read, write, tell stories, and memorize the meaning of words.
>
> **Spatial intelligence** involves the potential to recognize and adapt and use the varying types of space, such as wide space and more confined areas. (Smith, 2008)

Music and movement contribute to enhancing each of these intelligences. They are also interrelated to understanding the concepts of physics and mathematics for **logical-mathematical intelligence** and have connections to **interpersonal intelligence,** as music brings people together, and **intrapersonal intelligence** contributes to the development of the self. Music connects to **naturalistic intelligence** as it can be a significant way children relate to nature.

Contemporary views suggest that music for young children should be based on four elements. They include

- **Listening:** this requires children to have access to a variety of music including music from their culture, classical, and easy listening based on the interest of the children and at appropriate times;
- **Moving:** this requires children to have time and space to experiment with body movements and rhythm as music is played;
- **Playing:** this requires children to have access to music, instruments, and dramatic play props that will support children in acting out their interpretations of the music; and
- **Singing:** this requires children to have an early learning environment that supports them in having exposure to song, opportunities for singing and experimenting with words, and instruments and dramatic play props (Isenberg & Jalongo, 2010).

Morin (2001) indicates the need for early learning practitioners to develop a concept of play and how it relates to the musical learner. She identifies the need for early learning practitioners to examine the definitions of play. Littleron (1998) defines play as "pleasurable, freely-chosen, solitary, and absent of adult intervention" (p. 8). Jalongo and Stamp (1997) tell us that "play, like music, is symbolic, meaningful, active, rule-governed, and episodic" (Morin, 2001, p. 25). Littleton (1998) indicates that music-play episodes correspond to the general social and cognitive play categories of Parten and Piaget, as outlined in Chapter 2.

Morin (2001) categorizes music play as follows:

> **Cooperative music play** recognizes the role of socialization in children's learning and requires children to interact and communicate; **functional music play** encompasses exploring the environmental and musical sounds, sound production techniques, and resources that introduce musical concepts and ideas; **constructive music play** is an extension of exploration and involves creative idea development such as improvisation, composition, instrument-making, or sound recording; **dramatic music play** uses instruments or singing in role playing, make-believe, or story-telling contexts; **kinesthetic music play** involves the movement response to recorded music or instrumental or vocal sounds, with or without objects like streamers or scarves; and **games with rules** include more structured music experiences such as singing, clapping, or dancing games with predetermined actions and/or socially developed rules. (p. 26)

Early learning practitioners incorporate their knowledge about play and learning into the types of play experiences and strategies used to promote music and movement through exploration and discovery in the early learning environment.

## THE IMPORTANCE OF MUSIC AND MOVEMENT

The early years are critical for children learning how to unscramble the aural images of music and to develop mental representations for organizing the music of the culture (Davidson, 1985; Holahan, 1987). This process is similar to the young child engaging in the "language babble" stage necessary for language development.

Young children develop musically through a predictable sequence to basic music competence (see Table 11.1), which includes singing in tune and marching to a beat (Levinowitz & Guilmartin, 1996). Children are born with the potential to learn and develop musical skills and talents, just as they are able to develop art or

*Table 11.1*  *The Sequence of Music and Movement with Young Children*

| Infants' Developmental Sequence of Music | Infants' Developmental Sequence of Movement |
| --- | --- |
| • Is sensitive to loud and soft sounds<br>• Is soothed by soft, rhythmic, melodious sounds (Isenberg & Jalongo, 2010)<br>• The more lively the music, the more active the response—eyes or head turn toward music | • Respond to music using the entire body<br>• Infants who are sitting tend to bounce to the music<br>• Infants in an upright position may move from side to side or bounce up or down<br>• Infants turn body towards music, wave hands, and feet |

*continued*

| Toddlers' Developmental Sequence of Music | Toddlers' Developmental Sequence of Movement |
|---|---|
| • May imitate sound<br>• May try to make sound with toys or household objects<br>• Will react positively to music by clapping or bouncing to the music that the child is familiar with<br>• May hum sounds during play<br>• Is able to discriminate among sounds and songs<br>• Interested in musical instruments | • Respond to music using fine and gross motor skills with various body parts relevant to the music—arms and legs for some, upper torso for others<br>• Respond to the tempo of the music by moving body fast or slow<br>• Dance to music and produce some words with the dance |

| Preschoolers' Developmental Sequence of Music | Preschoolers' Developmental Sequence of Movement |
|---|---|
| • Begin to recognize the songs and sing the songs with accuracy (Day, 1988)<br>• Able to play a simple rhythm instrument such as bells or sticks<br>• Able to reproduce rhythm patterns<br>• Begin to recognize the sounds of different musical instruments such as horn, bells, flutes, etc.<br>• Able to sing familiar songs from beginning to end, some with basic musical concepts such as high/low, fast/slow, loud/soft<br>• Participate in group singing games and make up parts to songs with rhythm<br>• Participate in listening to music<br>• Begin to experiment with sounds | • Body movements become more coordinated and refined to music<br>• Movements such as heel to toe and tiptoes are evident<br>• Action songs completed with varying moves to music<br>• Songs are sung as movements take place<br>• Able to switch from one movement to another with speed and success<br>• Movements become more creative and varied among the children, using the whole body with the music to jump, hop, and walk |

| Kindergarten-Age Developmental Sequence of Music | Kindergarten-Age Developmental Sequence of Movement |
|---|---|
| • Able to illustrate pitch, rhythm, and melody<br>• Able to produce musical concepts of fast/slow, high/low on keyboard<br>• Able to reproduce sounds, tones, and patterns<br>• Able to produce a vocal range of five to six notes (Isenberg & Jalongo, 2010)<br>• Able to produce new words for songs | • Movements are well coordinated with music<br>• Combines two movements at the same time such as marching and keeping the beat with instruments |

| School-Age Developmental Sequence of Music | School-Age Developmental Sequence of Movement |
|---|---|
| • Able to sing "in tune" <br> • Begins to sing simple two-part harmony with role modelling <br> • Able to sing more complicated songs from memory <br> • Able to identify the types of music that are preferred <br> • Able to produce music on musical instruments | • Movements match musical characteristics <br> • Movements move simple to complex with ease <br> • Improvising of movements completed with ease <br> • Complex moves in dances achieved |

science skills. This development occurs in play environments that allow children to explore music and movement in a variety of ways.

Music and movement are important experiences and features for programming in play environments. They require thoughtfully planned experiences that meet the developmental needs and interests of the children. Music and movement should be transparent in both the planned portion of the program and in spontaneous play. The more opportunities children have to explore music through spontaneous play, the more likely they are to create music and engage in exploration (Morin, 2001).

Early learning practitioners often use the terms creative movement, movement, and creative dance interchangeably. Dance differs from movement. **Dance** is a more formal, structured movement. It integrates the mind and the body (Ross, 1994). Dance is generally based on a foot pattern and body movement that are used to depict the language of the music including the verbal message, beat, and tone. **Creative movement** refers to the process of children using their bodies usually with music to communicate an idea, a feeling, an image or a belief. It is a non-competitive activity. **Movement** refers to physical movement of the body that helps to develop skills such as balance, coordination, body awareness, and self-image.

Music is more than singing; it is a way in which children and adults communicate. Music and movement comprise a way in which culture is transferred from one generation to the next. In many cultures, children are introduced to music and movement through dance at a very young age. Often family and community gatherings have a strong focus on music, with the very young children joining in with song and movement. The Yamaha philosophy is that "music is a common language that unites people across international boundaries" (Yamaha Corporation, 1994, p. 295). Music, creative movement, and dance are interconnected. They include children singing, rhyming clapping, chanting, tapping, marching, and doing simple dances.

Many researchers highlight the benefits of music and movement on early brain development. The International Foundation of Music Research, based at the University of Texas, indicates that there is substantial evidence to suggest that music appreciation begins during pregnancy and continues as nurtured through childhood. They suggest that babies are aware of and respond to various sounds including music while in the mother's womb. At birth, a baby may turn in the direction of the voice of the mother. Newborns quickly recognize the mother's voice over other voices. They develop the skills to distinguish and respond to changes in a person's voice or pitch before their first birthday. Through the movement of their arms and legs and their babbling and cooing, they express their response to the voice and pitch changes. Enriching music and movement experiences contribute to aspects of brain development.

Don Campbell, author of *The Mozart Effect and the Mozart Effect for Children,* states: "Movement is an absolute necessity for a toddler, and music stimulates the best kinds of movement" (p. 102). As we think about the brain working by electrical currents, when children are engaged in movement, they are supporting the brain in replenishing the oxygen levels needed for functioning. The brain produces a chemical called endorphins. This chemical contributes to the child's energy level. Movement is one of the body's fuels responsible for developing the energy levels.

A study conducted by deVries (2004) indicates when young children are exposed to music and movement the following occurs:

1. Involvement in music activities allows children to release energy.
2. Motor skills are developed.
3. Music activities promote child socialization.
4. Music is a venue for children to express themselves.
5. Music is connected to dramatic play.
6. Music listening activities increase a child's ability to increase their listening skills focus in other play experiences.

Humpal and Wolf (2003) indicate that music is inclusive because "it offers varying levels of engagement—from simply listening to participating or even performing" (p. 103). Many children with atypical development exhibit an interest in music and develop music-related talents. For example, children who stutter are able to sing without stuttering. And school-age children are very connected to music not only for the sake of the enjoyment that comes from the music, but it is a social connection among children.

Morin (2001) "affirms that play is a significant part of music teaching and learning for young children" (p. 24).

Children's play is their work. Children should have opportunities for individual musical play, such as in a "music corner," as well as for group musical play, such as singing games. Children learn within a playful environment. Play provides a safe place to try on the roles of others, to fantasize, and to explore new ideas. Children's play involves imitation and improvisation (Music Educators National Conference, 1992, p. 21).

*Photo 11.1   Children engage in physical, social, and cognitive play with music and movement.*

Child's play includes opportunities to explore music and movement. Early learning practitioners and student practitioners think about ways to incorporate music and movement into the play of children. Because music and movement choices are so personal, early learning practitioners are challenged to listen to the children, offer them opportunities to explore a wide range of music, and to develop their preferences.

## WORDS OF WISDOM

Dr. Laurel Trainor, Professor of Psychology, Neuroscience and Behaviour at McMaster University and Director of the McMaster Institute for Music and the Mind, indicates that a study conducted on children between the ages of 4 and 6 years suggests that the brains of musically trained children respond to music in a different way from those of the untrained children. The results of the study also suggest that music training improves a child's memory. Children who are musically trained perform better in a memory test that is correlated with general intelligence skills such as literacy, verbal memory, visuospatial processing, mathematics, and IQ. The Canadian-based researchers determined this by measuring the changes in brain responses to sounds in children between the ages of four and six. This is the first study to identify these effects in brain-based measurements in young children.

"It is clear that music is good for children's cognitive development and that music should be part of the pre-school and primary school curriculum" *ScienceDaily* (September 20, 2006).

## Music, Movement, and Child Development

Music and movement contribute to the overall development of the young child, as identified in Figure 11.1. Early learning practitioners consistently observe young children to gain a sense of their developmental phase, interests, and capabilities. Examining children's interests and capabilities is of particular importance with music and movement because the child may express the interest in a variety of ways such as listening to music, moving to music, reproducing music, exploring different movements with body, or examining how musical instruments work.

Researchers continue to examine the relationship of music and movement to development. As new research becomes available, early learning practitioners will be required to examine the musical and movement attributes of the programming that young children are exposed to. For example, Kuhlman and Schweihart (2010) determined that "a child's timing—the ability to feel and express beat—is fundamental to both movement and music" (p. 1). They suggest that these skills affect a child's ability in sport skills, music performance, speech-flow, and performance of motor tasks. They indicate that children's ability to produce accurate timing has an impact on mathematics and reading achievement, self-control, and gross motor skills. When children are not involved in experiences and activities that will allow them to develop the timing/beat during the early years, it has a lifelong effect.

Wright and Schweinhart (1994) indicate that many children enter kindergarten and elementary school without the skills or the ability to identify and

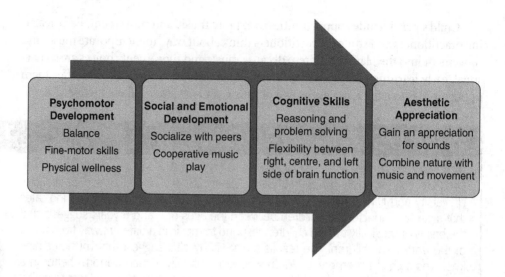

*Figure 11.1 Music, Movement, and Child Development*

express a steady beat. They cite one study that revealed that fewer than 10 percent of kindergarten children could feel or express the steady beat of recorded music. This deficit continues throughout childhood. Fewer than 15 percent of first graders tested had this ability and fewer than 50 percent of the children in grades 4 through 6 could walk to the steady beat of a musical selection.

Research has also revealed the relationship of cross-lateral movement to children learning how to read. According to Levinowitz (1998), the development of cross-lateral movement is required for the child's eyes to move from one side of the paper to the next—this is a brain function that requires movement from one side of the brain (right side) to the mid-section to the other side (left side). Early learning practitioners can provide numerous experiences that will have the children utilize both sides of their brain in the movement. Dancing with scarves, crawling like a baby, and, walking like a turtle or elephant can achieve this important movement. Studies such as these reinforce to early learning practitioners the importance of ensuring that children have opportunities to participate in a variety of music and movement experiences.

## Psychomotor Development

Music and movement constitute an important activity that supports the young child's psychomotor development from as early as three months old. For example, when babies are exposed to music, they move their arms and legs in response to the music. Toddlers begin to move their upper torso and their feet to the music. This enhances their ability to develop balance and to lift one foot and then the other. Preschoolers become more efficient in their movements. With music and movement they expand their balancing skills and their fine motor skills are enhanced as they begin to use musical instruments such as shakers. School-age children further expand their psychomotor skills when they combine physical activity in response to the music while producing music by singing or performing karaoke.

As discussed throughout this text, our children today require as many opportunities for physical activity as possible. Music and movement support children's physical wellness. Music and movement is an easy, natural strategy to use with children to incorporate movement into their daily lives. Isenberg and Jalongo (2010) suggest that if young children do not develop competence in movement during their early years, it may result in a poor body image and it may impact their ability or interest in participating in physical sports or other physical endeavours (Garcia, Garcia, Floyd, & Lawson, 2002). Through music and movement children develop the kinesthetic skills of knowing how their body movements work within their space and this is required to be successful in sports.

According to Levinowitz (1998), research has identified that there is a profound connection between rhythm and movement.

> The study of rhythm can be thought of as the study of all aspects of flow of music through time. We experience rhythm as the flow of our movement through space. From the developmental perspective, children must experience rhythm in their bodies before they can successfully audiate rhythm in their minds. The early childhood years are crucial for using the body to respond as a musical instrument in many ways to many different kinds of music. Real musical instruments, like tools, can then become simply extensions or amplifications of the body's ability to be musically expressive. (p. 1)

deVries (2004) indicates that by combining music and movement activities, children who struggle with movement will become more active and their motor movement becomes more developed. For example, he identifies that when children perform a motor skill to the beat while singing and moving from one motor movement to the next, such as jumping and hopping, the child's ability to expand to more complicated motor movements increases. As we think about psychomotor development, it is essential to recognize its importance in the lives of young children. Being exposed to psychomotor development opportunities contributes to the development of the child's ability to move their body, use their body, and to have confidence in their abilities to manoeuvre their bodies as they desire. Psychomotor development is effective when it incorporates listening, moving, playing, and singing (Isenberg & Jalongo, 2010) in various activities.

## Social and Emotional Development

Music and movement offer children another way to socialize with their peers. For example, when preschool children enjoy music, they will talk to each other about the music they like, they will identify the songs and games they wish to play, and they will share information about musical instruments.

*Photo 11.2 Children learn about their bodies, space, and beat though music and movement.*

When children are involved in music and movement, such as in chase songs/games, the children may call out the names of those who are being chased or they may provide words of encouragement such as "run faster . . . quick." These actions support one another; they introduce cooperative play and build self-esteem.

Dorman (1990) indicates that music-play interest centres are most effective when they are designed to support and encourage children's social interaction and decision-making opportunities. Music and movement extend beyond the group experience and the music and movement centre. It may become prevalent in the dramatic centre. Music allows children to enact different roles from the usual family-type familiar roles in the dramatic centre (although children will use music to rock the babies in the dramatic centre). When children become connected to music—and with props—the possibilities are endless, such as becoming rock stars in the dramatic centre. Musical instruments may be used for many parts of a child's dramatic play. For example, cowbells are used for police or fire truck sirens. Tambourines are used for doorbells, and clappers are used when playing "Three Billy Goat Gruff."

Early learning practitioners expand music and movement across the program as a way to support it in contributing to a child's social development. For example, children may note that there are various musical instruments in experience centres such as the block area. This becomes a conversational trigger and exploratory opportunity. Morin (2000) describes this rich play as **cooperative music play.** Children are communicating with each other to learn more about the musical attributes of items and experiences in the play space.

Think of the children that you may hear saying, "we will sing and you do the actions" or "let's play the song and do the actions." For many children, having exposure to music is an important strategy for them to express themselves and to become part of a group. Music and movement experiences that encourage the participation of young children will enhance the child gaining competence with peers, in groups, and in cooperative skills.

Littleton (1998) indicates that the application of social play categories, as described in Chapter 2, when applied to music and play, "strengthen the importance of socialization and its function in the music-play culture of young children and the importance of music-play to children's social development" (p. 13). When children have the freedom and respect of adults, they will engage in music play similar to other play. They will develop strategies for managing disputes and solve problems of noise on their own (Littleton, 1998; Smitherim, 1997).

## Stop . . . Think . . . Discuss . . . Reflect

When you think of music and movement in an early learning program, what does it look like to you? How is it different from the arts and science experiences extended to children? Why is it different? Is music a social or a solitary activity? Why? How do you support children with atypical development in becoming involved in music? Why would you wish to do this as an early learning practitioner?

Photo 11.3 *Children learn to play, problem solve, and discover how music and movement interests may be similar.*

## Cognitive Development

Researchers from the cognitive and neuroscience sectors suggest that music and movement experiences directly support brain stimulation and development (Jenson, 2006). The connections that are formed between the cells of the brain, known as synapses, are developed with stimulation. During the early years, it is important for the synapses to be strengthened through appropriate experiences. When children are not afforded experiences, such as music and movement, there is a risk that their potential in this area will have long-term developmental effects. For example, research suggests that one's singing voice generally develops during the first seven years of life. If children do not have any further exposure to music in their lifetime, their skills set that they acquired during the early years is generally what they have during adulthood.

Some researchers suggest that music and movement experiences increase a child's overall intelligence, as identified by Gardner earlier in the chapter. Researchers suggest that music and movement contribute to the development of one's attitudes, interest, motivation, and life focus. It also contributes to self-confidence and self-esteem. According to Bruner (1968), from a cognitive psychology perspective, children's abilities in the musical and kinesthetic domains tend to progress through three stages: (1) enactive, (2) iconic, and (3) symbolic. Bruner's enactive stage of development corresponds to Piaget's sensorimotor stage, as described in Chapter 2, whereby children benefit from experiences that focus on simple, repetitive movements with people and objects. During **the enactive stage,** predominantly experienced by infants and toddlers, the physical activity and music are linked (Mang, 2005). For example, adults will combine music and movement in their daily communication with infants and toddlers as they sing "Moving up and down" and as they bounce them on their knees. Toddlers and young preschoolers will share their delight as they sing and engage in action songs such as the "Eensey Weensy Spider" or "Head and Shoulders."

The **iconic stage** of development, experienced by primarily late toddlers and preschoolers, combines real objects with pictorial representations. During this phase, children require experiences that allow them to use their imaginations (Piaget, 1962) and assert their autonomy. Musical games such as "London Bridge Falling Down" encourages children to effectively incorporate music and movement as they use their hands and arms stretched out to make a bridge. Children experience the interconnectivity to music, movement, and language when early learning practitioners combine music experiences with action and words.

Children at the **symbolic stage** are usually kindergarten age and school-age. At the beginning of this phase, the children use abstract symbols, including language, to represent ideas. As they progress cognitively they use advanced abstract processes that may include "words, musical notation, and the movement and gesture of dance" (Isenberg & Jalongo, 2010, p. 157). This is supportive of Piaget's stage of development known as symbolic/dramatic play where children begin to express fantasy, use props, and take on roles other than being children.

When young children are exposed to music, early learning practitioners are providing them with the opportunity to develop "mentally the tonal aspects of rhythm and melody" (Isenberg & Jalongo, 2010, 168). For example, when children are able to participate in a song such as "Head and Shoulders" they are practising skills in linking words to actions and sequencing of what comes first, second, and third. As children gain more complex musical abilities, such as being able to play an instrument, they require higher-level thinking skills, such as application, synthesis, and evaluation, as identified in Bloom's taxonomy. Music is considered a language. Through music and movement children require and develop similar cognitive skills that are used in mathematics and literacy.

Music requires children to utilize both their memory skills and classification skills. For example, when children are exposed to music with instruments, they are required to classify the different sounds and rhythms that they hear. They need to use their memories to be able to replicate beat patterns. Singing songs adds to a child's language acquisition, as it introduces them to vocabulary and rhyme.

Recent data from the University of Texas suggest that children who are involved in arts education that includes a music component received higher Scholastic Aptitude Test (SAT) scores. Other studies show that music and movement support cognitive abilities, particularly spatial abilities, higher reasoning and motor skills, and higher achievements in math, language, and science.

The earlier young children are exposed to music, the more opportunity the brain has to respond to the various music tones. Because of developmental attributes that music and movement offer children, early learning practitioners incorporate opportunities for children to sing, improvise, move, and dance across the program.

*Photo 11.4 When children are exposed to various types of music and movement from a young age it becomes part of their lifestyle.*

# AESTHETIC APPRECIATION

Music and movement provide another venue for children to gain aesthetic appreciation. Early learning practitioners and students can pose questions to the children that help them listen to the various sounds, tones, and movement of the music. Practitioners can offer children music that introduces them to the various musical instruments such as bells, horns, cello, drums, etc. They also can offer music that is soft and gentle or more vigorous. Varying the music is important because this is how children learn to listen to the various attributes of the music and to determine how they feel about each type of music.

Aesthetic appreciation builds when music and movement are combined activities. Practitioners and children listen to music and move their bodies to the music. This contributes to children using their body within the spaces made available for music and movement. Movement and music assist children in devising ways to use their body differently in the space provided. This may require them to squish their bodies into small spaces or be as big as a giant. Think of a ballerina. Ballerinas develop the ability to listen to the music and have their body respond to it. They bring aesthetic appreciation to the eye.

Music and movement are part of our natural surroundings. When music is presented to children in the outdoor environment, the early learning practitioner and children compare aspects of the music to the sounds in the natural environment. For example, there may be music that has sounds of water or wind or birds. Children compare that music to the sounds present in their environments. This advances their connection to nature and aesthetics. It also assists the children in being able to reproduce new sounds with their voices or instruments. The natural environment combines music and movement opportunities into the child's world. Children are encouraged to combine sounds to movement. When they hear and feel the wind, children replicate the sound and the movement of the wind. These types of activities heighten the child's observation skills and their ability to appreciate the beauty of their environment.

Early learning practitioners ensure that the places where children experience music are appealing to them. Children require intrigue, which can be realized when the area is colourful and there are artifacts that pique the child's interests (Morin, 2001). This supports and models the importance of aesthetic appreciation.

## Presenting Music and Movement to Children

Early learning practitioners should plan music and movement experiences with children and support spontaneous activities. Music and song can be presented to children throughout the day in ways that support children gaining an appreciation for music. Music should be available at specific times during the day, not just at group experiences. Early learning practitioners can use simple, familiar songs to transition from one experience to another. Although young children should not be put in the position of needing to wait for activities or directions, at times this may occur. Music and movement are used at such times to make the waiting experience pleasant. Music brings children together at a group time experience and it is used to bring parents and children together.

Presenting music to children may be challenging for some early learning practitioners, especially those who feel they can't sing or are self-conscious to sing in front of their colleagues. As challenging as it may be, it is evident that quality programs offer children music and movement experiences. Early learning practitioners benefit from gaining practical knowledge about music and movement and to acquire skills that will support children in acquiring developmentally appropriate music and movement programming.

## Presenting Songs to Children

It is important that early learning practitioners have an understanding of what is meant by **pitch**, **pitch-matching**, and **vocal range**, as these guide practitioners in how songs are presented to children.

**Pitch** refers to the highness or lowness of the musical sound.

**Pitch-matching** refers to matching the musical sounds to the highness or lowness of the song (Kim, 2000, p. 153).

**Vocal range** refers to the distance between the highest and lowest notes the voice can match (McDonald & Simmons, 1989).

Early learning practitioners have a role in supporting young children in being exposed to a variety of music and ways to produce music. Often, the latter is done through group singing. Because many early learning practitioners do not necessarily have a background in music, one of the most common problems with young children singing in groups is that "some adults do not begin the song on a pitch that is comfortable for the majority of children" (Kim, 2000, p. 153). Many early learning practitioners use their own comfort singing range. This is generally too low for preschool children (Kim, 2000). Flowers and Dunne-Sousa (1990) indicate young children are more likely to open up their vocal ranges when adults model brief patterns rather than singing songs that demand the same range. Offering children opportunities to use high pitches through echoing and through imitation of natural songs supports them in their pitch-matching and vocal range.

Greenberg (1979) classified children's vocalization into five stages:

Stage I:    The first vocalization (birth to 3 months)

Stage II:   Experimentation and sound imitation (3 months to 18 months)

Stage III:  Approximation of singings (18 month to 3 years)

Stage IV:   Singing accuracy in limited range (3 to 4 years)

Stage V:    Singing accuracy with expanded range (after 4 years)

Greenberg indicates that it is not until the age of 5 or later that children generally are able to reach the higher tones with much accuracy. This is due to children not having reached the developmental level of being able to control the physical mechanism needed to produce these tones (Kim, 2000).

**Melodic contour** is the way in which each sound and silence connects along a curve.

**Lyric content** is the composition in verse which is sung to make up a song.

Barrett (2006) indicates that invented song is a common feature of young children's musical and life experiences. She suggests that there are three categories of invented song that early learning practitioners should be familiar with. They are identified as imaginative, narrative, and potpourri.

Imaginative song is where the child's focus is on the **melodic contour** rather than the **lyric content**. Narrative songs contain varied lyric and melodic content.

Nonsense words and phrases are incorporated into the song. Potpourri songs combine elements of songs they know with original melodic and lyric materials. Barrett (2006) suggests that when children have stimulating environments, invented songs will develop. As they progress in their invented song, they increasingly draw upon the musical forms of their culture to make "standard songs," "where known songs are adapted and shaped to the children's own purposes of play, expression, and communication" (p. 204).

Young children require songs that are simple, short, and repetitive, with only a few notes (Hendrick & Weissman, 2007). Traditional music such as "Twinkle, Twinkle, Little Star" offers early learning practitioners, students, and children with an introduction to music that is familiar and developmentally appropriate. As singing experiences are scaffolded, children between the ages of 4 and 5 years benefit from having many songs with a limited tonal range, and that have catchy tunes or tonal patterns. Young children master simple songs when they are repeated several times over several days. Early learning practitioners offer the first verse initially. Once the children have mastered that verse, then additional verses are added.

Children need the music experience to offer them a sense of curiosity and intrigue. Introducing instruments such as autoharp enhances the children's interest in the relationship of singing to the sounds of the instrument. "The advantage of using an Autoharp is that children can be invited to strum it in time to the singing, because all one must do to control the note is press down firmly on the correct key" (Hendrick & Weissman, 2007, p. 279). As children become more proficient with a song, building on both music and language, the early learning practitioner changes the words—some of which are nonsense words.

Singing songs from various cultures is a positive way to introduce children to the various cultures of the children in the early learning environment. If early learning practitioners do not have experience with music from different cultures, there are many child-appropriate recordings available. It is important that early learning practitioners become familiar with the material before introducing it to the children.

## The Value of Music and Movement to Children with Atypical Development

Music and movement experiences offer children with atypical development pleasure and opportunities to develop skills and a defined interest. Movement is a nonverbal response for children who do not yet have language ability. Some early learning practitioners offer children with atypical development enhanced music and movement activities because it supports children in developing or gaining skills that are particular to one or more children. Music and movement offer children with atypical development an effective communication strategy among adults and other children. Music and movement experiences allow for an extension of children's communication skills in a "socially inclusive manner as music is a universal medium" (Sharpe, Harris, & McKeen, 2010, p. 12).

# THE ROLE OF THE EARLY LEARNING PRACTITIONER

Throughout this chapter we have provided some examples of ways in which early learning practitioners can introduce music and movement to children. We know from the literature that there are a variety of factors that influence how the early learning practitioner incorporates music and movement into the early learning environment. These influencers include the level of training in music and movement, values and beliefs about the importance of music and movement to the development of the whole child, experience and confidence in presenting music and movement experiences, the physical space, the program, and the resources available.

## Stop . . . Think . . . Discuss . . . Reflect

When you think of children and music and movement, what are the key attributes that you believe an early learning practitioner must exhibit? How do early learning practitioners introduce music and movement if they themselves are not comfortable with it? How does your philosophy about music and movement fit with the information shared in this chapter?

When we think of the success of music and movement, it requires early learning practitioners to explore their values and beliefs about music and movement. Staff attitudes impact the quality of the experiences that are extended to the children. Often, when early learning practitioners suggest that music and movement are not their strong area of programming, it is because they do not have sufficient background and experience in the area. This leads to a general lack of confidence (de Vries, 2004). Initially, early learning practitioners may suggest that they do not have a repertoire of music and movement experiences to draw upon; however, music and movement include the performance of nursery rhymes and songs, finger-plays and action songs, alphabet and counting songs, and associated movement activities that emphasize beat and rhythm (Barrett, 2006), which most have experience with from their childhood.

Early learning practitioners have many roles and responsibilities in promoting music and movement in the early learning environment. One of the most challenging roles for early learning practitioners is to observe the child's play to ensure that the music and movement experiences remain "focused and evolve as musical play without deteriorating into random tag, rough-and-tumble, or chasing games" (Van Hoorn, Nourot, Scales & Rodriguez Alward, 2007, p. 287). As identified in the *Stories From the Field*, when music and movement are presented appropriately, it has a very positive impact on children and the feeling tone of the play space. When early learning practitioners use music to distract or entertain, it is merely just that. The potential of children being sparked to develop a sense of music will not occur.

Early learning practitioners examine the types of music and movement experiences introduced to the children and the reasons they are exposing the children to them. As in other early learning play opportunities, the early learning practitioner devises the music experiences based on the particular needs, interests, learning, and development of the children. For example, when children are playing in the rain, rain songs and props such as umbrellas are available. When early learning practitioners choose the musical experiences based on their own interests, and without children having a connectedness to it, it becomes teacher-directed. Children require opportunities to explore music and the freedom of improvisation with music.

Early learning practitioners ensure that children have exposure to singing and sing games, playing instruments, movement to music and moving to music with props, and listening to music. They may also include relaxation activities to music such as yoga.

Tarnowski and Leclerc's (1994) research on the roles of music-teaching styles provides early learning practitioners with important information on how they approach music and movement with children. Our method positively or negatively impacts children. They indicate that when early learning practitioners take on the role of observer, children will work independently. They demonstrate "the largest number of and most varied musical behaviours. Children without any 'teacher direction' also displayed the most complex dramatic playfulness and created the most sophisticated and eclectic scenarios" (Morin, 2001, p. 26). They suggest that direct teaching may inhibit the creativity, and the opportunity for exploration and discovery, of the children. When children have the freedom to explore music freely, they demonstrate more music abilities, explore more sounds, and engage in play longer (Smithrim, 1997), than when children are provided with structured musical experiences.

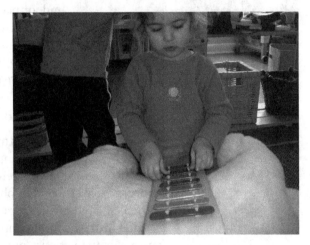

*Photo 11.5   Children explore music with exposure to musical instruments.*

## MUSIC AND MOVEMENT EXPERIENCE CENTRES

Early learning practitioners can incorporate a variety of strategies into the daily program that support young children's exposure to music and movement. The music and movement experience centre, similar to other experience centres, is designed to have materials that will trigger children's curiosity and allow them the opportunity to explore and create music. Movement will evolve from the music. For example, there may be a sound system set up with a microphone so that children may hear and play projecting their voices. There may be recording equipment so that they have the pleasure of singing and replaying their singing. Musical instruments such as drums, guitars, sticks, keyboards, and tambourines, and various shakers are rotated in the experience centre. Children make important discoveries about music when they have the opportunity to explore music boxes. The music experience centre "should function as a support to singing, listening, and playing that goes on among children and adults" (Watts, 1991, p. 75).

*Photo 11.6  Children love props such as dress up shoes and feathers.*

Music, culture, and dramatic play are interconnected. When the music and movement centre has dance costumes available, including scarves, headbands, and ribbons, along with a variety of music, children will create interesting play, dance, and dramatic play options. When children are given such opportunities to incorporate music into various kinds of play, children require the flexibility to move the materials to the appropriate play spaces. Children are provided with musical resources such as CD's and they are given materials and opportunities to make music in their own way.

Music centres are offered to the children both indoors and outdoors. When children have exposure to instruments such as drums outdoors, the sound and the overall experience differs from an indoor play experience. The dramatic play with instruments takes on new creative attributes when available outdoors. For example, children may develop a music experience in the park, or they may decide to have a wedding in the park. Musical instruments offer innovative experiences for the children.

## Musical Instruments

Early learning practitioners can ensure that there are a variety of musical instruments placed within the indoor and outdoor environment. Simple instruments such as keyboards, drums, rhythm sticks, tambourines, shakers, and autoharps offer children the opportunity to explore music, movement, and related concepts such as sound, rhythm, patterning, and creating. Musical instruments are important tools for children to experience as they develop an ear for the various sounds that each instrument makes. Children learn about musical instruments from experimentation. In order to provide children with this freedom to explore, it is advantageous to think about where children may go to bang on the instruments or increase the sound of the music. This is an essential part of them exploring music.

## When Early Learning Practitioners Have Limited Skills in Music and Movement

There are many resources available that will support and guide early learning practitioners in providing music and movement experiences to children. deVries (2004) indicates that early learning practitioners who have limited skills in music or lack of confidence to offer music should consider using pre-packaged resources with the appropriate sound recordings.

Other ideas include the following:

- **Use a variety of music to encourage children to engage in music and movement.** Expose children to different types of music, such as classical, contemporary, folk, or country. Encourage children to move to the music and have dialogue with them about how the music makes them feel.

- **Encourage versatility in their movements.** Use a variety of questioning techniques that will encourage children to move their bodies in different ways. For example, have the children move only their legs or their tummies, or their upper torso.
- **Offer items that the children may move with.** Use broom sticks, umbrellas, and feathers for use with a variety of music. Make musical instruments such as maracas out of plastic bottles.
- **Sing songs with the children.** Offer children a variety of songs to sing with you. Choose songs that move up or down the scale.
- **Invite children to discover music together.** Have children use musical instruments together to see what they may create.
- **Teach children songs with movement.** Teach children the song "Rig-a-Jig-Jig." Discuss with the children which movements are best suited for each verse (Morin, 2001).
- **Incorporate movement vocabulary.** Offer children exposure to daily discussions and activities with children using movement vocabulary. See Table 11.2.
- **Combine music and movement experiences.** Determine ways to combine music and movement experiences with other experience centres such as the art area, the dramatic play, and science.

*Table 11.2*   *Movement Words to Use with Children*

| Body Parts | Actions | Space |
| --- | --- | --- |
| • Head | • Swing | • Diagonal |
| • Face | • Push | • Shape |
| • Nose | • Pull | • Large |
| • Back | • Walk | • Tiny |
| • Ankle | • Gallop | • Far |
| • Heels | • Slide | • Near |
| • Toes | • Leap | • Beside |
| • Bones | • Rock | • Under |
| • Stomach | • Stomp | • Curved |
| • Elbows | • Crawl | • Round |
| • Spine | • Sway | • Zigzag |
| • Knees | • Bend, curl, flex | • In/out |

## OBSERVATIONS AND DOCUMENTATION

Early learning practitioners can learn important information about a child through observation and documentation. The observational and documentation tools used are intended to provide the early learning practitioners and students with information about

- the type of music each child enjoys;
- how the child responds to various types of music;
- how music and movement are incorporated into their play;
- the types of activities that sparked spontaneous music and movement play;
- the types of musical instruments favoured; and
- how the music is a social or solitary play experience.

Many early learning practitioners use charts to document the information. Others use video, as it allows the children to share the musical activity with their parents. As they continue to acquire information on the relationship of music and movement to development, early learning practitioners and children must become inspired to explore it to its fullest. Children require early learning practitioners to listen, to observe, and to know who they are so that environments may be prepared that will allow for active exploration, creative play, discovery, and exploration.

# SUMMARY

### Chapter Preview

- Music and movement involves children in physical, social, cognitive, kinesthetic, and communicative challenges.
- There is growing concern among researchers that early learning practitioners may not be emphasizing this area of programming to the extent of other programming areas.

### Historical Influences of Music and Movement

- The importance of music and movement was first identified by Jean Jacques Rousseau, followed by Herbert Spencer, Maria Montessori, and Carl Orff.
- From a contemporary perspective, Gardner identifies that music intelligence aligns with linguistic intelligence. Bodily-kinesthetic and spatial intelligence are needed for the movement portion of music and movement.
- Morin indicates the need for early learning practitioners to look at music and play. Children respond to music when it is associated with play.
- Morin categorizes music play into five categories: Cooperative music play, functional music play, constructive music play, dramatic music play, and kinesthetic music play.

### The Importance of Music and Movement

- Music and movement are important aspects of a child's whole development.
- Dance, creative movement, and movement are interrelated, but each has distinct characteristics.

- Through music and movement cultural aspects are transferred from one generation to the next.
- Music and movement are incorporated into a child's play and environment in a variety of ways.

## Music, Movement, and Child Development

- Music play supports brain development, psychomotor development, social and emotional development, and cognitive development.
- Bruner identifies that children's abilities in the musical and kinesthetic domains progress through three stages: the enactive stage, iconic stage, and the symbolic stage. These stages are related to Piaget's stages of cognitive development.
- There are various studies that suggest children who have had experience with music have high levels of spatial abilities, higher reasoning and motor skills, and higher achievements in math, language, and science.

## Aesthetic Appreciation

- Music and movement contribute to children developing aesthetic appreciation for music and their environment.

## Presenting Music and Movement to Children

- Music, movement, and song should be presented to children throughout the day in ways that will support children in appreciating music and movement.
- Being aware of the pitch that is used relative to the skills of the children, early learning practitioners can present songs to children.
- Greenberg identifies five stages of children's vocalization. He believes that a child is at least five years old before being able to reach higher tones with accuracy.
- Barrett indicates that invented song is common among children.

## The Value of Music and Movement to Children with Atypical Development

- Music and movement constitute an effective communication strategy for children who have atypical developmental patterns.

## The Role of the Early Learning Practitioner

- Early learning practitioners can provide children with play experiences that include a variety of music and movement opportunities, including singing, singing games, playing instruments, movement to music, and listening to music.
- Early learning practitioners should ensure that children have opportunities to explore music and movement similar to other play experience centres. The music centre is offered both indoors and outdoors, with a variety of intriguing materials including musical instruments and related artifacts rotated in the centres.
- There are a variety of music and movement experiences that early learning practitioners may offer children, even if they do not have a background in music.
- Observation and documentation helps early learning practitioners gain information on each child's interest and skill in music and movement.

# REVIEW QUESTIONS

1. Describe the importance of music and movement to the lives of young children.
2. How does the historical perspective of music and movement impact our practice today?
3. What does Gardner tell us about music intelligence, bodily-kinesthetic intelligence, and linguistic and spatial intelligence?
4. How do Morin's categories of play inform an early learning practitioner practice?
5. What is the importance of music and movement to child development?
6. How does music and movement impact brain development?
7. What are the key considerations that early learning practitioners must make when introducing songs to young children?
8. What is the value of music and movement to children with atypical development?
9. Describe the diverse role that early learning practitioners have in promoting music and movement in an early learning environment.

# MAKING CONNECTIONS

## Theory to Practice

1. You are working in an early learning environment where music and movement is secondary to other programming areas such as blocks, science, and art. What strategies would you put in place to advance the knowledge, skills, and opportunities of early learning practitioners and children in this area of programming?
2. Visit two early learning environments and do an inventory of the music and movement experiences that are offered children. What are they? How do they relate to a child's developmental needs? What is the role of the early learning practitioner?
3. You have been asked to design and implement a music experience centre. What would you put in the centre? On what basis are you choosing the materials? Why? How would you scaffold the materials? Why?
4. A parent comes to you to identify that he is concerned that his child is not musically inclined. How would you respond? What steps would you take to support the parent in gaining comfort in knowing what the child's musical interest is? Why?

## For Further Research

1. Tarnowski and Leclerc (1994) indicate that early learning practitioners impact children's music and movement experiences. What is meant by this? What research supports Tarnowski and Leclerc's perspective? How does the research inform your practice? Why?
2. There is a perspective that early learning practitioners do not have the same level of confidence or knowledge about music and movement as they do for other program areas. What research supports this perspective? Do you agree with this perspective? Why or why not?
3. Search for the work of Kemple, Batey, & Hartle (2004) on the internet. Find their article on creating experience centres for musical play and exploration. Using the ideas as inspiration, create your own centre and present it in class to other student practitioners or in an early learning setting with children.

# ADDITIONAL READING

Barrett, M. S. (2005). Children's communities of musical practice: Some socio-cultural implications of a systems view of creativity in music education. In D. J. Elliott (Ed.), *Praxial music education: Reflections and dialogues.* New York: Oxford University Press, 177–195.

Greata, J. (2006). *An introduction to music in early childhood education.* New York: Thomson.

Mang, E. (2005). The referent of children's early songs, *Music Education Research,* 7(1), 3–20.

Neeley, L. (2001). Developmentally appropriate music practice: Children learn what they live. *Young Children* 56 (3): 32–27.

Pica, R. (2009). *Music and movement: Birth to 8.* Belmont, CA: Wadsworth.

Smith, Mark K. (2002, 2008). "Howard Gardner and multiple intelligences," *The encyclopedia of informal education.*

Tsunady, M. (2001). Awaken the muse: Teaching music to young children. *Canadian Children* 26(2): 8–11.

# WEBLINKS

Importance of Music

**www.infed.org/thinkers/gardner.htm**

**www.musictogether.com**

**www.sciencedaily.com/releases/2006/09/060920093024.htm.**

# 12 Planning Play Space

## Stories from the Field: Practitioner to Student

When I began studying early childhood education I was required to create floor plans of how I would organize play spaces for the children. I looked at the floor plans that were included in a number of textbooks. This provided me with insight into thinking about space features such as wet and dry, quiet and noisy areas. I learned that there were government regulations for early learning centres requiring a minimum space for each child for their indoor and outdoor play. I also learned from observing space during my field placements that the way that the furniture is placed and the "special touches" within the environment impact the "feeling tone" for both children and staff.

After working in the field for close to 10 years, I believe from my observations that when a child's environment is organized, neat, and aesthetically pleasing, the children are calmer, they respect the environment more and they have more positive energy. Children and staff who are exposed to cluttered environments are more hyper and have more difficulty exploring the play options. This leads me to suggest to students that it is as beneficial to concentrate on creating an appropriate feeling within the room, as it is to ensure that the learning centres are placed according to a defined plan. In fact, I like to think, that by deviating from the traditional placements of learning centres, children will stretch play opportunities across centres rather than being restricted to the specified centre.

My advice to students and new early learning practitioners is to look at space options, materials, and interests of the children. There may not be a specific floor plan that should remain constant. Change brings new stimulation to staff and children.

*Wigwan, ECE Graduate, 2001*

# CHAPTER PREVIEW

Throughout this book we have outlined information on programming components that support children in their quest for quality play experiences. The program planning that children and early learning practitioners engage in is important to the success of each play episode. The environmental attributes of the play space are also linked to the success of a child's play experience. Ideally, the environmental conditions presented offer children a feeling of comfort, a sense of curiosity, and a desire to explore potential play options. It is the early learning practitioner, the child, and the environmental conditions that collectively impact the quality of the play experience.

Wigwan, in this chapter's "Stories from the Field," suggests that the feeling tone of the environment is as important as the placement of the experience centres. Early learning practitioners plan environments that "provide children with opportunities to initiate play, direct play, stimulate new ideas and levels of curiosity, and encourage them to take risks" (Dietze, 2006, p. 145). This requires the practitioner to be attentive to the environment daily.

As you begin to observe children in play spaces, observe the array of environments. Each environment will leave you with a different **feeling tone.** Some of the environments will make you feel alive and well; others will make you feel agitated and have an unsettling feeling or give you a sense of overstimulation. Others will have a calming effect and one that triggers you to want to explore new things. As you think about children in early learning programs, remember that many of the children spend more than 40 hours per week in the space. This is more time than they spend awake in their home environments. This leads us to explore throughout this chapter core questions such as: Are there places and spaces that offer children more comfort for learning than other places? Are there places that make children feel more alert than other places? If there is clutter in the space, how does that impact the child's play? Do order and routine impact children? What space makes children feel calm and what are the spaces that make them feel agitated or less calm? These environmental questions will affect each child differently. Early learning practitioners need to consider each attribute carefully when planning play space with children and colleagues.

This chapter does not specifically address how experience centres should be placed in an early learning environment. There are many ways to do so, and it is truly dependent on space availability. We do introduce principles that guide early learning practitioners in play space design. We also present an array of environmental attributes that impact children's play. These environmental attributes require careful consideration, as they are foundational to creating quality play spaces for young children.

# CHILDREN'S PLAY

As identified in Chapter 2, there are varying types of children's play that early learning practitioners observe and plan for from both an environmental and play perspective. The types of play—*sensorimotor play, symbolic play,* and *construction play,* combined with the children's interests, learning, and phases of development that each child exhibits sets the stage for planning play spaces.

*Photo 12.1 Children's play is influenced by their environment and the people in the environment.*

Let's take a few minutes to reexamine the characteristics of sensorimotor, symbolic, and construction play from a planning play space perspective. Children engage in these types of play in stages, moving from sensorimotor to symbolic to construction play. As children's life experiences expand, there is a shift in the types and duration of each type of play. The more exposure to rich play experiences and environments, the more advanced the play becomes.

Wolfgang and Wolfgang (1992) suggest that children between the ages of 1 and 2 years spend approximately 80 percent of their play in sensorimotor play, while the remaining 20 percent is in symbolic play. Children between the ages of 2 to 3 years spend about 50 percent of their playtime in sensorimotor-type play; 25 percent in symbolic play and 25 percent in construction play. Children 3 to 4 years of age reduce their sensorimotor play to approximately 30 percent, while there is an increase to approximately 40 percent symbolic play and 30 percent construction play. Children between the ages of 4 and 5 years spend approximately 25 percent in sensorimotor play, 20 percent in symbolic play, and 55 percent in construction play experiences (Hanline, 1999). Children between the ages of 6 and 12 years spend most of their playtime in construction play. These phases of play guide early learning practitioners in examining and designing play space that supports productive, quality play.

## Sensorimotor Play

During the first phase of a child's life to approximately 18 months the child learns through senses and interaction with people and things in the environment. Children's play spaces offer opportunities for repetition of sensory motor acts, many of which involve repetition of an action involving a child's body. Children flourish in environments that provide opportunities for their play to include materials such as pushing and pulling toys, grasping and shaking items, and materials that require the child to engage in trial and error experimentations. Children require intimate play spaces; yet, they also need sufficient space so that they may exhibit their need for autonomy.

## Symbolic Play

This phase of play is characterized by children using their imagination and role-playing to transform people, items, or events into various items or uses, depending on the play episode and needs that each child has to execute the play experience. Children scaffold symbolic play based on their developmental phases and life experiences. They begin with something that is familiar to them and that requires a real life object (Hanline, 1999). For example, a child may pick up the receiver of the telephone and pretend to speak to mommy. The child may use items interchangeably as props such as using a block for a bottle with doll play. As children progress in their play, they include various props as well as playmates. Children exhibit both **microsymbolic play** and **macrosymbolic play**. Children require a variety of play spaces and the materials in the environment are familiar daily living items.

**Microsymbolic** play refers to children using child sized materials that are replicas of objects such as a child's tea set or doctor kit.

**Macrosymbolic play** refers to children assuming pretend roles such as being a firefighter.

## Construction Play

During this phase of play development children begin to express an idea or construct items that represent ideas with various materials. Hanline (1999) suggests that construction play requires children to have access to both **fluid materials** and **structured materials** in their play space. Construction play progresses in phases. Each phase requires more time and more play space. For example, children first engage in play that focuses on mastering defined processes such as being able to complete a puzzle to gradually constructing realistic items such as a sand structure, a block structure of a castle, or a picture that expresses a life experience, such as the child's family or a community item such as the CN Tower in Toronto.

Play spaces are examined from the perspective of creating them, improving them, and ensuring that they are inclusive play spaces. In order to ensure that play experiences will be stimulating and advance the child's learning opportunities, play spaces reflect the interests and needs of children. Each play space decision is positively or negatively weaved into child's play.

**Fluid materials** refer to those materials that change in shape or by their use offer children opportunities to create items that can be altered in shape and form (Hanline, 1999). Examples of fluid materials include play dough, sand, water, paint, and paper.

**Structured materials** have predetermined characteristics that influence or guide the child in how to use the materials in construction. Blocks, puzzles, and climbing apparatus are classified as structured materials.

## THE ENVIRONMENTAL PLAY SPACE FRAMEWORK

Children's play is directly impacted by environmental conditions. Play opportunities for young children with or without disabilities require "the environment [to] be carefully planned to encourage children's active participation" (Hanline, 1999, p. 290).

Early learning play spaces are "a planned arrangement of ideas, people, time, space and resources" (McLean, 1995, p. 7). The way in which the play space is presented to children is directly linked to their abilities to function effectively within it. Adults who are concerned about children's developmental needs and children's interests create play spaces that offer children a sense of belonging and the freedom to build on their curiosity. The play space facilitates each child having a feeling of mutual respect and comfort with others in the play space. The adult–child and child-to-child interactions are nurturing and supportive.

Early learning practitioners consider a number of issues and perspectives when planning children's play space. Jalongo and Isenberg (2004) indicate effective environments include "all the influences that affect children and adults in early childhood settings" (p. 148). For example, think about the children who are in the outdoor sandpit digging. You notice that other children are frequently walking along the edge of the sandpit to get to the tricycles. This causes the children in the sandpit play to become upset. By placing a barrier between the sandpit and the tricycles, the early learning practitioner is planning an environment that is responsive to the needs of children. Not only does the barrier stop children from being distracted in the sandpit zone, it reduces the amount of intervention for redirection between the adults and children. It also reduces a potential safety issue. Think about the children who are consistently running out of floor space for their block construction. By rearranging the block centre so that there is adequate space, you are supporting children in being able to use the blocks in more creative ways. Without adequate space, children will not be able to expand their play options.

Play spaces responsive to the children's needs require practitioners to be observing and reacting as teachable moments evolve. For example, when children become interested in digging for worms, practitioners ensure that there is an experience centre outdoors that includes a book about worms and a magnifying glass so that the children can look closely at the worms and compare their findings.

As illustrated in the examples above, early learning environments are designed to support children's play and their senses. The experience centres and play options provide children with a variety of materials and facilitate many types of play and experiences (Hanline & Fox, 1993). Early learning practitioners plan play space that reflects how young children learn. Children learn best "when they deal with the real world—people, natural materials, problems to solve, their own creations" (Holt, Kamii, & Seefeldt, 1984, p. 20). If the environment is appropriate, children will exhibit their natural curiosity and playful attributes.

Greenman (2005) tells us that "childhood is when human beings should fall in love with the world and all its untidy and sometimes scary complexity, delights, and mysteries" (p. 2). He also tells us that as we reduce play options and the freedom for children to play, we are removing the meandering, the sense of journey, and the exploration "along the way"—all of which are essential parts to a child's play and discovery. Think about early learning environments. Do they currently provide children with the ability and the freedom to meander, to have a sense of journey and to explore "along the way" or are they places with clear schedules and routines that must followed? How do we build these needs into play space?

## Stop . . . Think . . . Discuss . . . Reflect

If it is important for children to have the ability and freedom to meander and explore along the way, why do early learning practitioners have schedules and timelines that they adhere to? What do we need to do to change the attitudes about schedules? How do we build in time for children to explore along the way?

Early learning play space is essentially the child's home away from home; therefore the play space is ideally designed to offer children a safe, caring, and nourishing place to be in and to play. Children require a play space that is designed to facilitate opportunities for them to be free to explore their environment and be comfortable within it so that they may engage in play to the fullest. The play space is reflective of children's developmental levels, learning styles, and interests.

Greenman (2005) encourages early learning practitioners to view early learning space as a full vision of childhood and family involvement. He describes full vision as including:

> Eating, drinking, sleeping, separating from and reuniting with loved ones, growing, changing, learning, falling in and out of love, getting knocked down and picking oneself up, feeling deep distress and then being filled with joy. (p. 3)

When we think of the full vision concept, from an environmental design perspective, early learning practitioners examine space on an array of characteristics including *feeling tone, aesthetics, learning and exploration options, space utilization,* and *adult–child connections.*

Dietze (2006) indicates that quality play space requires each segment of the environment to be examined and correlated with the needs and interests of the children. Play space is not fixed components; rather, it is fluid and emerging based on the children's input and interests. Examining and adjusting play space is a continuous process in order to accommodate the changing needs of children.

Much of the research indicates children learn best in play spaces that

- are appropriate for their age and stage of development;
- offer children the freedom and flexibility to support their needs to explore, experiment, and engage in play as required;

*Photo 12.2 Children will re-create play spaces to feel comfortable in their environment.*

- build a sense of community, respect, and trust among the individual child and groups of children and adults within the play space;
- are smaller spaces with cozy corners combined with sufficient space and freedom to move and are versatile to support various play opportunities; and
- are child-centred and play-based.

As we think about children and their play, early learning environments are created both on the components outlined in Figure 12.1 and on the following premises.

1. Children require play spaces that provide a variety of experiences. Children flourish in environments that stimulate them in exploring and experiencing new, innovative opportunities. Children benefit most when they are in environments that offer them opportunities to connect with a natural environment and one that is aesthetically appropriate for their age. Children need exposure to water, sand, things that move, things that they may dump and pour, and things that will allow them to build. Play spaces offer children new beginnings in their need for and sense of wonderment, experience, and exploration.

2. Children require spaces that provide them with the freedom to play. Early learning practitioners are constantly examining the environments to determine how they may encourage children to engage in play. Ideally, the

Supports children in
initiating play,
directing play,
exploring new play
opportunities, and
taking risks to
explore

Are inclusive

Supports children in
following their
interests and
curiosity that
stimulate new
learning options

Are safe, yet offer
children
opportunities to take
safe risks

Supports children in
developing positive
behaviours and
resiliency

*Figure 12.1*
*Characteristics of*
*Quality Early Learning*
*Play Spaces*

environment will offer children many options for their quiet and active play. This requires early learning centres to have a variety of props that will trigger exploration and play engagement.

3. Children require play space environments that are rich in exploration, role modelling, and learning. When the environment is organized to offer intrigue, reflection, exploration, effective role modelling, and coaching from adults, children engage in play and learning. When early learning practitioners use probing questions, dialogue, and documentation as foundational practices with children, the play moves from simple to complex and from surface to deep learning opportunities. Early learning practitioners "who stimulate more questions than they directly provide are truly teaching" (Greenman, 1988, p. 33).

4. Children require play opportunities that expose them to adults, children, and neighbourhoods. Early learning programs use the resources available to the children and families and seek out resources that will enhance the children's learning experiences. Children benefit from learning from our Canadian diverse population and they expand their knowledge and curiosity when learning options are provided in the early learning centre and in the community in which they live.

5. Children require play spaces that incorporate daily living responsibilities into the environment. Children live and play in early learning places. They, like the adults, flourish when they are assigned tasks that support daily living in the environment. Caring for plants, caring for their environment, and understanding principles of recycling help children to incorporate these skills into their dramatic play.

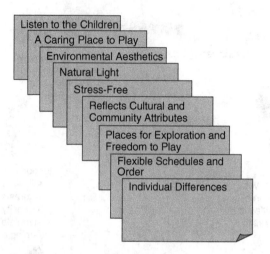

*Figure 12.2* *Characteristics of Responsive Play Spaces*

# CHARACTERISTICS OF RESPONSIVE PLAY SPACE ENVIRONMENTS

In this upcoming section, we will be introducing you to a number of characteristics, as outlined in Figure 12.2, that early learning practitioners consider when creating a responsive play space for children. These are in addition to the considerations needed for the overall physical play space arrangement. Often, these components that we are presenting seem less important to early learning practitioners than the actual placement of the experience centres. Research continues to examine these issues, and currently they appear to be as important as the physical play space design.

## Feeling Tone

**Feeling tone** is the way a child takes in experiences and physical sensations and processes them. These are filtered as pleasant, unpleasant, or neutral experiences (Dietze, 2006).

Early learning practitioners examine the play space and the overall **feeling tone** because together these two factors influence the quality of each child's play experience. The feeling tone is interrelated to the behaviours that children exhibit and the relationships among children and adults. The feeling tone also influences how the materials are used, which leads to the depth and breadth of the child's play experiences.

When examining the early learning space to determine how it supports relationships among children, adults, families, and community, there are many aspects to consider. For example, are the children grouped according to age ranges and divided into specific space? How beneficial is this to children and their learning? Is there consistency in the staffing model that extends security to the children? Is the indoor and outdoor floor space appropriate for the numbers of children and staff? Do the aesthetic attributes provide a sense of calmness?

Early learning practitioners incorporate ways to communicate value, respect, and understanding into the environment. This means that from the moment children, parents, and visitors enter the space, there is a sense of an inclusive, welcoming play space. A feeling tone is created by using soft music, materials that represent the cultural diversity of the families represented in the centre, and the natural light is used to complement the indoor and outdoor attributes and materials. When the environment is presented with care, there is a feeling of security. Conversely, if care is not taken to present a favourable environment, a sense of insecurity may be felt by children, families, and staff.

Environments that exhibit appropriate feeling tones show evidence of happy, active children. There is a humming sound of children engaged in play. Early learning practitioners monitor the noise levels and the types of noise levels because they affect children's learning (Tanner & Langford, 2003). When children are exposed to environments where yelling and screaming are permitted, or where early learning practitioners use loud voices as a child management strategy, the "feeling tone" of the play space is negatively affected. This type of noise level impedes children's abilities to effectively engage in play because they are not able to concentrate in the play space (Jalongo & Isenberg, 2004).

The feeling tone is built on many factors. As you review the upcoming sections and as you reflect on the environments that you have seen for children, think about how environments can support or detract from children having a safe, nurturing place to play, and to grow.

## Listen to the Children

As early learning practitioners prepare play space, one of their first roles and responsibilities in the process is to listen to the children during their play, observe children's play processes, and their interests. This helps practitioners and students gain insight into a child's point of view about the materials available relative to the child's stage of play and their experiences with the materials, peers, and overall environment. By listening to the children, early learning practitioners are able to

*Photo 12.3   New materials add new dimensions to the child's level of exploration and experimentation.*

match their observations and insights with their understanding of age-appropriate development (Bredekamp, 2004; Bredekamp & Copple, 1997). For example, when you listen to the play of 4-year-olds in the block centre, you may hear them using construction terms and wearing hats based on their role in the construction, such as the white hat for the supervisor. This information tells you that the children are ready to use signs in their play or produce signs for their structures. Or, you may observe younger children playing with materials that are familiar to them, such as a particular car or truck or doll. This reinforces the need for children to have access to materials that they are familiar with and the need to add new materials on a gradual basis.

Listening to the children helps us evaluate the quality and quantity of the conversations among the children, staff, and families. We also acquire information about how adults listen to the children. When adults listen to the children they gain information about children's thinking and learning styles. This information becomes the foundation for adults to formulate questions that will provoke children's thinking, which leads to them creating new ideas and learning. Listening to children and families builds a sense of a community of learning.

The most effective play space for children is created when practitioners take cues from the children. In so doing, you are, in essence, making decisions based on theory and research to inform your practice (Van Hoorn, Nourot, Scales, & Alward, 2007).

## A Caring Place to Play

Children require caring places to play. Children and their families come to us, all with different family stories and backgrounds. Early learning practitioners are cognizant of the varying cultures, beliefs, and values that each family brings to the play space. Some of the values may differ from our personal beliefs or our professional practice (Greenman, 2001).

The needs of families and communities continue to evolve. What one family may need or groups of families require today may differ significantly in six months or a year. Early learning practitioners respond to the changing needs of families and children. For example, you may be exposed to a centre where a large proportion of families requires services until after 6:00 p.m. or you may have a large group of children whose first language is not English. Based on the family population, policies and procedures may be developed or revised to support the needs of the families. Some centres examine their family dynamics and hire staff that will complement the family demographics.

Early learning centres need to be places where families connect. This increases the life experiences of the children and the overall connectedness among children, staff, and families. For example, think about an artist among the parents. This artist agrees to share some of her expertise with the children. As she works with the children to explore colour, she recognizes the incredible works of art that the children have created. She, the children, and staff decide to have a gallery showing the children's work. This extends a learning branch of the children's life experiences in new directions. Or, think of the new family from a new country trying to start a new life in this country. For many, the early learning centre is one of the first safe places in the community for them.

Creating caring environments takes time, acceptance of families, and space. For example, a place that welcomes families and empowers families to be part of the early learning place to play ensures that there is space that allows for family interactions. Displays of the children's documented play and learning are available as a way to share about play and learning. A caring place to play connects and engages families in the program.

**Environmental aesthetics**  is gaining more attention in early learning environments. It focuses on "the ways in which humans experience the world through their senses" (Carlson, 2002, p. 1). From a child's perspective this refers to how their perceptions and aesthetic preferences are experienced. Recognizing that children learn through their five senses; their environments need to include things that they may touch, smell, taste, see, and hear. This reinforces the importance of early learning centres exposing children to nature, art, and culture.

Aesthetic presentation means different things to different people. Each family and individual within the family develop their own approach to aesthetic appeal. Research continues to help early learning practitioners link the connection of the presentation of the environment to children's behaviour, resiliency, learning, and comfort within the environment.

Discussion about the aesthetics of the environment is not new to the early learning field. For example, Dewey (1990/1956) indicated that children require environments that provide "conversation . . . inquiry . . . making things . . . and artistic expression" (p. 47). He further identified that children require "large grounds, gardens, and green house." He advocated for children to have "open air" interiors with a variety of workspaces and the feeling of a "well-furnished home" (Upitis, 2005, p. 8). One way to achieve this is for early learning environments to provide children with natural products. For example, the table and chairs would be from wood, rather than popular coloured plastic furniture found in many early learning play spaces today.

Malaguzzi (1991) indicates that play-space aesthetics has a major influence on a child's comfort and security within their play space. Children engage in play more easily in environments where the feeling tone of the environment supports their needs and where they feel a sense of order (Dietze, 2006). Malaguzzi (1991) emphasizes the importance of early learning practitioners paying attention to the play-space aesthetics "because of its power to organize, promote pleasant relationships between people of different ages, create a handsome environment, promote choices and activity and its potential for sparking all kinds of social, affective, and cognitive learning" (p. 6). Reggio and Reggio-inspired programs view the "environment as a third teacher" (Gandini, 1998, p. 177). This means that early learning practitioners critically examine the play space environments to ensure that what is in the environment has meaning to the children and that what is displayed, is attractively presented. Spaggiari (2004) indicates that "the environment has a silent language, which interacts with the child and facilitates processes of living, of learning, and of relating to others" (p. 4). When the environment is meaningful and well organized, it acts like another adult in the room, providing support and encouragement to children's play experiences.

**Environmental aesthetics** focuses on how individuals experience their world through their senses, by incorporating their environmental perceptions and their aesthetic preferences in environments, cultures, and seasons (Carlson, 2002).

*Photo 12.4   Children and adults collectively determine how to create interesting play spaces.*

Olds (1998) indicates that children's play "is largely a response to variations in the environment . . . Environments must be consciously and lovingly created to uplift the spirit and honor of children's heightened sensibility. It is not sufficient that a setting be adequate. It must instead, be beautiful" (p. 124). Early learning practitioners and children work together to create their play space so that it is beautiful, appealing, and comfortable (Hendrick & Wiseman, 2007).

The aesthetic appeal of the environment is directly related to children exploring, discovering, and learning. When the aesthetic environment is correct, there is an increased level of sensory and perceptual activity. Language skills evolve and forming concepts through the various levels of problem solving occurs (Dietze, 2006). "Children make a series of interconnected discoveries about the physical, cultural, and social elements of their world" (Dietze, 2006, p. 160) in environments that offer the appropriate surroundings and venue for learning.

Environments may impact children either positively or negatively. One of the key influencers that impacts children's learning is the visual stimulation. Isahi, Ungerlerider, Martin, Schouten, & Haxby (1999) indicate that the way in which a child's brain deals with the visual stimulation is directly related to learning. They describe the circuitry in the brain's visual system responds to each visual stimulus that a child is exposed to. The more stimuli within the environment, the more the brain must process. The brain requires oxygen to process the images through the circuits. When children are exposed to cluttered environments, the brain uses energy to suppress the images. The more cluttered the environment, the more energy the brain requires to block out the stimuli. When the energy is used for this purpose, it increases children's activity levels and often leads to behaviours such as biting, hitting, and pushing. Environments that bring natural light and nature into play spaces and reduce the visual chaos and clutter, generally experience less overactivity by the children.

Many early learning and child care environments have not adequately incorporated principles of aesthetic appeal and appreciation into the play spaces. As indicated earlier, children do not flourish in environments where huge amounts of information are found on the walls or hanging from the ceilings. For example, if you enter a child's play space where many pieces of children's art is placed on bulletin boards placed at the adult eye level, with tape or tacks and with no semblance of order, you immediately may gain an uncomfortable, closed-in feeling. This discomfort is as a result of the presentation within the environment. Quality play spaces replace the commercial images, the permanent murals, and the overabundance of "stuff" in the environment because these images take valuable oxygen and energy away from the children's opportunity to use them for playing and learning. They focus their attention to how the natural light, the acoustics, furnishings, and materials are used to enhance the aesthetic attributes of the space.

*Photo 12.5    A child's environment incorporates community and culture.*

## BOX 12.1

### Beverlie's Story

Many years ago, in response to becoming aware of the importance of exposing children to beautiful things and aesthetic appreciation, we established a "beautiful things" experience centre. We placed a variety of items on the table, such as fresh flower arrangements in vases, pieces of pottery from our local artists, paintings, and fresh vegetables. As the children began sharing this with their families, adults would express concern about what would happen if their child broke something from the table. We explained to parents that it is during the early years that children begin to establish their aesthetic appreciation, based on their experiences within their environments. It is through such exposure that children develop the skills to touch and explore the items with care and appreciation. Children will live up to our standards. We need to share our faith in children with them. (Beverlie Dietze, 2010)

Aesthetic appreciation requires a balance of minimalism, natural products, and a sense of coziness. The materials and the aesthetic touches must have meaning for the children. Early learning environments are child-friendly and not overstimulating to the child. They do not project either too much clutter or too much sterility. Our experience tells us that children should be exposed to beautiful things.

## Natural Light

There are many advantages for young children to be exposed to natural light in both their indoor and outdoor play spaces. Research findings on the benefits of natural light reveals that natural light helps children concentrate, it keeps them focused and less distracted, and it improves academic performance and leads to improved attendance (Hathaway, 1995; Plympton, Conway, & Epstein, 2000; Richer, 2000).

There is a relationship of light to the physical well-being and health and wellness (Hathaway, Hargreaves, Thompson, & Novitsky, 1992). A number of studies suggest that exposure to poor lighting and/or fluorescent lighting is linked to hyperactivity and decreased productivity (Harmon, 1951; Liberman, 1991; Ott, 1976). Dietze (2006) indicates that "some studies suggest that children's language, social, emotional, and physical development progress more rapidly in outdoor play spaces than in indoor play spaces, due to increased freedom to play, access to natural light, and an increase in body movement" (p. 150). Early learning practitioners examine ways to implement strategies that will expose children to adequate natural light throughout our changing seasons.

## Stress-Free

How children feel in the environment impacts the intensity level and quality of the play experience. Early learning practitioners strive to create stress-free environments. When the environments are free from stressful feelings, children become more engaged in their experimentation and thinking. They also explore more ideas or things that are curious to them.

Stress occurs in environments when there is an imbalance between the demands on individuals or groups and human resources (Evans & Cohen, 1987). Creating a stress-free environment for young children today is imperative; as many of our children live in stressful home environments due to situations such as family relationships and dynamics, economic conditions, parental careers, or intergenerational responsibilities.

Scott (2008) indicates that there are many stressors hidden within a child's environment. Two prevalent stressors are poor diets and noise pollution. These factors impact how a child uses her play space.

- **Poor Diet.** Children who are exposed to an overabundance of convenience food or a diet that does not meet Canada's Food Guide may lack proper nutrition. This may contribute to a child experiencing mood swings, having a lack of energy, and not having the resiliency to deal with stressful situations.
- **Noise Pollution.** Some children are negatively impacted by the noise in their play environments. Noise pollution is caused by many factors. For example, too many children in a play space, the busyness of the environment, the adult/child interactions, constant music, and distracting noises from various toys. Noise pollution has the potential to decrease a child's

energy and ability to concentrate on exploring new learning opportunities. Children from noisy environments may suffer ill effects from noise pollution, which include less cognitive growth, delayed language skills, increased anxiety, the quality of one's sleep, and impaired resilience.

When early learning practitioners note that the noise level is escalating and the children are beginning to disengage in their play, steps are taken immediately to reduce the noise level. There are many ways to achieve this. The practitioner may wish to circulate among the children and experience centres, speaking softly to the children. The practitioner may engage in one-on-one dialogue with children who appear restless. Different experience centres may be suggested, or new materials that offer children new exploration may be presented. The objective is for the practitioner to change the noise level and find ways to have children re-engage in play.

Early learning environments are designed to positively influence the child's play and behaviour. When the environment meets the needs of children, there is a reduction in aggressive or negative behaviours. The more comfortable the children are with play space environment and the people in the play space, the more likely children will exhibit pro-social behaviours (Dudek, 2000). Stress-free environments support children feeling physically and psychologically safe and free from fear and chaos (Berner, 1992; Boss, 2001). When that feeling is not present, children build up an anxiety which, over time, has them feel and exhibit the fight-or-flight response to the children, adults, and the environment.

# REFLECTS CULTURAL AND COMMUNITY ATTRIBUTES

Similar to children gaining a sense about aesthetically pleasing spaces and beautiful things in their environment, quality play spaces provide exposure to culture- and community-specific items such as art, books, and artifacts. Early learning practitioners encourage families to bring forth culture-specific materials for the children to explore. The early learning practitioner builds in strategies to support children in gaining knowledge and experience with the cultural items in the correct context.

## Places for Exploration and Freedom to Play

Creating early learning play spaces that provide children with opportunities to explore and freedom to play requires discussion among the children and practitioners. Arranging the furnishings and assigning storage constitute one small aspect of the overall needs of children. More important is looking at the needs of children. When we think about the full vision concept introduced earlier in the chapter, we are reminded that children require space for exploration and discovery. They need places to run and jump. They need quiet places and noisy places. They need space

*Photo 12.6 Children's play is richest when it is hands-on.*

that will allow them to test their limits, to stumble and to fall. Throughout the text, we have provided overviews of programming specific attributes that support children's play. We encourage you to review the chapters on dramatic play, art, science and math, language and literacy, music and movement, and outdoor play. Then, think about how each of those programming areas requires places for exploration and freedom to play.

Experience-based, hands-on learning evolves in play spaces where children may choose experience centres that will engage them in their play for both long and short periods of time. These experience centres support the children's planned and spontaneous creativity, movement, and expansive play. Think about children going into an art studio—what would they see, what would they feel, and what would they experience? Or, if the children have opportunities to have a garden in their play space—what experiences will that provide them with? What are children missing in the world of play if a garden is not part of the play space?

Children require access to experience centres both indoors and outdoors. Experience centres reflect the children's interests and they offer them new options for exploration and learning. There are places for children to engage in scientific explorations such as places with kaleidoscopes, stained glass, sensory materials from their natural environment, and magnifying glasses. Children require flexible indoor and outdoor space to use natural products such as clay, paint, and paper. Children require places to dig and to pour and to "muck" about—to be free to explore the properties of mud, water, and sand. Children need room to climb, run, throw, jump, roll, and use their bodies in interesting ways.

*Photo 12.7* *Children require play experiences both indoors and outdoors.*

*Photo 12.8* *Children require a variety of play spaces.*

# FLEXIBLE SCHEDULES AND ORDER

Early learning practitioners recognize that the sense of security for children is formulated in environments that reflect the needs of children and, are familiar and predictable. Children require places that provide **ordered time** and space.

How a child's day is structured impacts play and exploration. The structuring of time requires early learning practitioners to establish a balance of the rhythms of children's needs and the predictable programming structure. Children schedules, similar to the play space, require flexibility, not rigidity, so that their needs and interests may be accommodated. For example, in order for children to have the freedom to play, flexibility is required in their daily routine. When children become absorbed in building a large box sculpture, the early learning practitioner observes the children's intensity in the activity. Early learning practitioners make judgment calls based on what is best for the children. Is it more important to allow the children to continue to be engaged in the structure or stop the play so that the children may return to the indoor environment for a group experience?

Greenman (2006) indicates early learning settings require an order that reflects the needs of children and early learning practitioners. He highlights the following four important considerations, which are necessary for order to be child-friendly:

1. The order is based on program goals and values. For example, if the early learning centre has as a goal for children to reach independence, competence, and development, then the materials within the environment are placed so that children may engage in a self-service model. Children have the freedom to use the materials as they require. Children develop a sense of the importance of using materials effectively and tidying the play space so that it is ready for the next child. The early learning practitioner develops strategies such as using photos to support children in replacing the materials to the appropriate place.

2. The order is restorable by children and adults. Early learning practitioners examine the skills and abilities of the children. Then, the methods used to restore order to the environment are determined. For example, the storage method with materials used with toddlers will differ from kindergarten children. Toddlers require photos of the materials both on the storage container and at the placement of the storage container on the shelf. Kindergarten children may have a combination of words and photos on the materials.

3. The order reflects the needs of the children and the changing conditions. Early learning practitioners recognize that the environment changes as the needs and desires of the children change. When children become familiar with the play space, there is a need to add stimulation to the space. Children and adults engage in changing the environment to meet the needs of the children. Change encourages new exploration.

**Ordered time** refers to an established framework that early learning practitioners and children follow to support children to anticipate the sequence and predictability of their daily routine.

4. The order reflects a sense of aesthetic appeal. The early learning practitioner and children determine ways to display materials that are reflective of an aesthetically pleasing play space. Harmony, size, and colour are considered.

Early learning practitioners listen to the children. In doing so, children will clearly send adults messages about their space, routine, and environmental needs. Early learning practitioners balance the play space with all of the program structural elements, which include "time, space, goals, organization, and people and creative problem solving to minimize negative side effects" (Greenman, 2006, p. 55).

# INDIVIDUAL DIFFERENCES

Not all children have the same needs or desires in their daily routine. There are differences in "stimulation and rest, for noise and quiet, and for interactions and privacy" (Dietze, 2006, p. 152). Practitioners examine the needs of each child and adjust environmental conditions so that the feeling tone may return to being one that is calming and pleasant. For example, some children may wish to have a quiet place when they first enter the early learning environment. This need is accommodated.

## Stop . . . Think . . . Discuss . . . Reflect

Is it really necessary for early learning practitioners to examine each of the responsive components outlined? If so, how do early learning practitioners gain sufficient knowledge and skills to be able to effectively carry out this task? How much of this is related to one's philosophy? Are we asking early learning practitioners to engage in so many "other responsibilities" that there is no time for play?

## Characteristics of Effective Play Space Environments

**The physical environment**    The physical play space impacts the quality of a child's play experience. Early learning practitioners invest a significant amount of time in planning an environment that will promote quality play experiences and the interpersonal relationships among children and adults, in the indoor and outdoor play space. For example, when planning the play space, early learning practitioners consider the space, the place, the play options, and the materials that will complement each child's chronological and developmental phase of development and their interests. If the materials are not correct or if the environment is not carefully planned, important play opportunities that support the various types of child's play may be jeopardized. As you examine this section, we ask that you consider how play space can accommodate fluid and structured play materials, child-initiated and adult-guided experiences, the indoor and outdoor required versatility, and sensorimotor, symbolic, and construction play options.

There are varying perspectives on the amount of space and play centres that should be made available to children. For example, Kritchevsky (1969) indicates that the most effective play spaces for children incorporate a minimum of 2.5 play spaces in each play zone per child. This means that for each group of eight children, there would be 20 different play spaces available. You may initially think that this is an overabundance of play space. However, as you develop knowledge about and observe children at play, you will discover that the various experience centres, such as blocks, science, literacy, art, music, physical play, math, and dramatic play, are all very important to each area of child's play. Generally, in child-centred play environments, children will have their play extend to two or three play spaces at any one time; they may change the play space a minimum of four times in any 60-minute period. The younger the child, the more frequent their change in play episodes.

One of the most effective ways for student practitioners to become familiar with how children use space is through dedicated observations. It is important to become familiar with the province or territory space guidelines for early learning environments as outlined in the respective day nurseries/early learning acts. Remember, these are minimum guidelines that licensed or approved facilities must meet.

Early learning practitioners consider many areas when planning play space. As you read about each of the considerations that follow, think about the impact on play if one or more of the items are not considered fully—how might children's play be influenced?

**Space** Planning for and providing interesting play spaces and materials for young children require careful observation and planning by the early learning practitioner so that the various children's needs are met, including opportunities for their social, emotional, cognitive, and physical development to flourish. For example, practitioners ensure that space for infants is bright, and that there is adequate floor space and materials available that will stimulate the child to begin to roll, creep, crawl, stand, and use their language capabilities. The practitioners provide additional space to toddlers to accommodate their needs for toddling, walking and balancing, pouring, dumping, and filling objects. Limited defined experience centres are created. The preschool child has additional space needs. The number of learning centres and array of materials are increased both indoors and outdoors. There is a need to accommodate space for advanced rough and tumble play, gross motor play with tricycles and bikes and overall running. The school-age space accommodates larger groups of children and it reflects their interests, which include group activities.

***Table 12.1*** *Perspectives on Play Space and Child's Play*

1. How does the play space support child's play?

2. What play space considerations are used to guide our practice?

3. What role do children have in designing the play space?

4. Are children required to play at experience centres for specified times each day or may they play at the centres until they have completed their play episode?

5. How does the play space support the versatility that children require to develop creative play experiences?

6. How does the play space support or detract from positive play engagement?

7. How does the play space help children to be competent in their play?

8. How active and engaged are children in the play space?

9. How does the play space accommodate inclusive play practices?

Early learning practitioners constantly examine the play space to determine how it is meeting the interests of the children, their changing needs, the materials, and the new opportunities for exploration that the practitioner wishes to incorporate into the environment.

Examine the questions in Table 12.1. These questions are intended to help you think about your perspectives on the play space and child's play.

The environmental design impacts the opportunities for the adult–child connections. Well-designed space ensures that children have space to play collectively and independently. There are places for the children to have discussions with adults and other children. There are places for both group and individual dialogue such as in cozy corners, window seats, benches, and near the garden space.

## Design Considerations for Effective Play Spaces

Early learning practitioners have a significant role in creating a responsive, effective play space that accommodates the needs and interests of the children. For example, early learning practitioners who take an interest in the outdoor environment are more likely to encourage children to engage in the variety of risk-taking play options that are possible in the outdoor play space. Practitioners who are passionate about the outdoor environment are more likely to encourage young children to explore, wonder, and appreciate the natural learning opportunities during their outdoor play. They interconnect the outdoor environment to indoor experiences by incorporating opportunities for the children to explore information about plants, water, surfaces, ice, flowers, trees, and other natural learning options in the daily life of children at the early learning centre.

Dietze (2006) identifies that there are nine design features (see Figure 12.3) of a responsive play space that early learning practitioners and children utilize.

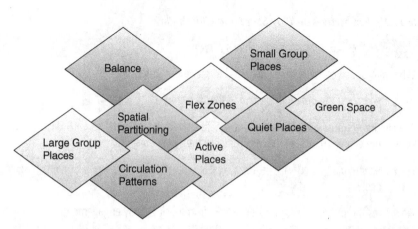

**Figure 12.3** *Design Features of a Responsive Play Space*

**Green space** The green space area is one where children have an opportunity to engage in a quiet and serene experience or active, gross motor play. It provides children with a calming effect and it rejuvenates their abilities to be resilient in play spaces where there is noise, stimuli, and other children. When children have opportunities to engage in long periods of gross motor play, it facilitates gross motor development and reduces stress and tension. Green space increases the quality of the air that children are exposed to. Ideally, the green spaces provide children with opportunities to play among trees, grasses, gardens, and other natural materials such as rocks and water. Early learning practitioners and children benefit from the green space being visible from the indoor environment. Green space and nature collectively enhance children's social and psychological well-being, which in turn has the potential to trigger wonderment, curiosity, and new play options.

**Quiet places** Quiet places provide children with a place to pause, reflect, reconnect, rejuvenate their energy, or plan the next areas of interest that they wish to explore. Quiet places accommodate children wishing to work on a project on their own or listen to music or review a favourite book. Quiet places are located both in the indoor and outdoor play space. They are cozy places where the child may watch other children play and these places may accommodate up to three children at any one time.

**Active places** Children require active places to play indoors and outdoors. Active places attract children wishing to play together. The children come together to decide about the theme of their play, their roles, and how the play will be executed. Active places are where children connect, they network, they observe skills of others, and they engage in group play. Active play spaces may be louder than other parts of the early learning environment and it is a place where exuberant play is most prominent.

**Small group places** These are located both in the indoor and outdoor space. They are used by small groups of children for a variety of play and exploratory experiences. It may include children gathering to hear a story, to engage in a focused experiential project and discovery, or to document previous play experiences. Early learning practitioners may use the small group places to display interesting items that children may wish to explore. Small group places provide children with a sense of security and belonging. It is often the space where children new to the centre will feel most comfortable until they adjust to their play space surroundings.

**Large group places** Early learning practitioners and larger groups of children may come together periodically for engaging in dialogue or group gross motor-type activities. Large group places are usually located both indoors and outdoors. Large group places offer the flexibility to be used by the children for a variety of play experiences, such as dramatic play, when they are not being used for group activities.

**Flex zones** Flex zones located in both the indoor and outdoor play spaces are designed to be child-friendly and their use is primarily guided by children. These flex zones allow children to use the same space in different ways and for different purposes. The furnishings in the flex zone are designed so that children may move the pieces as required. Early learning practitioners create opportunities for children to utilize the space in very different ways from one day to the next, as it is intended to offer children the vision of what can be and how they can actualize that vision.

**Circulation patterns** Circulation patterns are essential components for play space. The patterns provide children with opportunities to travel from one experience centre to another without purposely disrupting the play of other children. The circulation patterns are wide passages so that the children may move their bodies and their play materials with ease. As children move from one experience centre to the next, there may be times when they choose to pause along the circulation path to observe, think, or determine their next destination. The indoor circulation patterns try to accommodate children having access to the natural light and green space. This has a calming effect, and it also helps children regain a play focus.

**Spatial partitioning** Spatial partitioning is used to clearly define space for children and is of particular importance in play spaces that have an open-concept design. When spatial partitioning is done effectively, children are able to self-regulate how the space is intended to be used. This process allows children to competently move from experience centre to experience centre. More exploratory play occurs, peer interaction is facilitated, and positive child behaviour occurs because the child knows the boundaries.

**Balance**   Early learning indoor and outdoor play spaces require a contrast between their elements. As early learning practitioners and children create their play space, they are encouraged to have discussions about placing items that are thick and thin together, combining items that are hard and soft together, open with enclosed, long with short, dark with light, and thin with wide. As identified by Dietze (2006), by "juxtaposing different shapes within the overall space, action or lack of action occurs" (p. 158). Generally in early learning room designs, the larger spaces flow from the centre of the room. The smaller spaces flow from the periphery. Most often, the smaller spaces attract the children; this may be due to the feeling of security that it provides.

## Traditional Physical Play Space Considerations

Previously we introduced you to a number of considerations that early learning practitioners use to guide them in working with children and space designs. Below are 10 additional considerations that early learning practitioners use in preparing appropriate environments for children's play.

1. Safety and accessibility for all children guide the play space design.

2. Indoor and outdoor spaces are given equal consideration in all four seasons. When appropriate, children move between the indoor and outdoor areas freely.

3. The materials are placed in well-defined spaces both indoors and outdoors. The complexity of the materials is scaffolded from simple to more complex.

4. Provisions for environmental conditions are made, such as the ozone ratings in the summer and the colder temperatures in the winter.

5. The play space has a combination of defined and open space, which supports children in engaging in active and quiet play. The space is divided in a way that children feel secure (Caples, 1996, p. 15).

6. The experience centres and pathways are designed so that children may stop and observe the materials available in the centre or the play that is taking place. The pathways are organized to support children in moving around the play space without disrupting other children's play.

7. The experience centres are placed so that early learning practitioners have visual access to the play space for observing children and their play.

8. The children's documentation of their play is displayed in visually attractive ways in both the indoor and outdoor play space. Other materials displayed are chosen based on the meaning that they have for the children.

9. The indoor and outdoor storage units display materials clearly and attractively. They are designed to provide children with access to the materials independently. Other storage within the environment allows for unused materials to be placed and rotated as required.

10. The experience centres are placed based on wet, dry, noisy, and quiet designations (see Figure 12.4).

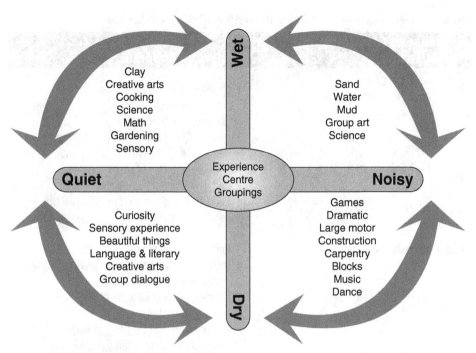

**Figure 12.4** *Experience Centre Groupings*
Taken from Dietze (2006) with permission

# HOW PLAY SPACES AFFECT CHILDREN'S BEHAVIOUR

As Table 12.2 illustrates, children are affected by the aesthetics of their play space and the people in their play space. The environmental conditions impact the feeling tone among children and adults. "Children and adults tell us how the room should be by their behavior" (Greenman, 1988, p. 136). Children are naturally good; but when the environment does not meet their needs, they become anxious, feeling overwhelmed, or experience psychological discomfort. Think of the 3- and 4-year-old children who have high activity levels. These children function best in large spaces and in environments where they may engage in physical activity and play—most often elements of the outdoor portion of the program. When early learning practitioners have expectations that these children will participate in indoor, small-spaced experience centres for long periods of time, children will react with behaviours that are not conducive to creating a harmonious play environment. It will take these high-energy children time to adjust to their environment. Or, think of the child who has a low tolerance for noise and clutter. If the play space has music playing constantly, if children and adults speak in loud voices, and the walls and the play space project a sense of clutter, this child experiences disequilibrium. Over time, children adjust to the play space in their own way; however, if the environmental conditions are not correct, it can impede a child's energy level, ability to problem solve, and ability to cope with the daily living behaviours required in early learning places.

*Table 12.2* *How Environmental Conditions Affect Children's Behaviour*

| Response to Environmental Conditions | Impact on Children |
|---|---|
| Anxiety | • Changes children's brain functions including processing mechanisms, coding processes, and memory function.<br>• Causes distraction and lack of concentration.<br>• Reduces ability to spend time on task.<br>• Impedes intensity of play experience.<br>• Reduces ability to be creative.<br>• Reduces social networking skills and pro-social behaviour. |
| Feeling overwhelmed | • Reduces attention span in play.<br>• Impedes ability to complete tasks or engage in discovery learning.<br>• Interferes with child's use of imagery.<br>• Is easily distracted.<br>• Increased agitation leading to negative behaviour such as biting, hitting, and kicking. |
| Psychological discomfort | • Reduces verbal interactions, language acquisition, and vocabulary expansion.<br>• Reduces social interaction and social networking.<br>• Reduces tolerance for adapting to environmental conditions.<br>• Reduces tolerance for cultural, gender, family, or atypical-development differences. |

Adapted from Dietze (2006) with permission.

The interactions among children, families, and early learning practitioners are influenced by the feeling tone or psychological comfort within the play space. Play spaces that have a sense of warmth, caring, and nurturing attributes contribute to an environment where the interactions are richer, language acquisition stronger, and children are able to verbally communicate their interests, needs, and discoveries. Children who do not gain a sense of comfort in their play space are more prone to exhibit inappropriate social interactions such as hitting, biting, or kicking. They may also regress in controlling their bodily functions, leading to wetting or defecating accidents.

The play space environment is intended to build respect among children and adults. When the environment is planned to support the needs and interests of children and families, there will be greater respect for differences such as culture, family units, skills and talents, and typical and atypical development. The early learning practitioner ensures that children and families have opportunities to use and experience materials, toys, and learning options that celebrate the diverse society that children and families bring to the play space. For example, early learning practitioners ensure that children who use a wheelchair for mobility may be as self-sufficient in having access to displays and materials as other children. Children who come from cultures that have different traditions and objects have opportunities to share these in the play space.

Early learning spaces are intended to offer children opportunities to play, to learn, to experience, to revise, to wonder, to reflect, to discover, to question, to connect new information, to create, and to discuss their experiences. To achieve these goals, early learning environments are rich in ideas, values, and aesthetics. The early learning practitioner values and encourages children to explore the environment, using their five senses. This contributes to children exhibiting a quest for knowledge. They will invent things in their play; they will make new connections between what they know, what they thought, and what they now have discovered. When the environment does not have the correct balance of aesthetics, space, interactions, and acceptance of diversity, children's behavioural patterns and learning processes differ markedly from the ones just mentioned. "Children require an environment that promotes new play experiences and provides the excitement of fresh perception; for like adults, children respond to the space they find themselves in" (Dietze, 2006, p. 163). Early learning practitioners have a major responsibility to plan and implement play space environments that meet the needs of the children.

# SUMMARY

## Chapter Preview
- Play space is linked to the quality and engagement of children in play.
- The environmental considerations are as important as the floor plan.

## Children's Play
- Each type of child's play requires various space allocations and materials to support the play.
- Children will gravitate between sensorimotor, symbolic, and construction play. Children benefit from having exposure to fluid and structured materials.

## The Environmental Play Space Framework
- Play spaces are responsive to the children's needs and interests so that they may engage in many types of play and experiences.
- Play space is not fixed components; rather it is fluid and emerging based on children's life experiences.
- Learning environments are built on offering children a variety of experiences; freedom to play; opportunities for exploration, role modelling and learning; exposure to adults, children and neighbourhoods; and opportunities to incorporate daily living responsibilities into the environment.

## Characteristics of Responsive Play Space Environments
- Early learning practitioners are guided by examining the following: the feeling tone, listening to the children, developing a caring place to play, environmental aesthetics, natural light, stress-free environment,

cultural and community attributes, places for exploration and freedom to play, flexible schedules and order, and individual differences.

## Characteristics of Effective Play Space Environments

- Early learning practitioners consider the space and the following design features: Green space, quiet places, active places, small group places, large group places, flex zones, circulation patterns, spatial partitioning, and balance.

## How Play Spaces Affect Children's Behaviour

- Children's behaviour can be positively or negatively affected by the play space.
- The interactions among children, families, and early learning practitioners are influenced by the feeling tone or psychological comfort within the play space. When the play space is not conductive to the needs of children, they may exhibit signs of anxiety, feeling overwhelmed, or psychological discomfort.

# REVIEW QUESTIONS

1. Why do early learning practitioners examine environmental conditions equally to floor plans?
2. Discuss four issues and perspectives that early learning practitioners consider when planning play space for children. What is the significance of each issue?
3. Greenman discusses a full vision of childhood and family. What does this mean for early learning practitioners when planning space and play options?
4. Why is it important for early learning practitioners to focus on the feeling tone of the play space and the noise levels? How do these two items influence children's play?
5. What is meant by environmental aesthetics? Why is it important for early learning practitioners to incorporate it into their practice?
6. Scott identifies that poor diet and noise pollution are hidden stressors within a child's environment. How do early learning practitioners respond to these stressors?
7. Describe what is meant by Greenman's perspective that the order exhibited in an early learning space impacts children. How do early learning practitioners incorporate order into their practice?
8. Why is it important for early learning environments to incorporate design features, as identified by Dietze, into their indoor and outdoor play spaces?
9. Describe how children's behaviour is positively or negatively impacted by their play space.

# MAKING CONNECTIONS

## Theory to Practice

1. You are working in an environment that you determine has a significant amount of clutter in it. How would you approach your colleagues to discuss this topic? What information would you highlight about clutter and children's learning? Why? What recommendations would you be prepared to share?
2. You have been asked to rearrange one of the play spaces in the early learning setting. How would you proceed in this? What research would you conduct? How? What areas from this chapter would you incorporate into your plan? Why? How?

3. Visit an early learning centre. Using the wet/dry, quiet/noisy guidelines examine the placement of the experience centres according to this guide. Would you recommend moving any of the centres? If so, why? How might your recommendations support noise reduction, behavioural issues, and play engagement?
4. Is there a place for cartoon-like characters in the early learning environment? Why or why not?
5. Research indicates that children's behaviours are impacted by their play space. What environmental conditions would you examine if a child began biting and hitting other children?

### For Further Research

1. Early learning practitioners are becoming aware of environmental aesthetics. Research the latest information on environmental aesthetics and then determine how it may impact play space for young children.
2. There is some research that identifies room colours used in early learning environments as having an impact on how children play and learn. Gather current research to determine how colour impacts children and their play. Then, visit three early learning centres to view the colours in their environment. Note how children are engaged in their play.

# ADDITIONAL READING

Curtis, D. & Carter, M. (2003). *Designs for living and learning: Transforming early childhood environments*. St. Paul, MN: Redleaf.

Greenman, J. (2005). *Caring spaces, learning places: Children's environments that work* (2nd ed.). Redmond, WA: Child Care Information Exchange.

Greenman, J. (2006). The importance of order. *Exchange: The Early Leaders' Magazine*. Redmond, WA. July/August.

Welsch, W. (2005). "Sport viewed aesthetically, or even as art," in: *The Aesthetics of Everyday Life*, A. Light and J. M. Smith (eds.). New York: Columbia University Press.

Zangwill, N. (2001). "Formal natural beauty," *Proceedings of the Aristotelian Society* 101, 209–224.

# WEBLINKS

Teaching Environmental Aesthetics, by Allen Carlson, at the *Aesthetics online* website
**www.aesthetics-online.org/articles/index.php?articles_id=17**

Inclusive Environmental Designs
**http://colormatters.com**

# 13 Taking Play to the Next Level

## Learning Outcomes

After exploring this chapter you should be able to

- address terminology issues and relate to the role of the early learning practitioner;

- reconceputalize a postmodern perspective;

- critically relate to values, beliefs, and images within the early learning and play environment;

- explain advocacy/activism and describe, in relation to children's rights, determinants of health and action research;

- describe the sustainability issue in early learning and play; and

- describe the difference between parent engagement and parent involvement.

## Stories from the Field: Author to Student

Throughout this textbook, you have had an opportunity to read stories from a diverse set of early learning practitioners. We hope that you have been able to hear the voices of these dedicated professionals and are able to relate to their stories. As the authors of the textbook, we will be using this final chapter to explore contemporary issues of play that may influence and scaffold your learning to the next level as you continue to think critically about, and reflect on, current thinking and theories about play.

Taking into consideration all the chapters you have read in this textbook, you may feel inspired to consider your own treatise on play—to contemplate your play mission or your vision for play for children. You may see it as a time to practice reflection and consider your values and beliefs. You may think about how to incorporate your ideas and new vision into your current and future practice in the field of early learning.

In each chapter we have attempted to share the voices of many early learning practitioners with you. We have tried to present stories, research, and information as objectively as possible. You may have detected our voice throughout. Yes, we have a vision for play and hope that you have seen ways in which we shared it with you throughout and in this final chapter.

## Diane's Story

When I began to practice as an early learning practitioner, I dismissed the theory that I had become acquainted with in my college courses. I focused programming for the children in my care on the theme approach. At first I was challenged and happy to be teaching young children but I became bored with this approach of program planning based on overriding weeklong themes. I knew that there was something more to teaching and learning. At the time, I was experiencing cognitive dissonance. "Deep understanding occurs when the presence of new information prompts the emergence or enhancement of cognitive structures that enable us to rethink our prior idea" (Brooks & Brooks, 1999, p. 15). I was increasingly uncomfortable with what I had once believed to be an acceptable approach when children displayed disinterest in a particular theme. It was not during the theme activities that I could see learning taking place. It was during play, when the children themselves were faced with cognitive dissonance, realizing that in order to build a bridge from blocks, a foundational structure was needed.

As the children in my care began to develop more abstract thought, my own development coincided with theirs. I started to ask questions and reconsider choices. I was seeking alternatives and deliberating. I can now see the correlation with my own development. Child development is considered a lifelong process characterized by stages or developmental milestones (Santrock, 2001). Teacher development is also a long-term progression or journey in which the teacher must pass from novice undergraduate to in-service practitioner (Katz, 1972). To become a teacher is to accept a process of education that is "guided by educational values, personal needs, and by a variety of beliefs or generalizations that the teacher holds to be true" (Eisner, 1994, p. 154). As beliefs and truths change, pedagogy is constructed and self-image is influenced (Kashin, 2009). It is my vision that early learning practitioners will reflect on values and beliefs, embrace theory, and actively advocate for play-based learning for all the world's children.

## Beverlie's Story

The first phase of my career was working with children in family settings. I learned from Anne and Jane and Brett and Kelly the importance of their freedom to play. They were happiest when they were playing in dress up clothes or in the garden making mud pies. They expressed a sense of wonderment when they observed butterflies or bees on the flowers. It was the simple environment where we played and talked and laughed and explored.

The next phase of my career led me to explore the importance of school-aged children having a place to play after school. There, in public schools, we organized play experiences that would allow children to "play"—I did not support children doing homework; rather I wanted them to run and to jump and to hop, and to skip. I wanted them to have a venue where they could engage in solitary or group play. My mantra was that children learn best through play.

I learned throughout my career that there are trends, there are thoughts, and there are preferred processes that the researchers and educators insist are best for the children. My values and beliefs are strong—children need play, they need early learning practitioners to listen to them and their play and they need environments that offer them a sense of wonder, exploration, experience, curiosity, and success both in indoor and outdoor places to play. Yes, that is my voice that you have heard so frequently throughout this book. My vision continues—open up the doors, let the children play!

# CHAPTER PREVIEW

Loris Malaguzzi (1998) suggested that children have a right to a new restored image that elevates their position to one of collaborator, communicator, and co-constructer with the adults in their lives. For early learning practitioners, the same parallel exists vis-à-vis their relationship to other educators. Early learning practitioners are also in extreme need of a restored image that elevates their position to one of collaborator, communicator, and co-constructer with educators from all other levels across the spectrum. For the many years that the field of early childhood education has been recognized as a distinct sector of education, those connected to it have been suffering from an image that impedes growth and development. If the image held is of glorified babysitters, the rights of children are compromised. A new image for both children and early learning practitioners should ascend in tandem. As the rivers are crossed and paths retraced, it is time to reconceptualize how we view the youngest learners and those charged with their care and learning (Kashin, 2009). We are committed to the philosophy that children learn best through play; therefore, collectively we have a commitment as early learning practitioners and other educators to bridge the gap and gain an understanding of the importance of play to a child's development and lifelong learning.

# TERMINOLOGY ISSUES

You may have noticed that throughout the chapters we have referred to those working in the field of early learning as early learning practitioners. There is a great debate regarding terminology in our field. There are many interchangeable terms, for instance, early childhood educators, child care providers, and child care practitioners (Ferguson, 2004). In addition to these terms, those who work with children are called or call themselves, day care workers, preschool or nursery school teachers, and caregivers (Kashin, 2009). To add to the confusion, kindergarten teachers working in the school system may also view themselves as early learning practitioners.

We have used the term early learning practitioner because it appears to be an inclusive term that best represents current contexts. We believe that it is important to focus on play and learning in the early years. We believe that learning in the early years must be based on the practice of learning through play. We also understand that the debate about terminology finds its root in the past and is a sensitive issue for many in the sector, as it reflects a desire to move beyond a specific and devaluing term, "*babysitter*," that has plagued those who have devoted their professional lives to facilitating the play and learning of young children.

Past and present contexts indicate that there is a funding link between the occupation and the devaluing term of babysitter. The tendency in Canada has been to concentrate on protection and bodily care when considering the educational needs of the youngest learner (Bennett, 2000). The term resonates with more meaning for early learning practitioners here than elsewhere in the world. Lack of government support connects to the predominant view of early learning practitioners and the corresponding terms used to describe them. In Canada, a national proportionate study conducted in 2002 found that child care has passed hurdles in public perception with 66 percent seeing it as a development service for children. Conversely, 17 percent saw it as babysitting (CCCF/CCAAC, 2003). While public perception appears to be improving, early learning practitioners, continue to struggle with their public and self-image. According to Tougas (2004), "there is always a deep feeling of impotence, frustration, dissatisfaction and fatigue that offsets the educator's pleasure and passion for their work with children" (p. 8).

Looking for a common, singular term that more aptly describes the role is the aim of many across North America (Caldwell, 2004; Ferguson, 2004). If care is considered less important than education, as it denotes a custodial function similar to babysitting, and education has more status in society, the question becomes where the emphasis should be placed (Ferguson, 2004). Caldwell (2004) sees the present-day terminology issues as an outcome of the merging of two fields. Early childhood education and care were once considered totally different from one another, mainly because of their different antecedents. Now, according to Ferguson (2004), the borders between care and education have become blurred. The dichotomous disparity in the field represents distinct images related to nursery schools and day care. Kindergarten programs and nursery schools are considered an educational service, whereas day care is considered a social welfare program. The half-day nursery school is usually privately funded for the middle class and affluent, whereas day care is often publicly funded for the lower class and poor. Kindergarten programs are most often delivered in school settings and are publicly funded. Nursery school is seen as a service for children and day care is considered a service for parents, providing institutional, custodial care, or babysitting (Caldwell, 2004). The impact of increased government funding towards the education of the youngest learner will see the terminology issues continually evolve (Kashin, 2009). We hope the utilization of the terms *early learning practitioner* and *early learning programs* demonstrate our desire to be inclusive. It by no means represents the final word on issues of terminology. There are other terms to consider.

In a study by Moss (2000), three basic options are identified regarding terminology within the field of early learning. The pedagogue, trained to work with children from birth to 6 years or older in non-school settings, has an equally important but different role than the school-based teacher. The early childhood teacher, trained to work with children from birth to 6 years of age within the education system, is viewed as occupying one branch or specialization within the teaching profession. Then there is a mixture of teachers working with children in the early childhood age range within the education system, as well as various types of child care workers employed in early childhood services in the welfare system. It is this last option that produces multiple and interchangeable terms. The final example is from the United States and illustrates that the origin of multiple terminologies rests in the connection between the field and the welfare system. The extent to which the system is split between welfare and education correlates, according to Moss (2000), with levels of training and funding. Denmark, home to the pedagogue, has a longer and higher level of training, substantial and sustained public funding, and a drive to recruit males to the field. The result has been the achievement of increased public recognition and status for the early childhood worker in that country. Rather than reflecting a dichotomous situation, a more holistic approach is necessary for early childhood care and education: one that would meet the need for children to be engaged in stimulating early learning experiences and the need of families to have high quality care for their children while they work. The field is moving toward strengthening the connection between care and education (Kashin, 2009). What the accepted terms will become remains unknown.

Is this field connected to care or education? Should care be implied by education, rather than having them be mutually exclusive? Educational researchers focusing on older learners call for education to be more caring (Noddings, 1992). Eisner (1991) recommended that all teachers develop an ethic of caring and create a caring community. Care embraces the roots of the field (Ferguson, 2004). What are the purposes of early learning programs and the work they undertake? Different understandings of early childhood institutions presume very different constructions of the young child, producing very different understandings of the early childhood worker (Dahlberg, Moss, & Pence, 1999). We believe that early learning practitioners are professionals working in diverse settings devoted to early learning. The professional practitioner is at the centre of a play-based learning program.

## PROGRAMMING AND CURRICULUM

You may have noticed in this textbook that we use of the term *programming* rather than *curriculum*. The Canadian early learning sector uses the two terms interchangeably (Crowther, 2003), even though they have different meanings (Dietze, 2006). Curriculum is the approach to education that is employed in the classroom. Specifically, it is the theoretical orientation and goals of the program in which domains of development are emphasized, such as the degree of structure in the program, the kinds of materials used, and the roles of the teacher and the learner (Howe, Jacobs, & Fiorentino, 2000). In a more traditional sense, curriculum is the plan of activities carried out by the teaching staff in order to help children acquire pre-defined developmental or subject skills (Bennett, 2000). However, contemporary views, such as those held by the educators of Reggio Emilia, see curriculum in a broader sense, as process-related and co-constructive (Dahlberg, Moss, & Pence, 1999).

Since the term *curriculum* has its origin in the educational sector and it primarily targets cognitive learning (Dietze, 2006), we use the word *program* for its broader focus. *Curriculum* has been associated with the traditional prescribed methodology used in classrooms (Dietze, 2006). The term *program* offers an alternative that we feel is associated with learning in a play-based environment. Rather than deliver a prepared curricula, early learning practitioners create co-constructively and deliver a program based on children's learning, interests, and development. By offering children play options rather than a prescribed curriculum, a process program approach evolves. A process-related program is by its very nature co-constructed by practitioners, children, and parents.

## Emergent Programming

The term *emergent curriculum* is used to refer to an approach that emerges from the interests of the learner and is co-constructed with the teacher (Jones & Nimmo, 1994). However, the process of emergent curriculum assumes a higher level of effectiveness when it goes beyond interests to a focus on children's thinking. It then assumes a transformational position that concentrates on personal and social change (Miller, 1993) and is based on the assumption that knowledge is socially constructed. *Emergent* and *curriculum* might be contradictory terms in some situations. We ask you to consider emergent programming as that which involves leading a child to new levels of thinking, scaffolding across the zone of proximal development within a social context. This social context is what Reggio educators consider the three subjects of education: practitioners, children, and parents. Integrating this theory into practice, the role of the practitioner becomes one that is accountable for facilitating an environment that is rich in play and learning. By demonstrating how play supports learning; making it visible and accessible, early learning practitioners respect co-construction in practice. The process has transformative possibilities. Emergent programming is the pedagogy of infinite empowering play and learning possibilities for children, practitioners, and families.

Figure 13.1 represents a cycle for emergent programming that begins with a play experience. Students and practitioners can observe children playing. With written observations and digital imagery the learning can be documented and related to development. By examining one's documentation, practitioners and students have the evidence to plan for play-based learning providing the necessary materials that will encourage scaffolding. Learning is made visible by offering children opportunities to represent and re-represent their learning either two or three dimensionally and in many languages. When the learning is made visible, documented, and displayed for others to review and reflect, collaboration

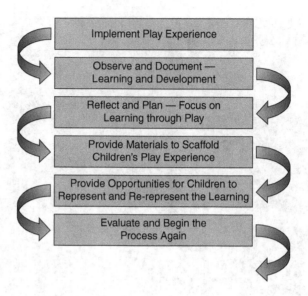

*Figure 13.1 Emergent Programming Cycle*

and co-construction are possible. With multiple perspectives informing practice, the process can begin again.

## Global Perspectives

**Globalism** refers to our interconnectedness with others around the world and globalization is the speed in which these connections occur (Marcus & Nyiszator, 2008).

The Reggio Emilia early learning programs have inspired this approach to programming known as *emergent*. With the globalization of early learning programming, worldwide examples of approaches to early learning are accessible. We felt that it was important to present global examples throughout the textbook and that you as a student practitioner consider the concentric circles that reflect the theories of Bronfenbrenner. Each circle represents a widening of perspective, from the micro to the macro view. We ask that you think about play, child development, and your role in relationship from a local and global perspective. By reaching out beyond our own contexts to the bigger picture, we can see that there are multiple points of view and perspectives regarding early learning.

## Postmodernism

The preprimary schools of Reggio Emilia are representative of one of the global examples presented in this textbook. These schools represent a worldview that is grounded in a postmodern perspective. "Postmodernists consider that there are many different kinds of voices, many kinds of styles, and take care not to value or privilege one set of values over another" (Penn, 2005, p. 28). A postmodern perspective in early learning is based on the assumption that teaching enacts power relations making multiple voices necessary to prevent privilege (Ryan & Grieshaber, 2005). Reggio may be postmodern, but Reggio educators resist the term because isms are too risky as they simplify and lock rather than inspire (Moss & Petrie, 2002). Inspiration for Reggio educators is the image of the child as having rights rather than needs.

A postmodern perspective evolves and is different from the modern romantic view of the child as espoused by Jean Jacques Rousseau (1762), the French philosopher who claimed that children are born weak and helpless and need strength, aid, and reason. We ask Geraldine Lyn-Piluso, an academic and a critical pedagogue, what words of wisdom she could impart to early learning students and practitioners regarding postmodernism.

## WORDS OF WISDOM

### Ask an Expert

**Geraldine Lyn-Piluso**

At the height of modern educational thought in the Western world, theories that emphasized ages and stages were rampant. Freud's psychosexual stages, Erikson's psychosocial stages, and Piaget's stages of intellectual development—they've all contributed to that lexicon of childhood. However, it's critical that we remind each other that such theories were developed and accepted by less than 20 percent of the world's population in a very small pocket of human history—the ideas are NOT universal and they do NOT stand the test of time. They analyze childhood as it is defined in the Western modern era. Postmodern thought provokes one to take a close look at how we know what we know, where that knowledge claim originated, and to ask why we should trust it. It challenges the structures on which we base our thinking and in fact challenges us to let them go and to rethink what we have come to accept all our lives. We are asked why we rely so heavily on so-called experts to explain the world. The postmodern educator accepts that childhood is a social construction—a concept that has been invented and that distinguishes a particular period of human life. It seems that there are multiple explanations for childhood—it's not defined by one single theory. It seems inevitable that our definition of childhood and the very existence of the concept will change and perhaps at some point in the future, disappear. This philosophical freedom—to let concepts change, flow, and even evaporate has the potential to improve the field of education and to help us stay relevant. Human thought evolves, it is not universal—we do not all think alike. We are forced to ask what ideas have we not yet considered and to ask specific questions such as, what is childhood, what is care, what is education and, in the spirit of this textbook, what is play (and "free play")? And here's the rub: postmodern theory won't answer that for you. You'll have to answer it yourself. Just as we often ask children to problem solve, to think creatively, and to think outside the box, postmodern theory challenges you to do the same.

## Voice

Ayers (1992) suggests that voice "is an essential part of the reconceptualization of the field of early childhood education" (p. 266). We ask that you find your voice as an early learning practitioner. *Voice* is "what people mean when they speak of the core of the self" (Gilligan, 1993, p. xvi). Voice can be seen as a metaphor of development extending well beyond the expression of a point of

**Critical pedagogy** is not a single concept so there are variations in its definition. Henry Giroux (1988) was one of the first theorists to develop the term, which has arisen from the foundations of critical theory. Critical pedagogy provides a conceptual tool in which to critique social, political, and equity issues within the classroom (Kilderry, 2004).

view. "Voice is a powerful psychological instrument and channel, connecting inner and outer worlds" (Gilligan, 1993, p. xvi). To have a voice is also relational; it depends on listening and being heard. Voice also reflects the empowerment possible when the voice is heard.

If you are purposeful in your role and provide children with multiple opportunities to experience play, a program evolves through a collaborative process of teaching and learning. It is your voice that needs to be heard alongside those of parents and children. You are without voice if you accept a prescribed curriculum. Who is heard and who is allowed to speak changes the power structure within the environment and ultimately the play experiences that children engage in. Play experiences impact the child's ability to have a sense of wonder, exploration, discovery, and reflection. When practitioners, parents, and children share in the learning process with voices heard and heeded, a shift in power occurs. Socially shared cognition, mediated learning, and joint activity can lead to your improved practice on many levels (Samaras, 2000).

The aforementioned quote from Ayers (1992) refers to the term *reconceptualization*. Reconceptualization involves critically examining the assumptions and knowledge base that has traditionally guided the field of early learning with the goal of reframing it (Pacini-Ketchabaw & Pence, 2005). In the spirit of looking at the world in new and creative ways, we ask you to critically think about what you have read in this textbook and the issues presented in this final chapter.

**Photo 13.2**   *Inviting a grandparent to experience clay with the children encourages the voice of others involved in the child's life.*

## THE RECONCEPTUALIZATION MOVEMENT IN CANADIAN EARLY LEARNING

Key elements of postmodernism include the openness to the presence of many voices and views. For early learning practitioners it means engaging other views and exploring a world of profound diversity. Process, engagement, dialogue, and co-construction take precedence over routines and prescribed best practices. The reconceptualist movement in Canadian early learning is just one facet of postmodern thinking (Pacini-Ketchabaw & Pence, 2005). In other parts of the world early learning practitioners are more prone to engage in reconceptualized discourse. According to Pacini-Ketchabaw and Pence (2005) it has kept a low profile in Canada.

In Australia, New Zealand, and Italy it has been more prominent. The work of Loris Malaguzzi has inspired many reconceptualized thinkers in other parts of the world. Pacini-Ketchabaw and Pence (2005) suggest that Canada's response to the programs of Reggio Emilia has influenced the discourse but not to the same extent as in other countries. "Rather than seeing the programs of Reggio Emilia and the words of their principal architect as revolutionary," in Canada the "field has seen them as evolutionary" (p. 14). In the United States the focus of the movement when it began was to critique DAP—developmentally appropriate practice (Pacini-Ketchabaw & Pence, 2005).

DAP represented a reform effort in the field of early childhood education when it came to prominence in the 1980s. The phrase has found its way into the vernacular of the field. For Bredekamp (1987) the concept of developmental appropriateness has two dimensions: age appropriateness, which uses human development research to guide practice according to predictable sequences of growth and change, and individual appropriateness, which encourages an inclusive curriculum. DAP curriculum is heavily influenced by the constructivist theories of Jean Piaget. DAP values child-centred, experience-centred, and process-oriented practices. For proponents of DAP, learning occurs in play-based environments, through developmental stages, with children able to understand, process, and construct knowledge at different levels and in different ways in successive stages (Raines, 1997). In spite of enthusiastic acceptance of DAP in the late 1980s and early 1990s, there has been criticism. Some of the criticism suggests that with adherence to developmental stages, the complexities of development are reduced to simplified and quantifiable representations. The objective is seen to override the subjective, which assumes that developmental theory is value-free (Dahlberg, Moss, & Pence, 1999). As well, it focuses on the individual child, rather than the child in a social, cultural, political, and economic context (Kessen, 1993). Advocates of play-based programs now suggest the focus move from the developmental level of the child to offering play-based experiences that build on the child's interests, capabilities, and experiences that support the development of the whole child.

## Critical Thinking

The DAP discourse is an example of practitioners, researchers, and policymakers thinking critically about an educational issue. Thinking critically is important for everyone, children and adults alike. Carr (1992) reminds early learning practitioners the importance of teaching critical thinking. Are you a critical thinker? What does it take to be a critical thinker? hooks (2010) reminds us that "one need not be either an intellectual or an academic to engage in critical thinking." Anytime that "we ponder the question of who, what, when, where, how, and why," we are on the path of critical thought (p. 187). This leads us to new places of thinking, learning, and practice.

> **Critical thinking** is thinking that is purposeful, reasoned, and goal-directed, involving solving problems, formulating inferences, calculating likelihoods, and making decisions. "Critical thinkers use these skills appropriately, without prompting, and usually with conscious intent, in a variety of settings. That is, they are predisposed to think critically" (Halpen, 1999, p. 69).

## Values and Beliefs

Balaban (1995) says, "Critical to truly seeing and understanding the children we teach is the courage to reflect about ourselves. Facing our biases openly, recognizing the limits imposed by our embeddedness in our own culture and experience, acknowledging the values and beliefs we cherish, and accepting the influence of emotions on our actions are extraordinary challenges" (p. 49). How do they impact your practice?

Carter and Curtis (1996) maintain that "play is of value in and of itself, but adults easily lose track of this fact" (p, 174). They suggest that children who are independently involved in play often are not noticed in the learning environment; rather, the children who are misbehaving acquire the attention. When there is no misbehaviour then practitioners often use the time to attend to other pressing needs in their work, such as housekeeping. When play is happening in the room but practitioners are keeping busy wiping tables and sweeping floors, do they really value play? Do you value play? What else do you value as important in the practice of early learning? How do your values coincide with your beliefs?

**Image**   Do you believe that children have rights as well as needs? What is your image of the child? What is your image of the early learning practitioner? The central notion for the philosophy of Reggio Emilia resides in the concept of images. By critically thinking about images, we can begin to see children and early learning practitioners from different perspectives. According to the Reggio Emilia philosophy, the image of the child is one where children are seen as strong, competent, intellectual builders of theories. Stremmel (2002) suggests that this image counters current perspectives of children as powerless, passive receptacles into which knowledge or skills are poured and suggests the Reggio image as an alternative. "Instead of fixing children by teaching them to memorize and be obedient, we should be helping them to develop dispositions of caring, fairness, and justice or how to engage in ethical reflection and live responsibly within a democratic society" (p. 43). Fu (2002) suggests that early learning practitioners too can be positively influenced by a reframed image much like that espoused for children. Early learning practitioners can be seen as strong, competent, intellectual builders of theories (Kashin, 2009).

Malaguzzi (1998) stresses the importance of early learning practitioners being open to change and reconstruction of themselves. Rinaldi (1998) affirms that when discussing the transcripts of children's work, early learning practitioners subsequently begin to question themselves and each other. This disposition on the part of Reggio early learning practitioners to question themselves and to change their interactions based on their reflections is behaviour that is valued and encouraged (Rankin, 2004). This role has resulted in the adoption of an image of the teacher as researcher (Hewett, 2001). So important is this image, that Malaguzzi (1998) suggests education without research "education without interest" (p. 73). Continual internal dialogues and discussions with others provide ongoing training and theoretical enrichment. Early learning practitioners can see themselves as researchers, preparing documentation of their work with children (Fu, 2002).

*Photo 13.3   The image of the child in a Reggio environment is one that sees him as a capable, competent builder of theories.*

Internal dialogues and discussions with others can lead to rethinking practice, which can lead to a shift from practices inconsistent with play-based learning.

## Rethinking Practice

Whardle (2007) asks, "Where do our practices come from?" According to critical theorists Ryan and Grieshaber (2004), our practices come from "research on white, middle class students, and from dead white men" (Whardle, 2007, p. 1). Whardle (2007) believes that early learning practices have been largely developed as a downward extension of school practices. She suggests that we rethink some of these practices from the schedule, to same-age grouping, to the exercise of the calendar. While the calendar seems to be an activity taught all over the world, Whardle (2007) wonders why given that "according to Piaget, preoperational children cannot possibly do the calendar activity in a meaningful way" (p. 2).

For Beneke, Ostrosky, and Katz (2008), using the calendar with young children may involve good intentions but they have gone awry. The morning ritual of a calendar circle may be one that some children dread and the experience can become unruly and distracting. It is hard to try to teach concepts to children who are not developmentally ready for the content, especially in a group setting. It is not an appropriate way to introduce the intended concepts. Beneke et al. (2008) have identified calendar concepts as time, numeracy, vocabulary (month, year, weekend), sequencing (yesterday, today, tomorrow) and patterning (Monday, Tuesday, Wednesday).

If young children participate in an activity frequently that they do not really understand, "they may lose confidence in their intellectual powers" (p. 15). Early learning practitioners who can reflect on practice and consider how children learn can "focus on calendar-related constructs such as patterning, sorting, and seriating during more natural and appropriate routines" (p. 16). We suggest that the most natural and appropriate time to learn concepts is during play. For some early learning practitioners it will be difficult to break the calendar habit, especially for those who have been using it as a morning ritual. Whether early learning practitioners are open to rethink this practice depends on their disposition towards change. Sometimes, such changes require early learning practitioners to examine the workplace environment and prepare to leave the security of the environment to join new colleagues who emulate a shared philosophical orientation.

# PROFESSIONAL DISPOSITIONS

In the process of research in practice, early learning practitioners can demonstrate a predisposition to critical thinking. Critical thinking is one of many dispositions that should be associated with the professional practitioner. According to Katz (1993), it is possible to have skills and lack a taste for or habit of using them. Knowledge as well can be acquired without having the disposition to use it. Early learning practitioners and students may have the skills required to be critical thinkers but may not be in the habit of using this skill. In turn, they may have

**Professional dispositions** include attitudes, values, and beliefs demonstrated through both verbal and nonverbal behaviours as early learning practitioners interact with children, families, colleagues, and communities (NCATE, 2007).

| Disposition | Description | Behaviour Indicators |
|---|---|---|
| Collaboration | The ability to work together with others | • Cooperates with others<br>• Makes contributions to the group effort<br>• Shares information, resources, and materials with others<br>• Assists/mentors others<br>• Supports group decision making<br>• Makes relevant contributions to discussions |
| Reflection | The ability to review, analyze, evaluate, and reflect on your experiences | • Accepts and incorporates suggestions<br>• Identifies own biases and prejudices<br>• Demonstrates self-analysis<br>• Uses reflective tools such as documentation in practice<br>• Uses reflective practices to set goals<br>• Recognizes situations that call for creative problem solving and collaboration |

**Figure 13.2**  *Two Examples of Professional Dispositions and Indicators*

knowledge about the importance of play but not the disposition to create and support a play-based learning environment for children.

If you were to create an inventory of the professional dispositions that you think an early learning practitioner should have, what would be on your list? In Figure 13.2, two examples are included along with associated behavioural indicators. If an early learning practitioner were demonstrating one of these dispositions, the list of indicators indicates the corresponding behaviour that should be seen or displayed.

## Stop . . . Think . . . Discuss . . . Reflect

What other dispositions do you think an early learning practitioner and student should be cultivating in their work with children? Aside from the dispositions identified, what else can you add? Add to the two examples in Figure 13.2. Identify the disposition, describe it, and then make a list of behavioural indicators. When you have completed this, compare and contrast the list with a peer or colleague. As a collaborative exercise, create a chart of all the dispositions identified by the group. Why is it important to examine this at this phase of your learning? How does it impact the work you do with cooperating practitioners? Why?

## Reflective Practice

In Figure 13.2, one of the dispositions listed refers to reflective practice. In 1987, Donald Schön introduced the concept of reflective practice as a critical process in refining one's artistry or craft in a specific discipline. Schön recommended reflective practice as a way to recognize consonance between individual practices and those of successful practitioners.

Research on effective teaching has shown that effective practice is linked to inquiry, reflection, and continuous professional growth (Harris, 1998). Tools for reflective practice can include portfolio development, action research, journal writing, and mentoring relationships (Ferraro, 2000). The ability of early learning practitioners to reflect on their own practices can provide them with feedback that nurtures their self-esteem and professional growth (Yelland & Cartmel, 2000). The greatest challenge to accepting an inquiry paradigm is transforming the image early learning practitioners have of themselves. If we see ourselves as already knowing, we are rigid rather than dynamic thinkers. Rigid thinkers are unlikely to see themselves as learners whose primary task is to grow. Without practitioners who are committed to growth, children are destined to have static and rather boring learning experiences (Kashin, 2009).

If we ponder the question of who, what, when, where, how, and why as suggested by hooks (2010) in relation to reflective practice, we can practice reflection. In Figure 13.3, you will see a cognitive organizer which will help you critically think about reflective practice.

> As defined by Schön, **reflective practice** involves thoughtfully considering one's own experiences in applying knowledge to practice while being coached by professionals in the discipline (Schön, 1996).

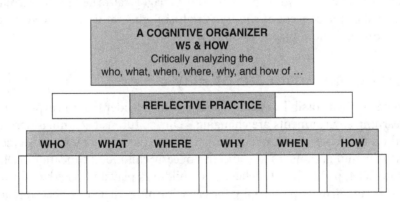

*Figure 13.3*    *A Cognitive Organizer for Reflective Practice*

## Children's Rights

In the Reggio Emilia view, the child has rights rather than simply needs. The child has a right to be a collaborator and a communicator. The child is seen as possessing strength, competence, and potential. This informs a view of the child as a protagonist, occupying a primary role in his or her learning (Hewett, 2001). The child as protagonist has the right to be a collaborator within a community of learners (Cadwell, 2003; Gandini, 2004).

To see children as protagonists of their own experiences of learning is to view children as having special rights. Children have the right to express their understanding of the world through many languages. Reflection on children's rights is an important exercise for practitioners and students.

As identified in Chapter 1, in 1989, the Convention on the Rights of the Child became the first legally binding international convention to affirm human rights for all children. World leaders decided that children needed a special convention just for them because those under 18 years of age often need more care and protection than adults. The leaders wanted to make sure that the world recognized that children have human rights too. The Convention on the Rights of the Child (CRC) is the first legally binding international instrument to incorporate the full range of human rights—including civil, cultural, economic, political, and social rights. It has achieved near-universal acceptance.

The provisions and principles of the CRC are the guiding force behind the mission of the UNICEF organization (United Nations International Children's Emergency Fund) as an international advocate for the protection of children's rights. The CRC spells out the basic human rights that children everywhere have: the right to survival; to develop to the fullest; to protection from harmful influences, abuse, and exploitation; and to participate fully in family, cultural, and social life. The four core principles are non-discrimination; devotion to the best interests of the child; the right to life, survival, and development; and respect for the views of the child.

The consideration of rights has propelled a worldview for early learning and shaped an empowering example in Reggio Emilia. How does the consideration of children's rights impact your view? Is your pedagogical orientation to children's play affected by the concept of children's rights? Rights rather than needs can scaffold our thinking about play to another level.

## Becoming an Advocate of Play

With such positive possibilities, it is distressing to consider that the expectations of early learning environments are changing. "Our culture is becoming increasingly focused on the achievement of functional skills (e.g. pre-literacy and elementary arithmetic manipulations) as the objective of early childhood education" (Oliver & Klugman, 2004, p. 22). If you believe that children's play and play-based learning needs to be the driving philosophy for early learning, then you need to consider becoming an advocate of play.

Advocacy is usually defined as the act of advocating for a cause. Oliver and Klugman (2004) suggest that if you want to speak out for play-based learning for young children, the first step is to clarify your own philosophy about how children learn best and most naturally. Advocacy begins with your own beliefs, values, and knowledge. We have already discussed values and beliefs. Expanding your knowledge involves reviewing the research about the role of play. Follow your exploration of the research literature with strengthening your communication skills, documenting what you know about the link between play and learning. For inspiration, let the words of Mahatma Gandhi serve as a powerful reminder to "be the change you want" and not to underestimate the impact of what you can do (p. 24).

Ebbeck and Waniganayake (2003) challenge this view by comparing advocates with activists. "Advocates and activists are very similar in that their primary objective is to advance a particular case or cause, usually on behalf of a powerless constituency, on an individual or collective basis" (p. 163). In order to effect change the suggestion is that going beyond advocacy which might involve a letter campaign to taking action by being activists. Acting collectively will lead to transformation.

## Action Research

Are there powerless constituencies in early learning? Some may consider children and early learning practitioners as needing empowerment. Ebbeck and Waniganayake (2003) recommend the use of action research as one of the best strategies of empowerment. Undertaken by practitioners, action research involves looking at one's own practice, or a situation involving children's development, behaviour, social interactions, learning difficulties, family involvement, or learning environments, and then reflecting and seeking support and feedback from colleagues. It is an approach to professional development in which early learning practitioners systematically reflect on their work and make changes in their practice (Borgia & Schuler, 1996).

There are three basic steps to action research (Smith, Willms, & Johnson, 1997). The first step is a willingness to investigate a problem that needs to be investigated. An example of a problem might be that children are having difficulty sitting still for the morning circle focusing on the calendar. The second step involves investigation of the problem and the collection of data related to the problem. Here an early learning practitioner's role might be to record instances of children's inattention to the daily rituals of the calendar. The final step is to take action. In this case, it would involve abandoning this daily rote exercise. The practitioner engaged in action research would then go back to the first step and should begin the cycle again. Action research has been referred to as opportunity to change. In the Reggio Emilia approach, action research takes place as a routine and expected function of early learning practitioners (Hill, Stremmel, & Fu, 2005). In a Reggio-inspired classroom, practitioners learn and relearn with children through observation, reflection, speculation, questioning, and theorizing (Kashin, 2009).

## Health Determinants

The World Health Organization (WHO) is the authority for health within the United Nations. The determinants of health are grouped into seven broad categories: socioeconomic environment; physical environments; early childhood development; personal health practices; individual capacity and coping skills; biology and genetic endowment; and health services. The fact that early childhood development is considered a determinant of health is significant. WHO has identified 10 facts about early child development as a social determinant of health listed in Figure 13.4. These provide you with more knowledge as to why it is important to advocate on behalf of children.

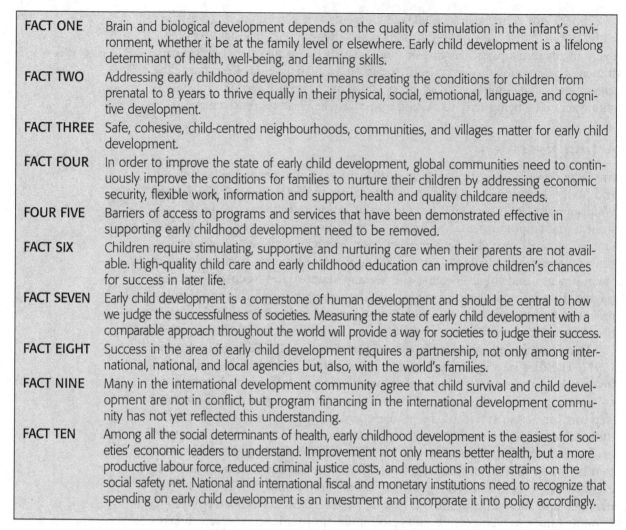

| FACT ONE | Brain and biological development depends on the quality of stimulation in the infant's environment, whether it be at the family level or elsewhere. Early child development is a lifelong determinant of health, well-being, and learning skills. |
| --- | --- |
| FACT TWO | Addressing early childhood development means creating the conditions for children from prenatal to 8 years to thrive equally in their physical, social, emotional, language, and cognitive development. |
| FACT THREE | Safe, cohesive, child-centred neighbourhoods, communities, and villages matter for early child development. |
| FACT FOUR | In order to improve the state of early child development, global communities need to continuously improve the conditions for families to nurture their children by addressing economic security, flexible work, information and support, health and quality childcare needs. |
| FOUR FIVE | Barriers of access to programs and services that have been demonstrated effective in supporting early childhood development need to be removed. |
| FACT SIX | Children require stimulating, supportive and nurturing care when their parents are not available. High-quality child care and early childhood education can improve children's chances for success in later life. |
| FACT SEVEN | Early child development is a cornerstone of human development and should be central to how we judge the successfulness of societies. Measuring the state of early child development with a comparable approach throughout the world will provide a way for societies to judge their success. |
| FACT EIGHT | Success in the area of early child development requires a partnership, not only among international, national, and local agencies but, also, with the world's families. |
| FACT NINE | Many in the international development community agree that child survival and child development are not in conflict, but program financing in the international development community has not yet reflected this understanding. |
| FACT TEN | Among all the social determinants of health, early childhood development is the easiest for societies' economic leaders to understand. Improvement not only means better health, but a more productive labour force, reduced criminal justice costs, and reductions in other strains on the social safety net. National and international fiscal and monetary institutions need to recognize that spending on early child development is an investment and incorporate it into policy accordingly. |

**Figure 13.4** *World Health Organization's 10 Facts about Early Childhood Development as Determinants of Health*

## Healthy Living and Sustainability

"Going green" seems to have become another catchphrase in the early learning community. The growing trend towards adopting "green principles" in child care services are part of a broader sustainability movement, which seeks to meet the needs of the present generation without compromising the ability of future generations to meet their own needs (McKay, 2009). To be sustainable in an early learning setting, it is not enough just to introduce a related theme of the week on the environment or to recycle as an isolated practice. Sustainability is not so much a "lifestyle choice" as it is a way of life and it should become part of daily practice (McKay, 2009). Davis (2010) suggests that everyone—children, families, and practitioners—take a whole centre approach to sustainability. Think of some commonplace toys that children play with or consider some of the consumable materials that are purchased for children's art experiences. Is there a way of reducing consumables? Again we can look to Reggio Emilia for an example.

In Reggio Emilia, the Reminda Centre promotes the idea that waste materials can be resources. They collect, exhibit, and offer alternative and reclaimed materials. These materials are obtained from unsold stock and rejects or discards from industrial and handicraft production, with the aim to reinvent their use and meaning. The educators in Reggio Emilia view the Remida Centre as a cultural project that represents a new, optimistic, and proactive way of approaching environmentalism and building change through giving value to these reject materials that would otherwise be considered worthless objects. The aim is to foster new opportunities for communication and creativity in a perspective of respect for objects, the environment, and human beings.

Do you have anything like a Remida Centre in your area? Davis (2009) states that internationally the early learning sector has been slow to engage in sustainability practices. Elliot (2010) suggests that sustainability practices need to be far-reaching and involve the children, parents, and community. Decisions made about sustainable practices are reinforced by decisions made about play materials and play spaces. For example, a dramatic play area could have purchased plastic pots and utensils and synthetic pretend food or cooking equipment collected from a second-hand shop and natural materials such as leaves or seed pods for pretend food. Involving children and parents as active participants and leaders in sustainable practices has transformative possibilities that can lead to true engagement in the learning process.

## FAMILY RIGHTS AND FAMILY ENGAGEMENT

If we are to continue to consider the three subjects of education: parents, children, and early learning practitioners concurrently with reframing our views, we need to revisit our image of parents. Some early learning practitioners consider parents too bothersome in their demands and look to involving families in limited ways. Including the input of others is essential in a reflective practice and families have a right to be included. The use of pedagogical documentation encourages and promotes inclusion. There are other ways as well.

Pushor (2007) distinguishes between parent involvement and engagement. You might recall a time when your own parents attended an event at your school. Most likely it was the school that set the agenda for the evening. This is considered parent involvement, where the focus is placed "on what the parents can do to help the school realize its intentioned outcomes for children, or on what the parents' hopes, dreams or intentions for their children may be or on what the school can do to help parents realize their personal or family agendas" (p. 3). With engagement early learning practitioners enter into a community to create with families a shared world.

In this final chapter, we hope that you have envisioned the possibilities for this shared world, particularly as they connect to play. We end the chapter with

**RIGHT TO PLAY**

**Mission:** To improve the lives of children in some of the most disadvantaged areas of the world by using the power of sport and play for development, health, and peace.

**Vision:** To create a healthier and safer world through the power of sport and play.

**Values:** Right to Play's values reflect the best practices of sport and play including

CO-OPERATION

HOPE

INTEGRITY

LEADERSHIP

DEDICATION

RESPECT

ENTHUSIASM

NURTURE

**Figure 13.5** *Right to Play's Mission, Vision, and Values*

**Photo 13.4** *All children have a right to play.*

information about an organization devoted to the transformative power of play. *Right to Play* is a leading international humanitarian and development organization devoted to using the power of play to build essential skills in children around the world. This organization is about taking action as a collective. Right to Play creates a safe place for children to learn and fosters the hope that is essential for children to envision and realize a better future. Figure 13.5 illustrates the organization's mission, vision, and values. Consider these in relation to your own developing vision for play. Can you imagine the world being a better place if all children had the right to play?

# SUMMARY

### Chapter Preview

- Early learning practitioners and children are in need of reframed images.

### Terminology Issues

- There are many interchangeable terms for both the field and the practitioner. Terminology issues have historical roots and can reflect different constructions of children and early learning practitioners.

### Programming and Curriculum

- The two terms can be used interchangeably, even though they have different meanings. *Curriculum* is the approach to education that is employed in the classroom. We use the word, *program* for it broader focus. Curriculum has been associated with the traditional prescribed methodology used in classrooms. Programs are co-constructed.

## Emergent Programming

- Emergent curriculum refers to an approach that emerges from the interests of the learner. When it goes beyond interests to focus on children's thinking, it assumes a transformational position.
- Emergent programming involves leading a child to new levels of thinking, scaffolding across the zone of proximal development in a social context.

## Global Perspectives

- Globalism refers to our interconnectedness with others around the world and globalization is the speed in which these connections occur. Reaching out beyond our own contexts to the bigger picture, we can see that there are multiple points of view and perspectives regarding early learning.

## Postmodernism

- A postmodern perspective in early learning is based on the assumption that teaching enacts power relations making multiple voices necessary to prevent privilege. It evolved from the modern romantic view.

## Voice

- Voice is what people mean when they speak of the core of the self. Voice can be seen as a metaphor of development.
- When practitioners, parents, and children share in the learning process with voices heard and heeded, a shift in power occurs.

## The Reconceptualization Movement in Canadian Early Learning

- Reconceptualization involves critically examining the assumptions and knowledge base that have traditionally guided early learning with the goal of reframing it. It is one facet of postmodern thought. Key elements of postmodernism include the openness to the presence of many voices and views.
- Outside of Canada the reconceptualization discourse is more prominent. In the United States, the discourse has focused on DAP—developmentally appropriate practice.

## Critical Thinking

- The DAP discourse is an example of thinking critically about an educational issue. Critically thinking involves pondering the question of who, what, when, where, how, and why.

## Values and Beliefs

- By facing biases openly and acknowledging our values and beliefs we can recognize how they impact practice,

## Image

- The central notion for the philosophy of Reggio Emilia resides in the concept of images. By critically thinking about images, we can begin to see children and early learning practitioners from different perspectives.
- Both children and early learning practitioners are strong, committed, intellectual builders of theories.

## Rethinking Practice

- Early learning practices have been largely developed as a downward extension of school practices. Rethinking the practice of the calendar requires critically thinking about its appropriateness as a way to introduce concepts.
- If young children participate in an activity frequently that they do not really understand, they may lose confidence.
- The most natural and appropriate time to learn concepts is during play.

## Professional Dispositions

- Professional Dispositions include attitudes, values, and beliefs demonstrated, both verbally and nonverbally, when interacting with children, families, colleagues, and communities. Indicators indicate the behaviour you would see demonstrated.

## Reflective Practice

- Reflective practice involves thoughtfully considering one's own experiences in applying knowledge to practice. Research on effective teaching has shown that effective practice is linked to inquiry, reflection, and continuous professional growth.
- Tools for reflective practice can include portfolio development, action research, journal writing, and mentoring relationships.

## Children's Rights

- In the Reggio Emilia view, the child has rights rather than simply needs. The child has a right to be a collaborator and a communicator.
- In 1989, the Convention on the Rights of the Child affirmed human rights for all children incorporating the full range of human rights—including civil, cultural, economic, political, and social rights. It has achieved near-universal acceptance.
- The four core principles are non-discrimination; devotion to the best interests of the child; the right to life, survival and development; and respect for the views of the child.

## Becoming an Advocate of Play

- If you believe that children's play and play-based learning need to be the driving philosophy for early learning, then you need to consider becoming an advocate of play.
- Advocacy is usually defined as the act of advocating for a cause. The first step to becoming an advocate of play is to clarify your own philosophy about how children learn best and most naturally.
- Activism is about taking action. The recommendation is to go beyond advocacy to activism, and by acting collectively transformation is possible.

## Action Research

- Action research is one of the best strategies to encourage empowerment. It is an approach to professional development in which early learning practitioners systematically reflect on their work and make changes in their practice.
- The three basic steps to action research are the following: (1) A willingness to investigate a problem that needs to be investigated. (2) An investigation of the problem and the collection of data related to the problem. (3) The final step is to take action.
- Action research has been referred to as the opportunity to change.

## Health Determinants

- The determinants of health can be grouped into seven broad categories: socioeconomic environment; physical environments; early childhood development; personal health practices; individual capacity and coping skills; biology and genetic endowment; and health services.
- The World Health Organization (WHO) has identified 10 facts about early child development as a social determinant of health.

### Healthy Living and Sustainability

- The trend towards adopting "green principles" in child care services are part of a broader sustainability movement. Sustainability is not a "lifestyle choice" but a way of life that becomes part of daily practice. Recommended is a whole centre approach to sustainability.
- Reggio Emilia provides an example with the Remida Centre, which promotes the idea that waste materials can be resources. The educators in Reggio Emilia view the Remida Centre as a cultural project.
- Decisions made about play materials and play spaces are two examples of how to reflect on sustainability issues.

### Family Rights and Family Engagement

- Revisiting the image of the family to be more inclusive involves pedagogical documentation.
- Parent engagement is distinct from parent involvement. With engagement early learning practitioners enter into a community to create with families a shared world.
- Play has transformational possibilities for this shared world. Children all over the world have a right to play.

## REVIEW QUESTIONS

1. What historical influences have resulted in terminology issues within the early learning field?
2. Describe the cycle of emergent programming.
3. Explain what is meant by a postmodern perspective and relate this paradigm to the reconceptualization movement in early learning.
4. What is developmentally appropriate practice and why has this approach received criticism?
5. Demonstrate critical thinking by apply the concept of image to a cognitive organizer—who, what, where, why, when, and how.
6. How do values impact practice?
7. What is a behavioural indicator for the professional disposition of flexibility in practice?
8. Distinguish between the concept of children's rights in relation to the concept of children's needs.
9. What is the difference between advocacy and activism?
10. What are the three steps of action research?
11. Explain the 10 facts about early development as a determinant of health.
12. What is sustainability? Give a local and a global example.
13. How does engagement differ from involvement?

## MAKING CONNECTIONS

### Theory to Practice

1. Write your own treatise on play which can become your play mission for the work that you do with children.
2. Observe a morning calendar circle experience. Reflect on your observations and think critically about the practice. Can you come up with ways to reinforce calendar concepts during play?
3. Identify five short-term and five long-term professional goals that you can identify for your further growth and development.
4. Identify and implement an action research project.
5. Develop a policy for sustainability that could be applied to an early learning setting.

## For Further Research

1. The United Nations Convention on the Rights of the Child sets out these rights in 54 articles and two Optional Protocols, which can be found at www.unicef.org/rightsite/237_202.htm.
2. The Convention of Rights has achieved near-universal acceptance. Which two countries have not signed on? Do some research to find out why?
3. Codes of Ethics and Standards of Practice are two ways to find out more about professional expectations for practice. In Ontario, the College of ECE is a groundbreaking regulatory body that aims to protect the public interest by focusing on quality and standards in the practice of early childhood education. Look up the Code of Ethics as Standards of Practice at www.collegeofece.on.ca. Do you think that anything is missing? Compare these to other Codes of Ethics or Standards of Practice that you can find on the internet—perhaps ones that are from your own province or territory.
4. The philosophy, theoretical foundation, and guiding principles of the Reggio Emilia approach offer ample research possibilities. Take one aspect of the approach, such as 1) the image of the child, 2) the environment as the third teacher, 3) the teacher as researcher, 4) pedagogical documentation, 5) transparency, 6) collaboration, and create a thesis statement and follow up with research to support your position. For example, *the image of the child as having rights encourages collaboration* would be an example of a statement. Can you create a five-paragraph essay that builds on this statement? Can you write your own statement? Your next step would be to find the research to support the statement. Once you have at least three possible paragraphs that you can write that will build your position, write an introduction and summary. If you approach this task with a critical eye you end up with many ideas for further research. May the quest for knowledge lead your journey.

# ADDITIONAL READING

Ayers, W. (2001). *To teach: A journey of a teacher,* New York: Teachers College Press.

Friere, P. (1970). *Pedagogy of the oppressed,* New York: Continuum.

Hooks, B. (2010). *Teaching critical thinking: Practical wisdom,* New York: Routledge.

# WEBLINKS

**www.healthychild.net/SafetyFirst.php?article_id=516**

**www.righttoplay.com**

**http://unesdoc.unesco.org/images/0015/001593/159355e.pdf**

**http://zerosei.comune.re.it/inter/remida.htm**

# References

Ahn, J. & Filipenko, M. (2007). Narrative, imaginary play, art, and self: Intersecting worlds. *Early Childhood Education Journal, 34,* No. (4), 279–289.

Ainsa, T. (1989). Effects of computers and training in Head Start curriculum. *Journal of Instructional Psychology, 16,* 72–78.

Alcock, S. (2000). *Pedagogical documentation: Beyond observations.* Occasional paper No. 7. Victoria University of Wellington, New Zealand.

Aldridge, J. (2005). The importance of oral language. *Childhood Education, 81,* 77–81.

Alliance for Childhood. (2004). *Time for Play Every Day: It's Fun—and Fundamental.* Retrieved January 15, 2010, from http://www.allianceforchildhood.net/projects/play/pdf_files/play_fact.sheet.pdf

Alliance for Childhood. (2004). *Tech Tonic: Towards a New Literacy of Technology, Alliance for Childhood.* College Park, MD.

Almon, J. & Miller, E. (2009). *Crisis in the kindergarten: Why children need to play in school.* College Park, MD: Alliance for Childhood.

American Library Association (ALA). (1998). New repost shows more libraries connect to the Internet, access still limited. *American Library Association— Washington Office Newsline, 7*(149). (On-line). Retrieved February 1, 2010, from http://www.ala.org

Anderson, K. L., Martin, D. M., & Faszewski, E. F. (2006). Unlocking the power of observation. *Science and Children,* September, 32–35.

Atlas, J. & Lapidus, L. (1987). Patterns of symbolic expression in subgroups of the childhood psychoses. *Journal of Clinical Psychology, 43,* 177–188.

Ayers, W. (1992). Disturbances from the field: Recovering the voice of the early childhood teacher. In S. A. Kessler & B. B. Weadener (Eds.), *Reconceptualizing the early childhood curriculum: Beginning the dialogue* (236–266). New York: Teacher's College Press.

Balaban, N. (1995). Seeing the child, knowing the person. In Ayers, W. *To Become a Teacher.* Teachers College Press. 49–58.

Barnes, H. (2008). The value of superhero play. *Putting Children First,* National Childcare Accreditation Council (NCAC) Issue 27, 18–21.

Barrett, M. (2006). Inventing songs, inventing worlds: The "genesis" of creative thought and activity in young children's lives. *International Journal of Early Years Education, 14*(3), October 2006, 201–220.

Beder, S. (1998). *A "community view," caring for children in the media age.* Papers from a national conference, edited by John Squires and Tracy Newlands, New College Institute for Values Research, Sydney.

Beneke, S. J., Ostrosky, M. M., & Katz, L. G. (2008). Calendar time for young children: Good intentions gone awry. *Young Children* May. 12–16.

Bennet, T. (2001). Reactions to visiting the infant-toddler and preschool centres in Reggio Emilia, Italy. *Early Childhood Research & Practice.*Retrieved May, 2010, from http://ecrp.uiuc.edu/v3n1/bennett.html.

Bennett, J. (2000, May 11). *Goals, curricula and quality monitoring in early childhood systems.* Organization for Economic Co-operation and Development, Consultative meeting on international developments in ECEC, Paris, France.

Benson, H. (2003). Glossary of math terms. *Young Children,* NAEYC. 1–2.

Bergen, D. (2002). The role of pretend play in children's cognitive development. *Early Childhood Research and Practice, 4*(1), 1–13.

Bergen, D. (2009). *Play and brain development as complementary nonlinear dynamic (chaotic/complex) systems.* Miami University, Osford: OH. Retrieved March 2, 2010, from http://jan.ucc.nau.edu/chap;x-p/docs/play2_bergen.pdf.

Berk, L. (2002). *Infants, children, and adolescents.* Boston, MA: Allyn & Bacon.

Berk, L. E. & Spuhl, S. T. (1995). Maternal interaction, private speech, and task performance in preschool children. *Developmental Psychology 20,* 271–286.

Berner, M. M. (1992). Building conditions, parental involvement, and student achievement in the District of Columbia Public School System. *Urban Education, 28*(1), 6–29.

Beyer, H. & Holtzblatt, K. (1997). *Contextual design: Designing customer-centered systems.* San Francisco, CA: Morgan Kaufmann.

Bilton, H. (2002). *Outdoor play in the early years: Management and innovation.* London: David Fulton.

Bloch, M. N. & Pelligrini, A. D. (1989). Ways of looking at children, context, and play. In M. N. Bloch & A. D. Pellegrini (Eds.), *The ecological context of children's play.* Norwood, NJ: Ablex Publishing Corporation.

Bloom, B. S. (Ed.). (1956). *Taxonomy of educational objectives: The classification of educational goals: Handbook 1, cognitive domain*, New York: Longmans, Green.

Bodrova, E. & Leong, D. J. (1996). *Tools of the mind: The Vygotskian approach to early childhood education.* Upper Saddle River, NJ: Merrill Prentice Hall.

Bodrova, E. & Leong, D. J. (2004). Chopsticks and counting chips. Do play and foundational skills need to compete for the teacher's attention in an early childhood classroom? *Young Children, 58*(3), pp. 12–19.

Boe, T. (1989). The next step for educators and the technology industry: Investing in teachers. *Educational Technology, 29*(3), 39–44.

Borgia, E. T. & Schuler, D. (1996). Action research in early childhood education. Urbana, IL: *ERIC Digest* Clearinghouse on Elementary and Early Childhood Education. (ERIC Document Reproduction Service No. ED401047).

Boss, S. (2001). Breaking out of the box. *Northwest Education Magazine, 6*(4). Retrieved January 4, 2010, from www.nwrel.org/nwedu/summer01/breakingout.html

Bosse, S., Jacobs, G., & Anderson, T. L. (2009). Science in the air. *Young Children*, November, 10–15.

Bouffard, M., Watkinson, E. J., Thompson, L. P., Dunn, J. L. C., & Romanow, S. K. E. (1996). A test of the activity deficit hypothesis with children with movement difficulties. *Adapted Physical Activity Quarterly, 13*, 61–73.

Bowen, C. (1998). *Ages and stages. Developmental milestones for receptive and expressive language development.* Retrieved February 4, 2010, from http://www.speech-language-therapy.com/devel2.htm

Bredekamp, S. (1987). *Developmentally appropriate practice in early childhood programs serving young children from birth to age 8* (Expanded Ed.). Washington, DC: National Association for the Education of Young Children.

Bredekamp, S. (2004). *Play and school readiness.* In E. F. Zigler, D. G. Singer, & S. J. Bishop-Josef (Eds.), *Children's play: The roots of reading.* Washington, DC: Zero to Three Press.

Bredekamp, S. & Copple, C. (1997). (Eds.). *Developmentally Appropriate Practice in Early Childhood Programs* (rev. ed). Washington, DC: National Association for the Education of Young Children.

Bredekamp, S. & Rosegrant, T. (1994). Learning and teaching with technology. In J. Wright, & D. Shade (Eds.) (1994), *Young Children: Active learners in a technological age.* Washington, DC: National Association for the Education of Young Children.

Brenneman, K., Stevenson-Boyd, J., & Frede, E. C. (2009). Math and science in preschool: Policies and practice. Preschool Policy Brief. *National Institute for Early Education Research*: March, Issue 19, 1–11.

Broadhead, P. (2006). Developing an understanding of young children's learning through play: The place of observation, interaction and reflection. *British Educational Research Journal, 32*(2, April 2006), 191–207.

Bronfenbrenner, U. (1979). *The ecology of human development. Cambridge,* MA: Harvard University Press.

Brooks, J. G. & Brooks, M. G. (1999). *The case for constructivist classrooms.* Alexandria, VA: Association for Supervision and Curriculum Development.

Brown, E. (1975). Developmental characteristics of clay figures made by children from age three through the age of eleven. *Studies in Art Education, 16*(3), pp. 45–53.

Brown, E. (1984). Developmental characteristics of clay figures by children: 1970–1982, *Studies in Art Education, 26*(1), 56–60.

Brown, M. R., Higgins, K., & Hartley, K. (2001). Teachers and technology equity. *Teaching Exceptional Children, 38*(4), 32–39.

Browne, D. L. & Ritchie, D. C. (1991). Cognitive apprenticeship: A model of staff development for implementing technology in schools. *Contemporary Education, 63*(1), 28–33.

Bruner J. (1972). The nature and uses of immaturity. *American Psychologist, 27*, 687–708.

Bruner, J. (1973). *Going beyond the information given.* New York: Norton.

Bruner, J. (1986). *Actual minds, possible worlds.* Cambridge, MA: Harvard University Press.

Bruner, J. S. (1968). *Toward a theory of instruction.* New York: Norton.

Burg, K. (1984). The microcomputer in the kindergarten. *Young Children, 39*(3), 28–33.

Butterworth, B. (1999). *The mathematical brain.* London: Nelson.

Cadwell, L. (1997). *Bringing Reggio Emilia home: An innovative approach to early childhood education.* New York: Teacher's College Press.

Cadwell, L. B. (2003). *The Reggio approach to early childhood education: Bringing learning to life.* New York: Teacher's College Press.

Caldwell, B. (2004). What's in a name? *Child Care Information Exchange.* Retrieved March 16, 2004, from http://mail.ccie.com/go/eed/0135

Campbell, D. (2000). *The Mozart effect for children: Awakening your child's mind, health, and creativity with music.* New York: HarperCollins.

Canadian Association for the Education of Young Children. (2006). *Play. Young children have the right to learn through play*. Retrieved December 9, 2009, from http://www.cayc.ca/pdf/playstmnt/playstatementrevision2.pdf

Canadian Child Care Federation (CCCF)/Canadian Child Care Advocacy Association of Canada. (2003). *What does the public want!* Fact Sheet 1. 1–2. Ottawa, Ontario, Canada: Author.

Canadian Child Care Federation (CCCF). (2005). *Early learning and child care in Canada: Moving toward a pan-Canadian system*. Ottawa, Ontario, Canada: Author.

Canadian Child Care Federation (CCCF). (2010). *Foundations for numeracy: An evidence-based toolkit for early learning practitioners*. Ottawa, Ontario, Canada: Author.

Canadian Children's Right Council. (2009). http://www.canadiancrc.com/default.aspx

Canadian Heritage. (2007). *Canadian Multiculturalism: An inclusive citizenship*. Retrieved May, 2010, from http://www.canadianheritage.gc.ca/progs/multi/inclusive_e.cfm

Canadian Institute of Child Health. (2008). *The first years last forever. The new brain research and your child's health development*. Retrieved March, 2010, from http://www.cich.ca/PDFFiles/FirstYearsEngWEB.pdf

Canadian Language and Literacy Research Network (CLLRNet). (2009*). National Strategy for Early Literacy Report and Recommendations*.

Canadian Standards Association. (2008). *Children's playspaces and equipment*. Mississauga, ON: The Association.

Canadian Toy Testing Council. (2001). *"I want that!": The impact of current trends and practices shaping the advertising of toys to children in the global market place*. Nepean, ON. Retrieved January 5, 2010, from http://www.toy-testing.org/images/bz_ms_intro.pdf

Canning, P., Courage, M., & Frizzell, L. (2004). *Overweight and obesity in preschool children in Newfoundland and Labrador*. Centre of Excellence for Children & Adolescents with Special Needs.

Canning, P., Courage, M., & Frizzell, L. (2004). Prevalence of overweight and obesity in a provincial population of Canadian preschool children. *Canadian Medical Association Journal, 171,* 240–242.

Caples, S. (1996). Some guidelines for preschool design. *Young Children, 51*(4): 14–21.

Carlson, A. (2002). Environmental aesthetics. In E. Craig (Ed.), *Routledge Encyclopedia of Philosophy*. London. Retrieved January 5, 2010, from www.rep.routledge.com/article/M047SECT1

Carr, D. (1992) Practical inquiry, values and the problem of educational theory, *Oxford Review of Education, 18*(3), 241–251.

Carter, M. & Curtis, D. (1996). *Reflecting children's lives: A handbook for planning child-centered curriculum*. St. Paul, MN: Redleaf Press.

Carter, M. & Curtis, D. (2008). *Learning together with young children: A curriculum framework for reflective teachers*. St. Paul, MN: Redleaf Press.

Cartwright, C. A., & Cartwright, G. P. (1974). *Developing observation skills*. New York: McGraw-Hill Book Co.

Cassell, J. (2008). *Children with autism may learn from "virtual peers."* Retrieved January 5, 2009, from http://www.eurekalert.org/pub_releases/2008-02/nu-cwa022908

Chaille, C. (2008). *Constructivism across the curriculum in early childhood classrooms: Big ideas as inspiration*. Boston, MA: Pearson.

Chapman, L. H. (1978). *Approaches to art in education*. New York: Harcourt Brace Jovanovich.

Charlesworth, R. (2000). *Experiences in math for young children*. Albany, NY: Delmar.

Chen, J. Q. & Chang, C. (2006). Using computers in early childhood classrooms" Teachers' attitudes, skills and practices. *Journal of Early Childhood Research, 4*(2), 169–188.

Chen, J. Q. & Price, V. (2006). *Narrowing the digital divide. A cross-country analysis of computer and Internet penetration*. Discussion paper #881, Yale University Economic Growth Centre. Yale University, new Haven, CT.

Children's Play Council (2004). *Children's Play Council policy positions. Risk and challenge in children's play*. Retrieved 15 May, 2010, from http://www.ncb.org.uk/dotpdf/open%20access%20-%phase%20 only/policyrisk_cpc_2004.pdf

Christie, J. & Wardle, F (1992). How much time is needed for play? *Young Children, 47*(3), 26–32.

Christie J. F. & Roskos, K. A. (2009). Play's potential in early literacy development. In Tremblay R.E., Barr R.G., Peters R., & Boivin M, eds. *Encyclopedia on early childhood development* [online]. Montreal, Quebec: Centre of Excellence for Early Childhood Development; 2009:1–6.

Church, E. L. (2003). Scientific thinking: Step by step. *Scholastic Early Childhood Today 17*(6), 35–41.

Clements, D. (2004). Mathematics and recommendations. In Clements, D. Sarama, J. & DiBiase, A. (Eds.), *Engaging young children in mathematics:*

*Standards for early childhood mathematics education* (7–72). Mahwah, NJ: Lawrence Erlbaum Associates.

Clements, D. (2005). Beyond "1,2,3. . .": Computers and mathematical thinking. Palmer, D. W. In *More than numbers: Mathematical thinking in the early years*, Redmond, WA: *Exchange*, 16–19.

Clements, D. H. (1999). Young children and technology. In G. D. Nelson (Ed.), *Dialogue on early childhood science, mathematics, and technology education* (pp. 92–105). Washington, DC: American Association for the Advancement of Science.

Clements, D. H. (1993). Computer technology and early childhood education. In J. L. Roopnarine & J. E. Johnson (Eds.), *Approaches to early childhood education* (2nd ed.), pp. 295–316. New York: Merrill.

Clements, D. H. (1993). Early education principles and computer practices. In C. G. Hass & F. W. Parkay (Eds.), *Curriculum planning: A new approach* (6th ed.). Boston, MA: Allyn & Bacon.

Clements, D. H. & Nastasi, B. K. (1993). Electronic media and early childhood education. In *Handbook of research on the education of young children*, ed. B. Spodek, 251–275. New York: Macmillan.

Clements, D. H., Nastasi, B. K., & Swaminathan, S. (1993). Young children and computers: Crossroads and directions for research. *Young Children, 48*(2): 56–64.

Clements, D. H. & Sarama, J. (2005). Young children and technology: What's appropriate? In W. Masalski & P. C. Elliott (Eds.), *Technology-supported mathematics learning environments: 67th yearbook (51–73)*. Reston, VA: National Council of Teachers of Mathematics.

Clements, D. H. & Swaminathan, S. (1995). Technology and school change: New lamps or old? *Childhood Education, 71*, 275–281.

Click, P., Parker, J., & Stone-Zukowski, D. (2006). *Caring for school-age children*. First Canadian edition. Toronto, ON: Thomson Nelson.

Click, P. & Parker, J. (2008). *Caring for school-age children*. Clifton Park, NY: Delmar.

Cohen, L., & Uhry, J. (2007). Young children's discourse during block play. *Journal of Research in Childhood Education, 21*, 302–308.

Cole, T. J., Belizzi, M. C., Flegal, K. M., & Dietz, W. H. (2000). *Establishing a standard definition for child overweight and obesity worldwide*. National survey. BMJ *320*:1240–1243.

Colvin, S (2005). Math milestones: Abilities of children of different ages. In *More than numbers: Mathematical*

thinking inn the early years, Redmond, WA: *Exchange*, 39–45.

Conrad, A. (1995). *Content analysis of block play literature*. University of Memphis, ERIC, pp. 1–27.

Copley, J. (2000). *The young child and mathematics*. Washington, DC: National Association for the Education of Young Children.

Corbett, B. (1979). *A garden of children*. Mississauga, Ontario: The Froebel Kindergarten Foundation.

Cordes, C. & Miller, E. (2000). *Fools gold: A critical look at children and computers*. The Alliance for Childhood, College Park, MD. Retrieved October 2009 from http://www.alianceforchildhood.net/ projects/computers/computers-reports.htm.

Cornett, C. E. & Smithrim, K. L. (2001). *The arts as meaning makers: Integrating literature and the arts throughout the curriculum*. Toronto, ON: Pearson Education Canada.

Craig, G., Kermis, M. D., & Digdon, N. L. (2002). *Children today*. Toronto, ON: Pearson Education Canada.

Craig, C. L., Cameron, C., Storm, Russell, S. J., & Beaulieu, A. (2001). *Increasing physical activity: Supporting children's participation*. Ottawa, ON: Canadian Fitness and Lifestyles Research Institute. Retrieved May, 2010, from http://www.cflri.ca/pdf/ e/2002pam.pdf.

Crossley, B. & Dietze, B. (2002). Opening the door to the outdoors. *Canadian Child Care Federation*. Available at http://www.cccf-fcsge.ca/practice/programming/ openingtooutdoors_en.htm

Crowther, I. (2003). *Creating effective learning environments*. Scarborough, ON: Canada: Thomson and Nelson.

Custodero, L. A. (2002). The musical lives of young children: Inviting, seeking, and initiating. *Zero to Three, 25*, 4–9.

Custodera, L. (2002). Seeking challenge, finding skill: Flow experience and music education. *Arts Education Policy Review, 103*(3) (February/March, 2002), 3–9.

Cutler, K. M., Gilkerson, D., Parrott, S., & Bowne, M. T. (2003). Developing math games based on children's literature. *Young Children, 58*(1), 22–27.

Dahlberg, G. & Moss, P. (2005). *Ethics and Politics in Early Childhood Education*. London and New York: Routledge Falmer.

Dahlberg, G., Moss, P., & Pence, A. (1999). *Beyond quality in early childhood education and care: Postmodern perspectives*. London: Falmer Press.

Damon, W. (1984). Peer education: The untapped potential. *Journal of Applied Development Psychology, 5*(1984), 331–343.

Danisa, D., Gentile, J., McNamara, K., Pinney, M., Ross, S., & Rule, A. C. (2006). Geoscience for preschoolers. *Science and Children,* December, National Science Teachers Association, 30–34.

David, T. (1999). Changing minds: young children learning. In T. David (Ed.). *Young children learning.* London: Chapman, 1–12.

David, T. & Weinstein, C. (1987). The built environment and children's development. In C. Weinstein & T. David (Eds.). *Spaces for children, 3*(18), New York: Plenum Press.

Davidson, J. (1996). *Emergent literacy and dramatic play in early education.* Albany, NY: Delmar.

Davidson, J., & Wright, J. L. (1994). The potential of the microcomputer in the early childhood classroom. In *Young children: Active learners in a technological age,* ed. J. L. Wright and D. D. Shade, 77–91. Washington, DC: National Association for the Education of Young Children.

Davidson, L. (1985). Preschool children's tonal knowledge: Antecedents of scale. In J. Boswell (Ed.), *The child and music* (pp. 25–40). Reston, VA: Music Educators National Conference.

Davis, G. A. & Keller, J. D. (2007). *Exploring science and mathematics in a child's world.* Upper Saddle River, NJ: Pearson.

Davis, J. M. (2009). Revealing the research "hole" of early childhood education for sustainability: A preliminary survey of the literature. *Environmental Education Research 15*(2), 227–241.

Davis, J. M. (2010). Early childhood education for sustainability: Why it matters, what it is, and how whole centre action research and systems thinking can help. *Journal of Action Research Today in Early Childhood,* 34–40.

Dempsey, J. & Strickland, E. (1999). Staff workshop teacher handout: The whys have it! Why to include loose parts on the playground. *Early Childhood Today, 14*(1): 24–25.

Derman-Sparks, L. & ABC Task Force. (1989). *Anti-bias curriculum: Tools for empowering young children.* Washington, DC: NAEYC.

deVries, P. (2004). The extramusical effects of music lessons on preschoolers. *Australian Journal of Early Childhood 29*(22), 6–10.

Dewey, J. (1934). *Art as experience.* New York: Minton, Balch, London: Allen & Unwin.

Dewey, J. (1990/1956). *The child and the curriculum and the school and society.* London: The University of Chicago Press.

Dickinson, D. K. (2001). Putting the pieces together: The impact of preschool on children's language and literacy development in kindergarten. In D. K. Dickinson & P. O. Tabors (Eds.), *Beginning literacy with language: Young children learning at home and school* (257–287). Baltimore, MD: Brookes Publishing.

Dickinson, D. & Tabors, P. (2001). *Beginning literacy with language: Young children learning at home and school.* Baltimore, MD: Brookes Publishing.

Dietze, B. (2006). *Foundations of early childhood education: Learning environments and child care in Canada.* Toronto, ON: Pearson.

Dietze, B. & Crossley, B. (2003). Opening the door to outdoor play. *Interaction,* (Fall) Canadian Child Care Federation.

Dietze, B. & Crossley, B. (Fall 2003). Two cultures/two approaches: Outdoor play in Jordan and Norway. *Interaction.* The Canadian Child Care Federation.

Donley, S. (1987). *Drawing development in children.* Retrieved January 5, 2010, from http://www. learning design.com/Portfolio/DrawDev/kiddrawing.html

Dorman, P. E. (1990). The importance of musical play centres for young children. *General Music Today, 3*(3): 15–17.

Downing, J. E. & Seigel-Causey, L. (1988). Enhancing the nonsymbolic communicative behavior of children with multiple impairments. *Language, Speech, and Hearing Services in Schools, 19,* 338–348.

Driscoll, A. & Nagel, N. (2005). *Early childhood education, birth—8. The world of children, families, and educators.* Boston, MA: Allyn & Bacon.

Druin, A. & Solomon, C. (1996). *Designing multimedia environments for children: Computers, creativity, and kids.* NY: John Wiley and Sons.

Duberry, K. (2001). Risk taking and achievements outdoors. *Early Childhood Practice, 3*(1), 67–70.

Dudek, M. (2000). *Kindergarten architecture: Space for the imagination,* (2nd ed.) Independence, KY: Spon Press.

Easton, F. (1997). Educating the whole child, "head, heart, and hands." Learning from the Waldorf experience. *Theory into Practice, 36*(2). EBSCO HOST Research databases No. 0040-5841.

Ebbeck, M. & Waniganayake, M. (2003). *Early childhood professionals. Leading today and tomorrow.* Sydney: MacLennan and Petty.

Eckhoff, A. (2008). The importance of art viewing experiences in early childhood visual arts: The exploration of a master art teacher's strategies for meaningful early arts experiences. *Early Childhood Education Journal*.

Edwards, C. P. (2002). Three approaches from Europe: Waldorf, Montessori, and Reggio Emilia. *Early Childhood Research and Practice*, 4(1). Retrieved May, 2010, from http://ecrp.uiuc.educ/v4n1/edwards.html.

Edwards, C., Gandini, L., & Forman, G. (1998). *The hundred languages of children—The Reggio Emilia approach—advanced reflections* (Second Edition). Greenwich, Connecticut: Ablex.

Eisner, E. W. (1991). *The enlightened eye: Qualitative inquiry and the enhancement of educational practice*. New York: Macmillan.

Elkind, D. (1996). Young Children and technology: A cautionary note. *Young Children*, 5(6), 22–23.

Elkind, D. (2004). Thanks for the memory: The lasting value of true play. In D. Koralek (Ed.). *Spotlight on young children and play* (pp. 36–41). Washington: National Association for the Education of Young Children.

Elkind, D. (2007, November/December), Preschool academics, learning that comes naturally. *The Early Childhood Leaders' Magazine*, 170, 6–9.

Elliott, S. (2010). Essential not optional—education for sustainability in early childhood centres. *Exchange*, March/April, 34–37.

Ellis, J. J. (1973). *Why people play*. Upper Saddle River, NJ: Prentice Hall.

Erikson, E. H. (1963). *Childhood and society*. New York: Norton.

Erikson, E. H. (1982). *The life cycle completed: A review*. New York: W. W. Norton.

Evans, G. W. & Cohen, S. (1987). Environmental stress. In I. Altman & D. Stokols (Eds.), *Handbook of environmental psychology* (pp. 571–610). New York: Wiley.

Fang, Z. & Cox, B. (1999). Emergent metacognition: A study of preschool literate behaviour. *Journal of Research in Childhood Education*, 13(2), 175–187.

Fenech, M., Sumsion, J., & Goodfellow, J. (2006). The regulatory environment in long day care: A "double-edged sword" for early childhood practice. *Australian Journal of Early Childhood*, 31(3), 49–58.

Ferguson, E. (2004). *What's in a name?* Ottawa, Ontario, Canada: Canadian Child Care Federation.

Ferraro, J. M. (2000). *Reflective practice and professional development*. Washington, DC: ERIC Clearinghouse on Teacher and Teacher Education.

(ERIC Document Reproduction Service No. ED449120)

Fischer, M. A. & Gillespie, C. W. (2003). One head start classroom's experience: Computers and young children's development. *Young Children*, 58(4), 85–91.

Fisher, E. P. (1992). The impact of play on development: A meta-analysis. *Play and Culture*, 5, 159–181.

Fisher, P. (2008). Learning about literacy: From theories to trends. *Teacher Librarian*, 35, 8–12.

Fjortoft, I. (2001). The natural environment as a playground for children: The impact of outdoor play activities in pre-primary school children. *Early Childhood Education Journal*, 29(2), 111–117.

Fjortoft, I. & Sageie, J. (2000). The natural environment as a playground for children: Landscape description and analysis of a natural playscape. *Landscape and Urban Planning*, 43(1/2), 83–97.

Flesh, R. (1955). *Why Johnny can't read: And what you can do about it*. New York: Harper.

Flowers, P. J. & Dunne-Sousa, D. (1990). Pitch-pattern accuracy, tonality, and vocal range in preschool children's singing. *Journal of Research in Music Education*, 31(2), 93–99.

Fox, J. E. (1993). Assessing cognitive development by observing children's outdoor play. In M. Guddemi & T. Jambor, (Eds.), *A right to play: Proceedings of the American Affiliate of the International Association for the Child's Right to Play*, September 17–20, 1992, Denton, Texas, (pp. 128–131). Little Rock, AK: Southern Early Childhood Association.

Fraser, D. (2000). Metaphorical pleasures; children's exploration of the self through writing. *English in Aotearoa*, 40, 27–33.

Fraser, D. (2000). *Curriculum integration: What it is and is not*. SET: Research Information for Teachers, 3, 34–37.

Fraser, D. (2000). *Danceplay: Creative movement for very young children*. Lincoln, NE: Authors Choice Press.

Fraser, S. & Gestwicki, C. (2001). *Authentic childhood: Experiencing Reggio Emilia in the classroom*. Albany, NY: Delmar.

Freeman, N. K. & Somerindyke, J. (2001). Social play at the computer: Preschoolers scaffold and support peers' computer competence. *Information Technology in Childhood Education*, 13, 203–213.

Freyberg, J. T. (1973). Increasing the imaginative play of urban disadvantaged kindergarten children through systematic training. In J. L. Singer (Ed.), *The child's world of make-believe*, (pp. 129–154). New York: Academic Press.

Friedberg, P. & Berkeley, E. (1970). *Play and Interplay*. London: The Macmillan Company.

Friendly, M. & Prabhu, N. (2010). Can early childhood education and care help keep Canada's promise of respect for diversity? Occasional Paper 23, *Childcare Resource and Research Unit*, January 2010, p. 28. Retrieved from http://www.childcarecanada.org/pubs/op23/crru_op23_diversity.pdf

Froebel F. (1889). *Autobiography of Friedrick Froebel* (E. Michaelis & K. Moore, Trans.). Syracuse, NY: Bardeen.

Fromberg, D. P. (2002). *Play and meaning in early childhood education*. Boston, MA: Allyn & Bacon.

Fromberg, D. P. & Gullo, D. F. (1992). Perspectives on children. In L. R. Williams & D. P. Fromberg (Eds.). *Encyclopedia of early childhood education*, (pp. 191–194). New York: Garland Publishing.

Frost, J. L. (1992). *Play and playscapes*. New York: Delmar Publishing Inc.

Frost, J. L., Wortham, S. C., & Reifel, S. (2008). *Play and child development*. (3rd ed). Upper Saddle River, NJ: Pearson.

Frost, J. L., Wortham, S., & Reifel, S. (2001). *Play and child development*. Upper Saddle River, NJ: Merrill Prentice Hall.

Fu, V. R. (2002). The challenge to reinvent the Reggio Emilia approach: Pedagogy of hope and possibilities. In V. R. Fu, A. J. Stremmel, & L. T. Hill (Eds.), *Teaching and learning: Collaborative exploration of the Reggio Emilia Approach* ( 23–35). Upper Saddle Tree, NJ: Merrill Prentice Hall.

Furedi, F. (2001). *Paranoid parenting: Abandon your anxieties and be a good parent*. London: Penguin.

Furman, L. (2000). In support of drama in early childhood education, again. *Early Childhood Education Journal, 27*(3), 173–178.

Gallahue, D. L. (1993). Motor development and movement skill acquisition in early childhood education. In B. Spodek (Ed.). *Handbook of research on the education of young children* (pp. 24–41). New York: Macmillan.

Gallahue, D. L. & Ozmun, J. C. (1995). *Understanding motor development: Infants, children, adolescents, adults*. Madison, WI: Brown & Benchmark.

Gallenstein, N. L. (2004). Creative discovery through classification. *Teaching Children Mathematics*, September, 103–107.

Gallistel, C. R. & Gelman, R. (1990). The what and how of counting, *Cognition, 24*(2), 197–199.

Gandini, L. (2004). Foundations of the Reggio Emilia Approach. In J. Hendrick, (Ed.), *First steps toward teaching the Reggio way: Accepting the challenge to change* (pp. 13–26). Upper Saddle River, NJ: Pearson.

Gandini, L. (1998). Educational and caring spaces. In C. P. Edwards, L. Gandini, & G. Forman (Eds.), *The hundred languages of children: The Reggio Emilia approach to early childhood education* (pp. 161–178). Norwood, NJ: Ablex Publishing Corporation.

Gandini, L. & Goldhaber, J. (2001). Two reflections about documentation. In L. Gandini & C.P. Edwards (Eds.), *Bamini: the Italian approach to infant/toddler care* (pp. 124–145). New York: Teachers College Press.

Garcia, C., Garcia, L., Floyd, J., & Lawson, J. (2002). Improving the public health through early childhood movement programs. *Journal of Physical Development, 27*–31.

Gardner, H. (1993). *Frames of mind: The theory of multiple intelligences* (10th anniversary ed.). New York: Basic Books.

Gardner, H. (1999). *Intelligence reframed: Multiple intelligences for the 21st century*. New York: Basic Books. Note date of Gardner (1996)

Garrison, M. & Christakis, D. A. (2005). *A teacher in the livingroom: Educational media for babies, toddlers, and preschoolers*. Menlo Park, CA: The Henry J. Kaiser Family Foundation.

Geary, D. C. (2006). Developmental of mathematical understanding. In W. Damon (Series Ed.), D. Kuhl, & R.S. Seigler (Eds.), *Handbook of child psychology: Vol. 2. Cognition, perception, and language* (6th ed., 777–810). New York: Wiley.

Gerbner, G., Gross, L., Morgan, M., & Signorielli, N. (1994). Growing up with television: The cultivation perspective. In J. Bryant & D. Zillmann (Eds.), *Media effects: Advances in theory and research* (pp. 17–41). Hillsdale, NJ: Erlbaum.

Gesell, A. (1940). *The first five years of life: A guide to the study of the preschool child*. New York: Harper and Row.

Gilligan, C. (1993). *In a different voice*. Cambridge, MA: Harvard University Press.

Gimbert, B. & Cristol, D. (2004). Teaching curriculum with technology: Enhancing children's technological competence during early childhood. *Early Childhood Education Journal, 31*(3), 207–215. Retrieved June, 2010, from EBSCO database.

Glasser, W. (1998). *Choice theory. A new psychology of personal freedom*. New York: Harper Collins.

Golinkoff, R. M., Hirsh-Pasek, K., & Singer, D. (Eds.) (2006). *Play=Learning: How play motivates and enhances children's cognitive and social-emotional growth.* New York: Oxford University Press.

Goncu, A. & Klein, E. (Eds.). (2001). *Children in play, story, and school.* New York: Guilford.

Goncu, A., Mistry, J., & Mosier, C. (2000). Cultural variations in the play of toddlers. *International Journal of Behavioral Development, 24*(3), 321–329.

Goncu, A. & Weber, A. (2000). Preschoolers' classroom activities and interactions with peers and teachers. *Early Education and Development, 11*(1): 93–107.

Goodenough, F. (1926). *Measurement of intelligence by drawing.* New York: Harcourt, Brace & World.

Goodyear-Smith, F. A. & Laidlaw, T. M. (1999). The price of safety at all costs. *Nuance, 1*, 15–21.

Gopnik, A., Kuhl, P. K., Meltzoff, A. (2001). *The Scientist in the crib: What early learning tells us about the mind.* Phoenix, AZ: New Ed edition.

Goswami, U. (2002). *The Blackwell handbook of childhood cognitive development.* Oxford, UK: Blackwell.

Greenberg, M. (1979). *Your children need music.* Englewood, NJ: Prentice-Hall.

Greenfield, C. (2003). Outdoor play: The case for risks and challenges in children's learning and development. *Safekids News, 21*, 5.

Greenfield, C. (2004). "Can run, play on bikes, jump the zoom slide, and play on the swings." Exploring the value of outdoor play. *Australian Journal of Early Childhood, 29*(2), 1–5.

Greenman, J. (1988). *Caring spaces, learning places. Children's environments that work.* Redmond, WA: Exchange Press.

Greenman, J. (2001). Beginnings workshop: What kind of place for child care in the 21st century? *Child Care Information Exchange* (November): 38–41.

Greenman, J. (2005). Places for childhood in the 21st century. A conceptual framework. *Young Children on the Web*, May, 2005.

Greenman, J. (2007). Just wondering: Building wonder into the environment in *Play: A Beginnings Workshop Book.* Redmond, WA: Exchange.12-16.

Greer, T. & Lochman, J. J. (1998). Using writing instruments: Invariances in young children and adults. *Child Development, 69*, 888–902.

Grieshaber, S., Halliwell, G., Hatch, J. A., & Walsh, K. (2001). Child observation in Australia and the USA: A cross-national analysis. *Early Child Development and Care, 169*(1), 39–56.

Guddemi, M. & Eriksen, A. (1992, Summer). Designing outdoor learning environments for and with children. *Dimensions of Early Childhood*, pp. 15–18, 23–24, 40.

Guhlin, M. (1996). Stage a well designed Saturday session and they will come! *Technology Connection, 3*(3), 13–14.

Gura, P. (1992) (Ed.). *Exploring learning: young children and block play.* London: Paul Chapman.

Guss, F. (2005). Reconceptualizing play: Aesthetic self-definitions. *Contemporary Issues in Early Childhood, 6*(3), 233–243.

Haight, W., Wang, X., Fung, H., Williams, H., & Mintz, J. (1999). Universal, developmental, and variable aspects of young children's play. A cross-cultural comparison of pretending at home. *Child Development, 70*(6), 1477–1488.

Halle, T., Calkins, J., Berry, D., & Johnson, R. (2003) Promoting language and literacy in early childhood care and education settings. Washington, DC: Child Trends; Neuman, S. B., Copple, C., & Bredekamp, S. (2000). *Learning to read and write: Developmentally appropriate practice.* Washington, DC: National Association for the Education of Young Children.

Halliday, M. A. K. (1975). *Explorations in the functions of language.* London: Edward Arnold.

Halpern, D. F. (1999). Teaching for critical thinking: Helping college students develop the skills and dispositions of a critical thinker. *New Directions for Teaching and Learning, 80*, 69–74.

Hands, B. & Martin, M. (2003). Fundamental movement skills: Children's perspectives. *Australian Journal of Early Childhood, 28*(4), 47–52.

Haney, M. & Hill, J. (2004). Relationships between parent-teaching activities and emergent literacy in preschool children. *Early Childhood Development and Care, 174*(3), 215–228.

Hanline, M. (1999). Developing a preschool play-based curriculum. *International Journal of Disability, Development and Education, 46*(3), 285–288.

Hardacre, J. (1995). Play and problem solving: What's the connection? *Canadian Children, 20*(1), 11–13.

Harmon, D. B. (1951). The co-ordinated classroom, *American Seating Co.*, Grand Rapids, Michigan.

Harris, A. (1998). Effective teaching: A review of the literature. *School Leadership & Management, 18*(2), 169–183. EJ 563–868.

Hatch, J. A. & Grieshaber, S. J. (2002). Child observation and accountability in early childhood education: Perspectives from Australia and the United States. *Early Childhood Education Journal, 29*(4), 227–231.

Hathaway, W. (1995). Effects of school lighting on physical development and school performance. *The Journal of Educational Research, 88*(4), 228.

Hathaway, W., Hargreaves, J., Thompson, G., & Novitsky, D. (1992). A study into the effects of light on children of elementary school age—a case of daylight robbery. *Alberta Education.*

Haugland, S. W. (1992). The effect of computer software on preschool children's developmental gains. *Journal of Computing in Childhood Education, 3,* 15–30.

Haugland, S. & Shade, D. (1994). Software evaluation for young children. In J. Wright & D. Shade, (Eds.), *Young children: Active learners in a technological age,* pp. *63–75.*

Haugland, S. W. & Wright, J. L. (1997). *Young children and technology.* New York: Allyn & Bacon.

Hawkins, J. & MacMillan, K. (1993). So what are teachers doing with this stuff? *Electronic Learning, 13*(2), 26.

Heath, S. B. & Mangiola, L. (1991). *Children of promise: Literate activity in linguistically and culturally diverse classrooms.* Washington, DC: National Education Association.

Hefferman, M. (1994). The children's garden project at river farm. *Children's Environments Quarterly, 11*(3), 221–231.

Heidemann, S. & Hewett, D. (1992). *Pathways to play: Developing play skills in young children.* St. Paul, MN: Redleaf Press.

Hendrick, J. & Weissman, P. (2006). *The Whole Child,* (8th ed.). Upper Saddle River, NJ: Pearson.

Hendrick, J. & Weissman, P. (2007). Total learning. Developmental curriculum for the young child. Upper Saddle River, NJ: Pearson Merrill Prentice Hall.

Hendrick, J. & Weissman, P. (2010). *Total learning: Developmental curriculum for the young child.* Boston, MA: Pearson.

Henniger, M.(2002). *Teaching young children. An introduction.*(2nd ed.). Upper Saddle River, NJ: Pearson.

Hermon, A. & Prentice, R. (2003). Positively different: Art and design in special education. *The International Journal of Art & Design Education, 22*(3), pp. 268–280.

Hewes, J. (2006). Let the children play: Natures answer to early learning. *Canadian Council on Learning.*

Hewett, V. M. (2001). Examining the Reggio Emilia approach to early childhood education. *Early Childhood Education, 29*(2), 95–100.

Hihiko, K. (2004). An introduction to active movement. *Sport and Recreation:* New Zealand, Wellington. Retrieved 16, May, 2006, www.sparc.org.nz/ education/active-movement/resources-and-tools/ introduction.

Hill, L. T., Stremmel, A. J., & Fu, V. R. (2005). *Teaching as inquiry: Rethinking curriculum in early childhood education.* Boston, MA: Pearson.

Hirsh, E. (1996). *The block book.* Washington, DC: NAEYC.

Hirsh-Pasek, K. & Golinkoff, R. M. (2008). Why play = learning. *Encyclopedia on Child Development.* Centre of Excellence for Early Childhood Development.

Holahan, J. M. (1987). The development of music syntax: Some observations of music babble in young children. In *music and child development,* edited by J. C. Peery, I. C. Peery, & T. W. Draper. New York: Springer-Verlag.

Holt, B., Kamii, C., & Seefeldt, C. (1984). Ideas that work with young children. Using worksheets in preschool. *Young Children, 40*(1), 20.

Holtzblatt, K. & Beyer, H. (1997). Getting started on a contextual project. *CHI97 Tutorial.* Atlanta Georgia: ACM Publications.

Holtzblatt, K. & Jones, A. (1992). Contextual design: Using contextual inquiry for system development. *CHI'92 Tutorial.* Monterey, CA: ACM Publications.

Holtzblatt, K. & Jones, S. (1995). Conducting and analyzing a contextual interview (Excerpt). In R. M. Baecker, J. Gudin, W. A. Buxton, & S. Greenberg (Eds). *Readings in HCI: Toward the year 2000* (2nd ed.) (pp. 241–253). San Francisco, CA: Morgan Kaufmann.

hooks, b. (2010). *Teaching critical thinking: Practical wisdom.* New York: Routledge.

Howe, N., Jacobs, E., & Fiorentino, L. M. (2000). The curriculum. In L. Prochner & N. Howe (Eds.), *Early childhood care and education in Canada* (pp. 11–65). Vancouver, British Columbia, Canada: University of British Columbia Press.

Huber, L. K. (1999). Woodworking with young children: You can do it! *Young Children, 54*(6), 32–34.

Hughes, F. (1999). *Children, play, and development.* (3rd ed.). Boston, MA: Allyn & Bacon.

Humpal, M. E. & Wolf, J. (2003). Music in the inclusive classroom. *Young Children, 58*(2), 103–107.

Hunt, T. & Renfro, N. (1982). *Puppetry in early childhood education.* Austin, TX: Nancy Renfro Studios.

Ihn, H. (1999). Analysis of children's equipment choices and play behaviours in outdoor environments. *Earlychildhood.com/articles.* Retrieved January 13, 2010.

International Play Association (Canada) (2006). The child's right to play. Retrieved January 13, 2010, from http://www.ipacanada.org/home_childs.htm

Isaacs, S. (1929). *The nursery years.* London: Routledge & Kegan Paul.

Isahi, A., Ungerlerider, L. G., Martin, A., Schouten, J. L., & Haxby, J. V. (1999). Distributed representation of objects in the human ventral visual pathway. *Proc. Natl. Acad. Sci. USA*. Retrieved January 5, 2010, from www.pnas.org/cgi/reprint/96/16/9379.

Isenberg, J. & Jalongo, M. (2010) *Creative thinking and arts-based learning: Preschool through fourth grade.* Upper Saddle River, NJ: Merrill.

Isenberg, J. P. & Jalongo, M. R. (2001). *Creative expression and play in early childhood.* Upper Saddle River, NJ: Merrill Prentice Hall.

Ivich, I. (1994). Lev. S. Vygotosky, *Prospects: The Quarterly Review of Comparative Education*, 24(3/4), 471–485.

Jalongo, M. R. (1999). How we respond to the artistry of children: Ten barriers to overcome. *Early Childhood Education Journal*, 26(4), 205–208.

Jalongo, M. R. (2000*). Early childhood language arts.* Needham Heights, MA: Allyn & Bacon.

Jalongo, M. & Isenberg, J. (2004). *Exploring your role. A practitioner's introduction to early childhood education.*Upper Saddle River, NJ: Prentice Hall.

Jalongo, M. R. & Stamp, L. N. (1997). *The arts in children's lives: Aesthetic education in early childhood.* Boston, MA: Allyn & Bacon.

Jensen, E. (1999). *Teaching with the brain in mind.* Alexandria, VA: Association for Supervision and Curriculum Development.

Jenson, E. (2006). *Enriching the brain: How to maximize every learner's potential.*San Francisco, CA: Jossey-Bass.

Johnson, J., Christie, J., & Wardle, F. (2005). *Play, development and early education.* Boston, MA: Allyn & Bacon.

Johnson, J. E., Christie, J. F., & Yawkey, T. D. (1987). *Play and Early Childhood Development.* Glenview, IL: Scott Foresman.

Jones, E. (2003). Playing to get Smart. NAEYC. *Young Children*, 58(3), 34.

Jones, E. & Nimmo, J. (1994). *Emergent curriculum.* Washington, DC: National Association for the Education of Young Children.

Jones, E. & Reynolds, G. (1992). *The play's the thing: Teachers' roles in children's play.* New York: Teachers College Press.

Jordan, B. & Smorti, S. (2010). Fearless science in the early years: Co-construction in a rural childcare centre. *The International Journal of Science in Society* (1) 4, 85–104.

Kail, R. V. (2002). *Children.* Upper Saddle River, NJ: Pearson Education, Inc.

Kamii, C., Miyakawa, Y., & Kato, Y. (2004). The development of logico-mathematical knowledge in a block-building activity at ages 1–4. *Journal of Research in Childhood Education*, 19(1), 44–57.

Kashin, D. (2009). *Reaching the top of the mountain: The impact of emergent curriculum on the practice and self-image of early childhood educators.* Koln, Germany: Lambert Academic Publishing.

Katz, L. G. (1993). Dispositions: Definitions and implications for early childhood practice. Champaign, IL: *ERIC Clearinghouse on Elementary and Early Childhood Education.*

Katz, L. G. & Chard, S. C. (2000). *Engaging children's minds* (2nd ed.). Norwood, NJ: Ablex.

Katzeff, C. (2003). Capturing playfulness in the design of digital learning environments for adults. *Share, Interactive Institute*, 2003-08–18. Retrieved January 5, 2010, from http://www.tii.se/share/downloads/Prestudy_PlayDesign.pdf

Katzmarzyk, P. T. (2004). Overweight and obesity mortality trends in Canada. 1985–2000. *Canadian Journal of Public Health*, 95(1), 16–20.

Kellogg, R. (1979). *Children's drawings/children's minds.* New York, NY: Avon.

Kessen, W. (1993). A developmentalist's reflection. In G. H. Elder, J. Modell, & R. D. Parke (Eds.), *Children in time and place: Developmental and historic insights* (pp. 226–229). Cambridge, UK: Cambridge University Press.

Kiger, J. E. (1994). *Relationship among the development of fundamental motor skills, basic timing, and academic performance in elementary school age children.* Unpublished paper, University of Wisconsin: Whiteater.

Kildberry, A. (2004). Critical pedagogy: A useful framework for thinking about early childhood curriculum. *Australian Journal of Early Childhood*, December, 1–2.

Kim, J. (2000). Children's pitch matching, vocal range, and developmentally appropriate practice. *Journal of Research in Childhood Education*, 14(2).

Kime, Z. (1980). *Sunlight.* Penryn, CA: World Health Publications.

King, J. A. & Alloway, N. (1992). Preschoooler's use of microcomputers and input devices. *Journal of Educational Computing Research*, 8, 451–468.

Kinnaman, D. E. (1990). *Staff development: How to build your winning team. Technology & Learning*, 11(2), 24–30.

Kirova. A. (2009). *Research in early childhood education course outline.* Retrieved June 5, 2010, from http://www.uofaweb.ualberta.ca/elementaryed/nav02.cfm?nav02=96422&nav01=99407

Klein, P. S., Nir-Gal, O., & Darom, E. (2000). The use of computers in kindergarten, with or without adult mediation: Effects on children's cognitive performance and behaviour. *Computers in Human Behaviour*, Amsterdam, Netherlands, 16(6), November 1, 2000, pp. 591–608. Retrieved May 2010 from http://web.macam98.ac.il/~nirgalo/a-publish&study/artical-klein%nir-gal&darom.htm

Korn-Bursztyn, C. (2002). Scenes from a studio: Working with the arts in an early childhood classroom. *Early Childhood Education Journal*, 30(1), 39–46.

Kostelnik, M., Stein, L., Whiren, A., & Soderman, A. (1998). *Guiding children's social development* (3rd ed.), Albany, NY: Delmar.

Kotsopoulos, D. & Lee, J. (Forthcoming) *Raising LittleCounters™*.

Krishnamurti, J. (2000). Educating the educator. Parabola. In Bello, S. (2002). Teaching children to express their inner world. *Encounter: Education for Meaning and Social Justice*, 15(3), 60–64.

Kritchevsky, S. & Prescott, E. (1969). *Physical space: Planning environments for young children*. Washington, DC: NAEYC.

Kritchevsky, S., Prescott, E., & Walling, L. (1977). *Planning environments for young children: Physical space* (2nd ed.), Washington, DC: National Association for the Education of Young Children, (p. 17).

Kuhlman, K., & Schweihart, L. (2010). Movement, music, & timing. Timing in child development. *High Scope*. Retrieved June, 2010, from http://www.highscope.org/Content.asp?ContentId=234.

LaFrance, M. & Meyer, A. (2009). Computers as barriers to or vehicle for equity response to "computer access equity." Southern Connecticut State University, *New Haven, CT*. Retrieved November 2009, from http://www.southernct.edu/organizations/rccs/resources/research/adap_tech/equity_access/

Labbo, L. D., Love, M. S., & Ryan, T. (2007). A vocabulary flood: Making words "sticky" with computer-response activities. *Reading Teacher*, 60, 582–588.

Landreth, G. L. (1991). Play therapy: *The art of the relationship*. Levittown, PA: Accelerated Development.

Landreth, G. L. & Hohmeyer, L. (1998). Play as the language of children's feelings. In D. P. Fromberg & D. Bergen (Eds.), *Play from birth to twelve and beyond*, (pp. 193–198). New York: Garland.

Lau, C., Higgins, K., Gelfer, J., Hong, E., & Miller, S. (2005). The effects of teacher facilitation on the social interactions of young children during computer activities. *Topics in Early Childhood Special Education*, 25, 208–217.

Lave, J. (1988). *Cognition in practice*. New York: Cambridge University Press.

Lee, M. W. & Houston, E. S. (1987). The advantages and disadvantages of microcomputers in early childhood education. *Early Child Development and Care*, 23, 263–281.

Lemerise, T. (1993). Piaget, Vygotsky, Logo. *The Computing Teacher*, 24–28.

Levinowitiz, L. M. (1998). An investigation of preschool children's comparative capability to sing songs with and without words. *Bulletin of the Council for Resear4ch in Music Education*, 100, 14–19.

Levinowitz, L. & Guilmartin, K. (1989, 1992, 1996). *Music together*. Cited in The importance of music in early childhood. Retrieved June, 2010, from http://www.musictogether.com.

Lewin, A. (1995). The fundamentals of the Reggio approach. In Cadwell, L. (ed.), *Bringing Reggio Emilia home*. New York: Teachers College Press.

Li, X. & Atkins (2004). Early childhood computer experience and cognitive and motor development. *Pediatrics*, 113(6), 1–8.

Liberman, J. (1991). *Light: Medicine of the future*. Sante Fe, NM: Bear & Company.

Lim, B. Y. (2004). The magic of the brush and the power of colour: Integrating theory into practice of painting in early childhood settings. *Early Childhood Education Journal*, 32(2) (October 2004), pp. 113–119.

Lind, K. K. (1999). Science in early childhood: Developing and acquiring fundamental concepts and skills. In American Association for Advancement of Science (AAAS). *Dialogue on early childhood science, mathematics and technology education*. Washington, DC: AAAS. 73–83.

Littleton, D. (1998). Music learning and child's play. *General Music Today*, 12(1), 8–15.

Liu, M. (1996). An Exploratory Study of How Pre-Kindergarten Children Use the Interactive Multimedia Technology: Implications for Multimedia Software Design. *Journal of Computing in Childhood Education*, 7 (1/2): 71–92.

Lowenfeld, V. & Brittain, W. L. (1987). *Creative and mental growth (8th ed.)*, New York: Macmillan Publishing Co., Inc.

Lupton, D. & Tulloch, J. (2002). "Life would be pretty dull without risk": Voluntary risk taking and its pleasures. *Health, Risk & Society, 4*(2), 113–124.

MacKay, G. (2009). Going "green" in child care services. *Putting Children First*, National Childcare Accreditation Council, Issue 29, March. 12–15.

Malaguzzi, L. (1991). (March/April). Not just anywhere: Making child care centres into "particular places." *Childcare Information Exchange*, 85, pp. 5–9.

Malaguzzi, L. (1998). History, ideas and basic philosophy. In C. Edwards, L. Gandini, & G. Forman (Eds.), *The hundred languages of children: The Reggio Emilia approach to early childhood education* (49–77). Norwood, NJ: Albex.

Mang, E. (2005). The referent of children's early songs. *Music Education Research, 7*(1), 3–20.

Marcus, B. & Nyisztor, D. (2008). *Balanced curriculum for young children.* Toronto, ON: Pearson.

Maslow, A. H. (1987). *Motivation and personality.* (3rd ed.), New York: Harper & Row.

Mason, J. (1982). *The environment of play.* West Point, New York: Leisure Press.

Mayer, K. (2007). Research in review: Emerging knowledge about emergent writing. *Young Children, 62*(1), pp. 34–40. January.

Mayfield, M. (2001). *Early childhood education and care in Canada: Contexts, dimensions and issues.* Toronto, ON: Prentice Hall.

McArdle, F. & Piscitelli, B. (2002). Early childhood art education: A palimpsest. *Australian Art Education, 25*(1), pp. 11–15.

McAuley, H. (1993). The relevance of early traditions of observation. *Early Child Development and Care* 92, 5–10.

McCain, M. & Mustard, F. (1999). *Early years study final report.* Toronto, ON: Publications Ontario.

McCarrick, K. & Xiaoming, L. (2007). Buried treasure: The impact of computer use on young children's social, cognitive, language development and motivation. *AACE Journal, 15*(1), 73–95.

McCune, L. & Zanes, M. (2001). Learning, attention, and play. In S. Golbeck (Ed.), *Psychological perspectives on early childhood education* (pp. 92–106). Mahwah, NJ: Lawrence Erlbaum.

McDonald, D. T. & Simons, G. M. (1989). *Musical growth and development: Birth through six.* New York: Schirmer Books.

McFadyen, C. L. & Doty Kirkland, L. (2009–2010). Early childhood visual arts curriculum: Freeing spaces to express developmental and cultural palettes of mind. *Childhood Education:* Winter 2009/2010; *86*(2), 87–91.

McLean, M. (1995, September). *Inclusion of children with special needs.* Presentation at the South Dakota Association for the Education of Young Children State Conference.

McLean, M. (1995, July). *Assessment of young children with special needs.* Presentation at the South Dakota Summer Institute on Early Intervention, Sioux Falls, SD.

McLean, M. (1995, May). *What do infants and toddlers need? An overview of recommended practices.* Presentation at the Effective Practices for Early Intervention Conference, Tampa, FL.

McNeal, J. (1992). *Kids as customers: A handbook of marketing to children.* New York: Lexington Books.

McVicker, C. J. (2007). Young readers respond: The importance of child participation in emerging literacy. *Young Children* Vol. 62, No. 3, Washington, DC: NAEYC. 18–22.

Media Awareness Network (2010). *Digital literacy in Canada: From inclusion to transformation. A submission to the Digital Economy Strategy Consultation,* July, 2010. Retrieved January 5, 2010, from http://www.media-awareness.ca/englilsh/corporate/ media_kit/digital_literacy_paper_pdf/ digitalliteracyp

Media Awareness Network (2010). *Special issues for young children.* http://www.media-awareness.ca/english/parents/marketing/issues_kids_marketing. cfm? RenderForPrint=1

Merrified, R. (2007) (Chair). House of Commons Canada Healthy Weights for Healthy Kids Report of the Standing Committee on Health. Government of Canada. Retrieved March 2, 2010 from www.sport-matters.ca/Images/2%20Support%20Documents/2 007/Home%20Page/391_HESA_Rpt07-e.pdf.

Mesher, P. & Amoriggi, H. (2001). Adapting to change: Can the Reggio Emilia approach help with the implementation of the new Quebec curriculum? *McGill Journal of Education, 36*(3), 239–250.

Miller, J. (1993). *The holistic curriculum.* Toronto, Ontario, Canada: OISE Press.

Miller, Toby, Nitin Govil, John McMurria, Richard Maxwell, and Ting Wang. 2005. *Global Hollywood 2.* London: British Film Institute.

Milone, M. N., Jr. and Salpeter, J. (1996). Technology and Equity Issues. *Technology and Learning,* 16 January, 38–41.

Mitchell, D. L. (1994). *The relationship between rhythmic competency and academic performance in first grade children.* Unpublished doctoral dissertation. Orlando, FL: University of Central Florida Department of Exceptional and Physical Education.

Monighan-Nourot, P., Scales, B., Van Hoorn, J., & Almy, M. (1987). *Looking at children's play: A bridge between theory and practice.* New York: Teacher's College Press.

Moore, G. (1987). The physical environment and cognitive development in child-care centers. In C. Weinstein & T. Davis (Eds.), *Spaces for children,* 41–72. New York: Plenum Press.

Moore, R. (1990). *Childhood's domain: Play and place in child development.* Berkeley: MIG Communications.

Morin, F. L. (2001). Cultivating music play: The need for changed teaching practice. *General Music Today, 14*(2), 24–29.

Morrison, G. (2004). *Early childhood education: Twenty predictions for the future.* University of North Texas. Retrieved November 23, 2005, from http://www.unt.edu/SuccessForLife/pdf/early_child_education

Morrow, L. (2001). *Literacy development in the early years: Helping children read and write.* Boston, MA: Allyn & Bacon.

Moss, P. (2000). Training of early childhood education and care staff. *International Journal of Educational Research, 33,* 31–53.

Moss, P. & Petrie, P. (2002). *From children's services to children's spaces: Public policy, children and childhood.* London: Routledge Falmer.

Music Educators National Conference (MENC). (1992). MENC position statement on early childhood education. *Soundpost,* (Winter), 21.

Nabhan, G. P. & Trimble, S. (1994). *The geography of childhood: Why children need wild places.* Boston, MA: Beacon Press.

Nastasi, B. K. & Clements, D. H. (1993). Motivational and social outcomes of cooperative education environments. *Journal of Computing in Childhood Education, 4*(1): 15–43.

National Association for the Education of Young Children. (1996). *The block book (3rd ed.).* Washington, DC: Author.

National Association for the Education of Young Children. (1997). Developmentally appropriate practices in early childhood programs. Washington, DC: Author.

National Association for the Education of Young Children Position Paper: Technology and young children–ages 3–8, (adopted April, 1996) *Young Children, 51*(6), 17–21.

National Childcare Accreditation Council (NCAC). (2005). Quality improvement and accreditation system: Quality practices guide. Sydney: Author.

National Childcare Accreditation Council (NCAC). (2007). A national quality framework for early childhood education and care. Retrieved May 1, 2010, from http://www.bing.com/search?q=National+Childcare+Accreditation+Council+(2007)&go=&filt=all&qs=n&sk=&first=11&FORI

National Council for Accreditation of Teacher Education. (2007). *Performance-based accreditation standards.* Washington, DC: Author.

National Playing Fields Association, Children's Play Council and Playlink. (2000). *Best play: What play provision should do for children?* London: National Playing Fields Association. Retrieved 15 May, 2010 from www.ncb.org.uk/dotpdf/open%20access%20-%20phase%201%20only/bestplay-cpc_20040115.pdf

National Scientific Council on the Developing Child. (2005). *Excessive stress disrupts the architecture of the developing brain:* Working paper No. 3. Retrieved February 5, 2010, from www.developingchild.harvard.edu

Neill, P. (2009). Put away the science activity books and tune in to your science senses! *Exchange Magazine,* November/December, p. 61–65.

Neuman, S. B., & Roskos, K. (1993). Access to print for children of poverty: Differential effects of adult mediation and literacy-enriched play settings on environmental and functional print tasks, *American Educational Research Journal, 30* (91): 95–122.

Neuman, S. B., Roskos, K., Vukelich, C., & Clements, D. (2003). *The state of state prekindergarten standards in 2003.* Center for the Improvement of Early Reading Achievement (CIERA).

Neumann, E. A. (1971). *The elements of play.* New York: MSS Information Corp.

New, R. (1991). Projects and provocations: Preschool curriculum ideas from Reggio Emilia, *Montessori Life, 3*(1), 26–28.

New, R. S. (1998). Theory and praxis in Reggio Emilia: They know what they are doing, and why. In C. Edwards, L. Gandini, & G. Forman (Eds.) (2nd Ed.), *The hundred languages of children: The Reggio Emilia approach—advanced reflections* (pp. 261–284). Greewich, CT: Ablex Publishing.

New, R. S., Mardell, B. & Robinson, D. (2005). Early childhood education as risky business: Going beyond what's "safe" to discovering what's possible. *Early Childhood Research and Practice, 7*(2). Retrieved March 20, 2010, from http://ecrp.uiuc.edu/v7n2/new.html.

Newman, L. S. (1990). Intentional and unintentional memory in young children: Remembering vs. playing. *Journal of Experimental Child Psychology, 50*, 243–258.

Nicholson, S. (1971) "How Not To Cheat Children: The Theory of Loose Parts", *Landscape Architecture*, v62, 30–35.

Nicholson, S. & Shipstead, S. G. (2002). *Through the looking glass (3rd edition)*. Columbus, OH: Merrill Prentice Hall.

Nikolopoulou, K. (2007). Early childhood education software: Specific features and issues of localization. *Early Childhood Education Journal, 35*(2), 173–179.

Noddings, N. (1992). *The challenge to care in schools: An alternative approach to education*. New York: Teachers College Press.

Nutbrown, C. (1994). *Threads of thinking: Young children learning and the role of early education*, (2nd ed). London: Paul Chapman.

Olds, A. R. (2001). *Child care design guide*. New York: McGraw-Hill.

Oliver, S. J. & Klugman, E. (2004). Speaking out for play-based learning: Becoming an effective advocate for play in the early childhood classroom. *Exchange.* January/February, 22–25.

Olsen, A. E. & Sumsion, J. (2000). *Early childhood teacher practices regarding the use of dramatic play in K-2 classrooms*. Paper presented at the Annual Conference of the Australian Association for Research in Education, December.

Oppenheimer, T. (2003). *The flickering mind: Saving education from the false promise of technology*. New York: Random House.

OECD (2008). Growing unequal? *Income distribution in OECD countries*. Retrieved June 1, 2010, from http://www.oecd.com

Ott, J. (1976). *Health and light: The effects of natural and artificial light on man and other living things*. New York: Pocket Books.

Oudeyer, P. Y., Kaplan, F., & Hafner, V. (2007). Intrinsic motivation systems for autonomous mental development. *IEEE Transactions on Evolutionary Computation, 11*(2), 265–286.

Oudeyer, P. Y. & Kaplan, F. (2007). The progress-drive hypothesis: An interpretation of early imitation. In K. Dautenhahn and C. Nehaniv (Eds.), *Models and mechanisms of imitation and social learning: Behavioural, social and communication dimensions*. Cambridge, U.K.: Cambridge Univ. Press, pp. 361–377.

Pacini-Ketchabaw, V., Pence, A. (2005). Contextualizing the Reconceptualist Movement in Canadian Early Childhood Education. In V. Pacini-Ketchabaw & A. Pence (Eds.), *Early Childhood Education in Motion: The Reconceptualist Movement in Canada*. Ottawa: Canadian Child Care Federation.

Paley, V. G. (1981). *Wally's stories: Conversations in the kindergarten*. Cambridge, MA: Harvard University Press.

Paley, V. G. (1988). *Bad guys don't have birthdays: Fantasy play at four*. Chicago: University of Chicago Press.

Paley, V. G. (1990). *The boy who would be a helicopter: The uses of storytelling in the classroom*. Cambridge, MA: Harvard University Press.

Paley, V. G. (2001). *In Mrs. Tully's room: A childcare portrait*. Cambridge, Massachusetts: Harvard University Press.

Park, B., Chae, J., & Boyd Foulks, B. (2008). Young children's block play and mathematical learning. *Journal of Research in Childhood Education*. December 22, 2008.

Parten, M. (1933). Social play among preschool children. *Journal of Abnormal and Social Psychology, 28*, 136–147.

Parten, M. B. (1932). Social participation among preschool children. *Journal of Abnormal and Social Psychology, 27*, 243–269.

Pascal, C. (2009). With our *best future* in mind. Government of Ontario. Retrieved January 5, 2010, from http://www.ontario.ca/en/initiatives/early_learning/ONT06_018867

Pear, Cohen & Gainer, R. S. (1984). *Art: Another language for learning*. New York: Schoken Books.

Pence, A. & Pacini-Ketchabaw, V. (2008). Discourses on quality care: The Investigating "Quality" project and the Canadian experience. *Contemporary Issues in Early Childhood, 9*(3), 2008, pp. 241–254. Retrieved February 2010, from http://dx.doi.org/10.2304/ciec.2008.9.3.241.

Penn, H. (2005). *Understanding early childhood: Issues and controversies*. New York: Open University Press.

Pepler, D. & Ross, H. (1981). Effects of play on convergent and divergent problem solving. *Child Development, 52*, 1202–1210.

Pereira, B., Fale, P., & da Guia Carmo M. (2002). *Playgrounds. Comparative study of six districts in the region of Cavado in the North of Portugal*. Paper presented at the European Conference on Educational

Research, University of Lisbon, 11–14, September, 2002.

Perry, B. (2004). *Maltreatment and the developing child: How early childhood experience shapes child and culture*. Inaugural lecture. Retrieved January 2010, from http://www.lfcc.on.ca/mccain/

Perry, B. D. (1997). *Incubated in terror: Neurodevelopmental factors in the "cycle of violence"* [online]. Retrieved May 2010, from http://www.childtrauma.org/CTAMATERIALS/incubated.asp.

Persky, S. E. (1990). What contributes to teacher development in technology? *Educational Technology, 30*(4), 34–38.

Peterlin, C. M. L. (1991). *Nurturing self-control through basic timing experiences*. Unpublished master's thesis. Rochester, MI: Oakland University Department of Human Development and Child Studies.

Petrie, P. & Poland, G. (1998). Play services for disabled children. *Children and Society, 12*, 238–294.

Phelps, P. C. & Hanline, M. F. (1999). Let's play blocks! Creating effective learning experiences for young children. *Teaching Exceptional Children, 32*(2), 62–67.

Piaget, J. (1962). *Play, dreams, and imitation in childhood*. London: Routledge and Kegan Paul.

Pintrich, P. & Schunk, D. (1996). *Motivation in education: Theory, research & applications*, Englewood Cliffs, NJ: Prentice-Hall.

Plowman, L. (2005). Getting the story straight: The role of narrative in teaching and learning with interactive media. In P. Gardenfors & P. Johansson (Eds.), *Cognition, education, and communication technology*, pp. 56–76.

Plowman, L. & Stephen, C. (2005). Children, play and computers in pre-school education. *British Journal of Educational Technology, 36*(2), 145–157.

Plympton, P., Conway, S., & Epstein, K. (2000). *Daylighting in schools: Improving student performance and health at a price schools can afford*. Paper presented at the American Solar Energy Society Conference, Madison, Wisconsin, June 16, 2000.

Poest, C. A., Williams, J. R., Witt, D. D., & Atwood, M. E. (1990). Challenge me to move: Large muscle development in young children. *Young Children, 45*(5), 4–10.

Popham, W. J. (2002). *Classroom assessment: What teachers need to know*. Boston, MA: Allyn & Bacon.

Provenzo, E. F. & Brett, A. (1983). *The complete block book*. Syracuse, NY: Syracuse University Press.

Public Health Agency of Canada. (2006). *Toward a healthy future: Second Report on the health of Canadians*. Retrieved January 5, 2010, from http://www.phac-aspc.gc.ca/ph-sp/determinants/index-eng.php

Pushor, D. (2007). *Parent engagement: Creating a shared world*. Invited Research Paper, Ontario Education Research Symposium, January 18–20, 2007.

Raffini, P. (1996). *150 ways to increase Intrinsic motivation in the classroom*. Needham Heights, MA: Simon and Schuster.

Raines, S. C. (1997). Developmental appropriateness: Curriculum revisited and challenged. In J. P. Isenberg & M. R. Jalongo (Eds.), *Major trends and issues in early childhood education: Challenges, controversies and insights* (71–89). New York: Teacher's College Press.

Ramsey, J. L. & Fowler, M. L. (2004). Using posters containing questions and general instructions to guide preschoolers' science and mathematics learning, *Young Children*, May, *59*(3), 88–92.

Rankin, B. (2004). Dewey, Piaget, Vygotsky: Connections with Malaguzzi and the Reggio approach. In J. Hendrick (Ed.), *Next steps toward teaching the Reggio way: Accepting the challenge to change* (27–35). Upper Saddle River, NJ: Pearson Prentice Hall.

Reicher, D. (2000). Nature's design rules: Leading the way toward energy-efficient schools. *Learning by Design*.Retrieved January 5, 2010, from www.asbj.com/ibd/2000/00inprint/00reicher.html

Reifel, S. & Greenfield, P. (1982). Structural development in a symbolic medium: The representational use of block construction. In G. E. Forman (Ed.), *Action and thought: From sensorimotor schemes to symbolic operations* (pp. 203–233). New York: Academic Press.

Resnick, M. (1996). Towards a practice of constructional design. In L. Schauble & R. Glaser (Eds.). *Innovations in learning: New environments for education*, Mahwah, NJ: Lawrence Erlbraurn.

Resnick, M. (1996). Beyond a centralized mindset. *Journal of the Learning Sciences, 5*(1), 1–22.

Reynolds, G. & Jones, E. (1997). *Master players: Learning from children at play*. New York: Teachers College Press.

Rinaldi, C. (1998). Projected curriculum constructed through documentation-progettazione: An interview with Lella Gandini. In C. Edwards, L. Gandini, & G. Forman (Eds.), *The hundred languages of children: The Reggio Emilia approach to early childhood education* (113–125). Norwood, NJ: Albex.

Rinaldi, C. (2001). Reggio Emilia: *The image of the child and the child's environment as a fundamental principle.* New York: Teachers College Press.

Rinaldi, C. (2006). *In dialogue with Reggio Emilia: Listening, researching, and learning.* New York: Routledge.

Rivkin, M. (1997). The schoolyard habitat movement: What it is and why children need it. *Early Childhood Education Journal, 25*(1), 61–66.

Rivkin, M. S. (1995). *The great outdoors: Restoring children's right to play outside.* Washington, DC: National Association for the Education of Young Children.

Robinson, L. (2003). *Engaging young children in computer activities.* Retrieved December 2009, from http://www.wiu.edu/users/mimacp/wiu/articles/engag.html

Rogers, R. & Russo, S. (2003). Blocks: A commonly encountered play activity in the early years, or a key to developing skills in science, maths, and technology? *Investigating Journal 20*(3), 17–21.

Roskos, K. A., Christie, J. F., & Richgels, D. J. (2003). The essentials of early literacy instruction. *Young Children*, Washington, DC: NAEYC. 1–7.

Ross-Bernstein, J. (2001). Observing children at play: Teachers as scientific inquirers. *Ithaca Prekindergarten Staff Development Initiative.* Cornell University. Retrieved March 1, 2010, from http://northernlights.vsc.edu/level_ii/0709/prekobserving_workshop.pdf

Ross, J. (1994). The right moves: Challenges of dance assessment. *Arts Education Policy Review, 96*(1), 11–17.

Ross, M. E. (2000). Science their way. *Young Children, 55* (2). 6–13.

Rubin, K., Fein, G. G. & Vandenberg, B. (1983). Play. In P. Mussen (Series Ed.), E. M. Hetherington (Vol. Ed.), *Handbook of child psychology,* Vol. 4, (4th ed., pp. 693–774). New York: Wiley.

Rudolph, M. & Cohen, D. (1984). *Kindergarten and early schooling.* Englewoods Cliffs: NJ: Prentice-Hall.

Rutherford, M. D. & Rogers, S. (2003). The cognitive underpinnings of pretend play in autism. *Journal of Autism and Developmental Disorders, 33*(3), 289–302.

Ryan, R. & Deci, E. (2000). Self-determination theory and the facilitation of intrinsic motivation, social development, and well-being. *American Psychologist, 55*(1), 68–78.

Ryan, S. & Grieshaber, S. (2005). Shifting from developmental to postmodern practices in early childhood teacher education. *Journal of Teacher Education, 56*(1), 34–45.

Saljo, R. (1988). Learning in educational settings: Methods of inquiry. P. Ramsden (Ed.), *Improving Learning: New Perspectives* (1988), 32–48, New York: Kogan Page.

Salmon, M. & Akaran, S. (2001). Enrich your kindergarten program with a cross-cultural connection. *Young Children, 56*(4): 30–32.

Samaras, A. P. (1996). Children's computers. *Childhood Education, 72*(3), 133–136.

Samaras, A. P. (2000). Scaffolding preservice teachers' learning. In N. Yelland (Ed.), *Promoting meaningful learning: Innovations in educating early childhood professionals* (17–24). Washington, DC: National Association for the Education of Young Children.

Sandberg, A. & Pramling-Samuelsson, I. (2003). Preschool teacher's play experience—then and now. *Early Childhood Research & Practice, 5*(1). Retrieved January 5, 2010, from *http://ecrp.uiuc.edu/v5n1/index.html*

Sandholtz, J. H., Ringstaff, C., & Dyer, D. C. (1997). *Teaching with technology: Creating student-centred classrooms.* New York: Teachers College Press.

Santrock, J. (2003). *Life-span development.* Boston, MA: McGraw Hill.

Santrock, J. W. (2001). *Adolescence* (8th ed.). New York: McGraw-Hill.

Sawyer, R. K. (1997). *Pretend play as improvisation: Conversations in the preschool classroom.* Mahwah, NJ: Lawrence Erlbaum Associates.

Saxe, G. B., Guberman, S. R., & Gearhart, M. (1987). Social processes in early number development. *Monographs of the Society for Research in Child Development, 52*(2, Serial No. 216), 153–159.

Scarlett, W. G., Naudeau, S., Salonius-Pasternak, D., & Ponte, I. (2005). *Children's play.* Thousand Oaks, CA: Sage Publications.

Scarlett, W. G. & New, R. S. (2007). Play. In R. New & M. Cochran (Eds.), *Early childhood education: An international encyclopedia* (Vol. 3, pp. 626–633). Westport, CT: Praeger.

Schirrmacher, R. (2002). *Art and creative development for young children (4th ed.).* Albany, NY: Thompson Learning Inc.

Schön, D. A. (1996). *Educating the reflective practitioner: Toward a new design for teaching and learning in the professions.* San Francisco, CA: Jossey-Bass.

Schwartzman, H. B. (1978). *Transformations: The anthropology of children's play.* New York: Plenum Press.

Scott, E. (2008). *The origin of the word play. How the word play entered the English language.* Retrieved February 2010, from http://languagestudy.suite101.cm/article.cfm/the_origin_of_the_word_play.

Scott, E. (2008). *Your child and stress: Causes of stress in your child's environment.* Retrieved January 5, 2010, from http://stress.about.com/od/studentstress/a/school_anxiety_4.htm

Seagoe, M. (1970). An instrument for the analysis of children's play as an index of socialization. *Journal of School Psychology, 8,* 139–144.

Seng, S. (1998, November). *Enhanced learning, computers and early childhood education.* Paper presented at the Educational Research Association Conference, Singapore. (ERIC Document Reproduction Service No. ED 431 524).

Shade, D. D. (1994). Computers and young children: Software types, social contexts, gender, age, and emotional responses. *Journal of Computing in Childhood Education, 5*(2), 177–209.

Shanker, S. (2009). *Every child, every opportunity: Curriculum and pedagogy for the early learning program.* Government of Ontario (Forward). Retrieved January 5, 2010, from http:www.ontario.ca/en/initiatives/early_learning/ONT06_023397

Sharpe, A., Harris, P., & McKeen, K. (2010). The place of music and movement in the curriculum settings— what do teachers think? *Faculty of Education, University of Wollongong.* Retrieved June 2010, from http://www.aare.edu.au/05pap/sha5231.pdf

Sheltz, K. F. & Stremmel, A. J. (1994). Teacher-assisted computer implementation: A Vygotskian perspective. *Early Education and Review, 5*(1), 18–26.

Shipley, D. (1998). *Empowering children. Play-based curriculum for lifelong learning.* Scarborough, ON: Nelson.

Shute, R. & Miksad, J. (1997). Computer assisted instruction and cognitive development in preschoolers. *Child Study Journal, 27*(3), 237–253.

Sivin-Kachala, J. & Bialo, E. (1994). *Report on the effectiveness of technology in schools, 1990–1994.* Washington, DC: Software Publishers Association.

Smilansky, S. (1968). *The effects of sociodramatic play on disadvantaged preschool children.* New York: Wiley.

Smilansky, S. & Shefatya, L. (1990). *Facilitating play: A medium for promoting cognitive, socio-emotional and academic development in young children.* Gaithersburg, MD: Psychosocial and Educational Publications.

Smith, L. (1999). *Decolonizing methodologies: Research and indigenous peoples.* Otago: University of Otago Press.

Smith, M. K. (2002, 2008). "*Howard Gardner and multiple intelligences*"—*the encyclopedia of informal education.* Retrieved January 5, 2010, from http://www.infed.org/thinkers/gardner.htm

Smith, S. J. (1998). *Risk and our pedagogical relation to children: On the playground and beyond.* New York: State University of New York Press.

Smith, S., Willms, D., & Johnson, N. (Eds.). (1997). *Nurtured by knowledge: Learning to do participatory action-research.* New York: Apex Press.

Smitherim, K. L. (1997). Free musical play in early childhood. *Canadian Journal of Research in Music Education, 4*(3):17–24.

Snowling, M. J. & Hulme, C. (2006). Language skills, learning to read and reading intervention, *London Review of Education, 4*(1), 63–76.

Spaggiari, S. (2004). The path toward knowledge: The social, political, and cultural context of the Reggio municipal infant-toddler centre and preschool experience. *Innovations in Early Education: The international Reggio Exchange, 11*(2), 1–5.

Spencer H. (1886). *The principles of psychology.* New York: Appleton.

Sperry Smith, S. (2009). *Early childhood mathematics.* Boston, MA: Pearson.

Spodek, B. (1993). *Language and literacy in early childhood education*; yearbook in Early Childhood Education. New York: Teachers College Press.

Spodek, B. (1993). *Handbook of research on the education of young children.* New York: Macmillan.

Stadler, M. & Ward, G. (2005). Supporting the narrative development of young children. *Early Childhood Education Journal, 33*(2). 73–80.

Stager, G. S. (1995). Laptop schools lead the way in professional development. *Educational Leadership. 53* (2), 6–13.

Statistics Canada. (2008). *Overweight Canadian children and adolescents.* Retrieved January 10, 2010, from http://www.statcan.gc.ca/pub/82-620-m/2005001/article/child-enfant/8061-eng.htm#3

Stephenson, A. (1998). Opening up the outdoors: A reappraisal of young children's outdoor experiences. Unpublished Master of Education, Victoria University, Wellington.

Stine, S. (1997). *Landscapes for learning.* New York: John Wiley & Sons.

Stokrocki, M. (1988). The development of children through clay modeling. *School Arts, 57*(9), 34–35.

Stremmel, A. J. (2002). The cultural construction of childhood: United States and Reggio perspectives. In V. R. Fu, A. J. Stremmel, & L. T. Hill (Eds.), *Teaching and learning: Collaborative exploration of the Reggio Emilia approach,* (37–49). Upper Saddle Tree, NJ: Merrill Prentice Hall.

Sutterby, J. A. & Frost, J. L. (2002). Making playgrounds fit for children and children fit for playgrounds. *Young Children, 57*(3), 36–41.

Sutton-Smith, B. (1997). *The ambiguity of play.* Cambridge, MA: Harvard University Press.

Swaminathan, S. & Wright, J. (2003). Educational technology in the early childhood and primary years. In J. P. Isenberg & M. R. Jalongo (Eds.), *Major trends and issues in early childhood education: Challenges, controversies, and insights* (pp. 136–149). New York: Teacher's College Press.

Sylva, K., Bruner, J., & Genova, P. (1976). The role of play in the problem-solving of children 3–5 years old. In J. S. Bruner, A. Jolly, & K. Sylva (Eds.), *Play*. New York: Basic Books.

Tamis-LeMonda, C. S., Bornstein, M., Cyphers, L., Toda, S., & Ogina, M. (1992). Language and play at one year: A comparison of toddlers and mothers in the United States and Japan. *International Journal of Behavioural Development, 15,* 19–42.

Tanner, C. K. & Langford, S. (2003). *The importance of interior design elements as they relate to student outcomes.* Dalton, GA: Carpet and Rug Institute. (ERIC Documentation Reproduction Service No. ED 478177. )

Tannock, M. (2008). Rough and tumble play: An investigation of the perceptions of educators and young children. *Early Childhood Education Journal, 35,* 357–361.

Tarnowski, S. M. & Leclerc, J. (1994). Musical play of preschoolers and teacher-child interaction. *Update: Application of Research in Music Education 1*(13), 9–16.

Timmermans, I. (2005). *The visual arts in early childhood education.* Brock University. Unpublished paper.

Topal, C. (2005) *Thinking with a line.* Worchester, MA: Davis.

Tougas, J. (2004). Who benefits from education and child care services and what purpose do they serve? Winnipeg, Manitoba, Canada: *Canadian Council on Social Development.*

Tough, P. (2009). Can the right kinds of play teach self-control? *New York Times Magazine,* September 25.

Tovey, H. (2007). *Playing outdoors: Spaces and places, risk and challenge.* Maidenhead: Open University Press.

Trainor, L. (2006). *First evidence that musical training affects brain development in young children.* Oxford University Press (2006, September 20).

Tranter, P. (2005, November). *Strategies for building child friendly cities.* Paper presented at the Creating Child Friendly Cities Conference, Melbourne. Retrieved June 2006, www.envict.org.au/file/Paul_Tranter.pdf

Trister Dodge, D., Colker, L., & Heroman, C. (2002). *The creative curriculum for preschoolers.* Washington: DC: Teaching Strategies.

Tyrell, J. (2001). *The power of fantasy in early learning.* London: Routledge Falmer.

United Nations. (1991). Convention on the Rights of the Child. Ottawa: Minister of Supply and Services Canada.

United Nations High Commission for Human Rights. (1989). Convention on the Rights of the Child. Geneva: UNCHR.

Upitis, R. (2005). *Architecture, complexity science, and schooling in the early years.* Hawaii International Conference on Arts and Humanities. Unpublished manuscript.

Van Hoorn, J., Nourot, P. M., Scales, B., & Alward, K. R. (2007). *Play at the center of the curriculum.* Upper Saddle River, NJ: Pearson.

Vasta, R., Miller, S. A., & Ellis, S. (2004). *Child psychology* (4th ed.). New York: Wiley.

Vergeront, J. (1988). *Places and spaces for preschool and primary (outdoors).* Washington, D.C.: National Association for the Education of Young Children.

Vieth, R. (2010). *Dark-skinned immigrants urged to take vitamin D.* Retrieved January 5, 2010, from http://www.cbc.ca/canada/ottawa/story/2010/02/12/ottawa-immigrants-vitamin-d.html

Vygotsky, L. S. (1976). Play and its role in the mental development of the child. In J. Bruner, A. Jolly & K. Sylva (Eds.), *Play: its role in development and evolution.* New York: Basic Books, pp. 537–554.

Vygotsky, L. S. (1978). *Mind in society: The development of higher psychological processes.* Cambridge, MA: Harvard University Press.

Vygotsky, L. S. (1981). The development of higher forms of attention in childhood. In J. V. Vertsch (Ed.), *The concept of activity in Soviet psychology* (pp. 189–240). Armonk, NY: Sharpe.

Vygotsky, L. S. (1986). *Thought and language* (A. Kozulin, Trans. Ed. and revised) Cambridge, MA: MIT Press.

Waite-Stupiansky, S. (1997). *Building understanding together: A constructivist approach to early childhood education.* Albany, NY: Delmar.

Walsh, P. (1993). Fixed equipment: A time for change. *Australian Journal of Early Childhood, 18*(2), 23–29.

Wardle, F. (1998). *Outdoor play: Designing, building, and remodeling playgrounds for young children.* Retrieved from http://www.earlychildhoodnews. com/earlychildhood/article_print.aspx? ArticleId=65

Wardle, F. (2007). Rethinking early childhood practices. *Early Childhood News*, Jan/Feb 2007.

Warner, L. (2005). Revisiting Bloom's taxonomy: Asking better questions. *Texas Child Care, 29*(3), 40–42.

Wassermann, S. (1992). *Serious players in the primary classroom.* New York: Teachers College Press.

Watson, R. (2002). Literacy and oral language: Implications for early literacy acquisition. In Neuman, S., Dickinson, D. (Eds.). *Handbook of early literacy research* (43–53). New York: The Guilford Press.

Weber, E. (1984). *Ideas influencing early childhood education: A theoretical analysis.* New York: Teachers College Press.

Weikart, P. S., Schweinhart, L. J., & Larner, M. (1987, Winter). Movement curriculum improves children's rhythmic competence. *HighScope ReSource, 6*(1), 8–10.

Weininger, O. (1994). *Understanding education play: An interview with Otto Weininger by Una Villiers, 25*(1), 4–6. Retrieved February 14, 2005, from: http://ercp.uiuc.edu/v5n1/index.html.

Weir, S., Russell, S. J., & Valente, J. A. (1982). Logo: An approach to educating disabled children. *BYTE 7,* (September 1982), 342–360.

Weitzman, E. & Greenberg, J. (2002). *Learning language and loving it.* Toronto, ON: The Hanen Centre.

Wellhousen, K. (2002). *Outdoor play every day: Innovative play concepts for early childhood.* Albany, NY: Delmar.

Wellhousen, K. & Kieff, J. (2001). *A constructivist approach to block play in early childhood.* Albany, NY: Delmar Thompson Learning.

Wheeler, E. J. (2004). *Conflict resolution in early childhood: Helping children understand and resolve conflicts.* Upper Saddle River, NJ: Pearson.

White, R. & Stoecklin, V. (2008). *Nurturing children's biophilia: Developmentally appropriate environmental education for young children.* Retrieved May 2010, from *http://www.whitehutchinsion.com/ children/articles/nurturing.shtml.*

Whitebread, D. (1996). (Ed.). *Teaching and learning in the early years.* London: Rutledge.

Whitehurst, G. J. & Lonigan, C. J. (1998). Child development and emergent literacy. *Child Development, 69*(3), 848–872.

Whiting, B. & Whiting, J. M. (1975). *Children of six cultures.* Cambridge, MA: Harvard University Press.

Wilder, G., Mackie, D., & Cooper, J. (1985). Gender and computers: Two surveys of computer-related attitudes. *Sex Roles, 13*(3/4), 215–228.

Wilson, R. A. (1999, March/April). Why nature? *Earlychildhood NEWS*, pp. 38–48.

Wiltz, N. & Fein, G. (2006). Play as children see it. In Bergen & Fromberg (Eds.), *Play from birth to twelve: Contexts, perspectives, and meanings* (2nd ed.). New York: Garland.

Wolery, M. & McWilliams, R. (1998). Classroom-based practices for preschoolers with disabilities. *Interventions in Schools and Clinics, 34,* 95–102.

Wolgang, C., Stannard, L., & Jones, I. (2001). Block play performance among preschoolers as a predictor of later school achievement in mathematics. *Journal of Research in Childhood Education, 15*(2), 173–180.

Wolfgang, C. H. & Wolfgang, M. E. (1992). *School for young children: Developmentally appropriate practice.* Boston, MA: Allyn & Bacon.

Wood, D., Bruner, J., & Ross, G. (1976). The role of tutoring in problem solving. *Journal of Child Psychology and Psychiatry, 17,* 89–100.

Worth, J. (1990). Developing problem-solving abilities and attitudes. In J. Payne (Ed.), *Mathematics for the young child* (pp. 39–61). Reston, VA: National Council of Teachers of Mathematics.

Wortham, S. (1992). *Childhood: 1892–1992.* Olney, MD: Association for Childhood Education International.

Wren, S. (2001). *What does a balanced literacy approach mean?* Southwest Educational Development Laboratory, Austin TX. Retrieved May 2010, from - www.sedl.org/reading/topics/balanced.html

Wright, C. & Schweinhart, L. J. (1994). *Social-academic and rhythmic skills of kindergarten children.* Unpublished manuscript. Ypsilanti, MI: HighScope Educational Research Foundation.

Wright, F. L. (1957). *A testament.* New York: Harper & Rowe.

Yaden, D. B., Rowe, D. W., & MacGillivray, L. (1999). *Emergent literacy: A polyphony of perspectives* (CIERA Report) Ann Arbor: CIERA.

Yamaha Corporation. (1994). Creating music for tomorrow: Young musicians speak. [Videotape]. Orange County, CA: Yamaha Corporation of America.

Yelland, N. & Cartmel, J. (2000). Rethinking professional practice: Narratives of the practicum. In N. Yelland (Ed.), *Promoting meaningful learning: Innovations in educating early childhood professionals*, (25–34). Washington, DC: National Association for the Education of Young Children.

Young, N. (1993). *Caring for play: The school and child care connection*, (Draft Edition) Toronto, ON: Exploring Environments.

Zacharos, K., Koliopoulos, D., Dokomaki, M., & Kassoumi, H. (2007). Views of prospective early childhood education teachers, towards mathematics and its instruction. *European Journal of Teacher Education, 30*(3), 305–318.

Zigler, E., & Bishop-Josef, S. (2004). Play under siege: A historical overview. In E. Zigler, D. Singer, & S. Bishop-Josef (Eds.), *Children's play: The roots of reading* (pp. 1–14). Washington, DC: Zero to Three Press.

# Credits

# Index

Note: Entries for tables and figures are followed by "*t*" and "*f*," respectively.

# NOTES

# NOTES

# NOTES

# NOTES

# NOTES

# NOTES